From Manchester
with Love

by the same author

ASK: THE CHATTER OF POP
NOTHING
WORDS AND MUSIC: A HISTORY OF POP IN THE SHAPE OF A CITY
JOY DIVISION: PIECE BY PIECE – WRITING ABOUT JOY DIVISION 1977–2007
JOY DIVISION: FRAGMENTS (with Christel Derenne)
THE NORTH (AND ALMOST EVERYTHING IN IT)
EARTHBOUND
I'LL NEVER WRITE MY MEMOIRS (by Grace Jones with Paul Morley)
THE AGE OF BOWIE: HOW DAVID BOWIE MADE A WORLD OF DIFFERENCE
THE AWFULLY BIG ADVENTURE: MICHAEL JACKSON IN THE AFTERLIFE
A SOUND MIND: HOW I FELL IN LOVE WITH CLASSICAL MUSIC (AND DECIDED TO
    REWRITE ITS ENTIRE HISTORY)
YOU LOSE YOURSELF, YOU REAPPEAR: BOB DYLAN AND THE VOICES OF A LIFETIME

From Manchester with Love

Paul Morley

The Life and Opinions
of Tony Wilson*
*aka Anthony H. Wilson

*Written in 51 sections that
prove how all dramatic truth
contains fiction*

faber

First published in 2021
by Faber & Faber Limited
Bloomsbury House
74–77 Great Russell Street
London WC1B 3DA

Typeset by Ian Bahrami
Printed and bound by CPI Group (UK) Ltd, Croydon, CR0 4YY

A CIP record for this book
is available from the British Library

ISBN 978–0–571–25249–7

MIX
Paper from
responsible sources
FSC® C020471
FSC
www.fsc.org

10 9 8 7 6 5 4 3 2

e.s.p.

Contents

List of Illustrations

Wilsonland

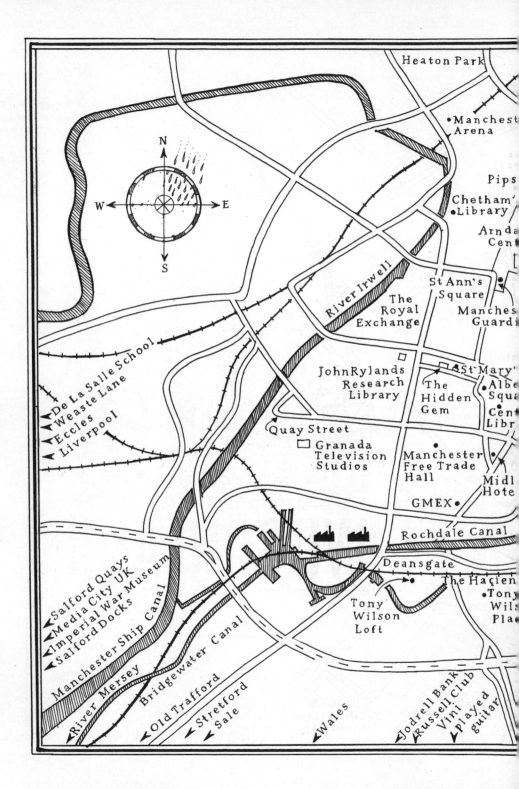

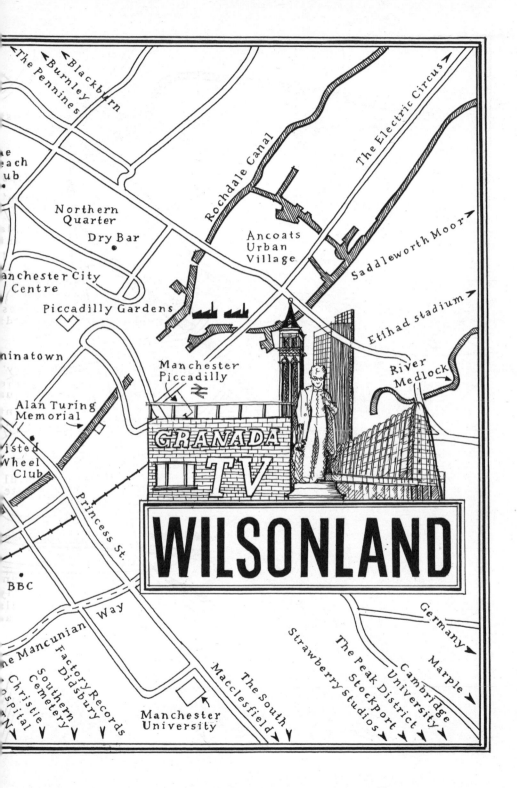

Exordium: Bringing the reader into the book

Aut non rem temptes aut perfice. (Either don't try at all or make sure you succeed.)
OVID

This book has, on paper, taken me ten years to write. Not that I have been working on it full-time for all of those ten years, and only working on it, hours a day, day after day, year after year. It hasn't been all I've done for ten years. There were other books I have written along the way while this one has been taking – and not taking – shape, which meant this book lived, or lapsed, or took on a life of its own at the back of my mind while I got on with other stories, lives and times. Some of those books took me far away from this book and meant to some extent every time I returned to it, I had to begin again. Some of those books were not necessarily me stopping work completely, just me temporarily thinking about something else. I might have been running away or conscientiously getting myself more prepared. One of these was a book that in many respects forms the second part of a trilogy set in the North of England, and in my life – a book actually called *The North*.

This biography of a great, resourceful man of the North, who filled my life one way or another – if only because I have spent a decade writing his biography and a good thirty years prepping for the task – becomes the third part of the trilogy. All three books, based in a North I lived through and then remembered or invented, piece together a history of certain events that I wanted to discover, and are about making sense of the world I found myself in. The first examined how my father, an uncertain man who was nevertheless sensationally certain of his fate, killed himself, and what that did to me, and my mind and future. The North, it seemed, was never good for the mental health of someone born in the South, and who never found himself comfortable in what appeared to him a faraway land. The second imagined how the North, as an idea, a sequence of events, a place I grew up in, came to be. The third is the official* biography of Tony Wilson, whom I first met weeks after my father killed himself, the story of a definitive, demanding, self-made man who liked to present himself as the brainiest person in Manchester. Perhaps even the all-time brain of the North, which for him meant the brainiest of them all.

Three books presenting my North, passed through the prism of me, my dad – a Kent-born southerner who found himself trapped in the dark, dank, ultimately dangerous North, what turned out for him to be a distant land which he needed to retreat from – and Tony Wilson, who perversely saw the marginalised North as an endless opportunity, the perfect location for spectacular self-advancement.

It may well be that I ended up writing this book about Tony Wilson because my father killed himself – and later on because of another suicide – and to insulate me from the shock of that death, the power of a self-murder which itself never died down, I wrapped myself in writing, which involved a continual sort of investigative problem-solving and a constant engagement with explanation and interpretation.

Writing first of all from inside the North, and writing about northern music in the late 1970s as it produced inside a few months Buzzcocks, the Fall, Magazine and Joy Division, with a lurking, disturbed Morrissey as shadowy immature audience member with ideas above his station, meant very quickly I would be getting to know Tony Wilson, another much less shadowy audience member keen on being something more and actually taking part in things. Here he was, taking shape, fast, leading from the mouth, learning by seeking and blundering, soon to form Factory Records – part record label and part fantasy – with an eccentric troupe of friends, drifters and wishful thinkers, the forceful music impresario, the imposing, eloquent North-West broadcaster, the superlative northern propagandist, the driven, unmanageable dilettante spinning yarns and truth, and last but not least the crafty, charming, unflagging bastard relentlessly urging everyone around him to pay attention to him or else.

* As official as this kind of thing can ever be.

One of his many mantras was a line peculiarly grabbed from the John Ford film *The Man Who Shot Liberty Valance*: 'When the legend becomes fact, print the legend.' He'd stolen that from the writer and broadcaster Terry Christian, but then all of us based in and around Manchester following his lead as journalists, presenters, designers, entrepreneurs, making a living from ideas, were all working for him behind the scenes, part of his writing room, his ideas machine, his publicity strategies, his randomly recruited, sometimes reluctant volunteers.

Over time I would get closer and closer to Tony. Eventually, by the time he died, thirty years after our first meeting, we were close enough for me to be his elected choice to write the biography of his life. There was no official confirmation as such, no grand ceremonial commission, no meeting to go through the details. He never directly asked me.

The suggestion he wanted me to be his official biographer was more to do with the way he behaved towards me over the years, supportively and aggressively, sympathetically and sarcastically, as though he was being both nurturing, generously urging me on as writer and cultural critic, and antagonistic, repeatedly testing me out to ensure I was up to the job. And then there were other possible candidates who he made very clear he didn't want to write it for one reason or another – or he was in the middle of a feud with them – which eventually left me as the last appropriate writer standing. Or sitting in front of my laptop, cursing him for blessing me with this task, which was both a privilege and a punishment. Sometimes all that was written on the screen in front of me was 'He was a bloody bastard.' There was the book, the testimony, the obituary, the summary. Five words. Or two words: 'Fuck him.' However much he embraced you.

And then another two: 'Love him.' However much he would reject you.

He was pushy and pushed me – and many others – around, just to see what happened. He loved to mess around in people's lives, one way or another, even if he wasn't so keen on being at the receiving end, very keen on deciding how to live his own life.

He challenged me without making it obvious, and sometimes making it too bloody obvious. Not so much like the father I had lost, but definitely like the older brother I never had. I had always wanted to be a writer, since I was thirteen, stuck in slow, ordinary and run-down Stockport a few miles south of Manchester, getting out and about in my mind by starting to read science fiction and the music papers, but I didn't really know what that was going to mean. I didn't think very far ahead. I certainly didn't think ahead to here, now, in my early sixties, still writing, about him for God's sake, someone who was actually the first media professional to tell me, 'You can write, you are a writer.' Perhaps in the end he was more colourful replacement father than imposing elder brother; he was also in his way lining me up for a long-term project.

He had already hired his preferred biographer, almost as soon as I started writing, back in the mid-1970s, even if we sometimes didn't talk for years at a time, even as he began to feature in book after book about the times, which would never have been written unless in the middle of it all there was Wilson. I was one of his discoveries, part of a greater collection, selected before I even knew he had his eye on me, before it seemed inevitable he would be important enough – or perhaps merely likely enough – to be the subject of a biography. The subject of a biography who always lived his life with his biography in mind, so that he lived with a certain grandness, adjusting and embellishing his life as he went along, even as he made it increasingly difficult to know the real life that was going on in his head while his public life, as hero and villain, unfolded.

All in all, it was a set-up. He trapped me. He arranged it so that I was, in his plan, whether he was talking to me or not, his approved biographer. He ushered me into position, amused, sometimes irritated but vaguely tolerant when I strayed from the subject of Manchester in my books and essays, knowing I would always return – and I never even realised it. He made sure Manchester was always calling my name.

Over the years, Wilson insisted that the best things I ever wrote were all Manchester-based, as he covertly encouraged me to write the ultimate Manchester-based biography, all about him, from Manchester with love, and other miscellaneous emotions. I never heard anything from him about my non-Manchester writing – even when, as benefactor, as part of the ongoing hiring process, he interviewed me in front of an audience about a book I wrote imagining a history of pop music. He never actually said anything for or against the book, somehow failing to mention it even as we talked about it for an hour. There wasn't much Manchester in it. He tolerated me writing about things set away from Manchester, but they weren't of much interest to him.

These were the pieces he considered some sort of preface to the book about him, all of them from and about Manchester:

1. The sleeve notes I had written in 1977 for a ten-inch compilation album featuring music from the last-ever two nights of one of his favourite Manchester venues, the Electric Circus, in the middle of edge-of-city wasteland, a nervy, rambling bus ride from the city centre into the coarse concrete void of Collyhurst. Almost overnight, after a few years as a more prosaic rock venue, this became a classic local punk club, which may have been tricky to travel to but which was wonderful once you got there. You really had to believe in something to become a regular. Outsiders suddenly found a place where they were on the inside.

As a legendary, perversely loved venue, it was made even more perfect by being shut down in 1977 by an alarmed local council – ostensibly for safety reasons – after inflamed, apparently city-threatening visits from the likes of the Sex Pistols, the Clash and the Damned, or possibly simply because the venue, as magnificent as it was for those of us needing to experience this urgent new music in the sort of venue that itself seemed built for chaos more than a reasonable night out, was so run-down it was falling to pieces. Floors were liable to sink, ceilings about to collapse, toilets gateways to stinking sodden hell; certain staircases and hallways led nowhere.

The building was perhaps only held together by the sweat – and spit – of the audience and the intensity of the performers. The compilation of music recorded over two nights of protest at the venue's suspicious-seeming shutting down was released on gimmicky blue vinyl as an early punk cash-in by Virgin Records, not sure how to package it all, so giving it a proto-new wave appearance. It featured the fast-forming sound of a new Manchester:

the Fall fronted by the murky, gnarly Mark E. Smith after mere weeks of performance already stumbling and grumbling across sound and sense in depraved distorted free fall like the Fall would forever sound, and the sound of Joy Division before they were even known as Joy Division, when as earnest, tentative Warsaw they were clumsier with their references, cruder with their music, and the bassist sported a moustache, while the strangely staring singer was starting to move like he really hadn't got much time.

2. My self-published *Out There* fanzine, which became my qualification for pop journalism, produced on the floor of my bedroom, and which took me a year to make and finish – during which time punk started. When I was eighteen, a year seemed as if it was ten years; many times it seemed as though *Out There* would never make it outside my bedroom.

3. An 8,000-word profile of George Best, the doomed football genius from Tony Wilson's beloved Manchester United, which I wrote for the first edition of *Esquire UK* magazine in 1991.

4. The memoir I wrote about my father's suicide, *Nothing*, set very much in my home town and Manchester, also featuring the suicide of Joy Division's Ian Curtis and the appearance of Factory Records, and therefore Tony Wilson, from Didsbury, south Manchester, a short bus ride from Stockport. He appeared in the book as someone inevitably up to something he shouldn't have been doing, in this case planning for the future, showing me the dead body of Ian Curtis lying in rest. He did this, he said – and I apologise to those of you who have read this in almost all the books I have ever written – because I was the one who was going to write the definitive story of Joy Division. And after that, I would be writing the story of Tony Wilson, and how he made his mind up about things, including what should be included in his biography.

5. An essay I wrote about Factory's graphic designer Peter Saville for a collection of his artwork published in 2003, *Designed by Peter Saville*. In

a biased review of the book, Wilson described Saville as the great image-maker and me as the great writer. Very nice. It was a part of his campaign to flatter me into position to be his biographer. He never had anything to say about anything else I did, never even complained to me that I was stealing some of his record label ideas when in early 1984 a record I helped make, 'Relax', by Frankie Goes to Hollywood, reached number one, never congratulated me when the follow-up 'Two Tribes' was number one for nine weeks. That merited the silent treatment. I don't know if he was pissed off, jealous or it just wasn't authentic enough for him. Anything, though, to do with Manchester, and a text would arrive, a phone call, a little compliment, an implied reminder not to forget to register the climax of the whole thing, of our relationship, the story we had shared, his story, made for a book, the story of his life. Some of the stories of his life.

He would consistently describe me as 'the greatest writer of his genera-tion', not necessarily because it was objectively true but to clarify to those whom it may concern that the person commissioned, or condemned, to write his authorised biography was of course the greatest writer of his gen-eration. No one else would do.

I caught him out once when he remarked that in fact the greatest rock writer was Greil Marcus. 'Ah,' he said, as I protested, typically within a split second coming up with an excuse, 'Greil is the greatest *American* writer. You are the greatest British writer.' So negotiated the man who was always split between Buddhist and Catholic, between sincere and insin-cere, tormentor and sweetheart, friend and enemy.

There was so much of him, so much that he revealed as he went about constructing himself first of all as a slightly unruly, jean-clad, undoubt-edly charismatic news-reading local television personality who stood out because his more formally attired television news colleagues clearly knew nothing about pop and art, and he did know something, obviously, if only because his trousers were slightly flared, his wide '60s tie a little devil-may-care loose, and his floppy, cavalier hair parted and hurriedly combed but covering his ears. At the time, around glam, before punk, longer hair on a TV talking head suggested you might, tantalisingly, be connected to the Grateful Dead and Janis Joplin even as you professionally read the local traffic news on a Tuesday evening about unfortunate congestion on the Bury New Road.

He didn't only read the news and host chat shows and game shows. He was so many things, an intellectual blur of action and acting up, which helped make it difficult to say what it was he actually was, to reduce it to a word, a particular occupation, although he was happy to describe himself certainly in the go-getting, go-faster 1980s, when the hippies he'd once been aligned with had been all but obliterated, as 'an entrepreneur'. (A caption presumably supplied by himself in a local newspaper under a photograph of him handing out prizes at a school competition in the late '70s said: *TV presenter, entrepreneur, Marxist, Atheist, Christian.*)

He became fascinated by the deal, and the deal-makers, whether those who had built Manchester since the early nineteenth century, or those who had created the music industry since the 1950s. His commitment was to make things happen, sometimes forcing them to happen, sometimes just putting random things together to see if anything happened, sometimes as delighted by those ideas that didn't quite come off as those that did. The failures ultimately created the circumstances that generated the successes.

The description of him accompanying the photograph by Withington-born Kevin Cummins that resides inside the National Portrait Gallery is *impresario, journalist and broadcaster* – fair enough to a limited degree. Wearing his velvet Shakespeare doublet, he would elaborate, 'What I do I liken to a "little touch of Harry in the night"' – Shakespeare's words for what Prince Hal does when he goes round the camp on the eve of the Battle of Agincourt. 'I'm good at nurturing people, I'm good at encouraging them, and I love doing it. I think it's a good job to do.'

Quite capable of being simultaneously self-effacing and self-aggrandising, he would say, 'I can't write songs, I can't design sleeves, but you could say that I was a Diaghilev figure' – Wilson naturally comparing himself to one of the great twentieth-century despot taste-makers, Sergei Diaghilev, the influential, alchemic, compulsively creative art critic, cultural patron and ballet producer with a knack for controversy, son of a bankrupt vodka-maker who remade himself as the greatest impresario of all time, forming Ballets Russes, which was part dance company, part art movement, reforming dance as elsewhere Satie, Debussy and Ravel were reforming music.

Diaghilev had a gift for collaboration – he worked with the ultimate all-star line-up of Picasso, Matisse, Cocteau and Satie on a (poorly received) cubist ballet, discovered Stravinsky, commissioned a young Coco Chanel. The opportunity to experiment was a greater motivation than finding stable funding, and he often found himself on the edge of bankruptcy even as he believed his taste and style choices were gospel. The greatest avant-garde artist of the early twentieth century was not actually an artist: no wonder Wilson saw parallels with his own activities, making art happen by somehow making room for it, losing money as if that in itself was a form of art.

When Wilson was profiled by *The Cut* magazine in the 1990s, their description was *TV talking head, pop culture conceptualist, entrepreneur and bullshitter*. He admitted it was very accurate, although he missed any reference to his academic side. Fundamentally regarding himself as an academic, analysing and interpreting cultural history through participation, he conceded that *bullshitter* probably covered his intellectual side and academic side.

Wilson's main task in life, the work he committed to the most, his single act of authorship, was as a futurist custodian inventing and displaying a new Manchester that evolved out of an old, ambitious, creative, industrial and scientific Manchester and that placed the city into a wider history. He imagined how the world's first modern city might become the world's first post-modern city. Faced with a city that had lost its way after its industrial heyday and a shattering war, he was committed to recovering its future. It was a mad city, but its madness was gallant. A beautiful city, but its beauty was grim. Chaotic, but everything that happened grew out of a need to solve a problem.

As much as Diaghilev, Wilson was also a descendant of the Fluxus patron, prophet, publicist and brand manager George Maciunas, who was perhaps the greatest outsider avant-garde artist, and non-artist, of the late twentieth century, regarding every object as an event and every event as having an object-like quality. The information-hungry, grandly impertinent Maciunas, expecting everyone to be as fully dedicated as he was to his amorphous movement, was a conduit through which ideas, possibilities and personalities flowed. Like Maciunas, Wilson could be described as beautiful, foolish, dogmatic, charming. Impossible.

Wilson was a figurehead, organiser and galvanising force more than an artist in the conventional sense, changing the world around him through sheer force of taunting, mixed-media personality. He didn't leave behind a physical body of work. His *oeuvre* perhaps consisted of the collectives and spaces which he set up and inspired and in a manner of speaking managed, the events and actions which he curated, the compendiums of works produced by his peers that he helped assemble and market with the instincts of a boisterous social revolutionary.

In one word, his occupation was 'Manchester'. A city big enough to matter in the world and small enough for you to matter in it. A city that could be left to its own devices, but when necessary could stand up if faced with an attack on its essence and instantly demonstrate in its own words its unique character, its underdog wit, its sense of itself. A prime site for dreams, if you happen to be a dreamer. Sometimes, when everything was stripped away, a city of terror.

Manchester was his canvas, and he used this canvas to make more of Manchester, which was also the gallery. It was the representation and the medium, the pencil and the picture, the chisel and the statue, the chord and the harmony. Cities are created by everybody, but some make more of a stand for the nature of a city. A city that for Wilson was always lying ahead. He knew more than many how it takes a community to raise an idea, and that Manchester traditionally contained the right sort of people to be part of that community: pioneers, trendsetters, hipsters, hackers, hustlers, trailblazers, inventors, heretics, creators, problem-solvers, optimists, obsessives, fire-starters, scientists, risk-takers, disrupters, game-changers, explorers and garage heroes . . . people like him, or people he modelled himself on.

After he died, once I had started writing this book, we got even closer, one way or another. Not close like family, or even friends, but close as players collaborating and clashing in the same sometimes preposterous-seeming story that he had set in motion, where he was the dashing lead actor, the compelling primary character. He was the star in a drama that may have been 'local' and based in and around Manchester, but which really was cosmopolitan and universal.

The three or four years since I had started the biography turned into five or six and then seven or eight, but eventually despite myself the book was very nearly finished – and then the problem became that the world had changed so much that a book written about Tony Wilson in 2018 needed to be very different from one written ten or even five years before. I began to think more of how the Tony Wilson of Manchester, of the twentieth century, was taking shape in the twenty-first century, how he would be remembered as a personality, as activist and entrepreneur, and in his own way as artist, academic and anomalous political campaigner, as anarchic champion of lost causes, especially as the longer the twenty-first century went on, the more he was becoming a distant historical figure.

The difference between one era and another – between a striving post-industrial Manchester that Wilson had helped manufacture and a confident post-digital Manchester – became much more distinct during the years I was working on his biography. The differences became particularly striking when a radical Islamist terrorist of Libyan descent set off a shrapnel-laden home-made bomb at the Manchester Arena after a pop concert in May 2017 by Ariana Grande, murdering 23 and wounding 139. Another Manchester instantly appeared, one that didn't contain Wilson and his influence as much as the Manchester that had formed since the 1960s, his contribution accelerating during his prime decades of activity, the 1970s, '80s and '90s, seeing the city as a place of connectivity, not simply territory.

The book had to take into account this new Manchester, which was replacing Wilson's ideal city with another version, a place where he was hidden but in plain sight if you knew where to look, and so there was another delay as I adjusted certain parts to make sure Wilson existed inside this violently remade twenty-first-century Manchester as much as his abstractly produced, modernised Manchester.

Wilson inside this post-bomb Manchester was becoming a figure from the twentieth century in the way that the great entrepreneurs, inventors, architects, scientists and artists from the nineteenth century saw their influence become more distant and less specific and visible during the twentieth. He was part of the city, because it existed in lots of ways because of how he impressed himself upon it and updated its radical, enterprising purpose, but he was also apart from the city as lived in and experienced by new, younger generations.

The influence of the nineteenth-century Manchester innovators was huge, their say over the city's future significant for better or worse, but their lives were very much from another world, another time. With Wilson, as a twentieth-century equivalent, I didn't feel this so much in 2010, when the twenty-first century hadn't really begun, but eight, nine years later, when it blew up in our faces, it was much more obvious.

The world he inhabited on the way to making up a new Manchester had become a very different place. Record labels and a certain sort of revolutionary zeal – and the agile marrying of entertainment with counterculture vision, performance with philosophy, an imaginative mutant intermingling of high art with low art – had themselves become period pieces, mashed into the shredded flicker of constant content and glory-seeking self-revelation the internet had become.

And then, as I was halfway through a sentence, the world stopped, as if tomorrow – a tomorrow that characters like Wilson had so passionately envisaged – had been closed. The world was made different inside a few months as a pandemic separated time and history itself into what happened before the event and what happened after. Manchester along with the rest of the world was about to change again, as much as it had during the nineteenth century and after the Second World War. Remembering, perhaps even immortalising someone like Wilson became something different again; history had been transformed with viral speed, and the book needed more attention, which led to more delay.

Of course, there would always be changes that would mean the book was continually being overtaken by events – at the beginning of 2020, one of Wilson's closest comrades at Factory Records, one of his closest friends, advisers and conceptual partners, the influential designer and artist Peter Saville, received a CBE, one step under a knighthood. (He was along with the more elusive and ethereal Alan Erasmus the last surviving member of the original Factory operation – Saville visualised the company, but it was Erasmus who was from the very beginning its ragged, glorious conscience.)

The grandness of Peter Saville CBE – he would no doubt want to re-design the award – was particularly absurd and weirdly splendid if a bit iffy to those few of us that were there at the very modest, sequestered beginnings of Factory. It started as a fanciful even delusional idea in the middle of an excursive, stoned conversation between friends, almost nothing more than a hypothetical talking point, a mad dream about doing something, somehow, that had never been done before, and might have gone nowhere if at least one of these friends hadn't made his mind up that the person who follows the crowd will usually go no further than the crowd. This led to a rough, unready, temporary venue in a cornered, dere-lict part of town elegantly and enigmatically promoted by posters Saville designed in a world of his own as though he was advertising the very soul of modernism – those of us there at the birth of Factory, where ideas were being manufactured, would be sniffily dismissed by prosaic pop star Noel Gallagher of Oasis, on the outside of this particular club, as 'arty types'. In Manchester of all places. What could be worse.

This CBE had to be folded into the book, because Saville was given his first break by Wilson in one of his roles as intuitive mentor, encour-aging the finest often unlikeliest of talents, and it was something else that helped measure as much as anything how far Wilson's work had travelled, as psycho-socio-cultural planner, even after he had died and become a shadow in time, even as the world was changing so rapidly. The idea that Saville had received such an award made you wonder if a still-living Tony

Wilson would eventually also have received an award; even been offered a knighthood, which perhaps he would have taken great delight in refusing. Or strange delight in accepting, the ultimate Manchester maverick socially tamed, if not politically, preparing the way for a few years as mayor of Greater Manchester, a job it sometimes seemed was his destiny, if only in a dream of Manchester.

Peter Saville CBE's love of typography and belief in design as a method of interpreting reality and fighting against ugliness helped change the appearance of things around the world, as filtered through commercial reality, because Wilson loved his obsessive commitment to the appearance of things. He hired him in 1978 at the very start of Factory to work on some posters and a record sleeve that may have been the extent of the project, before one thing led to another, and a Factory catalogue that would eventually include 501 products, events, scandals, asides, distractions, statements and follies. Number 51 – Fac 51 – was perhaps the most notorious of the 501, the Haçienda nightclub symbolising the implausibly adventurous spirit of Factory, which significantly adjusted the cultural and musical reputation of the city.

Wilson and Saville both believed that everything in the world is made just so that we can manage to live in the world. To them design in one form or another was part of everything.

Eventually, this strange, fruitful partnership led without their direct participation to the commissioning in 2015 of a grand arts centre in the city that would be called The Factory. The politician who was in charge of releasing the millions of pounds to finance it as part of a hopeful but ultimately futile 'Northern Powerhouse' attempt to boost the economy and prospects of the North, the then Conservative Chancellor of the Exchequer George Osborne, only saw the centre as a practical proposition when it was suggested it be named after the small, idiosyncratic, often quite contrary record label Wilson helped found. An arts centre in Manchester with an ordinary name didn't mean much to Osborne, with his own fond nostalgic memories of Factory and the Haçienda. Branding it with the Factory name – the name of a company that actually eventually stumbled to an unceremonious bankrupt end – was worth millions. It is worth noting that the friend of Wilson who originally suggested the name Factory, Alan Erasmus, was put out that this ostentatious arts centre was going to be called The Factory and not Factory. It was pointed out by Peter Saville CBE that this was because the new building wasn't going to be Factory, it was going to be The Factory, an entirely different prospect. Factory became what it became because of such disputes.

At times, it seemed like a race to see what would be finished first, The Factory Arts Centre or this book, and the delay in the completion of The Factory, as costs escalated and problems accrued, as if it had been infected by the chaotic spirit of Factory Records, led to another delay with the biography, based around an original plan that the book would end with the conclusion of this ambitious project. A whimsical regenerative civic gesture inspired by the ambition of Tony Wilson, a dramatic city-centre cathedral of the arts, a reach-for-the-skies symbol of Manchester's creative energy, built where the Granada Television studios once stood, where Tony Wilson presented television programmes which led, on the side, to his role in releasing records and running a nightclub, would be the end of this story of Tony Wilson.

Sometimes it seemed as though the slowness of a complex multi-million-pound construction project, the accumulation of missed deadlines and budgetary issues, and then the year of Covid, was infecting me, in my isolation; and in the late-night mania that occurs when working on a biography about someone like Tony Wilson I would begin to think I was somehow the cause of the problem. If I didn't finish, then the work on the building wouldn't be finished; if the building wasn't finished, then this book wouldn't be. Actually, it was all Wilson's fault, who even as his sense of destiny was unshakeable considered the perfect time for something to happen to be between haste and delay.

Eventually, if the book was to be real, there had to be a cut-off point, or I could keep on extending the deadline until, in fact, I reached a deadline of a completely different sort: something else that was happening as I worked on the book was that I had, without really noticing, drifted from what I could claim at the beginning was young middle age – youth vaguely spotted in the rear-view mirror – to what some would claim was more or less the beginning of old age, youth lost forever. Old northern cultural colleagues such as Peter Shelley of Buzzcocks, Mark E. Smith of the Fall, C. P. Lee of Alberto y Lost Trios Paranoias and Andy Gill of Gang of Four were dying around me. It started to look as though I might actually be running out of time.

And now that it is done, after all that, of course I have to explain myself, even if only to those in Wilson's orbit who had been waiting for ten years for this biography to appear. Perhaps even explain myself to Tony, who has been with me all the way, the most patient of anyone, who had put so much into the book, just by being alive, and then by dying. When I felt that the book had terminally fallen apart, I had no more to give, he would still pull me and it through with the sheer force of his personality, which death had done little to diminish.

And of course, this book would have been his favourite of all the things I have written. He would have loved that this book makes a case for his significant role in social and cultural history, where he liked to think he belonged. He would have been delighted that it was such a Manchester enterprise.

I did begin to sense that even he was getting a little ghost-twitchy as the bomb hit, and the virus spread, and the world held its breath, and reality was rearranged, worried that he might be forgotten in the fallout of it all as pre-2020 became an almost quaint long-lost alternative universe, one that might get replaced altogether by new forms of truth and post-truth. He needed to nudge me from beyond the grave, to get it sorted out, because the whole point of being the subject of a biography is that you don't want to be forgotten, whatever happens after you die. The man who went out of his way to make history does not want to be written out of history. The life of a man who loved books would not be complete without there being an official biography. He wouldn't let me give up, taking up space in my mind even in death.

One of Wilson's credos was that the best work was only worth showing when it was ready. Take as long as it takes. Really. He could think quickly on his feet and be completely composed in the middle of an important, complicated live broadcast, but he was quite understanding when it came to imaginative work being late. When it's ready . . . As long as it takes. In years to come, no one will care whether it arrived in time to meet its deadline, only that it was the best it could be.

'But surely, Paul,' I felt him whisper, or imagined a curt midnight text flying in from his present inexplicable location, urging me on even as the world took tumbles around me or entered a limbo so unprecedented that 'unprecedented' was nominated as word of the year. The world almost ended, maybe books themselves are coming to an end, who knows how long his kind of erratic, self-involved exceptionalism is permitted even in hindsight, after The Event the past will stay the same but people will look back at it differently, because they will be different, reality will be reimagined . . . 'this book must surely be finished. There is always history, one way or another. The biography must be written.'

And it now is. It's ready, Tony. You were right all along, of course. It was never in doubt. I had it in me. You knew it. Now I know it. Here you are, Tony.

It's here. It's what you planned all along. *Permitte divis cetera*. Leave the rest to the gods.

The readiness is all.
HAMLET

I believe in getting into hot water. It keeps you clean.
G. K. CHESTERTON

I would rather die of passion than of boredom.
EMILE ZOLA

What's beautiful is the voice of small groups having influence.
HENRI LEFEBVRE

Nostalgia is dead tissue.
MALCOLM MCLAREN

Part I: Before

One: The subject of this book materialises

Alea jacta est. (The die is cast.)
JULIUS CAESAR

I am going to try and write down a book I have been writing in my head for ages. It is about Tony Wilson, a lively, life-loving, individualistic expert in communications, imagination, people, history and media who combined a great many roles in his life, bringing together forces seemingly at odds with each other. Outspoken, stubborn and patriotic native of the North, Manchester through and through, loving a response whether love or hate to the things he did and said, Wilson raced through his life as if determined to escape the time of day, always in a rush to get somewhere else, doing something because he had an urge to do it, inventing the reasons later, and sometimes in my head the book begins this way: he was a mystery to himself.

Sometimes, it begins another way.

Fuck 'em: what the skilled quotologist and very quotable Tony Wilson would say about people who didn't like or get something he'd done, or simply didn't like or get him, with his surely fraudulent, bamboozling ways. Fuck 'em, said with a wrong-footing hardcore glint in his eye and a wide, sly, possibly fanatical grin set up to wind up the unconvinced, the sensitive, the boring, the po-faced, those standing in the way of his idea of a revolution.

This is a book, incidentally, that will mention the word 'revolution' over one hundred times. While I am at it, to help you get your bearings about what you are about to receive, 'intellectual' will appear over fifty times. The word 'praxis' pops up a few times as well. It was one of Wilson's favourite words, one often left hanging in the air as he held forth, or entertained an argument, or cheerfully confused an easily confused musician. Perhaps one of his greatest achievements was turning up in the Wikipedia page for 'praxis', explaining its possible meaning – 'action oriented towards changing society' – alongside Plato, Aristotle, St Augustine, Immanuel Kant, Søren Kierkegaard, Karl Marx, Antonio Gramsci, Martin Heidegger and Hannah Arendt – in whose company, making up his own reality, he liked to think he truly belonged.

He would love to define the word, if it became obvious to him that someone present wasn't sure what he was talking about, or he just wanted to show off. 'In Ancient Greece,' he would intone, '"praxis" referred to activity engaged in by free men. As Aristotle would say, [further warning: as it is written by me and it is about Tony Wilson this is the kind of music biography where Aristotle appears in the index] there is theory, where the end goal is truth. There is *poiesis*, where the end goal is production. And there is the practical – praxis, meaning "to do" – where the end goal is action. Some said Marxism was the "philosophy of praxis". There is no future without Marx, by the way. It will always be a mistake not to read and reread and discuss Marx. He's always there, waiting in the wings. Marxism is always open, because there are always new experiences, there are always new facts, including facts about the past. Anyway, essentially, what we're taking about with praxis is how do we get from *there* to *here*? How do we move forward?' Then he would get up and go and do something. He was always doing something, getting as near as he could to the heart of things, at least as they occurred to him.

Oh yes, the exceedingly quotable Marx, who himself was certain he was not a Marxist, mentioned in these pages perhaps as many times as Manchester, where he came to learn and work with his buddy Friedrich Engels on a proposal for the idea of communism, immersing themselves in books at Manchester's Chetham's Library, drinking for hours in pubs like the Grapes in Eccles: 'History is nothing but the actions of men in pursuit of their ends.'

Manchester will be mentioned, I will make sure of it – Wilson will – almost 700 times. He loved how it had in effect been invented out of very little, by a rousing collective of planners, dreamers, publishers, printers, builders, broadcasters, designers, schemers, writers, fantasists, feminists, drunks, addicts, scientists, commuters, teachers, enemies, critics and workers. It was as much as anything a city always experimenting with the idea of what a city is, and his personality favoured the experimental.

Fanaticism, Wilson would say, consists of redoubling your efforts when you have forgotten your aim. It's the only way to put an end to the doubts that constantly trouble the human soul; it's overcompensation for doubt, really. Whenever a clever phrase was wandering about in need of a good parent, he would adopt it, seizing on anything that glitters.

He could be terribly nice, and quite obnoxious. Very approachable, and an enemy of humility. A little mean-spirited, and entirely loveable. Bullying, and supportive. Cutting, and cuddly. Pompous, and pleasant. Black-hearted, and a heart of gold. Gentleman, and scoundrel. Family man, and emotionally unavailable loner. A damned nuisance, and irre-placeable. Minor celebrity – since he was twenty-three – and iconoclastic conceptualist. He found it hard to agree with what you were saying even if he agreed with what you were saying.

'I beg to differ . . .'

He could mix effrontery with patently insincere self-abasement, chuckling at his own insincerity, confident that candour would disarm all criticism, but not really caring if it didn't. He generated great energy from push-ing against something, from defying anyone who resisted his conniving charm. He was still having schoolboy crushes on things and people in his forties and fifties, right up to his last disintegrating moments alive, he's only fifty-seven, those last heartbeats, the epic last breath, catching him out as he realised he was taking it, savouring it and sickened by it, all that life coming to this, and is probably now enthusing to whoever will listen – what else have they got to do? – about the discreet, unfathomable length of eternity, how everything fits inside a single moment. Eternity as his lat-est fantastic discovery. He'll give it its own catalogue number, just like the records, and objects, and souvenirs collected on the record label that was a major part of what became a significant part of his life's work, the flawed, fantastic Factory Records, a record label somehow committed to avoiding all certainties. When he was alive he proved time and time again that he could keep an awful lot in his head. Why not now he was dead?

He liked detail but loved to keep things vague. Phony order bored even disgusted him. He furiously cultivated a renegade persona and seemed to welcome tension from wherever into the structure of his life. He was at peace with himself, and yet also at war with himself. He possessed a relentless fascination with how information gets distributed and interpreted. He could be defined as a reactionary plagiarist of the situationists, brazenly and tackily ripping off certain tricks of their trade, or a knowing, sympathetic inheritor of the radical traditions that the situationists themselves plagiarised. Deadly serious, and madly flippant. Running against the current, and running with the current. Jumping on the bandwagon, blowing up the bandwagon. The arsonist, and the firefighter.

He was a kind of influencer back when there was no such thing, or no such label. An influencer when they were few and far between, not an invasion, an influencer when they were operating in a much more rudimentary broadcasting system, when messages and opinions were transmitted as much by word of mouth and sheer force of personality as through instant technology. It was as though he was aware of and exploiting the notion that he was living in the final few years of the self-confident, self-certified creative individual being seen as an iconoclast, a special case, before they became the mainstream, before the world was full of stuff and energised, energetic, passionately misled sharers of stuff, and everyone could grab hold of a microphone and a keyboard and act like they knew things, if not everything, become a creative, a brand, an adviser, an instrument of their own promotion, sometimes even some sort of social therapist.

Born a Catholic, then wanting to become as good a Buddhist as he could, always with a desire for spiritual vitality, always looking for fulfilment and meaning, noting the common characteristics between the two, and also the differences. Buddhism offered a non-dogmatic and seemingly open-minded alternative to the Catholic Church's absolute approach to truth; it combined the mysticism he found appealing buried at the heart of Catholicism with a less organised, more illuminating mysticism.

A man of the people who was never quite a fan of the people, or vice versa. A daytime-friendly minor celebrity, and a stubborn, hectoring moral philosopher making a major contribution to the rampant regeneration of a city that had fallen on hard times.

A city mirroring our higher state, not just sheltering us from rain and wind, a place measuring time, on the make, full of people rushing in and puffing out of a station's mouth, a place always going somewhere even if just into itself, somewhere he decided could be built using language, design and music, 'built out of a poet's dreams', always faced with old threats, enigmatic enemies, dangerous others and the violence that takes us by surprise, hitting us like a shock wave, always a part of a great city's history.

'Living cities never stay still,' he would say, or someone once did, and he remembered and forgot to say it wasn't him who said it. A city is stimulating and agitating, entertaining and frightening, welcoming and cold; some are lost inside it, some know their way around. 'Living in cities is an art,' he read somewhere, and then forgot where. 'Whatever is done to a city, it will spring up again like magic.'

The city as wandered through and wondered about by Wilson was what it seemed to be, made up of shops, roads, stations, libraries, offices, bus stops, cafes, parks, canals, bridges, factories, skyscrapers, markets, halls, car parks, pubs and arenas, but it was also a poem, an hallucination, a series of philosophies emerging in the shadows, centuries of colossal history colliding sometimes even exploding in one street, radical energy secreted in darkness, over the border of legality, a place not only mapped out and organised by the politicians, businessmen, entrepreneurs, planners and academics, but by those progressive, iconoclastic, problem-solving thinkers, pleasure-seekers, artists, outlaws, vandals, psychedelic explorers and conceptualists who ultimately contribute the most to how things sound, feel, move, appear, warp and illuminate our lives.

He never made it easy on the way to getting across what he wanted to say, either because he didn't really know what he was doing and was making it up as he went along, or because there was resplendent method in his madness. His crusading, costumed, media-savvy, sound-bite-friendly enthusiasm for people, things, ideas and places could be contagious, and sometimes too damned chaotic and unmoored, too complex and ambiguous, his suggestions and recommendations, his general, non-stop philosophical bantering and polyglot obsession admittedly sometimes deliciously sensible, or utterly, annoyingly aggravating.

He never made it easy to work out who and what he was, and exactly what he was up to, even as it seemed unsubtle and obvious. Inconsistency was a central part of his belief system, something he relished and used as a way to induce creative vitality. He wanted even needed to plunge headlong into society, to feel its thrills, dangers and delights, its chaos and disorder, and from there edit events almost as soon as they had happened to suit his perspective, his views.

Here he is, holding court really for his own ends in a way that might in the end connect the earth-moving guitar-playing of his beloved Vini Reilly, who used his music to make endless spiralling maps of the cosmos, with the Renaissance and the sixteenth-century Polish astronomer, mathematician, clergyman and polymath Nicolaus Copernicus's formal introduction of the then very controversial idea that the sun, not the earth, was at the centre of our solar system.

He spoke in a kind of fruity, breathless rush, tinged with impatience that he could not simply beam his thoughts into your mind, a total conviction that you will of course agree with everything he had to say and be grateful he shared it all with you.

'What we think of as modern society,' explained Wilson, 'unfolded in the fourteenth, fifteenth and sixteenth centuries, with the idea of the Renaissance as the birth of modernity. It's all about the prototype of the modern world, as social patterns developed that were linked to a scientific outlook, social improvement and economic development, where individualism was discovered. You can draw parallels with Manchester in the nineteenth century as it moves in sixty years from being a modest market town to being at the centre of history. Copernican astronomy can be seen as the starting point of a secularised, rationalistic view of the state, tempered by bourgeois-humanistic notions of liberalism, individualism, human rights and democracy . . .'

Here he is, going back to his roots, lecturing one of the bands he managed, or one of the bands on one of his record labels, or someone who worked under or with him in some capacity, or talking to himself, or talking to a camera, which he would often find in front of him, something he was used to, at a time when talking into a camera seemed a specialist act, needing a certain sort of nerve and an actual form of expertise. Not everyone could do it. Just a few. Wilson was one of the few, and one of the reasons is because of how great a talker he was. He would start talking, and carry on for as long as necessary, for as long as anyone listened, or even didn't listen – *he* was listening, in love with his words, and once he was absorbed in something, an idea, an anecdote, a part of history, he would just keep talking. He talked in paragraphs. He talked in chapters.

Where did it all start for Wilson, the fabulous talker, the exuberant historian keen to explain everything and put it all in context, to dazzle you with knowledge, enterprise, determination? It started in Germany. The Manchester he came from, celebrated, sold and sensationalised was as much influenced and shaped by Germany and the Germans who came to the city to embrace its modern mills and captive workers at the same time as Marx and Engels were in town.

His mother's family were German émigrés, her grandfather Herman Maximillian Knupfer arriving in 1900 after a trip to America to avoid the conscription Germany introduced in 1899. One of the British places you would travel to during the Victorian era was Manchester, suddenly a city of significance, and its expanding surroundings. Whalley Range became known as Little Germany, its substantial houses built by German immigrants in the 1870s and '80s. Manchester's famous Hallé Orchestra, the world's first fully professional symphony orchestra, had been founded in 1857 by the German-born pianist and conductor Karl Hallé, friend to Chopin, Liszt and Berlioz, socialising with Wagner and Berlioz, fleeing Paris for Manchester in 1848 to escape the revolution. Not long after he arrived, he anglicised his name from Karl to Charles.

It was a Manchester calico printer who recommended Hallé come over to Manchester, considering him 'the fittest man to stir the city's dormant taste for the arts'. Thinking of himself as an educator as much as a musician, Hallé would become the first principal of the Royal Manchester College of Music, which he helped found in 1893, believing there was no reason Manchester couldn't become a musical centre of excellence.

Wilson once said he'd discovered that for many years at the end of the 1800s and beginning of the 1900s the only language you would hear during interval drinks at a Hallé performance was German. 'Manchester was a German town,' he would say. The German element was a major reason why Manchester was such a music city. 'The second was its openness. It would welcome music quicker than most places, from Hallé's classical music in the nineteenth century to pop, psychedelia, blues and soul in the 1960s, punk and disco in the '70s and Detroit and Chicago house in the '80s. We were never suspicious of the new. It's a city that was best when it looked outwards rather than inwards, so it would never become a backwater.'

Soon after arriving in Salford, Wilson's grandfather, his mother's father, apprenticed himself to a local jeweller and watchmaker. He inherited some money from his family in the small silver-mining town of Freiberg in Saxony, eastern Germany, and when the shop owner died purchased the shop. His brothers Karl and Edgar came to Salford to help out, and the brothers ran three jewellers called Knupfers distributed around the city. Wilson's German ancestry was important to him, and he once drove to Freiberg to see where his family came from. He had the address of a long-lost great-aunt. He knocked on her door, but no one answered.

Wilson once explained to me the roots of his and Manchester's Germanness. 'Up until the end of the nineteenth century Germans were the largest foreign minority in the country – and were the second-largest behind Russians and the Poles all the way up to the First World War . . . The German community in Manchester grew as the city did, they were attracted by the cotton and ancillary industries and were a striking presence in Manchester, central to the development of cosmopolitan Manchester. Wider political and philosophical ideals began to materialise out of their exile.

'It's in Mrs Gaskell's *North and South* – her cotton-mill owner talks of belonging to Teutonic blood, with much of their spirit, with life not being solely about enjoyment, but as a time for action and exertion – "our glory and beauty arise out of our inward strength, which makes us victorious over material resistance and over greater difficulties still".

'The German commercial community was the most significant cosmopolitan element in the bourgeoisie of Manchester up to the First World War, transforming the cultural and intellectual life of the city. German industrialists and merchants brought with them the sensibility of the educated middle classes of the German states, and they were a vital element in the establishment of cultural institutions in the city – they created a link between Manchester and Lancashire and the European mainstream, and as power in the country was decentralised during the Victorian era it was regional cities such as Manchester with this new outside injection and the creation of provincial elites that defined much of the idea of the middle class.

'The learned, cosmopolitan German presence helped reinforce Manchester's developing regional identity. The local radical sensibility identified with the struggles of liberals, progressives and reformers in Germany – it was a natural fit. A belief in the importance of local government, the sense that the new Manchester elite were battling for more control over their own affairs in an over-centralised state. It was something that Germany could warn them about, the threat to individual liberty from the state.

'There was a shared love for liberty, and there was definitely an absorption of German institutional templates . . . the reforming German approach to education was also an influence on local attitudes . . . manufacturing, mercantile and professional German families retained their connection through trading and holidays, and they continued to be influenced by German culture, which became strong in Manchester. The buildings, public and private, being massive and durable, that was the German influence on the city, to represent a certain kind of truth.'

Sometimes, when he was excited about something, when he felt he knew enough about whatever it was he was on about, you couldn't shut him up.

As the writer, critic, poet and one-time TV collaborator of Wilson, Clive James, once wrote from the clear, superior position of his own spiky, neatly summarising brilliance, Tony Wilson was brilliant . . . unfortunately there was no other word for him.

This could mean that any book about Wilson finishes here, wrecked by his incendiary and irreverent brilliance, which shone, and burnt, like the sun, which often goes dark, and how scary, and intimidating, this brilliance could be if you thought about it, and then had to explain it; really, this book *begins* here, with his complex brilliance, which dearly needs explaining, which involves finding other words, because it contained so many contradictions and such blarney, which made his relationships with friends, family, colleagues and enemies, with his work, his fame, his lovers, his bands, continually fraught, on a love-and-hate knife-edge between productive and catastrophic, and any explaining involves approaching the brilliance at something of an angle. He tore through people and their lives, leaving them at the side of his story, involved but apart, never entirely with him or even close to him, because it was hard to get close to someone always making a move, here, there and over there, always a few moves ahead, one step beyond, winning as much independent ground for himself as possible. They could only watch as he performed, and try in their own way to keep up, and work out what was happening, their lives very different because they were within reach, within the span of his life, and his lonely, intimidating mind.

He was always closely involved in the writing of his own story, an impulsive expert at taking control of the details, of the direction of a sequence of events, even if he rarely knew how things were going to turn out – and preferred it that way, loving, absolutely needing, the unexpected in his life, however disruptive. He was a hyperactive, hedonistic master of setting things in motion, whatever their possible value or virtue, just to see what would happen, conceptually planting the seeds of his own creation. He doggedly stretched reality as far as it could go without breaking when the facts didn't fit. To go beyond the stop-at-nothing brilliance, and everything else, which might be nothing else, to escape his hard-boiled interference, somehow, you have to take him, still mobile after death, still ricocheting through history, by surprise.

Wilson read the local news, interviewed politicians and pop stars and spoke into TV cameras like he was born to it, hosted quiz shows like it was beneath him but you've got to earn a living, managed pop groups as though it was an underestimated art form, stole and adapted the quips, quotes and views of others as part of the collage of his life, tackled community and personal problems with a politician's slickness and/or incompetence, became the spokesman for a record label that became a work of conceptual art in itself, all of it twisted into something greater, and rarer, because he easily combined all these apparently incompatible roles and created a character whose fundamental belief was that difficulties strengthen the mind. 'We cannot live better,' he would say, wearing a mask of Socrates, 'than in seeking to become better.' If he had somewhere along the line been asked the question 'Would you rather be divinely beautiful, dazzlingly clever or angelically good?' his answer would of course have been 'Dazzlingly clever.'

Two: Kindred spirits and family circumstances

Mutatis mutandis. (Once the necessary changes have been made.)

If you boil down the original names given to the writer, musician, essayist, satirist, novelist and intellectual exhibitionist Anthony Burgess at his confirmation – John Anthony Burgess Wilson – you can end up with Anthony Wilson, which can then become Tony Wilson. To get to one sardonic, self-mythologising, teasing, sneering, smart-alec, me-against-the-world prankster misfit Tony Wilson of Manchester, it helps to go through another sardonic, self-mythologising, teasing, sneering, smart-alec, me-against-the-world prankster misfit Tony Wilson of Manchester, and any other antic, boastful Tony Wilsons who might be lying around in the history of pop culture, exulting in and also resenting their outsider status.

First of all, there is the diversely talented, compulsively productive Burgess Wilson, born in 1917, not the subject of this book but one who paved the way, opened the door, a prince, a king, a champion of books, who began his life in humble Dickensian surroundings as part of a Catholic family above a tobacconist-newsagent in Harpurhey, three grimy, untended miles north of noisy, whirling, soot-blackened, rust-tarnished Manchester city centre, discovering the thrills of creative mischief as a solitary, intensely curious young boy, the avid student desperate to escape his social origins, the Lancastrian internationalist who never lost his young love for hotpot (a dish born of poverty and leftover scraps), whose work however conceptually removed from the city and century of his birth always pulsed with the civic socialism of Manchester, a thorn in the side of the Establishment, oppressed by the sterile demands of respectability, a hard-working, villainised Shakespeare obsessive who naturally aspired to know everything, a fierce appreciator of the innovations of modernism who believed in bold, persistent experimentation, believing, like his hero James Joyce, that geographical peripherality is the precondition of cultural centrality, who thought that over-planning was fatal to creativity, who lived on and off but mostly on for music, loving to set the needle crackling on side one of his favourite record, whose first volume of autobiography was called *Little Wilson and Big God*, enlightenment and insight bolting everywhere.

However hard he searched, he never found a remotely successful metaphysical substitute for the Catholicism that limited and liberated him, and couldn't shake off the insane feeling that his soul was stained indelibly with sin. Once a Catholic, you are always a Catholic, whatever else happens to you, however much you learn, fight, evade, spend your life negotiating with how you were taught that pleasure is a bad thing, finally defeating the crushing, irrational notion. Catholic forever. Even if you come to the conclusion that the Catholic Church is the greatest hoax ever perpetrated on a gullible mankind. You have found faith. It has found you, and it will not let you go. As a Catholic, you feel marginalised because you are in a minority, but also superior, feeling in possession of the transcendent truth, something pressed inside you since before you were even born. What chance did you have? And from an early stage as a young child you learn all about the power of art, all those church paintings and icons of Christ.

There was no such thing as heaven, Burgess Wilson decided, but there was very definitely a hell. His stamina, developed with a striver's respect for honest toil, was immense.

In the wickedly prophetic and transgressive world of Burgess Wilson's most famous novel, *A Clockwork Orange*, his most widely read book in the white light of Stanley Kubrick's incandescent film transformation, this gratified consumer of eighty cigarettes a day with a qualified approval of the smoking of cannabis renamed cigarettes 'cancers'. At a literary festival in 1992, presenting a talk on translation thirteen months before his own death at seventy-six, fourteen years before the death of Tony Wilson, a flashy, dashing life suddenly cut short by cancer at fifty-seven, Anthony Burgess wryly announced that he himself was 'shortly to be translated'.

So it goes.

*

Burgess, this other Wilson, once said, as though speaking, roughly speaking, on behalf of them both, 'I am a pessimist but believe that the world has much solace to offer: love, food, music, the immense variety of race and language, literature and the pleasure of artistic creation.'

It was as if he was aware if only in a dream of the younger, counterfeit Wilson, who always acted with the unshakeable, self-appointed authority of an insatiable intellectual, tangled up with a curious journalist's driven need to entertain and inform and an egoist's desire to try and mould public opinion even as he flew in the face of it. A younger, equally ambitious, post-war Tony Wilson, born thirty-three ruinous years after Burgess, a few rain-soaked pungent-smelling bombed-out smoke-stained tram-lined people-jammed miles away from his own unsavoury inner-city birthplace, not far from the factory making sewing thread in Weaste where the twenty-two-year-old Fred Engels was sent by his rich businessman father in 1842.

Burgess and Wilson once met, in this or some parallel universe, but then Tony Wilson as personality and impresario met a lot of famous people in all walks of life, so you could begin to believe it did actually happen. He really did meet Sophia Loren, and flirted a little with her about the ladder in her stockings, and he met the Pope, for God's sake, and flirted a little with him about papal infallibility, so why not Anthony Burgess? He flirted a little with him about moral conscience, and how far you can take individual freedom before it destroys the freedoms of others.

This meeting to some extent is why Tony Wilson became Anthony Wilson – and then needed to slip an 'H' in between for further clarity, or perhaps further superiority. Anthony Burgess was known to those that really knew him as Tony – and of course to some extent this meant he also was a Tony Wilson.

One Tony Wilson felt that he needed to put some distance between himself and the other, especially because the other had a definite international reputation, and so he became, on a whim, Anthony Wilson. To further confuse things, after making a local name for himself as Tony Wilson, he then became Anthony H. Wilson. He could do this a little more easily than most people because as a television presenter his name would regularly appear in the credits of programmes he had appeared on. He could suddenly decide, as he did, that he now wanted to be known as Anthony H. Wilson, and his name could appear this way at the end of his programmes, shows and bulletins. The majority of people would have to work a lot harder to abruptly and successfully change their name, without this visible and somehow official way of saying, from now on, 'I am someone else.'

When he did this, it seemed to those in the city and region where he was most known a complete confirmation of the ego and eccentricity of someone who was both abused and admired, often by the same people. As Tony so suddenly became Anthony H., jaws hit the floor. Plenty were tickled by the idea that he had extended and glorified his name, plenty were given further ammunition for how and why they mocked him, feeling superior to the man in town who acted the most superior. It was difficult to take seriously, the way he upgraded his name in much the same way he would upgrade his cars, so that he jumped from the battered, stained Ford he would drive in his early twenties to the shiny, fuck-off Jag he would drive in his early thirties. Status meant a lot to someone who in other ways was deeply opposed to the oppressive nature of status.

'Tony' had come about, against his wishes, when he was at Cambridge. It was his first byline when he had an article published in the university's student magazine, *Varsity*. Oddly, two sets of deflection; Anthony was the basic getting-stuck-in northern lad, Tony the rare Salford-born stuck-up Cambridge scholar. To his regret, he got labelled with 'Tony' through the 1970s and most of the '80s, until he had the power and sufficient local glory to change it back. He was asked at the time whether he thought a name change might harm his career. 'I don't have much of a career,' he replied, quite happy with the thought. And just in case he was developing something as ordinary as a 'career', a sudden name change might knock it a little out of shape.

On one of the television programmes he was working on at the time he asked for his name to be changed in the credits, so that it would say 'Presented by Anthony H. Wilson', and his producer, now having to call his presenter by a different name, made sure that every single person in the credits also had an 'H' inserted in their name. The people he was working with, who actually liked even loved him, certainly enjoyed working with him, couldn't take the idea seriously. Who else would ever consider such a thing?

Most people would have given up trying to become this new person, but he stuck at it with typical stubbornness and a typical indifference even relish for the irritation it caused in people. He never had a fear of being wrong, and even when he declared himself wrong, deep down he knew he was right. He never changed his mind just because people were offended or irritated.

Over time, Tony became Anthony H., but was still, really, Tony – Anthony H., the character and personality with some front, designing his life as he went along, and Tony, who loved dressing up and playing up. 'A Tony by any other name', announced the headline in the *Manchester Evening News*, reporting on his indulgent rebirth with a little smirk.

I asked him at the time why he had made the change. He knew, he said, that it would wind people up. So what? He never gave a damn about what people thought. 'You know me, Paul. I can't resist winding people up. It's always been one of my favourite things.' Teasing was his way of flirting with the whole world, of exhibiting power and control, of deliberately creating desire.

Also, he admitted, coming down a little from the arrogance he would playfully paste over his personality, gently turning to more of the truth, Anthony was what his mum had called him, dead for quite a few years when he made the change. Sometimes he would joke she never called him Tony or Anthony, so frustrated with his chosen way of earning a living that she wilfully forgot his name. Tony was too slick and see-through. 'No Tonys like being called Tony. Most Tonys find it rather undignified.' Anthony had a greater presence, an unabbreviated purity that really showed what he was made of.

The name Anthony came from the deep love his mum had for her son, which was bigger than even his ego and the reputation he had in his city, which mixed up the buffoon and the brainbox. The love of his mother meant he was alive and could play around with the idea of being alive, as if he was artist, which he never really was, even though he thought like an artist. Or at least thought he knew how artists think.

Thanks, Mum, thanks for everything, thanks for believing in me even as a Tony, knowing in the end I would always be your Anthony. And the 'H' was something even the great Anthony Burgess didn't have, even though he had the Wilson. The 'H' could put him out on top. The 'H' was the real wind-up. The 'H' was the extra splash of defiance that really got under some people's skin; where the 'H' might stand for Howard, history, heavenly, humble, humanist, hack, hex, han, hothead, hauteur, Huxley, horsing around, hyped, host, Hamnet, help, heuristic, honey-tongued, hector, has-been, him, habit, halcyon, Hegelian, high-minded, humility, Hardy, hellion, ha ha ha, hegemonic, hippy, hot air, H from Steps, Horace, hoop-la, hearer, headliner, hybrid, Homer, Haçienda, hero, hope, hands-down, hysterical, hallelujah, holistic, hacker, holier than thou, hapless, halo, hydra-headed, Hidden Gem, honourable, horror, heart, high as a kite, honest, honesty, honestly, hamartia or nothing at all.

Maybe in the end he changed from Tony to Anthony because – so the story goes, put around in the first place by Wilson, who once queued up for an audience – the Pope himself challenged Tony about why he was using the frivolous diminutive version of St Anthony of Padua's name, the great thirteenth-century preacher who once famously said in a sermon, 'Actions speak louder than words; let your words teach and your actions speak.' (When St Anthony was exhumed some 330 years after his death at thirty-six in 1231, his body had totally decomposed, become dust and bones, but his 'incorruptible' tongue was still life-like and intact.) Wilson changed his name because Pope John Paul II of all people suggested he should. Of course.

There was a character called Tony Wilson played by Rock Hudson – an anguished, multilayered role originally meant for Laurence Olivier and turned down by Marlon Brando – in a 1966 psychedelic noir film, *Seconds*, directed by John Frankenheimer, the final part of an unofficial 'paranoia trilogy' following *The Manchurian Candidate* and *Seven Days in May*.

Superficially, *Seconds* was about a boring burnt-out banker called Arthur Hamilton who is jaded with life, sex, work, desperate to fill the empty void of his life. He doesn't want to be himself any more. He finds a shadowy Kafkaesque organisation called The Company that can stage his death and allow him to begin his life again surgically and psychologically transformed, with a new, younger, smarter body, a brighter, sharper mind and a new name. A 'second'. He becomes the suave, successful artist Tony Wilson, an archive of his own bestselling art instantly supplied for him by The Company. The film combined the approaches to reality of Arthur Miller and Philip K. Dick, of Alfred Hitchcock and *The Twilight Zone*'s Rod Serling.

Ahead of its time, or simply of its time, with movie-star Hudson stepping – floating, crashing – outside his accepted, often camp but indelibly heterosexual, full-colour, light-comedy zone, where he was usually smooching with Doris Day, adding to the film's general disorientation, it's a black-and-white Lynch-like dark fantasy that weirdly savours the bleak, inescapable emptiness of modern life. Rock slips from Day into the darkness.

It investigates with near-documentary matter-of-factness the sadness and sickness of imagining that plastic surgery can offer a second chance at possibly eternal life, as though a pseudo-perfect appearance symbolising youthfulness can compensate for deep, alienating anxiety. Can you replace yourself and therefore produce a new you, with a new name, a new life and ultimately a new reality? There is a hint that there is, or was, a real Tony Wilson, someone Hudson is now impersonating, or being, but the possibility of there being a real Wilson, and what might have happened to him, remains a mystery.

Industrialised celebrity Hudson, not his real name, an invention not known for playing complex roles in experimental films, is himself being replaced in the film by another invention, a vividly rendered pop-art version of the Hollywood fantasy. Hudson, craving credibility in the agitated, agitating, turned-on mid-1960s, appreciating more than most with a performer's survivalist instincts how the flawless matinee idol he personi-fied had become outmoded, attempts to rebrand himself – to make himself new – by taking a brave new artistic direction. Expected to always play the easy-on-the-eye big-screen dreamboat, here he tries to come out as Hamlet.

Somehow, the name given to this lonely, tormented 'second', this reflec-tion of the nature of second chances, of the desire to be someone else, to be different, to lead another life and achieve personal freedom, of how a person is nothing if not an accumulation of time and memory, and their previous selves, is Tony Wilson.

Tony Wilson. Who liked to say, while wearing a mask of V. I. Lenin, 'A lie told often enough becomes the truth.'

Songwriting genius Brian Wilson of the Beach Boys is said to have decided for some reason to see *Seconds* during its initial West Coast theatrical run in 1966 while in the middle of a particularly potent acid experience. He turned up late for the showing, so that the first line he hears leaping into his tender mind as he enters the cinema is 'Come this way, Mr Wilson.' The fact a film about a conspiracy to undermine identity seemed to be directly talking to him and reflecting his fragile mental state through warped cine-matography triggered a response that led to him abandoning the album that would have been *Smile*. This was due to be the glittering follow-up to *Pet Sounds* and his response to the rapidly evolving, enriched art entertain-ment of the Beatles, holed up in Abbey Road, St John's Wood, north-west London, working on their own hallucinatory, historic, world-fixing British showbusiness response to Wilson's feverish Californian pop grandeur.

Wilson was under considerable pressure to complete *Smile*, the record-ing sessions hampered by his intensifying perfectionism, competitive anx-iety, manic overreaching and levels of exhaustion that were coalescing into provisional mind-shredding schizophrenia. It was due at the beginning of 1967, based on the simplistic showbusiness idea that the writing and delivery of gorgeous, timeless, money-making pop songs was still a mere craft, a swift, glib, crowd-pleasing process, a hoodwinking of a susceptible, easily fooled teenage audience, rather than a newly developed, technologically evolving, increasingly competitive advanced art form wringing the most out of life; still about the creation of astute, attractive novelty rather than a mobile expression of deep, dark emotions in the tangled middle of all the inevitable commercial trappings.

The process of faking your death and remaking your life to get rid of your demons as depicted in *Seconds* apparently infected Wilson's thinking over the next few months. He imagined that rival producer Phil Spector, inventor of many of the innovative recording techniques he was now elaborating on and desperate to improve, who he feared was out to kill him, had instructed the producers to make the movie specifically to mess with his mind. In Wilson's music-mad mind, the God-like Spector obviously had the power to behave this way. He sensed that Spector was quite capable of killing someone.

It was certainly a good if irrational excuse Wilson could use to escape the impossible commercial *Smile* deadline and avoid having to finish what needed, if only in his mind, to be a sound-changing, Beatles-beating, Spector-outwitting, pop-defining masterpiece. In a way he did fake his own death, and became another version of himself, a 'second' lost to himself, although he lived to see the album reconstructed as far as possible in a less pressurised, post-vinyl 2011, when its impact could only be safe nostalgia, the mystery of creation, the marvel of innovation, completely tamed by time.

The myth has it that one of rock's great lost albums, its most legendary failures, a kind of negative triumph, one that more or less broke up Brian Wilson the genius and replaced him with an undead paranoid recluse, was caused by the exposure of someone on a bad trip to the cinematic depiction of a bad trip taken by one real and unreal Tony Wilson.

Make of that what you will.

Tony Wilson – the real one in this book – is at sixteen, when *Seconds* appeared, hitting grammar-school sixth form as an industrious, driven, non-sporty and quirkily eloquent northern boy stumbling into discovering like many others at the time how cleverness can be a ticket out of a dead-end life, education a way of escaping your class, of finding a new you, of discovering the wonders of the world even if only inside your own head. He starts to love talking, and over time learns to love the sound of his own voice and becomes known for being talkative to the point of excess, as if talk is the one thing that makes him tick. He would open his mouth and show the world what was on his mind.

He's thinking of becoming an actor, like his exuberant dad Sydney Russell, who began acting in the army, gay it turned out, with a very proper speaking voice. It was a time when what would commonly be described as 'over-groomed' homosexuals with their 'fussy dressing and suede shoes' still carried a considerable stigma and dealt with the danger of arrest, shame and threats using exaggerated camp and a language all of its own, filled with code words and slang. Means of oppressing known homosexuals, like secret and secretive Manchester war hero and computer pioneer Alan Turing, included aversion therapy and even chemical castration. For some, like Turing, state torture could lead to suicide.

Sydney was hiding from polite society inside a marriage of some convenience with the indomitable Doris Emily Wilson – they married in 1948, when she was forty-four, the war weighing heavily on the imagination – helping her run the homely back-street tobacconist and card shop she had bought with money her father had left her. She'd been married once before, in her mid-twenties, to someone Tony described as 'the love of her life', who died of a brain haemorrhage straight after their honeymoon.

Her marriage to Sydney, he would conclude, was really about friendship. His mum knew about Sydney's sexuality but at the same time didn't know at all or put it safely to one side, away in a drawer. In one story, perhaps started by Wilson himself, elaborating for kicks, Tony conclusively found out about his father's homosexuality some months after his mother died in 1975, when he was twenty-five. He was parking his car on Quay Street near the Granada Television studios where he worked, and he spotted Sydney entering some public toilets. He waited in his car to say hello, and he was still waiting half an hour later when his dad finally emerged, his shirt askew, looking a little harassed, perhaps a little pleased with himself. There was another man exiting at the same time, and a few words were exchanged as they parted, and a telltale touch of the arm and a knowing smile that gave the game away.

In another telling, maybe closer to the truth, Sydney abruptly came out to Tony on the day that his mum died. Within weeks, his father has burst out from under the cover of his marriage, and he's visibly displaying himself around town, out and about with boyfriend in tow. Released into the wild.

Tony would describe his relationship growing up with his dad, certainly when his mum was alive, as a little off kilter. Nothing you could put your finger on, just different from his pals and their dads. 'No matter what your father is,' Doris would regularly tell him as he grew up, when this difference became an issue, 'he is a very kind man. Always remember that.'

Her brother Edgar lived with them as well, make of that what you will, and Tony is a child surrounded by three adults who all adored him: a watchful, loving mum, a shadowy, enigmatic uncle – whom he is the spitting image of – and an extremely self-conscious dad, whose key role in life was mostly getting used to erratic family circumstances. A mummy's boy to the power of three.

To some extent becoming an actor like his dad would have meant becoming an out-of-work actor, certainly once the war ended, but always acting in the everyday, letting every room and space he found himself in be a stage, a place to make believe, and make up rules. Invent reality like Nabokov's harlequin.

Because of his dad, the performer in life of a life in order to function in what were the dark ages for non-straight men, certain layers of camp become permanently impressed into Tony's being, into his performance both in life and on screen. This light, ethereal campiness, which emerged in the soft, often high-handed sing-song phrasing of his voice and the flighty dance of his public mannerisms, put him at some significant distance from the standard local hard-man image, where basic protective swagger pushed, pulled and often drove you through life. Tony conceived a very different form of defensive and/or tough, offensive northern swagger. Something northern you wouldn't particularly label as obviously northern, because it came mixed up with so many other facets and peculiarities, and an innate tendency to never want to fit in.

His mother's influence might have come through the fact she cheerfully rode a motorbike, a feisty Royal Enfield Bullet, and the police were very aware of her, an unusual sight charging around 1950s Salford. As she rode into Manchester from Eccles there was a particular roundabout with a regular traffic police presence, where the bobby on duty would always wave her through, knowing she was a little unsure of the bike's brakes and accelerator. She got her own way.

Tony was quick to outgrow the general adolescent point of view that authentic reality and all of history began with himself, and that what long preceded him was irrelevant. With his German family behind him, he developed a precocious interest in history. He fell in love with the ideas that gave us Western civilisation at the same time as he was falling in love with rock music, and the two things got tangled in his mind and ambitions. Ideas stirred him, books inspired him, he was partial to wayward tyrants, and he loved finding obscure or obvious iconoclastic mentors to guide him. It was a golden age of such fervent, constructive interaction, for the making-up of yourself out of the character and perceptions of writers, musicians, thinkers and artists you found and admired, as though they belonged only to you, part of a private church.

Three: Some Wilsons, some influences (1) and some Manchesters

Vita in motu. (Life is in motion.)

Tony grew up with clear signs that Wilson, however plain, was a leader's name, a passport to some kind of greatness. Harold Wilson, a northern-born modernising moderate socialist with brittle hints of the wry and sly, and his own camouflaged brilliance, was the British prime minister between 1964 and 1970 – almost all of Tony's impressionable teenage years – leading a Labour government that abolished capital punishment and was committed, in the era of the 'white heat of the technological revolution', to liberalising laws on censorship, divorce, abortion and homosexuality. In 1964, Wilson had an unworkable majority of four seats. A snap election in 1966 led to a much healthier majority of ninety-six.

He became prime minister again between 1974 and 1976, the difficult years between Prime Ministers Edward Heath and Jim Callaghan and between glam rock and punk, when there were three-day weeks and inflation was heading skywards.

There were also clear signs in another Mr Wilson that the name brought with it a certain measure of potential to become someone. A (young) Wilson could definitely make a name for himself. There were Wilsons setting an example. The twenty-five-year-old working-class autodidactic non-Oxbridge writer Colin Wilson wrote a book published in 1956, *The Outsider*, with a kind of prescient punkish energy that made him a combination of pop star, pin-up and cult philosopher, hailed as the young British equivalent of Albert Camus and Jean-Paul Sartre, as though such a thing was possible.

(Colin) Wilson proposed that modernity had created a new type of person, and a new kind of knowledge, and set to work defining this new person and new knowledge. In a dark, frustrating post-war period such extreme forward-looking thinking was bold and exciting, truly a brightness, an investigation of how the ordinary could become the sublime, a way of furiously rejecting conformity and the mechanisation of mass society. For a brief period of time, when all things had broken down and nothing yet had replaced the smashed, distorted spaces left by the war, it was even possible for an Englishman to become, or appear to become, an intellectual, and boyishly, brazenly propose that it was ideas and thinking that were going to remake the nation and a world it once ruled and was now careering to the edge of.

The Outsider was not necessarily academically stable, and definitely written from a place outside the literary mainstream, but the ambition and style were a hint of the self-important, cosmically reinforced psychedelic rock thinking to come ten years later. Wilson as a haywire existential impresario introduced a fantastic cast of writers and thinkers in one racing, riotous and glamorous place. It was an awestruck celebration of rebellious genius, and of bright, often young stars burning themselves out: Blake, Van Gogh, Hemingway, Dostoevsky, Nietzsche, Kierkegaard, Kafka, Eliot, Hesse. For many it was a first fantastic introduction to a number of these writers and artists, written about as heroes and practical, weirdly accessible creatures, which was more important than what the book was actually saying – a guidebook to thinking that led you to other mind-blowing guidebooks to thinking.

According to Wilson, 'the outsider', those who don't fit in long for a way they can live fully and generate some tremendous synthesis of being where they create their own religion and live in harmony with the god inside them. Needy, dreamy, knowledge-hunting teenagers and adolescent dream boys and disguised girls melodramatically feeling cut off from the rest of society would come across this intoxicating and elevating book for decades as it was repackaged and re-marketed to suit different generations, from skiffle to post-punk. They would identify with its manifesto for a rejection of dullness and routine, as though this was also a manual that could teach you how to express yourself, how you could, in the words of Blake, 'go out and develop the visionary faculty'.

For two or three decades before other intellectual fashions took over, it still had momentum as a rough field guide to the dynamic energy of human thought, but eventually what had once seemed so timely and time-less became fixed in the 1950s, along with the beat poets, the Angry Young Men, cool jazz and James Dean. It was a souvenir of an age when the cultural mood was shifting, when the mode was for younger people to react to their stunted surroundings by wanting to be smart, find out things, make new connections, on the way to a series of youth-led revolutions in the 1960s, but many of the new formats, fashions and functions, and technologies that would amplify this mood were not yet established.

The Outsider was for better or worse more an early popular culture arte-fact than any grand new philosophical theory; on the way to John Lennon, Jim Morrison and Pete Townshend, and later Ian Curtis of Joy Division, rather than Sontag, Kristeva and Foucault. Ten years later, with those sorts of thoughts Colin Wilson might have formed a group or managed one: The Thinkers. He might have started an independent label specialising in experimental pop: Exist.

Its popularity led to Colin Wilson's Wellesian downfall, although his problem was not that he could not get books published but that he wrote too many, none of them as useful as a guidebook to different thinking as *The Outsider*. As time passed, a lot of *The Outsider* behind the star names would seem a little loopy, with Wilson obsessing over a crowd of white men, and a general tone on the occultist edge of what now seems alt-right; the original provocative intellectual star transformed into a marginalised, peevish and undervalued English eccentric with dubious even freaky interests.

But at the time and deep into the 1960s, before he offended various gods and plunged back into obscurity, here was an influential Wilson confident in his own genius, with an unquestioning belief in his own significance. With a boyish enthusiasm for ideas that need to be categorised and decoded, infuriating the conventional intellectual Establishment, grandly if not naively demanding a new sort of religion, he announced with unfettered grandiosity that the way forward leads you into more life and that you must always live with the same vividness that you do when approaching death.

It was this sort of vividness that helped energise pop musicians in the 1960s, heading straight into a new world appearing all around them, alive with immense, necessary energy, with the war right behind them and the reality of nuclear war closing in all the time, one foot in hippiedom, in protesting and imagining, one foot still in the Depression, or the Blitz, in wacky, frenetic, artistic and vaudevillian ways of escaping their intrusive horrors. As we move further into the twenty-first century, it seems clearer that pop and rock music, which all seemed so present and crucial at the time, so permanent and exceptional, was a very particular period of repair, rejuvenation and revolution between the end of the Second World War and the age of the computer, helping set up the recyclable content that would be required by the insatiable internet.

To find another version of Tony Wilson, where he seems fused with nineteenth-century political thinker Karl Marx, twentieth-century urban theorist Rem Koolhaas and centuries-old time traveller Dr Who – as if these caped crusaders and messianic builders of mind-blowing new worlds were aware of each other, even drank and smoked together, chatting about the magic of change – you can visit some Otherworld, one created in a graphic magazine storybook by the former video games journalist and self-described 'dodgy fanzine kid' Kieron Gillen, who now works, and plays, at twisting the fates of various superheroes and their long-running meta-narrative universes for Marvel and DC Comics.

Gillen has such a spirited mouth, and an endless diagnostic ability to whip up and spin myths, that he could out-mouth and out-myth Wilson in a heavyweight counterculture concept clash on some fantasy battle-ground somewhere in space. Wilson, though, is a mentor, one of the reasons Gillen thinks so deeply about ways to communicate complex human mystery through the careering, connecting channels of popular culture.

To some extent, he's what Wilson might have been if he'd been born twenty-five years later than he was, born into games, comics and computers as much as English Lit., television and the Sex Pistols. Their minds would meet somewhere in the baleful, meta-north, partially disgraced area of the Smiths, and the kind of idiosyncratic anti-business indie thinking that Wilson helped dream up, as the policy-issuing commissioning editor,

49

metaphysical entrepreneur, propagandist, part artist, part conman, dictatorial chairman leader of the Factory Records label/committee/system/playground he helped form in the grey, fomenting Manchester of 1978. A never fully tamed Manchester he considered to be without doubt at the heart of the universe; and there he was, never fully tamed, at the heart of Manchester.

This was a city described as a 'bellwether for social change in Britain', a centre for movements and ideals such as universal suffrage, female suffrage, the co-operative movement, communism, Victorian liberalism, the Manchester School, the Anti-Corn League and the Manchester Chartist 'sons of freedom', leading to trade unions and the *Manchester Guardian*.

As a lively, hungry music city in the 1960s, climbing out of the reduced and straitened 1950s, keenly moving with the times, which saw teenagers finding their own independent space, there were scores of beat clubs and coffee clubs playing jukebox music, livening up a dowdy city centre that was almost abandoned at night, getting around the licensing laws by serving coffee; the birth of what became known as northern soul spinning out of the enthusiastically managed mid-'60s Twisted Wheel club and the rare, transformative, post-gospel/doo-wop, pre-funk, speeded-up American R&B records played there; the Twisted Wheel's 'show runner' Roger Eagle's influential mid-'60s *R'n'B Scene* fanzine illuminating the novel concept of an articulate, insightful young pop music obsessive; Eagle opening the unlicensed but drug-fuelled late-'60s Magic Village club when his love for music tripped into the new underground psychedelic music, another sort of soul music altogether; the abrupt change in lifestyle of the Hollies' singer Graham Nash from impoverished, bombed-out, over-occupied post-war Salford slums with outside toilets just around the corner from Salford Lads Club to golden California dreaming and Joni Mitchell's bed, her fireworks at the end of the day, to fighting with colleague Stephen Stills over Rita Coolidge and hanging out with Jimi Hendrix; the first major blues show in the country in October 1962, the American Folk Blues Festival at the Manchester Free Trade Hall, featuring the then sacred-seeming Muddy Waters, Howlin' Wolf, T-Bone Walker and John Lee Hooker, which was attended by devoted fan boys Brian Jones, Mick Jagger and Keith Richards a few weeks after their very first show as the Rolling Stones – hiring a minibus to drive up the exciting new motorways from the South to get close enough for the first time to their gurus and their guitars – as well as a trio of connoisseurs, Alexis Korner, Jimmy Page and local lad John Mayall, influencing the British blues boom and all that followed, including the white re-exporting of the blues with an edgy, fantastic English extra back into America; the American Folk Blues Festival in Manchester playing a significant role at the very beginning of British rock; Chris Wright booking more and more new bands as the social secretary at Manchester University in 1964 as student unions became key venues for the rapidly growing rock music, at twenty becoming one of the biggest music promoters in the country on the way to forming Chrysalis Records; and the legendary booing and Judas heckling of Bob Dylan in May 1966, again at the Manchester Free Trade Hall, for blasphemously introducing electric guitars and dark satanic amplifiers into the apparent progressive, pastoral purity of folk.

For the record, the times they are, etc., the electric Dylan Free Trade Hall concert took place the day after the Beach Boys' *Pet Sounds* and Dylan's *Blonde on Blonde* were released. Elsewhere, on the same day in 1966, poet, dictator and demi-god Chairman Mao issued the May 16th Notice, warning that enemies of the communist cause had infiltrated the party with the intention of reinstating capitalism, marking the beginning of the chaotic, brutal Great Proletariat Cultural Revolution. This made the real principles and guidelines collected two years earlier in the Little Red Book, a revision of Mao's original ideological field manual for soldiers, 'a spiritual atom bomb', which pointed out that a revolution is not a dinner party, or writing an essay, or painting a picture, or doing embroidery . . . Every problem in life could be resolved by referring to Mao Zedong thought.

Manfred Mann's joyfully charged pop romance 'Pretty Flamingo' was the number-one single that week, a Bruce Springsteen favourite written by a musical director of *The Banana Splits* TV show who wrote for the Monkees and the Archies, with bass played by Jack Bruce, soon of superpower trio Cream, his only appearance on a number-one hit. The Rolling Stones' *Aftermath* was the number-one album, the only number one that year that wasn't the soundtrack to *The Sound of Music* apart from the Beatles' *Revolver*. Two of those albums were of interest to the sixteen-year-old Wilson, the Little Red Book ultimately more so as a fashionable accessory, a modish commodity, a scandalous symbol of radicalism and revolution emitting a sacred aura.

There was a certain fashionable infatuation with Maoism among leading French thinkers in the 1960s (with a few reservations), as though Mao really was a friend of the oppressed and exploited, a vital catalyst in a global wave of upheavals fighting capitalist greed and inequality by youth, students and workers. All this was a big influence on Wilson, turning eighteen in 1968, the year of the May civil unrest in Paris, of the Prague Spring in Czechoslovakia, the student massacre in Mexico City, and his subsequent compulsion always to be at the forefront of the latest intellectual chic, for reasons that seemed all at once cheerfully superficial and intensely serious.

He would be very comfortable indulging in this radical chic over the years, cheerfully expressing and defending a certain sympathy with Colonel Gaddafi's murderous assault on the Libyan middle class, 'as a member of the middle class myself'. He had a similar indulgent fondness for Pol Pot – 'he couldn't have been all bad' – quite enjoying the fact that one of 'his bands', New Order, following the enforced shutting down of Joy Division due to the suicide of their singer, one of the great, tragic, ultimately exploitable events in Wilson's life, were named after a *Guardian* headline referring to brutal revolutionary Pol Pot's mass-murdering Khmer Rouge and the 'new order of Kampuchea', not enjoying so much the fact that Hitler and the Nazis had also used the name New Order, which called for a more nuanced defence, especially after Joy Division with their to-some-sinister name rooted in German concentration camp history.

In a 1990 interview with *MoneyMaker Magazine* headlined 'The New Order of Success', Wilson claimed Gaddafi – seizing power in Libya in 1969 at twenty-seven, Ronald Reagan's 'mad dog of the Middle East',

Nelson Mandela's 'one of the greatest twentieth-century freedom fighters' – as his 'number-one hero for his sense of style and sense of achievement, his struggles against the barriers of prejudice'.

In the carefree, if careless, often foolish days before the crushing, unforgiving internet made an improvisational assembly of an eccentric personal ideology based on mischief a natural, common-or-garden process, Wilson approved of Gaddafi's 'epic revolutionary image'. He saw him as a serious, visionary nation-builder working to free the entire continent of Africa from Western imperialism, before he became caricatured in later life as a weird, excessively eccentric dictator. He admired Gaddafi because he didn't play the game by the international rule book – he was 'mythology made flesh'. To be truly revolutionary one way or another, those committed to bringing about vast change will always appear as a form of formless madness to those who believe in institutionalised and regulated political systems and classes.

Perhaps Wilson was undermining how he was being profiled as a fine, upstanding if unorthodox capitalist in a strait-laced financial magazine. He needed to add a dubious dash of perversion, an unstable point of view, play the disruptive businessman who made up his own rules. Then again, the rare, disordered cool of Tony Wilson existed because he was never afraid of appearing deeply uncool, apparently wrong and completely antithetical. He was a one-off combination of the happily naff, the politically loopy and the extremely knowing, and his enthusiasm and passion for the unorthodox and deviant meant he opened himself up to ridicule.

Wilson once began one of his after-midnight television shows with the largely improvised monologue he always liked to deliver, a fan of irreverent, disreputable American talk-show hosts, mixing smooth Johnny Carson patter with more wayward musings, deciding this time to present his thoughts on the Tiananmen Square Massacre of 1989, the violent retaking of the square by Chinese authorities from pro-democracy protesters. 'Yes, of course,' he pronounced, as if he alone knew the absolute truth, 'you should not go around shooting innocent protesters, but it is of course more complicated than that, this is an ideology and a regime that has by following its path whatever the obstacles and difficulties educated hundreds of millions and taken them out of their backward rural existence . . .' He might have believed it or was looking for an argument. He might have been checking if anyone was awake or testing the limits of what he could get away with. Perhaps he was bored that day with the millions of words he would speak on television that went nowhere, that meant nothing. Really, just playing. Checking out what happened if you put one thing with another: a glib, smiling, late-night television presenter with a part-time, psychedelically minded, forensically analytical firebrand.

Right or wrong, the mid-'60s Manchester heckler accusing Dylan of outrageous betrayal symbolised a definite defiant local we-know-best spirit, where even one of the greatest musical minds of the twentieth century was not above criticism and an uppity sectarian form of spiritual instruction.

Tony Wilson's patient acceptance even approval of the sometimes friendly, sometimes not, heckles, abuse and cursing that often accompanied him on the streets of Manchester and beyond is perhaps based on the view that it was a compliment, coming in the city where even Dylan – as he made an audacious change in his music, leaving authentic, gritty folky steam behind to go cosmic rock-star electric – was jeered and taunted for arrogance, a vainglorious rising above his station. For Wilson, based on the unshakeable evidence that Bob Dylan plugging in and playing really loud was not the end of Dylan but a monumental transformation, being insulted by locals was a sign that he must be doing something right. Being insulted – so absolutely noticed – also clearly helped make history. Of course, his basic assumption, written all over his demeanour, that in some artistic spheres he was travelling near the same orbit as the likes of Dylan was part of the problem that led to the leery small-town derision.

Ten years on from Dylan being labelled a Judas in vigilant, judgemental Manchester, a certain set of historical circumstances created a unique local reality that could be read as emerging from an alliance of radiant common sense between Shelley's poem 'The Masque of Anarchy', inspired by the Peterloo Massacre at St Peter's Field in Manchester in 1819, when peaceful protesters demanding universal suffrage were charged by soldiers on horseback, leaving hundreds injured and fifteen dead; *The Condition of the Working Class in England*, based on mid-nineteenth-century evidence collected by philosopher, journalist and businessman Friedrich Engels from touring Salford and Manchester's filthy, overcrowded 'hell upon earth' slums, anticipating the grim future of capitalism and the industrial age; and the Sex Pistols' song 'Anarchy in the UK', rhyming 'pissed' with 'anarchist' and based on a ferociously energetic desire provoked by 1970s poverty and political breakdown as predicted above to prove you were much better than society's standard, inhibiting estimation of your worth. Thirty-five years later, these historical circumstances would influence a comic book where the star turn was not Engels' world-changing Manchester collaborator Karl Marx, the transcendent poets Percy Bysshe Shelley or Bob Dylan, or the incandescent word slinger Johnny Rotten, but glib, gabby television presenter Tony Wilson.

Tony Wilson, wearing a mask of his own face, liking to point out that 'Great minds think alike . . .'

The mind of a Tony Wilson born in 1975 would have found himself influenced by the provocative, mind-stretching fun and games the Tony Wilson born in 1950 liked to have with the role art, television and music played in people's lives, because of the Beatles, the Sex Pistols and, beyond that, the first album released on Factory Records, Joy Division's *Unknown Pleasures*.

Kieron Gillen was a games obsessive who formed comics rather than bands and who realised that Factory, as imagined by Tony Wilson and his equally if differently driven co-workers, was a logic-twisting, multilayered puzzle, as much about local identity, the energy of a city, the importance of independence, the removal of rules, the depths of art, the otherness of music and the drama of discovery as it was about simply the business and culture of rock and pop.

Factory Records created a spiralling, numbered universe that went from 1 to 501, packed with its own myths and conflicts, in the same way a Marvel series did. A music release on Factory, and the other objects, conversations, buildings, lawsuits, occasions, furniture, paperwork, phantoms, accessories, fragments, horseplay, dossiers, random asides, sales talk, art works, slogans, obscurities, accounts, interviews, contracts, badges, buckets, dental work, behaviour, red wine, white wine, *Just say no to London* and *From Manchester with love* T-shirts, Christmas gifts, salons, bits and pieces and memorials and coffins were the equivalent of an issue of one of the comics that expanded through time, space and various media over decades, mostly of interest to a small, transfixed audience of single-minded geeks and freaks but ultimately with a much wider influence.

Wilson and Gillen, both gamesters in their own way, appreciated how reality and history were forms of fantasy you could move inside and treat as material for stories and dreams, as a way of channelling your own confusions, ambitions and revelations. Both began their projects from a position of 'What if . . .' and a perception that pop culture is difficult to take seriously and yet the most important thing in the world.

Gillen created the sadly short-lived *Phonogram* with artist Jamie McKelvie, a comic book about pop music where music is actually magic, something which can transform you or destroy you, and records contain superpowers, controlled by 'phonomancers'. The seven issues were inspired by the Pipettes, Cansei de Ser Sexy, the Knife, Robyn, the Long Blondes, Camera Obscura and TV on the Radio.

The Gillen series *The Wicked + The Divine*, also constructed with Jamie McKelvie, is another vital, critical, post-music-paper response to the addictive, transitional energy of the pop music that began with seven-inch 45 rpm singles, born in the 1950s and creating enough momentum to spill over into the first two decades of the twenty-first century, almost thirty years after the format disappeared. Ancient gods are reincarnated as twenty-first-century pop stars modelled on Prince, Bowie, Rihanna and Kanye West, who have two years of fame, of being 'loved and hated' before they die. Their music is something you can reinvent again and again by connecting it to your own life, wherever and whatever you happen to be. Ninety years later, the cycle repeats itself. Everything has been done before, but things that have happened before are always different according to the new context in which they happen.

Marvel's *Journey into Mystery* series began as a pulp science-fiction/monster magazine in the 1950s, and in 1962, up to its eighty-third issue, Stan Lee and Jack Kirby, original creators of the Fantastic Four, X Men and the Hulk, introduced the Asgardian Norse god superhero, the Mighty Thor. Two years later, Thor's evil adoptive brother Loki, the god of mischief, was introduced – the character played by Tom Hiddleston in the Marvel cinematic universe sixty years later, once the legions of superheroes were officially part of the life-and-death-explaining electronic folklore of America.

Hyper-prolific Gillen wrote some Thor issues for *Journey into Mystery*, numbers 604 to 614, and then concentrated on remaking the dead Loki, giving him life, and transforming him from malignant trickster villain into a buoyant young hero, Kid Loki, who saves rather than destroys the world through his lies and mischief. With flaming Wilsonian grandiosity, Gillen used his stories and mixtures of fact and speculative fiction to explore the whole idea of superhero comics, and the meta-realities of being a fictional villain in a Marvel universe, as though that could unlock the secrets of the human universe. Wicked Loki was reincarnated as a hopeful young boy who wanted to prove he could be different, he could be better. He could change.

In *Journey into Mystery* issue numbers 639 and 640, gods appear as walking versions of industrialised nineteenth-century cities. A character called Master Wilson, resembling Tony Wilson as a superhuman flight of fancy – 'I'd prefer Mister but it seems the Gods have forced a position of power on me' – is the eminent arch druid of the Manchester gods, representing the spirit of the Industrial Revolution and progressive modernity, fighting a war of ideas, magic versus science, the cold analytical mind versus a sense of wonder, and the rural agricultural life versus the urban industrial life. 'I call my beliefs urban pantheism,' intones Master Wilson, bearing down on reality like a quintessential romantic, a Blakean saviour, a liberating force for freedom, and in this case ghostly robotic hero, 'but that's just me being pretentious. Ah pretentious. A lovely word. A verbal tick of the dull and slovenly, a whip to lash those who have ideas above their station. I don't have much time for people being stuck at their stations.'

Manchester is defined quite logically as the first city of the future in a supernaturally rendered England, and there is a sense that in this numinous, mystic world Tony Wilson is 'Will's-son', as in William Shakespeare, who is often given credit for creating the first modern man, Hamlet, who unites in himself so many different elements.

Or the first modern man could be the writer, essayist and nineteenth-century art-critic-as-artist William Hazlitt – also a travel writer, memoirist, political commentator, painter, philosopher, tireless self-promoter, and a specialist in the great general drama of the human spirit. He was writing in the first decades of the 1800s, when technological advancements were bringing newspapers to an increasingly wide audience and setting up the mass media to come. Reaching a wider audience, exposed to opinions and flights of fancy other than their own, he provoked many enemies, who disagreed with him and the way he couldn't help placing his ego at the centre of his work, unable to keep his mouth shut or his mind modest. Tony Wilson can easily also be this fiercely radical, scurrilous proto-media star Will's-son. 'The more we do,' Hazlitt said, 'the more we can do.'

And then there's poet, painter and engraver William Blake, born 1757, another early example of a multimedia artist, born in unpretentious, moderate surroundings, living a peaceful, pleasant childhood, avoiding formal schooling, developing unique, even alarming mental powers, living through and artistically feeding off the revolutions in America and France, working to bring about a change in the social order and the minds of everyday people. Blake predicted all kinds of theories in science and art, but as much as he was looking into the future, he was also looking deep into the present.

Thirsty for all kinds of knowledge, with a supremely questing mind, he assumed the role of bard and prophet, proposing a balance between energy and reason, believed that true faith was incompatible with institutionalised religion, holding that all religions are one. He wasn't interested in writing or drawing for 'the many' but completely believed his writings were of national importance, was treated with both praise and derision, dismissed as probably insane, had trouble earning money, determined not to sacrifice his principles in order to reach a wider audience. 'Remain just and true to our own imaginations,' he demanded, believing that the imagination is human existence itself, over time influencing how a succession of artists viewed reality. 'Improvements make straight roads; but the crooked roads without improvements are the works of genius.' Tony Wilson was perhaps the only early-evening television newsreader with a loyal following of enamoured tea-drinking older ladies you could make a case for saying was this Will's-son, or the only one perhaps taking to his professional heart Blakean words like 'The road of excess leads to the palace of wisdom' and 'If the fool would persist in his folly he would become wise.'

So Tony Wilson is a spin-off from the mental cosmos of Anthony Burgess, who ran all-knowing rings around language and refused to be held back by low, condescending expectations of the intellectual capabilities of a provincial boy. Tony Wilson shares the name of a character played by Rock Hudson in a film that increasingly makes sense as time passes and a growing number of people pursue a second life, another version of themselves, by altering their appearance, changing their minds and vainly chasing eternal youth. He is a metallic, metaphysical, unsleeping but still dreaming Manchester Time Lord battling cosmic forces of banality and ignorance rising from the South and the forces of evil emerging from inside and outside the mind. He is Wilson, part of an abstract family of famous, notorious Wilsons and Williams who didn't seem content with merely interpreting the world but wanted to change it, possibly even turn it upside down. He sees poets and prophets, seers and sages and one or two priests as great warriors. Wearing a mask of Gaddafi, he muses – about to read the news, about to interview a member of the Cabinet, about to snort cocaine with Shaun Ryder of the crooked pop group Happy Mondays, about to lecture an audience about the poetic, practical and persistent glory and generosity of Manchester – how 'power is hallucinogenic'.

Four: Salford, Marple and busy being born

Ubi bene, ibi patria. (Your homeland is where your life is good.)

Superficially Wilson was a provocative liberal arts entertainer, minor music-industry player, capricious cultural theorist, abstract, self-celebrating know-it-all and self-appointed urban planner, born in Salford but professionally based in Manchester, in his absolute reality-arranging pomp during the late 1970s and '80s, when the idea of Salford had been almost completely absorbed by its more exhibitionist next-door neighbour, Manchester.

Few outside the area would have known that Salford was a city separated from Manchester merely by a shared river, once one of the filthiest stretches of water in Europe, and a few bridges, a city stretching from Manchester city centre to the borders of Wigan and north Cheshire; the cities were right next to each other, connected, twinned, one city with a great historic name kept alive by its football teams – one of which, United, was over the border, actually outside Manchester – and its educational establishments, one city brutal and run-down, buried under its oppressive industrial history and a melancholy sense that its past, present and future were ghostly and whose famous ones tended to morph into being of Manchester. Friedrich Engels lived in Salford on and off for over a quarter of a century, working at his dad's mill not least to support Karl Marx as he worked on his *Communist Manifesto*, but this too would disappear into the idea of Manchester.

'I come from Salford,' Wilson would say when it suited him, when he fancied the company, from the lowest to the highest, anonymous dodgy ruffian to sublime, roundly modernist composer Peter Maxwell Davies, or he needed to emphasise an authentic working-class background, which was actually, on his mother's German side, a more upscale retail background, 'but by the mid-'80s we came from Manchester. It meant something different then. For years I would have denied coming from

Manchester. Until about 1980, when people asked, "Where do you come from?" I would say, "I come from Salford." And people would go, "Ah, Manchester." And I'd explain, "No, it's fucking Salford." Albert Finney would have said that to you, Ben Kingsley, Alistair Cooke – we come from Salford – and there's a real pride about it . . . Salford is what it is. It was *the* working-class city. But the word "Manchester" came to mean not just the centre of Manchester, it came to mean "the project", being the rebuilding of this whole northern territory, including Salford and south Lancashire. Manchester was shorthand for this mission. So I'd be happy to say, after all, that I was from Manchester. Manchester and Salford are a bit like Minneapolis and St Paul, two sides of the same city.'

In the 1960s and '70s, when I was growing up in Stockport, six miles south from Manchester city centre straight down the bus-battered, weather-stained A6 through Ardwick, Longsight, Levenshulme and Heaton Chapel, Salford in the sooty distance seemed dead, gone, discarded, the very drizzly, degraded essence of the grim 'up north' tag used by enemy forces to keep the North locked up inside a sort of moaning, self-pitying, perpetually cloth-capped smallness. Stockport could still seem tangled in the nineteenth century, but Salford still breathed its air. Coming to populated, enterprising life during the nineteenth century, one of the greatest cotton towns, granted city status in 1926, separated from Manchester to the east by the River Irwell, it suffered most from the after-effects of the Industrial Revolution it had been a driving part of as much as its more celebrated next-door neighbour.

It was the *Manchester* Ship Canal, that audacious competitive inland retort to coastal Liverpool's natural nineteenth-century maritime superiority, but it was the busy, efficient *Salford* and Manchester Docks at the canal's upper reach where mighty, towering ships from around the world were loaded and unloaded. Of the nine docks, only one was within Manchester itself.

As the canal and the wonderfully anomalous inner-city docks outlived their usefulness during the twentieth century, finally shutting down for good in the early 1980s, Salford withered faster and more dramatically than the esteemed fighting city it was jammed against; even Manchester in ravaged post-war, post-industrial decline, where solid things and places had turned to air, did not shrivel up as comprehensively as Salford.

It was described in the nineteenth century as fetid by Engels, shocked by its polluted, densely packed appearance, rivers running purple with bad-smelling dye, vast piles of buildings full of windows rattling and trembling all day long, almost all the workers there doing all the dirty work for the rich, living in wretched, damp, filthy cottages, and subsequently seemed in the popular imagination permanently slummy and doomed. It was as though the city could never recover from Engels' description of a man of about sixty living in a cow stable 'which had neither window, floor nor ceiling, with the rain dripping through his rotten roof. This man was too old and weak for regular work and supported himself by removing manure with a hand-cart; the dung heaps lay next door to his palace.'

A hundred years later, insensitive post-war refurbishment and rampant slum clearance apparently promoting new civic order replaced devastated terraced slums and scars on the landscape with inappropriate sub-avant-garde concrete tower blocks that quickly became new slums. Salford became increasingly disconnected from any flow of money or energy. Blighted tower blocks blotted the skyline, randomly dumped among grimly standardised maisonettes arranged in forlorn patterns.

Even as the city's clustered, bypassed and inarticulate griminess was given poetic dimension through Ewan MacColl's loving lament 'Dirty Old Town' – Salford as his Athens of the North, one way or another – Tony Richardson's black-and-white 1961 film *A Taste of Honey* featured different kinds of adventure and stress, and by being the original, strangely near-sensual source of lingering *Coronation Street* iconography, Salford sank further under a ton of bricks, forgotten sensations, devastated ambitions and a maze of narrow, neglected streets – all very like one another, inhabited by people equally like one another, in Dickens' words – into unemployment and squalor, leading to its wealthier residents migrating away.

Salford seemed so encrusted in its be-sooted past, so slammed into deprivation, it would surely never break free of its soiled image. Even the adoption of supreme but patronised northern artist L. S. Lowry as prized local symbol emphasised to the outside world lowly cobbled stick-man quaintness and the weird vestiges of the past rather than impressive imaginative grandness.

As Salford fell away from or into exiled history, a dirty word for decades, a dirty old footnote, Wilson pragmatically identified with Manchester, also drifting but with a certain unbreakable glory, a city that became more and more of a brand during his heyday, not least because he could make so much of the city, and its history, which was really the battling, striving history of lots of distinct districts, towns and regions including Salford piled up around the city centre.

At the time Wilson was beginning his reign, his role as conceptually minded cheerleader, the region had all become Manchester, and as he committed to the city – the city of Manchester, and the abstract idea of a city – Salford was becoming even more broken up and lost. Manchester, in his eyes, and in his biography and manifesto, was the special birthplace of capitalism and of communism, of computers, women's rights, trade unions and social compassion, and, in his dreams, hinted at a tantalising immaterial utopian space promising a release from the unstable and unsatisfactory present. He made Manchester his playground, complete with swings, roundabouts and sandpit.

He could easily switch allegiances. His attachment to Salford was largely romantic, and mostly based on his grammar-school years, when he attended De La Salle in Weaste Lane and continued visiting the stolid family shops stuck in Salford time that still traded there. He only actually lived in Salford for his first few years; enough to make him from the age of eight a lifelong Manchester United fan, his local team, of Stretford in the borough of Trafford, just over the water from the Salford Docks, a team given world-renowned mythical qualities after the Munich air disaster decimated their prized young team in 1958. United would become international, owned by distant and indifferent Americans, its fans scattered worldwide, but for Tony the team would always belong to the people of Stretford, Urmston, Old Trafford, Chorlton and Whalley Range.

He began watching United reserves just a few months after the air crash, his favourite match of all time against Sunderland in 1964 – 3–1 down with ten minutes to go, pulling back to 3–3 – and his all-time favourite player was feisty no-nonsense Scottish wing back Pat Crerand. Tony drove down to see United win the 1968 European Cup Final against Benfica in his dad's car. In 1995, when United's volatile hero Eric Cantona launched himself kung-fu-boot-high into the crowd after he had been sent off at Crystal Palace, striking a fan who had shouted at him to 'Fuck off back to France,' Wilson was naturally on the side of Cantona, whom he saw as the victim, calling the Palace fans on television 'obnoxious Croydon wankers'. For a while he presented a show for the Manchester United channel MUTV, *Masterfan*, based on *Mastermind*, for next to no money, just because he loved United and loved talking about them.

He saw his last United match in May 2007, in the last weeks of his life, deep in thought in the pouring rain, watching them against relegation-fighting West Ham United, not sure if he was leaving home or heading home but always at home at Old Trafford. They lost the match, surprisingly, and there was no final United goal to take to his grave even after Cristiano Ronaldo came on as a second-half substitute, but they were once more under Alex Ferguson Premier League winners. When Tony died his team were the English champions.

In 1955, when he was five, after a short time at an independent prep school in Worsley his family moved about as far south as you can from Salford – and Lancashire and Manchester – before you slip into Derbyshire and leave the North-West altogether. His mum and dad, Doris and Sydney, and the ever-present Uncle Edgar, king son and his doting three parents, moved to Marple, a modest, tranquil town surrounded by the kind of bucolic views estate agents swoon over, perched at the edge of the country's first-ever national park, the Peak District, officially established just four years before, after the passage of the 1949 National Parks and Access to the Countryside Act by the post-war Labour government.

On a clear day, from its highest point, the brooding moorland plateau Kinder Scout, it's possible to see into Manchester city centre, and in 1932 a mass trespass was the culmination of a campaign led by politically motivated working-class ramblers from industrial Manchester and Sheffield to be allowed access as free people to the uncultivated moors and hills. Previously, they had been guarded by gamekeepers armed with sticks beating away the intruders. Landowners had traditionally refused ramblers seeking a respite from cramped, smoky towns and cities the chance to wander unhindered across their land, and the mass trespass as a significant act of social activism became a key event in the access-to-the-countryside campaign. Seventeen years later, after the Second World War, as part of the post-war reconstruction plans, and as a direct result of the pre-war protests, the countryside was made available to all.

Marple sits at the unhurried southernmost tip of my sprawling home town, Stockport, at the southernmost tip of what would become in 1974 Greater Manchester – up until 1936, and local-government reorganisation, it had been part of Derbyshire, slipping into Cheshire when Stockport was very much of Cheshire, until 1974, as Stockport was folded into Greater Manchester, and therefore Marple was as well. Compared to Salford, in the 1950s it was very definitely a pretty Cheshire village, an appealing image it likes to hold on to, even though it is now of Greater Manchester.

The railways had reached the town on Victorian cue, meaning its heyday as a location was reached in the late nineteenth century, when it had mainline importance as a stopping and connection point, with lines radiating from the central Manchester stations London Road, Victoria and Central out to Liverpool, Sheffield, Stockport and Derby. It was also a stopping point on the train that by the 1890s could travel from Manchester to London St Pancras in an astonishing, world-shaking 4 hours 20 minutes. Thousands of people started to use the line halfway between Manchester and Sheffield to pour into suddenly accessible Marple, on works outings and school trips to local beauty spots.

By the early twentieth century, an increasingly fuelled world speeding faster and faster, Marple was bypassed as a main line, falling back to the slower margins of things, part of a gentle scenic route, an occasional destination rather than a centre of discovery. The beauty spots were still there, but not as rare and special as they once were when the railways were opening up possibilities. Passing through one day by train, the neat Victorian railway station with even in the 1920s a sense of aged dignity gave Agatha Christie the name for her shrewd, elderly, freelance and childless detective Jane Marple.

Wilson's mum was fifty-one when they moved to pastoral Marple, because there had to be more to life than rattling, slumping, perpetually filthy Salford, as much as Tony would romanticise it later. It was a way of getting Tony away from the toughs, the bad boys that she felt he would be drawn to, a sucker from an early age for roguish dirty tricks. She worried there was something in her lively, inquisitive only child that was attracted to the kind of ruffians and ne'er-do-wells who might lure Tony into temptation. She would have nodded knowingly about his eventual enraptured attraction to the Happy Mondays; it was exactly why she moved to Marple, to escape the sort of seductive monkey business that would always lead to no good and from there go from bad to worse.

A staunch Tory, she worked hard, liked to save as much money as she could and plan for a better life, for herself and Tony and her husband and his brother, who was coming along for the ride and helping her fulfil her dreams, completing this unusual post-war family unit close to but far enough away from the dingy, scarred streets of Salford.

She had her only child at forty-six, in austere, bureaucratic 1950, when the general social attitude to someone getting pregnant so relatively late in life was that you had to have an abortion – having a baby in your midforties was medically extremely dangerous and socially very unseemly. It was her last chance to have a child, as if the war had got in the way and she could finally return to normality, to being a woman and not merely a survivor, and she was prepared to do whatever it took, somehow knowing that she had it in her to create something special. It was her way of saying the war is over, when its miserable legacy was still everywhere to be seen.

The coronation of Queen Elizabeth II in 1952 was an extremely imperial occasion, the monarchy steadily recovering after the pre-war abdication crisis. The largest immigrant group at the time was the Irish, and there were fewer than 140,000 Blacks and Asians in 1951 Britain. The mostly southern-based media was dominated by newspapers, with the BBC broadcasting from the superior-sounding South-East, far away from appreciating how different the language and the humour were in all areas of the North.

The wartime spirit of 'make do and mend' was still prevalent. Staple foods were still rationed. An attempt to make sweets and chocolates more freely available in 1949 had to be delayed because the demand was so great. Sugar was eventually de-rationed in 1953 following intense pressure from sweet manufacturers. Food rationing finally ended in 1954. In those disorientating years following the rotten war, children were a way of making things new, of beginning again after atrocity and devastation, of magically reintroducing untainted energy and generating a fresh start. The pregnancy didn't look as though it was going to naturally run its full course; it all became very touch and go. There was a slightly unorthodox and bold, possibly reckless doctor, Eric Hall from Didsbury, who performed a then-rare emergency caesarean – under 3 per cent of all births in England at the time – the safest option in the circumstances but terrifyingly all-or-nothing for both mother and baby. The operation was, for all the risk, brutality and fear, a success. New little Wilson appeared, at bloody speed, out of nowhere, the inside of everything, into all that tremendously sudden light and noise, missing the trip down the birth canal, dramatically, wetly, loudly, mouthily plucked from oblivion.

Falling, exploding, fragmenting into the world, flung into limitlessness, boundaries collapsing, suddenly, there he is, already an outrage, howling in favour of being. Born a troublemaker.

Boom, baby!

'Untimely ripped,' he would say – as with Macduff in *Macbeth*, not necessarily 'born' but self-born. His birth had to have in his telling heroic reverberations. It was as though he had organised the move himself – it was all his doing, launching himself from inside the dark womb into the whirlwind of the great outdoors, already taking control, and then spending much of his life recreating the phantasmagorical canal trip he never got to make. Looking for some way of compensating for missing out on such an adventure. He found himself in Salford, but long before he could work out why, he was moved somewhere else.

Stockport is set in its ways at the bottom of a depressed valley within sight of the forbidding Pennines, biding their time until all this fussy, silly human interference passes, under what always seem to be bruise-coloured skies and murky drizzle, even though the sun does occasionally shine. Cutting through the valley there's a classic 110-foot-high, 27-arched, brick-solid Victorian viaduct, built to make sure the early steam trains from increasingly important Manchester could get to the South, with a late-twentieth-century motorway now indifferently blasting through its conveniently sized arches.

The timeless, deeply melancholy viaduct, which drifting, collecting L. S. Lowry loved for the deep-set spirit of loneliness contained inside this carefully compiled deadweight mass of bricks, is the reason why a few minutes after the train to London sets off from Manchester, really wanting to pick up speed and get on with things, it has to stop; a by-law dictated that trains were only allowed to cross the viaduct if they made a stop at Stockport's Edgeley station – since 1967, simply Stockport – and this ruling, even if now less legally enforceable than in the nineteenth century, still endures, helping Stockport through the lean, leaner, leanest years to be a little more relevant than its mostly struggling lower-class football team, declining, non-central position and general depleted reputation might otherwise have permitted. The vast viaduct stopped it being completely overshadowed by its master, the famous, strident city to the north, which nourished it but also kept its distance. The trains kept stopping; Stockport still existed, its people still fighting and despite it all laughing and sometimes singing.

Underneath the looming viaduct, Stockport's town centre is formed at the edge of where the River Tame from Yorkshire meets up with the River Goyt travelling through Marple from Derbyshire to become Wilson's beloved River Mersey, the historic border between Lancashire and Cheshire.

'Every phase of my life,' Wilson once wrote, 'has been touched, sprinkled religiously perhaps, by the waters of the River Mersey. No surprise since I think of myself as a Lancashire lad, and as a Lancashire lad, it is this river which rises in the black-brown moors to the east and kisses the Irish Sea in the west that flows right through my homeland. I look back to a 1950s heyday when Regent Road where I first appeared in the world was one of the great shopping streets of the North. And why? It could hardly be unconnected with the fact that less than half a mile away, just down Trafford Road, were the magnificent gates of the docks of the Port of Manchester, the designated terminus for the equally magnificent Manchester Ship Canal, built by Manchester men to combat the hegemony and high taxes enjoyed by the port of Liverpool. Without the Mersey Bay, there would, of course, have been no logical entrance for the great ships that went on to cross the fields around Warrington and made it to the very edge of Manchester. Eastham, on the south, Wirral side of Mersey Bay, the western end of the Ship Canal, was indeed the entrance to Manchester. It was our Ostia, the harbour port gateway to Ancient Rome. Salford and in particular Cross Lane Corner where I was brought up were the intentional and alternate universe to the great port of Liverpool.'

A fleshy, life-lined L. S. Lowry with his smoky mind would drift in heavy charcoal suit and ever-present homburg tethering him to the nineteenth century down one of the twisting cobbled slopes which dropped matter-of-factly into Stockport's town centre, near the mundane source of the Mersey before it was coldly built over with concrete, bus stops and commerce. He would be searching for something surreal washed up from the past to paint, a perversely beautiful crooked lamp post, some mysterious steps that stand in for the eternal, a charred thin chimney obelisk poking up into the glum sky, a cheering glimpse of the stoical viaduct as indifferent to passing time as a mountain. He was a landscape painter; it was just that many of the landscapes he painted were littered with chimneys and packed with brick. Lamp posts were spindly trees.

At the top of one slope, along a narrow lane that in Chester would be charming and filled with tourists but in Stockport was roughed-up, run-down and boxed-off, he would pass an anonymous outlying dirty red-brick building where, years later, Joy Division recorded their *Unknown Pleasures* album for Factory Records, a label more or less originally funded by money left to Wilson by his darling mother, an irresponsible and/or inspired investment of £10,000. Inside, under weirdly strict sometimes lunatic conditions, tech man, one-time sound engineer and bass player for hire Martin Hannett with his carefully chosen newfangled electronics made the music he called gothic dance music, and he should know; catalogue number Fac 10, for those who like to count and collect. This was Strawberry Studios, formerly Inter City, designed and owned by 10cc, a smart-alec and romantic Manchester pop group that emerged in the smoke and damp, and the times that were changing, between the northern dream harmonies and Beatling beats of the local Hollies featuring Graham Nash and the visiting punk rock that led, once it had gone round a few terraced houses, and a few local minds, to Joy Division, whose music, more than most rock and pop, always sounds like it has just been composed, just thought of.

Stockport takes you to Buzzcocks, October 1976, formed a few months before, rehearsing and making early recordings that, oddly, would make a difference to Manchester and to the entire history of pop, proving how funny and astounding the North and pop music could be, singing about boredom as an ultra-modern, artificially created method of social control, tucked together a few feet above the most anonymous and ordinary of streets, underneath grey slates surrounded by bricks in an attic room somewhere along the Bramhall Lane, where somehow extraordinary creativity and intuition had insinuated itself into an unpromising physical space. The attic had been turned into a primitive four-track recording studio, owned by a professional engineer who had worked with the Who, Andy McPherson, but it was the cheapest place the group could find, just so they could hear what they sounded like without having to play at the same time. Forty-five quid, job done.

For young drummer John Maher, unceremoniously jammed into an airing cupboard to play the basic studio kit, these demos – leaked by the brother of the band's guitarist Pete Shelley, becoming the bootleg known as *Time's Up* – accidentally became the best album Buzzcocks ever made, their original spirit of accelerated adventure captured by the skin of its teeth. Their entire repertoire of ten songs was recorded in four hours, any mistakes uncorrected, no time, becoming part of the composition, truly a record made as a record of time and place, early instincts made buoyant by sheer exhilaration.

The band had met at Piccadilly bus station and travelled south to the studio on the 192 bus, which never stops linking in an industrious straight line the stratified layers of Stockport and eventually one of its posher southern borders, Hazel Grove, with the centre of Manchester. Somehow, you can hear in the recordings that they'd arrived by bus, as though some of the songs were thought of on a local bus, the soon-to-be-legendary light speed of their songs thought of when the bus really accelerated between traffic lights and with rare freedom attacked one of the city's most hard-working main roads. Dead-end ordinariness poetically transforms into something extraordinary.

Stockport takes you to Durutti Column, looked after by invisible band member Tony Wilson as eager, post-Epstein boy-band manager, except this boy band is one boy, really, Vini Reilly, using the guitar to fly in and out of himself, as if jazz was invented in Wythenshawe, his group named with mistaken Factory loftiness from a wrongly spelt situationist reference – two 't's instead of two 'r's – after an almost mythical anarchist group of militants formed during the Spanish Civil War by Buenaventura Durruti.

The *Return of Durutti Column* album, Fac 14, came sleeved inside lumpily glued sandpaper, one of Wilson's besotted, mischievous homages to the sarcastic, experience-spinning, near-imaginary situationists, inspired by a 1959 book, *Memoires*, the result of a collaboration between two original members of the Situationist International, artist Asger Jorn – a Danish professional bookbinder who proposed replacing the term 'art' with 'experimental action', possessing a sensuous, irrational Scandinavian situationism that was ultimately more conventionally shamanic and exotic than the central French methodology – and the group's assumed mastermind Guy Debord, with his more authoritarian, and more dominant, approach; plus of course the contribution of Danish printers Permild and Rosengreen. 'The artists can only rarely do without the help of a printer,' the more romantically minded Jorn had stated, never as committed to severely self-examining abstract theorisation as Debord. Wilson always appreciated a good printer, and Factory often needed a very understanding printer.

Memoires was a book inside a sandpaper-wrapped auto-destructive jacket, to be handled with great care, designed to damage books placed next to it on the shelf and any polished wooden tables it might be laid on, filled with fragments taken from other sources. The sandpaper for the Durutti Column anti-record, which contained the un-roughest music imaginable, was sourced by the industrious, single-minded, perpetually obsessive Wilson from Naylor's Abrasives of Bredbury, a couple of unexceptional miles east of Stockport town centre, birthplace of the comedian and impressionist Mike Yarwood, whose successful 1970s career was largely based on his meticulous take-off of Gannex-raincoat-wearing, pipe-smoking Prime Minister Harold Wilson droning on about 'the pound in your pocket', who made the final decision for Britain to move by 1971 to a decimalised currency, from ten-shilling notes to fifty-pence pieces, from tanners and threepenny bits to new pence.

A hundred years before the Wilsons moved out to the farthest south-eastern edge of the industrial North-West, the nearby industries clustered around the Mersey in central Stockport – one of the many little Manchesters orbiting the mothership – had created enough momentum to reach sleepy, remote Marple, previously almost untouched by civilisation, and wake it up in the late 1700s, ready for the radical changes of the nineteenth century.

As industrial energy waned in the twentieth century, Marple didn't keep growing, but it didn't completely go back to sleep. It settled down into itself, as a nice place to settle, with views of the green, restful stillness that make more sense the older you get. Wilson never made much of his time in this emptier, prettier North, but it was as much a part of him as the more obvious city-centre history and setting, and as much a part of the music released on Factory, as cut through with absence as it was with presence. Joy Division themselves, one of the greatest 'works' he was connected to, and helped make happen, were made up of this combination of the arcadian and the urban, with singer and drummer coming from calm, edge-of-rural Macclesfield, surrounded by light, and guitarist and bass player coming from grimy, industrial Salford, where the light seemed to have disappeared. The distinct time and place, light and dark attitude and vision that helped produce the particular Joy Division dynamic included this combination of unruly inner-city strangeness and ominous edge-of-world, woodland shadow, two very different places where life comes and goes, and leaves lingering traces on a scale somewhere between epic and mundane, between astonishing and menacing.

There was still history all around him as he grew up, not least because of the River Goyt, which streams through these parts on its way to becoming the Mersey fast enough to power some of the mills and factories that drove the Industrial Revolution. The Industrial Revolution began alongside such rivers, and there were fossilised signs of early industrialisation all around young, roaming Wilson, in the canals, the bridges, in old buildings, some of which had been reduced to ruins or completely retaken by the peaceful nature the Industrial Revolution had once so abruptly disturbed. Before the industry, there were also signs of much earlier times; Mesolithic, Neolithic, Bronze Age, Iron Age, Roman Britain and medieval days.

A print works was established in the last few years of the eighteenth century, near where the Wilsons' home was, still functioning well into the 1900s. The surreal tall chimney that rose above the surrounding trees was eventually ceremoniously demolished in 2007, a few months before Tony died.

Two nineteenth-century employees of the Strines Printworks keen to demonstrate how rural communities were up to date with mainstream intellectual and scientific thought started a journal based at the works, very much in the spirit of Victorian self-improvement: *A Monthly Magazine of Literature, Science and Art*, a single handwritten, hand-decorated issue filled with essays, articles, illustrations and poems which they shared with fellow employees, friends and associates. By the early 1850s, they were including photography, extremely new and rare at the time, long before people in portraits had the teeth and desire to smile, in case, as Mark Twain said, 'a silly, foolish smile was fixed forever'.

The forty-seven journals that were produced between 1852 and 1860, and the Strines printing company's considerable private library, are previews of the artistic ambition and eccentrically learnt enterprise – and his love of exquisite, innovative, limited-edition printed matter, and his whimsical community-minded commitment – that Wilson introduced into his Factory over a century later.

There was also a classic, self-made local benefactor, responsible for remaking the area's natural landscape and surrounding districts, the kind of adventurous entrepreneur Wilson fancied himself as a psychedelic, post-modern update of. Not far from Wilson's clean, comfortable family home lay the lost remains of what was known as Mellor's or Bottom's Mill, built between 1790 and 1792 by the aspirational merchant who dragged Marple, of all placeless places, into the modern world.

Stockport's Samuel Oldknow had the kind of dreams to make a difference, which meant he ended up as some kind of visionary, thinking big not just to make money and grab power but to produce almost utopian micro-societies, with high-reaching ambitions to supply moral guidance and nourishment to his workers. Out of the resourceful plans of such irregular regional visionaries emerged the Industrial Revolution. For Oldknow, changing the world meant first of all changing his immediate surroundings, however isolated and unfancied they seemed.

The greatest symbol of this was the mighty 400-feet-long, six-storey mill he built along the Goyt, powered by a massive 22-foot-diameter waterwheel, simultaneously showing off his clout and anticipating the bold, aspirational shape and look of a new world. Oldknow had become one of the country's leading muslin manufacturers thanks to a loan from Samuel Arkwright, who had recently revolutionised cotton spinning with innovative new machines. Boldly investing his profits in a new mill that would use Arkwright's world-changing machinery, Oldknow, fancying something extraordinary, organised the building of the world's largest cotton mill, the template for the kind of solid, multi-storey mill that rapidly took over the entire region.

In the middle of what was effectively nowhere, a building materialised with the height and heft of something usually belonging to the aristocracy or the Church. Soon, sturdy buildings like this would be everywhere, initially hugging the rivers for power, and then moving elsewhere when power came from a different source, and then, finally, running out of use when the world was upgraded yet again.

Oldknow was a major shareholder and supporter of the Peak Forest Canal, and along the banks of this new water system he built the Marple Lime Kilns to burn and transport limestone, determined to make them not only functional but elegant as well, as if a factory could resemble a palace or a monastery, bringing northern magic and a strange calm to its location even as it released clouds of smoke into the sky from its Gothic-style chimneys. To harness the Goyt's power, he had built an intricate system of waterways, canals and reservoirs that would be romantically named the Roman Lakes, which, set in the Goyt valley near Wilson's childhood house, in the early twentieth century, complete with outdoor dance floor, became a wonder that remains high on a list of local places to visit – for free – on day trips.

The audacious, innovative Oldknow couldn't cope with the smash-and-grab volatility of the cotton industry, surviving only with the help of the more practical and organised Arkwright, and by the 1820s was bankrupt, with debts in the hundreds of thousands. When he died, his estate passed to the Arkwright family. A great mind was not necessarily a great businessman.

In 1892, the mighty, prototypical Mellor Mill was burnt to the ground, and the Lime Kilns were left to deteriorate after their closure in the early twentieth century. There would be little left of his imagination other than haunting ruins sinking back into the woodland, nature taking back, puzzled over by archaeologists, while enthusiastically run tourist sites and smart newbuild houses found new ways to make use of the environment and the view, which hadn't been undone by the passions and initiatives of Oldknow. Marple had been somewhere, tried the outside world, and then, over time, it decided it preferred a quiet life. The yearning entrepreneurs could try their chances elsewhere.

Wilson's mum was happy to forget the dire visible impact of the noisy Industrial Revolution, which had pummelled Salford into submission and coarsened the sensibilities of its population. His parents went the opposite way from those who had originally moved from the countryside to Salford as thriving Lancashire became a central industrial location in the nineteenth century. Now that it was almost off the map, lacking opportunity, community spirit threatened, the Irwell clogged with waste and worse, they moved towards trees, fields and hills where the canals didn't look wretched but near-picturesque, and almost as a relief, nothing much happened and the past knew its place, and the future went through the motions.

They settled in a well-turned-out cul-de-sac with more than a hint of southern comfort, just off Strines Road, near the tiny village of Strines, one of the many passive, self-contained villages that fringe the Peaks, a short walk from Marple town centre. Strines would make it seem, with its cobbled lane built for horse and carriage leading to its little station, like nothing much had changed since the nineteenth century, in a good way. People had come for the recuperative 'healthy air' in the nineteenth century. The air was still seen as non-city healthy in the 1960s, and it's the same now.

It seemed a much better place to bring up their precious, precocious son than soiled Salford, which in the late 1950s seemed to be emptying out, of people and possibility, leaving little behind but street after street of sullen-looking, grey-topped terraced houses and trapped, frustrated but hardy people doing their routine best as the rain kept falling and few came calling. A city shaped by industry and reshaped by its collapse. Built, and then ruined. Unimaginable that it would ever be reshaped again, pockets of it regenerated by post-industrial initiatives and post-modern architectural flair, where the defeated canals almost completely stripped of industrial legacy would become attractive water features, overlooked by museums, theatres and a sprawling purpose-built media campus, becoming by the second decade of the twenty-first century one of the greenest areas in England.

Five: Start saying Granada, from the North and some influences (2)

Fiat lux. (Let there be light.)

Tony Wilson making a meal of Manchester, who can also be described as:
- combining punk snottiness with snooty pseudo-intellectual pretension
- a sponge for popular culture
- a real genius for processing the discoveries and inventiveness of others
- a cosmopolitan who ran the risk of becoming provincial
- like Faust, greedy for knowledge and ready to trade punishment for it
- sectarian cultist
- lounge lizard
- needing to keep interested
- when he liked something he really liked something
- indulging in a series of unfortunate flings
- romances not entirely sanctioned by the legal and marital circumstances of those involved
- giving himself constantly away
- bankrupt, twice, for not paying his taxes, which was either because he couldn't afford to, never making the money he should or could have, suffering from some sort of Catholic anxiety, or Marxist diffidence, or was enacting some sort of sloppy situationist prank
- courting an image of himself as social dandy but fiercely private about his private and family life
- well-spoken, well-dressed heartthrob
- dope-smoking mystic
- coke-snorting maniac
- meta mind-fuck jibber-jabber
- putting everything from the early '70s inside air quotes

- reaching Istanbul at eighteen alone and scared and hungry. 'I found a kebab place. They served me meat stuff with yoghurt on it. Yoghurt! On meat! It was so alien I was almost sick. Since then, it's become one of my favourite foods'
- sitting in someone's front room earnestly teaching a member of a lesser-known Manchester band how to do Rubik's cube
- a magnet for creative expression
- never able to avoid thinking about the kind of world he belonged to
- consulting Camus, synthesising Marcuse, mulling over McLuhan
- taking the greatest pleasure in being what he was

Tony Wilson became a shy, well-behaved ten in 1960, the perfect age to hit all the beats that were to come in the 1960s and disrupt that shyness and reserved childhood religious obedience. Perhaps he acted a little older and seemed older than his years in his twenties and thirties because his mum was nearing sixty when he became a teenager. To some extent, he also needed to be the one grown-up male in the house.

What made him think differently was made up of things he stumbled across that just happened to be of interest to a kid, a teenager, a student, forces and forms that were as inescapable as the presence, individually and together, of his honest, careful mum and gregarious, argumentative dad, his uncle making his life a pure, or impure, soap plot, of the God he was compelled to surrender to from an early age without having any idea who He was.

Forces and forms that were as inescapable as the trams that mono-tonously rattled and rolled along the damp, cobbled, shop-jammed streets outside his cold, tiny bedroom in his first few years, the noisy, rowdy, happy-sounding people coming out of the boisterous Salford pubs at clos-ing time, the dream-like, mountain-sized ocean liners towering above the terraced streets as they passed along the Ship Canal just down the road, intensifying his emerging sense of local pride. In his early days, before the move into the countryside, he never dreamt of any landscape but this one. Lowry's landscape, with chimneys juxtaposed with the otherworldly visitations of those serene mighty ships, towering above his world. Embedded in Salford but in touch with the world.

Then there was the miserable, magnificent rag-and-bone man with his hard-working, melancholy, clip-clopping horse, whom you could hear coming from the next street as he shook his bell and bellowed like a rocka-billy mutant, 'Raaaa booownaa.' If you had any rags or scraps for him, he'd give you a colourful balloon, maybe a donkey stone for your mum to scrub clean the front doorstep of Salford smoke and grease. Not quite treasure, but a sort of memorable, irregular theatre. You took what you could find.

Eventually, using what he found outside the home, the church and the school that was an extension of the church, he came to the decision that God, what there was of Him, wasn't telling you to go to church and pray every day and everything will be fine. He was saying, 'Go out and make the changes that need to be made, and what you decide there is of me, which parts you could possibly believe in, will be there to help you.' Wilson's philosophical underpinning, though – making unlikely connections, gen-erating a union of opposites, the inherent impulse of life to assert itself – goes back to his Catholic upbringing and exposure to scripture; 'I am the Lord doing all these things,' forming the light and creating darkness, bringing prosperity and creating disaster . . .

He came across alternatives to the Church that could become their own churches, with enough independent power and constructive momentum to balance out the immense, oppressive presence of Catholic traditions: pop music, science, football, literature and television, with their own exciting, illuminating rituals, costumes, gossip and glamour, their own venues and icons, their own gods and monsters.

Voices coming through the television when it was still a strange, special part of the home had an early impact, and ultimately influenced what became, in the middle of everything else, his career, how he earnt a liv-ing, and how he first learnt to use his mouth and mind to reach people. Granada Television was a huge influence on him, and he started to pick up its attitude from a young age, long before he ever worked there, never really thinking of it as a possible career.

If you can ever say that you are lucky to be born where you are born, especially when at first sight the surroundings and prospects seem particularly uninspiring and inhibiting, then he was lucky that he lived inside the transmitting reach of Granada TV, which started broadcasting when he was six years old, and soon entered what became known as its golden years – which came about because of a swashbuckling, precocious, self-opinionated, insufferably arrogant approach the owners and consequently the programme-makers took to making television.

Wilson ended up at Granada either because he possessed these innate qualities from sudden bloody birth, or because he developed these qualities as an impressionable, unfulfilled teenager by being exposed to the channel in the important early years when it defined and developed its distinct and adventurous identity. Living in the area, you would sit down and watch Granada TV from a young age, often simply because it was on, without even realising what an impact it was having on how you enjoyed, understood and related to the world, without appreciating what an unconventional, enterprising, even ideologically forceful channel it was. You'd begin your very provisional preparation for what you were going to become while being exposed to a channel that was like no other channel, with a name like no other regional channel.

Commercial television first gained serious momentum in the 1950s, after the Tory general election win in 1951 put a halt to the great radical and reforming post-war Labour government led by Clement Attlee, whose modest self-deprecation had been a necessary antidote to the Nazi-beating wartime bombast of Churchill. After Britain won the war, Attlee's attitude was 'We must now win the peace.' Eventually, winning the peace was not as dramatic as winning a war, it was mostly policy and process, however progressive, and there was a longing for the more visible, and audible, triumphalist methods of Churchill, presumably to make Britain great again.

Cecil and Sidney Bernstein were owners of the palatial, kitsch Granada Theatres, most of them in the South, and were initially more interested in extending their brand to the North than in television itself. Granada was a name they had chosen after a memorable walking holiday in Spain. It was a word they thought sounded continentally exotic and which reminded them of the architecture and monuments they'd loved, especially the Alhambra, the city of Granada's fourteenth-century Moorish palace and fortress complex, which looked to them like it belonged in paradise. There was little as exuberantly fantastic in Britain, and they thought there should be and tried to introduce some of the wonder through the ornate design and decor of their theatres. (A 1930 advertising campaign for the first cinema they owned to be branded a Granada, in Dover – they were Kent men – featured a poster around town that announced with a cryptic, Factory-like quality, 'Start saying Granada.' If Granada had been catalogued, the poster would have been Gra 1.)

The Bernsteins were politically more to the left than the other founding contractors of the new Independent Television regions. Opponents of the brothers' more liberal views even accused the more outspoken, innovative and flamboyant of the brothers, the jovial, authoritarian Sidney, former business partner of Alfred Hitchcock, of being a communist. Not a fan of the idea of commercial television, fearing its influence on people could easily fall into the wrong hands, Sidney's attitude was, if there was going to be such a thing, they wanted to be involved. They naturally took the position that they were in no way the wrong hands.

In 1959 Sidney gave a speech in which he presented the reasons why they had applied to run the northern ITV region: '. . . the North is a closely knit, indigenous, industrial society; a homogeneous cultural group with a good record for music, theatre, literature and newspapers, not found elsewhere in this island, except perhaps in Scotland. Compare this with London and its suburbs – full of displaced persons.' He added with a knowing smile, 'And, of course, if you look at a map of the concentration of population in the North and a rainfall map, you will see that the North is an ideal place for television.'

Granada's evidence to the Pilkington Committee of Enquiry into Broadcasting in 1961 made a more formal argument for their decision to submit for the northern franchise: 'The North and London were the two biggest regions. Granada preferred the North because of its tradition of home-grown culture, and because it offered a chance to start a new creative industry away from the metropolitan atmosphere of London.'

Initially, the Bernsteins intended to run Granada from London, which seemed the most practical idea – beaming programmes up from the South. This, though, would have meant breaking the terms of their licence. They were required to be located in the North. They needed to be northern. Manchester was chosen as their base.

From the point of view of London, the city was relatively remote in the 1950s; churning, chanting steam trains took over four hours to get there, just as they had seventy years before. It was even a little difficult to get through on the telephone, like you were calling back in time. Manchester was still Bible-black, packed with uncleared bomb sites smothered with rubbish, broken glass and weeds, lined with once-proud, monumental buildings that now looked neglected and adrift with no clear purpose. It was a cold, wet city of blank, defective spaces that needed filling, often seeming cut off, with nothing but stillness and emptiness and therefore a kind of distilled menace. The thought of a television station miles away from London amidst such disarray seemed to some faintly idiotic.

Faced with the reality of the North, the Bernsteins took the task, and the city, extremely seriously, with showbusiness entrepreneurs' flamboyance, quickly appreciating the new technical issues at the heart of local broadcasting. Not only did they have to overcome the reality of being regional and therefore apparently inferior, they also had to convince many that the idea of breaking up programmes every few minutes with adverts wasn't annoying and vulgar. Many thought television spoilt by constant advertisements selling you stuff was never going to last. How could advertising breaking into your home and nagging at you to buy things possibly catch on?

The Bernsteins had enough time between being awarded the contract and going on air to build the first purpose-built TV studios in the country. They were constructed just off Deansgate, on a former industrial site surrounding an old Manchester Ship Canal basin, along Quay Street, near the River Irwell. One of those murky, disabled city-centre spaces that needed filling. The building was designed by architect and social idealist Ralph Tubbs to a comprehensive brief from Sidney, a keen architecture fan and allegedly skilled draughtsman who was notorious for paying attention to the smallest detail.

Used to designing their cinemas as incongruous, grandiose set pieces introducing some resplendent continental magic into depressed English towns, they took the same approach to their Manchester TV centre. The Bernsteins' public-spirited entrepreneurial activist feelings that a unique Granada HQ must be built and be a living, breathing part of the city's psyche were recreated a quarter of a century later when Tony Wilson, guided by his contrarian Factory colleagues Rob Gretton and Alan Erasmus, for wild, idealistic reasons of their own, financed with socialist dedication by the record sales of Joy Division, started work on a preposterous-seeming post-modern nightclub inside a community centre inside a private members' club inside a folly, in an area of the city that seemed on the edge of the map even though it was a few minutes by foot from the large BBC centre. It backed on to an ignored sludge-filled canal, opposite the railway line that dutifully headed out from Oxford Road station north and west into the outer reaches and coastal areas of Lancashire. Even in the early 1980s such a club seemed as far-fetched as basing a television channel in a purpose-built setting in a soiled 1950s city, but there were still plenty of those post-industrial abandoned spaces, post-war ruins and neglected corners that needed attention.

The Haçienda, a mile or so to the south of Granada HQ, the other side of the Town Hall and the Free Trade Hall, a short walk from where the Twisted Wheel had been, opposite the fire station at the end of Whitworth Street, initially a dream mess, eventually generating its own hyper-local, internationally minded aura, was an irrational descendant of Granada and the Bernsteins' love of the idea of a town-centre pleasure palace.

It was inspired by the conceptual, post-modern instincts of Wilson and his cohorts during late-night thinking sessions, considering that each new situation requires a new architecture, that other cities run down by time and neglect had such independent, non-specific, almost ungoverned places where creativity, the trying-out of new ideas and connections, could thrive.

Why not Manchester? Wilson was, like Sidney, a fan of architecture, with a particular interest in the quixotic urbanist conceptual art of starchitect Rem Koolhaas and the way he mixed fantasy and pragmatism. (If there were two kinds of 1960s, one a modernist, avant-garde side inherited by Koolhaas, the other an Anglo-Saxon, hippy-ish, political side, Wilson the pop culture utopian swung both ways.)

Before the Second World War a young Ralph Tubbs had worked with the notorious architect Ernö Goldfinger on his visionary minimalist white modernist houses on Willow Road, north-west London, austerely piercing the standard rows of proud red-brick Georgian houses by the Heath in Hampstead. After the war Tubbs had designed the flying-saucer-shaped Dome of Discovery as the centrepiece of the 1951 Festival of Britain on the South Bank, a spirit-raising celebration, a treasure trove, of British arts, science and technology.

The Festival was organised to give Britons exhausted by the war an optimistic sense of recovery and a belief in a brighter future, and to promote better-quality design in the necessary rebuilding of the nation's cities and towns. Like the other austere-seeming, playful, even enigmatic-seeming buildings designed for the Festival, Tubbs' vast concrete and aluminium dome was coldly sold for scrap by Winston Churchill's new 1951 government. Only the more obviously functional and therefore more usable Festival Hall survived the cull. Such solemn, hard-edged buildings, clearly making a confident futurist break from London's more traditional rococo past, were seen by Tories as a worrying symbol – 'three-dimensional propaganda' – of Attlee's determined socialist vision.

By choosing Churchill and his gigantic, self-made history over Attlee and his bold sense of the future, the voters didn't appear ready yet for a modernist-minded, concrete-coated brave new world, or perhaps the hopeful summer fun of the Festival was too little, too late before an autumn election to make up for 1950s post-war shortages, continuing rationing, high taxation and a constant dreary sense of austerity. Expectancy was not enough, however constructive and practical.

Labour would remain in opposition for thirteen more years, between Gracie Fields and Vera Lynn and Lennon and McCartney, between Max Miller and Peter Cook, before a man called Wilson led a return to a relatively radical, modern-thinking and liberalising government, beating Alec Douglas-Home's morally broken Conservative Party. Some say the Labour Party was finally helped into power by the positive, open-minded wit and very un-Tory, un-square pop beat of the Beatles, who were soon 'rewarded' with MBEs.

Tubbs' Granada studio and office complex was a less aggressive version of his mentor Goldfinger's assertive brutalism. It's said that it was designed in such a way that if commercial television failed – and who knew at the time if it would work – it could easily be converted into a hotel. A brawny, eight-storey block of granite and glass, it was the first post-war commercial building in Manchester, a vital part of the city's staggered regeneration, and had its own forward-looking symbolic presence in a very Victorian city that at the time was mostly made up of worn-out, solid and static buildings from a decaying industrial past. The new building was a post-Bauhaus descendant of the once-mighty mills and workshops that grimly hung on all around Manchester, most of them emptied of use and reason. A grand illuminated sign announcing 'Granada' in red all-caps Stymie Bold Italic lettering – a sunshine name for a rainy place, like the Haçienda – was placed as a definite iconic gesture on top of the building, a reassuring, optimistic presence in a mostly gloomy-seeming, cramped city centre which at night would quickly become deserted.

Over time, art-loving sophisticate Sidney would line the walls of the Granada offices with paintings taken from his extensive personal collection – a Chagall, a Modigliani – and he even hung a nightmarish Bacon 'screaming pope' in the foyer, indifferently oozing decay, an intimidating representation of existential anguish next to a sign proclaiming Granada as the greatest independent television company in the world. The abstract horror pope made up of a melting mind and body looked down on those coming in for job interviews, making them understand how this was definitely not the BBC and that it will want something else from you.

The building's entrance and the corridors and offices inside emphasised how Granada became the intellectual core of the city, especially after the *Manchester Guardian* dropped the *Manchester* part at the end of the 1950s.

There were portraits in every office of the kind of showmen Sidney favoured, including nineteenth-century American circus owner, entertainment impresario and ground-breaking self-publicist Phineas T. Barnum, because however serious your work, you must never forget the showbiz razzle-dazzle, and however local you are, never forget you are also international. Barnum was an integral ingredient in Granada's approach to communication, which was somewhere between the Wild West and the Global Village.

At another extreme, but also an influence on its approach, there were portraits of the influential newsman and broadcaster Edward R. Murrow, whose pioneering work in television journalism and defiant breaking of the hold Senator Joseph McCarthy briefly had over America would become part of Granada's DNA.

With a building embodying its ambition that was like a physical manifestation of its progressive intentions and its collective love of enquiring minds, Granada Television became a unique institution by allowing creative and opinionated people to flourish as it set out to compete with the monopoly position of the established, formal BBC, although on the opening night of broadcasting one of its first programmes was in fact a generous tribute to the Corporation. It inherited some of that organisation's more eccentrically idealistic public-service principles, but added a new zesty, open-minded vision and passion for the new medium of television and a belief that television was definitely the future and a way of communicating positive, provocative ideas and interpreting even shaping the modern world as much as merely simply pleasing, informing and comforting people. There was also a tribute to Lancashire, boxing from Liverpool and Val Parnell's *Variety Spectacular*.

The fears were that independent television financed by advertising was going to undermine the nation's values, erode traditions and kill conversation; Granada's philosophy was built from the very beginning on the almost insolent idea that it could elevate people's spirits in an intelligent even spiritual way. The Bernsteins didn't want to simply react; they wanted in the right circumstances to act first.

To calm fears, especially from the Labour Party, that ITV broadcasting adverts to viewers unused to them would mean people spending money they didn't have, there was an opening announcement that was itself like an advertisement for advertisements – selling commercials as entertaining, informative and 'a guide to sensible buying that will help you get value for money. We hope the names [of these products] will become as familiar to you as the names of your family and friends. You can use Granada advertisements as a trustworthy guide to wise spending. Wise spending eventually saves money. And saving money can help with one aspect of our country's economic problems.'

Granada raised almost £15,000 from advertising on its opening night.

Being based in the North-West, at the centre of an artistic revolt against a largely complacent southern-based Establishment impervious to defiant, grinding northern lives, meant that the local channel and its energetic, youthful new staff paid attention to the so-called angry young men in theatre, literature and cinema and those writers in the developing world of cultural studies with robust views about post-war social development. Various working-class intellectuals – Richard Hoggart, E. P. Thompson, Raymond Williams and Stuart Hall – were committed to working out what 'culture' was becoming in a country, and outside world, where everything was changing. They were attempting to maintain some kind of sense of what a new moral and political authority could be at a time when things seemed to be in limbo, when, as Marx had predicted, there was a more intensive commodifying of everyday life.

This was when a remaking of the rules of art and entertainment and modernising social aspirations were running in parallel with the accelerating, alluring presence of popular music, an upstart, impetuous relative of film and theatre, much of it initially coming from America. The 1950s and '60s were no time for nostalgia; there was nothing to look back on but bombs and chaos; rationing and other after-effects of the war still lingered. There were new problems threatening a still fragile, nervous world – the Bomb, the Suez Canal, the developing mysteries of the Cold War, jet aircraft affecting geographical and psychological distances between countries. The energy spiralling out of pop music, less conservative cinema and theatre and the cultural-studies blend of literature, sociology and a certain disciplined moral fibre reflected an urgent need to create a future. A future that would reflect new, flexible, progressive ways of thinking and feeling, the dramatic acceleration in the international transmission of words, documents and people, unprecedented forms of working-class opportunity and affluence, and a democratised craving for the novelty of pleasure.

There was a cultural revolution in the 1950s, featuring the rapid, haywire expansion of mass consumption and mass society, a sudden increase in the means of communication, an influx of people from Commonwealth countries and the expansion of an Americanisation of British culture. Britain was no longer an imperial power, with all that meant in terms of its identity; a new cultural and national identity was required to cope with this combination of a breakdown of the old order and the presence of unprecedented new social and commercial forces. New styles of study, and new forms of media, were required, ones that acknowledged the tension and difficulty of these converging new energies.

Committed to realistic drama and early forms of authority-challenging investigative documentary-making, Granada also imagined clever new ways of covering current affairs, and from an early stage applied itself to an incisive form of serious political journalism, covering the annual Trade Union Congress from Blackpool in 1957. The impertinent new channel's coverage of the Rochdale by-election in 1958 seemed for better or worse to change the nature of democratic politics by supplying new methods for voters to decide who to vote for. It was a successful, direct challenge to the idea that such questioning programmes would be in breach of the 1949 Representation of the People Act. (In October 1959 Granada Television sponsored a set of lectures in London's Guildhall on the subject of communication in the modern world. Bernstein's hero Edward R. Murrow delivered a speech titled 'Television and Politics'. Using a phrase which summed up Granada's vigorous approach to political television, he said, 'When the politicians complain that TV turns their proceedings into a circus, it should be made clear that the circus was already there, and that TV has merely demonstrated that not all the performers are well trained.')

The Granada approach to programme-making was also rooted in Sidney's understanding of the influence and responsibility of the new medium, a commitment to extending the experience of its viewers, to examining and defining the North's larger social identity, and his belief that you could make intelligent programmes without being sensationalist or vulgar. There was also the fact that in return for the substantial income it received from advertising, broadcasting regulations insisted that a proportion of the programmes made must perform a public service, and at Granada this manifested as a commitment to taking current affairs seriously.

The boldest reflection of its attitude towards what television should and could be was the talent it hired, in front of and behind the camera.

Granada TV resolutely reflected the North back at the North, something the deeply southern and conservative BBC, with its deferential but ultimately insipid and stubbornly southern 'one nation' policy, was not doing. It wouldn't know where to begin. Granada hired northern writers and artists and made a point of recruiting local voices and accents as its main presenters and newsreaders. You didn't just see the North, you heard it.

One of its first slogans was 'From the North' – just as Richard Hoggart's *Uses of Literacy*, John Braine, Keith Waterhouse, Alan Sillitoe and Stan Barstow had been, and Morecambe and Wise, and soon the Beatles, forever impressing the wit and wildness of northern-ness onto popular culture, and eventually, inevitably, beyond. 'From the North' was a definite, inspirational, three-word manifesto, with a logo featuring an arrow pointing up from the South, towards where the action now was.

Mixing shrewd, empire-building public relations and a self-branding form of psycho-geographical invention, the Bernsteins and their team created the alluring abstract idea of Granadaland – those areas in the North of England that could receive Granada TV, including all of Lancashire, the epicentre of its concept, with Salford and Manchester at the heart of that, and Liverpool as an allied if vaguely pissed-off and self-reliant territory. Sidney's commitment to the pan-northern idea of Granadaland as a kingdom meant that, as the 1960s unfolded, you could not only get your local news from Granada, you could rent the TV you watched from Granada Rentals, watch films at Granada Theatres, and even eat out at Granada motorway cafes, all with an arrow pointing out the way.

In 1960 the channel's offices were filled with eager, mostly northern-born and -bred programme-makers encouraged to think differently and impress their demanding but open-minded bosses, who combined a businessman's prudent profit-seeking straightforwardness with a versatile research-and-development mentality. This led in 1960 to Tony Warren's *Coronation Street*, an idealised dramatic version of the closely packed, grey-roofed terraced Salford back streets Tony Wilson was born into, filled with faces and accents that still seemed nineteenth-century. Influenced by the monochrome kitchen-sink social realism and classic cobbled-street North-ness of Shelagh Delaney's 1958 play *A Taste of Honey*, of the idea of gossip as a way of producing a form of internalised domestic self-control, initially shown twice a week the programme became the ultimate emblem of the imaginative northern spirit of Granadaland, and of the Granada principles of entertaining but also moving, informing and inspiring. A fiction loosely but conscientiously based on a real place and the desires, dreams and daily routines of real people, *Coronation Street* was destined to outlive the Granada channel, and the shrewdly piloted Granadaland empire, a final lingering sign of Granada's proud, principled, from-the-North methods.

As well as the challenging dramas, documentaries and news reporting, there were the ordinary but individual faces of Granada, and its quickly defined style, the journalistic presenting of serious issues in a popular package, which became part of the background of Tony Wilson's early life. The cultivated, welcoming voices of Granada's presenters, many of whom sounded like your next-door neighbours or work colleagues rather than minor members of the royal family, meant that eventually he would work there, very much at home, patrolling the corridors and studios of Granada TV as one of the most idiosyncratic consequences of Sidney Bernstein's own idiosyncrasies and his expedient and idealistic commitment to creative northern energies and public-service integrity. A channel that was renowned for its inspirational, troublesome qualities nurtured the troublesome, inspirational nature of one of its greatest characters.

Wilson wasn't perhaps quite what Bernstein had in mind, especially when his presence led to programmes being put together in a haze of marijuana, girls in studio audiences wearing swastika armbands and a sinewy, self-flagellating Iggy Pop swearing for his life with a horse's tail protruding from his backside, but Wilson was perhaps the perfect result of Bernstein's methodology, his love for unorthodox showmen and incisive, stimulating journalism and the Granada reputation for attracting talent, anticipating trends and tolerating an informal office culture. Sidney never quite got *Coronation Street* either, but appreciated its importance and the money it made. Wilson himself could readily identify with the motto Bernstein adopted when he was made a life peer in 1969: 'If I rest, I rust.'

These talented Granada voices and faces that set the tone, helped give television a new, human dimension and ultimately led to Tony Wilson included the smart, graceful Irish writer and historian, and one-time editor of *The Spectator*, Brian Inglis, who wrote and presented the very first edition of *What the Papers Say*, once it was obvious with only a few hours to spare that Sidney was not going to get his typically audacious first choice, Orson Welles. Inglis's low-key but addictively instructive presentation of *All Our Yesterdays*, reviewing events from twenty-five years before – leading to the Second World War years – ensured his stint on the programme beginning in 1961 lasted for eleven years. For many it was how the war was watched, how a later generation began to process it, and there was something about the pace he spoke at, the pauses he left between words, that allowed the viewers to find their own space to think and reflect.

Well-informed studio talk using relaxed, expert presenters, mostly journalists, and intelligently chosen images was a classic Granada format;

cheap to produce, but making a consistent impact, and enhancing the broad-minded, forward-looking reputation of the channel. The reputation for taking risks and a kind of black-and-white-era blue-sky thinking meant it attracted some of the best minds in the country. Granada became the kind of centre of excellence, in this case for broadcasting, that traditionally usually ended up being in the capital city.

What the Papers Say was a rotating selection of journalists who would select some newspaper articles to review, write a pithy script and read it out, with voice artistes reading the newspaper extracts. It was oddly compelling, almost soothing, even watching, as I did, as a bemused ten-year-old, as if it was somehow compulsory, or just because it was the only thing on. Journalism, the serious and the comic, came alive in these understated but magnetic weekly few minutes.

Brian Trueman was one of the many local Granada recruits in the late 1950s who more or less fell into newsreading, and he turned out to be a natural, which would lead to different forms of reporting and presenting. He described working for the Bernsteins as like living with a benevolent despot crossed with a Jewish mother. They put enormous trust in the people they hired and effectively threw into the fray, letting them get on with it once chosen, and it paid off.

The suave, extrovert but highly composed and ever-smiling Mike Scott was a prime example of how Granada created different, flexible roles for its journalists – often as producer–performers: slick and appealing in front of the camera, but also responsible for what they were saying, and meaning, giving their appearances, however benign, even cosy, a refreshing, egotistical, self-assured edge. Scott also directed the early ground-breaking live by-election broadcasts, and some early episodes of *Coronation Street*, which he didn't think would work outside the North-West. Eventually, despite that, he became the channel's programme director, although he never lost his cautious, suspicious approach to the new and untried.

The breezy but still trenchant and campaigning Sale-born Bob Greaves was a more straightforwardly beloved and enthusiastic Mr Manchester before that title passed over to Tony Wilson and got a little warped by knowledge of the Flying Burrito Brothers and Colin Blunstone and the untypical argumentation of Boethius.

Greaves began his screen life in 1963, joining as an eager recruit from the *Daily Mail*, and ten years later Wilson appeared on the teatime news half-hour *Granada Reports* as a sidekick to the extremely experienced and in his own amiable way not-immodest Greaves, teasing him by calling him Dad. Wilson definitely picked up some of Bob's mischievous if beige-coloured teatime approach to hosting and presenting, his ability to read the purely information-conveying news in a way that was necessarily neutral but still very human, so that with Wilson something cheeky and engaging got weirdly mixed up with the cerebral and pushy.

A new style of professional television presenter rapidly emerged in Granada's early years, as a collection of smart, devoted talents made the rules up as they went along, in front of and behind the camera. Mostly journalists expecting a fairly anonymous life, they found a strange kind of fame in their new surroundings, appearing on screen five days a week and becoming a part of the family throughout a region suddenly presented with its very own stars. Unlikely, regular-looking blokes with no immediate signs of charisma such as Scott and Greaves would be mobbed on the streets of Manchester.

Thoughtful, conscientious journalism with an intellectual flair and a laid-back seriousness, with a brisk, sophisticated method of making the complex appear understandable, became a part of the local 1960s atmosphere, as Manchester entered its final years as an industrial city, heading into unknown territory, possibly terminal decline. A few of these energetic, quick-witted performer–producer–celebrities passed through Granada, almost an alternative, anti-elitist educational establishment, and went on to become national broadcasting legends.

The intimidating, steadfast Bill Grundy, Chorlton-born, Pennine-loving son of a factory worker, originally a geologist, worked as a newsreader from Granada's first days in 1956, when he was thirty-three. He flourished inside the new building in this relatively novel and still primitive medium, becoming one of its first favourites and an early Granada great, developing natural skills as a forensic interviewer, spontaneous, self-possessed presenter and shrewd, devil-may-care producer who would be passed on through the Granada generations and into wider television history.

He relished the freedom being on a less-scrutinised local channel provided, but never acted as though it was provincial or inferior. It was simply pure television, an exciting, stimulating new journalistic craft, even an art form, that required an unprecedented situational awareness. As an interviewer, he would dare people to go further than they had planned, needling them to reveal more about themselves. It was this technique that would become famous when on live television the Sex Pistols were dared to go further, with no idea of who Grundy was, who had no idea who they were.

Grundy was responsible along with other Granada workers for developing an accessible, intuitive, often quite bolshie ITV way of doing things, very different from the BBC, but which would ultimately lead to a necessary response, an acknowledgement and appropriation of this different way of doing things. Grundy was thoroughly ITV, provoking and challenging in a way that could verge on the punkish and living a personal life that often meant he needed a vital recovery sleep minutes before interviewing defensive, high-powered politicians with clear-headed precision. Colleagues would talk of a Jekyll and Hyde personality – but how a few hours with an on-form Grundy were worth the few hours of the other, darker Grundy. Both sides were present when he had words with the Pistols.

Barnsley-born son of a mostly out-of-work miner, Michael Parkinson was another inquisitive, insightful journalist joining the multi-accented, multi-talented Granada TV in its first few years and finding ways to adapt his resourceful writing and cultural and sporting interests to the still-unstructured new medium. He learnt his craft, like a number of Granada workers, on the other side of the Pennines, at the *Yorkshire Post*. Starting work on its producer training scheme, Parkinson described the atmosphere at the unformed channel positively as a kind of creative anarchy.

95

The fact that someone as skilled, ambitious and informed as the young, unflappable Parkinson wanted to work at Granada shows that in the early 1960s it was the place to be.

Such conviction flowing into Manchester then flowed out into the city, leading to something Tony Wilson once said, or he heard someone say and then said himself, or a character based on him said in a film: 'This is Manchester. We do things differently here.' What that difference was emerged as much within Granada as within the city's people and history. The self-reliant energy and pioneering approach contributed greatly to the tone and purpose of the city and those who represented it through music and other media for decades to come, long after Granada itself was absorbed into the greater body of ITV, losing its original independent and intrepid approach even as an increasing amount of television was made and based in the Media City complex in Salford – thriving media replacing industry in the old dock area, an island of placelessness in the North, but not of the North.

Parkinson worked as a researcher and producer for Grundy in the early 1960s, and when he was inevitably encouraged to try out on screen by Granada executives always searching for fresh new faces, it was Grundy who gave him advice on appearing in front of the camera. Very basic, almost Zen, but liberating, he simply told Parkinson to imagine as he spoke to the camera that he was telling a story to his wife, Mary. Move in towards the camera, and make sure he slowed everything down to counteract the adrenalin that would inevitably surge through him as he appeared on live television. And when you're finished, never forget to say thanks to the guys on the floor: the cameramen, the sound man, the make-up, those on the lighting grids. They're the ones who matter the most, because to be any good on TV you need those people the most, before you think of anyone else. They're the ones who put you on television, after all.

It was a message that passed through the Granada presenting ranks all the way to Tony Wilson and the many presenters he himself mentored, from Richard Madeley to Mark Radcliffe and BBC economics editor Faisal Islam. Whatever was thought about him in the outside world, just for being Wilson, few if anyone had a bad word to say about him among the Granada studio staff. 'Thank you, darling,' he would say as soon as he finished a shift, flouncing off to another of his lives, or to St Mary's church, the 'Hidden Gem' a few hundred yards the other side of Deansgate, which he would visit perhaps not so much to pray – this atheist who believed in God – as to find some peace. God bless.

The history of St Mary's went back to Henry V giving permission for a parish church in 1422; four years later, papal confirmation was given by Martin V. After a few nomadic centuries, the church, the first Catholic Mass centre to be opened in Manchester following the Reformation, found its permanent location in 1794 to tackle Manchester's deepest-troubled area, which lay between Deansgate and Albert Square. Over the next few decades the isolated church would be joined by the Town Hall, John Rylands Library, the Central Library, a rapidly growing city centre, and it became an important refuge for the thousands of Irish moving to Manchester from the middle of the nineteenth century. In 1869, Father John Newton commissioned carvings of saints and angels and decorations of the walls and high altar, the detail of which led to Bishop Vaughan, second Bishop of Salford, founder of the Catholic St Bede's School, to give the church its nickname: 'No matter on what side of the church you look, you behold a hidden gem.'

Parkinson went on to be one of the great British broadcasters, combining a journalist's ability to ask questions and construct a structured interview that unfolded coherently in real time with a way of talking intimately to the camera that came from those early Granada days. When he left Granada in the mid-1960s, on the way to establishing his famous chat show and himself as proto-national treasure, he was replaced by an affable young Cambridge-educated presenter from Anglia TV, Chris Kelly, one of the first signs of new talent coming from within television itself, not from print journalism.

The easy-going Kelly – being this amicable on television was a difficult skill Wilson appreciated, and adapted to suit his own approach – would become nationally famous for presenting *Wish You Were Here . . .?*, *Food*

and Drink and the kids' film quiz *Clapperboard*, but for years his definitively reassuring voice made him the main narrator of the audaciously
eclectic, troublemaking investigative current affairs programme Granada
started in 1963 with a definitive modern media title, *World in Action*.

Conceived by brash thirty-five-year-old Australian producer and ex-
Daily Express subeditor Tim Hewat, a contemporary at the Australian
Anglican Geelong Grammar School of Rupert Murdoch (motto: *Christus
nobis factus sapientia* – For us, Christ was made wisdom), *World in Action*
brought ground-breaking abrasive tabloid simplicity to television. Hewat
contributed an often reckless, campaigning dynamic to the Granada DNA
that was too volatile to be seen as biased either to the left or the right
– although Margaret Thatcher on becoming prime minister considered
Granada to be overrun by 'Trots' – and he was a significant influence
on most of those who would later shape British broadcasting, including Jeremy Isaacs, chairman at the beginning of Channel 4, and Gus
Macdonald, joint editor of *World in Action*, a presenter of *What the Papers
Say*, later a life peer and a minister in the Blair government.

Wilson became *World in Action*'s first on-screen host in 1980, while
another part of him was running Factory Records. His time there was
among his favourite TV work, when the programme was still perpetuating
insubordinate Hewat principles, the absolute essence of Granada's artful
approach to combining entertainment, opinion and information. By the
time he made it to the serious, respected *World in Action*, there were other
distractions taking up his time, forcing the powers that be to question his
commitment, the late hours and the ways he achieved those late hours, if
never his professionalism. Once or twice he turns up to Granada with his
Factory face on, and sometimes he handles Factory business as the serious
journalist, forgetting who he's meant to be.

There was less Granada hiring being done from radio, as though in the
rush to create something new it would be a backward step to look at what
now seemed old-fashioned and stilted. Irish broadcaster Gay Byrne was an
exception. He began working in advertising in Ireland in the 1950s and
did continuity announcements for Radio Éireann, ambitious to become

a broadcaster like his smart, smooth hero, the discreet showman Eamonn Andrews, eventual definitive presenter of *This Is Your Life*.

Hired by Granada because of the compelling quality of a classically engaging Irish voice that emerged from the tinny little speakers on rudimentary black-and-white TV sets like it had fallen from heaven, and because of a gently subversive, investigative edge to his calm, collected manner, Byrne would do a full working week in Manchester for Granada, and then fly back to Dublin for a weekend of radio shows and to present *The Late Late Show*. He took talking for a living in his stride, like it was what he was born for. Talking to you through the screen as though he was in the room with you. Wilson inherited this effortless-seeming informality, with a little added flicker of nihilism, of irrepressible cheek, coming from a different sort of knowledge.

Byrne hosted Irish institution *The Late Late Show* from the early 1960s to the late '90s, and his way of handling both the comforting and the controversial, the showbusiness and the contentious, the genial and the coldly inquisitive helped make it one of the most successful talk shows in the world – a continually transmitted social history of Ireland through a particularly turbulent period, passed through his forceful, accessible imagination. His broadcasting style, combining the serious and the playful, the thoughtful and the frivolous, was part formed at Granada, where he was allowed to test the limits of what you could do and say as a broadcaster without alienating your audience. What became very mainstream, almost middle-of-the-road in terms of capturing the popular imagination began in an experimental setting, where new rules were being invented for making television programmes.

Parkinson, Byrne and Grundy all worked on the magazine programme *Scene at 6.30*, produced by Johnny Hamp, and Byrne was the presenter of another varied if less groovy Granada nightly news show Hamp also produced called *People and Places*. Hamp would eventually get a nickname that also could easily have been handed on to Tony Wilson – Manchester's Mr Showbusiness. He was responsible as head of light entertainment for shaping Granada's coverage of popular music, at a time when British pop music was mostly a pale, high-spirited imitation of American styles, not least because the Beatles hadn't yet happened, and added something very English to imported rock 'n' roll, from Lewis Carroll to the Goons, and the accent and dissent of Liverpool, thirty-five miles up the road, river and miracle canal across Lancashire and Cheshire from Granada HQ.

Hamp had started working for the Bernsteins in their opulent theatres in the mid-1950s, working behind the scenes in various capacities on concerts, from Frank Sinatra to Cliff Richard. A valued member of the post-music-hall, pre-TV, theatre-running staff, he started working at Granada in its new Manchester television headquarters from the very first day, finding celebrities for quiz shows and guests for a London-based variety show. While scouting for talent, he soon became a northern clubland regular, promised land of sharp, mercurial comedy gold, another great source of the essential, smart-arse northern brass with hard-boiled knobs on that would infuse the Manchester to come. Sidney encouraged him to produce programmes, which sent him into the rapidly growing pop scene when it was just an extension of music hall, often a slightly chaotic part of the working men's club circuit.

Programmed by his work on the quiz shows to be always hunting for the new and fresh in whatever form, he had seen the Beatles in a sweaty Hamburg club in the company of soon-to-be-notorious agent and bullying manager Don 'Mr Big' Arden of Cheetham Hill. This was when the group was a necessarily overstimulated, rough-and-nearly-ready version of what we think of as the Beatles. Arden was hooked, and under his abrasive, threatening management style the Beatles would have been part of a very different history of pop; it was Brian Epstein, as a modernising, marketing-minded update of the shrewd old music-hall administrators and talent-spotters, who took steadying control of the Beatles, while Arden ended up with the less historic Animals, Small Faces, Move and ELO.

Hamp thought the Beatles were scruffy, even a couple of shades too unrefined, but he liked the beat, a solid, repetitive pounding that relentlessly drove you forward and held together what often verged on distorted amplified chaos. Back in the early '60s, the beat was what counted most for those working out what they liked and didn't like among this raucous new-sounding music that didn't necessarily have much of a future, that seemed to be a part of showbusiness but coming from somewhere else altogether, somewhere possibly at the edge of reason.

Against internal Granada feelings that the Beatles were too coarse and common, and therefore surely unprofessional and not very conventionally showbusiness, Hamp put them on *People and Places*, and on 17 October 1962 Granada's Gay Byrne became the first broadcaster to introduce the Beatles on television. The band's television debut on Granada was five days before John F. Kennedy spoke to a panicked nation as America and Russia seemed to be heading towards certain nuclear conflict. British pop music was rapidly changing shape as the American president dealt with the Cuban Missile Crisis and impending Armageddon.

The Beatles' television debut was also just four days before the American Folk Blues Festival at the Manchester Free Trade Hall attended by Mick Jagger, Brian Jones and Keith Richards, up from London for the day, and almost running into their imminent rivals in a pub along Deansgate. A couple of years later, Mick would pragmatically tell Granada that he felt the Stones would probably only be together for a couple more years. How far could you go with those particular chords, and songs about teenage love and basic lust? Would-be economist Jagger had probably calculated the ways and estimated their lifespan.

In 1967, a year after Jagger made that flawed estimation of his own destiny, following three very anxious nights in Brixton jail for possession of drugs he was persuaded by John Birt, an ambitious new twenty-two-year-old Granada production trainee, to take part in some filming for an edition of Granada's current-affairs crown jewel *World in Action*, in which unorthodox, forceful approaches to campaigning investigative journalism occasionally spilt over into gimmickry. (Some of the programme's aggressive approach to creating situations and causing reactions anticipated what would become known as reality TV.)

The newly free Jagger landed in a helicopter on the grand manicured lawn of a stately home to have a discussion about drug use and youth culture with various predictable members of the Establishment, including a token bishop and William Rees-Mogg, editor of *The Times* and father of Jacob. The contrived happening was hyped as a combative meeting between generations; already showing signs of the cultural control-freak tendencies working at Granada could amplify, Birt, on his way to ruthlessly ruling and reforming the BBC in the 1990s, advising Tony Blair and becoming a baron, was perhaps surprised that Jagger, the economics scholar on his way, after all that, to a lifetime of the Rolling Stones and a knighthood, was about as truly revolutionary as Rees-Mogg, on his way to a peerage. Everyone, really, was in the same business – promotion and publicity and defending their faith – just bringing to it different approaches to colour, shape and content.

Hamp grew into his role as producer – more importantly, a discerning Granada producer with a fresh, exploratory attitude to television, that it wasn't only about reacting, but acting on hunches and new possibilities – treating the job not just as a way of covering pop music as a superficial teenage fad, but as a means of anticipating trends, interpreting emerging genres and generally treating the new music as something serious, of appeal to a new sort of discriminatory fan. He started to build his own little fiefdom within Granada, a result of how the channel worked, allowing individuals considerable autonomy as long as they delivered, something Wilson would exploit once it was his turn, until he took it all too far.

In the early 1960s, the idea of 'light entertainment' was being stretched to include ground-breaking new acts and suddenly emerging pop scenes, before it became obvious that they were no longer simply a part of light entertainment, and certainly not just for kids, as much as there were many in the media mainstream who liked to keep them there. Until it was too late, and they reverted to being pretty much nothing but light entertainment in the early twenty-first century, when 'kids' were anything between ten and seventy.

Hamp had been aware, once the world had been saved, of how the 1962 American Folk Blues Festival at the Free Trade Hall had accelerated the British blues boom, and of an equally influential follow-up concert in 1963 featuring Muddy Waters, Sonny Boy Williamson, Otis Spann and Memphis Slim. With his director Phil Casson, Hamp persuaded the Granada bosses to allow him to film some of the acts appearing on the tour – convincing them by acting as though this was just some new light-entertainment talent from America, not the strongest, hardest sort of modern music, aggressively amplified in ways that a few years later would so upset the delicate ears and snowflake stomachs of Dylan's proto-hippy folkie fans.

On 18 December 1963, *I Hear the Blues* was broadcast in a low-key, minimally decorated Granada studio in front of a small, devoted audience, for whom the wonders of the blues and of television were as exotic as each other; Spann, Slim, plus Willie Dixon, Victoria Spivey, Sonny Boy Williamson and Muddy Waters played some of the very first blues music to be broadcast on television in Britain, an event that also had a political quality.

Granada through Hamp and Casson was opening eyes and minds to a different kind of music that reflected quickly responding Manchester fans' early love of this music and also its connections to the Civil Rights movement in America. It was classic Granada – of local interest, because these musicians were playing locally, to fans who knew what they were talking about, but complete with an international, documentary dimension.

A year later, the same year the local mod-filled, music-mad Twisted Wheel club started its R&B all-nighters, Hamp took the blues coverage even further, becoming a creative part of the new music process – taking the blues out into the damp, chilly Manchester air, filming Waters, a revelatory Sister Rosetta Tharpe and Sonny Terry and Brownie McGhee at a disused railway station in Chorlton, four miles south-west of the city centre on the way to Didsbury, as if it was somehow a central blues location – Chorltonville – existing at the same time in Granadaland on the banks of the Mersey and the Deep South along the mighty Mississippi.

Granada was broadcasting rare, exhilarating music shows that influenced local sensibility and excited national interest, and which became important archive material. Some of these artists were barely filmed for television; Hamp had an instinct for capturing unheralded performers but knew the importance of also filming more established legends. In 1964 he was producing *It's Little Richard*, a year after that *The Bacharach Sound* and *The Music of Lennon and McCartney*, a prescient Granadaland celebration of adventurous Granada boys the Beatles as infinitely interpretable world-class composers. Granada was making pop music history, a body of experiences that can be passed on and that make a difference, from the very beginning.

Six: Songs, shows and behind the scenes

Aut viam inveniam aut faciam. (I shall either find a way or make one.)

The first pop concert Tony Wilson saw was at the Free Trade Hall when he was twelve, but it wasn't the 1962 American Folk Blues Festival tour – he didn't claim to have been at anything that significant and historic, knowing no one would believe even he had been so bold at twelve, and he never claimed that he was at the infamous 1966 Free Trade Hall battle between a loud, busy-being-born Bob Dylan and some deeply wounded folk-forever fans. (For years the bootleg album from his 1966 tour was mistakenly known as *Bob Dylan Live at the Royal Albert Hall*, as though such a momentous occasion could only have happened in London, and that somehow this was diminished by the heckling being in Manchester. A tape of it was one of Tony's favourite things to play in his car.)

Wilson didn't feel the need to make anything up and claim a more legendary or revolutionary first gig. In a way, in this case the truth was more interesting than retrospective pretence, revealing a boy midway between being a child and a teenager about to discover new interests and getting an early taste of music that for all its surface lightness was about something more than comforting entertainment.

His first was during those 1960s years, when the majority of the concerts at the Free Trade Hall were by the hard-working Hallé Orchestra, ageing sign of the city's once-buoyant prestige, instigated during its industrial heyday, with occasional, slick interruptions by Shirley Bassey, Matt Monro, Duke Ellington, Kenny Ball and His Jazzmen, Ray Charles, Ella Fitzgerald and Gerry Mulligan. Pop music as we would know it wasn't yet actually popular enough to fill such a hall; it hadn't yet been revolutionised by the early great leaders, the Beatles and Bob Dylan. The teenager as a concept, an amorphous social movement, hadn't yet fully materialised, or at least music for teenagers was yet to take over the world.

Wilson went to see Peter, Paul and Mary in 1962, three Greenwich

Village-based folk music activists – two singers and a left-leaning come-dian – managed by Bob Dylan's Albert Grossman. They'd been carefully nurtured by Grossman and had a hit with a post-war protest singalong song co-written by folk activist Pete Seeger and originally sung by Seeger's group the Weavers, 'If I Had a Hammer', an anti-war song to satisfy the grown-ups with its discreet socialist pull, sung as though for children and with enough orderly shine for mainstream pop radio, although it was blacklisted during the anti-communist scare in the early 1950s. It became closely associated with the American Civil Rights movement, and Peter, Paul and Mary sang it before Martin Luther King Jr gave his 'I Have a Dream' speech at the historic March on Washington in August 1963.

The twenty-two-year-old Dylan was up to his second album, *Free-wheelin'*, after a mostly ignored, even derided, abrasive debut, and the folk was already a little fucked. It was Peter, Paul and Mary that took *Freewheelin'*'s opening track, the surreally stirring folk spiritual 'Blowin' in the Wind', into the charts, as a sort of friendly but still steadfast advance guard for the more enigmatic, challenging and off-puttingly furtive, even menacing Dylan.

Peter, Paul and Mary willingly sang their hearts out; Dylan, possibly lack-ing a heart, or possessing two, was welcomed as a compelling original song-writer into a world where he could soon drift out into the exotic wildness of time and space like a galactic ghost seeing a connection between Frank Sinatra and Arthur Rimbaud rather than a plain, plodding rock star, confi-dent that behind him was always this hopeful, world-famous and reassuring anthem, initially delivered by the safe hands and bland, pale-skinned har-monies of Peter, Paul and Mary in their suits and ties and glittery dresses. The song believed that every question possesses a power that does not lie in the answer, but they sang it as though it was filled with happy endings.

Wherever Dylan travelled, however far out, whatever happened to his voice, that magnificent mind, however many times he shattered the mel-odies of his best-loved songs, refused to smile and perfected a bohemian avoidance of resolution, he was always the man who wrote this song, as though he really did know what the answers were to all our questions. Or just knew another question to ask, always seeking knowledge in a way Wilson would love. Geniuses have a knack for raising new questions, which can mean that they are either admired for their creativity or detested for disturbing our daily peace of mind.

At the time, this sort of acoustic folk-singing with a social conscience was about as radical and progressive as you could get in a pop setting – hence the shock and fear when Dylan, obeying nothing but his diabolical imagination, replaced the serious, relatively comforting acoustics with trivialising, sense-ripping pop electrics. The folk era led on to Wilson's hippy-era taste in music, deep down his constant favourites, from Neil Young, Jackson Browne, Gram Parsons and most of all Leonard Cohen, through to Bruce Springsteen, one of his last great solemn, denim-clad American crushes before English – and Manchester – punk handed him a different kind of key.

As a sucker for a slogan, and always loving, and loving to spot, or be seen to spot, the next big thing, Wilson inevitably fell for the Jon Landau, *Rolling Stone*-sparked Springsteen 'future of rock 'n' roll' hype in 1974 which launched a 'new Bob Dylan' into rock. *Rolling Stone* was a Wilson bible, and Landau one of its leading critics, and later he would produce and manage Springsteen – a seamless move from one role to another that showed Wilson how being a journalist didn't have to fix you in one place. Wilson was definitely the only early-evening newsreader on television in the mid-1970s who would announce to his viewers with breathless excitement, wearing over his shirt and tie a Bruce Springsteen T-shirt he'd bought in San Francisco, that he had just seen the future of rock 'n' roll. In the North-West we assumed other regions' teatime newsreaders were similarly inclined to impulsively express their infatuations on live television, but in fact only Tony Wilson was acting like this. He was sowing doubt even as he sat behind a TV desk as though he was seriously invested in the status quo. He wore a jacket and tie, stayed mostly loyal to his autocue script, but he was actually a dream chaser.

At the time, pop on TV was tucked into one or two safe, orderly and/ or vulgar places, and rock was filtered through the gentle, wholesome and strictly anti-hype mind of bearded, square freak Bob Harris. Based on pure enthusiasm, and a little amazement that no one else in his position was picking up on these things, Wilson was transmitting peculiarly mixed signals out into the North-West.

To many, especially those living in the more remote parts of the region outside the cities and the larger industrial towns, those not in touch with a local independent record shop or a hippy bookshop packed with disruptive underground energy and left-wing pamphlets, watching Wilson on Granada was like coming across a teacher smuggling tantalising information into the middle of the usual dull lessons. He might be getting it wrong, and there was something a little unstable even unreliable about his presence, but that didn't matter – it wasn't the detail, it was just the fact that something different was happening, something that didn't happen anywhere else.

Springsteen was a definite descendant of the sociopolitical anger of Peter, Paul and Mary – a culture of rebellion forged in the Joseph McCarthy witch-hunting 1950s – with their processed theological connections to Dylan and Pete Seeger, if not their general light-heartedness and sweet, hearty singing.

Two years after seeing the trio at the Free Trade Hall, young Wilson bought his first LP, a double-album souvenir of the group's live show, *Peter, Paul and Mary in Concert Volume 1*, which opened with a brand-new Dylan song, 'The Times They Are A-Changin'', a pretty protest song, conceptually if not cynically but definitely historically blending the formulaic and the eternal. Dylan had spotted how history was changing, and then made sure himself that history was changing in other ways. Tony bought the album possibly because they were such generous, or Grossman co-ordinated, Dylan deliverers, or more likely because among their well-organised folk, gospel and political songs there were very catchy songs for children, including the sweet, possibly naughty 'Puff the Magic Dragon', which may have been an early, sneaky metaphor for drug use but more likely was inspired by Ogden Nash's children's poem, 'The Tale of Custard the Dragon'.

Ultimately, 'Puff' is about a little boy who likes to fantasise and play pretend, and then the day arrives when the boy has to wake up and leave his little-boy daydreams behind and find his place in the grown-up world and behave himself in adult society. And Wilson the pretend grown-up's interest in Peter, Paul and Mary was more to do with manager Albert Grossman than the group. As the first album he owned, *Peter, Paul and Mary in Concert Volume 1* points forward to how what most intrigued him about music was those who put it together behind the scenes, those who formed the groups, styled them, gave them opportunities, even their names, prepared them for the commercial world, fought nasty battles with the greedy, unimaginative and cynical in order to create artistic space. The impresarios. The movers and shakers.

Grossman was one of the early masters, known as the 'first modern manager' and quickly controversial because of his early materialistic-seeming ambition to commercialise folk music and its serious, radical-message music. Peter, Paul and Mary had never played together until Grossman created the group, spotting a way to sell anti-commercial folk as commercial pop music.

Wilson would end up more interested in how these formidable, tough, ingenious deal-making characters functioned, what their role was in making the whole thing happen, and where other people might look to Dylan's snarky, masquerading, hyper-touchy persona as displayed in D. A. Pennebaker's documentary *Don't Look Back*, Wilson would look to where it probably came from: his ever-present, challenging, condescending, high-handed and sometimes cruel manager. Dylan got the cryptic and mercurial as much from Grossman as anyone.

These were the individuals Wilson liked to study: how, say, Grossman got into the music business after going to university and getting a degree in economics, running a club in late-1950s Chicago showcasing forward-sounding folk that became the hippest venue in the city, gathering talent as he moved from club to record business to management, Chicago to Greenwich Village, the centre of a hip, messy new kind of cultural heat, of a new form of exciting, influential pop literacy.

Determined to take his personal taste out into the world, into the mainstream, winning huge success without sacrificing credibility, Grossman was one of those early operators who knew there was change in the air, based around the energetic new minds, voices and instruments of those starting to fuse folk with rock with blues with drugs with youthful idealism with recreating the world – articulating and rewiring the epiphanies and indulgences of the teenage baby boomers – and he wanted to work out how to reach people so that the change happened in a big, mainstream way. There was change in the business as well: he was one of the first to recognise the profitability of music publishing, where the money could flow and sometimes become a flood.

There was all this art, and because of it, because of those changing times and a new buying young, there was going to be all this money. How do you turn someone as revolutionary as Bob Dylan – whose commercial potential could be restricted by ideals that made his words and melodies so transcendent – into an international pop star? How did Dylan and all that thinking make it into the charts on his own terms, without diluting any of the mystical power? This balancing of the business with the creative took its own genius, and its own emotional violence, and was a major contribution to the establishment of rock music as a cultural phenomenon.

Grossman was one of the first to appreciate how music made by the young with a radical, rebellious edge was rapidly becoming an industry, a force in its own right with enough of its own energy to compete in the more traditional grown-up world. Dylan was the artistic revolution; Grossman – like Epstein with the Beatles – was the one without whose negotiation, promotion and organisation the revolution wasn't going to happen, without whom the music wouldn't make any kind of real impact.

Eventually, Grossman got a little greedy, for the limelight as much as anything, for empire-building, and he wasn't so happy to stay in the background. He fell out with his acts, who were like his children, Dylan included, who got really pissed off – not least with the 25 per cent Grossman was taking, which led to one of the longest and nastiest of music-business court cases – and lost interest in music.

Wilson loved these sorts of stories. Musicians were just a part of the history, and possibly often got in the way, had little exciting to say outside their songs, and didn't really appreciate the myths and energies spiralling around their music, and how they emerged, often accidentally or because of tragedies, crises, chaos, triumphs, images that you could never anticipate or create but which you used to your advantage after the event.

Wilson recognised the worth of true mysteries like (the tone-deaf) Tom Parker of Elvis, Epstein of the Beatles, Peter Grant of Led Zeppelin, Andrew Loog Oldham of the Rolling Stones, Guy Stevens of Mott the Hoople, Tony Defries of David Bowie, Tony Secunda of T. Rex, Robert Stigwood of the Bee Gees, Joe Boyd of Witchseason, John Reid of Elton John, pioneering rock promoter Bill Graham of San Francisco, Jon Landau of Bruce Springsteen, David Geffen of Asylum Records, Chris Blackwell of Bob Marley and the Wailers, Jake Riviera of Elvis Costello, Malcom McLaren of the Sex Pistols. And, closer to home, Richard Boon of Buzzcocks, and Rob Gretton, with a lazy, wary grin Lewis Carroll would have swooned over, whose taste was really northern soul, of Joy Division and New Order, the groups who really made the money that enabled Factory to build all sorts of things, from records to clubs to offices to tension and myths. And, at the very extreme, of Don Arden, operating as though managing was as much about acting, occasionally for real, like a gangster as much as a mentor and money man, or between Grossman and Gaddafi.

These were the ones. The ones who managed and ran labels and guided careers, doing the deals, coming up with ideas and scams, fighting with lawyers, former friends and clients, not really to be trusted but totally committed to their artists until they weren't, the ones who get called 'bastard' and worse because of how they protected, or neglected, or even exploited their musicians, the ones who acted like none of this – from Dylan down – would have happened without them. They were Wilson's real heroes. He believed in them.

You could say his first gig, then, wasn't Peter, Paul and Mary. It was Albert Grossman.

Seven: Debating, grammar school and the Beatles

Gladiator in arena consilium capit. (The gladiator is formulating his plan in the arena.)

Tony Wilson the harum-scarum motivational speaker, who can also be described as:
- preferring to spend more on the design of a record sleeve than on the production of the music
- 'There are many people who'd like to hit me, and many people who'd like to chat with me for an hour. They are generally the same person'
- flicking through a rack of albums in Piccadilly Records, Manchester's longest-running independent record shop, while standing under a *Tony Wilson is a wanker* T-shirt
- 'Today, I've done 73 meetings, 100 phone calls, two interviews, five photo shoots and before I go to London, and I must go to London tonight, I've got to go to Wigan, fucking Wigan, to talk to 50 kids about why rock 'n' roll is a fantastic business'
- straight man
- confidence trickster
- loving, absolutely adoring all the things he knew
- not easily placed in a captionable context
- a restless conjuror of images
- live by the sword, die by the sword
- irresponsible on a grand scale
- up himself
- passionate advocate
- a gobby sort
- too big for his own boots
- civic, Catholic, contrarian, charming, cunt and other 'c'-words (copyright Richard Boon)

Wilson, the cradle Catholic, the duteous young soldier of Christ, was a proud altar boy at his nondescript Roman Catholic school in Marple Bridge, St Mary's, slowly coming to life through the learning he took to with ease, especially mathematics, having no problem with whatever the pace of teaching was. Tony was never a particularly naughty boy. The worst thing he would be picked out for was talking during class. At the back of the class, always with something to say, the mouthy bugger, already thinking his ideas were worth sharing.

He remembers being infatuated with nuclear physics when he was ten, which was in fact a Manchester thing as well. When Wilson would come up with his list of things that Manchester did first, making pretty much everything, including computers with the help of Alan Turing, his claim that the splitting of the atom first happened in the city – just off the surely dead-ordinary Oxford Road – seemed one of his more outlandish local boasts, alongside his suggestion for the original location of the Garden of Eden as Longsight – near the studios where *Top of the Pops* was initially based from 1964 – and the first Marks & Spencer shop in Hulme; the formation of the Shakers in 1747 by Ann Lee of Toad Lane (now Todd Street, near Manchester Cathedral and Chetham's Library), the illiterate daughter of a blacksmith and a mill hand craving something more emotional and personal than the Church of England; the world's first commuter towns in Altrincham and Sale, meaning Manchester had the first commuters as well as the first computers; the formation of the National Union of Journalists by staff at the *Manchester Guardian* and the *Manchester Evening News*; the birth of vegetarianism in Salford; that Manchester students Alcock and Brown were the first to fly across the Atlantic Ocean; Frankenstein and Sons of Newton Heath's role in the design of the first man on the moon's spacesuit; and Didsbury near the Factory Palatine Road offices was the birthplace of Israel.

The nuclear age did begin in Manchester, though, during a meeting of the Manchester Literary and Philosophical Society on Tuesday 7 March 1911, formally announced by New Zealander Professor Ernest Rutherford, thirty-nine-year-old head of physics at Manchester University, former student at Trinity College, Cambridge. How to unlock the secrets of the universe and work out how everything in it is put together was in the Manchester air, circulating around many of its university buildings and therefore through the centre of the city.

For some in the early twentieth century Manchester was an unlikely place to come for science – smoky, dirty, born in a noisy, messy, nineteenth-century flash, very much not as genteel, established or intellectually reputable as Oxford and Cambridge – but there were numerous institutes, committees and societies, and during the nineteenth century there was a constant surge of riveting intellectual interaction – science, like fire, was put in motion by collision – culminating in Rutherford's exploration and revelation.

Inside seventy years, as Manchester made some people fortunes and condemned others to a living hell, it had also become an eminent scientific location, renowned for invention, progress and discovery. The well-equipped physics laboratory at Manchester University was the one thing in the city that interested Rutherford – the Hallé Orchestra, built on the municipal German model and thriving local theatres, held no attraction. He arrived in 1907 and quickly put together a crack team of scientists including Hans Geiger – who had developed a method of detecting and counting the emitted particles of radiation – Niels Bohr and Ludwig Wittgenstein that was the very beginning of nuclear science.

The first president of Israel, pioneering scientist and statesman Chaim Weizmann, lived in Manchester for thirty years, an almost random choice of city, initially describing it as frightful and 'beyond description'. He arrived in 1904 to read biochemistry at the university, becoming part of the second-generation Jewish immigration into industrial Manchester, initially seeing it as a stranger as 'a hellish torture for an intellectual to live in the English provinces'. He grew to like and understand it, relishing how it was 'brimming with liberalism', moving from being an exile to being at home, happy to be removed from the petty rivalries of London Jewish politics. He found intelligent company and support from *Manchester Guardian* journalists, including its editor C. P. Scott, the philosopher

Samuel Alexander and Simon Marks, who would help turn Marks & Spencer from a local family business into a national retail giant.

Weizmann formed and led various Zionist societies, and audacious plans for a Jewish state began in the sort of sturdy red houses in Didsbury and Fallowfield where later Factory Records and Roger Eagle's *R'n'B Scene* fanzine were conceived. (Roger Eagle paved the way for Wilson as specialist fan and entrepreneur, before rewiring his love of music in Liverpool after moving in 1970, leaving a space in Manchester to be filled.) This was the city Wilson loved, where knowledge, expertise and inventiveness were passed on haphazardly with unanticipated often controversial consequences from generation to generation, where local thinkers exploiting the diversity and vigour of the city became figures of national even international significance.

While Ernest Rutherford was at Manchester University, Weizmann was a senior lecturer in chemistry. He described Rutherford as young, energetic, boisterous, and he talked 'readily on any subject under the sun, often without knowing anything about it'. He would hear him coming down a corridor after his lab results were particularly promising singing 'Onward Christian Soldiers'.

Rutherford wrote a book in 1904 called *Radio-activity*, which, what with one thing and another, seventy-one years later became the title of the fifth Kraftwerk album, which featured a track called 'Uranium' by the affluent, delicate techno-prophets of future musical, personal and social feelings, singing softly of constant decay, of the radioactive ray created by uranium. Rutherford had performed many experiments studying the properties of radioactive decay, coming up with the terms 'alpha ray', 'beta ray' and 'gamma ray'. On 'Blue Monday', New Order would sample the sweet, doomed choir sound from 'Uranium', featuring a different sort of decay – sound decaying in a certain amount of time to nothing at all – which Kraftwerk originally made using a Vako Orchestron, an obscure, fragile-sounding alternative to the more mainstream Mellotron.

The secretive, colour-coded sleeve for the twelve-inch-only 'Blue Monday', representing a floppy disk to symbolise the tech that helped make the record, was designed by Peter Saville, believing in science as much as art. The first record he bought for himself was *Autobahn*, the fourth album by Kraftwerk, released in 1974. Saville came from a steady, suburban, northern middle-class family in refined Hale, with two elder brothers, a Twisted Wheel dance freak and an Afghan-coat-wearing dope-smoking acid-taking hippy, who brought all sorts of records, from Santana to the Chi-Lites, into their house so he didn't have to buy any of his own. Until Kraftwerk, beyond pop, his own thing, beyond disco, beyond hippy, another kind of music, outside of everything, which left his brothers behind.

He'd heard the title track of *Autobahn* on the radio, edited down to three minutes – for some sort of safety, as though its mysteries could be neutered by turning it into an abbreviated novelty record – but still sounding like it was creating an infinite dimension. He adored it and was then told by a friend at the Manchester School of Art whom he'd known since school, Krautrock fanatic Malcolm Garrett, that the track on the album actually took up one whole side of the LP. His mind was blown. 'I'd never bought an album until *Autobahn*, and it brought me in contact with some kind of European canon. I didn't know such a thing existed, I didn't know the meaning of the word "canon", and it opened up European modernism, this journey they were recording you just knew went past power stations and cathedrals, a history of European civilisation. For me, the music was my life, as it was then, a continuum and a state of being.'

The sound of it, and the stark, graphically radiant sleeve the record came in, were like crossing unlimited space and time, and Saville took the techno-transcendent spirit to his sublimely non-representative, mostly unmarked sleeve for 'Blue Monday', which became as much a part of the record as the astonishing track, which by the 2020s was perhaps the greatest example of an anthem for the nervous system of a city that became what it became because of connections between people, time, minds and machines, that constantly left traces of itself throughout history. It was a song that could only have existed because of Factory, because of Manchester – an unbroken chain of events and ancient experiences flowing one out of another – and, even though he was distant from its composition and

116

production, busy in the shadows, because of Tony Wilson, who could make things happen often just by existing, and by making connections that made no sense to anyone until they did. Everything was linked, as far as he could see, especially in Manchester, where disorder created connections and a glorious resonance.

The song, which somehow could describe just about any situation – from love to death, from thinking to dance, loneliness to togetherness – was a melancholy turning of time into tune, loss into momentum, memory into rhythm, suicide into sensation. It wondered aloud what Kraftwerk would sound like if they were produced by Giorgio Moroder, influenced by Joy Division and came from Manchester. Which, because music could cross space and time, was in New Order's mind a part of New York. 'Blue Monday' as a key part of the soundtrack to this story of Tony Wilson explains how in this story everything fits, everything is in its place. How Manchester became more Manchester in the most unlikely of ways because Tony Wilson needed to feel connected with the purpose of the city, where as far as he was concerned everything happened first, even if it didn't.

While working in Manchester, Rutherford discovered the nuclear atom, and in 1917 was the first person to create an artificial nuclear reaction in laboratories at the university, initiating the field of nuclear physics and helping instigate the great theories of quantum theory – the atom was not the smallest particle in the universe, it was itself a miniature universe in which the mass is concentrated in the nucleus surrounded by planetary electrons. Science was changed, the world was changed, Einstein would call him 'a second Newton', and Manchester was the host city for such genius. A young boy's dream of becoming a nuclear physicist was as much a Manchester – or Salford – dream as playing centre forward for United or City.

In 1961 Wilson earned a scholarship to the boys-only De La Salle Catholic Grammar School in Salford. His parents had been worried their easily distracted son wouldn't pass the eleven-plus, an examination that meant at ten and eleven years old hemmed-in British children in a seen-and-not-heard world still worn out from the war were being funnelled one way or another via the competitive whims of a series of crude, weighted tests of ability into a form of education that had the potential to decide their whole lives. For many, education was destined from an early age to be a form of bondage; failing this mysterious exam, given so much importance during these years, could make you feel stupid for the rest of your days. The eleven-plus principle was based on the decades-old national belief that a test at this age could accurately predict what a child might go on to achieve, as if this enigmatic obstacle measured innate intelligence.

It worked for Wilson: the heavy brown council envelope containing the test results that would finally drop through the front-door letterbox containing pretty much your immediate destiny had very good news, a sign that his parents' decision to move to charming Marple to allow Tony to concentrate on school and exams had worked after all. According to his results, he was one of the clever boys he talked about who came in to De La Salle from all over the region – Oldham, St Helens, Stalybridge – what he liked to call the 'Catholic diaspora', never expecting to be challenged about what he actually meant. He even claimed he eventually found out that of the 750 or 1,000 entrants for his year – the story naturally tended to change depending on whom he told it to – he, of course, had the very top results.

Some 50 per cent of the boys in his year were scholarship pupils taking advantage of the selective system, to the relief of their parents, avoiding the alternative, a plunge into the disadvantaged 'secondary modern' channel, where you were in the second tier, with opportunities and teaching standards immediately reduced. On both levels, grammar and secondary modern, there was streaming, children separated into A, B and C classes according to alleged merit, meaning that education was based on division and segregation at every level, a reflection of the wider schisms of the enduring and rigid English class system. The lowest were treated as beyond help and were driven even lower. Breaking out of the cycle took luck, pluck, a kind of unconscious determination or, occasionally, unstoppable, ageless genius activated by accidental contact with random writers, artists and musicians, and positive, loving parental influence.

At his primary school and then his grammar school, Wilson was definitely A stream. Some of those who found their way into the so-called superior grammar schools like De La Salle found themselves out of their depth, at a loss how to deal with the rules and regulations and an intimidating culture of bullying. Not Tony. He developed enough confidence to deal with his new surroundings and expectations and worked out how to fight against all kinds of bullies, from classmates to teachers, using words, the power of persuasion and a rapidly developing charisma.

'He was a gentle soul and he was definitely bullied at school,' said his old friend Neville Richards, 'but he didn't fold when faced with this kind of rejection. He found ways to use it, to be motivated by it.'

Wilson would talk about how, by thirteen, he was already inventing a persona, a lower-middle-class kid's 'protective blanket of righteous rightness. It all starts there, perhaps. I think I found being clever a bit embarrassing and dealt with it by becoming the classic class joker, slightly the fool. The fools in Shakespeare, though, are the only ones who have read the entire play. They know where they are, they are aware they are a character in a drama. The secret of the successful fool is that he's no fool at all. I liked that. I got behind that, and then it developed.' He became a licensed jester in the Shakespeare style, getting the respect of the king, with an element of danger lurking beneath the surface of the smile, permitted to say the unsayable, to make the forbidden joke, to outwit the terrible forces of disorder in the world.

The other 50 per cent taken into De La Salle, part of the social levelling the grammar schools were meant to achieve, were the sort of intrepid locals Wilson never lost his fascination with, the 'Salford heavies', the weakest of them much tougher than the very toughest boys in Marple, a different breed altogether. For Tony, tucked into the soft underbelly of the underwhelming lower middle class, the working-class toughs, greasers, rockers, skinheads, football hooligans, casuals, whatever their current fashion status, were a constant embodiment of an uncelebrated avant-garde, often in their own way with their resentful airs generating a sensationalist form of surreal reality. They could be clever in different ways to Wilson and were a constant source of mystery to him.

It was the Salford lads at his school who tended to have the gumption to duck into the city-centre clubs of Manchester – into what was known as 'town' – and bring back exaggerated reports of the life and soul happening there, the dancing all night at Rowntree's Sounds. It was a non-Salford De La Salle boy, though, who got expelled for selling purple hearts at the Twisted Wheel.

De La Salle was a rugby-playing school, a sport guaranteed to boost the strength of the toughs, a sport that permitted, even encouraged, formalised violence; soft-centred Wilson spent most of his time working out strategies to avoid having to take part. He is so wooden and stiff when he does find himself playing rugby, the ball bouncing off him when it is thrown his way, he gets the nickname Plank.

At the other extreme, the skills required to become head boy didn't particularly interest him either. He didn't wear the cherry-red De La Salle blazer with the kind of neatness – maybe just a hint of rumpled camp insouciance – that suggested he was organised enough to be given those kinds of responsibilities. Or, in his correcting memory, the position of head boy was abolished as soon as he was old enough to be given the role; he did become form captain, though, taking the responsibility in his stride. He was just naughty enough to occasionally get in trouble and be labelled by the Latin teacher his 'problem child'.

Part of getting into – or out of – trouble was his ability to argue. In 1964 he enters a public-speaking competition organised by the Catenians, established as the all-male Chum Benevolent Association in 1908 by the Bishop of Salford, anxious to see working-class Catholic communities break free of lack of opportunity and limited influence. The name derived from *catena*, the Latin word for 'chain' – each member a link ensuring the strength of the whole organisation, representing a continuity of brotherhood. A version of the Freemasons, and still in existence, the Catenians have often been accused of being a secret society with obscure ceremonials and oaths, which the association puts down to lack of publicity rather than anything intentional.

Young Wilson gives a speech about the Socratic paradox – *I am the wisest man alive, for I know one thing and that is that I know nothing* – and wins first place, smart enough to know there was so much stuff he didn't know, or smart enough to pretend he thought that when really he was also fancying himself for knowing things. He was beginning to learn the skills of stirring controversy, already loving to know things that other people didn't.

Inevitably, Wilson joined the De La Salle sixth-form debating society, not only because of his big mouth, competitive urges, comprehensive reading and evolving argumentative self-confidence, but because school debates meant competing with other schools, some of which you would travel to, some of which contained an exotic species his school terribly lacked: girls. Debating would also nurture in him the sort of sophistry – 'There is no such thing as truth or lies, only what I say' – that would deliver plenty of entitled, obnoxious, fraudulent Eton and Oxbridge boys to the top of the political world.

Wilson was endlessly enchanted even obsessed by the local grammar schools, which for some were at the time in the middle of a golden age. His enchantment was due not least to these grammar schools producing four fifths of the Factory cabinet. These being boy schools, and mostly Catholic, with all that means in terms of women's subordination to men, rooted in Jesus' choice of his college of twelve apostles and their choice of collaborators, Factory was very much boys only, men being men.

Wilson liked to greet and label his male friends with a sing-song, grammar-school 'Mister', and Mr Gretton was of Catholic St Bede's in Whalley Range; other alumni included Peter Noone of Herman's Hermits, playwright Trevor Griffiths, venerable local folk singer and broadcaster Mike Harding, Buzzcocks drummer John Maher, the sixth Dr Who Colin Baker and radio and television presenter Terry Christian. Mr Hannett was of Catholic Xaverian College, run by a teaching order of unordained monks in Rusholme – where Anthony Burgess went between 1928 and 1935, publishing some of his first writings and art works – and Mr Saville went to St Ambrose College, an independent Catholic grammar school in Hale Barns, Altrincham, as did Lonnie Donegan and Saville's fellow designers Keith Breeden and Malcolm Garrett. (The non-grammar Mr Erasmus would be described by Mr Wilson as 'the only black boy on the Wythenshawe estate, which is why he was so fucked up'. Those weren't the days.)

No hint in Wilson's rather glib memories of De La Salle of the consequences of such institutions' fear that state interference in education was leading to the decay of religion and the growth of immorality. The misuse of adult authority in relation to children, the casual sadism, low-grade dread and fierce sometimes brutal strictness that others talk of. Discipline with strong religious undertones, at its best a quaint and funny weirdness, the gothic grotesquery involved at such a school, combined with what some pupils refer to as 'monk dodging'.

None of it happened to him, or some of it did but he learnt to take his punishment without flinching, and he couldn't be bothered carrying baggage with him from the past or becoming some kind of victim. Move on. Onwards, darling.

His description of those years was that he kept his distance from potential issues and threats, talked his way out of trouble, avoided traps, certain secrets were kept, and academically he thrived. 'It was a wonderful school,' he cheerfully remembered, because after all he went there, and academically he sailed through. Perhaps he got the luck of the draw, getting teachers less likely to make it an unnerving experience. He studied English, Latin and history for A level, revelling in the sixth form, loving these subjects, worshipping Yeats especially, and his initial thought was to become a teacher – he taught English, drama and history briefly at a comprehensive school in Oldham, a little hint of an alternative future making good use of his room-dominating raconteur skills.

Years of being taken to Stratford to watch Shakespeare with his actor dad had shaken away his childhood ambition to become a nuclear physicist;

language and what you could do with it, what you could invent and change with it, the splitting of words as though they were atoms, harnessing semantic energy, was an increasing interest. Shakespeare rhetorically split the atom three centuries before the fact. Wilson found a different way of putting things in motion. Talk could make such a difference. The imagination, the force of the human spirit, most distinctly represented by poetry, connects the mind with the world and creates the world as a living entity. He loses interest in putting numbers into equations and in his late teens begins putting words into poetry, those immeasurable equations of human emotions. He moves from mathematics to poetry, a sort of inspired rhapsodic mathematics. Not necessarily because he wanted to be a poet, but because of the spells words create, how they help you think, and find your voice, and create a world of your own.

Previous pupils at his school included the literary scholar, cultural theorist and bold and unrestrained defender of Marx, Terry Eagleton, born in Salford in 1943 to third-generation working-class Irish immigrants, the school inspiring in him a more sophisticated world view, if not an enduring loyalty to Catholicism – the overall plan was to project you into secure middle-class-ness, and prepare you for a wider, more cosmopolitan world than the local Irishness traditionally set you up for. 'Successful revolutions,' he wrote in his book *Why Marx Was Right*, 'are those which end up by erasing all traces of themselves.'

There was also another old boy from De La Salle called Terry, the ventriloquist creator of Lenny the Lion, Terry Hall, who had a television show starting in 1962, *Pops and Lenny*, which featured on 20 May 1963 the second BBC TV appearance by the Beatles, seven long months after their Granada debut on *People and Places*.

This was when pop music was still, in the eyes of most of the media, especially the stubborn and cautious BBC, something only for children. The idea of youth, of hostile, self-centred and creative teenage energy, hadn't yet fully come into focus. Childhood segued pretty quickly into the routines and responsibilities of adulthood; youth had not yet begun to create its increasingly elastic partition between one and the other. It still seemed unlikely that pop music would ever be of interest to mature grown-ups, even something those over twenty would stay connected to.

The Beatles performed their third single and first 'authorised' number one 'From Me to You' for Lenny the Lion, and a quick run-through of a song that was only two minutes long anyway, 'Please Please Me', their second single, which had been a number one in the *New Musical Express* and *Melody Maker* charts – it reached number two on the independently audited *Record Retailer* chart, which would controversially be used after the fact as the official 1960s chart, even though it sampled only thirty shops while the *New Musical Express* and *Melody Maker* sampled over a hundred. There was no official UK chart before February 1969.

The first UK pop charts based on record sales rather than sheet music were compiled by the *New Musical Express* pop magazine; its enthusiastic editor Percy Dickins, copying the exciting-looking chart system of American *Billboard*, rang around twenty record shops for a list of their bestselling songs. Initially, it was an awkwardly shaped, non-decimal top twelve, but the addictive idea of a number-one song, a chart of favourites creating glorious hits and shadowy misses, changed more than just music and the industry. The erratically coordinated early market research of the 1950s top ten becomes the vertiginous, mega-monitoring and manipulative twenty-first-century millions of songs; the sorting, sharing and rating of music spills beyond reason. By the 1960s, there were a handful of national UK charts, published by rival music papers, including a BBC average.

Before the pop charts and the accelerated routine of new sounds and constant, competitive changes in style and tempo there was no independent space for teenagers to occupy, to find themselves and for better or worse begin to take control of their own destinies and locate their own events, opportunities and places of worship. The charts as a system of estimation and self-serving commercial bias were discriminatory in all sorts of ways, the basis of the commercially, ultimately ideologically selective mainstream music industry, but they left room for glitches and the introduction of surprises, oddities and even actual signs of disruption. Around the exhilarating idea of a universally agreed-upon hit song, the unquestionable, fascinating existence of a definitive chart-topper, new ways of knowing that would not have happened without the cherished grooves of two-sided hit records, secret and spectacular teenage life uncoiled, monitored and maintained by a controlling record industry.

At the end of *Pops and Lenny* the Beatles sang a song with Terry and his b-b-b-bashful puppet – created from a fox-fur mane and a golf-ball nose. Manager Brian Epstein had been building his version of the Beatles out of his desires and demands, throwing a little of his voice into them, scrubbing up the Hamburg/Liverpool bohemian Beatness into a cuter, suited, less-threatening unit. The muted, suited and booted moptop model wouldn't last long, but it worked for now. After all, here they were on kids' TV, finally on their way. Winning over the kids first of all, including prepubescent girls abruptly alighting on something uncanny, creating the template for all boy bands to come.

Wilson would say he was the perfect age for the Beatles when they first broke through with a spirited pop music expertly designed for new teenagers fast developing their very own media and musical, and now directly catered-for emotional and sexual, needs – thirteen – and watching Lenny the Lion operated by a De La Salle old boy help the Beatles on their way to history, talking about it in the De La Salle playground the next day, excitedly thinking about a change in hairstyle, one involving an impertinent fringe flopping into the eyes that would annoy the hell out of his school masters, many of whom started teaching before the Second World War and clung to Edwardian values. Pop groups were well on the way to becoming more famous – and even more sensational – than talking lions. On their way to becoming something you would want to put a religious amount of effort into following, collecting and experiencing.

Young people had found a way of letting off steam and imaginatively dropping out of the system, even if only tentatively, or briefly. It was a clear sighting of a new sort of independence for the young, an unknown, unmeasured collective, at a time when the post-war world was moving from a culture of necessity – buying things to survive – to a culture of desire – buying things simply because they are wanted. Popular culture was not fully understood by the Establishment or the mainstream media, and was yet to take it over and sell it to the world. There was a little gap in proceedings that was destined to remain intact for about as long as there were vinyl records.

This was when rock 'n' roll and pop defined young people as being different, as being separate – the dawn of the pop culture teenager, discovering something still rooted in the spirit of the outlaw, the rock 'n' roll revelation of liberated sex. For Wilson, looking back, as always making up history, 'Please Please Me', as the first top ten hit for the Beatles, their first real number one give or take some bureaucratic cock-up, beginning the process of generating if not uniting a generation, was a supreme *political* moment. One springing from outside the system, even initially outside the commercial world, producing a whole new set of rituals and experience, even new erogenous zones. Prior to the 1950s the young had been slaves, tools, the property of others, and now they were on the verge of winning some form of independence by revolting against their very non-existence.

Tony followed one Terry out of De La Salle to Cambridge, and one Terry into television showbusiness.

Eight: Jesus College Cambridge, Coleridge and *Tristram Shandy*

Mens agitat molem. (Mind moves matter.)

Tony kept passing exams, and in 1968 at the end of this successful run he got into Cambridge University as a working-class grammar-school scholarship boy. He was a living representation of the social history of the time, an example of what was a classic narrative when university education was an elitist privilege and working-class and even lower-middle-class participation was minimal. After the war, social class continued to play a major role in educational achievement, and in the early 1960s education had become a vicious fight between those who were happy to preserve the status quo and those who knew it was important to radically change it. Education was a key component in post-war regeneration and rebuilding, and change helped Wilson make it to Cambridge.

Prime Minister Harold Wilson had been determined to increase the number of university places and create a revolution in higher education, but also questioned the efficiency of the eleven-plus. His first Labour Party conference speech as leader in Scarborough in October 1963 was where he talked of a new Britain being forged in the white heat of a technological revolution. It was described by political journalist James Cameron as 'political science-fiction'. A new age, with no place for restrictive practices. 'He who rejects change is the architect of decay,' Wilson said. 'Everyone should have an equal chance, but they shouldn't have a flying start.'

Jesus College is one of the 'old' colleges among the thirty-one at Cambridge, founded in 1496, 287 years after the university was founded, and one of its wealthiest. Its full name – College of the Blessed Virgin Mary, Saint John the Evangelist and the glorious Virgin Saint Radegund, near Cambridge – came about because it was outside the original town limits, while its usual title derives from Jesus Chapel, originally built in the twelfth century, its name based on a cult which was then achieving wide international popularity. Queen Elizabeth I declined to visit the college on her visit to the university in 1564 because it was too far away.

The college was founded by a Yorkshireman, John Alcock of Beverley, an architect who may have contributed to the college's design, and the Bishop of Ely, briefly the lord chancellor of England, whose rebus was a cock standing on a globe. Surrounded by the open spaces of Butts Green, Jesus Green and Midsummer Common, with a medieval cloistered court-yard, the college retains a monastic sense of isolation from the rest of the university. Its buildings reveal the layout of the Benedictine convent of St Radegund, which originally existed on the site. By the time Alcock replaced it with the college, only two nuns remained; another reason for shutting down the nunnery was the rumour it had developed a disturbing reputation for licentiousness.

The long, narrow, high-brick-walled passage that takes you to the por-ters' lodge at the entrance to the college is known as the Chimney, from *chemin*, French for path. Wilson had travelled from a soiled, stubborn northern landscape covered with chimneys to this single, fancy, metaphor-ical chimney, the dramatic dream-like entrance to a very different life.

He would be following the footsteps along the Chimney of one of histo-ry's greatest writers, Yorkshire's Laurence Sterne, writer of one of the North of England's, and the world's, great books, the relentlessly self-conscious and slippery novel and anti-novel *The Life and Opinions of Tristram Shandy, Gentleman*. While rooted in the cornucopian energies of Renaissance prose and steeped in the ornate literariness of Rabelais, Montaigne and Burton, based on a model by Cervantes, Sterne's dazzling, quizzical and self-reflective conception all at once invented or influenced Balzac, De Quincey, Dickens, Tolstoy, Lautréamont, T. S. Eliot, Thomas Mann, Thomas Bernhard, Flann O'Brien, vaudeville, Romantic autobiography and how to fashion a nar-rative self, surrealism, Proust's great works of intellect and intimacy, the many planes of narrative in Joyce, the shifting perspectives and tricks of memory of Virginia Woolf, the many feigns of storytelling in Burgess, meta-narrative, existentialism, structuralism, deconstructionist theory, sit-uationism, all forms of literary shoplifting, i.e. plagiarism, the idea that what goes on in our heads is literature, Marvel comics, the songs of Bob Dylan, the films of Charlie Kaufman, the television of Vince Gilligan, the rhythms of Björk, the fourth-wall-busting flair of Phoebe Waller-Bridge and Michaela Coel, and ultimately remains hard to place. 'I write not to be fed,' Sterne once said, 'but to be famous.' He was attracted by the very idea of celebrity, and by writing a book that announced so early and so brilliantly that all writing relies on other writing this provincial parson was suddenly handed the strange, challenging glories of fame.

Tony Wilson would say, wearing a mask of Laurence Sterne, 'What a large volume of adventures may be grasped within this little span of life by him who interests himself in everything.' He would also appear in a film, loosely speaking, that the director Michael Winterbottom made about trying to make a film of Laurence Sterne's novel, *Tristram Shandy: A Cock and Bull Story*. Winterbottom skilfully, lovingly adapted three Thomas Hardy novels, expressing a mature love for Eng. Lit., but the Sterne film accepts that it is impossible to make a film about a book that is notoriously impossible to film but also seems impossible to write, and it is therefore a smart, daft film about the film-making process and about impossible dreams.

Shandy and Shandy's father are played by an intense and shady Steve Coogan, who also plays himself, to some extent. Coogan played Tony Wilson in a film about Factory and its place in Manchester and its place in pop culture – 'from the dawn of punk to the death of acid' – that was really a farcically artistic film about Tony Wilson, who could never be separated from his work, and was always playing himself.

Middleton, Manchester, comedian Coogan played Wilson as an antagonistic, awkward, too-clever-by-half-wit, using many of his own moods and mannerisms in the portrayal, and also a fair amount of his most famous character, the wretched, sad and unwanted, slightly smutty TV and radio personality Alan Partridge, so that Wilson, whose comic timing was not perfect, is played by a comedian with immaculate comic timing pretending to have slightly wonky comic timing. Hilarity – and hokum – ensues.

In *A Cock and Bull Story*, Wilson plays himself, a moderately famous regional television reporter interrogating with a generally well-played sense of 'I'm having none of this' a drained, bamboozled and self-important Coogan; to some extent, by interviewing Coogan, Wilson is interviewing himself. For obvious reasons Coogan inevitably gets to say in this setting that the book the film is ultimately not based on 'is a kind of post-modern masterpiece before, er, there was any modern to be post about'.

The bendy Shandy film is to some extent the sequel – or prequel – to the raucous, unusually successful rock biopic Winterbottom made about Tony Wilson in 2002, *24 Hour Party People*, this one sailing between the eighteenth and twenty-first centuries in the way *24 Hour Party People* sailed between the Shandean vanities of Coogan and Wilson into a Manchester of powders and pills, thrills and spills, celebration and impersonation, night and day, success and failure, life and death. Both were bawdy films about a liberated spirit who acts as though he is God's gift to mankind, about chaotic play, about being busy being born and a certain sort of debauched, astonished-by-life sentimentality.

Wilson once complained that the unreliable, demented fictionality of *24 Hour Party People* was great, but that Coogan played him as a pretentious prat. It was pointed out to him that he would often be heard in meetings, whether about pop records, TV shows or comedians, quoting Proust at everyone – 'Happiness is beneficial for the body, but it is grief that develops the powers of the mind.' And, of course, pretentious quotations are the surest road to tedium. But then again, in quoting others, we cite ourselves. To the regular accusation that he was a pretentious prat, he had a ready answer: 'Fine. I don't think great literature and great art is pretentious, so I do talk about things like that to people. If that makes me a prat, so be it.'

Steve Coogan, comedian, actor, impressionist, writer, 'Alan Partridge', 'Tony Wilson'

It's too simplistic to say I played Tony simply as Alan Partridge, even a weird, avant-garde Partridge. I know Tony was nervous about a comedian playing him, as if it would be a satire just mocking him, but I wanted to honour him as well. He quite liked the idea of someone famous playing him, because he was like a child when it came to knowing famous people. He absolutely loved it. It was probably why he went into television, and then into music, so he could keep meeting famous people, and of course he loved finding out what it was like to be famous, seeing the distracted look of the woman serving you in the newsagent's who has seen you on television.

We went out for dinner and he was initially a little distant. I said, 'We are not going to deify you, but you are going to come out of it a good guy.' I wanted him to hear me say that. He paused for about a minute, and he said, 'Well, I don't believe in interfering with anything artistically.' He started to hang out on the set, which was a bit weird at first. There was a scene where, as Tony, I was doing a big fat line of coke in the Granada offices, and he said, 'Well, that never happened, not the way you're suggesting, but I don't believe in interfering with your vision, so carry on.' He saw we were doing his story with our own form of integrity, and he ended up coming on tour in America to help promote the film. That was his way of making it a new project, something contemporary that he was part of, nothing nostalgic. He would hold court, and I loved being with him. He took me to a bookshop in New York and bought me a load of books he said I should read. The ultimate Wilson compliment.

Wilson himself writing the novelisation of the film, for a little bit of inevitable whiplash post-modern zip, was another way of turning the venture into something contemporary and adding something capricious, the self-conscious creation of a conceptual cash-in version of an autobiography. He wrote about himself in the third person, as if it was all nothing to do with him, even though it couldn't have happened without him. He took it as an opportunity to appear to reveal some truths while actually staying in hiding.

'Purposefully shoddy,' said his friend, the writer Jon Savage. 'He wouldn't go deep into his own psyche. He would never go deep because that was not what he was interested in. The book tells you why he didn't go deep precisely because it doesn't go deep and buys into the wanker thing, which was more distraction, because in truth he was many things, but he wasn't a wanker.'

Richard Madeley, television presenter, author

About three weeks after I joined Granada Television in 1982, I started to present programmes with him and Judy, a three-presenter line-up, which was very unusual in those days. Richard and Judy and Tony. It actually worked really well. And at that point, all across Manchester, it lasted about two years, there was graffiti done in the same spray-can style, same font, same silver-grey colour. And it said, 'Tony Wilson is a wanker.'

Wherever you looked in the city centre, it was on every available flat surface! 'Tony Wilson is a wanker.' You couldn't miss it. It became part of the city. I hadn't really spoken to him much before, and I asked him, straight out, 'Don't you mind? You can see it everywhere. Look out the window, you can see one of these messages right there.' He said, 'Why should it bother me? Would it bother you?' I said, 'Well, actually, if all over my home city it said everywhere, "Richard Madeley is a wanker," yeah, I think it might fuck me up a bit.' And he looks at me as if I was mad. And he said, 'Well, it doesn't bother me. Because I am.' I said, 'You are?' He says, 'Yeah. I am a wanker! So are you!'

I said, 'Sorry?' He said, 'Right. So you like being on telly. I know you do, because I've seen you.' Yes, I do. I couldn't deny it. He says, 'Well, that makes you a wanker. If you actually enjoy the process of putting yourself out there in public as if you have some sort of importance, you are a wanker, by definition. I love being on TV, therefore I am a wanker. I fucking love it! I fucking love being on telly! I'm a wanker!

'It's fair comment,' he said, 'and anyway, if you put yourself out there, people can say what they like. I don't give a fuck, people can think I'm a wanker, great. I don't care, because I am.' It was a masterclass really in not taking yourself too seriously. If you're going to be in this mad, stupid business of television, do not think it confers any kind of status on you because it fucking doesn't, you're a little wanker and never forget it.

People will come after you just because you're on telly, you know, and you have to deal with it and not mind about it and accept it, embrace it, and that's what Tony did. And that was a very important lesson early on in my career from him, which stood me in bloody good stead later when we started This Morning *and we got all the criticisms – you know, trivial candy-floss television. Bored gossipy daytime TV for bored housewives and all that shit. We didn't give a fuck, we didn't care what anyone said. That was what they thought, which was fine. We were confident in what we were doing. That attitude came from Tony.*

Judy Finnigan, television presenter, author, co-founder of the Richard & Judy Book Club

The thing about Tony was he managed to walk this incredible tightrope between being really big-headed – and he was, he was really big-headed and knew it – and at the same time totally self-aware and not pompous about it. He was incredibly sort of almost God-like in this appreciation of his own superiority and his own intellect and what he had to offer and his own creativity and all the rest of it. He didn't underrate that at all, but at the same time he was quite able to say, 'I'm a complete wanker.'

Steve Coogan

One time I was walking to the set in a shaggy long-hair Wilson wig and a '70s Tony shirt and denim bell-bottom pants. He saw me at the end of the corridor, and he was on the phone and he went, 'Hang on, I'm gonna have to call you back.' And he was just staring at me. It was just me and him in the corridor. He put the phone down. I told him it was 1977 all over again. He came up to me and just stared at me for ages, his arms folded. Didn't really know what to say, but he stared at me for a long time and then he would displace it by talking about other things, a distraction. 'Interesting thing about that time, blah, blah, blah, blah.' Like, displacement conversations. He did that a lot. He never really talked about his feelings. I think it was very bittersweet for him, looking so hard at his past, at him.

Another thing for Wilson to moan about with *24 Hour Party People* was that he thought it was far too kind to him, even if some thought it mocked him as much as it martyred him. He would grumble that it didn't get across how mean even vicious he could be. He didn't mind being portrayed as the twat, the poseur passing joints, quoting philosophy, admiring his own dishevelled reflection, sleeping around, acting the goat, taking one pratfall after another, he certainly didn't mind the braiding of the truth, but he didn't want to be portrayed as a soft-hearted teddy bear. He knew his own temper could be a terrible thing, rooted in his quest to make a difference, to get things right, and he missed seeing it in the film. You messed with his demons and you got the devil in him. His family knew that side of him, and he wished Winterbottom had shown a little bit of that in the film. Like the time during a Christmas dinner when his daughter was supposed to be helping and forgot to bring something to the table. 'The gravy, Isabel, the gravy,' he snarled, with a sudden scorching tone. The rest of the meal would be eaten in silence.

There was another, much gentler, more serious film featuring Tony Wilson and a ghostlier Manchester, with no sign of miscreant Happy Mondays and no orgies and cocaine parties. *Control* was a stark, soul-searching black-and-white biography of the short life and early death of Ian Curtis, a singular portrait of a tortured artist. This wasn't a rock 'n' roll cartoon; this was an attempt to make a work of art about art.

Director Anton Corbijn channelled his memories of meeting Joy Division as a naive young artistic Dutch photographer arriving in coarse, grainy and damp late-1970s Manchester, experiencing a moody combination of wasteland and wonderland. If *24 Hour Party People* was the Factory as frayed farce, here was the devastating domestic tragedy. Corbijn's penetrating late-1970s photographs of the group – and their shadows, which tended to explain everything – helped fill in some of the missing information that spread around the group. Manager Rob Gretton felt it best they didn't do too many interviews, because before Ian died they didn't really have the words, and for quite a while after as New Order they definitely didn't have the words.

Later, there was an eerie, slightly nutty, posthumous Anton Corbijn video for the solemn, hymn-like 'Atmosphere', a grand pop song about human goodness and eternal darkness which imagined Phil Spector producing Kraftwerk featuring Roy Orbison singing about the absence of God. Very Manchester, actually, if not for Noel Gallagher. Gretton told Wilson the surviving members of Joy Division hated it, especially when a cluster of midget monks carried a monumental photograph of a crestfallen Curtis across a deserted beach. In fact, they loved it, appreciating the black humour. Rob didn't take to it, because part of his modus operandi was sowing seeds of doubt, just for the hell of it, to make things happen, and sometimes not happen.

In *Control* there is a softer, vaguer Wilson, hinting at a certain helplessness as life gets out of control, morally adrift, another Wilson that was really nothing like Wilson but was more or less related. These fictional Wilsons would flatter and disturb him at the same time and put some kind of block between him and the future, turning him into a caricature he wasn't in control of even as he tried to take control of everything.

Control appeared in his final few months, just before he added to the Factory death toll, when the sombre, elevated dirge of 'Atmosphere', recorded twenty-eight years before, seemed written specifically for Wilson's funeral march. Five years earlier, he had expressed frustration that *24 Hour Party People* was consigning him to the past, as though his great deeds were done, and that it was a kind of memorial, even if refreshingly mutant. There was now nothing but the past.

He once left a message on my phone a few minutes after we had talked about *24 Hour Party People* for the *Guardian*. He was worried that we had only talked about the past, because that was what the film was about. He wanted to make sure that in my piece I would not conclude that the making of the film meant the end of his journey. He insisted he was actually only just beginning. 'There are the things I am doing that make the movie irrelevant to me,' he said, sounding like he was on the move, although he was always on the move even when he was sat down, 'big development projects in Liverpool, lots of things in Manchester to do with moving the city on. I really want to get across that just because they are making a movie about your life it doesn't mean that it's all over. Life does go on. OK. God bless. Bye, love.'

'One has to pay dearly for immortality,' he said, wearing a mask of Friedrich Nietzsche. 'One has to die several times while one is still alive.'

He tried to turn the nostalgia upside down by adopting what he called his new slogan, from *The Tempest*: 'What's past is prologue,' spoken by Antonio in Act II, Scene i, trying to persuade Sebastian to murder his sleeping father so he can become king. What has happened until now only sets the stage. Everything that came before doesn't matter. Wilson had to believe that there was still a new and glorious future stretching before him. See *24 Hour Party People* and afterwards think, *The king – or the fool – is dead. Long live the king. Long may the fool make merry.*

Watch *Control* and think, *No one is dead while their name is still spoken.*

At Jesus College Cambridge, to his evident delight, following one of his heroes, the great Salford writer and broadcaster Alistair Cooke, Wilson would study in rooms named after another Jesus boy, Samuel Taylor Coleridge, who as a fresh-faced, dreamily handsome teenager Wilson slightly resembled, both possessing a nice head of hair and a searching, melancholy, vaguely challenging air and what Coleridge himself described as 'an almost idiotic good nature'. William Wordsworth described Coleridge's often one-sided conversations as 'like a majestic river, the sound or sight of whose course you caught at intervals; which was sometimes concealed by forests, sometimes lost in sand; then came flashing out broad and distinct . . . you always felt that there was a connection in its parts, and that it was the same river'.

In a lecture Coleridge delivered in 1818, insisting as an ingenious literary thief himself on *Tristram Shandy*'s greatness, he noted that Sterne's humour was where 'the little is made great, and the great little, in order to destroy both, because all is equal in contrast with infinity'.

William Hazlitt – also very much on the side of Sterne – wrote an awe-struck piece about his first meeting with Coleridge in 1798 that gives you a sense of what Wilson felt a couple of hundred years later the first time he met Shaun Ryder of the Happy Mondays and the song '24 Hour Party People': 'I was at that time dumb, inarticulate, helpless, like a worm by the wayside, crushed, bleeding, lifeless . . . that my understanding did not remain dumb or brutish, or at length found a language to express itself, I owe to Coleridge. I could not have been more delighted if I had heard the music of the spheres.' Hazlitt also said of Coleridge, 'If Mr Coleridge had not been the most impressive talker of his age, he would probably have been the finest writer.'

Coleridge was at Jesus between 1791 and 1793, in his last year winning the fifteen-guinea Sir William Browne Gold Medal for an ode in Latin or Greek for his poem 'On Astronomy', hailing Urania, queen of the night. Coleridge practised astronomy, a huge influence on the rhythm and imagery of his poetry, part of his Enlightenment belief in a universal science.

The Browne prize was handed out on and off into the twenty-first century, but not during the time Wilson was at Cambridge. The winner in 1932 was Wagner fan, Nietzschean and dazzling classical scholar John Enoch Powell, who would go on to have an interesting life. In Birmingham as Conservative shadow minister for defence in the momentous year of 1968, a couple of weeks before the May student demonstrations, strikes, occupations and widespread civil disruption in France, Enoch Powell delivered his toxic, horribly memorable 'Rivers of Blood' speech, presenting his apocalyptic vision of bloody racial conflict. For many Conservatives he was the leader they never had, the British prime minister that never was, a prophet but, not least because of the blood he conjured up, ultimately doomed to become an outcast.

On 20 April 1968, like the Romans he saw 'the River Tiber foaming with blood'. Powell the detached scholar was quoting Virgil. He later said his one regret was that he had quoted Virgil in translation, which he felt possibly exaggerated the fierceness of the image and helped create the damning headlines, the newspapers not looking for nuance. Racists were enlivened by his demand to end immigration; almost everyone else, from the far left to the conservative Establishment, was appalled. Powell's florid, uncompromisingly eccentric intellectual brilliance had ruined his future prospects. He decided to retire in 1974, to pursue among other things his theory that Shakespeare had been written by committee, but kept a parliamentary platform until the late 1980s as the Ulster Unionist MP for South Down. Asked in his seventies how he would have wanted his life to be different, he replied, 'I wish I had been shot in the war.'

The day of Powell's rant would have been Adolf Hitler's seventy-ninth birthday. The number-one single in the UK charts the same week was 'What a Wonderful World' by Louis Armstrong, which would stay there deep into the month of May, which in 1968 was the month of revolution. In the October weeks when Wilson started his life at Cambridge the number one was 'Those Were the Days' by Mary Hopkin.

Coleridge was one of the famous 'big six' Romantic poets, along with Wordsworth, Blake, Byron, Shelley and Keats – definitive heroic individuals using the imagination to address the meaning of truth, knowledge and selfhood, roaming across the temporal boundaries of past, present and future, convinced that consciousness can set one free of the ruins of history and culture. One of the first things Tony sees when he arrives in Cambridge is a line of William Blake from 'Proverbs of Hell' laid out in thick white paint along a brick wall in Silver Street, making him realise he has landed in the right place – 'The tigers of wrath are wiser than the horses of instruction.'

He inhales the words, feels time take a tumble, as if something from a centuries-old dream is talking straight to him and giving him advice, and imagines a Manchester where the graffiti on the endless brick walls quotes Blake. 'Rouze up, O Young Men of the New Age!' The everyday environment inscribed with the spectral presence of Blake.

After Cambridge, Wilson would be walking, working and playing in Manchester like he still existed inside the Romantic period, as though it started with the invention of print and would only truly end with the establishment of the internet, which was always going to be tough on romance and true romantics. He ran his label and club, presented his television programmes, ran his conferences, managed – and mismanaged – his musicians, spun his tales, goaded his colleagues, minions and enemies, formulated his theories, drove his cars, smoked opium-tainted cigarettes like he had spent time with these great poets whose presence never seems to fully decay, through the ages continually asking each other vital questions about humanity's future, their relevance somehow increased during times of immense social trauma.

Cambridge seemed not only 168 miles from 1970s Manchester, but also 168 years away, impossible to access without the combination of intellect and flamboyance of someone like Wilson, so it was difficult to understand the nature of the adventures Wilson actually had there. Those who went to Cambridge were generally an exotic, opaque species. I for one knew no one at the time who had gone to Cambridge and was removed from my grammar school in Stockport at sixteen as a complete waste of time and space, because those who showed little aptitude for an Oxbridge future were quickly weeded out.

In 1970s Manchester, our only clear evidence about what Wilson got up to at Cambridge and which ghosts and students he interacted with was his swooping self-confidence, his bearing and his ability to impersonate a Romantic sensibility as brilliantly as the great Romantics, who of course were themselves superb at impersonating being Romantics. This evidence seemed to suggest to outsiders like me that one of the things you got to do at Cambridge was hang out with Romantics, enacting glorious homosocial sessions of talk, companionship and competitive banter, talking about everything under the sun in flats, pubs and other venues. Sometimes these discussions could last all night – the open-ended idle chatter of students, as if it could genuinely be part of a general attempt to rethink political, social and cultural praxis. Getting high, and hungrily devouring Coleridge, De Quincey, Rimbaud, Marx, De Sade, Breton, Joyce, Lautréamont and Hegel.

Wilson brought back to Manchester such an attitude, and to some extent set up equivalent worlds in different northern settings where he could continue such conversation and engagement – Granada TV, Factory, the Manchester In the City music conference he founded in the early 1990s based on the New York New Music Seminar he loved talking at and barging into so much in the 1980s.

At Cambridge, Wilson discovers new modes of sociability. He starts to learn what it is like to feel you are at the centre of the universe, surrounded by lots of other bright people with boiling brains, having constant stimulating conversations about subjects he thought he knew, at exactly the time Vietnam, May '68 in Paris and broader cultural contexts were rapidly radicalising students. Left-wing sensibilities were exploding, even – sometimes especially – among the other, still worlds of Cambridge.

Wilson didn't continue the consistent exam-passing academic brilliance he had demonstrated up North. He had to fight away a form of diffidence that struck him amid all the whirring, combative cleverness of Cambridge, but more importantly for him, he was opened up to wide-ranging political and intellectual stimulation, to the sorts of arguments and debating skirmishes that could lead to better ideas and learned positions. He dived into the depths of knowledge.

Nine: Professor Williams and the television personality

Patientia comes est sapientiae. (Patience is the companion of wisdom.)

Wilson studied English under the immensely influential thinker, writer and critic Raymond Williams, from the small village of Pandy, on the South Wales border with England, on a route used by the early railways. (His work tended to be concerned with borders, and crossing frontiers, how they obstruct action and movement, and how they are penetrated.) The son of a left-leaning working-class family who encouraged intellectual pursuits, Williams grew up in a community where there was nothing wrong with being bright. Cleverness didn't disqualify you from being a man, from respect as a horny-handed worker.

His kind of brightness led to Cambridge in 1939. Identified as talented at King Henry VIII Grammar School in Abergavenny, he was almost indecently packed off to the university before he knew what was happening to ensure the Welsh couldn't complain they were being excluded. While there, he felt like an outsider, confused where the borders were that needed to be crossed. He immediately joined the Socialist Club, was a member of the Communist Party for a while, but left in 1941, rejecting Stalinist simplicities in politics, art and culture.

Adrift from the political and academic mainstream in the unformed 1950s, Williams returned to Cambridge as a lecturer at Jesus College in 1961, becoming one of the great social, cultural and political theorists, rewiring critical thought, treating learning as an everyday activity, not something remote and repetitive. He was quick to discern that the 'disbelief, boredom and contempt' of a new kind of post-war youth would be a challenge to the listless orthodoxies of mainstream '60s society.

His work in the 1950s studying how 'culture' was defined in the post-war world culminated in an autobiographical and analytical essay, 'Culture Is Ordinary', which featured his move from the country to Cambridge, taking a bus through the Black Mountains on his way to the university, and two books, the humanist Marxism of *Culture and Society* in 1958 and *The Long Revolution* in 1961. In *The Long Revolution*, using the label 'the slow reach for control', he put forward the idea that cultural, social and political transformation – the taking control of our own lives that the revolutionaries and radicals demanded come immediately – was coming, but over a long period of time.

He dominated cultural studies throughout the 1960s and '70s as one of the originators of the field, along with Richard Hoggart, E. P. Thompson and Stuart Hall. This was politically committed teaching searching for an independent critical space that tellingly began outside the universities, which were too set in their ways to initially allow such transformative ideas. Williams himself was convinced that popular culture was not only worth studying in a new way but that it could be a dominant force for change. He and his fellow thinkers believed that the world could be changed without a revolution; the revolution would come through thinking, exploring, explaining, approaching ideas from a new perspective. If they were the Beatles of cultural studies, analysing the effect the Industrial Revolution was still having on the working-class environment, Williams was the John Lennon.

Williams' socialist intellectualism was an alternative to Harold Wilson's much less flamboyant centre-left technocratic belief that society and industry could be controlled by an elite of technical experts – an old communist idea in which the proletariat are in power but administration is left to the experts.

So Tony Wilson was exposed to one of the greatest twentieth-century thinkers, a founding father of cultural studies who popularised a radical and critical approach to mass media, which combined social radicalism with an emphasis on cultural change at a time when revolution was in the air, and Williams was one of the high priests of the marching students. The *May Day Manifesto* of 1968, the year Wilson arrived at Cambridge, had been Williams' idea and was drafted in Coleridge's old rooms. Williams relished the tension between the dominant culture and the emergent energies which resist it, and attempted to unite different radical factions and leftist organisations, local issues and international interests into one anti-Labour left-wing force.

Williams was active and involved in working towards change and new directions, committed to community and social unity, as well as being an innovative theorist, teacher and world-class critic. Being exposed however indirectly or occasionally to such a combination of theoretical and practical energy made an enormous difference to Wilson's thinking, particularly the way Williams alternated between his isolated working-class homeland and rarefied Oxbridge, monitoring the fine calibrations between intellect and experience, exposing high culture to 'ordinary' people, but deeply suspicious of the majestically static Cambridge intellectuals imposing their cultural assumptions on the so-called unlearned masses.

Williams was inevitably a formative and formidable intellectual influence on Wilson, an amplification of the enriched literary and intellectual Cambridge spirit but also a necessary, realistic modern correction and redirection of its historical, almost escapist qualities, taking into account the effect on human interaction of what became known as popular culture. A few years before, there had been no interaction between literary history and the movement and influence of popular culture.

Williams was not close to his students, never really read or marked a student's paper, and Wilson never became any kind of collegiate son – as his De La Salle predecessor Terry Eagleton had, becoming Williams' teaching assistant but eventually rebelling against him, frustrated by his lack of rigour, and then returning to the fold, appreciating more his long-term strategies. Eagleton remembers Williams' lectures as being delivered by 'someone with a human voice', which was relatively rare at Cambridge, where there remained a certain kind of distance and obscurity.

Wilson was shyer, working out his role and position at Cambridge in a more cautious way, feeling excluded by the humbling, painful condescension of the ex-public-school students with their domineering, confidence-stuffed, ruling-class accent. It was a piping, self-glorifying sound guaranteed to make a provincial boy seem inferior however much he fought the feeling and didn't actually believe that a way of speaking brings with it natural superiority and razor-sharp perception, merely loathsome entitlement.

Wilson struggled to reconcile life in Marple, Manchester and Salford with his unfamiliar and extreme new setting full of ancient and modern temptations, puzzles and surprises, but couldn't avoid the powerful force of Williams, a down-to-earth but complex thinker who himself had felt the sting of university snobbery. Those excluded by the dominant upper-class culture would have been defensive and have looked for people and language they could identify with. Williams would have been recognis-able to Wilson as such, as pressing forward with ideas that drew together all sorts of performance, media, systems and institutions into one new, responsive cultural space, into 'culture'.

Cambridge happened in mysterious ways: you were both on your own and surrounded by thousands of near-like minds and very different minds, and you were expected to piece things together and make sense of a series of almost fragmented perceptions and presentations. Its ulti-mate point amidst what could seem structure-less was to encourage you to find your own voice. Make you understand the importance of educating yourself and refining your own judgements, but ideally without rejecting Cambridge decorum.

For Williams there was no point in separating the idea of education from the new media of broadcasting and television, and more established media such as film and newspapers – they should work together. The post-war world that people inhabited could not maintain the notion that education remained apart from what was happening in the world, either as straightforward training or the perpetuation of an indoctrinated elite which situated and fixed people according to the limited, particular needs of one particular element of society. What was happening in the world – and how it was beginning to reach people through the media, not through the narrow, patterning channels of traditional education – was becoming a large part of how people were now being educated. And it would produce a tremendous number of independent, spontaneous minds, the kind of original minds mainstream education often worked against producing.

Contemporary realities had to be taken into account, and Williams as an anti-elitist could immediately see that people were being exposed to new forms of information and new kinds of communication, and that this was, for better or worse, education as well. The thing to watch out for was that education didn't become a form of shepherding, that it was directed towards creative enquiry more than simply passive acceptance. The new forms of culture were a basic part of society, but also a potential means for social transformation. Culture should not be divorced from the world around it, which it undeniably had an influence on, and was influenced by, or it was nothing. To carry on teaching certain subjects such as literature without taking into account the new ways ideas, thinking and language were being distributed seemed irresponsible.

Wilson certainly took away from his exposure to Raymond Williams the notion that everything could and should be mixed up, from the highest culture to the lowest, from a great novel to an episode of a cop series, from Shakespearean drama to a television quiz show. He also experienced seeing how someone engaged with the world and serious about progressive change could work to make things happen through his personality, opinions and presence, through manifestos, argument and example. He could observe at close quarters the theatrical way in which this deep-thinking and in many ways reserved social philosopher made his intellectual presence felt.

Williams became a television critic for the BBC-managed review weekly *The Listener* while Wilson was at Cambridge, hired by perceptive cultural impresario Karl Miller, and was one of the first to approach writing about TV as an art form as much as entertainment. Williams helped to invent the idea of modern television reviewing, along with another Miller hire, Clive James, taking it seriously, criticising its conventions, connecting it with real life and personal experiences, and making the response itself a work of art. He applied critical techniques learnt studying literature to TV programmes, treating cop show *Softly, Softly* and antiques programme

Going for a Song with as much care and attention as Dickens and Hardy. He talked of television's daily flow, the constant juxtapositions of different energies, subjects and ideas, its increasing contribution to a widespread reorganisation of social and individual space.

Television was creating a different kind of reality, in effect changing everything because of how reality was now passing through this machine, this apparatus, to reach people in a new form. Anything that didn't pass through television would increasingly be left in the dark. (Fifty years later, those in the dark are those on the outside of social media – and Zoom, Skype, TikTok, YouTube and Google Hangouts – which is now operating on reality more aggressively and unforgivingly than television.)

Williams observed what happens to ideas of travel, science, sport, crime, gardening, antiques, science fiction, food and children's entertainment once they are filtered through television, as a technological invention, a method of communication, a propaganda system, a new way of being creative and, most importantly, an increasingly permanent and switched-on part of everyone's living room. He was quick to notice and be intrigued by how television relied on a new breed, the 'personality', to show us around, as though we would not understand anything at all without their comforting, easy-going presence, their essential unthreatening pretence. The ever-present presenter was being turned into the whole point of television, the person who made television human, who gave it speech and charm, but presenters were also a puzzle, an intrusion, often a complete annoyance, intruding their personalities and opinions into what they were talking about, making themselves more important, distorting the world in one way or another, even if they did so with the best of intentions, a pleasant smile, a little knowledge and a nice line in archly managed self-deprecating humour.

Irish presenter Eamonn Andrews was one of the originals of this miscellaneous new breed – his relaxed, amiable, off-the-cuff style influencing broadcasters from Terry Wogan to Tony Wilson. A keen amateur boxer whose working life began as an insurance clerk, he was a boxing commentator on the BBC before moving to the game show *What's My Line?*, and made his name presenting *This Is Your Life* between 1955 and his death in 1987. He also had a spoken-word novelty hit record in 1956, a 78 rpm produced by George Martin, unknowingly preparing for the sequence of extraordinary novelty hits he produced for the Beatles a few years later.

Noting his unlikely new television-conceived fame, Andrews remarked, 'I became, almost overnight, a face. I acquired that new, meaningless description for people who can neither sing nor dance nor juggle nor play the harp – a personality. A television personality.'

Raymond Williams once wrote about the biography as a form:

> *It is a common experience when reading the biography of a selected individual in a given time and place to see not only his individual development but a more general development in which, within the conventions of the form, other people and other events form around him and in this crucial sense are defined by him. This is a relatively satisfactory reading experience until we read other biographies of the same time and place, and realise that the displacements of interest, perspective and relation, which we must now be conscious of, but which, with the first biography, we had almost unwittingly taken as natural. The momentary minor figure is now the very centre of interest; the key events appear and disappear; the decisive relationships shift.*

Williams died, aged sixty-six, in 1988, thirty-five years after starting to formulate unprecedented arguments and radically define culture in ways that were by then largely accepted, even completely obvious.

So it goes.

Ten: Secret transmissions, situationism and the friends of Lautréamont

Possunt, quia posse videntur. (They can because they think they can.)

Being at a university at the exact time Wilson was also means that much of the education he was receiving or had access to would have come from outside what Williams was introducing, even someone as engaged, driven and audacious as this unorthodox professor. Other ways of piecing together knowledge and constructing an abstract new sensibility would have been inspired by what was happening around the world – the student protests and civil unrest in Paris as radical youth increasingly found a political as well as artistic voice, the London anti-Vietnam protests, left-wing actions and attitudes breaking out in all sorts of ways around the world.

The students around him, suddenly feeling at the centre of the world, or at least at the centre of the news, were responding to these events, some of them in more specific and actively involved ways than others. Williams identified with the grievances and commitment of the students, but completely separate from how his students would have been accessing and sharing the moments among themselves.

This was something locked inside the esoteric student system, and as part of Wilson's contact with students interested in radical activity, a general awareness of what was happening, Wilson would have picked up on the secret transmissions. Those involved in radical pursuits, engaging in the kind of revolutionary thinking that traditionally never takes permanent hold within an English setting, that prefers the complaint rather than the action, would have appeared very enticing and glamorous to hungry, growing Wilson with his own awareness of northern radicalism. He never had an assassin's instincts, but he was becoming increasingly intrigued by the forbidden and the indiscreet.

This curiosity would bring him as close as he ever got to actual contact with the Situationist International, a mysterious, near-mythical anarchist avant-garde movement formed in 1957, critically and competitively materialising out of the ruins, dreams and nightmares of other protean subversive twentieth-century movements, including surrealism and Dadaism, to drag their visions and ventures through Marxist concepts of commodification, reification and alienation.

Surrealism to this provisional collective of abstract utopians was mere prettiness, its works oddly a little too organised, too planned and completed, not fanatical, or farcical, enough. The confrontation, mechanics, mockery and savage, scamming sarcasm of Dadaism, the pillorying and hijacking of everything, its cultural terrorism, was much more the situationist style. The situationists, primed by the tips, slashes and collages of Dada, didn't make art so much as use it, with montage methods and incongruous juxtapositions becoming tools of discovery. They identified with the Dadaists' fascination with and exploitation of new media, their aggressive delight in provoking the complacent using outrageous statements, actions and 'poster-poem' collages, their mixing of manifesto, oratory, comedy, their devious satirical impulses, their lack of interest in disciples.

The Dadaists were barely in favour of themselves, had a central lack of unifying style, and the DNA of Dadaism was self-destructive. They were the most pungent critics of their own movement, determined not to be the stars of any revolutionary movement, wanting their ideas to be notorious, not themselves. Ultimately, their belief was in a romantically conceived order in the universe that stood above human activity and manifested itself as flux and chaos. Meanwhile, they wanted to abolish art and preserve it at the same time. The Dadaists had named themselves, their own anti-movement, selecting a word at random, and they were all for 'foolery extracted from the emptiness in which all higher problems are wrapped'.

Michèle Bernstein was a founding member of the Situationist International, yet another male sect that had a troubling blind spot in its radical vision when it came to women. (Thérèse Dubrule, the partner of another founding member, Raoul Vaneigem, once observed, 'I never saw Guy Debord do the dishes.') She was the writer of one of the few

149

female contributions to the movement, *All the King's Horses*, a fund-raising mock teen-romance novel about a pair of avant-garde activists in an open marriage in late-1950s Paris based on her and her libertine husband Guy Debord.

They lived together in a dark, miserable room with no lights at all, but the radiance and excitement of their actions came from their thinking and research. Debord would say he got by without any money by 'living off my wits'. Bernstein would do horoscopes for racehorses that were then published in racing magazines to help find winners. They split up in 1967 after a few years of living as the ultra-subversive Burton and Taylor.

She once noted how their Dada ancestors were 'finishing off art . . . declaring in the heart of a cathedral that God is dead; plotting to blow up the Eiffel Tower . . . the domain we meant to replace was the real scandal . . . Everyone is the son of many fathers. There was the father we hated which was surrealism. And there was the father we loved which was Dada. We were the children of both.'

Dada influenced all avant-garde and mischievous art movements that came after it – from action painting, pop art, Fluxus and happenings to punk, post-punk, YBA/Brit art, Turner Prize art and Banksy, most of it without the rebellious content and divested of its original transgressive nature. Some say Dada was the point when modern started to become post-modern, so almost as soon as there was mechanical-era modernity, there was post-modernity, from one set of disturbances to another. Through all post-Dada art movements, and through existentialism, structuralism, post-structuralism, deconstruction and naturally situationism, Dadaism is rethought, remade, always seen as an ancestor, a precedent, its reputation growing over time, shifting from a mere early-twentieth-century side-effect of expressionism to the art sun at the centre of everything. Situationism is Dada's favourite child, even though it had no favourites, and possibly, after all that, no children.

The situationists were made up of playful, insurrectionary and poetic close friends, lovers, chancers, artists and enemies – 'people of the future'. There were only ever about seventy of them, and never more than around twenty at once. They made the Beats look like babies – they dismissed them 'as the right wing of youth revolt' – hippies seem pointless, appeared to be cynical fatalists but possessed a strong utopian drive, were antisocial but with a social mission. They determined to transcend the easily controlled and institutionalised categories of art and culture and make them part of everyday life. To change the world you had to, in the words of Arthur Rimbaud – the juvenile figurehead of this artistic revolution – change life, live dangerously, break through its repetitions and systems and open everyone up to possibility, replace the sterile constraints of reality with a sacred poetic institution of the infinite. Theirs was a kind of sophisticated, often ridiculous naivety, with an eye on a brighter, better, if blurred future.

The situationists, because they stayed fiercely loyal to the genuinely transgressive, also had a much greater influence than their limited actual output, as a sort of volatile, innocent–corrupt micro-society, climaxing and quickly shrinking as a social and revolutionary force in the 1968 Paris riots – when 'imagination seized power', and Paris, briefly, astonishingly, fell, as if outside capitalism itself. After their dissolution the situationists' influence reached deep into the commercial, artistic, musical and theoretical spheres through provocative slogans, designs and a generally radiant, often spitefully idiotic sense of mischief. 'Our thoughts,' as they said, mixing art with arrogance as one of their many aesthetic blends, ultimately mixing analysis with entertainment, propaganda with fury, theory with mockery, 'are on the minds of everyone.'

By the late 1960s there was nothing much out there of their 'work', or nothing that could necessarily be found that easily, and they constantly fought among themselves, fewer and fewer members avoiding coups, exile and expulsions as enigmatic anti-survivors until there was nothing left. And yet there was a lot of information and instruction to take, once their thinking was bound, archived and translated, not least because of how much they took from other places and minds, reworking and replaying previous ideas in different post-war and post-modernist forms and contexts. In their world, this was known as *détournement*, a turning-around, subverting elements of the mainstream mass media, the rerouting of images and events into a radical new space, the deflection, integration, diversion, distortion, misuse, misappropriation, hijacking or general taking of one piece of artistic or commercial production and giving it another purpose, another meaning, often some extraordinary new life. The source and the meaning of an original work could be inverted or perverted to create something new. The conventional purpose of neutral mainstream images could be superimposed with revolutionary values.

In their eyes it was a way of making things right, of transforming the failures and banal ordinariness of the everyday into art through a form of imaginative conviction – taking what was made for ordinary or banal reasons and forming a new, stimulating ensemble. The situationists exist here as the pissing link between Duchamp's *Fountain*, a porcelain urinal set sideways and signed by 'R. Mutt' that becomes a work of art in a new setting and a new context, and Jamie Reid's poster for the Sex Pistols' 1977 single 'God Save the Queen', in which the head of the royal family is portrayed as a member of an international terrorist group engaging in guerrilla street theatre by mixing up various visual codes, including the placing of a safety pin through the Queen's lips. The safety pin references the very last painting by Marcel Duchamp, *Tu m'*, short perhaps for '*Tu m'emmerdes*' (You annoy me) or '*Tu m'ennuis*' (You bore me), Duchamp's attitude as he left painting behind.

The situationists weren't interested in making money, just questioning everything, generating confusion and inspiring a revolution that resulted in people doing activities for the sheer joy they bring rather than supporting accepted capitalist interests. They proposed that authentic experience could be found in moments of artistic expression, political struggle and self-absorbed play. In 1968, at Cambridge, as the rumours of this suddenly visible, rigorously maintained, dangerous–sexy secret society spread through those students eager for new ways to oppose the Establishment, there was a tantalising occult glamour about its members, as though they were related to the Romantic poets, to Marx, Mao and Lenin, and the most exciting rock, art and film stars. Never mind that situationism was an ideology that the situationists were unanimous in rejecting. This strange incognito clique was largely invisible but had such a great image. They did to theory what Hendrix was doing to the electric guitar and Dylan to rhyme and reason.

At Cambridge, Wilson would attend what was titled with very gentle sub-situationist mischief the Kim Philby Dining Club, named after the upper-class ex-Cambridge spy, Britain's most notorious Cold War traitor. Here was someone who was seen as having done the most in recent times to humiliate and wrong-foot the Establishment, using his high-level contacts and insider status to evade suspicion. The club's name, a little sliver of *détournement*, was destined to upset very few other than the easily affronted right-wing press, and was little more than a place where leftish students of all hues from unaffiliated to moderate to Trotskyite would meet for some food, wine and general, relatively friendly but deadly serious debate. 'We wanted to destroy the system,' explained Wilson years later, exaggerating what was probably more like boisterous wishful thinking, 'but didn't know how.'

It was a time when discontent among the young hadn't yet been atomised by the internet into a mosaic of grudges, hashtags and complaints, aimed at specific, often temporary subjects, issues and targets, rather than the fundamental, whole nature of capitalist society, which in the 1960s was still perceived as a construct rather than the natural order of things. Rejecting so-called bourgeois life and forming collectives, clubs and committees wasn't merely an alternative lifestyle choice, a curation of virtue in a vacuum. It would seem much more essential, and world events that suggested revolution was spreading from city to city, student to student, were almost instantly transmitted via television news. Paris 1968 was the very first televised mass insurrection, not so much changing the world as changing how the world would be accessed and interpreted. What was turning the world into a prison of images was also capable of encouraging viewers to work out escape methods.

Instantly knowing what was happening in other countries through TV was still relatively new, and had the effect of linking communities and campaigns, and producing an international sense of a common cause. Immature students clothed as free spirits were involved in a serious mission to teach stupid grown-ups a thing or two about how to make the world a better place. It was naive, it was necessary. Student conversations were rooted in a refusal to adapt to what school and family, work and state, their traditional, inflexible morality said was the only way. It seemed vital to head towards change, even if ultimately there was no obvious way to turn an attitude of resistance into anything other than talk. But the talk would lead to certain intellectual choices that would deepen a nascent rebellious spirit, and once that reached a certain level, it would always be there.

Some more serious and elusive members of the Kim Philby wine and cheese club looking for assistance in destroying the system would bring news of situationism and the graffiti techniques of the Paris riots. (Many of the most infamous slogans scrawled on Parisian walls during this time were lifted from situationist writings; *Free the passions*; *Never work*; *Live without dead time*; *It is forbidden to forbid*; *Long live the commune*; *Boredom is counter-revolutionary*; *Create or die*; *Run for it, the old world is behind you*.) Speech had become savage and inscribed itself on city walls; it wasn't restricted to what had been approved by the state or put there by advertising agencies selling stuff and town planners explaining things, all of it representing the Establishment. The walls of the city could be a free art gallery.

Posters and pamphlets designed and distributed collectively as part of a significant use of political graphic art were seen as 'weapons in the service of struggle . . . Their rightful place is in the centres of conflict, in the streets and on the walls of the factories.' On one occasion the police were summoned to deal with the silk-screening machines the students were using to create the posters; such machines were deemed to be weapons, and the police came armed with their more orthodox weapons: tear gas, guns, clubs. The students defended themselves, in an act surrealists and situationists would heartily endorse, by barricading themselves in using valuable paintings taken from the walls of their school. The police, it being France, were compelled to retreat. Here was student revolt in creative action, which to the polite, and occasionally not so polite, Cambridge students offered some sort of way forward, a practical antidote to paralysing conformity.

The comedic *humour noir* element of situationism would also have been an attraction, indirectly connected as it was to the absurdist, meta-satirical Cambridge comedy of Footlights as manifested through Kenneth Horne, Peter Cook, Jonathan Miller and the Monty Python members. Situationist slogans could seem like fine, lunatic one-liners as much as dynamic calls to arms. They could also seem like they had fallen out of songs by Bob Dylan, Syd Barrett, Frank Zappa, the Fugs and the Velvet Underground. You didn't necessarily buy into a philosophy that was tricky to work out anyway, but it had elements, on the surface and inside its organism, that you could tap into and easily make part of your own interests, and your instincts when you wanted – needed – to step outside a life manufactured for you by others whom you resented.

Some Philby attendees were closer to barricade-storming Paris than others; some had visited the city during May. They'd been there. They'd seen it happen. Witnesses to what appeared to be the high point of modern revolution, and what in the end could be seen as the high point of situationism. Paris 1968 was situationism's biggest hit, its greatest engagement or most successful campaign, before the group fell away into spite, bickering, expulsions, rivalry, fallings-out and what the SI dismissively called 'recuperation' – the actions of those inspired, influenced, seduced or bullied by situationism into copying, remixing, distorting or honouring through reprinting, contesting, regurgitating and/or analysing its strategies. Recuperation at its worst was when subversive actions and activities were appropriated by the mainstream media; most of the internet and social media is the consequence of recuperation.

Some of those Cambridge witnesses to the Paris events, impassioned by the idea of social justice, were motivated by their closeness to revolutionary anarchism and libertarian activism to take their grievances to the most obvious example of the Establishment facing them – Cambridge University itself, borrowing some of the ideas of Strasbourg University's Campaign Against Assessment: sit-ins, occupations, disruption of lectures, graffiti and forced debates. And some would go on to translate the writings of two key situationist strategists: Guy Debord, written into history as the last and greatest champion of situationism, and Raoul Vaneigem, written out of history as 'the other situationist'. Debord was asked at an event at the London Institute of Contemporary Arts in 1961 exactly what situationism was all about. 'We are not here to answer cuntish questions,' he replied – up there in the top ten of the things that influenced certain parts of Wilson's character. As was the Vaneigem observation 'The work of art of the future will be the construction of a passionate life.'

There were two pamphlets issued from within the without walls of situationism that particularly caught the attention of Wilson and a couple of university friends, John Fullerton and Paul Sieveking, who later formed a London-based informal pro-situationist group, BM Ducasse, also known as the Friends of Lautréamont, which included Wilson, if only for a meeting or two, or even less, maybe just a lukewarm half of shandy in a grotty Soho pub followed by a vomit in the toilet.

Perhaps the pub involved merely a handover of some LSD, as Wilson would later suggest that the person who introduced him to situationism was his acid dealer – or perhaps it was the other way round – as though it was situationism and its desire for a high-energy, free-wheeling culture and anti-authoritarian psychic liberation that led to the next, stronger, bolder drug. Grass wasn't the gateway to acid, but the SI pushed you from being mellow social outlaw to cosmic fugitive, from mild, buzzing kicks to an intense and unremitting dose of bacchanalia. As Aldous Huxley said, you didn't want to be in your right mind. He also said that the only completely consistent people are those who are dead. In 1956 Huxley was searching for a name to call the new hallucinogenic drugs he had been introduced to by the pioneering psychiatrist Dr Humphry Osmond. Huxley attached mystical significance to mescaline in his book *The Doors of Perception* – where the Doors got their name from.

Osmond was interested in hallucinogenic drugs as a potential treatment for psychological problems and mental illness, inspiring the founder of Alcoholics Anonymous with his theory that they could shock alcoholics out of their addiction. He first suggested 'psychedelics' as a name for LSD and mescaline at a meeting of the New York Academy of Sciences in 1957, years before they were banned – psychedelic, combining two Greek words, *psyche* and *delos*, meaning 'mind manifesting'. Huxley had sent Osmond a rhyme containing his proposal for a name – 'To make this trivial world sublime / take half a gram of phanerothyme,' rooted in the Greek for soul – but Osmond was not impressed. He replied, 'To fathom hell or soar angelic / just take a pinch of psychedelic.'

LSD was a situationist drug of choice, needed by some in the movement to create new situations, to dissolve received opinions and inherited models of behaviour and information processing. Imagination sparked by LSD. It accounted for some of its play, if not the serpentine theory, and the possibility that everything you know is wrong. Acid was the logical next stage after experiencing situationism, rather than it being pot that took you there. Its smoking, tripping, exploring, protesting, driven followers lived a life that embodied the social changes they desired, believing that the cities would be renovated, institutions remade, the downtrodden uplifted, equality about to happen. The world seemed alive with possibility, and those who were part of the protest, the young radicals and rebels, were confident that, in the words of Lautréamont, 'the storms of youth precede brilliant days'.

Lautréamont was the pen name of Isidore Ducasse, born 1846 in Montevideo, Uruguay, dead under mysterious circumstances twenty-four years later in Paris, disappearing into an empty space, a proto-rock star anti-hero. He was embraced as an ancestor by dogmatic surrealist manifesto writer and gothic Marxist André Breton, choosing his antecedents carefully, who fell for the morbidly romantic, bitter, twisted and sadistic pitch-black humour of Lautréamont's obscure, sole surviving complete book, *Les Chants de Maldoror*, and what was almost the founding sentence/slogan/sound bite of the surrealist spirit, 'as beautiful as the chance meeting on a dissecting table of a sewing machine and an umbrella'. By the time surrealism became a broad church, just another by-product of realism, this became almost as reproduced as Dalí's soft clock, Magritte's hats and Oppenheim's fur teacup and saucer.

Surrealism was packed with influences, precursors, stalkers and fellow travellers, but Lautréamont was definitely a special case, a touchstone of authenticity, and his abusive presence and absence reached through their skin and bones to the situationists, stealing, rubbing themselves in, regurgitating the slime, shit and juices of his artistic powers, exquisite corpse and strategies of horror, inspiring them to think things they shouldn't be thinking. He wrote, 'Poetry must be made by all. Plagiarism is necessary: progress implies it.'

One of the pamphlets Wilson, Fullerton and Sieveking found under the counter in some off-the-beaten-track bookshop, sparkling with subversion, was entitled 'Ten Days That Shook University Life', or 'On the Poverty of Student Life', an English translation of the militant Tunisian Mustapha Omar Khayati's brutal, coruscating and wildly comic attack on mundane modern university life, produced as a collaboration between the Situationist International and a group of students at Strasbourg University elected to the French student union. The twenty-nine-page publication was originally titled 'De la misère en milieu étudiant considérée sous ses aspects économique, politique, psychologique, sexuel et notamment intellectual et de quelques moyens pour y remédier'.

There was also a four-page comic called 'The Return of the Durutti Column', by André Bertrand, which presented some of the dense, complex situationist ideas, proposals and theories in an accessible, impudent visual style, especially appealing to those French students who had grown up reading European comics like *Asterix*, Hergé's *Adventures of Tin Tin* and *Lucky Luke*, the last set in the American Wild West and featuring a cowboy who 'shoots faster than his shadow'.

The Strasbourg students illegally used 5,000 francs of university funds to produce an initial run of 10,000 copies of Khayati's brochure and 5,000 copies of the comic, which were distributed on a student open day, leading to various disruptions and occupations of buildings. The university asked for a court order to stop the protests. The judge ruling on the case said:

One only has to read what the accused have written, that these
students, scarcely more than adolescents, lacking all experience of
real life, their minds confused by ill-digested philosophical, social,
political and economic theories, and perplexed by the drab monotony
of their everyday life, make the empty, arrogant and pathetic claim to
pass definitive judgements, sinking to outright abuse, on their fellow
students, their teachers, God, religion, the clergy, the governments
and political systems of the whole world. Rejecting all morality and
restraint, these cynics do not hesitate to commend theft, the destruction
of scholarship, the abolition of work, total subversion and a world-
wide proletarian revolution with 'unlicensed pleasure' as its goal.

This sounded more like a seductive manifesto for change – 'unlicensed pleasure' – than a reprimand and had the opposite effect to what the judge imagined. The Strasbourg scandal and the popularity of the 'Poverty of Student Life' pamphlet, necessitating a further printing of 10,000, resonated throughout the universities of France, copycat occupations and obstructions lighting a fuse that eventually helped ignite the events of May 1968.

The bigger myth is that situationism alone incited the French revolt as a mass spontaneous outburst without any specific leaders, and Debord's small, obscure, oddly media-friendly unit of loyal followers gained enough publicity to achieve international notoriety, as much as they appeared to resist being hyped up. More realistically, the SI was perhaps a cultural component of the general collective consciousness, made more prominent by the clique's purposeful and accidental techniques of manipulation, its rhetorical talent, its hard-edged parodying and corruption of mainstream marketing tactics. The situationists greatly exaggerated their role, but they were believed and made it true by saying it, using devious social media techniques long before there was social media.

For something against selling, the SI sold itself very well, but then it needed to as part of its campaign to produce knowledge outside the usual institutional channels. It couldn't be totally invisible. The situationists needed to be seen, by hook or by crook. They also believed that legends are as important as history – one of their main forms of influence on students at the time, and then eventually on popular culture in general, and on Tony Wilson. You never knew who Guy Debord really was, but you developed a very good idea of a character named Guy Debord who had been appointed by the media as a leader of the revolt. This was a Debord who had a life of his own that was nothing to do with the actual Debord and whatever his poor, addicted, cantankerous life consisted of.

Wilson was attracted to them as a kind of infected, sinister public relations company successfully making its presence felt which happened to be influenced by Marcel Duchamp. Duchamp in turn had been influenced by prototype existentialist and individualist anarchist Max Stirner's 1845 *The Ego and Its Own*, or *The Unique Individual and His Property*, which made Duchamp realise that the ego is always there in everything – 'I am unique' – and Stirner was not necessarily interested in political change, only personal liberty.

Stirner's proposed union of egoists, where the individual is the measure of all things, was also an influence on Karl Marx and a precursor of the situationists in its romantic, or infantile, attack on how the modern world was increasingly dominated by oppressive social institutions. The proposal advocated the existence of small, personal arrangements that evolve fluidly without much structure to them, cells lacking formal ties but communicating and working together to fix certain perceived problems. Individual autonomy, according to Stirner, must be allowed to flourish. This was another of the top-ten influences on Wilson, and on the workings of Factory.

The events in Strasbourg and Khayati's pamphlet particularly inspired students and Kim Philby Dining Club attendees John Barker and Jim Greenfield to consider introducing the technique and tactics of the SI to Cambridge. They were increasingly disillusioned even embarrassed by being students at such a corrupt, decadent place, forced to fulfil the expectations of government, industry, media and the academic system itself. Exposure to new ideas made it increasingly apparent that what they were compelled to trust was deeply flawed. Fresh from Paris during May and what they perceived as the failed Grosvenor Square demonstration against the Vietnam War, they felt Cambridge was distorting even destroying their identities, forcing them to conform to traditions, rules and categorisations that were limiting their potential freedom and intellectual powers. Their campaign of rejection reached its logical conclusion in June 1969, when Barker and a few like-minded colleagues tore up their final exam papers, dropped out of the reviled university system and headed with real purpose into the wider world.

Nothing much changed at rich, settled Cambridge, which could sail through such callow, stagy gestures, but Barker and Greenfield were set to continue their ambition to radically rebalance society, rethink and redesign politics, fight oppression and transform countercultural principles into something far more relevant than dry debates, hippy dreaming and mere marching.

As well as 'On the Poverty of Student Life', on Wilson's reading list there was former teacher and Belgian-born Raoul Vaneigem's *Banalités de base*, rendered by its translators as *Totality for Kids*, written in 1962–3, when revolutionary writing was taking over art production and miscellaneous artistic activities as a central method of situationist myth-making. In this Vaneigem had demanded that the dispossessed seize their own lives, five years before the spirit of situationism broke to the surface in a Paris that for a moment was completely turned upside down. It was Vaneigem's lyrical, feverish lament *The Revolution of Everyday Life* from 1967 that Wilson's comrades Fullerton and Sieveking would translate six years later, their translated title turned around from *Traité du savoir-vivre à l'usage des jeunes generations* for the benefit of the young generation.

Wilson would read the thirty elliptical sections of *Totality for Kids* in his modest rooms at Cambridge, loving that it was so hard to make any sense of what was being said, knowing it was as important as anything else he was reading. Perhaps he detected a link between situationist '*dérive*' – the flow of acts and encounters described by Debord as 'a technique of transient passage through varied ambiances' – and Romantic associative drift – 'a world without a centre, like the new prefabricated cities that are its decor. The present fades away before the promise of an eternal future that is nothing but a mechanical extension of the past.' Wilson's methods, intentionally or not, derived from '*dérive*', with its Latin root *derivare*, meaning to divert a flow, and the sense of following channels, eddies, currents, and also drifting, sailing or working against the wind, sometimes sure where you were heading, sometimes leaving it to chance.

In 'On the Poverty of Student Life', which in its English translation had the subtitle 'If you make a social revolution, do it for fun', Wilson found himself being instructed to 'indulge untrammelled desire'. These were words and sentiments that you felt rather than necessarily immediately understood.

Debord was the elusive, snide and dictatorial leader of a leaderless priesthood who became a prophet, because others said so, of spectacular capitalism. He was, because others said so, and he would have denied it, like he denied everything, the Nostradamus of post-modernism, and what happened to it after the internet turned everyone, knowing it or not, into a descendant of Dada, a sibling of situationism, mostly pouring forth an aimless trafficking in freedom, identity and argument without the intended, ingenious, subversive intentions.

In 1967, a decade after the materialisation of the situationists, Debord writes what becomes considered, a little traditionally, as his masterpiece, or as simply unfathomable, the dialectical prose poem *The Society of the Spectacle*, a critical elaboration of the thinking and rejection of society he experienced as a twenty-five-year-old in 1957, the twisted, bastard, sick and sickened distant relation of Colin Wilson – a teenybopper next to Debord – and the cultural studies Fab Four. He came from a bohemian world that often leads to art, music, poetry, novels, but rarely this sort of incandescent theory, conceived as though it can have the qualities and power of avant-garde art.

It is made up of 221 numbered 'theses' which would have a heady, abstract influence on post-'68 counterculture after the failure of hippy culture and the ongoing permutations of the wilder edges of popular culture

– once they were packaged in introductions to the movement alongside the doctored cartoons, fan worship and fractious graffiti of the Situationist International. Thesis number 207 plagiarises Lautréamont's 'plagiarism is necessary' note on plagiarism, which of course plagiarised someone else, possibly Coleridge, who took it from Sterne, who took it from Robert Burton of *Anatomy of Melancholy*, the world's first psychiatric encyclopedia, a compendium of thought with references to almost every aspect of seventeenth-century culture, sprinkled with classical allusions, possibly the maddest book ever written, and Burton took it from the essays of Montaigne and the satire of Erasmus of Rotterdam, the most influential humanist of his day, who said, 'The highest form of bliss is living with a certain degree of folly,' and 'A good portion of speaking will consist of knowing how to lie,' who took it from Cicero, Socrates, Plato, St Thomas Aquinas, Aristotle and Dante, and so on, and so it goes.

The Society of the Spectacle is a vivid, volatile and poetically intellectual remix of Marx and his belief that work is needed to externalise what is good inside us, distilling the best part of us, our rigour, creativity and logic, increasing our own pleasure and pleasure for others – the bringing into existence of something wonderful; the penetrating of the world with something marvellous.

Debord's remixed Marx responded to new, mass-media-defined post- and de-industrial conditions, a world filling up with celebrities and visual communications, with 'the spectacle' replacing the commodity at the centre of capitalism. Images and information had replaced money. Images were now capital, shrewdly and cynically used to trap people in an economic system very much not of their making and very much not in their best interests. Capitalism manifested through media, technology, transport, urban planning, information and then, possibly finally, definitively, computers controlled the very conditions of existence. Capitalism with consumerism not production at its heart.

Spectacles, imaginary representations, were generated by advertising and consumerism in order to render capitalism's customers, its lined-up victims, compliant and receptive. These spectacles were used to dominate and exploit people, to dictate how they enjoyed their leisure time. Reality was replaced by another, narrower, duller, meaner reality, one that suited those whose interests were profit, control and their own continuing power.

Debord (and co.) advocated combating these images, fantasies, promises and spectacles with reckless, riotous, beautiful alternative imagery, connected not to the regulated, entangling selling of product, which was becoming a nightmare, but to the reawakening of the imagination, spontaneity and dreams. Anarchic, cryptic, art-fired marketing with a superior moral and emotional quality generated to confront the bland, repetitive marketing of industry, politics and education, the actual commodification of existence.

One of the most inspiring aspects of Debord and the SI for students was how they constructed and executed their theories and challenges in a very personal, playful way. Debord was the mutant, even vicious, dark side of the university professor, but as intellectual, as knowledgeable, as interested in passing on information and learning. If the situationists' irregular but perversely inexhaustible optimism was missing from traditional politics, their emotion and wit was missing from traditional education. Ultimately, missing from both was a kind of lyrical innocence and devotion to difference that resonated with young people being forced to swallow whole either the oppressive system or an unexceptional, unrealistic and certainly unexciting opposition to the system. 'We think the world must change' was guaranteed to appeal to restless, dissatisfied students in the late 1960s. And to change the world, they were realising, you had to change life. For some, the thing that was changing life the most in the 1960s was popular culture and rock music.

Access to the situationists at the time would have been limited to occasional pamphlets and articles, their rareness giving them extra, magic powers. Prime vagabond anti-hero Debord was for some at the opposite end of the situationist spectrum to Vaneigem – the sensual rather than the cerebral, the poetic as opposed to the polemic, the ecstatic more than the ascetic – and both published major works in the same year, not knowing what the other was up to, connected but apart.

Guy Debord can be summarised, to his grave-spinning disgust, as a saint of the negative: reclusive, destitute, alcoholic and rarely photographed – which encouraged the situationists' carelessly cultivated air of mystique – hanging out with the marginalised dangerous, never a hired hand, never owned by an institution, university or corporation, at various times the film-making equivalent of John Cage – theorist, writer, hypergraphist, metaphysical guerrilla, cultural saboteur, creative destroyer, a dogmatist without dogma, a 'doctor in nothing'. He improvised his life like one long theatrical act, until his suicide in November 1994, aged sixty-two.

He shot himself in the heart, as if his whole life and vision were destined to end this way: a violent death mirroring the violent death of his ideals, the awful prospect he might become some sort of minor celebrity, turned against his will by stupid popularity into a stupid, populist figure. The social revolution he had worked, played and drank for ended up being controlled and gutted by the very forces he was fighting. His suicide was the ultimate, vain, transcendent self-critical act of a great critic, the ultimate moment of completion for someone making their whole life a work of art; it was the ultimate spectacle. Through everything that he did, for real and in hiding, he always cultivated the idea that he had the right to erase himself.

Abruptly, the Debord that lived an obscure life collides with the myth of Debord lodged into the grain of popular culture – the life slammed into the legend – and he becomes perhaps what he wanted to be all along, a ghost, an absence, haunting the confines of collective memory, connected to Karl Marx's portrayal of history itself as a ghost. But then that was how it was always destined to end; the trick was to hang on to some sort of awareness and expression that it was happening, and why it was happening. Until it was all over. If we were not seeing the real world, only the world we were conditioned to see, it was up to the individual, and the situationist, to do as much as possible to reveal glimpses, or more, of the real world, and what might be left of it. Until it was all over.

So it goes.

*

Wilson found himself at Cambridge officially tutored as a good, conscientious student by Professor Raymond Williams and abstractly, unofficially influenced – and therefore, as Williams would admit, actually educated – as a discreet, developing but still deferential student rebel by Guy Debord via early spellbound, attractively righteous and ultimately committed university adopters of situationism.

Williams and Debord inhabited very different worlds, recommended very different syllabuses and pulled out of Marxism very different decisions and conclusions, but to some extent were exploring the same territory: the way people were now relating to each other via the media, an alienating filtering of reality producing a bombardment of pseudo-realities, a splintering of competing truths. One was prone to fierce debate, and the other to violent argument; a quiet revolution versus a noisy revolution. One was waiting for a distant revolution, the other anxious to reinvent life in the here and now. Their worlds very rarely touched each other, their supporters and disciples fussing over their legacy and enduring star power occupied very separate camps, but Debord and Williams, like Catholicism and Buddhism, with their monks, meditation and prayer beads, had a lot more in common than seemed immediately apparent.

Debord the adventurist may have called the radical transformations of his time 'the spectacle', and the drier, more academically precise Williams may have called them 'the exponential presence of dramatic simulation on everyday experience', one may have been French working class, erratically educated, roaming his own space and time and self-designed mystery, the other Welsh working class, formally educated, tucked inside the protected bubble of Cambridge, the London media and the various, conventional and conventionally unconventional wings of the British left, but they were both talking about the conquest of the world by insidiously irresistible images.

In one place Wilson would be exposed to Williams' view that dislocated and disembodied industrial/post-industrial life had shaped us into spectators of a world out there, caught in an 'unfinished, transient, anxious relationship' with ourselves and others as we search and wait for the news from the outside that will create and confirm our identities. And then there was Debord, very much not waiting for the news: 'Fragmented views of reality regroup themselves into a new unity as a separate pseudo-world that can only be looked at.'

But both were talking about being cut off from the world out there, a vast inaccessible reality that can never be questioned, so that people's attentions were being directed towards some things and away from others. And Williams' definition of culture gives us one viewpoint of the notoriously elusive situationists: culture as the peculiar and distinctive 'way of life' of a group or class, the meanings, values and ideas embodied in institutions, in social relations, in systems of beliefs, in mores and customs, in the uses of objects and material life. Culture is the distinctive shapes in which this material and social organisation of life expresses itself. Culture is the way the social relations of a group are structured and shaped, but it is also the way those shapes are understood and experienced.

(There was another new direction the susceptible Wilson discovered at Cambridge. One of his best friends there was Patrick Gaffney, who had connected spiritually at the university with the charismatic Tibetan Buddhist teacher Sogyal Rinpoche; later, after the mask of benign positivity slipped off, or was ripped off, the description would become 'the controversial teacher' and 'dubiously charismatic Rinpoche'. At the time, such a presence, bringing news of otherworldly Tibet but at ease with Western routines and habits, was rare and even glamorous, something guaranteed to intrigue someone like Wilson needing answers to all sorts of questions.

His friendship with Gaffney, Rinpoche's favourite student, helped steer Wilson away from hierarchical and dogmatic Western religion into more ethereal, spiritual areas, as it did many impressionable or mentally flexible hippies at the time. Rinpoche would win them over with his idiosyncratic methods of teaching, described as 'crazy wisdom'. Later, the wisdom would appear crazy sinister, but this was after Rinpoche lost his reputation as one of the most revered Buddhist masters of the twentieth century and became widely regarded as a cult leader who had abused an ancient spiritual tradition for the sake of power, money and sex. Oddly, he died on the day I was writing this paragraph, so that one minute he was alive according to Wikipedia and then seconds later when I checked back he was dead. He 'leaves this world', as his followers dutifully reported, those unconvinced by the accusations of greed and corruption, on 28 August 2019.

So it goes.

Gaffney would collaborate with religious scholar Andrew Harvey and Rinpoche in the writing of million-selling spiritual manual *The Tibetan Book of Living and Dying*, published in 1992. It was based on Rinpoche's oral teachings concerning death, his editors working hard to capture the particular rhythm of his thoughts and insights. The book would make Rinpoche the best-known Tibetan Buddhist teacher after the Dalai Lama. Gaffney also edited two of the Dalai Lama's books. Eventually Rinpoche's personal assistant would be dragged into the scandal, judged to have known of the allegations and instances of abuse against students. 'We may idealise freedom,' Sogyal Rinpoche would say in *The Tibetan Book of Living and Dying*, 'but when it comes to our habits, we are completely enslaved.')

Whether or not Wilson understood what was going on around him, there he was, caught in some sort of web created where the thoughts of Guy Debord and Raymond Williams met, the irresponsible, abusive, mental fucker of situationism and the responsible, beloved guru of cultural studies, seasoned with the cosmic scrutiny, or narcissistic deceit, of Sogyal Rinpoche. Some of it rubbed off on Wilson, determined or contaminated his psyche, as he grew increasingly eager to be enchanted by new ideas and ideology, even though he might not have known it himself for a few years.

Wilson left few signs of being any kind of rogue or serious radical while at Cambridge, or few signs of being anything at all. He was intrigued by anarchy and those who discussed it with him but kept a safe distance. It never possessed him. He was certainly not any sort of situationist, outside of immature flirtation in college clubs, some absurdist theatre and overexcited drinking and smoking sessions. At a conference on the legacy of situationism held at the Haçienda in its last months in 1996, notable mostly for Wilson merrily squabbling with the sour situationist sceptic Mark E. Smith of the Fall, the virulent anti-Wilson scoffing at all this poncey intellectual distraction, he admitted that in 1969, as a child of the left, he mainly liked the slogans. (Meanwhile, after the famous protests and revolutions of 1968, attention in 1969 would turn to the first human beings walking on the moon and the Woodstock Festival.)

He did wonder whether his incurable infatuation with situationism – or perhaps with its enchanting inner circle – was the reason, just another example of his zealous flippancy, why he inserted into Factory contracts with artists, 'The musicians own everything, the company owns nothing, all our groups have the right to fuck off.' This meant that when he tried to rescue Factory from bankruptcy in 1992 by selling the company to the major label London Records of Phonogram, it turned out Factory didn't actually own a record company's most valuable asset, the recordings made by the label's groups, including its biggest sellers, Joy Division, New Order and the Happy Mondays. Wilson's show-off grandstanding, which made Factory such a great game for self-styled anti-capitalist heroes, was always destined to backfire. 'Oh well,' he muttered when the mistake was pointed out to him, not with nihilistic situationist glee but a deep sigh of resignation. At that point he needed the deal, needed to be rescued.

Any interest in anarchy and university friendships with those who took it a little or a lot further was probably something he was destined to leave behind as a temporary student infatuation while he made his mind up about what he wanted to do with his life. At some of the more newsworthy moments that took place during his time at Cambridge, he was somewhere else, making his mind up, attracted to mischief but not enough to make it a way of life.

Eleven: The Angry Brigade, *Varsity* and virginity

Non nobis solum nati sumus. (We are not born for ourselves alone.)

On a sunny spring day in 1970, Cambridge student Peter Freeman, a self-styled libertarian, made a whimsical, highly hippy, end-of-innocence film called *The Silver Wheel*, a documentary covering unreal events mixing Celtic, Nordic and Greek myths and solemn gaiety. It's a Syd Barrett daydream of a wedding party set in a dreamy, sun-dappled, illogically tilted Cambridge. Freeman assembled a cloaked and costumed amateur dramatic cast from earnest university and college students.

Wilson's superficially Situ friends John Fullerton and Paul Sieveking are among the students enjoying themselves in the sun, pretending to play dead and be reborn, playing Druids, angels, clowns and gods. Fullerton and Sieveking, along with what Freeman called a 'unique array of future poets, politicians, philosophers, jailbirds, journalists, academics, captains of industry, eminent surgeons, admen, diplomats, cider farmers, judges, therapists and chefs', give us an idea of who Wilson was living alongside during his years at Cambridge. These include sculptor of the *Angel of the North* Antony Gormley, Augustus John's grandson Phineas John, advertising guru Chips Hardy, father of actor Tom, and Arianna Stassinopoulos, later Huffington, founder of the *Huffington Post*.

No sign of Wilson. He's either slept in, thinks all the play-acting is a bit southern soft, or he's having his own myth-mad daydream. Maybe he was embarrassed that, despite his early ambitions to be an actor, he wasn't really good enough – or he thought such frolicking was actually beneath him. Or he was frustrated, unable to stand out like he wanted to because everyone was eccentric and clever at Cambridge.

Tony's not fully worked himself out, but he demonstrated his interests were shifting towards journalism and writing by briefly editing the oldest of the university's student newspapers, *Varsity* – as many famous names did while at Cambridge, including broadcasters Jeremy Paxman and David Frost and the television presenter mostly known for being the original host of *Countdown*, the first programme broadcast on Channel 4 and possibly the last, Richard Whiteley. Contributors had included Sylvia Plath, J. G. Ballard, Germaine Greer, Clive James and Charles, the Prince of Wales, who graduated from Trinity, Cambridge, in 1970, which meant he was sometimes within some sort of reach of Wilson.

During the late 1960s *Varsity* was very much the traditional student publication, a little self-consciously trying to work in the necessary sex, drugs and rock 'n' roll, and ending up on the softer side of that mantra, the doomed peace, love and understanding. Those identifying more with the radical energies being unleashed around the world rebelled against *Varsity*'s perceived staid qualities, as if in this small world it was the Establishment to resent; they produced magazines more in line with an underground sensibility and a belief in student power, such as the short-lived *1/-*, the title coming from its break-even cover price.

The *Shilling* – 'the journal of the socialist society of Cambridge' – emerged out of an experiment in open education called the Free University, organised by left-wing students and certain professors during the demonstrative summer of 1968, the ultimate branded year of revolt. Doing its alternative press job well as a voice for all sorts of independent views, its exact authorship never clear, the *Shilling* became one of Cambridge University's most controversial student newspapers, initially for failing to register itself as a newspaper at the Post Office, later for using its pages for basic, volatile Marxist messages as though the death knell of capitalism had sounded, for anti-imperialist statements, fierce support for the abrasive French social revolution and sundry complaints about petty college restrictions, stopping reasonably short (in the English style) of advocating violence and actually breaking the law.

A few months before *The Silver Wheel*, on Friday 13 February 1970, there is a brief, explosive sign of adult-hating, system-deriding 1968 student disturbances making it to Cambridge, something angrier and more authentically chaotic than Freeman's sweet, meandering little film. A formal dinner to promote tourism to Greece at the Garden House hotel along the peaceful, drifting, punt-packed River Cam was gatecrashed by banner-waving students protesting against the anti-communist and torture-loving right-wing military junta known as the Regime of the Colonels, which had been ruling Greece since 1967.

Shilling's twenty-one-year-old editor and later Granada Television producer Rod Caird was outraged that at the height of a brutal dictatorship in Greece local travel agents were using Cambridge to promote the country as a place to visit on holiday, so the paper issued an open invitation to what they described as 'Greek fascists holding propaganda party'. Around 400 students accepted the invitation, thinking all they were going to do was stop people attending the dinner, get a little abusive and enthusiastically proclaim, 'Down with fascism.'

The larger-than-expected protest became violent; the dining room was invaded, and a few brave souls made it onto the roof. Underprepared police and provoked students fought; bottles were thrown, and the hotel was damaged, curtains torn and windows smashed. Students mostly playing at the idea of being actual violent protesters were suddenly becoming (moderately) violent protesters. A minor skirmish ended up being called the Garden House Riot by a media alarmed that such an unruly protest had actually happened at sedate Cambridge. The occasion, as is usually the case, was not labelled and therefore styled by those involved, but by those on the outside, what you might call the opposition, who by definition are required to present such events as antisocial.

Caird and five others, initially arrested among tens of others for relatively minor offences, found themselves accused of more serious assaults and leaving 'a hooligan trail of wreckage, injury and terrified women', and were jailed for between six and eighteen months. Relatively tame offences were treated as more serious because they were part of general public disorder, numbers exaggerating the impact of impulsive, individual misdemeanours and turning them into what was described in court as mob violence. Long-haired troublemaking lefties were usefully made an example of.

Even conservative commentators and the university authorities were shocked by what they considered the severity of the sentences, delivered with the intention of issuing a warning to potentially rebellious students, especially those at Cambridge, where radical students were still in the minority, that any sort of 'riot' would lead to extremely serious punishment. The Greek protest became the peak of certainly internationally-minded internal Cambridge dissent.

Those who had dropped out of Cambridge – Barker and Greenfield – continued their fascination with a vicious, sarcastic, situationist-inspired approach to resistance and dissent, less interested in situationism as convulsive theory or radical play, more as a series of ideas and concepts to adapt about social revolution, surrealist campaigning and emotional power. They appropriated the SI not for graphics or slogans but for its fluid, spontaneous philosophy, the assault on reason and the commitment to action as much as rhetoric.

They entered an underground period of communal living, radical local politics, grassroots organising and an anti-Establishment campaign that evolved into something as violent as any modern English urban guerrilla group has been – perhaps along the way motivated by the extreme judicial reaction to the Garden House Riot and the jailing of some old friends from the Kim Philby Dining Club, sentences that were in their eyes a form of legitimised institutional violence.

The group became known as the Angry Brigade, an anonymous group bombing politicians, government offices, police and Establishment figures, without any deaths or much injury, mainly in the first few months of Edward Heath's new Conservative government. They could not legitimately be labelled terrorists as they never killed anyone, but they were hunted down as though they were, as though their forceful intellectual threat was as concerning as anything truly violent. A natural anglophone scepticism about 'intellectualism' – and any accompanying radicalised romanticism – meant that the police and others investigating, chasing and prosecuting the Angry Brigade were especially fired up.

With SI-motivated outlaw perversion, the Angry Brigade used a series of arch nicknames to brand their attacks and sign their incendiary communiqués before the Angry Brigade label stuck. Their name and methodology were somehow classically English, somewhere between daring and madcap, well organised and a little DIY, with romantic hints of the Angry Young Men of the 1950s, of irritated, neurotic, middle-class commuters losing their brollies on trains that were always late, but also more seriously echoing contemporary European guerrilla groups. Germany's Baader-Meinhof Red Army Faction, the Enragés of 1969 Paris and the Red Brigades in Italy formed an international phenomenon furiously demanding a new order.

Active English revolutionaries almost seemed a contradiction in terms, and their anomalous, confusing, amused-seeming existence as much as their insurrectionist manifesto and strategic violent methods inspired in the Establishment deep hatred leading to a frantic, concerted effort to destroy the Brigade. At the end of 1972, suspected members were subjected to a particularly long trial that seemed as much for show as anything conventionally legal. The trial was an example of how the Establishment used illusion – the spectacle – to further its cause, countering the underground self-made myth of the Angry Brigade with its own version, its own illusion, one it could shape and speak through.

The Angry Brigade, insisting at all times that they could not and should not be pinned down, turning into clichés of anarchic student rebellion, of the freedom-seeking swinging sixties, were pinned down and seen to be pinned down by their enemies. Pinned down by being labelled and then arrested, tried, convicted and jailed, the slippery Establishment with its own dark mischievous roots highly experienced in making a mockery of those who tried to make a mockery of it.

Revolting un-English behaviour had been chopped off at the knees. Here was another apparently quixotic Anglo-failure of a revolution, its instigators' subsequent marginalisation meaning they were all but wiped out of existence, leaving just enough residue to make it clear they did not succeed, or at least came to their own conclusion, timing their own finish. All of their hope for change, their belief that power in society could actually pass to the underdogs, the impotent, the idealistic and the artistic, smashed into another wall. The Angry Brigade was an upgrade from the Garden House Riot, the consequences for those jailed graver, but both resulted in the petering out of an ebullient militant spirit that for a time seemed to be genuinely disconcerting the powers that be.

A few months after the Garden House Riot, chaste if perhaps mildly stoned students are virtuously prancing around in fancy dress, often near naked, in *The Silver Wheel*, and the *Shilling*'s more militant, libertarian presence and any connection to members of the Red Brigade who might have been involved, or turned up to the Kim Philby Dining Club for fevered debates, soon fade away. Cambridge remains Cambridge, the weight of history and custom crushing anything that threatens its stability, its steady way of doing things. (Democracy eventually returned to Greece in 1974.)

Tony Wilson was not of *Shilling*, and did not take part in the *Shilling*-generated Greek protest or distribute provocative pamphlets and posters with Barker and Greenfield before they dropped out in a scowl of glory, but like others who stayed at Cambridge and played the game, fulfilling their immediate duties however conscientiously, haphazardly or mischievously, he was aware of the role Cambridge students played while he was there in local disturbances and national terrorism. There was excitement, even an intellectual prestige, about it, but ultimately, as far as he was concerned, in this form dissidence was futile.

Wilson liked the play, the flirting with danger, the rubbing dull, cautious people up the wrong way, the romantic association with scandal and scoundrels, but never felt that throwing his all in with marginal, and marginalised, spirits would suit him. He liked knowing about them, but they were just a part of what influenced him, the way they made life more interesting by experimenting with the conditions of existence even if never succeeding in taking control of those conditions. The influence was aesthetic – what was decried or reluctantly tolerated within the SI system as 'recuperated', a softening, a diluting, worst of all in their eyes a popularising of basic tenets.

Wilson was an innocent fan, not a committed fanatic, although as a fan he could skilfully impersonate the fanatic. He developed an understanding that a way to stand up to what was defined as the Establishment, the state, with its centuries-old ability to create events and ceremonies that generated a certain sort of reality, was to produce alternative versions of these events and ceremonies. Pop music and pop culture were areas where increasingly these kinds of alternative illusions could exist – not as conventional acts of revolution, but as ways of opposing the tactics of the Establishment to control people through its manufactured distractions. Not revolution, perhaps, but the kind of education that can lead to changes in social conditions and intellectual awareness.

Wilson was a witness to the continuing failure of any English revolution to get outside the state enough in order to break it down. Opposition always remains inside the system, made real because of the response of exactly what it is trying to undermine and dismantle. It relies on the state for its very existence. Disruptive youthful optimism even when it becomes violent and unpredictable, and for a moment almost verging on the successful, is somehow still enclosed inside the Establishment, which can then absorb it and render it harmless, or at least shred it into mere incidental noise. But opposition from within art and entertainment can sometimes be so different, so dissident, so experimentally, fluidly ceremonial, it can avoid being almost instantly co-opted. It generates a different sort of energy, is outside the political, but is inside the minds and imaginations of its followers, where it can resist being interfered with.

By necessity, during their guerrilla activities the Angry Brigade had been secretive, and for decades after they maintained that secrecy. They were interested – after situationism – in publicising ideas, methods and effects, but not themselves. The Angry Brigade's uncompromising reluctance to mythologise and simplify their efforts and achievements in hindsight so as not to reduce their campaign to brief, diminished history – complying with the mainstream interpretation – also means that their years of activity become almost ghostly, folded into the system they reviled.

In 1972, with an 'official' membership of almost zero, a consequence of their habit of constantly quarrelling and insulting just about everyone, the SI dissolved itself in its own acid as any kind of focused and/or hot-headed going concern. This was also the year SI disciples Barker and Greenfield were jailed for the bloodless Angry Brigade bombings – as if, perhaps, all that '60s fury and discord had run its course, and lost its way, and been wrapped up and filed away by the steady, ever-watchful Establishment.

For some of us about to emerge into pop culture and rock music, born at the other end of the 1950s to Tony Wilson, becoming teenagers in the 1970s, on the cusp of glam rock and colour television, the underground hopes and dreams, fantasies and efforts, struggles and endeavours that peaked in 1968 and then fell away into disrepair and despair might as well never have happened. We grew into a whole new set of conditions and surroundings, as if everything was beginning anew.

So it goes.

A revolution that has failed is a revolution that never happened. Or it is a revolution that has been hidden by those who tell us what is going on in the world, those who, as our friends, enemies and combatants the situationists explained, control what we see of reality by being masters of illusion, terribly competent at making everything including resistance and revolutionism a component of bourgeois culture.

The revolution never happened, so it needed to happen again.

When Wilson was editor of *Varsity*, the offices were a tiny, cluttered room on Bridge Street in the north of central Cambridge, next door to some public toilets and near the twelfth-century round, medieval Church of the Holy Sepulchre and the thirteenth-century St Clement's. The office walls were decorated with old *Varsity* articles and mock-ups of new pages.

Wilson had been attracted to the thirty-seven-year-old history of the paper and his exciting antecedents who had gone on to become national names. He dedicated himself to what most of the time was drudgery, writing stilted, relatively passive articles using dented manual typewriters, gathering copy, editing, working on layouts, taking the material out to the printers, returning at dawn, all in between delivering essays and attending lectures, if he could be bothered. The editorial skills he picked up at *Varsity* lasted him all the way through Granada and Factory.

He would also gain experience working with other ambitious minds working out how to make their presence felt and game the system on the way to their own kind of greatness, or not. Eventual highbrow populist and cultural historian Sir Christopher Frayling, rector of the Royal College of Art, chairman of the Arts Council, would write film and theatre reviews for *Varsity*. He wrote so many he would send in some under pseudonyms – his real name for serious films, another name such as Ray Fling when it was a blockbuster. At the end of Wilson's time he confessed that he wrote under different names. 'Don't you think I knew that?' replied his editor.

Wilson credited the time he spent at *Varsity* – traditionally just one term – as the reason why the northern brilliance that had carried him into Cambridge didn't result in a good degree. There was no leeway given for being editor. That was the choice you had made, nothing to do with your course work, and it was up to you to make up the time. Depending on how self-deprecating he wanted to be, how rock 'n' roll, and who he was talking to, Wilson left Cambridge with either a lowly, merely competent 2:2 degree – the same as Prince Charles, himself the subject of 'twat' and 'prat' and worse insults – or possibly an almost criminal, and in that sense actually poetic, third-class degree, complete with a romantic whiff of scandal. Something to show off, really, making it to Cambridge, but being too much of a bad boy to bag the golden double first, even if not enough of one to rip up his exam papers and walk out of his finals. So what had led to such a sudden plunge in his exam reliability?

Obviously, whatever his result, it didn't undermine his sense of his own intellectual powers. To some extent, it was a form of proof. A lower second was a bit bland, but in the way working at *Varsity* put him alongside entrepreneurial broadcaster David Frost and prophetic futurist J. G. Ballard, a third put him in the company of poet W. H. Auden, TV giant David Dimbleby and supreme journalistic provocateur Christopher Hitchens, who all got thirds at Oxford and then went on to get firsts in life. Coleridge never even received a degree from Cambridge.

And for Wilson at Cambridge, what would have seemed among the most important forms of new knowledge, of re-education, a sudden truly individual freedom? A rational increase . . . and the removal of something

Manchester Town Hall by Alfred Waterhouse. Completed in 1877, painted in 1900.

Left: Manchester Free Trade Hall, Peter Street, Manchester, 1900.

Right: Staircase inside the John Rylands Library, Deansgate, commissioned by Enriqueta Augustina Rylands.

Top left: Baby Tony.

Top right: Young Tony preparing for battle.

Above:
Little Tony holding hands with his mum and dad, Marple, early 1950s.

Left: Granada Television Studios in 1965, now the location of The Factory.

Below right: Granada Television founder, chief and art collector Sidney Bernstein.

Bottom: Granada logo.

Top: Tony wins with the
De La Salle debating team, 1967.

Above: Cultural revolutionary Guy
Debord at the 3rd Conference of the
Situationist International, 1959.

Right: Between illusion and reality . . .
Tony, Cambridge University,
graduation, 1971.

Jesus College
Founded A.D. 1571

Top: Tony and leather blouson on the set of *So It Goes*, 1976.

Above: All things must pass – Tony and George.

Left: Malcolm McLaren, 1976, because fashion is never wrong.

Above: Buzzcocks at the Lesser Free Trade Hall remembering the
Sex Pistols at the Lesser Free Trade Hall two years earlier.

Below: Vini Reilly and a mind full of guitar, 1980.

Opposite: Peter Saville, Tony and Alan Erasmus at work, 1978.

Top: Martin Hannett at the controls in Strawberry Studios, Stockport, with Tony and Alan Erasmus, 1980.

Above: The author telling Richard Boon he's started a book about Tony Wilson, the Haçienda, 1982.

Fac 50: New Order's *Movement*. Fac 51: the Haçienda Nightclub (plaque, right). Fac 52: A Certain Ratio's 'Waterline'.

that, the longer kept, the less its worth? He loses his virginity. He gets rid of it, at last.

He's nineteen. It makes all the difference. The desperate hope and wonderment finally over. Flinging it away with a nameless she, under a full southern moon, shooting for the stars, by the river, the deep black water, spectral cows mooing on the green. Or one astounding afternoon, after cheap cider and a smoke. Or was it during his poetically self-flagellating water-only period, in a grubby bedsit made for fumbling starring an ash-tray overflowing with cigarette ends, displaying his 'wit' to the strong, frag-ile sound of fellow university dreamer Nick Drake, channelling through late-'60s Cambridge the watery poignancy of Coleridge and Wordsworth.

His first actual experience with the elusive mysteries of the birth canal. It happens at Cambridge, another classic initiation ritual for a male stu-dent transferring from adolescence to adulthood, from masturbation to manliness. A story he would be very happy to pass on to any of us who happened to be there when one of his informal presentations took an autobiographical turn somewhere between boasting and dissimulating, without giving much away about the girl who helped him find a new way of loving life.

Teenage (late) sex at Cambridge; theatrical, the curtains opening, the stage beckoning, acting well his role, and all that rubbing.

Another reason for the late nights and newly animated lusts that led to that delinquent, almost aristocratic third.

Twelve: The news and the newsreaders

Multa paucis. (Say much in few words.)

Tony Wilson the Cambridge snob, who can also be described as:
- bona fide genius
- orgasm addict – he's always at it
- knobhead
- shaky tennis player
- enthusiastic wind sailor
- basically, 'praxis' means learning: a cycle of theory, action and reflection that helps us analyse our efforts in order to improve our ideas and transform the world
- cultural intermediary
- skilled networker
- flawed deal-maker
- evangelising for disruption
- this expert at forging connections between people in a pure and organic way
- his sense of his own charm can be overconfident
- wife number one, 1970s – his drug dealer: 'He did say I reminded him of his mother, because I was quite domesticated. I would dye his shoes and cook his meals for him. Apparently I peeled potatoes like his mother did, on newspaper. I became a bit of a domestic slave, but not by choice'
- wife number two, 1980s – the mother of his children: 'I was not in the music business, and I think he was looking for someone to ground him, away from the madness'
- 'wife' number three, 1990s – the beauty-queen entrepreneur with political ambitions, the one he would be happy working with, to be seen working with, introducing her at meetings as his partner, his work partner, making up for never seeing the women he worked with

or even lived with as equals: 'In the end he was quite a simple man who was a bit star-struck'
- it's like there's a hook in his mouth when he falls in love with a woman and you just can't get the hook out
- posturing as an enemy of class, privilege and vulgar capitalism while living the high(-ish) life
- restless alchemist
- lunatic enabler
- permanently followed by a dog called Ego
- shameless shaman
- getting on approximately everyone's nerves
- acutely conscious of historical change and acutely aware of how to stage himself in relation to his historical moment
- man with a plan

Time for work, this son and grandson of solid, conscientious Teutonic–northern workers, ending his time at university as a charming good boy for all his love of getting high and enjoying himself, for all his contact with the voices and forces of the far left, the decadence, depravity and secular spirituality of poets and artists. He didn't want to let his mum down as she neared seventy back in Marple. 'Be a good person,' she would say to him, which he once said was the best advice he had ever received. Whatever happened in his life, his regular visits to church, taking his kids to Midnight Mass every Christmas, were his way of keeping a connection to his mum. From his mother he learnt good manners, which entered his personality as a form of graciousness that would be present even when a darker, nastier side was spiking. He could be very formal even as he was losing his cool.

He'd come through the '60s as an armchair or pub-stool or library revolutionary, at best only vaguely politically active among the loitering heirs of Cambridge, a lover and analyst of film, books and theatre, a convert to the mystically practical promises of Buddhism, where mediation came before doctrine. Buddhism complemented the acid better than

Catholicism. Coming out of university with the unchecked exuberance of Keats as an earnest fan of yearning soft rock, he developed a long-haired, flared-trouser taste for the enlightened folk/psychedelic US West Coast wing comprehensively covered by the scholarly hippies and new journalists tracking down greater truth at *Rolling Stone* magazine – the serious writer no longer meaning primarily 'novelist'; writers were finding new kinds of topics and subjects that could be appropriate to journalism and not just fiction.

This sensibility took him to the freak philosophies and complicated karma of Allen Ginsberg, Timothy Leary and Ken Kesey – tapping into the vastness beyond their conditioned selves, widening the area of consciousness, conceiving their own scenes and ceremonies – as much as to the far-fetched French post-structuralist revolutionaries Deleuze, Barthes, Foucault, Debord, Derrida, Baudrillard, Lefebvre, Lyotard and Kristeva; probably loving both sets for being great marketers apart from anything else – shrewd, manipulative managers of their own faith, sects and fortune-telling.

He was inevitably committed to the idea of questioning authority, but was, for now, quietly constructing his own, personal method of learning to think for himself, mostly more of an observer, a fan, a collector of ideas and ideologies. The things he took away from his dabblings in situationism were the classic, clichéd drifting, the observing, the gathering, the abrasive, even abusive juxtaposition of apparently incompatible data and ideas. The moving from one thing to another in whatever order came to mind, in whatever order seemed for now the most attractive. And, perhaps, a fascination with the art of the insult, a love for argument and dispute, a habit of raiding the past to find material to make new in a different context, as part of a constant rebuilding of the world.

Others he had come across while at Cambridge flew off the handle, set off for inevitable Establishment success or glorious failure, made a name or a pseudonym for themselves as provisional revolutionaries, or directly engaged with perpetuating and distributing the words, spats and scandal-mongering of the situationists, as if to do so was to make themselves an accredited part of the cult, the religion or perhaps the business strategy.

Tony's Cambridge friend John Fullerton is soon translating more French texts by Raoul Vaneigem, including one written in the year Joy Division's *Unknown Pleasures* is released, appearing in English four years later as *The Book of Pleasures*. Jon Savage's review of *Unknown Pleasures* in *Melody Maker*, ten months before singer Ian Curtis hanged himself in his cramped, lonely kitchen, uses a quote from Vaneigem: 'To talk of life today is like talking of rope in the house of a hanged man.' This is where pop music had gone, just a few years after Cliff Richard and the Shadows and their living doll.

By 1979, Vaneigem had been for many years a former SI member and was pursuing a belief in the power of pleasure to subvert oppressive cultural norms, articulating his desire to live a life full of joy and spontaneity that broke through the passivity of contemporary society. *The Book of Pleasures* was another manifesto, echoing or articulating his emerging subconscious desires, translated by an old friend, for Tony Wilson to plunder and remake.

It was Vaneigem who considered the dreadful possibility that the elusive radical pursuits of situationism would inevitably be absorbed into the mainstream culture it resisted as simply another failed revolutionary outburst: 'What prevents what we say on the construction of everyday life from bring recuperated by the cultural Establishment is the fact that situationist ideas are nothing other than faithful developments of acts attempted constantly by thousands of people to try and prevent another day from being no more than twenty-four hours of wasted time.'

Wilson hated wasting time; the rest of his life wasn't going to last forever.

'Society,' Wilson would suddenly announce, although I swear we had been discussing his hatred of the Ramones, 'is a battleground of representations.'

Wilson had made his mind up what he wanted to do next, and editing *Varsity* was part of the solution. Something to do with words, but also something to do with pictures, preferably pictures that moved. A synthesis of text and graphics; something else taken from the SI.

At Cambridge, a university centre of the universe for companies and corporations scouting for groomed, highly equipped new talent, you would be aware of the very best career possibilities. Wilson, his self-confidence blossoming after three years at Jesus, had his eye on the two highly prized general traineeships available at the BBC, but – according to him – they were cancelled the year he graduated. He applied for the six news trainee-ships there were at the BBC, six Thomson regional newspaper traineeships at Cardiff, two traineeships at Reuters and two at ITN in London. He realised the competition for these positions was formidable, and not just from Cambridge – from other universities around the country, hundreds if not thousands of candidates aiming to secure one of these important, even glamorous chances to enter the media, which had the world at its centre and was getting closer and closer to the centre of the world.

He went for his ITN interview feeling he had failed at his meetings with Reuters and the BBC. He'd been too nervous, too polite, and he needed to do more to compensate for his dubious degree. At this interview he was asked if he thought there was anything the relatively new, moderately innovative ITV news providers could do better? Wilson, looking back at how he answered from a position of becoming rampaging Mr Manchester, claims he was already in full-blast flamboyant mode, taking on the world, or at least a formal interview board, and said how as a twenty-one-year-old taking pop culture very seriously he was disappointed with the brief, almost condescending way ITN had covered the death of Jimi Hendrix – as if it was all about drugs and scandal, not about the death of an impor-tant and unique artist.

He felt he had nothing to lose, it was his last chance, so why not be honest to himself and his principles, as bizarre as they might have sounded to suit-and-tied mainstream journalists not quite used to the idea that young people had their own ideas how the world should be interpreted and presented. The death of Hendrix, Wilson intoned, should have been treated as something serious and tragic, not as a minor event in the appar-ently irrelevant and trivial counterculture. His interviewers were perhaps hoping for some insight into how British television news could catch up with covering foreign news, which at the time was still mostly the territory of newspapers, but he gave them something else to consider.

A few days later a telegram arrived addressed to his room at Cambridge to tell him he had been selected as a trainee at ITN. The northern brilliance still existed, enhanced by official tutor Williams, scabrous tutor Guy Debord, the Catholic neutralising acid of Buddhism – through the strength of their beliefs – as well as by ghostly tutors Keats and Coleridge, Sterne and Huxley, accompanied by Jimi Hendrix and Leonard Cohen.

Entering broadcasting and in particular ITN, he reflected, was one of the key moments in his life, setting him on a course he would never deviate from, as much as he could help it, even as he did all those other things to do with Manchester, music and messing for good and for weird with the minds and destinies of as many people as he could.

ITN was a better place for Wilson to begin working than the BBC, which in essence was an extension of the strait-laced systems and hierarchies of Cambridge. Independent Television News had been set up in 1955 as part of the new ITV, which would broadcast its programmes, and the company instantly set itself apart from the discreet, formal BBC by actually naming its newscasters and reporters, and giving them unprecedented freedom to investigate and interrogate and even think a little spontaneously.

ITN was motivated by the same principles as ITV: to fulfil its tightly regulated public-service remit, but also reach as many viewers as possible. It mixed a rigorous, uncompromising news-gathering and presenting style with innovative ideas like interviewing ordinary people, often in the street, and mixing hard news with more entertaining, so-called human-interest stories. The ambition was to be as scrupulous and informed as the BBC, but not as boring or rigid. BBC newsreaders were still wearing bow ties and communicating like a hybrid of butler and public-school headmaster.

Interviews handled by the uncompromising Robin Day in the company's early days alarmed politicians, who were used to the fawning, diffident style of the BBC. Day dived straight in with a bullish purpose that never left him throughout his career, treating the MPs he interviewed as responsible for their actions, needing to explain and defend their decisions and views rather than allowing them to go through the motions and repeat empty, scripted platitudes as though they sat above everyone else. He never allowed them to simply say what they wanted or what they had prepared without being challenged.

Wilson joined the company four years after it had been commissioned to supply a thirty-minute daily news programme to be broadcast every night at 10 p.m., initially on a thirteen-week trial to mollify those within ITV who didn't believe its viewers would appreciate uninterrupted news and mostly static talking heads. Previously, the news on ITV had gone out just before nine, and lasted only around twelve minutes – almost an aside to the main scheduling, an interruption more than an integral part of viewing.

Without sacrificing its news coverage, actually adding to the detail of their coverage with vivid on-the-spot reports from around the world, the new *News at Ten* used two presenters, was made as entertainment as well as a serious, factual programme, and some bulletins started to feature in the top ten television ratings. By the time Wilson joined, audiences regularly reached 12 million. This was the heyday of national communal viewing, and ITN had managed to convince viewers that the news was as much a part of the flow of television that Raymond Williams had written about as comedy, sport and drama.

Within three years, the BBC, traditionally worried about giving individual newsreaders too much power, still wary of suggesting its presenters had actual independent personalities and opinions of their own, even, God forbid, charisma, was forced to respond with its own *Nine O'Clock News*. In its own sober way, the BBC had adapted to the idea boldly conceived by ITN that the news could actually be a show with some borrowed American razzamatazz without risking its carefully measured sense of objectivity.

News at Ten became popular as much for the regular exposure of its eccentric, amenable, sometimes attractively sombre newsreaders as much as for the way it packaged and rethought the news. Its small pool of newsreaders became as famous as any voices and faces in the country by being on screen almost every night, and for being more or less the sole deliverers of national and world news. They came across as being as important as the news they transmitted, and in a world of very few channels were a habitual part of daily life. Safe, dependable and definitely commanding, nicely turned-out men with warm, reliable voices and a calm, methodical manner established a manner that was a combination of journalism and showbusiness, analysis and performance. (This was the 1960s and early '70s, so it was all white southern middle-class men, as though that was the only way to convey authority, just as it was, with precious few exceptions, in the counterculture. Granada's Anna Ford would become the first female newsreader for ITN in 1978, with Reginald Bosanquet publicly pleased to be joined by someone he had heard 'was a very professional and competent lady'.)

The roster of *News at Ten* presenters, for many years a bulletin of males, included Alastair Burnet, Gordon Honeycombe, Sandy Gall, Andrew Gardner and Bosanquet, mixed up in very un-British American-style presenting couples. This was not so much to create tele-friendly double acts, but so that while one presenter was on screen, the other could be preparing for the next segment, enhancing the feel of speed and spontaneity. For most viewers, though, the relationship between the two newsmen became a reason to watch.

The most appealing of the newsreading duos was imposing, unruffled, aristocratically proportioned Gardner and spirited, hedonistic Bosanquet – who had the family roots to actually claim a seat in the House of Lords – wearing a skittish toupee accompanied by louche sideburns and possessing a shaky, idiosyncratic, lopsided delivery that some suggested was due to alcohol or a recent stroke, and which he claimed was the result of the anti-epilepsy medication he required. There was also a hint he may well have been driven gently mad by years of broadcast journalism, a peculiar job that nonetheless hands you a tremendous feeling of power. (A Benny Hill parody in 1971 renamed the company NIT and captioned the newsreader 'Reginald Boozenquet'. Gardner and Bosanquet established a reputation as the Morecambe and Wise of news, and by coincidence Bosanquet's death in 1984 at fifty-one was overshadowed by the death the following day of Eric Morecambe.)

The combination of impassive straight man and mischievous-seeming partner – broadsheet depth with tabloid directness – was irresistible and generated a particular kind of trust in what they were saying to the nation during a turbulent time of political strife, wars, disasters, hijacks, terrorism and economic chaos. Plus the *News at Ten*, which began with the dramatic opening bongs of Big Ben and a portentous theme tune, established a way of finishing the news, however alarming or taxing, with a frivolous flourish, some feel-good fluff – the 'And finally . . .' coda, delivered with added chuckle and twinkling eye, that proposed however grave, scary and tense the world was, life goes on, and we're all in this together. And – something the BBC was forced to catch up with – 'And finally . . .' made it clear that the newsreaders were human, not just machines to read words, to pass sanctioned messages through.

Wilson's first task at ITN was to contribute to the scripts that these famous screen regulars would read, quickly learning from some of the nation's most experienced newsreading experts the techniques of writing informative, accessible and intelligently lucid summaries of complex events for live broadcast that also introduced original touches of insight.

Alastair Burnet in particular, a former editor of *The Economist*, could compress an extraordinary amount of unruly information into the few precise words a news script required. This quickness and flair influenced Wilson as much as the great storytelling Bosanquet's relish for the drama of live television, the ability to deal at a moment's notice with something going wrong in the studio and maintain complete composure during a live broadcast, knowing that if you said the wrong thing, your entire career, even your life, could blow up in front of you. Wilson's flair for storytelling, for transmitting authority through the screen whether introducing Blondie and Iggy Pop or interviewing leaders of political parties, begins with Burnet and Bosanquet. He falls in love with the tremendous rush of live television, this technological method of being compelled to live off your wits.

Wilson was also rapidly learning from the inside about the power of television to influence events and distribute images and meaning on one of the most innovative television news programmes in the world. For many at the time, as worldwide communications were being transformed by satellites, television had become their single source of information. Those interested in power, sometimes even greedy for it, quickly realised during the 1960s and '70s that television was the most influential tool ever invented up to that point.

Wilson, playing up the impact of ITN to boost himself, but this time with more than a grain of truth, later claimed that it was at this point the second-best news organisation in the world, behind only CBS, pointing out how impressive this was considering CBS's history and resources, and its iconic, influential and responsible newscasters Walter Cronkite, Edward Murrow and Don Rather.

Dangerous, changeable reality was being carefully but speedily packaged for popular consumption, information was being constantly processed, simplified and recycled, but Wilson from inside the system appreciated the skill necessary to manipulate and mould information for a large audience without being cynical or condescending. He was working from inside the production of Debord's spectacle, as both a believer in the process and a sceptic. He wasn't a seditious activist lying low within the Angry Brigade, launching splinters of resistance into the Establishment alongside his Cambridge peers, but he was writing the script about their antics for the national news. The observer as participant, if not wholly *the* participant.

He developed his own technique, somewhere between hypocritical and intellectually supple, of appreciating there was a kind of art, even poetry, to being so close to the idea of how reality was channelled through the technology and choreography of television without completely distorting the news or disorientating the viewer, and somehow allowing a little space for them to question even challenge what they were being told.

Wilson was at ITN for almost two years, making the occasional appearance on some of the lighter items, getting a little restless with the work he was doing. He was looking for some adventure, wanting to report himself, possibly from exotic or even dangerous foreign locations. The intention was not so much to appear on television, which wasn't something he initially aspired to, but to become part of the scrupulous and prestigious ITN tradition of tele-journalism, which put him close to the centre of the world, or at least in a place where world events came to him and sometimes even relied on his judgement. He liked the idea of that. Something about him was attracted to the power it gave him. Eventually, being on TV would become like a drug to him, and whatever else he did, he never wanted that to be taken away. He wanted more and set out to make sure there was always more.

Too impatient to pass through the established ITN system, his thinking was not to head straight for Granada, the station he eventually seemed a natural part of, as if that had been his ambition since childhood, but to move into regional television anywhere in the country, train as a reporter on a local magazine show and then return to ITN. He thought of the company and *News at Ten* as his home, and his aim was to become an ITN reporter, hopefully a foreign correspondent, go on the road, visit war zones and troubled, threatened places, and then move into the job that was, to his surprise, actually higher up the chain of command: the news anchor.

He would claim in years to come that he wasn't looking to become famous. He was interested in the task, the technique and the connection he could make with the moment, another word for the 'situation' or the 'spectacle'. The newsreader was one of the first points of contact, certainly the first visible point of contact, with situations and events as they developed around the world. Wilson could use what he had picked up from the situationists from within. Seeing close-up the grand masters of *News at Ten* – Burnet, Gardner and Bosanquet – he noticed how there was an element of acting as well, the kind of acting he thought he was capable of, drawn from his dad, playing a role, in this case the role of a newsreader, dependable, precise and very confidently informing the nation of exactly what was happening in the world, like you'd just thought of the details yourself.

Getting used to the idea he was inventing his own life as he went along, the first job he saw advertised was at Granada, for another role. As he loved to do, he said that he made a mess of the interview, but he was

offered a job as a reporter, coming from the outside, from London experience and the well-respected ITN, but returning home, perhaps temporarily but soon discovering that Granada was where he belonged. He made
the opposite move to what most did at the time – leaving to go to London.
He left London to come to Manchester, initially on a two-year contract.

Thirteen: An aside, arguments, acid, Richard and Judy, making friends and getting married

Nemo autem regere potest nisi qui et regi. (No one is able to rule unless he is also able to be ruled.)

The bonkers-bright Tony Wilson, also known as Anthony H. Wilson, as well as Mr Manchester and him off the telly, can also be described as:
- irritating dilettante
- pretentious charlatan
- Salford son
- chairman of the North
- mad Tony
- Alderman Wilson
- great red
- wind-up merchant
- arrogant bastard
- Factory boss
- fat-Tory boss
- infuriating bighead
- huckster extraordinaire
- bullshitter
- a sucker for modish philosophies
- as bloody-minded as William Blake
- a genius who will do anything to get attention

While interviewing for this book two close colleagues of Wilson from Granada TV, Judy Finnigan and Richard Madeley, who achieved sizeable end-of-the-twentieth-century television fame with their agile and friendly, husband-and-wife presenting of ITV's mid-morning daily show *This Morning*, I told them that I was thinking of calling the book *Self-Division*. Richard, as a switched-on TV energy and celebrity definitely influenced by Wilson, was appalled. It's a nod, I explained, feeling pinned to the ground by Richard's sure fury, to Tony's many overlapping personalities, his Nietzschean capacity for self-invention and the band he was most associated with, Joy Division. 'Oh God, no,' said Richard. 'Oh no. No, no, no, no.' Another characteristic he shared with Wilson; confidence is like a hydra where for every head cut off two will grow back.

Richard and Judy knew, worked with and were influenced by Tony Wilson the sparkling TV personality, who had an easy-going knack for winning over – and sweetly teasing – audiences and negotiating with nerveless composure the complexities and pressures of live television. The thrill of live television was one of his addictions.

They knew his family, went on the school run together. They had less experience of the other side of Wilson, the one who ran an experimental, fiercely independent record label with a sensibility as connected to the Italian Renaissance humanist, author, artist, architect, poet, priest, linguist, philosopher, cryptographer and ideal citizen Leon Battista Alberti as to positive, maverick record-label bosses like Richard Branson of Virgin and Chris Blackwell of Island. Alberti would write, 'A man can do all things if he but wills them,' and believed the city was a necessary component of civilisation.

Richard and Judy were not so aware of the Wilson who was in charge, more or less, of a Manchester nightclub that was more, or less, than a nightclub, which began the 1980s as an overambitious venue for cultish indie bands, a deviant drinking club, at times barely existing, and became famous by the end of the decade as a post-modern dance club that more accidentally than not gave substance to Wilson's dream of rearranging Manchester's entire reality let alone its music scene. The Wilson whose life was a series of artistic turning points and sociopolitical discoveries as much as it was a mapped-out television career that followed a, more or less, logical route after university.

They had only a distant understanding of Tony's zealous commitment to the ideal of devolution for the North, his aggressively idealistic belief that the North-West of England should exist as an independent state, his raging disgust with how the Establishment, controlling the nation from small, self-serving sections of the South, consistently ignored the North, neglected and underestimated its beauty, energy, innovation and talents. His opposition to the eternal inequality built into the North–South divide was once an eccentric proposition, his belief in an independent North-West verging on revolutionary. By the 2020s, the idea was not so far-fetched.

Richard and Judy's Tony was mainly the lively, lovely, admittedly cocksure man off the telly, a near neighbour of theirs in Didsbury, south Manchester – the south of Manchester being more related to the affluent north of London, the North being like south London – who had a kind of hobby to do with music and young people, almost a form of giving back to the community, which, charmingly, he never quite grew out of.

So Richard was very 'No, no, no, no' when I mentioned *Self-Division* as a possible title. He vigorously shook his head to emphasise the idiocy of the idea. 'No, no, no, no.' After a minute or so of the noes I changed my mind, although I made it clear I was not going to call it *Mr Manchester*. Or *Mr Madchester*. Richard was right about *Self-Division*. But then, in the universe of Wilson, so was I. His opinions might change, but never the fact that he was right.

Richard Madeley

Actually, I had an argument once with Tony about Joy Division. We sat at the same desk at Granada, and one day he had been on the phone making some sort of deal with or for Joy Division. After he hung up I said to him I didn't think Joy Division was a very good name. 'Actually, I think it's a mistake.' 'Do you mean commercially?' he asked. I said, 'No, morally, because we all know what the name refers to, but their fans might not, and if they do know and they don't mind then that's wrong. You're talking about poor women who were sent to concentration camps and screwed for extra rations. That's the reality of it.' I didn't think it was appropriate. We had a bit of a ding-dong about it, a good old argument. And at the end I remember him saying, 'OK, you're fucking right. Sorry,

you're fucking right. But I'm fucking right as well and that's where we're
going to leave it, all right?' That was Tony.

Alan Erasmus, friend, ex-friend, Factory director 1978–92

I met Tony for the first time in 1974 at some party. He was regaling
people, of course everyone looking his way, putting him where he liked
to be, at the centre of attention. Before then I just knew him from the
television. I remember thinking while I was watching him, just from
the look on his face, Wow, if I ever met that guy I'd end up fighting
him. *It actually became the friendship from heaven, if then one not so*
wonderful. It turned out we had the same sense of humour and ended up
being so close some people thought we were in a relationship. He would
confide in me before his wife Lindsay! She hated that. We'd smoke and
talk and smoke and talk and go all over the place, and at the weekends it
would be acid, which meant other places altogether.

Neville Richards, close friend, traveller, Buddhist, prison chaplain,
raconteur

We never had a cross word for thirty-five years. None of that shite that
went on with his business partners. We met at a party at the house of
the radio personality James Stannage. He was this confrontational disc
jockey, like an early shock jock, for Radio Piccadilly in Manchester, and
his wife went to art school with my ex-wife. Me and Tony got talking
about Bruce Springsteen, who had just put out his debut, Greetings from
Asbury Park, *so it's early 1973. He was so excited about that record,*
and we became friends from then on. He appeared straight, although
he also appeared not so straight, and I soon realised he was a bit of a
freak. I had been on the front line in Wythenshawe, it was a war zone
in the '50 and '60s, and it definitely gave you an edge, and you had to
have a bit of a head on your shoulders to make sure you avoided the
nick. You either fought or boxed clever. I boxed clever and got out, went
abroad, all over the world, discovered different religions, was walking
around Wythenshawe in the late '60s in a white dress with paint on my

forehead – that meant taking a lot of fucking shit, believe me. Me and
George Harrison were the only northerners into Hare Krishna. I was in
the same class as Erasmus, and the racism at the school was terrible –
the geography teacher would point out Africa on the map and go, 'Oh,
Africa, you know all about that, don't you, Erasmus?' He had been born
in Wythenshawe, lived there all his life! Tony was attracted to things he
hadn't experienced, and I was a bit wild, had an edge. He was a posh
boy really, his decorous mum's son, but he always fancied a bit of rough
– a bit of rough who was into Hinduism and Springsteen.

Richard Boon, friend, manager of Buzzcocks, Rough Trade, rational
irrationalist, librarian

He once said to me, 'Richard, have you read Ulysses?' 'No, Tony, I
haven't read it.' He had because it was probably a set text at Cambridge.
'Right,' he said, 'here is my copy, and here is a concordance, an index
in alphabetical order to all the words in the Bible. Read them both
together,' he said. I tried and gave up, and he said, 'You should have
read Ulysses first and then the concordance, and then go back.' I gave up
many times. It seemed a lot of work, when I believe we had been talking
about record distribution. I tried again many decades later and got stuck
in the brothel scene. He was always wanting to give bits of information
to people he thought might benefit from it. He wanted people to be as
clever as him. It's not like he was keeping it all to himself. It was like
with Buzzcocks – I was so pleased we got 'Ever Fallen in Love' into
the charts with a sleeve based on Marcel Duchamp's fluttering hearts
serigraph. We all wanted to get content out there in a world that at the
time was largely content-free.

Steve Coogan

The generation of parents who were married before the 1960s might
as well have been married sixty years before that. So my generation – I
was born in 1966 – and my parents' generation straddle this cultural
precipice. My parents are pre-rock 'n' roll – my dad likes Glenn Miller

and brass bands. My parents weren't teenagers. They left school and got a job. My parents didn't want to be young and hip. They just wanted to be responsible. These days parents even grandparents have tattoos, right? That absolutely wasn't the case then. My older brother influenced and turned me on to new things. 'You shouldn't listen to those bands; you should listen to these bands.' I remember going out and buying Siouxsie and the Banshees, you know, and I was hit just for ordering it from Boots. Right, remember? But as soon as something would chart, he'd drop them. Love it at number seventy-five, under the radar, hate it at number one, mocking me for still listening to it. I remember him arguing with my dad, who was screaming at him downstairs because he'd dyed his hair blond. 'What is wrong with you? You look like a girl. Why are you dressing in a way that I'm not even sure if you're a man or a woman?' I didn't know what was happening. He used to work at a clothes shop in the Arndale called Clobber, this was about 1979, and he wouldn't come home while his hair was blond. My father couldn't understand how you could ever be someone's father looking like that. And that was really heartfelt. Tony Wilson was in the eye of that storm, in a way. He was in no-man's-land. He was a bit too old to be hip, but he wasn't so old to be like your parents. He was like a sort of intergenerational figure, legitimising something that was so new – the idea of the teenager, but then the teenager taking those interests through their life. It had never happened before, and he made it not seem reckless but quite noble.

I think he made it all right for working-class men to read books. Be working class and macho but aspire to something else. It's a little bit quaint, looking back. At the time I was into a very anti-emotive, anti-rock 'n' roll thing, deliberately into music where the word 'love' was not used in songs. At the time it wasn't ironic or anything, it was genuine, it was a time to take things seriously. Tony pushed that in Manchester, as a progression from the past, but not looking back, looking forwards. There was that period in the early '80s, a period of feeling that this is kind of important. You didn't think very far ahead, but it seemed to be *about the future. And also, being at school, knowing that there's the music that everyone else likes and there's the music that people who are in the know like. And I'm with these people. Image and emotion went hand in hand. And being slightly elitist, in some ways, but I don't care. But even so it was like there's somewhere for us to go. I remember in the late '70s, it was post-punk, when Tony started Factory really being quite aware that this was an exciting time. Being aware of it, being existentially aware. It seemed a noble thing, to want to break out. You know, everything gets assimilated these days. Anything that is remotely interesting, it sort of has the life sucked out of it by commerce almost immediately. Because of the speed of things. If punk rock happened now, it would last about week.*

Fourteen: Home again, *Granada Reports*, 'What's On', falling in love and driving Jags

Fata viam invenient. (The fates will find a way.)
VIRGIL

Wilson never went back to ITN. That part of the plan was replaced with something else, which itself would then be replaced with something else. Granada pulled him in and gave him a chance to play, and territory to roam, splitting his time between the more straightforward presenting and a more interventionist cultural role that crept discreetly towards the subversive.

He got happily, if sometimes frustratingly, stuck at Granada, and by being regularly on screen with a definite flirtatious approach, watched throughout strongly branded Granadaland during a limited time of only three TV channels, he started, to his surprise, to become well known. A friend had warned him that by being regularly on the television he would become famous, but he didn't believe it. Being known only locally, enclosed inside the North-West, made the fame even more intense and, nationally, strangely lopsided. Being known meant being liked, and also being definitely disliked, because he couldn't hide who he was and the volume and strength of his opinions.

He quickly learnt how he could play with the role, be more than just someone off the telly. He didn't care for being neutral, and somehow he got away with it. There's more he wants to say than just what he's given to read. He uses his regular screen presence to rile fans of Liverpool FC, rivals to his beloved United more than City. In 1974 he was in Liverpool on the day their legendary, adored and surely permanent manager Bill Shankly resigned, the man who had changed the entire culture of the club and turned them into European giants. Wilson went out onto the streets with a hastily arranged camera crew to tell local fans – all sharing the same effeminate, wavy glam hair as him – that Shankly, without any notice, was going, leaving them in total shock and complete disbelief. Their whole world falls apart, and a gleeful Tony can't believe his luck that he's the one to tell them. This is definitely his kind of job; he's in control of the out-of-control.

Being a part of Granada, travelling the region for stories and interviews, meant that he soon came in contact with great figures such as Shankly, even spent time with them. Devoted United fan he might have been – the club had its own powerful and innovative Scottish manager, Matt Busby, responsible for rebuilding the team after the Munich air disaster, guiding them to the European Cup in 1968 – but he considered the idiosyncratic, philosophical hard man Shankly the greatest manager of them all. And Shankly would call him Tony, like he was a friend.

He once asked Shankly how he managed to control his players. Shankly told him that after he had worked with them for a couple of weeks he would grab them by the collar, look them in the eye and tell them in his ball-busting Scottish accent, 'I know you . . .' Wilson said the way he said it turned him to jelly. He was also delighted to hear that in the 1950s Shankly used to feed his players amphetamine sulphate in order to get the best from them, like a low-down scheming manager of a rock group achieving results whatever it took to get a performance. He also liked how Shankly considered team spirit a form of socialism. 'Everybody working for the same goal and everybody having a share in the rewards. That's how I see football, that's how I see life.'

Despite Wilson's admiration for the charisma, strength and style of Shankly, he never failed to use his position to wind up Liverpool fans, whom he usually mockingly categorised as 'our cousins down the East Lancs road'. He once presented a Granada show wearing without any explanation a rosette of the team they would soon be playing in the 1978 European Cup final. The producer had asked him not to say anything about the imminent match, and he didn't, just sat there eyes twinkling, wearing a Club Brugge rosette.

Workers from Granada in Manchester finding themselves in Liverpool were used to having to pass on to Wilson basically the same disparaging insult from disgruntled locals, sometimes meaning it as a kind of back-handed compliment. By the time he was not only one of the most famous television presenters in the Granada region, but the Factory boss, landlord of the Haçienda with his (fucking) photograph hung up at the entrance, and also making such a play for Manchester being the centre of everything, some lads in Liverpool had had enough.

They stole his pride and joy from outside the Granada studios, the brand-new Jaguar he had bought to show off his early-'80s anarcho-aristocratic-celebrity-entrepreneurial status. He travelled by train to pick it up from where the police had found it and drove it back to Manchester. A few hours later, the symbolic Jag was back in Liverpool. The thieves had followed him to Granada and stolen it again with a tempestuous sit-uationist flair he had to admit was impressive, even in its own way an act of affection, provocatively throwing his symbolism, and his teasing, back at him. Others at Granada less familiar with the marching-to-a-different-drum ways of Wilson's world didn't understand when he explained this meant he must be doing something right.

Lindsay Reade, first wife, writer, Factory collaborator, co-manager early Stone Roses, A&R executive

I'd seen him on the TV and had this thought that I would get to know him but didn't imagine how I would. And then I met him three months later at this party. I was with someone, he was with someone. I didn't fancy him at all, I wasn't interested. But I ended up selling him some drugs. I'd been living with this guy for two years, he sold drugs, and he knew this dealer in London who got this Thai grass, the best grass I ever had in my life. Two hits and you would be in an altered state. My mum had given me a thousand pounds when I was going to marry someone before Tony, and I had this thought to spend it all on this grass – because it wouldn't be around for long. Someone said, 'Tony would really like this,' and I happened to have a lot of it. I got his phone number, and we met at this pub car park in Disley, south of Stockport. He drove this blue souped-up Ford Escort which seemed to match the blue of his eyes,

*and I immediately fell for him. We drove a little way and had a smoke. I
was staring at the patches on his jeans, thinking, I don't want to be with
anyone else. I just want to be with you. That was that. Smoking dope,
listening to music, him writing me letters filled with quotes from poetry.
For six weeks it never rained, the sky was always blue. I couldn't believe
I was with this guy. It seemed like paradise. Once I got to know him the
shine wore off it a little – and vice versa for sure.*

Judy Finnigan

*Tony used to drive me home from work sometimes; we lived close
to each other. He used to stop at a florist on the drive home. He was
bonkers about fresh flowers in his house. I was in awe of him because
he seemed the epitome of cool. He had this reputation at work of
getting away with anything. Nobody would get in his way. They'd try,
but nothing fazed him. He'd put all these flowers in the back of a car,
playing 'Sexual Healing' on a cassette, and he'd smoke a joint, sometimes
steering with his head on the steering wheel as he took a puff. It was
always a mystery to me how he drove in daylight through Manchester
and never got pulled up by the police. His self-assurance somehow gave
him immunity.*

Richard Madeley

*I didn't copy the joint or the steering with the head, but I was impressed
with him getting all those flowers. I've done that ever since, possibly
because of Tony. It's lovely filling the house with flowers. And he copied
me, because when I joined Granada in the early 1980s, and Judy was
assigned to look after me on day one, I had a Mark 2 Jaguar. I still had
it when Judy and I got together. Tony coveted that car, he really loved
it, he would just stare at it. I wrote it off when I had to swerve to avoid
a cyclist knocked off his bike and I hit a car coming the other way. I
got another temporary car, not a Jag, and I was parking it at Granada
when the gate opens, and this absolutely beautiful dark green Mark 2
Jaguar rolls up with Tony behind the wheel. He saw me looking and very*

guiltily rolled down the window and said, 'I couldn't do it while you had one. It would have been too much both of us driving one, and I wanted one all my life.' I said, 'That means I can't get one now.' 'So it goes, Richard,' he said. 'So it goes.'

Terry Christian, disc jockey, writer, presenter of *The Word*

When he turned up for the first time with that Jag, I said, 'Bloody hell, Tony, that's a bit flash. I thought you were broke.' 'It's all borrowed money, darling,' he said.

Oliver Wilson, son

Honestly, when I think about Dad, I think about his car. We were always in his car driving somewhere. He rolled spliffs on his knees at 120 miles an hour on the motorway. That was his thing. He had a body kit on the Jag fitted in Germany and low-profile tyres. It looked amazing, and we'd go all over the country for gigs and theatre and meetings. We'd drive across Europe over the Alps for holidays and not book a hotel, just see where we got to at the end of a day. There was always this great spirit of adventure with how my dad did things. His car was littered with demo tapes, and he had this notepad on a suction cup attached to the window so he could write notes. He'd always be gesticulating and muttering to himself, coming up with speeches and pieces to camera.

He becomes a part of the team for the 6 p.m. magazine programme *Granada Reports*, which came out of previous shows such as *People and Places* and *Scene at 6.30*, made by young people desperate to get on and impress the Granada hierarchy, giving the show a specific, changeable energy that Wilson revelled in. Six in the evening was when the ITV network showed local programming, with each area of the country getting its own news and its own faces. Wilson was being sent out on the road, all over Lancashire and Cheshire, doing trivial items, investigative films, gamely playing the fool in silly stunts, getting more and more used to being on camera.

With his own form of living poetry, Wilson had managed to lure Thelma McGough née Pickles away from her husband Roger McGough, a poet famed for his wit, his novelty pop hits with light-hearted deep thinkers the Scaffold, featuring Paul McCartney's brother Mike, and his Merseybeat association to the Beatles, which wasn't quite as intimate as Thelma's, a former girlfriend of both Paul and John. Tony's first real love was one of the Liverpool Beat girls, girlfriend of John Lennon as arty, sassy beatnik in 1958, briefly dating Paul McCartney a few years later as the Beatles were becoming famous. Just to confirm, because this must be stressed: Tony Wilson's first real girlfriend had previously dated both John Lennon and Paul McCartney, something which instantly inserted him in his own mind into pop culture history, into greater historical importance.

At Cambridge, enraptured by a famous living northern poet, Wilson had started a fan club for McGough, and back in the North-West he would sometimes camp outside McGough's house and in the morning hand him a poem he had written. One day Thelma answers the door, and there is an instant attraction between the famous poet's wife and the romantic ex-Cambridge student balancing the obvious charm of someone who believed in himself and a certain forbidden danger. Charm is always genuine; it may be superficial but it isn't false. With Thelma and Roger's marriage existing as some kind of virtual separation inside the same house, Thelma and Tony begin an affair.

As a Granada reporter, he makes sure he gets as many stories based in and around Liverpool as he can, sometimes as many as four, making it back for the live evening show with minutes to spare. While he spends secret time with Thelma, the crew have to drive forty-five minutes around the block. Roger eventually finds out, and one of Tony's proudest moments is when he receives a poem from McGough, still one of his idols, telling him to leave his wife alone. He writes a poem back, explaining himself. There is no charm like courage. Roger is not charmed. The fan club is dissolved.

Thelma would be with Wilson when he recorded some of his kamikaze stunts – a slot dreamt up by producer John Slater. These were making Tony locally famous. She made Wilson a sweatshirt with *Kamikaze* stitched on it.

Watching him at work, seeing what outrageously entertaining, usually daft thing he'd do next, he made it all seem so effortless, and, she noted, he never seemed to do any research. He would tackle almost all of the stupid stunts that were handed to him, failing only at water-skiing, which brought out the De La Salle plank in him. Thelma going on shoots with Wilson led to her own career at Granada, working as a reporter from the Liverpool office. She quickly realised none of it – the research, filming, presenting – was the breeze that Wilson made it seem. Another great result of the Granada system, she went on to be a producer on Granada's highbrow puzzle-quiz *The Krypton Factor* and her old Cavern pal Cilla Black's *Blind Date*.

Thelma started working at Granada in 1974, after an earlier guest appearance as an artist experimenting with fashion. Wilson was the perfect person to know inside the building in terms of his contacts and inside knowledge, whisking her down the art-lined corridors between studios, edit rooms and offices. He would say to Thelma, while accepting his slapstick role as kamikaze king, that one day he would work for *World in Action*, Granada's political and intellectual peak, one of the channel's most glamorous programmes. 'They're the serious film-makers. I'm going to be like them one day. I'm going to make serious films.'

Tony had the capacity never to be boring, which for a few years Thelma found irresistible, until not being boring became something you could overdose on; it seemed he wanted to woo her for eternity, which tends to get in the way of actually living in the present. He seemed really interested in other people until it became clear that this meant he was only really interested in himself. She finished the relationship in 1976 and broke his heart. The split agitated the sensitive soul to a few tears. He much preferred to be the one breaking hearts.

Wilson's immediate ambition was to link *Granada Reports* from behind a desk in the studio, still with the aim of returning to ITN, but those first jobs send him out into the region to gather film news, where he perfects his skills at dealing with the wild and the wacky, and all sorts of people in all sorts of emotional states doing all sorts of things, from the trivial to the important.

Covering the 1974 election of Harold Wilson to his second stint as prime minister, Tony Wilson is reporting on local results live on location, and his producer, new to working with him, realises that while she is getting more and more tired as they work into the early hours, Tony is becoming more and more awake, and actually sharper. By 2 a.m. he's flying. She asks their sound man, 'How on earth does he do it?' She's flagging, can barely keep her eyes open, and Wilson seems to be getting increasingly energetic and enjoying himself almost too much. He's nothing less than professional, just adding something a little helter-skelter to the idea of professionalism. The soundman smiles and tells her the truth, 'He takes drugs . . .'

There was a moment when his original plan almost did lead to a return to London, a completion of his original intention to get some on-camera experience in the regions and then return to national television. In 1977 he landed a job on the BBC's *Nationwide*, which would have taken him to much greater recognition, perhaps on the way to an eventual return to the *News at Ten* at ITN. There's even a place in London where he thinks it would be cool to live: Ladbroke Grove, in Notting Hill at the end of its hippy years, before its million-pound years.

He drives down to London to prepare for his new role, but the further he gets away from Manchester, the more uncomfortable he feels. Something doesn't seem right. He's either nervous about working in London, where he is less likely to stand out, no longer a big fish in a small pond, or he feels the historical pull of Manchester, which since he returned from Cambridge had got under his skin. You can easily lose yourself in London; in Manchester you are in control of your own destiny. Plus, the drugs – getting them and taking them – might be more of a problem.

His unease increases the closer he gets to London and the South. A few miles from the city, perhaps just north of Watford, where for many in London the North begins, he has a sudden change of heart. He finds a phone box and calls his boss to check whether his old Granada job is still available. Absolutely, he's told. He jumps back into his car, turns around, and heads back up north. That was the last time he ever considered making any kind of full-time move away from Manchester. 'Darling,' he announced to some friends gathered to welcome him back, 'you don't get rid of me that easily.'

His on-screen slickness, and possibly his gently batty quality, gets him appointed as one of the four elite rotating presenters of *Granada Reports*, along with Trevor Hyett, Gordon Burns and Bob Greaves, all of them wearing the monstrous coloured ties and jaunty wide lapels of the early 1970s, as though they would never go out of fashion. Of the four, only Wilson presents the programme with an expression that lightly suggests it is all a pose, a part of some greater game, with the long hair of a rebellious sixth-form fan of Crosby, Stills, Nash and Young.

Every Thursday *Granada Reports* featured a fifteen-minute 'What's On' section covering locals arts and entertainment, and Wilson felt this could be his way in to less hazardous and more influential studio presenting. He was interested in music, movies, theatre and in featuring musical guests; he had, after all, an arts degree; in his mind he seemed a natural.

The presenter at the time left for some other department, and Wilson took over, bringing with him not only his rapidly developing skills as a presenter, but also his tastes and musical interests, and instincts as a producer, even though formally the presenter was meant to have little influence on the items and the slot's sensibility. The presenter may have had a certain sort of editorial vision and cultural knowledge, but the real power lay with a programme's producer. Wilson wanted that kind of control, the ability to shape policy, but also the satisfying power he was realising came with presenting, being seen, using his mouth and how that was connected with his mind. One of his bosses at the time would say that Wilson did not produce 'What's On', but enthusiastically 'enhanced' it.

Elsewhere at Granada, much of its regular music coverage – the local equivalent of the BBC's *Top of the Pops* – was run from the children's department, firmly controlled by Muriel Young, former actress, presenter and the first continuity announcer on commercial television when it started in 1955, and also once of Granada's *People and Places* alongside Gay Byrne and Michael Parkinson. Her experience of TV music programmes had come via making shows that featured folk singer and former skiffle musician Wally Whyton, guitar educator Bert 'play the guitar in a day' Weedon and a series of glove puppets that accompanied her all the way to Granada, including impudent Scouse owl Ollie Beak, in school cap, and shaggy cockney mongrel Fred Barker, voiced by Ivan Owen, also the voice of rascally fox Basil Brush.

After Granada's early-'60s adventures the more conservative view had taken over: pop music after all was actually a branch of light entertainment, something for the kids shown at teatime, so it needed talking puppet animals, while rock music was too wrapped up inside the fading notion of the counterculture, so covering it was a potentially political act.

Young's pop shows began in the late 1960s using neo-hippy cabaret singer Ayshea Brough as the presenter of *Lift Off*, previously known as *Discotheque*, which by 1972 had become *Lift Off with Ayshea*. Ayshea was also 'Operator 2', in form-fitting nylon catsuit, in TV series *UFO* and a favourite of surreptitiously watching dads and older brothers, and an extremely rare example of a British Asian on 1970s TV. The daughter-in-law of the 1950s radio ventriloquist Peter Brough, with his famous dummy Archie Andrews, through her marriage to record producer Chris Brough, her brief engagement to Roy Wood of the Move and Wizzard became official when he wore an 'A' on his forehead on *Top of the Pops* and as one of his backing singers she had an 'R'.

Lift Off occasionally smuggled unexpected music into the living rooms of teenagers and, because of the puppets, even younger children, so that during the five years the show ran, to 1974, as well as the lighter, novelty chart performances, from Ken Dodd and Charlie Drake to the New Seekers and Cliff Richard, there was also a chance you might come across, at five o'clock, because they were in the charts, Black Sabbath, the Move, T. Rex and the first TV performance of David Bowie's 'Starman'.

The pop shows produced by Muriel Young following *Lift Off* were presented by manufactured boy bands of the day – the Bay City Rollers' *Shang-a-Lang* and the Arrows' show, *Arrows*, with a similar chart-led policy, meaning a lot of Gary Glitter, David Cassidy, Showaddywaddy, Cliff and Slade, and few if any surprises. A gesture was made towards informing the shows' young viewers – Big Jim Sullivan was the resident guitarist on *Shang-a-Lang*, bringing with him an oblique history of pop through the songs he'd played on, which included rhythm guitar on the original John Barry recording of the James Bond theme, Gerry and the Pacemakers' 'Ferry Across the Mersey', Cilla Black's 'Anyone Who Had a Heart', the Small Faces' 'Itchycoo Park', Serge Gainsbourg and Jane Birkin's 'Je t'aime', Sandy Shaw's 'Puppet on a String', Peter Sarstedt's 'Where Do You Go to (My Lovely)?' and Thunderclap Newman's 'Something in the Air'.

This teatime teenybop sequence continued with the whimsical, poignant *Marc* series, which because of Marc Bolan's personality, part cosmic teenybopper, part psychedelic trickster, had an unavoidably off-beat, non-kiddie quality. It began in the punk era, and featured a few less obvious, post-T. Rex acts like the Damned and the Jam, and abruptly concluded with Bolan's final appearance on television, a few days before he died in a car crash. He hosted old friend and Granada regular David Bowie, now a real-world version of the 'Starman' he had sung about five years before on another Muriel Young show.

Despite being broadcast only an hour or so after Young's shows, Wilson's 'What's On', using Bruce Springsteen's 'Born to Run' as its theme tune, began to assume the relationship to her kitsch, well-intentioned, kid-friendly pop programmes that the BBC's more worthy, grown-up and deliberately less exuberant *Old Grey Whistle Test* had to the contrived, commercially packaged spontaneity of its chart show *Top of the Pops*. Made for the same company in the same building but coming from completely different ways of thinking about and presenting music for young people, Muriel's shows were for teenybop readers of *Jackie*, and Tony's was for reverential readers of the *NME* and *Rolling Stone*, with occasional, unlikely, and because of that wonderful, crossovers. Wilson figured that the children of the 1960s, of which he was one, would love the sort of music he was putting on, but 'It turned out by the early '70s they had all become solicitors, trainee teachers and accountants. They all despised me. Their musical tastes had stagnated.' He needed to find another audience.

Broadly, music had fractured into pop, consisting mostly of commercially crafted, radio-friendly singles made without any real consideration that they might have cultural or even artistic value, versus rock, mostly albums that came with a general association with an experimental underground, an artistic vision and a countercultural spirit – worlds that the Beatles and David Bowie and precious few others could combine. A world of trivial fun up against a world where music articulated and transmitted a deeper sense of reality, and life, and, to those willing to suspend disbelief, simmering, inspiring strangeness.

Wilson presented and influenced 'What's On' as though it was all his idea, even if he still had to convince those working on the show that this was the way to do it. He possessed it from within, and when he moved on, the next producer to work on it admitted his intention was to remove some of the unconventional even wacky ideas Wilson had introduced. Ideas that made little sense if they weren't presented by the passionate, proselytising Wilson, and which meant little to the more moderate and cautious staff at Granada still not convinced that popular culture was something to take seriously.

To gig-going readers of music papers and the underground press these ideas were not particularly far-fetched or freaky, not least because this was where Wilson was getting his information and finding out about the newest music, but within the confines of conventional early-evening local television – and even late-night national television – there was nothing like 'What's On'. Wilson was one of the few figures on television who took seriously what at the time was still being treated tentatively or condescendingly by mainstream culture – in fact, would be for decades to come. For Wilson, there was no question rock music and pop culture were a part of the arts, with their own internal balance between the highbrow and the lowbrow. When they were highbrow, they obviously belonged with 'official' high and fine art, with poetry, film and theatre.

Wilson was becoming a visual, discreetly educational version of a disc jockey, not quite achingly cheery early-morning Tony Blackburn, not quite offhand savant late-night John Peel, but something unclassifiable in between. A little bit shiny, over-talkative travelling salesman – selling his own presence – a little bit irascible, subtly subversive hippy, the two sides connected by an unthreatening flippancy.

As much as possible Wilson encouraged the booking of musicians who reflected his own interests, and in the process reanimated some of the early ambitions Granada had when it came to acknowledging and archiving important new music. Rock was still developing, still progressing, and he was interested in recording the changes from a position of enthusiasm if not knowledge. At the time enthusiasm was knowledge. There was also an ideological separation between the covering of music that had settled into something formulaic, mostly shadowing the charts and the commercial wishes of the music industry, and the covering of music to showcase unconventional styles and new ideas.

Muriel Young's prosaic approach, a metaphor for the unconvinced mainstream media in general, was to treat pop as though the late 1960s hadn't happened, as if moptop pop had never been romanced by the avant-garde, paralleling countercultural concerns and more cosmopolitan even intellectual interests; Wilson was very aware of what had happened during the late 1960s, and how that entered into, sometimes charged into rock music, producing the kind of drama that could actually make an impression on reality. He was a believer. He had found another new faith, and the television studio was where he practised and occasionally worshipped.

As a believer, being involved as presenter and creatively as unofficial producer on 'What's On', with the local-community fame he was quickly realising could be an unexpected bonus, he found a place where he could feel important, and also, excitingly, actively involved with the rock business. This importance and involvement, as local as it was, put him in contact with representatives of the music industry who wanted to get their acts onto the show while they were playing in Manchester. This sense of importance, and the fact the outside world was coming to him, quickly meant he lost any urge to return to ITN.

Working at ITN, he might well have swiftly risen through the ranks, fulfilling his original dream of becoming a national news anchor, but he wouldn't have had this contact with music, with the arts, with the things he was most interested in, which allowed him an element of self-expression. It wasn't poetry, film or music, it wasn't acting, but he had stumbled into a way to have a voice, and because he was the only one doing anything like his combination of entertainment and the arts, he stood out. At ITN he would not have been allowed the opportunity to speak his mind and indulge his interests. Tony was also pleased to be back in the North, close to his ageing, ailing mum, seventy in 1974, even if she felt working on television and often acting up wasn't a real job, was somehow a come-down after the heady heights of university. There was something a little unsavoury about working on television.

His parents were never convinced by his career, which they saw as superficial and empty of real purpose, and not at all what they thought would happen after Cambridge. But then his mother felt that Cambridge had ruined him, bringing out the bighead, lifting his sometimes reckless self-confidence dangerously sky-high. Maybe it was the acid he'd started taking as much as the place, the situationism and Buddhism, the intima-tions of independence and the irradiating expressiveness of his new heroes as much as the learning. Doris would leave notes for him at their Marple home, explaining their position. 'Your father and I have had a discussion and we want to pay for you to train as a priest, teacher, doctor, something useful to society rather than being a TV presenter, which is just being a parasite.' She never lived to see him manage bands and run a nightclub, but that might also not have been in her eyes 'useful to society'.

In a way, his mum was right. Wilson wasn't too good for television; it was more that he was too quick-witted and imaginative, too intellectually aware of its process, absorbing how it worked from his time at ITN quickly enough to imagine new ways of making it work and changing how it was presented. He didn't want to be only the efficient reader of an autocue, and he always aimed to make his outside reporting more than simply stringing together a few basic facts. Making, presenting and producing television was almost too easy for him; he had to find other ways of being challenged. He was also something of a daredevil, never wanting things to be too comfortable, always inventing new ways of keeping himself interested. He knew his stuff, was extremely qualified and experienced, and could therefore deconstruct some of TV's techniques and play around with many of its traditions.

He was, perhaps, the first of a looser new post-rock 'n' roll generation to enter mainstream British television, which in other areas mostly continued to do things as they were done in the 1960s even '50s, mostly in a very lightweight, literal way, if occasionally, in the hands of Robin Day and Bill Grundy, with an acerbic kick. Wilson was Bill Grundy if he'd been influenced by the Grateful Dead and Ken Kesey; Robin Day as a disciple of Timothy Leary.

Wilson's unorthodox reading of the properties and possibilities of television – forty-odd years before linear-disrupting streaming, before the infinite fragments of YouTube – was the kind of experimental but accessible sensitivity that came after Richard Lester's slapdash Beatles film *A Hard Day's Night*, the *Monitor* arts documentaries of Ken Russell, John Berger and John Schlesinger, after Bob Rafelson and Jack Nicholson's fourth-wall-demolishing Monkees film *Head* – which begins with a suicide – and after *Monty Python's Flying Circus* and one of its influences, the logic-warping *Q* of Spike Milligan. He breaks into Granada Television because he has been trained at ITN's centre of excellence, but he is very much the broadcaster who broke into ITN because he thought they'd underestimated the cultural importance of Jimi Hendrix.

Sometimes he could play a television studio with the mercurial virtuosity of a broadcasting Hendrix, strangely tapping into a comparable expressiveness even as he was presenting a factual report for a teatime magazine show. When he went out to make his films for *Granada Reports*, unlike other reporters he would approach each one more as a film-maker than a mere deliverer of a piece to camera, however trivial the subject – and even with his braininess, early in his Granada days he was generally steered towards the light-hearted and non-political. He wasn't trusted with the important interviews until much later.

Time was always tight, as something filmed during the day would be needed, tidy and brightly coherent, by the evening's live broadcast. Wilson would be in the editing room loudly issuing instructions to the editor – 'Cut this, move that, swap this and leave gaps for my commentary.' If he wasn't at the edit he would pass on his notes – X, Y and Z followed by B, A and C, and it would all fit together beautifully. And he would always have a good angle, the right opening line and a snappy conclusion. He could visualise how a four-minute news film fitted together better than most; at what in the end is a superficial construct he was a master, his darting autonomous energy perfect for this disposable kind of television.

Sometimes he wouldn't quite be finished with his film: he still needed to do his scripted voiceover, and the studio director would have a script outline filled with blanks and some timings. Tony would tell him not to worry as he arrived for the night's live programme, would calmly take his seat in the studio, and as his film went out, would read his commentary live, filling in the gaps at just the right time, indicating to the director when he was going to speak. It seemed like chaos to those in the studio, but anyone watching at home wouldn't have noticed, and his films were usually perfectly put together. He had it all in his head, and it didn't matter to him how he got it out, as long as he did.

He could walk into a studio seconds before a live show, racing past those anxiously waiting for him and loudly announcing, 'The meat has arrived' – American inside slang for the on-screen talent. He'd sit down, comfortably on a knife-edge, cleanly present a script he had never seen before, and then immediately leave the studio as though it was no big deal. It was amazing. It was infuriating. He'd say seconds before a broadcast, having sorted out some mess production had made, knowing how good he was, 'The trouble with you lot here is you are all fucking amateurs. Sometimes on television these things happen.' This was where he was an artist, even though what he did lacked any greater meaning – the reason why he searched for meaning elsewhere. Wilson would sometimes take his young son Oliver to watch him from the back of the studio, giving him an earpiece so he could listen to the directors. 'They were giving him hell,' says Oli. 'It just seemed to spur him on. For me watching him rehearse shows, with the way he would speak and move on the stage, this amazing presence, he was like a Shakespearean actor. I remember Frank Sidebottom came and sat next to me one day and took his head off, which totally freaked me out.'

Through sheer force of personality Wilson stamped himself all over the 'What's On' segment, and within a couple of years had interviewed Paul McCartney and George Harrison of the Beatles, Bill Wyman of the Rolling Stones, Emmylou Harris and Leonard Cohen – for Wilson the unabashed groupie-fan a sign that his new role could give him direct access to his heroes and, just as attractively, his villains.

Andy Harries, started at Granada TV, producer of 'What's On', producer of *The Royle Family*, *Cold Feet*, *The Deal* and *The Crown*, received an Academy Award nomination for *The Queen*

The pattern was always the same on 'What's On'. We never worked on Friday much. On a Monday we'd have a meeting to decide what was going to be on the Thursday show. We'd already booked the bands and I'm thinking about what other films would be in, who's in the North-West. We wouldn't even start to write a script until Wednesday evening. This eccentricity and spontaneity in television has completely disappeared. After Wednesday's Granada Reports, he would come back to the office and he would start to write his script, rolling a joint or two or three or four. We'd have a sandwich and then I would leave. 'Fuck off,' he'd say with a smile. I would come back in the morning about seven and he would be fast asleep under the desk. My job was to make him a cup of tea and shake him awake. He'd get up and have a shower and we'd knock Thursday's show into shape. And then it would all start again.

After working on 'What's On' for a couple of years, he was finding a way to indulge the music fan, the liberal arts thinker and chaotic artist of no fixed abode embedded in his character, while savouring the modest but intense power of presenting the local news. He was good at making and appearing on television, getting better all the time, and 'What's On', where his style was positively described by a slightly nonplussed Granada TV press office as 'bizarrely eccentric', evolved into the first thing he would be noticed for nationally, his first specifically creative act, *So It Goes*. By the time he got to *So It Goes*, he had already been experimenting with television formats, with his teatime arts show nudging into a more off-beat, Americanised, even surreal approach. He was no comedian, but 'What's On' had a loose, funny side, a remnant of the late nights and stoned inspiration.

A little worried about his unpredictability, finding ways to channel his unruly passions, the Granada hierarchy mostly let him do what he wanted, within reason. When they didn't, which started to coincide with the emergence of punk, where his goonish wackiness flipped into something politically a little edgier, he made his feelings known. He sulked. He argued. He cajoled. After one incident when he acted like he was above the rules, they made it clear that from then on he did what they said, because they paid his wages. He agreed to calm down a bit, and then carried on as usual.

He once got a slightly panicky call from headstrong local broadcaster Terry Christian, then pugnaciously presenting Channel 4's *The Word*, a scurrilous, self-consciously outrageous tabloid-weighted descendant of the programmes Wilson was making twenty years before, in the 1970s. Christian was frustrated that, even though he was the face of the show, his suggestions about which bands and guests to invite were being ignored. 'Everything it seemed to me had to go through that Home Counties posh kid media prophylactic, and if what they put on was shit, I felt that was damaging my brand, as they'd call it now.' He asked Wilson how much say, as the presenter, you should you have in the programme's content. He didn't like asking Tony for specific advice, there was an unwritten rule that this wasn't done, but he was desperate.

Wilson thought for a moment, and then, sounding quite serious, said, 'Hmmm, 11.5 per cent, that's exactly it – 11.5 per cent, I'd say.' 'Jesus, Tony, what does that mean – I get to choose my own shirts?' Wilson was quiet, a sign that he had finished this part of the conversation. He meant it, and of course he didn't mean it. He was keeping his secrets, or there were no secrets to keep. Ultimately, the advice was, not as much freedom as you would really like, and sometimes you had to put up with it.

Granada viewed him as their joker in the pack, a token radical, and as long as they could fit him into their usual routines they allowed him a certain amount of freedom. They knew they couldn't tame him, and certainly up to the early 1980s, when his attention was increasingly wandering because of Factory and then the Haçienda, they learnt how to treasure him as a secret weapon, even though they were never going to use him to the limits of his ability. They made sure they didn't lose control of him. They would let him off the hook, but always find a way to rein him in. 'He was their undeployed silent missile,' said Richard Madeley. 'The bosses and executives viewed him with a kind of bemused exasperation. They knew he was a real asset and a great person to have around, but they were also wary about his tendency to go rogue.'

He still did things his way, though, but never forgot, however often and far he strayed from the broadcasting, where his main income came from. He couldn't really do what he wanted, but he found the spaces to do things that few others had the chance to do, keeping his bosses more or less happy, believing he was a Granada man, however extreme.

Fifteen: Punk and local accents

Testis unus, testis nullus. (One witness is no witness.)

Tony Wilson, keeping his bosses more or less happy, can also be described as:

- egotistical gadfly
- modern idler
- smiling polymath
- walking bibliography
- his favourite Gallagher? Rory
- perpetually immature
- he's an only child, remember
- the golden one
- even his turds were polished
- quite an actor
- a monologue of self-activation
- a monologue of achievements
- unhidden persuader
- tacky thief of situationist elan
- surfing the physical internet of TV shows, gigs, meetings, debates, interviews
- signing the contract in the City Arms pub between his label and Joy Division in 1978 in blood 'as a joke. You just prick your finger and let it onto the page, and then take a dry pen nib and write through it'
- 'I protected myself from selling out because I had nothing to sell' – a line he stole from a fictional version of himself and made his own
- gassy
- curious optimist
- twisted humourist
- who the hell does Tony Wilson think he is?

Before punk rock in 1976, Tony Wilson could be spotted at the bigger gigs in Manchester, mostly at the Free Trade Hall, a safely substantial nineteenth-century concert venue in the more intact part of the city centre. The silky, grinning newsreader permanently wearing TV make-up and surely hairspray in his lively sandy locks looked totally out of place, too old, wearing grown-up, vaguely hippy clothes, no doubt in for free, spoiling it for the rest of us just by being there. He seemed so sure of himself, which to those of us who could never imagine a day when we would have such sureness seemed a particularly annoying trait.

At twenty-six, he seemed older than was decent for those of us who felt that music was a liberation from elders and authority. At the start of punk, when he started turning up with a foolish, ungainly presence in the city centre, at smaller clubs, it appeared even more offensive to see this other creature, from another world, elbowing his way in, for free, the freeloading bastard.

On television the facile smile seemed understandable, part of a necessary, crowd-pleasing small-screen shtick. Watching John Cale and Pink Floyd at the Free Trade Hall or venturing into new, unclassifiable, even risqué clubs tucked under the time-worn streets of the city centre, where exciting new networks were forming, the smile seemed creepy if not downright sinister.

Was he spying on us? Or wanting us to spy for him? Recruiting us in some underhand way for some obscure task? Or were we just jealous of him for the ease with which he seemed to move around town, the connections he clearly had with worlds that would surely always be beyond us?

Those on the television on the three sparse channels that existed in the early 1970s seemed a breed apart, almost alien, untouchable, however approachable they seemed. They had a form of soft power and sociable aloofness that seemed unattainable by those on the outside. There was something uncomfortable about him standing around in clubs at a time when the world was clearly going to become very different and leave the likes of him behind. But we had no idea how stubborn, how determined and how thick-skinned he could be. Something was happening, and there was no way – as campaigning journalist, as unquenchable fan, as unconventional local historian on the hunt for new, revitalising energy – he was going to miss out.

Getting onto television seemed impossible, some kind of magic act; television people living ordinary lives seemed fairly improbable. Seeing Wilson burst from the telly into the real world, as irritating as it was, seemed to lend him an impenetrable aura of titanic individualism. His mutant largeness set him apart, even if he was ultimately a garrulous proto-geek and current-affairs wonk with a cheeky smile and distinct sense of superiority, an otherness and an attractively soft, bouncy, quasi-posh accent, lower middle class on the make to be both working class, to claim some sort of authenticity, and upper middle, to demonstrate how socially mobile he was. He was unknown to most of the nation, and gamely acted the jester for a captive North-West audience in silly little novelty items meant to give you a little chuckle after the hard, heavy main news.

He was a local star, and stars didn't hang out in everyday places. They had their own places to go. It was embarrassing to have him interfere in our business. This is perhaps why the booing started, the jeering that would greet his arrival in the early 1970s at Manchester rock concerts, often as he sauntered to the front of the queue like he was showing off that he was somehow on the inside track, before many of us even knew what a guest list was. (My first use of a guest list was to see MOTT – Mott the Hoople without original front man Ian Hunter – at Salford University in 1977, and it did feel like smooth magic: say your name, get in for free.)

The booing came from a kind of fear and ignorance that spilt over into lively rancour, and maybe sometimes it was good-natured joshing. What was he doing, this grinning newsreader off the TV who resembled an off-duty policeman, or perhaps a cop going undercover and wearing badly chosen fashionable clothes in order to mix with those who might be doing something illegal? He seemed to be slumming; he was an intruder, an interloper, poking his nose where it didn't belong.

The American novelist John Updike once wrote that appearing on live television made you feel like yourself, only more so. You felt stretched, turned into an exaggerated version of who you were, as though there were parts of you that you never usually knew were there, which suddenly erupted when you were in this strange new mind-napping position of being self-consciously alive, and thinking of what you are saying after you had said it. You became more aware of yourself, and the nature of thinking, and talking, and coming up with coherent sentences that at the very least made sense even if you could never lock together the thoughts you were having and the things you were saying. In the way you could when you talked in less pressurised circumstances, and certainly in the way you could when you wrote.

Tony Wilson got to appear so much on television that, as with other TV personalities who spend a lot of their time talking into a camera, his situation seemed the reverse. He was larger than himself in the real world; he fitted into television because he understood how to make it seem like the artificiality of it all, the lights, make-up, studio, desk, the freakily compressed time, the constant pressure, was his natural habitat. It was in the outside world that he felt like himself, but more so. Speaking into the camera, passing on important news, wholehearted opinions and random, time-filling nonsense, rapidly, bossily interviewing celebrities, politicians, musicians, specialists, local personalities, people on the street, he was at ease, or extremely adept at pretending he was at ease. In the outside world, as he himself became news, and was interviewed, he exhibited a form of sometimes defensive awkwardness that he covered up with a different sort of ebullient pretence.

On TV he didn't seem to be performing. Off TV he was always performing, at least as he made his way through Manchester and through its history, and gathered people around him who might help him with developing and sustaining his performance.

In the summer of 1976 a few Manchester music fans of a certain age had gone all punk and already provisionally post-punk and got involved, if not in groups, then in writing about groups, photographing groups, putting on shows, forming labels, just looking for something to do, in order to *be*,

searching for an identity in what seemed to be a country and a world slipping and sliding into circling nowhere. This nowhere actually turned out to
be a dismal, disappointing, dangerously constant, counterculture-wrecking,
even horribly infectious Thatcherite universe, where you were driven into
competing for territory and attention whether you liked it or not.

Wilson was always searching out new things with a local TV journalist's
nose for news, serious and silly, and for usefully eccentric and filmable
emerging personalities. In those final months before the slick, Saatchi-
inspired election of a new kind of political product, a different sort of No
Future as styled by those who styled Margaret Thatcher, a different sort of
outsider, he noticed that punk was something that could easily be turned
into a movement. He had learnt that change comes from the margins of
society, since people on the margins invariably develop their own media
because they need their own voice to put across their own point of view.

Punk was followed by those feeling stranded and lacking direction
who were looking for a way forward out of a post-war – and post-'60s-
revolution – limbo that wasn't the way forward soon to be proposed by
the unreflecting, unrelenting Margaret Thatcher. There were those who
felt that the rebels and voices involved in early punk – seeping out of
night-time New York and then seedy, secretive central London, reported
on in the music papers – acted like they might be saviours. This is how
important music and its associated energy seemed at the time – a matter of
life or death, because music was the one place where the making of reality
seemed as if it was truly under the control of idealists and artists, dreamers
and philosophers.

There was a loose, loosening energy about punk that the overemo-
tional, public-spirited Wilson relished; he might have been temperamen-
tally, even sentimentally, a hippy, and practically speaking an opportunist,
even a little Establishment in terms of his regular television hours, but
he was also a kind of rootless, anti-institutional outlaw and pushy academic rogue unafraid of adopting unpopular ideas and pursuing trends
in unlikely places. He willingly fell for those committed to shaking up
the world by shaking their own minds awake and developed a passion for

those suspicious of homogenisation, mass, competitive culture and mass design, especially those with enough of an uncompromising attitude to risk their own safety. He yearned for the countercultural ambitions and actions of the late 1960s that hadn't really gone anywhere but into the sweet and/or sour voices of his favourite singers and into the pockets and mouths of other incorrigible agitators looking for distinctive new action.

Punk came a few years after the revolutionary times of the late 1960s, but Wilson could see the connection and understood that punk wasn't the impatient break with the countercultural past its first wave liked to claim it was, but a spirited continuation. Punk was actually an out-of-place soundtrack to the protests and anger of the late 1960s, to the actions in 1968 Paris and international student demos, but arriving a few years later. It took time for the emotions and disruptions to make it into music. Different clothes, different haircuts, a different way of using rhyme and reason, but essentially the dislocated sound of resistance, the fury and sarcasm of Paris '68 mixed up with the romantic outsider noise of Vietnam- and Nixon-damaged Americans and a fired-up Establishment mocking British unease.

Wilson was an insider, to an extent, loving to operate from a position of power, but also very much an outsider, loving to complain about the corruption of those monopolising authority (he was also an assiduous combination of amateur and professional), and he desperately wanted to be thought of as a battling outsider more than a smug insider, if only because outside was where the more interesting people were, those who hated the idea of mediocrity. He wanted to feel more alive, and just at the moment when he might perhaps have been settling down into a career he was very good at, with a future that could very easily have seen him become an amiable mainstream national figure even a treasure, something came along that completely rekindled the unruly, trend-chasing, semi-reckless, lustful and radical teenage rebel inside him, and it never really let him go.

Punk in Manchester, for a short while, was a small, fast-moving, grass-roots movement, a distinct offshoot of the seductive combination of energy and image that had arrived via downtown New York, obscure, offbeat London pubs and clubs, the responsive music press and occasional anomalous televised happenings. The music had the look and sound of something that took the world seriously, and was searching for freedom or at least some separate space where life seemed something you could make up for yourself.

The ragged haircuts and broken, borrowed clothes worn by this scattering of curious new creatures seemed separated by centuries from what had happened over the last few years, whether that was arch, showy chart glam, heavy-metal denim and leather or the soft, glowing flow of California's singing dreamers. Punk songs were short and to the point, and even if they weren't, and took time to make their point, they didn't operate with the ponderous pace and estranged virtuosity of progressive rock. They were still emphatic, and impulsive, full of buzzing, fretting invention and momentum, the actions of fierce minds raging away, intent on becoming a part of the very atmosphere that surrounds and directs us.

Punk was generally motivated by a political, artistic or just plain musical defiance, and part of its appeal was how open it was, as if its main purpose was to influence others and change things that way. You could copy the haircuts and even the intensity and purpose of the music without having to be a professional or even know anyone professional. You could do it yourself. Cut your hair so that it was many lifetimes removed from hippy length, which had ended up seeming aristocratic. Pick up an instrument and make a noise, make up your own sense of order. Sing some words based on what *you* thought was exciting, or frustrating, or inexplicable, and your own desire to express this knowledge whether anyone would hear it or not. Punk wasn't just about music, about listening to records, following trends and putting posters of your favourite stars on your bedroom wall. It brought out the critical, criticising, creative best in insular, determined young North-West minds with a long, healthy tradition of distrusting the Establishment, defying conventional wisdom and rejecting the status quo.

In what was effectively a small town, I was one of those inspired by punk as a movement – more than simply music – whom Wilson quickly became aware of, because he was looking for something to cover on the television, was genuinely interested in local activity or was just pleased even relieved that there was some sign of dissident youthful energy on his beat. If radical, protesting Manchester had gone quiet since the sons of freedom, since various activist uprisings in the early twentieth century, since the dissatisfaction with Dylan in 1966, it appeared to be returning.

I made a fanzine, *Out There*, which Wilson found – or a friend found for him – in a local shop, possibly 8 Days a Week, a crammed, ramshackle head shop selling pungent incense and locally printed underground literature like the *Manchester Free Press* and *Mole Express* near the university buildings along Oxford Road, where I'd managed to leave some copies, overcoming my fear and nervousness. I'd planned and written *Out There* in my bedroom, and there is a world where once I had finished it, I didn't take it outside my bedroom, which involved dealing with parts of the outside world that were a complete mystery to me. The mysteries I faced up to with the fanzine were all about music, and writing.

Mole Express, materialising out of a classic haze of dope in the early 1970s, and the monochrome, militant *Manchester Free Press* were a big influence on *Out There* – as well as Paul Krassner's New York-based *The Realist*, first printed in 1958, the ground zero of the anti-Establishment satirical and radical underground press. Not so much the content and ideology of the *Free Press* and *Mole Express* but simply their existence, emerging into Manchester from somewhere inside Manchester. There were no punk fanzines when I started planning mine, but at around the same time as *Out There* appeared, other home-made magazines emerged, because what was happening one fast, furious song at a time needed to be covered one pasted-up page at a time by those within it, feeling the same urge to make and do and say something.

Manchester's music-makers in the 1960s and early '70s never created a distinct scene that was going to make history, like the city's near neighbours in Liverpool had. Manchester wasn't any kind of stand-out pop city, in spite of, or because of, Herman's Hermits, Freddie and the Dreamers and Sad Café. The Hollies or 10cc never really lifted Manchester with them into the charts in the way the Beatles had lifted Liverpool with them and to some extent replaced the fallen British empire with an unlikely, effervescent alternative. It had great clubs, inheriting the city's working-class lust for a lawless, liberating kind of nightlife that could be represented by cheeky, scandalous comedy, by the imported, travelling glamour of television entertainers or the latest sounds from America, but nothing that had become as internationally known, and therefore a clear part of cultural history, as Liverpool's Cavern.

Those in Manchester who hit a freakier spot, reflecting jazzier, heavier record collections, like C. P. Lee's Greasy Bear, with Martin Hannett on bass, and Alberto y Lost Trios Paranoias or the Purple Gang, would never rise above being busy, enterprising local attractions finding ways to live a little but making little noise in the South. In the early '70s the Albertos were playing what they called 'guerrilla' gigs, spontaneous happenings featuring poetry, music and film, a little hint of what was to come, but they remained largely local, with little desire or opportunity to travel too far. Manchester had never alerted the world that something special was happening around the first few meandering miles of the ageless flowing Mersey. The Mersey magic, the internationally famous Beat, was all at the non-stop Liverpool mouth, where it poured out via the Irish Sea into the rest of the world, lifting local accents and attitude with it.

By 1976, the dissident musical energy that had built up in Manchester during the 1960s had all but petered out. 'The tide had gone out,' remembers Richard Boon, who was then compiling 'very thin' music listings for the local equivalent of *Time Out*, the *New Manchester Review*. 'There were just a few rotten corpses left on the beach.' It was a city in trauma waiting for music that dealt with the trauma, the sound of the young explicitly or cryptically doubting themselves but aiming at something.

I'd started my fanzine simply wanting to work out for myself what it was to be a writer, about music, about ideas, not particularly thinking it had anything to do with Manchester, and at that time what became punk hadn't yet been officially named, and to an extent instantly tamed, made easier to mock, package and undermine by those on the outside. 'Punk' as a name for what was happening had come from New York, and it didn't necessarily suit the British activity, which shared some musical influences, but also had its own uniquely English quirks and desires.

I included in my fanzine some brief, rhapsodic last-minute notes on the Stranglers, the Ramones, the Sex Pistols and their first visit to Manchester, and – at the very last minute – an appropriately breathless, rushed response to the frenetic, smart, local-looking but surely art-mad and pop-sure Buzzcocks, supporting the Sex Pistols on their second, life-changing visit to Manchester. Without this late news flash there would have been nothing local at all in *Out There* outside of the local venues where outside music visited.

Looking for something more abstract than the still not settled 'punk' label, something fluid enough to resist outside classification, I called the music 's' rock – 's' for surge, for secret, spirit, sabotage and sensation. For Patti Smith. For Sex Pistols. For that 's' at the end of Buzzcocks. The 's' quickly dissolved; this new music was after all called punk in the national music papers, because the word punched into the moment like the music did and rattled the mainstream rock network with its suggestion of some-thing damaged and aggrieved.

A new music of Manchester, featuring local accents, shorter hair and a different way of holding and playing the guitar, made it into my magazine in ways that didn't seem very likely in the weeks before the Sex Pistols visited. My small, exhilarated entry about Buzzcocks was at the bottom of the originally blank back page of *Out There*. I had left it blank as if to say, 'For what happens next, fill it in yourself.' And then something happened, so I filled it in myself. I'm still filling in that blank page.

Sixteen: So it goes and so it goes but where it's going no one knows

Post hoc, ergo propter hoc. (After this, therefore, because of this.)

Viewing him as their 'pop' expert, Granada gave Wilson the chance to create an alternative to the BBC's successful *Top of the Pops*. The pilot Wilson made was inevitably not quite what they imagined or wanted, more of a discordant magazine programme than a pop show. They were thinking of a straightforward chart show with a little Granada kink, but they gave him a late-night slot to take his ideas further.

So It Goes was Wilson's attempt to create a rock television show to rival the BBC's staid, reliable link to the underground and album rock, *The Old Grey Whistle Test*, with added humour and opinion, and an experimental sense that rock music was not just about music. It was about images, technology, fashion, spirit, style, satire, politics, and expressed the playful part of Wilson as critic and consumer who both revered and mocked popular culture – and by mocking it he was paying a wary tribute to its spreading power.

The title came from Wilson's girlfriend at the time, Jane Buchan, who was working on the show as a researcher and was an avid fan of Kurt Vonnegut. She had just read Vonnegut's *Slaughterhouse-Five*, his psychedelic, non-linear, black comedy anti-war classic about witnessing at twenty-three years old the Allies firebombing Dresden in an air attack that instantly killed 130,000 people – more than Hiroshima – and destroyed the city. He'd finished it in 1968, the year of assassinations, rebellions, sieges and the Tet Offensive in Vietnam, the year of the coming-of-age of the post-war baby boomers rebelling against their parents and their parents' values.

'So it goes' follows every mention of death in the novel, however personal and obscure or however massive the scale. All deaths are simple moments that exist in time, and then life goes on. The central character,

Billy Pilgrim, can go back and forth in time, 'unstuck in time' as a result of shell shock, with 'no control over where he is going next'. He never knows what part of his life he is going to act in next. The book reflects in its own way how history repeats itself; and some books need to be read and reread.

'So it goes' is eventually used 106 times, keeping count of the mounting presence of death throughout the book and articulating the essential inevitability of death whoever and whatever you are, and the idea that death, like time, is illusory. The three simple words increase in force through the book, turning into something that can be infinitely interpreted, from being simply a form of punctuation, of comic relief, and of pause to consider the immensity of death, to being a mantra, a form of meditation – it's a kind of prayer, an amen; it means life goes on, enjoy it as much as you can, we have to accept life for what it is; it's a way of saying that the death of someone is the end of a life that could be told in greater detail, but that's a story for another time; it's something that we will all experience, but it doesn't mean the end. Life is impermanent. Everything that starts ends. Everything that ends starts.

As the abstract name of a rock show that perhaps said nothing but hinted at a message worth following, it worked – and at about the same time there was a single with the same name by ingenious rock troubadour Nick Lowe on the cusp of pub rock and punk, which gave the show a hint of now. The title had a randomness and a deeper sense of otherness than was immediately apparent. There was a greater meaning, even if you had to know the literary connection to get it. It was *The Tony Wilson Show* in masked disguise.

Wilson was, again, the show's presenter, not the producer with ultimate power over content, but his personality and sensibility completely influenced the policy of the programme – an unstable, mildly radical wing-and-a-prayer mix of Cambridge-incubated smartness, outsider underground press irreverence, forensic New Journalism attitude, haywire broadcasting brains, situationist-stained slapstick, confidential northern sass and weekly-music-paper energy, combining oblique talent-spotting, spoof and analysis.

For something that became so identified with punk, the first series began with its head happily in the clouds of the 1960s, reflecting a mid-'70s rock world that had plenty of characters, history, virtuosos and dreamers, but no particular direction. It was in a kind of free fall, full of itself, increasingly well organised as a business, as a system of delight and discovery, but disconnected from the social and philosophical movement rock music had been directly and indirectly driven by in the first few years of its existence.

Beginning in July 1976, *So It Goes* was accidentally timed to record the radical shift that was about to take place between the rock music that was spilling over from the invention and scenes of the 1960s and the rock music showing its first signs of life in the more abrasive, anti-pomp margins of British pub rock and in the artier, minimalist downtown parts of New York.

There was something on the way that was going to provide direction, and change everything, but at the beginning of series one of *So It Goes* there was barely any sign of this. Wilson subconsciously wished there was, and the warm-up speech he gave to a polite, unsure studio audience before the first show reveals a desire for change that wasn't immediately obvious. The music that was around on major record labels wasn't going to be part of this brave new rock programme. 'This is not just a music show. If you don't like the music on *The Old Grey Whistle Test*, you won't like the programme. We aim to make *So It Goes* good entertainment even if you don't like the music.'

Musically, the pilot show was more *Old Grey Whistle Test* than *The Old Grey Whistle Test*, as though those long-haired early '70s were destined to drift right through the decade without interruption; the abstract light metal of Wakefield's Be-Bop Deluxe was as radical as it got, with the lighter vocals of Linda Lewis, the even lighter guitar of Gordon Giltrap and the even lighter pale rock of Gallagher and Lyle showing how denim the show was in its provisional state. Any extraneous entertainment for those not impressed by these almost middle-of-the-road bookings was supplied by the amused and amusing satirical editorialising of Clive James and the non-rock music of a violinist and pianist playing some Spanish classical music – for Granada! 'It was like *The Old Grey Whistle Test* gone mad,' says Andy Harries. 'Bob Harris sped up, with a chiffon scarf.'

Wilson watches the first *So It Goes* at home with his latest girlfriend, Lindsay, and to celebrate the fact he now has his own music show, they drop some acid. The show would never have existed without his discovery of LSD, the angelic soaring. He would take it, never quite working out when it had worn off, assuming, sort of knowing it had, that nothing was fixed, especially reality, which it turned out was only one of many, and was limitless. There was a world where a television programme could be the same, in a limited way.

Tony waits for the phone to ring with some congratulations for his splendid audacity, his changing of the rules. No one calls. Perhaps you needed to drop acid to get into the show's oblique rhythms, and it seemed none of the viewers or any of his friends had. They were in the wrong reality.

The gawky, garrulous intensity of Wilson, whose peculiar trying-too-hard presence, a hippy who was too groomed blended with a newsreader who was too scruffy, a kind of grown-up playing at being too groovy, speaking from the countercultural margins with a fruity professional broadcaster's voice, made little sense to those outside the Granada area unfamiliar with his charged, wonky cheeriness and suspicious of his sloppy-seeming eclecticism. The early reviews were almost universally dismissive, shoving Wilson into a shell, feeing unloved and humiliated.

Years later, he would agree the first series was not very good. It was a pile of shit, Tony would admit, embarrassed by the initial indifferent, even angry response, although he believed in it at the time, not really caring it didn't have a particular direction; and coming from the North it seemed, of course, to a condescending South unused to Wilson's elliptical, ingratiating ways, somewhere between crude and cute. At the time, he was proud of what he'd done, breaking through into a new way of presenting music on TV, of approaching the overlapping, developing worlds of popular culture.

In the first few shows, it was the more obscure music that revealed Wilson's intentions, when there just wasn't the music to fully reflect them, or it was just beginning. He wanted to book unusual, generally disregarded performers outside the range of *The Old Grey Whistle Test*, even beyond John Peel, so before the punk that gave him his new unknown there was the riveting Croatian theatre singer Bettina Jonic singing Dylan as though he was an influence on Weill and Sondheim, and the curious, intricately cross-cultural spiritual music of Stephan Micus, played on bells, flower pots and Japanese flutes, plugged onto the show by the avant-garde wing of Virgin Records, Caroline, an oblique, subdued world of its own and an influence on the lesser-known works of Factory.

Micus later released records on the visionary Munich-based label ECM, where the sounds, textures and history of jazz and classical were being constantly remade, the one label apart from Factory that could have released the Durutti Column; Factory, on the quiet, at the back of the cupboard, in the dusty corners of its catalogue, was in many ways a dream northern English relative of the northern European ECM, with an equally commanding graphic identity, an enchanting commitment to the interior design of music and its packaging. Micus played a world of music in a classically influenced, experimental post-folk place, one that would eventually be called world music, as if all these sounds and instruments could be held in the one pure, simplistic place.

The show's musical line-up made no sense, on paper, in a cautious TV sense, but in Wilson's mind it all made perfect sense; when and where you least expect it will emerge the most wonderful sounds, the strangest ideas.

He had become a considerable supporter of local interests, but it was combined with a culturally internationalist outlook – you didn't have to be from Manchester to be from Manchester. This early *So It Goes* was also an ancestor of the international remit of the Manchester International Festival thirty years later – it was a place for the avant-garde to pass through and leave their rarefied messages, and it added to Manchester's reputation for welcoming the experimental and provocative, so that it didn't sink back into its post-industrial internment. Make Manchester if not a place you come from then definitely a place you want to visit – for its own history and the history of those drawn to the city.

Within weeks, signalled by the appearance of the brilliantly de-centred Patti Smith – still coming from the breakthroughs of the 1960s and the spirit of *Rolling Stone* magazine, but gazing into the future, drunk with utopianism, with a fiercer, more urgent tone and presence, targeting transcendence – the programme starts to react to the changes, and keep up with them. Patti Smith was closer to Jonic and Micus than it might seem but more fashionable, and had Lenny Kaye on guitar, curator of the *Nuggets* compilation of American garage bands, which became a 'how to play punk' manual. This was a scholarly understanding of the deviant, unwritten rules and regulations of rock given theophanic surfacing.

Wilson's peculiar, messy, almost unclassifiable project was moving erratically with the times, and only years later can it be seen how quickly things moved musically during the summer of 1976, as it switched between before punk and during punk. *So It Goes* series one started one way, and what with one thing and another ended somewhere else, a television music show that was up for changing its mind until it found itself.

Unlike most working in television, and apart from John Peel and one or two others in radio, Wilson was living in the moment, ready for the change as an avid reader of the music press, a child of the '60s, believing in the magical transformation of art, on the hunt for heroes to recruit, and also as someone with an interest in the local community ready to use his rock programme to mix up artists from elsewhere with regular coverage of Manchester music.

When that coverage begins on early *So It Goes* shows, it is Alberto y Lost Trios Paranoias, with their roots in late-'60s comic psychedelia, a south Didsbury Mothers of Invention, and within a year it is intense pop-punk Buzzcocks, inductive post-punk Magazine, early Wilson favourite John Cooper Clarke – good-natured, enigmatic Salford poet nimbly sidling from post-beatnik pre-punk obscurity playing local folk clubs to unlikely punk fixture, his words and appearance a perfect fit – and the furious alchemy of the Fall, as bitterly fresh as the dead-on Manchester moment, all of them quick off the mark following punk coming to town. The second series started to connect with the Granada history of not only covering music – it featured clips from the blues music Granada had smartly captured in the early 1960s – but of actually discovering new music, of becoming part of history, not simply watching and recording it from the outside.

For those weaned on the worthy approach of *The Old Grey Whistle Test*, on the idea of rock music being about technical competence, with an orderly view of its history and development, there was something repellent about the apparent lack of technique demonstrated by the punks and post-punks, but also an ignorance of what they were actually communicating, and what they represented as social thinkers and antisocial activists. Wilson's understanding of this was more sophisticated than that of conventional producers and commissioners – who believed that punk was a musical aberration and a cultural flash-in-the-pan – and responded to how the meaning and message of punk was more disenchanted and engaged than most mainstream rock.

His musical instincts at the time were correct – he talked of his understanding of what was happening in modern music being at its best between 1976 and 1981, and it's true that this is when his musical taste and desires meant his choices for both his television shows and later his clubs and label revealed a discrimination he would never have again without assistance from others. His choices were often based on the recommendations and discoveries of others, but for a few years he was at his sharpest in responding to something he saw as being of the moment, even if he wasn't totally convinced himself – the signing of a guitar-less even drummer-less electronic duo from Liverpool, for instance, called Orchestral Manoeuvres in the Dark, whose first machine-built Factory single 'Electricity' non-musically but ingeniously reversed a Kraftwerk melody to find its own melody, was a long way from the soft, sunny, West Coast guitar idealism and sensitive American folk lyricism he had long favoured.

Orchestral Manoeuvres came from an idea Roger Eagle had about putting a double twelve-inch single out on a label based around the Factory club, two groups from Manchester, two from Liverpool. When Erasmus saw OMD at the Factory, he loved them, even before they started playing, for the bright, bold fluorescent tubes they used for their lighting. The stark lights and then the radiant electronic rhythms instantly separated them from the rock status quo. Wilson didn't really like their music – he was always fundamentally a guitar man – but he liked the idea that his main designer, Kraftwerk enthusiast Peter Saville, did, and that the sleeve Saville made for the record was in some sort of code, the kind of subversive code Tony liked cracking and making part of his chaotic factory of dreams. And anyway, he would nurture and manage and develop a lasting obsession for the Durutti Column, the glistening sound of star-kissed otherness coming out of the head, hands and absurdly fluent guitar-playing of Vini Reilly, which made it appear as though broken, bruising Wythenshawe, home to the largest council estate in the world in the 1950s, was within touching distance of golden Malibu, which itself was within touching distance of Mars, the freezing northern Moors touching the vast Pacific.

Durutti Column were Wilson's south Manchester West Coast, a weirdly perfect manifestation of electric guitar music solidly pleasing to mind and ear that connected Reilly to guitar poets such as John Fahey, John Abercrombie and Jerry Garcia, ultimately magically independent of their time, even though by being on the Factory label they seemed vaguely connected and somehow punk, or at least post-punk, and definitely mysteriously energised; and elsewhere, he liked the music that was beginning to appear not so much because of the music, but because of what it represented, and what it meant, its interim way of raising a low subject.

The music happening at this time was the kind of music he had been craving at the end of the 1960s and through the early '70s – music that made more sense to someone with an interest in revolution, situationism and subversion, with a more abstractly political and militant edge to it, and a sense of experimentation and even a kind of roughed-up spiritualism. But in the end still pop music.

Wilson wants high-art pop beauties Blondie on *So It Goes*, but he is overruled by his producer, showing that the presenter, ultimately even Wilson, lacks the power of the producer. It's a sort of democracy, but one in which sometimes Wilson has the final say and sometimes the producer. Wilson instead gives them their first appearance on British TV on 'What's On', still an option for him even as *So It Goes* is being made, and as a taste-maker, someone scouting for what the next thing is, he is proved right.

Devo are on British television for the first time on Granada via Wilson at around 6.25 in the early evening, in a casual introduction for many to the most surreal pop they would have encountered at the time if not all time. He introduces convulsive crooner Elvis Costello on 'What's On', booked to play his recent hit 'Less Than Zero' but instead playing a song he had written just a couple of days before, 'Alison', and Tony feels he's at the centre of things, putting Manchester at the centre of things, and he likes the feeling.

Blondie would have been a great *So It Goes* booking, as part of what ended up in its however random two series being a much better judge at the time of where music was and where it was going than *The Old Grey Whistle Test*, which, through the almost monastic diffidence of Bob Harris and his attachment to an illusory notion of authenticity, cannot cope with the disruption and ultimately damage punk is doing to his standards. The old guard misses the point, or doesn't care, that this is where the music of the 1960s and any connection to the counterculture had travelled, to a very different 1970s, with its need for a different kind of protest. Two separate parts of history find a way to collide.

Wilson comes into contact with a new breed of musician at just the right time. Working in and around music at this time meant you could with the right instincts have access to the tremendous changes that were happening, and this means that when Wilson comes to begin the idea of Factory at the beginning of 1978, as a club, and then a label, and then beyond that, he has a unique set of experiences, with a distinctive set of ideological and cultural sensitivities influencing his idea of what a label could be. Having a label was like producing and presenting a TV show, releasing music and artists that he loved in the way he had booked them for his shows.

So It Goes was a TV anomaly, produced by the very different history and structure of Granada Television, its unorthodox internal systems combining with the methods, interests and enthusiasms of Tony Wilson, his very grown-up ITN experience, the fastidiousness he learnt at Cambridge and his musical taste coinciding with a rock otherness emerging in the late 1970s. The lack of interest shown by the network in *So It Goes* proves that no one there believed in it or understood it, and mostly just dismissed it as pointless self-indulgence, one of those programmes that didn't become anything, that didn't go anywhere. The fact that it was taken up by only three ITV regions – Granada, Yorkshire and London – and shown late at night in what was more or less a graveyard slot, remaining pretty much a local programme, reveals the then dominant mainstream media attitude towards rock and pop culture. It is seen to be of marginal minority interest, and in the case of *So It Goes* very much of the arts – as in too strange for popular consumption but without any apparent actual artistic content.

Wilson in Granada's eyes was useful as a lively, attractive presenter who added unusual local glamour to his programmes, but who was a bit wayward and erratic as a programme developer, a mixture of too naive and too ideological.

Wilson was responding to punk as a distinct hybrid of newsman, journalist, fan and art critic, one who found himself temporarily in the unique, almost uncensored position of being able to put his interests and insights directly onto television. *So It Goes* tapped into something that was happening as it happened, as though it was news, as though it explained the mysteries of life, because of the instincts Wilson had developed at ITN, the instincts of someone also fascinated by Romantic poets and situationist spite. He reacted to punk as current affairs, which suited what was happening, and selected music not because of its popularity or even its potential popularity according to the industry, but based on what he thought was socially and culturally important.

The final show in the first series directly connects with the Granada Television that first broadcast on television the most significant pop group of the 1960s; the ninth *So It Goes* means that Granada TV is the first television company to broadcast the most significant pop group of the 1970s. In fourteen years, rock music has gone from the Beatles to the Sex Pistols, two different, very English reactions to what rock and pop, and entertainment, and love and pleasure, social conscience and experimental vigour could be. Granada TV happened to be paying more attention than most because of one or two people working there who could see what was coming. Wilson, on behalf of Granada, which had no idea what was happening, worked hard to make the Sex Pistols happen on air, deciding it was his job to transmit the news of the moment, even if for conservative music fans they surely couldn't be taken seriously. The Pistols, of course, were not really about music. Believers and non-believers could agree on that.

There was only a little resistance to putting the Beatles on television for the first time in the early 1960s, when they weren't really the Beatles, just a gang of lively, dirty kids from thirty-five miles away playing the American rock 'n' roll and soul they loved, speeded up with a Scouse accent. There was no clear evidence they were destined to dominate the 1960s. Resistance to putting the Sex Pistols on television for the first time was much greater. Wilson had to change suspicious Granada minds, because to those not paying attention or too old to be in the right mood they really did seem to be a mob of dirty, aggressive hooligans. For Tony, they perhaps seemed to be pissing on the altar of rock 'n' roll, but they were still paying homage to the Church. They were saving rock 'n' roll even as they seemed to be destroying it.

A few days after the Pistols' first appearance in Manchester at the Lesser Free Trade Hall, where he was both present and not present, according to whom you believe – and why wouldn't you believe Wilson, even though no one remembers him being there? – he took a *So It Goes* researcher to see the group play at the Assembly Hall in Walthamstow, east London. Perhaps he had heard what had just happened in Manchester and realised he had missed something special. He needed to make up for it very quickly; or in his world, where he certainly had been at the first show, for once modestly hiding at the back or leaving early for some other apparently equally compelling engagement, he was dutifully following up as soon as he could on what he had seen.

On a bright summer's evening under a cloudless blue sky, they walked into a completely dark hall, where the group were already playing. There was some distance between Johnny Rotten and a small semicircle of curious, possibly nonplussed onlookers. Wilson realised it was because they were standing out of range of Rotten, who was seeing how far he could spit into the audience, as if anointing them. To the researcher they seemed like hoodlums possibly on the verge of turning on each other; the world wavered and quivered and threatened to burst into flames. Actually, he just saw a group of Bash Street Kids making a bit of an echoey, rocky racket with their skinny, sneering singer gobbing furiously at the audience, looking just like the kind of characters likely to swear at length on live television, but Tony heard something calling. He felt a passionate, desperate hunger, as though inside these raging louts was the secret of his own regeneration. He stared in wonder.

At more than music. Argument. Struggle. Poetry. Love, if you knew what it really was. Class struggle. Nameless pleasure. The realms of freedom. Praxis! Oddly enough, venture capitalism. At a gang of glorious odd ones out building a world where they could be at home anywhere. As if by magic. He had to have them. He had to be the one to introduce them for the very first time to a TV audience.

He stormed into work next day, marvelling at what he described as 'nothing less than an epiphany, the most exciting thing I had ever seen'. *Another Wilson infatuation*, his colleagues thought, but they shrugged, 'OK,' because Wilson could put obscure, eccentric things on his shows as if they were going to heal a wounded world, and sometimes he even seemed to know what he was doing. He delivers one of his speeches, a couple of centuries tripping off his tongue, setting out the entire innovative history of Manchester, the great pioneering city, what it has taken to be such a city – the people, the location, the buildings, the science, the art, the *Manchester Guardian*, the weather, the humour, the sneer, the sheer bloody-mindedness, and who came from the outside, from Ludwig

Wittgenstein to George Best, for it to be such a city – not forgetting the Bernsteins themselves giving the city the building they were standing in. 'And that's why we should put the Sex Pistols on Granada!'

His boss looks at him with a mixture of awe, fear and not a little contempt. He finds himself saying the only thing he can say after such an onslaught of knowledge, hogwash and supplication. 'All right, then,' he sighs, holding his breath, not sure if Wilson is just wonderfully naive or a little disturbing, giving him permission just to get him out of his hair.

When Wilson was forced to defend the programme to his bosses, usually when there was swearing on the show, usually from Iggy Pop, the mythical American suddenly given television space like an invader from the future, his attitude was that what he was doing was covering the arts and featuring artists. He was reporting on the new world, where what was being said, and who was saying it, had social and cultural value. This music had a special charge, whatever your feelings were about its commercial potential or whether you enjoyed it or not. It was a long way from what Muriel Young was doing, but then so was John Berger's *Ways of Seeing* from *Blue Peter*. Television could take it all in, because TV could take in the whole world.

To the petty, prudent ITV guardians, and the particularly cagey programme controller of Granada, Mike Scott, much of *So It Goes* was not popular music, it was not music of the charts, and there was seen to be something suspicious about the musicians and artists featured, as though their relative obscurity and their ugly intensity and visible difference rendered them ideologically suspect. Scott orders the *So It Goes* set to be destroyed after the first series, after a performance by the Pistols that to this day is one of the few TV occasions when the television screen itself seems threatened by danger, of cracking, allowing in other dimensions. The Sex Pistols mean that the second series leaves the studio and is all on film. It is produced with certain promises a diplomatically apologetic Wilson – increasingly accustomed to prostrating himself before furious bosses – makes about no more swastikas and no more swearing. He's still hoping this will be a long-running series.

Maybe, the Granada bosses begin to think after the first series, which to the safety-minded ended in farce, they had given their young firebrand from Cambridge, who was amusing within the confines of 'What's On' and even likeable as part of the *Reports* team, far too much leeway. The sort of leeway that can get an entire channel taken off the air.

So It Goes lasts for just two series, ripped from his heart just as Wilson is beginning to perfect its style. A wormhole that only Wilson with his odd position at Granada could have dreamt up, something that anticipated, in a sudden few months, musical and cultural changes and liberations over the next forty years, is blocked up, the show cancelled.

The bad reviews helped set music television back for decades, the so-called more serious pop programmes after the demise of *So It Goes* reverting to an insipid combination of worthiness, curatorial caution and orthodox, very literal direction. Its influence tended to be on arts and culture programmes daring to feature the experimental and temporarily indefinable, daring to work around commercial structures and the obvious guidelines of the charts.

So it goes.

Part II: It Happens

Seventeen: The Sex Pistols, Malcolm McLaren and giving meaning to one's life

O, tempora! O, mores! (Oh, the times! Oh, the customs!)

The Sex Pistols change the direction of *So It Goes,* and Manchester music, but in the same way Wilson's first concert was Albert Grossman not Peter, Paul and Mary, it is the Pistols' manager Malcolm McLaren who changes the direction of Tony Wilson. McLaren's capricious, pugnacious, entrepreneurial blend of performance, persuasion, playfulness and perversion helps Wilson work out what he can do and be.

It all brings disparate elements of the 1960s that never came to any kind of fruition and mostly seemed to be heading towards final irrelevance into sudden focus, a clash between music that had something on its mind and ways of expressing and presenting this music, so that involved in the design and distribution of this music were ideas that emerged out of the underground and alternative press, independent, left-wing promotion, avant-garde art, anarchic pamphleteering, intellectual philosophical developments and experimental ideas about design and typography.

Wilson possesses all these wide-ranging influences, starting with his mum, Doris, who brings him to Manchester, via Germany and Salford, with the timing to become a teenager in the 1960s, and whose death leaves him with a lot of space to fill and releases him from having to limit some of his wilder, weirder elements for fear of upsetting her. There's God, which initially takes some disbelieving, and the arcane rules and regulations, pains and pleasures of his Catholic grammar school to accept and reject, leaving him with the faith that never leaves his soul, mingling with the Buddhist rules of life, one of which is to live without rules. There's Jesus College Cambridge, from Raymond Williams to his acid dealer bringing him access to mental adventure and equally trippy, reality-rearranging situationist rants and visions. There's the inventive 1960s Manchester and North-West of Granada Television, brought to life by the brashness and boldness of the Bernsteins. The words Wilson reads, from Shakespeare and the Romantics to the Beats and the music press. The getting drunk with Leonard Cohen and feeling some life-defining divine intervention. The existentialist advice which tells you after being abandoned in the world to look after yourself completely. The intensely lucid paternal and journalistic influences of the live TV voices and faces of ITN. His fulsome hero worship of singers and musicians and of course their cunning, conniving, culture-shaping managers in the fast-moving 1960s and early '70s.

All of these scattered strands exist inside his head, none of them particularly connected but all contributing to his distinct approach to television and the media in general. Some of these strands were perhaps due to dissolve, as such things often do as you get older and face different issues and demands. In the mid-'70s, in your mid-twenties, having some kind of self-involved fannish interest in rock music looked a little immature.

Ultimately, as he enters his late twenties, making good use of his unlikely position at Granada TV in order to learn more about making and presenting television shows, he seems to be settling into a role where his future is very definitely in television, and increasingly serious television. He's having fun, but soon the knot in his tie will need to be neater, the hair tidier, the heretic glint in his eye will need extinguishing. Those who enjoyed looking at him read the news for the amount of subtext he slipped into it – the nods and winks and little twitches around the mouth – would be disappointed as this disappeared under a necessary new slickness.

He is heading towards perhaps being the kind of figure who would ultimately be an iconoclastic Michael Parkinson, a psychedelic Bill Grundy, a compelling showbusiness interviewer with a solid journalistic background or a highly paid, highly visible newsreader at ITN, leading towards becoming a Jeremy Paxman, front man of serious news programmes like *Newsnight* with a little light presenting work on the side, or a mature, ever-reliable political broadcaster like David Dimbleby or Andrew Marr.

It would have meant relinquishing much of the music and arts work he enjoyed doing, his locating of spiritual power in unusual, obscure places, but there was a sense at the time that his destiny was as a major national broadcasting figure, the type who eventually becomes known as a (in some cases slightly edgy) national treasure, and that his time at Granada was a form of apprenticeship. He would soon be moving on to bigger things, coming alive on live TV, filling the nation's screens from general election to general election, interview to interview.

And then along came mouthy hawker Malcolm McLaren, anchored in carnality, swanning into Manchester like a manic missionary – Manchester often made into something new by those coming in from elsewhere, from Marx and Engels of Germany and Richard Cobden of Sussex and the Anti-Corn Law League to the displaced 1950s West Indian immigrants and Guyanese Clive Lloyd of Lancashire Cricket Club, from Alan Turing to Manchester United's Matt Busby and George Best and Manchester City's Malcolm Allison and Rodney Marsh, some sticking around, adding to the city's mongrel intensity, finding that it is a place where great and active minds can flourish.

The city relishes – and naturally scorns if its integrity seems suspect – crusading showmanship, fancy footwork, big-mouthed self-belief and a gutsy, confrontational smartness. The big personality is respected, however flawed or unstable. Manchester considers arrogance a key component in its make-up, and it trusts the single-minded, as long as they conform to specific local desires.

Those who come from outside bringing their own energy, influence and ambition into Manchester have always been as important in the construction and modification of its history and image as those born and bred within. The city is formed by a succession of those restless pursuers of greatness, sure of their own minds, who use its fluid historical momentum and the revolutionary intention lingering in the atmosphere to help establish their own position and personality.

McLaren, rushing in and out on a temporary visa, made sense of the numerous different sides of Tony Wilson, contained his disorders and gave them form, as though that was his main purpose in coming to town. Constructed out of his own many clashing contradictions, he hit some kind of nerve in Wilson – always susceptible to enchanting new mentors, alert to whispers – and shouts and demands – being passed from generation to generation. McLaren connected in Wilson the dissident with the populist, the communicator with the fan, the provocateur with the raconteur, the genius with the buffoon, the gentle, nurturing mentor with the impatient know-all, and brought them all into one place, making one very new kind of absolutely original person.

After meeting, and experiencing, McLaren there is for Wilson a moment of recognition. Suddenly, there is the future. One that you can make up after the fact, shaping the story how you want to fit your agenda. He learns from McLaren the art of what the French so beautifully call *l'esprit d'escalier* – hindsight, the ability to make it look as though you knew what you were doing all along even as one thing just led to another, and all you really did was talk a lot, throw the dice, believe that it was always time for a change, for a new thrill, a new idea, beyond the control of those in power.

'In the course of giving meaning to one's life,' said Malcolm McLaren, wearing a mask of Jean-Paul Sartre, 'one fills the world with meaning.' And then, wearing a mask of Yves Saint Laurent, 'I prefer to shock rather than bore through repetition.' And then, wearing a mask of Andy Warhol, 'Art is what you can get away with.' And then, wearing a mask of Sol LeWitt, 'Ideas alone can be works of art; they are in a chain of development that may eventually find form. All ideas need not be made physical.'

McLaren like Wilson grew up in the 1950s, part of another misshapen post-war family – his father left home when he was two, and he was raised and home-schooled by a vehemently anti-royalist, slogan-loving grandmother in conditions that resembled creative chaos. He moved into his teens in the 1960s, as popular culture started to make the fluid, challenging ideas of art and otherness accessible to all, allowing a new generation to – perhaps – take control, or at least have a say, using its own new language. Destiny, a chance inheritance, meant that the post-war generation, part of an unlikely recovery, could do what it wanted with its youth. For some kids this meant stealing – and singing – the blues, and giving it a right British kicking. For McLaren, it meant stealing all he could get his hands on.

His England was an England of liars and pirates telling long shaggy-dog tales, queering the script, scamming the innocent, bluffing their way through, world-class in the culture of deception, so deceptive they can never be straight. He committed himself from a young age to creating new and strange perspectives on the past and the present, always on the hunt to challenge history and break the rules in order to change the future. He relishes finding himself around as popular culture takes hold of the world. Everyone can access it. Everyone gets a bite of the cherry.

Uncommonly clever like Wilson, with a head equally always full of information and gossip, he's a student during what he called 'the winds of change' in the late 1960s. As an embryonic artist, smart alec without portfolio and then a buyer and seller of fashion, he picks up the principle of copying others as much as you like, taking other ideas and making them bigger, one eye on Warhol and pop art, one eye on the radical philosophers and loose cannons that led to situationism's heyday, structuralist decon-struction and student revolt. Eventually, his raiding, appropriating, rewir-ing sensibility would lead to the copyright-trashing, truth-rearranging worlds of sampling and social media.

McLaren enters the music business via his contact with situationist adventurers, his shops and his love of clothing, while Wilson comes to it through his broadcasting and love of literature, both bringing unprece-dented, chaotic, intellectual, artistic and critical energies into rock and pop music. The King's Road shop McLaren runs with Vivienne Westwood becomes the no-nonsense, no-nostalgia Sex, dingy and graffiti-sprayed, with elegantly degenerate clothes falling from the minds of alert deviants, forcing some people to explain why they wanted to own an item. It wasn't enough that you could afford them, or they fitted you. You had to under-stand them, believe in them as an ideology, a whole belief system.

Regular and accepted rock 'n' roll clothing is replaced with nastier, less easily adaptable, more fiercely sexualised body-fitting, or body-mocking, outlaw styles, and the restless McLaren begins putting together his own model of the New York Dolls. Not so much because he's interested in music in the way that say the presenter of *The Old Grey Whistle Test* or the drummer in Genesis would understand it, but because he's interested in how pop music can carry ideas, art, even psychic forms of power and dispute, and indeed sell his clothes and lead to unlikely adventures, to the great state on the border of who knows what, of what the hell. In this approach, truancy, flippancy and delinquency are more important than chords and melodies. Uplifting pop melodies will come out of a certain facetious madness, out of the overall performance, out of essential style.

In the end, if a group looks like a group, it is a group. It becomes a group. The greatest groups of all time always looked like groups, based on the early templates of what a rock group was, once there was this idea of there being a guitarist, a bassist, a drummer, a singer, a poet, a daydreamer, a fighter, a lover; the music comes after, a lucky accident, or a basic part of the fate, influences, location that brought the three, or four, or five together to become a group and all that means in the first place.

McLaren comes up with the name for his take on the Dolls, the Sex Pistols, imagining a gang of potential assassins. They begin for real not with a song or a sound, or even as a name they've chosen for themselves, but with three ne'er-do-wells hanging around Sex who seem to look the part, a couple with the untamed look of furtive small-time crooks constantly suppressing wild energy. Steve Jones, Paul Cook and Glen Matlock are brave enough to come into the flashy gloom and prepared sleaze of the shop, not necessarily to buy anything, but maybe to nick something or experience the disconcerting nightclub atmosphere and soak up the information that makes the shop like nothing else in London.

McLaren's first thought for Sex Pistols vocalist is to import another of his of-the-moment Lower Manhattan crushes, Richard Hell. A ragged-haired, lyrical and sardonic post-hippy New Yorker, co-founder of free punk group Television with Tom Verlaine before SI-style expulsion, Hell patches together a dangerous and anomalous mid-1970s hybrid of sordid Baudelaire, sullen Beat and intense, minimalist, jazz-pierced garage rock, and presents it all like it's a whole lot of avant-garde art. His 'Blank

Generation' is an anthem for those who hate anthems, a teenage anthem written when he was twenty-seven. He was ripping holes in his T-shirts before the ones they were selling at Sex and had a shredded haircut that seemed to come from the sewer more than the salon. McLaren sees the present in Hell, often harder to do than seeing the future.

When Hell declines to become a plaything, part of an obvious set-up, out of place in London, McLaren sees nothing wrong in stealing the racket, the wrecked jackets and the safety pins, the short hair, even the idea of anthemic anti-anthems. He even thinks of kidnapping a New York Doll, Sylvain Sylvain, and sticking him on a plank in front of his thieving, drunken Pistols. His age, background, sensibility and hair length would be totally wrong, but McLaren is having difficulty finding the final piece, the most important piece of his fake group – the face, voice, hair, pose, something the world at large would have difficulty making heads or tails of. There's a brief glimpse of a solution with Peter Perrett, known now almost solely for one dream of a song, 'Another Girl, Another Planet', but for all his vagabond talents, he is seen more as an almost conventional if hedonic singer/songwriter than McLaren's preferred easily moulded lowlife with nothing to lose. McLaren is like the head of some surreal offbeat stage school: he's looking for a dirty street version of a stage-school kid.

He needs a perfect contrarian to front his brainchild, and after hearing rumours of someone who looks the part and turns out to be punk-christened Sid Vicious, who eventually replaces Glen Matlock as the more visually ideal brattish bassist, it's shy, pent-up and undernourished north Londoner John Lydon who ventures into the shop with badly dyed hair, rotten working-class teeth and a near limp, wearing an *I hate Pink Floyd* T-shirt. It was a T-shirt that said, forty years before the rock festival would once and for all ruin the idea of music as a partial critique of the old world and its values, 'Rock festivals are nothing but the celebration of the triumph of a neo-imperialist assault on the cultural consumption of youth trying desperately to appear as the success of the revolt of youth. The hip lifestyle reproduces the consumerism it imagines it opposes.' It was a T-shirt that said, 'Never trust a hippy.'

His rough and blackened teeth say neglected urchin, and give him his pirate nickname; his hair is more Hell than Doll; the self-styled T-shirt says he has an ideology, even if ultimately it means he's the sort of deep-thinking, discriminating music fan who leads the Sex Pistols to become something more than conceptual-clothes-shop living mannequins and actually, temporarily, a fantastic musical act as well as an oblique piece of avant-garde merchandising. Lydon's restless curiosity and askew intellectual energy stop the whole thing from becoming a master and his apprentices, combining Warhol's Factory with a medieval workshop where assistants obediently carry out instructions. The battle for authority, for leadership, becomes part of the story, creating something more significant than what the Pistols dare to imagine in their wildest dreams.

He's on a different timeline to McLaren, but one that occasionally coincides. Rotten's hatred for bland, product-line music means a love for the experimental that leads him to the wonder worlds of Captain Beefheart and Lee 'Scratch' Perry; McLaren's loathing of the dreary and conformist leads him deep into his childhood love for fast, raucous and roughly dramatic rock 'n' roll, one step removed from the circus, from theatre, from pop art. Ultimately, this meant that John Lydon's Sex Pistols influenced music and musicians, even if just spiritually, and Malcolm McLaren's Sex Pistols influenced marketing, art, fashion, publishing and – in how he gleefully and chaotically chased major-label money and clout and sabotaged the system – independent record labels, although the influence on musicians needed the paranoia and precision of McLaren, and the non-musical influence needed the emotion and seriousness of Lydon/Rotten.

They both feel a need, from different points in time and different forms of education and desire, to make something happen and to assault general cultural apathy. They weren't in sync, they weren't heading in the same direction, but they were both interested in the altogether different. Where and how they aligned, in temporary grace and gracelessness, along with the other unruly states in the band, created enough momentum to get through a short series of operatically interventionist singles, a fucked-up album and some riotous shows, and for them to become a cultural spectacle that could only end with collapse. A collapse that quite properly included death, misery, squalor, lawsuits and resounding mediocrity.

All great groups have their extra members, the ones not in the group who contribute ideas, visuals and concepts that complete the image and confirm the meaning and the message, even when meaning is not actually a requirement. As well as grand mentor and project leader McLaren, extravagantly and egotistically elaborating on the showbusiness idea of what a manager is and does and approaching the designing of a pop group as though it was an art event, creating the blueprint and then handing over the production to others, there was the artist, designer and situationist sympathiser Jamie Reid. Reid's Sex Pistols was where the Pistols of McLaren and the Pistols of Rotten – and the rest of the rabble – connected.

Reid was in McLaren's eyes one of the discerning few, using his small south London printing press to distribute ideas and thinking to the converted, with little interest in reaching the distant, indifferent masses. No one was being upset. There was a kind of safety, a loneliness, in his approach to broadcasting subversive ideas, or perhaps a patience, a marginal version of the 'long revolution' of Raymond Williams. Eventually . . . McLaren, a developing specialist in the still relatively early days of pop culture, when everyone was within reach – the whole point – was interested in creating something that was popular *and* inflammatory. Why leave all that popularity, all that potential audience, to the ordinary and the unadventurous? Why leave marketing and advertising to those using its tricks and techniques only to make money, not to push new ideas?

He pitches to Reid his idea for a version of the Bay City Rollers, the teenybop group of the day, with some added blasted bohemian Hell/Doll/Mob-like art and menace. His Pistols, he claims, are younger, better-looking, sexier than the Rollers, and would look ripe for attention – ripe to hype – in Sex clothes. He's imagining a depraved boy band. He loves how the fans of the Bay City Rollers wear the same clothes, seeing in this total confirmation of the link he's always seen between music and fashion, image and emotion.

Reid isn't interested; the idea seems safe and easy to him. He encourages McLaren to consider that if he really wants to fuck up, and fix, popular culture, he should really fuck up popular culture. Don't compete with the Bay City Rollers, a minor temporary fragment of pop; compete with the whole history of popular culture. Reid and Westwood persuade McLaren to think bigger. Rotten will be thinking like that anyway – recreate in a modern setting how when rock 'n' roll music first appeared, and went through its adaptations, it was a cultural, aesthetic and social risk to look that way, sound like that, wear those clothes, and act like they knew something beyond the everyday.

Using *l'esprit d'escalier*, the hindsight that comes once the experiment, the fun and games, has finished, once the Pistols stopped firing, McLaren will take to talking about them as an 'art event', as an experiment in pop culture appropriation or a kind of living billboard for the Sex shop, but at the beginning he's just acting like the promoter of an eccentric new group, doing an extreme amount of hit-and-miss ducking and diving to get them gigs supporting mid-level pub rock acts in small pubs and colleges around London. He's constructing an adventure, and everyone has to start somewhere.

Conversations night after night in a central London pub where he meets the band with Jamie Reid develop the blueprint for the look, sound and content of the group. McLaren has assembled an idiosyncratic, neo-anarchist inner circle. The theories and policies of Debord and his fellow situationists are passed through this ad hoc social setting, and end up being distilled into pure visceral lyrical and performance energy by Rotten. Theory becomes action. Delinquency and antisocial behaviour – the petty-criminal wing of the Pistols – clashes with the artistic and intellectual, as channelled through Reid the anarchic printer and McLaren the piratical philosopher. Two different forms of snotty, provocative behaviour. Ironic anger combines with self-righteous arrogance. Slogans and tactics that culminated in 1968, and had sadly disintegrated by the early 1970s, the idea that youth were the agents of real social change, aristocrats of disobedience, are still working their way forward towards wildly varying destinations.

McLaren marvels that Lydon in particular, starved of knowledge, of information about like-minded spirits, manages to soak up all this highfalutin and intellectually opaque information, all this new blood and thinking, and transform it into something so direct and unpretentious, an Anglo-Saxon avant-garde. It's English, London, Soho, conceived inside a noisy, smoky pub on Cambridge Circus, but the ideas are boundless and borderless, the equivalent of the self-conscious late-night Cambridge University conversations in which Wilson and cohorts, some of whom flew close to the situationist sun, would discuss cultural revolt, freedom of choice, how capital shapes culture and society, and how it accumulates to become an image. From pub plotting and wild planning, some ideas on how to organise a preposterous event materialise. No one's really thinking how to make it work, just thinking if only there was such a thing, such a moment. A fuse is lit before time is called and the punters are kicked out.

The Sex Pistols, as an act with some worked-up songs of their own and a few familiar covers to point out that they are a pop group, begin by meaning something to a few of their friends, to customers, employees and associates of McLaren and Westwood's shop, to some estranged, extreme kids from the suburbs who don't need to defend why they want to buy and wear Sex clothing – they were walking adverts, their own clothes fitting in well. Some non-Sex customers come across the Pistols playing in the middle of nowhere having come from nowhere, supporting acts that suddenly look old and irrelevant. A handful of those in the know become forty, fifty, a hundred. A hundred here, a hundred there. A mention here, a mention there in the music papers. The word carries. Some come into the shop and strike up conversations, asking McLaren if he would be interested in taking his group up North. Would they come and play in Manchester?

Maybe. What's in it for us?

Coming up to Manchester leads to their first TV appearance, a cultural jolt in time made apparent by Tony Wilson, who lures them in; what's in it for him is making his series leap from novelty art show to a piece of broadcasting history.

Part of the Pistols' strategy is heading out of the city to the North, to where there are even more urgent needs. They arrive in Manchester, make their way to the famous Granada studios and are surprised by the character who greets them – not what they were expecting, neither a boring old fart making some sort of mistake asking them on his show not really knowing what he's getting, nor a younger type with the look of something punkish about him, knowing a good thing when he sees it. They are met by an eager, slightly shambolic hippy, wearing the creased clothes of someone who attends a lot of meetings and maybe sleeps in his car, slightly to the left of completely focused, obviously a fan, and obviously attracted to their manager.

Tony meets Malcolm, Malcolm meets Tony, both of them buzzing at different frequencies, but sort of connecting, and so it goes. Wilson, explains Sex Pistols biographer Jon Savage, soon to be Wilson's colleague, became McLaren-damaged. Damaged enough that a year or so later he's fighting with McLaren himself, pupil voice already turning into pupil action. He's been chasing McLaren because he wants to put the Pistols on TV again in a *So It Goes* special – 'Don't just tour to reach the kids, use television!' – and he's pissed off because he feels he's being ignored. He wants to give them a whole show, using McLaren's preferred director, Julien Temple – a chance to reach an audience of three million. 'Because I think your methods are seven-eighths correct I'm offering my metaphysical anus to be *used*.'

He's hearing nothing back, or being told to fuck off like he's some sort of hippy irritant, and he's not happy. He lashes out on paper with a few phrases that show how much he reads the music papers – the writing of Nick Kent, Charles Shaar Murray and Lester Bangs. The experienced television personality usurps the overexcited fan, but the idealist doesn't go missing. His usual way of sorting out his thoughts, Wilson types out one of his rants in the form of a three-page letter. He's not only angrily complaining at what he sees as McLaren's humiliating treatment of him – 'it's a lot like dealing with the Rolling Stones or any other fucked-up rich man's band who treat media lackeys like me with the same amount of contempt' – but also defending his own credentials as a serious, anti-corporate, community-minded journalist and producing a manifesto for a new kind of music organisation without really knowing that's what he's doing. He's attacking the system by getting things out of his system.

'First off, more important than you, safety pins or Steve Jones' rapidly improving guitar playing are the kids, all those youngsters with new reasons, new thoughts and new excitements. You were the first band to show them the potential in stepping outside the dried skin of the music world.' He soon turns to what he describes as 'commodity theory' – whether the Pistols have been some highfalutin scam, or whether 'we really are talking about "the poverty of everyday life" and the avoidance of spectacular existence and the divorced sense of reality, etc etc . . .'

By the last paragraph, he is really picking up speed, as TV personality, entertainer, academic, writer, theorist, dope smoker, bored ex-teenager, trainee provocateur, Mr Angry of Granada, eccentric punk acolyte and slightly patronising, slightly self-important teacher (a couple of years later this sort of thing would be getting a Fac number):

> *Whatever went wrong with music in the past, in 58–62 or 70–76, although it can be seen as the prevailing culture buying itself a piece of the revolution, and draining the blood out of it by so doing, it is also the history of the artist's proximity to his audience; Keats had this thing about the artist being a fairly irrelevant tool just like this typewriter, and he compared it to an Aeolian harp . . . a Greek stringed instrument that was played by the action of the wind blowing over it . . . for wind read mass consciousness, the audience, the Zeitgeist or whatever . . . all I'm trying to say is the audience is the important factor and in telling me to take a running jump you are saying exactly the same thing to all those kids in Aberdeen, Wigan and Slough who aren't going to get to see you but deserve to.*
>
> *Those are my arguments, you know them anyway, but it helps to exorcise a little of the anger I feel at having being quite considerably fucked around.*
> *Tony Wilson*

PS If you're going to be so damned purist about not doing So It Goes *at least do me the favour of being equally purist in other fields and avoid all the other crap . . . and get the fucking LP out . . . and make it cheap.*
   Nice talking to you.

The Sex Pistols *So It Goes* special never happened. McLaren had other things on his mind – or perhaps he'd decided even before Keats and the Aeolian harp that pontificating Tony's mission wasn't quite his mission. And Wilson has come to the realisation that McLaren's methods are not quite his methods. They didn't fall out, though, not for long. In a way they loved each other a little bit more. Disagreement was all part of the relationship.

It was the same with Granada TV, his place of work, the source of his early power, where he felt comfortable by never feeling comfortable and always testing the limits of the relationship. 'They don't know what we're fucking doing here,' he rants to his Granada colleague Andy Harries, who's still smarting after a Clash shoot for *So It Goes*, where his job was wiping the spit from the camera lens as it rained down on the group, dripping off the microphone, saturating singer Joe Strummer. 'In years to come this will be history, it's outrageous not to film this stuff and create an important archive.'

He tried to persuade Granada to allow him to film a documentary of the Sex Pistols' time in Manchester, just as they were about to become national headliners.

'He was so angry they didn't go for it,' recalls his Granada associate. '"They're such dullards," he said, "the footage would be priceless." They thought it would be a waste of money, but Tony argued they would make tons of money from it over time. It wasn't pop music, it was history. He knew he was right.'

To get on with things he had to know more than Granada, and more than McLaren, even get tired of his heroes, the ones that came to save him – turn them into enemies, to motivate him, fuel his fire, even as he still needed heroes as he grew older.

258

Eighteen: The greatest gig of all time and various consequences

Exegi monumentum aere perennius. (I have made a monument more lasting than bronze.)

The pop world was changing in so many ways, but in Manchester what was almost immediately important was that instead of Manchester being a place bands from other places came to and then moved on from, there were local bands with distinct local elements in their music who were part of whatever suddenness there was as symbolised by the Pistols. If there was a revolution in the air, and the look and sound of the Sex Pistols suggested there might be, Manchester with its long-standing campaigning tendencies was quick to join in.

As Tony Wilson once said, wearing a mask of yippie, self-conscious rebel and social clown Abbie Hoffman, the wild and crazy Jewish stepfather he never had, the only way to support a revolution is to make your own. If you don't like the news, make up your own.

The past is the past and sometimes you don't want to touch it. Other times you want to grab hold of it and make it into something else. Put things in a different place. In a different order. Allow chronology to shiver a little. Shred it even. Act like the past hasn't yet happened and you are still to experience it. 'The only way to fight nostalgia,' said Tony Wilson, wearing the mask of New York journalist Pete Hamill, who wrote the sleeve notes for the original cover to Bob Dylan's *Blood on the Tracks*, 'is to listen to someone else's nostalgia.'

Because I start writing for the *NME* from Manchester in the few weeks after the Sex Pistols came and, more or less, told many of us what to do next – including some abstract instructions issued to an alert and susceptible Tony Wilson, half Peter Pan teenybopper, half theory-mad intellectual – I end up writing about much of this for forty years, as pop and rock become increasingly a matter of anniversary and nostalgia, of more and more stuff, simply about content rather than discontent, looking back at something that worked so spectacularly in the first place because it announced so aggressively that there was no point in looking back and merely wallowing.

Over time, the role of a kind of historian seizing and organising the past, battling against my instincts to keep looking forward, wins through. Hopefully, it's a way of making the past influence the present, of still being active, of observing influences being passed creatively from generation to generation, energy amplified and reordered, not just sentimentally recreated. I have refined my recollection of the Pistols and their two summer Manchester 1976 concerts and what happened next in the city to the hopefully not-too-sentimental following, although it remains a work in progress and something I will be coming back to until their fiftieth anniversary, maybe even beyond that.

Google 'Sex Pistols Lesser Free Trade Hall 1976' or simply 'June 4th 1976' and you can use the resultant 10,700,000 pieces of information to piece together a crudely helpful history of (a) Manchester music, (b) the birth of indie music and (c) the 'greatest gig of all time' that 'changed music forever'. None of this is necessarily true, but it's not exactly inaccurate either.

'All truth is simple,' said Tony Wilson, once more wearing a mask of Friedrich Nietzsche. 'Is that not doubly a lie?'

The fact that if you google simply 'I swear I was there' you come across more details about that Sex Pistols performance emphasises the show's reputation, not least because, and this has become an integral element in the ensuing mythologising of the gig, there weren't that many people who bought the 60p ticket, but thousands now claim they did. Those that like to nourish the legend favour an estimate of around 40; other less romantic minds suggest a number closer to 100.

The small lecture hall at the side of the larger Free Trade Hall up a few flights of stairs contained around 150 seats and had been booked by Howard Devoto and Pete Shelley of Bolton College of Technology's suddenly formed Buzzcocks, who weren't quite ready to support as planned – as it turned out, making this sort of noise with feeling required a certain preparation. They asked another band from the college to fill in for them, and so Solstice, long-haired hippies in flares who played faithful cover versions of dope-drenched songs by Man, the Welsh Grateful Dead, made the gig seem at first as though it was absolutely nothing new, in fact total proof that nothing much of note was happening locally and probably never would.

Howard and Pete had been to see the Sex Pistols support nutty novelty rock act Screaming Lord Sutch in High Wycombe, because a review in the *New Musical Express* had suggested here was a British group influenced by Iggy and the Stooges, which seemed instantly a welcome, wonderful hint of The Future. They were looking for something to tune in to. Reality as a radio: you could turn the dial and pick up signals. They'd been to Sex at the end of the King's Road in London's Chelsea, driving down in Pete's car, meeting their friend Richard Boon, who was studying art in Reading. They introduced themselves to Sex owner and the Pistols' colourful manager, Malcolm McLaren, flamboyantly of the fashion trade, who was rather excited that news of his raggedy young protégés had made it all the way to distant Manchester.

They weren't the Sex Pistols we think of now. There was no real plan. They were a pitch, a hobby, a joke, a project, a scheme. A scam. *What an adventure*, thought McLaren, *what a prospect, to see if anyone was actually interested in what they were up to all those motorway miles from home. Could their racket, their shakedown, mean anything outside a few square miles in the South?* It was the beginning of a plan. Something that needed a little more organisation than usual.

The Pistols travelling north set the precedent for the new punk groups to head out of London, previously their comfort zone, deep into the provinces. They discovered the most extraordinarily sympathetic and aroused audiences, small but frenzied, grateful that the latest thing was not limiting itself to the energy-sapping capital city. Local energy and visiting energy combined to produce a new kind of new.

Devoto, Shelley and their studious, experience-hunting sidekick Richard Boon, who was to become the Buzzcocks' manager, although his real role required another name – Richard would say 'mismanager' – chose a venue never really used for rock music, adding to the oblique specialness of the occasion. The venue was next door to the Free Trade Hall, a large concert hall named after an economic principle, and a grand symbol of once-mighty Victorian civic pride, original home to one of the world's first city-based orchestras, organised to sell a city's superior class, where bands like T. Rex, Black Sabbath and Little Feat usually played.

I was there, I was a witness, although not enough of one to notice at the time that what was taking place was 'history'. The day began like any other day and ended pretty much the same, give or take a racing mind. I had no idea I would talk and write about the gig for what is turning out to be the rest of my life, as the 1970s turn into a bygone era, finding new ways to point out from anniversary to anniversary that the evening was something of a revelation because it instantly suggested that (a) there were other people interested in music that made you feel, think and want to do/be something radical/individual, (b) you could make music without the usual support systems of London record companies, promoters and showbiz managers and (c) there was an exciting way to effectively and importantly assassinate Yes, Emerson, Lake and Palmer, and Genesis, who indifferently perpetuated various demoralising and bloodsucking forms of alienation, elitism, pomposity and complacency, building musical palaces covered with the clotted gold of unreal feelings. This music came across as the kind of kitsch you could die from.

Something else seemed urgently needed. Music at the time was a matter of life or death because it seemed to exist to save your life from straightness, from sameness, from blind authority, from simply following your parents into various oppressed emotional and financial cul-de-sacs.

I'd gone on my long-haired nineteen-year-old own, having no idea what to expect. The review Devoto and Shelley had read in the *New Musical Express*, along with everyone else who had bought a ticket, said the group was not really about music but chaos. A perfect, seductive response to the times, and a further hint, intended by the group or not, that this was more a splattering blast of art than simply more merely decorative songs. More information was constantly being delivered through the music papers to suggest that nothing like this had ever happened before. Some reviews were like warnings – *Careful, look over your shoulder!* Some suggested the group, guitar gangsters, had stolen their equipment from the Rolling Stones or David Bowie, that they were as much of a joke as Screaming Lord Sutch, better known for his eccentric electoral campaigns representing the Monster Raving Loony Party, an anarchic ancestor of Nigel Farage.

One relatively, temporarily fashionable, anti-prog art group, the Doctors of Madness, who thought they were creatively splicing dark rock with extreme theatre and inventing a new form of pop, said that before they began one of their shows supported by the Sex Pistols, they were the hippest thing around; immediately after the show, witnessing the Pistols not so much fuse music and theatre as smash them together, they were as old-fashioned as skiffle, and to rub it in a Pistol or two had stolen some cash from their dressing room. And within a few days of these reports coming up from London, the actual thing, named like a revolutionary gang where the exploited were taking on the exploiters, was coming to Manchester. They were on the march. Well, they were looking for pockets to pick and possibly guitars to steal.

Manchester was traditionally a very good host and was very good at fans – its greatest, most original performers of the 1970s were not necessarily bands but dancers, especially the Twisted Wheel and northern soul dancers and those dressing up for the glam and local street theatre of Pips, and its independent, import- and bootleg-stocking record shops meant the record collections of the locals were famously eclectic and knowing – but its rock music scene consisted mostly of derivative, pseudo-international, non-northern music that was rarely going to travel.

The city's people loved, needed to be entertained, to be shown other ways of being and acting, or simply sung to, joked with, made to feel part of something they were in control of. Great music always came to Manchester, to the great halls in the embellished city centre, the enterprising student unions and the dingy underground clubs in the derelict margins, but there had been nothing like this. And this was coming to one of the great city halls, originally Victorian and rebuilt after the war as though suddenly it was at the fantastic edge of the world. Or, suddenly, from the puzzled and/or enraptured pages of the music papers, where there was still a sense it all might yet be a stupid non-musical scam, the Sex Pistols were stepping right into the middle of things.

I'm not sure what I actually recall or what I filled in using data acquired later as the gig was talked up into legend, each new subsequent Manchester movement and scene amplifying its importance. I seem to recall lots of empty seats, an audience split somewhere between agitation and anomie, and the Pistols solemnly if savagely covering the Monkees and the Troggs, turning perky pop into an act of provocation. One of their songs seemed like a combination of something by the Move – surely a buggered-up version of the frenzied riff of their 'Fire Brigade' – and a fervid anti-republican chant. Was this ordinary, or extraordinary, music, or something closer to a happening?

Rough pictures, as if photography had just been invented, of Johnny Rotten from the show, some kind of evidence of the flatter, unfiltered truth of the evening, now suggest a boyish, highly amused, almost frail presence; in the sickly flesh, he was magnetic, alien, victim and victor, seething with a thinly veiled theatricality that was part corrupted vaudeville and part emerging from his belief that through music you can briefly glimpse the entire magnitude of existence.

He appeared to be single-handedly bringing to life – and knowing he was doing it – the thoughts and feelings of those who are usually ignored by the Establishment and the corporate media. The Pistols seemed to have completely bypassed a music industry that funnelled things through to us to suit its own agenda, and without engaging in any form of market research were perfectly pitched to appeal to a certain age group at the perfect time. And Manchester turned out to be the perfect place.

It was mostly males watching him watching us watching him, the straight kind that felt an abstract erotic tingle when they listened to Iggy Pop, although there were women starring in the exotic Pistols entourage – all part of the performance, also featuring their manager, the grand

evangelical barking circus misfit, berserk merchandiser and cultural loi-
terer Malcolm McLaren, of the 18, 19 and 2060s, putting the 'Sex' in Sex
Pistols to promote his London clothes shop, running everything like it was
half circus, half political demo, with the hungry, preoccupied-looking face
of a dealer that suggested he could sell and tell you anything and you'd buy
and believe it. For now.

The women came costumed in a ripped, pinned and fishnet style that
to long-haired flared-trousered still fairly cobbled barely Roxy'd scruffily
Bowie'd northerners of the time was somewhere between Fosse's *Cabaret*
and clockwork Kubrick. What the hell was going on in London? Why
were parts of it sending people back from the future?

The Pistols were clearly wearing the avant-scruffy clothes they'd travelled
in, and were unabashed by their overall ugliness, but were somehow the
most glamorous, extravagant performers seen around town since the Bowie
of another, earlier – and in some ways later – London town passed through,
leaving behind infectious traces of his mind, clothes and perfume.

As well as understanding even with their limited experience how to
put on a show, the Pistols seemed more intuitively aware of Manchester's
original nineteenth-century status as the world-shaking 'shock city' and
the radical origins of the building they were inside than the audience.
They seemed a lot more connected to the shock art of Dada as well, no
doubt via the accidental or not strategies of the shit-stirring shock showman McLaren, and once you pass rock music – and what it had become
inside about thirteen years – through such a filter, everything will change,
as if everything is beginning again. They wouldn't have sounded like they
did without the Who and the Stooges, even Slade and the Troggs, all that
riffing and banging, but they sounded like nothing that had come before.
They appeared to be singing about anarchy and the IRA, not cars and girls.
They were those who light the fires, not the fire brigade putting them out.
If there was any romance, it was violent.

We, the yokel audience, strangers to the destinies of each other, were
mildly retarded, isolated, avant-garde music fans motivated by John Peel
and the weekly music papers to constantly search out new music as if it

transmitted sacred power; tribe-less fans of the Stooges, MC5, the Velvet Underground, maybe Can and Eno, dub and definitely the guitar-armed amped-up riff-mad garage bands of Lenny Kaye's *Nuggets* compilations. The Pistols shooting into the city like a draught of fresh air made it seem as though music was not something you merely reacted to and simply enjoyed and collected; it gave you a sense of being of use in the greater scheme of things: you could be a part of life, not merely observing it.

Many audience members have since become well known. So well known it now appears that the show was attended by a host of rock celebrities – members of Joy Division, New Order, the Fall, the Smiths, A Certain Ratio, Ludus, Simply Red, Buzzcocks, Magazine, John Cooper Clarke, Martin Hannett, Kevin Cummins. It was in fact attended by unassuming non-entities drawn to the gig from within a fifteen-mile radius of Manchester city centre, perhaps because they were frustrated by their stranded non-entity status and craving purpose, but not really expecting to find blatant clues about how to break out of that post-war, post-'60s, post-industrial breakdown limbo. The Sex Pistols' deviant pop art rage and indignation, actually fighting their way out of the war, the '60s, which seemed so long ago, and deindustrialisation, were an immediate clue. They were making history by tearing it apart. They didn't so much bring light into the city as lightning.

I seem to recall no one looked as though they were in a music group and ever would be, because of course at the time no one (a) local, (b) regional and (c) provincial who looked a little ordinary even dull and dressed a little second-hand, a little charity shop, formed pop groups. This was to change quite quickly, because the Sex Pistols themselves did not look like a band, not as bands were perceived at the time, whether that was Genesis, or Mott, or Free, or even those early hints of a certain sort of energising cultural and musical correction that was about to take place, the down-town New York, leather, black-and-white Ramones or the dishevelled, straight-from-office-work-clothing, black-and-white Dr Feelgood.

Would another group of forty have ended up forming the kind of groups that got formed because, suddenly, there appeared these perverse educators,

266

these militant cultural critics possibly influenced as much by Marcel Duchamp of Dada and Guy Debord of situationism as the Small Faces and the Who, sensationally branded by offended and wound-up tabloids as grubby nuisances, bringers of vicious punk rock and associated loutish scandals? Or were they obviously the obvious forty or so who would end up forming those bands and labels – and writing these words/taking photographs/designing sleeves/managing/roaming/making what forty years later would become known, sadly, as 'content' – because they attended the gig in the first place, and had agitating within them all those songs, ideas, words, images, plans, beliefs, manifestos, and just needed some sort of cabalistic psychic trigger, a dressed-up sign, a fearless look in the eye, as delivered by the haughty and entertained intellectual hooligan Johnny Rotten.

I came away more sure than ever that I wanted to be a writer and pass on the information I had just received in my own words, following the motivation as I searched to name this new music in my fanzine 's' for Sartre, whom I was all over at the time, as though it was the law of the land that all secluded *NME*-reading teenagers embrace existentialism, that it is better to be a good journalist than a poor assassin. I was in the mood to change my Christian name to Verlaine, because of the French poet – 's' for the soul that is shaken by new feelings – and because of the New York guitarist – 's' for it seems so perfect, I see no evil – and because I felt like a new person, one finding all this fantastic stuff as though it was right in front of me, there for the taking in the distant, badly treated, apparently hopeless North. It was making it there on paper, in pages, on the radio, on TV and film, now and then in astonishing person.

Six weeks later, on 20 July, the Pistols returned, stronger, faster, harder, darker, on the way to becoming officially nationally notorious, tabloid tearaways, shambolic generators of magnetic queer space, with Johnny up front more experienced in the arts of taunting and leering and even at one point giving the audience a slow handclap, because we were slow, and backward, or because Malcolm, at the back of the venue, was encouraging him to do so. Or maybe he was copying Johnny. What came first – the genius of the singer or the genius of the manager? Or the genius of the audience . . .

I now had friends to go with, as if they had appeared in the few weeks since the last show, because we were part of a movement. I'd cut my hair short. The Lesser Free Trade Hall was now full of more-knowing fans already with shorter hair and narrower trousers and a lot more sectarian self-confidence paying a pound to see the ready, fiercely smart Buzzcocks and rowdy, not so smart Wythenshawe post-glam chancers Slaughter and the Dogs of Rabid Records. They'd got their name by telescoping Mick Ronson's solo album *Slaughter on 10th Avenue* and Bowie's *Diamond Dogs*, and that supplies all the information you need to imagine how they sounded, without the, you know, imaginative transcendence.

Somehow, Slaughter and the Dogs had got themselves above Buzzcocks on the tickets, as though they were more important. You can now see representations of one of the tickets to this show made into an art piece on the wall of an up-market Manchester city-centre hotel. Believe it or not, the five-star hotel exists in many ways because of this ticket, as if the new, high and hectic Manchester of the twenty-first century materialised magically around this scrap of paper.

There actually was, relatively speaking, someone famous at this show: passionate Cambridge-educated local TV personality Tony Wilson, obsessed with Manchester's pioneering and progressive credentials, looking more like a teacherly outsider snooping for some unspecified professional reasons than someone about to spike their hair and shed obvious floppy signs of the now reviled, soft-centred world of hippiness. He always claimed he had also been at the first show, because how could he have missed it if he knew what was happening? But it would have been impossible to miss him in a crowd of forty. He would get angry with those who pointed out he definitely hadn't been at the first one, perhaps even threatening the author of the book about the show, *I Swear I Was There*, that if he revealed what in this instance was unbendable truth, 'he'd never work in this town again'. Wilson did, though, manage to see them before their second Manchester appearance.

But mostly it was still a crowd of unknowns, including the reserved, deep-thinking, it turns out flash-tempered out-of-towner Ian Curtis, meeting people he had something in common with and totally ready to let the dead-ordinary but uncanny Rotten inspire him in what turned out to be the last four years of his life, as time spiralled dangerously out of control. The evening ended with some of the people he came across at the show deciding to form a group.

Because, as is obvious once time has passed, one surprising thing leads to another, the first Pistols show led to the second Pistols show, led to the most historic part of Wilson's eccentrically experimental pop arts TV show *So It Goes*, to bored, alive Buzzcocks' 'Spiral Scratch' – things starting from scratch – on the New Hormones label, Org 1, as an austere, beautiful emblem of the secret, principled and intelligent modern thinking that helped produce the very birth of indie, DIY thinking landing in the present, to Org 2, Linder Sterling and Jon Savage's *The Secret Public*, with glistening hints of the feminine sublime, because it wasn't all about the music, there was all this other stuff, told with images, graphics and oblique written clues, there was the meaning, the mythical, broken up and hidden and divine. To the endless, amodern and tentacular Fall, always falling in and out of shape, rockabilly rebels high on anarchy, flaunting their ragged independence, to Liz Naylor and Cath Carroll's all or nothing editions of *City Fun* furiously poking fun at the fucking cheek of fucking Wilson, the sick sacred monster the white male monolith a recuperated spectacularised revolutionary with his fucking political spin, his unremitting patriarchal authority, his shady bossiness, his Factory men, his demi-guild, his haute bohemian, architectonic packaging of dissatisfaction, desire and dissent putting up new barriers of exclusion, Liz and Cath having their own desire to 'occupy the factory', to release the children, feed the workers, create their own situations, to be listened to, to be important, leaving red-ink-stained tampons in the Haçienda men's toilets, I'll show your illustrious Lordship what a woman can do, feeling that one set of orthodoxies had merely been replaced by another, with an erasure of the queer spaces, a denying of their glorious peculiarity that the Pistols, the Slits and the Banshees had introduced to Manchester, to John Cooper Clarke nosing around inside language and the everyday somewhere between Allen Ginsberg and Victoria Wood, to Linder Sterling's Ludus songs of menstruation and her unmade menstrual egg timer (Fac 8, a glimpse of another Factory that never appeared), to the empty canvas Durutti Column primed with an overall hue of music, to the epic, neo-minimalist northern voodoo of the Passage, to the sinister-silly mock big head of Frank Sidebottom, to Magazine absurdly, fabulously using pop music to examine consciousness, to Factory, initially almost merely a late-night debating club, a drug den, and its sublime collection of misfits, anti-heroes, martyrs and prodigies, to the Haçienda performance nightclub as a gift rather than a commodity, as a shed in the backyard to hide from the missus, as so much playground space to lose yourself in because at first there were only a few loners setting foot inside, that fucking trendy place becoming an unlikely internationally minded emblem of the new post-industrial Manchester, as a new centre twenty years after the Twisted Wheel for white Manchester kids to dance to black imported house music selected and played by a new breed of local music expert, this new Manchester dancer going fucking mental to A Guy Called Gerald's 'Voodoo Ray', black Manchester darting into the party, showing off its own secrets, underpinning the Haçienda's own local anthem, 808 State's 'Pacific State', as high as the Haçienda got before the inevitable crash, people trying to sneak into the club through the air vents, before notoriety translated into celebrity, marginality into the mainstream, until it was driven out of business by bad books and lurking crooks, and turned into flat-pack designer living quarters, to those with something going for them for whom recognition did not come (the Worst, the Gay Animals, the Distractions, Dislocation Dance, Eric Random, the Diagram Brothers, Property of . . ., Spherical Objects, Cath Carroll, God's Gift, the Mothmen . . .), to the musical mind meld of guitar dreamer Johnny Marr and sweet and sour Morrissey, to their meltdown, to politically toxic headstrong Morrissey as punk's Rudyard Kipling, to Madchester as one crazy tabloid-friendly addition to modern thinking, as though the whole city was marinated in Ecstasy, to the Stone Roses at Spike Island gener-ously turning their fans into the real performers, to the aborted fucked-up drug-dealing bovver-pop fun times of the Happy Mondays, for Wilson somehow the missing link between Shakespeare and Bernard Manning, to the Gallagher brothers of edge of Stockport Burnage retro-roughing up modern thinking and coughing up the past, coming after all that to a pallid straight male, cocksure conclusion, representing the continuing dominance of all those white heterosexual local boys and boy groups that as Cath Carroll pointed out had 'never got over their first erection', a comprehensive crushing of the queer spaces vibrating from the Lesser Free Trade Hall to the pre-commodified dance hall of the Haçienda, but writing a song that became Manchester's 'My Way' as much as anything by Joy Division or the Smiths, to Carol Morley's *The Alcohol Years* – along the imaginary line, the fantasy catalogue, from the never-known Factory of Linder's unreal egg timer – picturing another phantom Haçienda as a bent, de-centred community in between paradise and purgatory, between remembered and forgotten, release and recovery, girl and voice, the one that must be built but didn't quite exist, to Manchester historically confirmed as a powerful pop city, with the paved heritage trails and endless anniversaries that follow, to a slapstick Dada *Carry On* film chronicling how this all happened leaning towards the view it was all based around the unhinged, accidentally unifying ego of Tony Wilson, who started looking like the whole city, or the city looked like him, to a post-modern, re-enchanting brand of civic pride, a scattered community of friends, the Haçienda officially demolished and replaced by a residential development, and what with one thing and another to *I'm a Celebrity . . . Get Me Out of Here!*, and not forgetting a lot of death, and more life, and more hotels, and the city becoming international one Monday night in May 2017, because of pop music community and violent vicious change out of extreme nowhere. Manchester had an immediate answer to a terrorist – and/or a catastrophically criminal – bombing, an answer that came as much from its musical history, a history of its people, its listeners, fans and makers and performers, as its political, social and radical history. It had its own way of doing, and saying, things, constantly alert to the pull and pressure of abrupt historical interruptions, from one kind of revolutionary thinking to another.

Part III: After

Nineteen: Meeting Tony Wilson off the telly

Fronti nulla fides. (Do not trust the appearance.)

Tony Wilson always finding something else, who can also be described as:
- able to drive and roll up at the same time
- improbable entrepreneur
- icon of hipsterism
- pub landlord
- Salford nancy boy
- a slap in the face of the ordinary
- keeping ideas of social change symbolically alive if nothing else
- well endowed with charm
- dad
- bad dad
- amazing dad
- permissive dad
- amoral dad
- given to employing esoteric jargon and impenetrable syntax
- acutely conscious of historical change and acutely aware of how to stage himself in relation to his historical moment
- as though Alex DeLarge as played by Malcolm McDowell in *A Clockwork Orange* was reading the news
- interviewing Victoria Wood at the Opera House and trying to make some small talk with her about a Neil Young concert there in 1973 and she has no idea what he's talking about
- the stubborn self-conscious myth-maker who used social media techniques to generate attention and distort reality decades before there was social media, believing that new social relations always demanded a new space, and vice versa, who felt that panic and failure generated their own kind of useful energy, that theories were just tools to use in the production of knowledge, a thinking man

ahead of his time – truth does not exist! – and knowing it and making something of it
- possessing a flawed and/or perfectly reasonable theory that pop music unfolds in predictable thirteen-year cycles
- nothing if not a follower of fashion
- emotional vampire
- merry prankster
- playboy philosopher
- financially strapped
- devious auteur
- gregarious loner
- acid casualty deciding, wearing a mask of Max Weber, that if science, modernity and rationalism disenchanted the world and swept it clear of gods, spirits and magic (or problematised believing in them), then psychedelics offered a potential way out of the ensuing existential impasse
- bloody-minded sensationalist
- halfway to megalomania
- a scarred veteran of the age of revolution
- banging on about his pet subjects like a broken record
- perpetually hosting a masterclass in the art of being Tony Wilson

He was the first person off the television I ever met, at a time when that seemed an impossible thing to ever happen.

He was the first person off the television I ever became friends with, and then sort of fell out with, and then just knew on and off until he died. As long as I knew him, whatever happened in his life and between us, I never really lost that vaguely star-struck, unnerved feeling, all rooted in being initially stunned that the well-known Granada television star would come to my house in the first few months I got to know him.

I can't remember the exact first time I met Wilson, which is strange because I'd watched him on television for years and seen him hovering suspiciously at pop concerts, hovering in the distance like an exotic wild hunting animal. Somehow, out of nowhere, and off the telly, he was part of my life. The force of nature crept into my life. It was perhaps one of his conjuring tricks: slipping past the initial wariness you might have felt, ultimately flattering you because he expressed an interest in what you were doing, and then, there he was. Using you maybe, but also, undoubtedly, helping you.

I can't remember how it happened, and what we said — although I imagine he said a lot to me, and I said very little, not yet used to speaking to anyone outside my immediate environment, let alone someone famous, with a mouth that could drink the Mersey. I imagine I was so shy, faced with the fame from the telly, that I said next to nothing to him as he threw words and razzle-dazzle all over me, or I was drunk and tried to keep up with him, as if I could use words too, and had some dazzle of my own. I don't believe I ever had a comfortable face-to-face conversation with him, because I wasn't sure if he was playing a game I didn't know the rules of, or I was playing a game I didn't know the rules of, because I thought that's how you had to behave in his company.

I lived within a couple of miles' walking distance of a pub called the Oaks. Here, where Didsbury bordered Chorlton, almost as soon as mysterious new London groups were forming, eager local lad Rob Gretton would be booking them to appear. This meant in 1976, in the weeks and months after the Sex Pistols showed up in town with something never seen or heard before, groups like Siouxsie and the Banshees, the Adverts and the Slits were playing the small upstairs room on a stage so tiny it wasn't even a stage, giving a few intrepid locals a sense of what it must have been like to encounter the Velvet Underground play their very early shows in New York ten years before. The experience was, again, something other than music. It involved performance and appearance, a rearrangement, an intensification, of reality that seemed a continuation of what David Bowie had been proposing, mixing witchcraft and rhythm as he shuffled identities and styles in the early 1970s.

I'd walk home on my own from the Oaks after a performance that had been closer to a dream I once had than a rock gig, mind racing, working

out what had just happened, feeling I had been allowed in on some wonderful secret, something I would keep to myself and yet somehow share.
As I walked through deserted streets, I made plans about what to do next,
and what might happen next, which would become the thoughts I had
about what had just happened, which would turn into writing, which
would turn into belonging.

My late-night walks making sense of changing times and a changing
Manchester would, via the *NME*, take me to Stuttgart in Germany, into
a small room backstage at some anonymous hall where I would meet and
interview Patti Smith, something I was just about prepared for having
encountered Siouxsie Sioux, Gaye Advert and Ari Up of the Slits inside a
grimy, nondescript pub in Chorlton, suddenly given psychedelic properties which would stay with me once I had walked back home.

It would all be transformed into a weird new confidence, embellished
by my time with Patti Smith, which would lead to another meeting when
she was in Manchester to film a performance on *The Old Grey Whistle Test*.
I was taken to a room in the kind of Manchester hotel I had never previously had the nerve, or money, to enter, and she emerged through a door
as if she had been discussing Celtic culture and the British lack of interest
in philosophical debate with the ghost of Engels. At least, that's what I
thought as I walked home ears ringing, brain buzzing from seeing the first
shows played by local bands with names like the Fall, who as soon as they
began playing seemed to know exactly what they wanted to do with noise,
words and rhythm, and how they would make themselves known.

Manchester had changed, and by May 1977, as if I had made some
sort of move from rags to riches, I was writing for the *NME* about how
Manchester's very particular take on punk had created what could only
be described as a scene. The best of the new Manchester groups sounded
nothing like the Sex Pistols, or the Slits, or the Clash, or Television, or
any of the other punk groups coming to the city, but they were as much
of a shock to the senses. I had for real become a Manchester writer and
needed to open a bank account to pay in the cheques I was being sent from
London, mainly for listening to records and going to gigs. This wasn't the

path a careers adviser at school would have suggested for how to become a journalist.

A review of the Buzzcocks in a run-down hall along Deansgate near the inscrutable John Rylands Library was the first piece I had published, in the magazine I had set my heart on writing for since I was thirteen, a magazine which from the outside seemed full of outsiders and which regularly whispered in my ear, reaching into my brain, *This is the way to step outside*. It all made complete sense – Buzzcocks in Deansgate, the centre of Manchester, an instant update of local history, this linking of minds and music inside the sort of mythical Manchester Wilson contained and explored inside his imagination – but wouldn't occur to me for years, decades even.

Wilson, though, was looking, and could see what was happening, and couldn't wait to get involved, and for all I knew was even making a lot of these things happen. Up to then, he'd felt chained, famous but contained, charging around Manchester looking for something to do, even though he already had plenty to do – a full-time job, a secure career – so something else to do, to fill a head that needed so much stimulation and newness. He found security through getting something done; accomplishing something made him feel worthwhile. Once that was done, something else. 'Knowing is not enough,' he would say, wearing a mask of Johann Wolfgang von Goethe; 'we must apply. Willing is not enough; we must do.'

One day I came home from some random task or aimless wander through the shopping precinct – or, in my stunning new role, an interview with a transgressive New York rock poetess – to be told by my mum, even more star-struck than me, that Tony Wilson off the telly had been round, turning up out of the blue, knocking on the door and asking if I wanted to come out and play, and he waited for a while before he had to leave, to look for someone else to play with, to bother – who knows – to offer some cryptic opportunity to.

He even helped her try and fix the leaky tap in our badly soiled kitchen sink. Or was there a plumber already there, so awe-struck by the sudden arrival of someone off the holy telly that he made a hasty retreat, or finished the job and left without asking for money, rewarded enough by the sight of someone famous? Even in our house, the facts of the event got twisted in truth-testing Tony time, as if Wilson had this effect on those around him, changing reality, or our perception of it, as he passed through.

Did Linder Sterling, who created and collaged the mysteriously masked and sexualised covers for fantastic early records by Buzzcocks and Magazine and became muse to an infatuated Morrissey, or vice versa, come along with Tony and sketch some detail of our front room, where on faded, peeling, moss-green wallpaper that seemed to have been there since before the Second World War I'd pinned a 'Holidays in the Sun' Sex Pistols poster?

My mum was excited enough to act as though she had just been visited by Burton and Taylor, adorning the mundane back streets of Stockport with shocking glamour, and was forgetting the details within hours but remembering the event. Oddly enough, she said Wilson reminded her of Mike Baldwin, a character from *Coronation Street* – a charming cockney wide boy who happened to be the boss of the underwear factory.

'I made them a cup of tea. He was lovely. We had a lovely chat. I told him that my dad was a lifelong pipe smoker. He told me how his mum taught him to make perfect mashed potato by whisking them in front of an open door.' It all seemed a bit odd. What were Tony and Linder doing together? Wasn't Linder with Buzzcocks singer Howard Devoto? What did Tony call my mum – her name, Dilys, or Mrs Morley? Darling? Because he could go through life never calling you by your real name, and 'darling' came easy to him. Odd indeed.

It made my mum's day at a time when little could, what with the recent death of her husband and a general collapse of everyday reason. (I think of my recently widowed mum being old when he popped round for tea, but she was only forty at the time, with perhaps grief adding some years, the sort of time which cannot be measured and which you never recover, and a face that didn't know whether to laugh or cry from moment to moment.)

The fact there was a Pistols poster on the wall featuring a safety-pinned Queen was perhaps the one vivid demonstration that my dad was very much no longer around. In many ways, his timing was extraordinary – punk rock could not have happened in my house in the way it did if he had still been around, what with visiting musicians treating the place a little like a squat and a general sense of domestic anarchy. The thought of him meeting Tony Wilson is as unlikely as him meeting Harold Wilson, and someone who reacted with distaste to much of what he came across on *Top of the Pops* while I sat there watching like I'd seen the light would have considered the Sex Pistols to be a revolting, temporary aberration. In some senses he was correct.

My dad left before we had to have any sort of conversation about my new preoccupations, departed with a permanence that put everything in perspective, even though I put off acknowledging that for a while, more particularly what came next, which I very quickly and possibly before anyone else called 'post-punk', which was a more successful name for something than my previous 's' rock, if only because my new name was in the pages of the *New Musical Express*.

My mum smiled about the day Tony visited for the rest of her life. Wilson of course moved through the public, his viewers, fully aware of the near-priestly powers he had, years before he crossed over as Factory boss into being more widely famous, and more fanatically received, if only in the music papers and non-broadcasting spheres of cultural provocation. Even if what was left of our family forgot the details, we knew it must have happened, because Linder left behind her poetic sketch of our unpoetic front room, as though it might be something that had somehow been made into history, even if the very distant, ragged edges.

Wilson emerged as a responsible if slightly irreverent face of television as it rapidly replaced religion as a central national source of mental and spiritual support, at practised softening, perhaps condescending ease, while his slightly awed parishioners were barely able to look him in the eye. This was a time around Manchester when people would stand to attention when a local TV presenter walked into the room, as though they were royalty, not ultimately a journalist, a breed that usually didn't impress people so much. They were celebrities in the way pop stars were, even if they wore the ties of politicians and the sweaters of ageing sportsmen. There are hundreds of thousands of such characters inside the millions of moving panels making up YouTube. In the 1970s there were just a few eccentric examples making themselves at home in your home.

Bless you, my child, but do not be overwhelmed by my outsized smooth-skinned TV-given grace. I come from the illuminated heavens of television, but I'm completely down to earth, actually really from dark, cramped rooms above a humble local corner shop infused with an earthy, damp aroma selling Woodbine, Swan Vesta and St Bruno ready rubbed. I may seem holy but actually I'm quite homely. Milk and two sugars, please, and yes, I'd love a custard cream, darling.

'If you have charm,' Tony Wilson would say, wearing a mask of the author of *Peter Pan*, James Barrie, 'you don't need to have anything else; and if you don't have it, it doesn't matter what else you have.'

Of course, knowing where I lived – in a drab, run-down house stuck on a gloomy street – and how I lived, in what conditions – suffering from the inescapable consequences of a suicide in the family – made me feel he had a certain power over me, and that if life was a game, and of course in his eyes it was, then he would always have the advantage over me because of his understanding of where I came from. Another reason to be oddly anxious in his presence. Come to think of it, I would feel the same sensation standing within a few feet of the Sex Pistols as they blasted me in the face using guitar riffs as revolutionary banners, a feeling that, when it came to life, even though I had just been very close to death, I didn't know the half of it. I had so much to learn.

So it goes.

Vini Reilly, Durutti Column guitar poet, permanent Factory act, friend

We didn't watch television in our house until my dad passed away. He didn't want a TV in the house, but as soon as we got one me and my sister would be watching Tony Wilson, hosing down elephants, doing parachute jumps, somehow cool and funny. Very different. I saw him for

the first time at the Wythenshawe Forum when Slaughter and the Dogs played. I didn't speak to him. There was no chance I would approach him, he seemed from another world. I'd known Alan Erasmus around Wythenshawe and Moss Side, and I was at Alan's place one night and Tony came round. I was very depressed at the time. I'd had two spells of bad depression, and I was in one of those stages when I wasn't interested in anything. People were irrelevant. Not even the man off the telly suddenly turning up made any difference. I didn't even say hello to him. I think this intrigued him.

Steve Coogan

When I was growing up, he was just part of the landscape. So I would see him all the time on the television, which is where he seemed to belong. And then he actually came to a party at our house. My auntie used to be a make-up artist at Granada TV, and she borrowed my parents' big house in Middleton to throw a party for her twenty-first. Me and my brother were sat on the stairs looking at people arrive, and he came through the door, and I remember turning to my brother and saying, 'Oh my God, it's Tony Wilson.' There was Lewis Collins and Diane Keen from the sitcom Cuckoo Waltz. Granada royalty. Thirty years later he came to the house for a series he was making called Celebration about local people made good. He was interviewing my parents, and as he came through the door he said, 'I'm sure I once came to a party near here.' And my mum said, 'It was this house.'

Carol Morley, film director, writer, Haçienda regular in the early to mid-1980s, fan of the early Happy Mondays, sister of the author of this book

When I first met him, or Tony first met me, I was fourteen, and so it was post-Joy Division, and I think it was pre-New Order. They hadn't got a name yet, and there was a rumour they were doing a gig in Rochdale, at Rochdale Art College. Me and a few friends went there, not many in the audience, and Tony was on the mixing desk, and I went up to him, and I went, 'I'm going to be on Factory Records when I grow up.' And

*he went, 'Good girl, good girl.' He was famous, and he was in Rochdale,
with the rest of us. Somehow it was both odd and ordinary.*

Terry Christian

*The first time I ever saw Tony Wilson in the flesh, in the late 1970s, he
came down to a local club I was at to do the raffle, dressed like your
dad as though he thought he was cool. He'd had Steel Pulse on one of
his TV shows, and he'd plugged a gig they were playing which I then
went to, and I went up to him and said, 'You should put more reggae
on TV.' I'm some snotty-nosed little kid wearing a '70s-style suit like my
mum has dressed me for Mass and I'm having a cheeky dig, but he's still
paying attention to me. This gave me a weird idea of what people in the
media would be like, because he wasn't stuck up at all. He would seem
interested in what you were saying even if he had something else on his
mind. You could rib him, and he didn't seem bothered.*

Gonnie Rietveld, Quando Quango programmer, academic, writer

*I came to Manchester from Rotterdam in 1979, '80, with my boyfriend
Mike Pickering. We had formed a band together, and it was a complete
culture shock for me when I arrived. It's all obvious, but it was boring,
it was cold, I didn't think there would be much of a difference – it was
European after all. I was a middle-class Dutch girl, and it just seemed
really conservative, and there didn't seem much going on. And I was just
amazed at the amount of carpet everywhere – pubs, shops, homes, even
those making weird avant-garde music had homes covered in flowery
carpets, with little dishes hanging on flowery wallpaper in the hall. You'd
go and watch Bauhaus in some mucky little club in town and you'd be
standing on sticky carpet. It made no sense. Unlike others in the North
I first saw Tony in the flesh, not on TV, because we were non-paying
lodgers at his friend Rob Gretton's house, and he would pop round –
some guy I was told ran an interesting local label, like it was just one of
those things. And then I saw him on television reading the news, and I
was like, 'Is that Tony?' Everyone would laugh – for them, he was almost*

like on a pedestal; for me it was like, 'What's that bloke Rob knows doing on TV?'

Jon Savage, *Sounds* journalist, Factory collaborator, friend, author of *England's Dreaming*

I was training to be a solicitor in London, still living with my parents, but I fell in love with Manchester punk because London punk had burnt itself out by 1977. I wanted to do something other than what my parents were desperately leading me towards, and I called Tony Wilson from an office at the solicitors where I worked, and he invited me up for an interview at Granada TV. I got a job as a researcher, and before you know it I'm helping out Tony Wilson, living in his house for a couple of months while I found somewhere, and I remember the first thing he said to me was, 'We're not like London – we smoke dope and we like the first Public Image album.' I thought, Well, I can do that. *He was fantastically glamorous to me. He was a golden boy with this floppy hair, a few years older than me, clearly in the know about a lot of things. There was something homoerotic there, I'm not denying that – and we had one thing in common which was very rare then: we had both been to Cambridge University, but we were interested in pop culture, obsessed, you could say. That was incredibly unusual. He could be very careless about people and he could be a bully. But he was quite Warholian at that time, in that he provided an outlet for people – he was a catalyst, and he provided an arena which allowed for possibilities, for experimentation.*

Andy Harries

I'd grown up in Peterborough, went to university in Hull, and I remember when I first came to Manchester in 1976 – it was very late 1976 – one of the things that most thrilled me was there was a pizzeria. In fact, there were two pizzerias in town. I mean, I thought this was fantastic because there were no pizzerias for sure where I'd come from. It's weird to think now it was such a big deal. I was twenty-two years old, I think, when I started working with Tony at Granada. And he seemed incredibly

*charismatic, he seemed incredibly smart, he was very funny, he was very
eccentric. I became very friendly with him, but it was quite hard to really
get close to Tony because he will never really sit down and tell you about
his life, and I was always a bit baffled by his endless girlfriends and I
think, sexually, he was quite strange. I'm not saying he was in any way
gay, but he had a certain fluidity about it that was very unusual, a little
uncertain. When his dad came out it was tough for him to handle, and he
would always process these things in his own way.*

Andy Spinoza, writer, publicist, Wilson collaborator

*I'd come to Manchester because of the writing and photographs of what
was happening in the late 1970s – that had to be the place to head to. I
was a student in the early 1980s, and on the student union noticeboard I
saw a subtle little notice for the Fabian Society advertising Tony Wilson
and some local MP talking about the media. It was in someone's house,
someone's front room. We were ushered in and there was a dozen or so
people, say, on sofas. I remember him sat cross-legged on the floor, and
he was talking about how when he writes reports about the IRA for
Granada he always called them Irish freedom fighters. 'It would always
be changed back to terrorists,' he said, 'but you must never forget that
there is more than one way of seeing things.' Afterwards I asked if I
could interview him for the student newspaper, and he gave me twenty
minutes, already helping out when he didn't have to. When I got home
the tape was ruined and you couldn't hear him, which was a sort of
metaphor for a Tony fuck-up.*

Twenty: History, libraries and brotherhood for a better world

Felix qui potuit rerum cognoscere causa. (Blessed is he who has been able to know the causes of things.)

When he lived in Marple as a boy, Tony was ten miles from the centre of Manchester, connected by labouring bus and rail still following strict, tidy, Victorian routes, nearby but apart, and the idea of Manchester could slowly form in his mind, be made up from occasional, inspiring visits to music venues, shops, museums, Old Trafford and magical libraries as he grew into his teens. It was a place his mother loved, passing on her pride and knowledge of the city to her son, telling him stories, planting the idea in his mind. His mum and dad, on their visits into town from Marple, made him think from a very early age of Manchester as 'a groovy city. I remember my mum and dad coming home with a programme after seeing *West Side Story*. We were the pre-run of London's West End in the early '60s. My mother loved going into Manchester to see friends, have coffee, sit in the grand Midland Hotel, queen of all she surveyed.'

For a long time, Manchester was somewhere he visited, as an outsider, building it up as he went along, the Big City, Lancashire, where the modern world began, the dream destination, all that history and endeavour. His future. He would make it there. Act like he owned the place. Become part of its story. Make sure that story was printed one way or another.

Once he'd made it there, and it became his home and mission and he began burying his memories there, to find later or leave for other people to find, Wilson appreciated how the ruined spaces in the 1970s city were like haphazard images that recombined as though in a dream, how random buildings built in different centuries standing in curious relationship to each other possessed an indefinable emotional charge. It was a place where fortuitous accidents could take place – turning a corner might change events, produce unexpected meetings – with something of a magical quality. As French activist and poet Ivan Chtcheglov wrote, in a growing city 'three steps cannot be taken without encountering ghosts, bearing all the prestige of their legends'.

Around the bus-packed commercial city centre, where the destruction was intermittent, and you could frequent the relatively orderly comfort of Woolworth's and John Lewis, pass underneath a modest smattering of metropolitan sky-scraping modernism, and stroll through Piccadilly Gardens, which actually became more blighted in the twenty-first century, there was a ring of ruins, wasteland and derelict spaces, cul-de-sacs and vacant lots smothered with weeds, rubbish and broken glass, emphasised to the south by the clustered ghost houses and crumbling ghost estates of shattered, dilapidated Hulme, Moss Side, Longsight and Rusholme. Places no one would choose to live in, where you just found yourself, stunted streets packed with rows of uniform dull red-brick houses grinding together, loaded with surface tension and hidden networks, laced with camouflaged spaces incubating the sort of intensive, insider, sometimes desperate creative activity that would one day make it to the city centre and help remake the city. It seems impossible to talk about such places without using the word 'edgy', and I'm not able to avoid it now. Eventually, a jump in continuity and the less impacted, leaf-lined, decent brick houses of Chorlton, Whalley Range and Didsbury, some of them villa-sized, take over, more congenial but still concealing secrets, sedition and freaks.

In the more ruined areas, bordered by tatty blankness and the end of days represented by uneven pavements and tired brick walls, on the way to concert halls, ad hoc venues and punk clubs in locations where the city seemed to have fallen apart, your senses would be weirdly jolted, your sense of the present disrupted by powerful sensations from the past not yet extinguished by monotonous but clean new buildings and a general cosmetic tidying-up and reordering. The music at these venues seemed more heightened and all-consuming by being at the end of often nervous, isolated walks, on bombed sites and inside collapsing boundaries where relentless capitalism, warfare, defective town planning or general political indifference had resulted in desolate or possibly deviant spaces, many of them doomed to disappear in time. The music, all of this determination and concentration, the making of transcendent mental spaces, was what could save us from the crippled, treacherous world.

Some of us came to this understanding years after the event; Wilson seemed aware of it all in the 1970s, in his twenties, or more aware than most – tuned in to the massed haunted ruins of the twentieth century, the matter out of place, the spilling over of mystery and the esoteric, the marginality associated with transgression, the consequences of certain social and cultural processes, with particular attention paid to the weird mixtures of materials and substances, objects and illusions, absence and presence in and around Manchester.

The sturdy, stoical Town Hall on Albert Square was at the centre of the many routes Wilson would take as he marched through the compact city centre on some urgent errand or other, striding through time and criss-crossing his own emerging destiny, sensing a city yet to come, engaging in illegible improvisations. To me in the mid-1970s the Town Hall was simply an old building that exuded little but dense permanence and a cryptic internal functionality. *Mind your own business*, it seemed to be saying. *Nothing here for you. Move on.* For Wilson the building expressed a mood, a collection of moods over time, all the time it had been standing there, and what had happened around it and would happen around it in the future. It was like a few verses of a poem that was still being written, constantly being compiled in different volumes as new buildings and a succession of pasts and presents stacked up around it.

The foundation stone was laid in 1868, and it took nine years to build; a hundred years later, nine years would take Tony Wilson from boyishly starting as prodigious educated local at Cambridge University to the punk-hinged second series of his innovative television pop show *So It Goes* – still contemporary-seeming in its ragged, whimsical mix of signals and signatures when it was shown again forty years later.

Wilson saw the beauty, soaked in history, of a building ingeniously fitted into an awkward triangular plot, created by an arrangement of pleasing angles and deliberately arranged ornamentation, conceived in the

Victorian Gothic revival style featuring appropriated aspects of thirteenth-century England. The exterior is dominated by a 285-feet-high clock tower and decorated with carvings of significant local figures. It seems to be solid stone but is brick-clad with hard Yorkshire sandstone known as Sprinkwell Stone from quarries near Bradford, the other side of the Pennines. The Town Hall's eminent architect, Alfred Waterhouse, specialist in Victorian Gothic and responsible for the Natural History Museum in London, explained that he chose these materials because he needed to combat 'the evil influences of the peculiar climate of Manchester'. The intention was for the stone to resist what was already being described as acid rain – another first for Manchester, as the industrial pollution of the time rapidly caused stones and bricks to crumble. The glass for the windows and skylights was also carefully chosen to allow the most light into the building on the North-West's regular dull days.

Inside, past statues of great locals and coats of arms of Manchester's former trading destinations, surrounded by the utilitarian corridors that reflected the municipal function of the building, there was the richly decorated and baronial Great Hall, one of the great public spaces in Manchester, where Waterhouse commissioned some daring murals from Ford Madox Brown. Brown shared the ideals of the Pre-Raphaelite Brotherhood, a Victorian avant-garde artistic movement that combined meticulous precision and heightened majesty, fascinated by medieval culture, preferring the volatile sense-spinning detail of art before the softening elegance of Raphael and the Renaissance. Millionaire businessmen in Manchester looking to bring art and culture into the raucous upstart city, to demonstrate there was class among the foul, belching, money-making and lung-wrecking smoke, particularly liked this epic, ostentatiously colourful style, and another brotherhood, the Ancoats Brotherhood, helped Brown get the commission to paint the walls of the Great Hall.

The Ancoats Brotherhood was formed by local socialist councillor, philanthropist, social reformer and art dealer Charles Rowley, based on a popular series of Sunday lectures and rambling and cycling clubs he organised. An enlightened, idealistic member of the Free Libraries Commission,

Rowley aimed to introduce the struggling, densely packed working people of Manchester to poetry, art and literature.

Ancoats, to the east of the city centre, is often credited with being the world's first industrial suburb. Cramped back-to-back houses built on a Georgian grid plan over former corn fields and garden cottages were set alongside new factories and workshops. It was the first residential area intended to be occupied solely by the new urban working class, and its residents suffered the consequence of industrial expansion before most: a squalid, nasty, brutish and short life. The first industrial suburb quickly became Manchester's first slum, described by Engels as 'a densely populated and unlovely tract'. Not quite the 'fullest classic perfection' that he claimed could be achieved by the proletariat in the city.

People, whatever the squalor of their lives, Victorian philanthropic thinking went, must in some mysterious way become possessed of a desire for beauty, even if it was filtered through middle-class standards and tastes. Bringing culture to the people was deemed to be one way of inspiring that desire. This nineteenth-century socialist dream of the cultural elevation of the working class, what Rowley called 'the best in way of art and recreation for the people', is one hint of the subsequent growth of popular culture, in which socialist do-gooders have competed often forlornly with an aggressive leisure industry for the attention of the working class.

For figures such as Rowley, popular culture was too important to be left solely in the hands of the promoters of commercial entertainment, who excited appetites and created fictitious needs merely to generate and then exploit consumers. The working class must not be left to find all its pleasure in the crammed pit of a madcap music hall before returning to gruelling, mindless toil. What about the acquisition of knowledge and a true, liberating freedom from the drudgery of work? Pleasure – true and rational pleasure – as the end and aim of existence.

The Ancoats Brotherhood, a small band of enthusiasts, planned all sorts of ways from the fantastic to the futile to raise the intellectual tone of the workers of Manchester. Poet Matthew Arnold, 'giving some taste of the best that has been thought, done and said', was one ancestor of Factory

Records, the ragged and illogical manifestation of Wilson's plans. Arnold was a key Victorian proponent of the belief that the value of art lay in its ability to effect moral or social improvement in the viewer.

What became Wilson's awkward squad of schemers, dreamers and activists heralding new attitudes was definitely a brotherhood: former insurance man, fanzine writer, combative band manager, martial arts enthusiast and knowledgeable, discriminating music enthusiast Rob Gretton; absurdly erudite designer and typographical stylist Peter Saville, soon mostly on the phone from London; radically introspective, deviant producer Martin Hannett, self-obsessively turning loneliness, estrangement, threat into echoed sound; and elusive, creative facilitator and tangential motivator Alan Erasmus. Joined together by the man off the telly, who was excited about creating something or just excited about being excited, whose acid experiences had led to the sort of bodacious head trip in which, as much as he could, he would put things back into the stream of history and of human consciousness. Wilson had learnt his trade in television, and put together his outfit like a television production crew, everyone with a specific role: cameraman, sound man, graphics, researcher and, fronting everything, all mouth and espousing, the presenter/producer.

'We cannot seek achievement for ourselves,' he would say, coming down from a trip during which he imagined he had interviewed the American Latino folk hero, Civil Rights activist and labour organiser César Chávez, 'and forget about progress and prosperity for our community.'

The Factory brotherhood began with a depressed phone call. Wilson's friend and drug-taking partner Erasmus was not making much money from acting, and was looking to do something more than just look for work and daydream. On the stag night for Wilson's first marriage, in a Failsworth pub, fuelled by Dutch speed, they saw a covers cabaret band, a bunch of eighteen-year-olds called Flashback; at the beginning of 1977 this was already a rewind-sounding name for a new group needing to seem ready for punk with its rigorous artistic standards. By the time they'd become the not-much-better Fast Breeder, as if they might con their way into fashion, Erasmus was their manager, on the hunt for extra forms of income, an unsung expert in not being entirely sure what he was looking for. Fast Breeder weren't anything great, he knew, but you've got to start somewhere. The group started to write their own songs, and one or two sounded like they might be on to something.

On 24 January 1978 – which is why many Wilson-associated businesses were named after 24 January – Alan rang Tony to tell him that he'd been muscled out of the group along with two band members: drummer Chris Joyce and guitarist David Rowbotham. He wasn't sure what to do next and was feeling frustrated. Alan and Tony often had the best conversations in the world while the city slept, time beautifully squandered as whole worlds were formed and forgotten. This time the conversation drifted towards some sort of purpose.

Wilson, busy enough but with time on his hands, at that moment unintentionally and reluctantly talked himself into the music business by suggesting, just to cheer his friend up, that they form a band around the two remaining members, adding gentle star-gazing local lad Vini Reilly, the uncommonly talented guitarist from daft punks Ed Banger and the Nosebleeds – a temporary stopping point for Morrissey. One thing led to another, and Wilson found himself managing a band – more of a flexible assembly of disparate freelance musicians – that he called Durutti Column.

'We are not in the least afraid of ruins. We who ploughed the prairies and built the cities can build again, only better next time. We carry a new world, here in our hearts' – railway worker and trade unionist Buenaventura Durruti, definitive working-class hero symbolising the insurrectionist spirit of Spanish anarchism during the Spanish Civil War.

When the new group needed a place to play, Erasmus asked the alleged owner – 'some white gangster hipster' – if they could rent a grimy but lively late-night club set up for the mostly black neighbourhood that he went to in Hulme, little more than a low-slung brick shed surrounded by run-down houses and estates, isolated as though permanently from Manchester. The

Factory nights began there on 19 May 1978 – Durutti Column supported by Jilted John, the alias of madcap local drama student Graham Fellows, on the verge of an eponymously titled teen-drama novelty hit on Rabid Records. This was the first hit produced by Rabid's Martin Hannett, soon to become Factory's house producer; Factory was in the process of emerging from Rabid, one very pragmatic, hard-boiled, hustling Manchester being replaced by an oblique, provisional one, one always ready to be formed.

There was a scruffy poster announcing the opening night, with at the top 'The next music begins at The Factory' and at the bottom a line taken from a situationist pamphlet: '*Je me promène. Principalement je me promène.*' I drift. Mainly I drift. This drifting, this reflective drifting, being open to the unexpected – and the re-enchanting of scorned, marginalised spaces like Hulme – was the beginning of a new Manchester. The poster does not look like it is announcing a new Manchester, although later posters put together by Peter Saville would, as if their job was to imagine changing the look of a city and to influence the future, not advertise some obscure group with a target audience of about sixty in a one-storey venue in the bricked-up back streets of the back and beyond where time, most of the time, stood still.

Chris Joyce would later become the drummer in Manchester's biggest chart act of the 1980s, Simply Red. Dave Rowbotham, an eccentric, reclusive character who contributed to great records by the Mothmen and Pauline Murray and the Invisible Girls, was found dead in his Burnage flat in 1991, bludgeoned to death with a plasterer's hammer. Everyone who had known him was questioned by the police, including a shocked Tony Wilson, who had long lost touch, and an unshockable Shaun Ryder, who wrote a Happy Mondays song called 'Cowboy Dave' about the unsolved crime. Erasmus says he knows who did it, and they got away with it.

So it goes.

Factory began preliminary operations – based on various daydreams, all-night discussions, messy arguments and smoking late-night theories about what the perfect nightclub or record label could be – in a flat on Mersey Road where Erasmus lived with Charles Sturridge, who at twenty-eight, a last-minute replacement for Michael Lindsay-Hogg plucked from *Coronation Street*, directed *Brideshead Revisited*, Granada's lavish eleven-part series based on Evelyn Waugh's reflective 1945 novel about a rapidly disappearing world and how the dreams of youth change with time and you have to face up to sterner reality as you grow up. *Brideshead* would win an Emmy for its graphics, and Wilson would make a point of how those early Saville posters and *Brideshead* both came out of the same flat. 'Genius,' he would say, wearing a mask of Vladimir Nabokov, 'is finding the invisible link between things.'

Factory's premises soon became the scruffy but large-roomed second-floor flat Erasmus moved to at number 86 Palatine Road in Didsbury, 'home to professionals, drug dealers and musicians for fifty years'. Palatine Road crosses the Mersey, and therefore exists in both Lancashire and Cheshire; Factory was north of the river, inside the Lancashire part, in an unpretty house that in the 1970s seemed solidly, neutrally planted in time, but which would gradually be reached by the city's creeping gentrification.

As things got more serious at Factory, once the brotherhood had started organising itself into an almost perfect anti-organisation, the working day starting at ten with a joint, those who ended up, because it was the way things were done then, making the coffee and answering the phone were left out of the photos and the history but had their own dreams and plans and feeling of involvement. There was Rob's future wife Lesley, Tony's then wife Lindsay, and informal receptionist Tracey. Without whom there would have been no Factory, but there was no space for them among the musketeers loudly shouting and noisily, or quietly, making themselves up. Perhaps the women were too grown-up and self-aware to bother with the immature games the men seemed to be playing, so obsessed with music and art it could seem naive and adolescent. Nerds *in extremis*.

Perhaps the women were shoved out of the way by those who took it for granted they were the authors, and the rest were merely assistants, at best one-step-under collaborators. Girlfriends. Wives. It was a failure of imagination, even though it would never have occurred to the men that this was the case, so thoroughly were they socialised, even in the times' more fluid, precocious cultural margins, to go along with how things were. Gallantry, sometimes love, perhaps sex, would, they vaguely felt, somehow compensate for their ignorance.

This was a time when Norman Mailer would describe Susan Sontag as a 'lady writer', when Johnny Cash would introduce Joni Mitchell on his TV show by saying 'how lovely' she looked. Imagine him introducing Dylan by saying he was looking mighty pretty. The girlfriend of the guitarist in early, ferociously uncompromising Birmingham punk racket the Prefects, part of the Clash's 'White Riot' tour, was tasked with wiping off the spit that smothered his guitar following the inevitable shower of gob.

Until the Slits, Poly Styrene, Siouxsie and other fe-punks took advantage of the punk resetting of musical history to zero, when, between amateur and art, imagination and energy were as important as conventional musical knowledge, female singers and all women rock bands were still labelled, as though they were in on it, 'chicks'. As Tony Wilson might have said, if he'd been thinking about it, wearing a mask of bell hooks, 'When it came to issues of gender, men who might be radical thinkers in other ways were as sexist as their conservative cohorts.'

Even before it was certified as the first Factory headquarters, the Didsbury flat already existed as a great place to hang out, the ad hoc south Manchester beginnings of the city-centre Factory-run clubs, venues and bars to come, somewhere to meet up, listen to music, smoke dope continually, take acid and have visions, and talk about what could happen next.

'At the time you would take acid to understand the mind as much as anything,' said Tony's close friend Neville, an oft-consulted invisible energy at the edges of Factory. 'This was in the spirit of the Beatles going to India, the Stones going to Morocco. It was freaky before it was New Age. Fifty years later it would end up with Spice being all over Manchester, crushing the mind, sapping the will, but in our day it was all about opening the doors of perception, finding difference, seeking truth and hanging on.'

A boys' club, for sure, and it could have stayed just as fanciful boy talk, but the talk almost to everyone's surprise turned into action. Individually, the brotherhood could only get up to so much, but together, somehow, they produced a different kind of activism from their drifting and dreaming, phoning and listening, and occasional tripping and giggling, watching and organising. They didn't think they were ignoring the values and virtues of the women; they just felt that in this setting their friends, making these sorts of plans, sharing these kinds of secrets, getting close because of ideas not feelings, were men. Alan and Tony making plans for Factory became the history, whereas Lindsay and Tony's plans, which to Lindsay were the same sort of talk, made on the same sort of drugs, were never acknowledged as being for Factory. That was just pillow talk.

'Of a perfect society,' Wilson would say, wearing a mask of Montaigne, 'friendship is the peak.'

Ford Madox Brown, another Factory ancestor, another Shakespeare obsessive like Wilson, an egalitarian celebrator of the endeavours of the victimised working class, moved his family up from London to create the twelve murals in the Great Hall of the Town Hall. New to the city, he identified with its energy and dissident spirit and found it a good place to live and work. Researching Manchester history, he came across numerous events and subjects that connected with his own understanding of the dignity and drama of the rapidly progressing new human society.

The murals, a lively, subversive series of scenes in historical order representing constant change and continuity, from Roman Manchester, battles with the Danes and the arrival of the Flemish weavers through to the monumental opening of the Bridgewater Canal and its industrial present, imagine a momentous history of Manchester. This is a sweeping drama, climaxing with how Manchester in a matter of years had gone from a marshy, sparsely populated market town in the late eighteenth century to the cotton, the machines, the canals, the factories and the steam – and the bosses and the workers, the muck and the brass, sun-blocking brick and rickets – becoming the most densely populated area in the country, the nation's second city.

The paintings blend the real and the dramatised, exaggerating some of the events, discoveries and great personalities to boost, or define, the emerging international importance of Manchester, projecting backwards to make sense of the working nineteenth-century miracle of Manchester. They're full of wit, playfulness and a non-conformist spirit – Madox Brown painted himself into one of the scenes as the Archbishop of Canterbury – and are a precursor of the socio-surrealist myth-making comic books of Kieron Gillen.

A few hundred yards from the Town Hall, across Albert Square, in the mid-1970s as much a busy, unflagging bus terminus as Victoria and Piccadilly, past and present very visibly clashing, a walking Wilson, generating a rhythm of stability, with and without purpose, complete with ubiquitous saddlebag slung nonchalantly over his shoulders, would quickly reach the John Rylands Library. This was one of his absolute favourite Manchester buildings, for its structural eccentricity and world-class contents. The kind of building that could intoxicate the church-loving, godless but spiritual Wilson at a single glance, once a daydreamy wanderer through the fixed, honoured past and ambiguous present of the colleges, libraries, chapels and alleyways of Cambridge University. The space inside a church, inside a library, could never be like any other space. Inside Manchester such spaces became a miraculous suggestion of other dimensions.

John Rylands sat along the busy, shop-lined Deansgate like a mysterious miniature cathedral, almost blessing through its gaudy originality the mostly neutral commercial surroundings, close to a very different sort of dream space – the pioneering Kendal Milne department store, known locally as Kendal's, then the now closed-down House of Fraser Manchester, originally opened in 1796 by a Didsbury farmer, rebranded as Harrods when it took over the shop in the 1920s, before patriotic local resistance demanded a return of the beloved Manchester name. (After Engels arrived in Lancashire, he would work in his family's Victoria Mill in Salford, and also in the company's office in Deansgate, which would eventually be transformed into the perfume counter of Kendal's.)

The library, a neo-Gothic masterpiece designed by Basil Champneys, renowned for a number of Oxbridge buildings, took ten years to build and was one of the first Manchester buildings to be constructed with electric lighting as part of the design – installed by plumbers before there were such things as electricians. It was finally opened to the public on 1 January 1900.

When it was built, its size and fancy splendour would have been even more striking and hallucinatory. This was a time when Deansgate was dominated by squalid, precarious slum housing and tenements where workers and their families squeezed into dangerously damp and dark rooms, sometimes just holes in the wall, so the design of the library didn't allow you to see out from the interior splendour into a filthy, cacophonous part of Manchester you were happy to escape; the biblical-seeming light flooded in through thick, coloured high windows, assisting all-important concentration. Although in grey, ugly Manchester you were somewhere else, far away, in another time, perhaps on another planet, as soon as you walked past the large decorative columns at the entrance, there to separate you from the miserable soul-crushing outside and launch you into bewitching imaginative space.

Since 1653 and the first free public library in England, opened using money donated by wealthy local Humphrey Chetham, libraries have been a constant Manchester corrective to the uncomfortable, even deadly environment, built to encourage ordinary workers to educate themselves. Eventually, by the time it was a key part of Wilson's route around the city in the 1970s, John Rylands was positioned more importantly in the unofficial civic area of Manchester, within minutes of the crown courts, the magistrates' courts and the Town Hall.

The exterior – as much as I would have seen in the 1970s, when it seemed completely outside my school-hating, pop-saturated world, the columns a complete barrier to entrance – can look a little dark red, an ornate Hammer House of Horror, but inside it is a work of art, and Wilson, with his Cambridge-induced confidence and energised out-of-town sophistication, loving this form of stepping back in time, or across it, was particularly familiar with the majestic, long and high-ceilinged reading room. He was also familiar with the vast collection of manuscripts and rare books inside – more time travel – including a third-century fragment of Homer's *Odyssey*, early editions of John Milton's

Paradise Lost, the first book ever printed in Manchester – John Jackson's 1719 *Mathematical Lectures* – Dickens' serialised novels in their original wrappers, a first edition of Shakespeare's *Sonnets*, a first edition of James Joyce's *Ulysses*, the second-largest collection of works by the pioneering printer William Caxton, first and second editions of the Caxton-printed *Canterbury Tales*, the theories of the early-modern scientific discoverers Galileo, Copernicus and Newton, the records of the Jodrell Bank radio telescope a few miles away in the Cheshire countryside, and the personal papers of John Wesley, John Dalton and Elizabeth Gaskell. There is also the original manuscript in four bound volumes of *The Manchester Man*, an 1876 rags-to-riches novel by proto-feminist Isabella Varley Banks, charting through one heroic cotton lord – Jabez Clegg, the 'Manchester Man' – the rise of the city at the heart of the Industrial Revolution, featuring vivid portrayals of the Corn Law riots and the Peterloo Massacre of 1819. Isabella mainly wrote under her married name G. Linnaeus Banks – in those days, a woman's identity would be hidden behind her husband's name.

Located in an upper gallery, the reading room is lined with statues of the cultural, historical, political and scientific figures Wilson worshipped as much as twentieth-century musicians, writers and artists. Here he would be surrounded by Shakespeare, Wesley, Francis Bacon, the revolutionary inventor of printing Johannes Gutenberg, who along with Caxton shattered the monopoly of knowledge held until the mid-fifteenth century by priests, creating an 'infinite number of volumes' so that books would become an extension of memory, the foundation of consciousness, establishing the very idea of the mind.

Printing brought the Bible to the masses – a few centuries before, St Anthony of Padua would have travelled with the Bible as something to be remembered and spoken, myth and matter springing from his mind in front of an occasional audience; the Gutenberg Bible is the first complete book to be printed using moveable type, in an edition of about 180 copies, and the John Rylands Library has a copy printed on paper, one of six in Britain and around forty-eight that exist in the world. It also holds a small, deeply mysterious, centimetres-wide fragment on papyrus of the *Gospel of John*, originally discovered in Egypt in 1920.

Calculated to have been written in the first half of the second century, just a few decades after the death of the Apostle himself, possibly the last living eyewitness of the living Jesus, it is one of the earliest known fragments of the New Testament in any language. Such early evidence of words and phrases that existed in the Bible fifteen centuries later suggests there were few changes over time from the original; generations of copying had not corrupted the text. The myth-making, it appears, was there from the very beginning, undiluted by later additions to the legend.

The papyrus has seven lines written on both sides, and features a significant conversation – or cross-examination – between Jesus and Pontius Pilate, before the Roman orders Christ's crucifixion. On the second side, after Jesus explains that 'Everyone who belongs to the truth hears my voice,' Pilate asks, 'What is truth?'

In an era when museums and galleries have become more visible and celebrated, a theatrical, real and surreal antidote to a purely digital and levelled-out world, the Rylands Library has become one of Manchester's most cherished and visited attractions. Wilson could see this coming when it was more obscure, even hidden, because to those who didn't take the time to understand, it seemed a relic of a discredited past rather than a living, changing part of the volatile present. Intellectually ravenous, he could see past the 'oldness' into the heart of the modern intentions behind such a building, and the timeless, esoteric and eclectic glory of the words and ideas inside.

The contents – including the precious fragment of the *Gospel*, an astonishing early version of world-changing journalism, and the works of Shakespeare, inventing the human – would be part of Wilson's idea of what Manchester was: electric with energy, lush with fictions, packed with pasts that were once presents, an archive of human imagination. It included all of this – and Madox Brown's prototype comic-book representation of how Manchester became Manchester, his 'Journey into History' Town Hall murals. And so the confidence Wilson had in the idea of Manchester as a home to the kind of local history that had changed the world, which seemed so inflated in the city's run-down, injured 1960s and '70s, was based on this appreciation. It didn't then seem like the kind of city to make people think, *Wow, I really want to live there*, or *Let's go there for a holiday*. It wasn't Rome or Florence with their classical loveliness. At best, it was one of England's other, workaday cities, overshadowed by London, permanently tarnished by its location, its nineteenth-century boom time long gone.

Wilson knew better. He was prepared to do the exploring that was required to find its beauty. He had the imagination to find its brilliance under the ugliness, the city that had been lost and needed to be recovered. Where it seemed abandoned and ruined, dense with the nineteenth century, undone by decay, he could see majesty. It had a lot of stories to tell, and there were clearly more to come. This energy and ingenuity could not be allowed to dwindle to nothing. The Manchester he had inside his head was gloriously vast and made up as much of the imagination and imported texts and the answers to all questions that books contained, the solutions to all problems, as of the prescribed, official city history. Inside his head was a city that could astonish the world, or at least a city that could make a noise and stand up for itself.

He saw deep inside the city a progressive, enterprising Manchester that most of the rest of us making ourselves up through music, books and entertainment had no idea about. The scary, disconcerting alertness in his eyes, his evangelical verve, came as much from what he knew lurked deep inside the libraries of Manchester – almost everything, to some extent, all of it belonging to him, because he belonged to the city – as it did from his ego, pretensions and passions.

Peter Saville CBE, Factory director, designer, artist, creative director of the city of Manchester

In the nineteenth century Manchester was, for a period of time, perhaps the most important place on earth, so people of all kinds of interest were drawn to it. When a place is like that, it doesn't matter what the

weather's like, or the food's like, it doesn't matter, you eke out something
that works for you in this unpromising environment. It was a very
important place. I think simply as its significance in global thought and
progress declined, its ability to retain progressive thinkers diminished,
year on year, decade on decade, generation on generation. With every
generation of young people, you're losing the best, because people go to
centres of excellence, that's where they go, and after the war Manchester
was less and less a centre of excellence. Manchester was one of the
world's great centres of excellence in the late eighteenth and through the
nineteenth century into the early twentieth century, and people would
come here. By the 1970s, people would leave, and Manchester needed
people to come because the people who leave are taking something with
them – their talent and energy – that the city needs. How to do that?

With culture, with activity, with services for the people who are there.
If you're not finding a bookshop, a bar, a restaurant, a cafe, a pub, a club,
a gallery, if you're not finding it, it's because there's not enough people
there for that and people there offering it. That's it. It's the ongoing
impoverishment, not of the people born there, because talent and ability
are born everywhere, in every walk of life, it's how to hold on to them.
Tony didn't leave, as he easily could have, and that does shift the balance.
If he had left with all the talent he had, it would have left a huge hole.
It used to be a city that the talented and enterprising went to, and he
decided because it had been once it could be that again. And he helped
with that by building from within.

Jon Savage

That's the first thing I have to say about Tony: no matter what happened
to us later, and we did fall out, because with Tony it's inevitable, he
changed my fucking life. He got me the gig that I wanted. He got me out
of the fucking law. He got me out of London, into Manchester, which
was a whole, unbelievable education. I think everybody, every Londoner,
should go and live in the North-West. What I felt about it was that, at
that point, Manchester was desperately poor and so was Liverpool, and

previously I had no idea. It really sharpened up my politics, and at that point made me a Labour voter. Bits of London were very poor, but they still had the basic wealth of the city around them. But fucking hell, Jesus, I mean, this was poverty. You needed to have some imaginative strength to imagine as one person you could actually change things.

Richard Boon

What was he looking for? A better world. We were all in Manchester at the same time, which had to count for something – I was an incomer, from Leeds, and when I got there Manchester was just dreadful. Having been the cradle of capitalism, it was very much in the midst of an endless lull, or so it seemed. What was he after? Who knew? But he was clearly at the centre of something, because of the TV. I would go for a drink with him, and as he walked along the street everyone had something to say to him, either some random insult or 'Hey, Tony, how are you doing, love?' because this was Manchester, and people called each other 'love'. He wore it very lightly. What was he after? He would always say, 'It's always just for the art of it,' but I think he had some thought early on that there could be some edgy cultural development of a new Manchester. I don't think he particularly saw himself as the focus of it, until a little later.

Elliot Rashman, friend, Simply Red manager

We're very funny in Manchester. We're always talking about Manchester, and not many cities do it like we do. That probably came from Tony. And Manchester always wants to be somewhere else. This week Barcelona, next week New York. What about Paris, Madrid, Milan? Liverpool just goes, 'We're Liverpool. That's it. We're just Liverpool.' Manchester became that modern city thing that Tony wanted, and it was a curse and a blessing, because his idea of a modern city is not necessarily what the council thinks it is.

Twenty-One: Manchester smoke and making connections

Omne ignotum pro magnifico. (Everything unknown seems magnificent.)

The knowing-he-was-right Tony Wilson, who could also be described as:
- sent half crazy trying to set a good example to the world
- simultaneously sublime and ridiculous
- loving to the point of groupie status celebrated and influential people
- sometimes saying outrageous things just to hear what they sounded like coming from his mouth
- appearing as an after-dinner speaker at his high-school alma mater. He wears a white dinner jacket featuring a substantial red-wine stain down one sleeve. When asked why he hadn't had the jacket cleaned, Wilson explained that Leonard Cohen had spilt wine on him in Montreal in 1974. He couldn't imagine how cleaning the jacket would improve it
- true-ish Renaissance man
- businessman who did whatever he wanted
- insecure amateur intellectual
- someone who decided to separate the two sides of his life, one that pays the mortgage and looks after his family, the other that allows him to do what he enjoys, such as hosting a staff party for Granada TV employees in 1979 that featured the haywire Hulme glum funk of A Certain Ratio and sundry other less-than-cheery and/or decisively non-singalong Factory acts, which was greeted with shall we say a certain paper-hat-wearing-audience disappointment
- surreptitious faker
- arriving for a meeting or an interview – being interviewed himself or interviewing someone – wearing a baggy linen suit, sandals, carrying a bulging briefcase, his toenails, sometimes just the big ones, painted a rich plum colour

- taking acid at a bullfight
- never bullshit a bullshitter

He smoked as well, scarily to me clearly something other than tobacco, something which helped add to how he performed off screen – and, now and then, perhaps more, on screen, because even as he got serious with national political issues and social concerns, and cleverly, sensitively interrogated the high and mighty, or the low and vulnerable, there was always a hint of something incongruously playful, with traces of something even more incongruous . . . something spiritual or just plain, sweetly stoned.

For someone who loved thinking and who was intensely inquisitive and often pretty wound up about one thing or another, cannabis would inevitably be a drug of choice, at least before he got infected by a drug more associated with the 1980s, and entered another zone, to keep up in a world made faster by cruel politics, hectic, hyperbolic video edits, economic mania and general end-of-century anxiety, a world where drugs were more publicly dangerously exotic.

Dope could make you think you were thinking, really thinking, more deeply than you ever had before, and maybe you were. Thinking about thinking. Thinking you were in control of the actual act of thinking, thinking you had what it takes to be someone and do something. It helped him feel he could be, or even was, the king of everything, with a deep insight into how others felt, what made them tick.

He is the second person I remember seeing rolling a joint, smoking like a maestro, skinning up with diligent, almost intimidating, self-absorbed agility, and then putting it to his mouth and sucking on it, creating a hissing sound which you could imagine was a close cousin to the fizzing sound made as the needle dropped onto a record before the song started. The first was the wild-haired, wild-minded and sound-addled producer Martin Hannett in the pre-punk days, when he was a part of Music Force with Anthony 'Tosh' Ryan-Carter, Bruce Mitchell and others, the Manchester music cooperative keenly seeking out new venues, postering the city and renting out equipment, loosely linked to the Workers Revolutionary Party.

(Wilson indicated an interest in joining but was rebuffed, this bumptious man off the telly not cool enough at all – another frustrating little rejection that he turned into inspiration.)

Hannett rolled up as we chatted, his mind on something, eyes fixed on the task at hand. It was a ritual, and as he finally put the neatly sealed roll-up to his lips and took a healing draught, eyes shut, head raised like he was hearing some rhythm in his head, it seemed that we were in deepest Peru rather than in some grubby first-floor premises on Oxford Road.

This was when I encountered Hannett behind a desk in an office, feet up, phone to his ear, as someone who arranged gigs and found new places for bands to play, before he became the fabulist, clairvoyant producer of a diverse techno-divine Manchester sound. Finding ways to make use of a fantastic record collection, an obsession with new technology, and constant drives after dark through the city into the outer suburbs and beyond, the everyday steeped in otherworldliness, often seeing no one else and no other cars for miles and miles. Once he had learnt about delay and dynamics in a recording studio, quickly working out how studios worked technically and emotionally, he experimented not only with how far you could push, stretch, invert, pierce and launch sound but also how far you could push the people making the sound – most dramatically through Joy Division, Durutti Column, using the name the Invisible Girls working with John Cooper Clarke and Pauline Murray, with other less celebrated, ultimately more abandoned, Factory records, and on music outside the Factory with Basement 5 and U2.

His sound emerged out of the spaces and non-spaces, and spaced-out minds, and inexplicable presences, damp and decay, form and character, textures and patterns, apparition and essence, temper and love, streaks of night rain and shards of sunlight, rooms and machines, of a smoking city, with, under noiseless clouds at the very edge of things, wonderful wilderness, surrounded by the dark of night, the sky cracking, the ageless Moors, the isolated Peaks and the unearthly Pennines existing as an uncanny, spacious background cut through by the serpentine Snake Pass. The desolate places a few miles from the city centre were the destination of many of his drives through empty streets, letting his favourite music fill his car, wondering what Neu! would sound like if they were from Salford and were fans of Wishbone Ash, what Black Sabbath would sound like if they were from Macclesfield and were fans of Pere Ubu.

Eventually I would see the Factory four smoke together, getting on like a house on fire, opening up all sorts of rabbit holes between them, and leaving me behind, their conversation taking on a diseased acuteness. The sight of them lighting up never made me want to join in, ritualistically passing the joint around in a circle safely made of boys, music playing, and there's Alan now, he's just thought of something else, places to go, people to see, an idea wrapped up in the mad and the perfect, and there's soul-mad Rob, sharing another joke with himself, with his all-knowing wind-up smile, the third and fourth I see lighting up, and then the sight of them relaxing into what happened next, smiling to themselves, a cult of secrecy, criminals against the state, surrounded by a smoke screen, appearing to be receiving inexplicable messages, achieving some agreeable personal clarity, experiencing time in a very different way, disappearing into another tunnel, wondering just how far dreams can reach, a wonderland of peace and possibility. But also feeling vaguely, sometimes not so vaguely, anxious. I decided if I joined in I might go somewhere else and never find my way back. I found other ways of joining in, to achieve a certain sort of stress relief and social courage.

I was still in awe of drugs, fascinated and a little horrified, when I first came in contact with those who were very much part of a Manchester notorious for generating new ideas and associations, as much because of drugs as anything else. This was a great drug city, its various music scenes and movements breaking new ground at the edges of life and initially in the shifting shadows of the night always based around a specific drug, a magic potion, influenced by and then influencing the soundtrack of the time. In the 1960s it was as though the drugs, and those taking them – smoking, popping, sniffing, in and around the inner-city beat clubs of Manchester that were the few after-hours signs of life – were keeping the city centre alive, with underground colour and energy, when it all seemed to be grinding to a halt, dead quiet and weighed down by a history starring war and economic decline.

Drugs were a way of discovering something that was outside the city, including the future, and bringing the outside in. It was a way of re-enchanting the world, which was suffering under relentless attack from industry and government, from the recurring, punishing ordinariness of the everyday. The police were horrified, angered and confused by this strange new world – the clubs to them were filthy, badly lit, crowded, the 'music' loud to the point of distortion; the clientele wore exaggerated clothing and were known as 'beatniks, mods and rockers' – but the drugs, and the discoveries that came with them, never stopped. To the police it was the end of the world. To those taking part it was, apart from anything else – the thrill of the chase, the connection with the music and the musicians that made it – the end of the war, even if it was the beginning of the drug wars.

And always, whatever other drugs came and went, speeding people up, slowing them down, enhancing the imagination, tackling tension, cleaning the mental channels, those that rolled up and skinned up, all fingers and thumbs, were part of a very special dope-fiend joint-action kinship, a private revolt against society as well as a form of liberation. They were in something together. Feeling what each other felt. Inhaling a particular way of dressing, talking, acting, certain attitudes. Sharing thoughts. Sharing smoke. Sharing a part of yourself with the smoke. A reprieve from dead time, school time, television time, punch-the-clock time. Happy to be losing the same, or different, memories. Perhaps it was all they had in common.

This smoke didn't stain the city's buildings like the Victorian factory smoke, but this smoke made a difference to the soul of the city, doing the rounds, connecting Wythenshawe with Levenshulme with Salford with Didsbury with Urmston with Fallowfield with Chorlton with Stretford with Middleton with Swinton with the four Stockport Heatons with Gorton with Collyhurst with Crumpsall with Cheetham with Prestwich with Hazel Grove with Hyde with Altrincham with the centre of the city. With San Francisco, Berlin and Greenwich Village. All those doors leading somewhere, into other rooms, with other doors, hidden from plain sight.

I was aware at the edge of my fraying innocence that 'it' went on, and at school that some of my friends had a look in their eye, and a strut in their walk, that suggested they were familiar with lighting up and losing themselves. Or thereabouts. It was nothing like the look in Tony Wilson's eyes, as he played to the crowd, even though there was only you and him, as if he knew exactly the effect he was having on others, because of the effect life, and everything in it, was having on him. I was intimidated, perhaps, because I didn't know how to respond to him. There was no one else like him, no guidance in how to deal with him.

Sometimes he was scary, because he made me do things I never thought of doing or didn't even want to do. I didn't think I would end up talking on television and the radio, and designing a record label, because I wasn't built that way, with nothing like all that thick-skinned all-seeing Wilson hoof and heft, and I knew it, but I did those things because he made it seem possible that you could perform different functions at the same time. Slip from one art to another, blurring lines, crossing borders, intensifying one skill by trying another. He opened doors for me, just by being who he was and doing what he did, just round the corner, on the television every night, with his love for setting up situations, showing off his knowledge and creating rivalries, but sometimes I didn't realise what was on the other side.

I would do the sort of things he would do – host concerts, chair discussions, appear on panels, dispense apparently expert opinion – but could not imagine he suffered from the same kind of anguish and doubt I did after the tasks were done. He was made for this kind of life – or made himself ready for this kind of life – bouncing from performance to performance, broadcast to broadcast, controversy to controversy with this impervious belief that he had nothing to prove to anyone. He acted like he was in a battle, and he was keeping his foes confused. They were never certain who he was or what he wanted, and they wouldn't know what he was going to do next.

He never let a negative voice creep into his head and drown the hundreds of positive voices that were often all his. When people did their best to upset him, he had this ability to laugh at them. He could flaunt himself like few others, and he seemed to get high on the noes he would open himself up to hearing; they were a sign to him he was getting closer to a successful life. He was being paid attention to. And if venturing forth and making things happen, making all sort of claims and counterclaims, did cause him anxiety, not to venture forth meant losing his sense of self.

Twenty-Two: Betrayal, the 'Factory Sample' and Vini plays guitar

Memento audere semper. (Remember always to dare.)

Tony Wilson the impenetrable performer, who can also be described as:
- feeling the only people who should have a say in the North of England were from the North of England
- leaving behind a broad trail of broken hearts, shattered expectations and empty wallets
- the greatest political interviewer of his generation
- talking about books as though they might rise up and attack him, especially fond of quoting Auden's remark that books read us as much as we read them
- the man who wore a fur coat while interviewing David Cassidy on television
- when he does business seminars, Tony Wilson (yours from the Society for Business for £2,500 a night) likes to quote Sid Vicious. Sid was once asked his opinion of the man in the street. 'Fuck the man on the street,' he replied. 'The man on the street is a cunt'
- calling up a record shop in Harlem in 1981 and asking if he could sign Grandmaster Flash, and being told, 'Fuck off, whitey'
- meeting the Space Monkeys for the very first time in 1995, and before he even introduces himself or says hello he rolls out one of his well-oiled record-biz chat-up lines – 'I want to sign you. I can't make you rich or famous but I promise I will let you make the music you want and we will have a lot of fun.' The band ask, 'Where do we sign?' and Tony drives off in his Jag before it gets nicked
- in the early 1980s lending two young friends, Liz Naylor and Cath Carroll, £150 to make a fanzine, and they hated it because they printed it in colour, they fucked it up, they knew it, but he was

amazingly unfriendly about it and over twenty years later is still
moaning about how they ripped him off
- a detective without a lead
- cock of the North
- semiological guerrilla
- king of aimless serendipity
- rhino charging out of a thicket

Wilson, believing that the North was the best place in the world because
he was born there, never forgave me for leaving Manchester in late 1978,
one consequence of me seeing the Sex Pistols at the Lesser Free Trade
Hall. Never. He could really sulk when he wanted to. In personal terms,
he could keep it up for years, quite happy to drop anyone once they were
of no use to him or didn't conform to his expectations of what the relationship was.

He saw me leaving Manchester as a complete betrayal of his standards, even though he had left the city to pursue his dreams, first of all
for Cambridge, a journey into uncharted outer space for someone of
Wilson's background, and then from there for London and a good job at
ITN, world leaders in the relatively new pseudo-objective packaging and
distribution of international news, not returning until he was twenty-
three, and not necessarily because it was part of his plans. He had become
national, even international, and fully intended to carry on that way. But,
he would say, he returned. He had seen enough of the outside world to
learn things that would be of use in Manchester, which he came back to.
And when he had been tempted to head back south, to a national job, he
had resisted the call.

When he heard I was going to leave, not least because I had been
promised full-time work by the *NME*, he made an attempt to keep me in
Manchester by trying to get me a job at Granada Television. I was never
sure if it was a generous even philanthropic offer to make sure I earned
enough money to stay in the North, or an attempt to keep me under his
influence – tucked inside Granada, his own personal territory – but I did

as I was told and turned up for an interview with Scottish-born Steve Morrison, who had risen very quickly through the Granada tiers since joining in 1974, from *World in Action* to editor at *Granada Reports* and then head of Granada's regional programmes, making more than twenty-five hours of television a week on a tiny budget. He would keep rising, producing a number of Granada feature films, including *My Left Foot*, until he became Granada Media's chief executive.

One of Granada's great inspirational and demanding disciples, loving how unusual a place it was, a station where boldness was encouraged, in the late 1970s he persuaded the editor of the TV page at the *Sunday Times* to preview that week's programmes as though he lived in Granadaland and not the South. The *Sunday Times* did it for one week only, flipping the usual London bias, and the usually obscure regional programmes no one outside the North-West had ever heard of were suddenly given star billing. Those working inside Granada – the very best journalists, producers, editors, presenters, many of whom would become national and international award-winners, never losing their quixotic Granada instincts – considered that it should have been this way every week.

Morrison was a little nonplussed as to what I was doing in his office and seemed very unimpressed with both my meagre qualifications and also my lack of preparation for the job, which I was told was as a researcher on local magazine programmes, something I knew nothing about. It was the kind of position that could lead to great things – producer, director, executive. Wilson of course had not explained to me what would happen, the kind of competitive world I might be about to enter, and that this was actually a serious interview at what those inside quite rightly considered to be the best place in the country to work if you wanted to enter television.

Eventually, exasperated, clearly with much more important tasks to attend to and more talented people to collaborate with, Morrison asked me if I knew that over 2,000 people had applied for this particular position. People would kill to get this job. It could set them up for life. I did not know this. I did not get the job. I was abruptly dismissed, Morrison probably chalking the pointless meeting down to one of Wilson's regular whims, some of which were worth following, others not so much. I left for London. Wilson brushed off my failure and told me, 'You'll be back soon, London isn't for you.' It seemed Granada wasn't either.

Once it became clear I was not going to return from London, he quietly punished me, needled me, tested me, even as he also encouraged me.

I left the North because I had been offered my dream full-time job at the *New Musical Express*, my own journey into space. I was never officially a staff member, but my name was put in the staff box as part of the paper's weekly credits. This was my Cambridge and ITN and Granada rolled into one. I didn't leave to go to London, which actually meant very little to me. I left to go to the *NME*. As far as I was concerned it wasn't even in London. It was everywhere and anywhere, and could include London, and could absolutely include Manchester, because my writing included Manchester. I took Manchester with me, into everything I did. That is where it had begun, and it was never going to leave, however far away I moved, whatever I wrote about.

Wilson didn't want me to go, because by then he had Factory Communications, which included Joy Division, and he was managing Durutti Column, and his PR mind knew it was important to have a local writer for a national music paper on hand to publicise the shows they were promoting and the records they might get to release. While I was still in Stockport, sending my articles down to *NME* HQ by post, collecting singles to review from the parcels office at Piccadilly station, he badgered me for weeks, close to begging at times, to review their first record release, 'A Factory Sample', a delicious compilation of weirdly patterned outsider music that at the time seemed it might be a one-off, Factory's single artistic act.

An equivalent of the very first New Hormones record by Buzzcocks, 'Spiral Scratch', the 'Sample' was a four-act souvenir of a brief moment in time, the chronicling of some intriguing post-punk activity, the running of a converted club in record form, and it might not have been followed up at all. It had evolved from Roger Eagle's original idea of a Manchester/Liverpool double twelve-inch, after he approached Erasmus to fund it. Erasmus had used all his spare cash to replace Fast Breeder's equipment, which had been stolen from the back of their van. Tony had his inheritance from his mum, and they got it costed out, not as a plan for a record label, but to make this one piece, this one-off project.

Once Wilson had the shiny, oddly substantial finished product in his hands, once it existed, because he was now such a media personality he could not bear to do something that wasn't noticed. Plenty of people plugged him to get their acts and musicians on 'What's On' and *So It Goes*. He knew how it all worked. He knew how to make connections. Once it was noticed, he might want to do more, but first it had to be noticed. He was used to getting attention in the North-West; at times he would even actually be at the centre of attention. It was the kind of thing that always kept him eager. The next challenge was to get attention from elsewhere.

The 'Sample' was the first Factory record, but its catalogue number was Fac 2, something else that suggested that with Factory nothing would ever be what it seemed. Fac 1 was a poster designed by Peter Saville for the four opening shows Wilson and Erasmus had organised at the Russell Club in Moss Side. The stark, striking poster was in black and yellow, prefiguring the Haçienda colours and using an appropriated stylised illustration of a man with his fingers in his ears advising 'Use hearing protection'. 'Russell' was spelt wrong, with one 'l', as it would be on the next Factory poster. The details, the facts, weren't quite as important as the tone, the space between letters, the principle that here were the clean, ordered, visual values of Bauhaus planted into inner-city debris, as if the poster was making an argument for intellectual and social order in the most unlikely setting.

It advertised a series of Factory presentations at the end of May and the beginning of June 1978, beginning with the 19 May Durutti Column and Jilted John show, when Factory officially opened for business. On 25 May the Russell Club hosted Manicured Noise, scratching out from punk a more cerebral sound, and festive make-believe noise freaks Big in Japan from Liverpool, hinting at an alliance between Manchester and Liverpool that never went beyond conversations between Wilson and Bill Drummond of Zoo Records and later KLF, and his partner Dave Balfe, and an open-air concert in Leigh, halfway between the two cities, which featured Zoo and Factory acts.

Wilson would implore Drummond not to sign his highly desirable early Zoo groups Teardrop Explodes and Echo and the Bunnymen to major labels down south. They should stick together, he said. Drummond pointed out that Wilson had a well-paid job at Granada, while they were all on the dole. He could afford to be radical. It was all very well for Wilson with his adopted Cambridge swagger and steady Granada income. Zoo were secondary modern and/or three failed years at art college. No contest, as things were and it seemed always would be. Wilson's argument that record labels were really just moneylenders charging interest rates worse than the banks made little sense to the Liverpool wing. The sentiment was both reasonable and entirely unreasonable. They had no experience of generating business plans and asking impatient, flat-faced officials for bank loans, and absolutely no sign of a helpful inheritance from the family. Their route was always going to be major record labels, the traditional romantic working-class dream of signing a record deal, as subservient as this might make them in Wilson's superior eyes.

The third show on 2 June again featured Durutti Column, with Cabaret Voltaire of Sheffield, the fourth show the following week the first appearance at the Russell Club by Joy Division, playing with the Tiller Boys. This was when the club was settling into its position as idiosyncratic community club, when a few more people had made their way to its obscure, unpromising setting, getting used to the odd sight of the man off the telly floating around the place. A skittish seventeen-year-old Liz Naylor, learning how to navigate the nooks and crannies of a broken city, would creep through a side door during the sound check and stay inside hidden in the shadows until the evening. It was a broken city where broken people could find a way towards something. 'It was desolate,' says Liz, 'but in a way I loved it. It was very accessible to me as a woman in a very man-made city. I didn't feel threatened in that environment.'

The poster arrived too late for the opening night, which created a sense of timing that was never absolutely corrected as Factory released more product and processes and made more promises. This would eventually lead to many record sleeves featuring no text or band names, not just because *Unknown Pleasures* had proved you could do this – as Hipgnosis had done with Pink Floyd, as Island/E.G. had done with King Crimson, as Andrew Loog Oldham had done with the Rolling Stones, album sleeves disguised, or actually existing, as non-commercial conceptual concerns – but because the sleeves often took so long to design and produce they were not made for a particular group or record. Music would sometimes be attached to a pre-existing sleeve, even if it hadn't been intended for that group.

Saville was perhaps the only person Wilson had ever met who was more sure of himself and his approach than he was. Saville's mantra about the work he did for Wilson and Factory, which began when he was a nobody and his lateness might have jeopardised a working relationship that hadn't even begun, was 'It takes as long as it takes.' Wilson would adopt this when it suited him. This meant Saville's work was sublimely free of commercial pressure, even when it became in its own way commercial, but also meant that he never became a dominant force in graphic design in the more practical, and nervous, world beyond Factory. Only Factory could afford, by not really affording it, to give him the space and time to imagine product design as though it was art.

When discussing with Wilson the logo he had created, taking his time, for Fac 51 – the catalogue number of the Haçienda – Saville explained, 'There is commercial art, which you will have to correct every two years, and then there's what I do, which will never need correcting.' He never got paid the Jony Ive Apple millions, but he knew his own worth, which ran into the abstract millions.

At the beginning of 1978, the certainly late Peter Saville, twenty-three, art-school graduate, was keen to equal the advancement his close art-school friend Malcolm Garrett had already achieved in designing record sleeves for Buzzcocks. Their manager Richard Boon mentioned to him that Tony Wilson needed a graphic designer for various projects he was planning. Wilson knew Factory's first non-Saville attempts to create imagery that matched their aspirations, usually just relying on briefing local printers, were 'shit', like cheap, not nasty or knowing enough Jamie Reid. Factory wanted to take a different, daring sense of style, and anti-style, of believability out of situationism, from using design to ask people to do something and behave in a certain way, and then reward them for it.

Wilson was also perhaps jealous of Richard Boon, who in Garrett had his own Manchester School of Art student, his skilful apprentice, creating work that imaginatively borrowed from Dada, Bauhaus and a history of traditional and experimental typography to produce a Manchester look that inherited nothing at all from previous pop and punk, or indeed anything from any previous Manchester music scene. (Org 1 and Org 2, a record and a pamphlet produced by New Hormones, could be seen as the first phantom Factory numbers, as if it all started from minus; the Factory catalogue grew from less than zero, from a New Hormones plan based on Wilhelm Reich's idea of orgone energy generated by orgasms – sex meets anarchy – and out of long technical and emotional conversations about process and production Saville and Garrett had had as students sat in Garrett's car outside his Rusholme house, which was too scruffy for Saville to enter.) Wilson wanted his own student, and Saville was summoned – or, perhaps, the stories quickly spiralling, he summoned himself for an audience with someone he knew from the television, who might have some work for him.

At their first summit meeting the solemnly highfalutin, floppy-haired Saville auditioned for charming floppy-haired Wilson in the Granada canteen, surrounded by cast members of *Coronation Street*. Saville had no work to show him, but cleverly flattered Wilson by showing him a minimal palate of specialised design preferences: 1940s Penguin book covers, 1920s constructivist posters and 1960s pharmaceutical catalogue covers, the lettering and spacing of which he elegantly if slowly grafted onto the first, delayed Factory poster. Wilson had given him a chance, asked him to design a poster just to see what he would come up with. The poster's style had no relation to the music and the groups it was superficially promoting, but this was absolutely no problem for Wilson. The incongruity was its beauty. The words, the letters, the shapes became the image, the communication, building up from subtle zero a radical way of presenting pop music.

The music – and Manchester – must live up to these ideas, this collection and interpretation of influences, this imageless presentation of obscure emergent music being played in a shabby club in a dilapidated part of town but creating a very different illusion.

The illusion would last, overcoming the reality, which was never the point in the first place. This self-contained approach, between sleight of hand and fastidiously forensic, would be distilled into the minimalist monochrome poster for the Joy Division Factory/Russell Club show on Friday 20 October 1978, basic information stripped so far back into itself, so categorically separate from the conditions and clichés of the city, and from the rapidly evolving sound of the group, it discreetly glowed with an autonomous determination that was another, antithetical way of saying, 'This is Manchester.' A Manchester that could do, as it always imagined it could, anything. This one left Bauhaus behind, because Garrett had claimed that first. Saville swept into classical typography for his own untrammelled inspiration, a different, madly exquisite route into a new Manchester, taking a detour from punk into another dimension.

Wilson would swoon over how the lettering was 'perfectly set in the centre', as if this meant his dreams were coming true, dreams he didn't even know he had until Saville showed up, treating every letter in the alphabet as a god, treating typography as a foreign language he alone understood. The analytical, almost antiseptic reasoning spilt over into the Factory 'Sample', but this piece of Factory needed to be sold, at least if there was any prospect or intention of making something else. Wilson naturally hit the phone. He had my number. He had everyone's number.

This was another odd thing, the colossally self-reliant TV man asking me for something. Me, from my lonely bedroom, from the streets of nowhere, not yet fully understanding how it now looked to the outside world – the small, insular, inter-sniping pop music world of Manchester, which in my music-loving innocence I never fully came to terms with – that I now wrote for the *NME*. In Manchester I *was* the *NME*; I had power. I had no idea. At the *NME* I was a shy kid from up north who occasionally was of service because, after all the bedroom studying, I knew a lot of music and was in the right place when Manchester started to become one of the great punk cities, with its own style, its own mission, and indeed its own vocal and sometimes not so vocal leaders and agitators.

I had trouble getting the Factory 'Sample' into the *NME* – it was local for a start, which still counted against things then, as if that made it automatically inferior. Not so much that it was from the Manchester of the Hollies, Freddie and the Dreamers, Sad Café and 10cc, but that it had not been certified as somehow official by being on a major, southern-based label. The Beatles may never have made it if they had insisted on making records for a Liverpool label.

Also, perversely, because this was Factory, and from the very beginning they had a late-night, what-if allergy to travelling down routine grooves, the record was neither an album nor a single. It was seven inches, but there were two discs, so it didn't fit into the rigidly defined singles column. It contained four acts and didn't really fit into the album reviews section. There was that provocative lost 'r', so that it was a sample, not a sampler, which irritated the more literal-minded, not getting the factory reference. It was a sample presenting the label's work, not a record label sampler.

The sleeve by Saville, an extension of the posters, was absolutely, almost suspiciously beautiful, a multilayered sheathed-silver construction, but that also counted against it, as if it was more art than music, or perhaps the vanity publication of some minor local celebrity, the equivalent of a brisk, pushy Radio 1 disc jockey making a novelty record, even if this one had its show-off roots in the avant-garde rather than the end of the pier. In fact, it might be better to treat it as a kind of book, a pamphlet, a Fluxus box of tricks, a subversive summary of cultural prognosis. The sleeve required assembling by hand, as if in an artisan factory located in some out-of-the-way narrow back street – a romantic connection with what felt like the giddy wonder of actually putting a record out, truly savouring it as an individual object as opposed to mass-produced product – and it contained a set of irrationally expensive stickers representing each of the acts. If this was going to be Factory's one and only product, mediocrity was not an option.

It was perceived down south as vanity publishing, not as imaginative and insurgent but as the self-serving act of someone promoting their own little career in a small corner of the world. There might have been a grain of truth in this, certainly from the point of view of someone a long way from having any knowledge of how the Factory 'Sample' had been conceived – of the North, because the North is rising, bringing with it a new kind of community spirit. A spirit emerging from some new place midway between an underground vision and a scruffy flat in Didsbury where Factory was based, not far from the Mersey, and conceptually not far from another Factory, in New York City. And it was not a single and not an album, and was packaged in a smart post-minimal way that might have made sense after the invention of the iPod but looked a little blank at the time, if you weren't that way inclined and knew and loved, say, your Lucio Fontana. Or your Bauhaus. My editor didn't. He was more of a ZZ Top man, an ex-*Daily Mirror* sub. With Wilson ranting at me down the phone, I was ranting at my editor about necessary anti-corporate excellence, and he was worrying about how many words to allocate to the new Fleetwood Mac album.

I could have quoted Wilson about why it was so important that this record looked as though it belonged in an art gallery – or at least the gallery shop – more than a record shop: it was, just in case it really was the only record Wilson ever had anything to do with, a carefully conceived object that worshipped the very idea of the record, and therefore that itself asked to be worshipped. 'Why was packaging so important to Factory?' Wilson would say. 'Because the job was a sacred one. Music had transformed our young lives, children of the '60s all. And now we were in the privileged position of putting out records ourselves. Does the Catholic Church pour its wine into mouldy earthenware pots? I think not.'

I thought it best not to run that past my editor. Nor the possibility that Factory as a record label was selling things it truly believed were too good to be actually sold, that they were in open if usually stoned agreement with the situationist disappointment with those who turn their lives into the meaningless pursuit of commodities. Perhaps I would have done better if I had explained that he should think of the silver sleeve as something that could in the history of the glamour of pop be placed next to the silver dress Debbie Harry wore around that time and the transparent X-ray sleeve used for the first Faust album.

The 'Sample' *NME* review was in limbo, not accepted by my editor, something made worse because if you didn't know about the Russell Club Factory nights, where art clashed with punk and generated new desires, there seemed no rhyme or reason to the acts collected on the release. There was experimental electronic music (Cabaret Voltaire, listing as aesthetic technicians their machinery on the sleeve), at a time when such a thing seemed almost anarchic, a group that was perhaps punk but sounded too gravely literate (the recorded debut of Joy Division, with nothing to say on the sleeve, Gretton from the beginning keeping the group at a distance, because 'the music speaks for itself'), hard-to-categorise instrumental guitar music (Durutti Column, with a situationist-inspired list of when group members had left) and some comedy (John Dowie, vaudeville Dadaist). It was a goddamn wonky variety show!

My editor at the time, not necessarily in the spirit of new punk, or even in the spirit of music being any kind of revolution, or even the soundtrack to a revolution, found the whole thing near insulting, possibly verging on the fey. And, worst of all, provincial. This was in a period when the first feature I wrote about Buzzcocks still referred in a patronising headline to cloth caps, whippets and clogs, as if they were the sons of George Formby and Gracie Fields, not Iggy Pop and Can; it was always going to be, for many southerners, grim up north, cock.

There also seemed to be no firm release date; the record in many ways contained the DNA of the label itself, as curated product, as an inscrutable, discreetly voluble indie endeavour packaged as a luxury item, but also something that existed to create culture, not just distribute music, and because of complex manufacturing issues and missed deadlines, it was constantly delayed, missing its naturally perverse Christmas Eve 1978 release date. Eventually, my editor relented. The *NME*, after all, should not turn its back on something just because it didn't fit into the established grid. Perhaps he suddenly had a gap to fill in that week's paper. My short review of the 'Sample' just about slipped into *NME* print, weeks before the record actually made it into the world. I was on time; Wilson and co. weren't. But then some of the music on the record had a way of stopping time.

> *Incorporating the diversity of Rough Trade with the sharply eclectic marketing processes of New Hormones, Factory Records is run by co-directors quicksilver actor Alan Erasmus and ingenious graphic designer Peter Saville. With the ever-enthusiastic Tony 'So It Goes' Wilson inevitably involved, it will release an attractive double EP sampler of acts and artists who have appeared at the club over the last few months. A devious sampler out to both seduce and introduce, its packaging is thoughtful and unusual, its implications exciting. It is provisionally set for mid-December release, priced an irresistible £1.50.*

Pleading to the point of bleeding, Wilson had got what he wanted, and why not? That was my job. And it was his job to tell me it was my job. And then it was on to whatever was next.

What was next – and who saw this coming – included a sandpaper sleeve for an album of delicately captured instrumental music arranged by Hannett, closer to sonata form than pop music, an extension of the ways Durutti Column explored tense, sense and absence. Factory's virtual house band, set up by Wilson and Erasmus, based the album on a series of studies and sketches by vulnerable, vivacious Vini Reilly, tenuously searching for clarity and light.

Vini Reilly

I was in bed one morning, always a good place for me when I was feeling down. I'd been told that a recording session was going to happen by Tony, maybe Alan, but I didn't believe it. There were often plans that came to nothing. But Martin [Hannett] knocked on the door to collect

324

me, and I got up and got dressed. We drove to Rochdale, to Cargo Studios, and Martin was talking all the way about astrophysics. I didn't say a word.

I had a hand-made Gordon-Smith electric guitar, and Martin fiddled about plugging things in and out, looking for the sound he wanted. While he was doing that, I was ranting at him, just moaning, feeling depressed for a change, ha, and all he said was, 'You're being a bit unreasonable.' I was a bit thrown by that, so I just got on with playing bits and pieces on my guitar.

I started improvising, going through ideas, memories of music I had played to myself, and he started treating the sounds as I went along, as if we were a sort of jazz duo. I played something, it just came to me, and he said, 'Play that bit again.' I didn't know which bit, so I played what I hoped was the part he meant. He twiddled some knobs, and later he would do overdubs. It became 'Sketch for Summer', but I didn't know what it was going to be until I heard it later.

I did maybe thirty-five pieces on the day, and eventually I'd played everything I could think of, so I went back to being depressed. Martin looked after the mix in his own time. Tony and Lindsay arrived at my house a few weeks later with a white-label test pressing, and I couldn't believe it. That one day of me and Martin circling each other, doing things in our own world in the same space, had turned into a whole album?

I had all these ridiculous ideas for a sleeve. I don't know what I was thinking, but it was the time of punk, and I thought, Well, it's my music and I want it my way. *The funny thing was the more I made my mind up about what I wanted, the more Tony wanted me. Me being difficult never put him off. The sleeve turned out to be sandpaper, a long way from my ideas about colours and shape. I thought the sandpaper was funny because it was a total contrast to the music.*

I don't know who was dafter, me or Tony. He was very protective of me, very fatherly; he knew I didn't have a dad. He warned me that the album would change things for me in terms of losing half my mates in

Longsight, Burnage, Levenshulme – hard areas. I was known as Skinny Vini, or Oxfam, stood out a bit among all those toughs. He said they would be jealous of me making a record. They'd make fun of me. He was right. When it came out one lad said I must have had to sleep with Tony to get a record out. 'Yes,' I said, 'and it was great – you should try it.' But without Tony I don't know what would have happened to me. I was very lucky to be able to have this setting to make records, because who else would have let me do it in this way?

The second album I did at my mum's house, next to her bedroom while she was asleep. Made it in about three hours with my guitar, a cheap drum machine and a Roland Space Echo, onto a four-track. I was just making some random stuff for Tony to listen to in his car, really. It clarified how I made music, which began with Martin but could now take off without him, now I knew how a piece of music could be made from a series of impressions, from just playing along with my own thoughts. When I think of a piece of music that lasts for, say, five minutes, I hear it all at once. There's a tiny prick in my brain, and then the piece is all there in one go and I just have to play it out, letting it reveal itself. It's impossible to say a feeling, but music can do that. I could go in the studio with nothing to play, but feeling a lot, which became the music.

Tony had a listen and he said, 'Well, it's an album.' It also came out of nothing, and cost next to nothing, half a day in Graveyard Studios to mix it. This was LC, more my album this time, whereas I think of the first as being Martin's. He was great at pulling people's minds into different shapes. He knew how to handle me when I was depressed, which was most of the time. I remember once when I was really down he got a big ball of cannabis resin and put it on the mixing desk and said, 'Come back when you've smoked that.' It was too big for me. It ended up on my mum's mantelpiece for two weeks. People would come and go, look at it and have no idea what it was.

Tony always used to say he liked managing me because there was nothing to manage. You couldn't exactly promote me or put me in a

video. I didn't have to sell myself, and he never minded. He knew I
thought that pop groups ended up having to be salespeople. He also
liked that I was blissfully unaware of any other music at the time. I lived
in my own world, and that seemed to suit Tony just fine. It meant my
music didn't seem connected to any other music.

He would always be there for me when I needed something, even
a guitar. I was in this musical instrument shop in Cheadle, Stockport
– Sounds Great, run by a guy called Gary. He would go to the States
and buy special instruments, and I didn't know that he had these great
guitars. I just walked into the shop, and I saw this Fender Stratocaster
on the wall, and it looked really good. I asked to have a go, and Gary
didn't say anything, just passed it to me. It played itself, so sensitive, so
responsive, it was mad – and I thought, This is mine. *Gary then told me*
it was the most expensive instrument he had ever had in the shop. Three,
four grand, even at the end of the 1970s; it would be five times that
now. I immediately rang Tony. He had a real thing about Fender Strats
as opposed to Les Pauls; he was disappointed when I once said I wanted
a Les Paul because he loved Strats. I said, 'I have just seen the best Strat
I have ever seen.' He said, 'Well, you should have it.' I passed the phone
to Gary and walked out of the shop with it. Tony came to some kind
of deal. I never knew the details. I don't think Lindsay was best pleased
when she heard. Yes, Tony looked after me.

'It appears clear and certain that music is so much a part of our nature that
we cannot do without it, even if we wish to do so,' said Tony Wilson, listening to those first two Durutti Column albums, wearing a mask of Anicius
Boethius, a sixth-century Roman senator, consul, scholar and philosopher,
renowned as the best-educated Roman of his time, who believed that the
universe is ruled by divine love and that true happiness can be achieved
not through power and money but by turning to otherworldly virtues.

Twenty-Three: Life, death, love and tears: Joy Division, to the centre of the city from the ends of the universe

Pulvis et umbra sumus. (We are but dust and shadow.)
HORACE

It took nearly three years to get from the Lesser Free Trade Hall Sex Pistols call-to-action performance manifesto to the first Joy Division LP, *Unknown Pleasures*. From one kind of intensity to another altogether. The two events were centuries, or continents, apart, but both in and of Manchester. First of all, there had to be a meeting of some of the characters who eventually would belong together in history.

At first, nothing much happened in the months after the Sex Pistols transformation, as bands formed because punk was for all, and rehearsed, and became something, in secret, in their bedrooms, inside some of the derelict buildings around the city centre that looked out through broken windows over stifled urban Manchester to the clouded wildness beyond. Out-of-use buildings finding a new use. Abandoned warehouses that seemed lost forever became rehearsal rooms where echoey bricked-in sounds tentatively strived to resemble Bowie's *Low*, Iggy's highs, Patti's power, Lou Reed's *Berlin* or even the Sex Pistols' fury. The early, frantic speed of the new music would start to evolve into a different kind of speed, fierce fastness becoming more wrung-out, New York and London punk becoming Manchester difference.

The players in the game had not yet made it into the same story. That happened one night in April 1978, when two London labels ventured north following the Pistols' trails and a notoriety that had coursed through the country, making them apart from anything else the latest new thing, a musical and cultural sensation and also a tabloid one. There were rumours that the northern cities were coming up with something of their own. Where there's noise, there's brass.

Stiff Records, quick off the mark putting out the Damned's gloriously nasty debut single 'New Rose', as if it might even become known as the first bona fide British punk record, and pub rock specialists Chiswick Records, hoping to keep up to speed with this newfangled rock, put on an audition night, dangling the promise of an actual record deal in front of those Manchester bands that had formed with little idea of what to do next. This free-for-all talent show called the Stiff/Chiswick Challenge was held in Rafters, another one of those intoxicating Manchester clubs reached by heading downstairs, next door to the grand Manchester Palace. It held around 200 people, jammed in tight, and at the time was a venue for the likes of Pere Ubu and Wilson favourite Elvis Costello, bringing different, useful-sounding messages to locals from far-out places, because rock music was on the turn, towards the frenetic, the experimental, the adventurous.

Lost among a dozen or so new groups auditioning in an old-fashioned way for the exploitative enemy down south, this was the first time Joy Division appeared as Joy Division, having been Warsaw for a few months until a name change was required because of a band called Warsaw Pakt. The new name they chose was much better, with shady, dismal roots in the concentration camps of Nazi Germany, but one that when recontextualised in a different time and place had a dark, sombre glow, a broken beauty about it that meant the earnest, generic music of Warsaw was not appropriately demanding even demonic enough.

Warsaw had been well-intentioned but lacking in zest. Months of determined rehearsal added stranger, dissolved power to their basic speed and energy, so that by the time they were Joy Division the same four-piece sounded like a completely different group. They'd made a record as Warsaw, 'An Ideal for Living', which made them look and sound like an earnest minor band with no distinct image – except for an unhealthy fascination with Second World War imagery – who would never get to make another record. (I was due to attend the recording session, performing some function or another, but a hangover caused me to miss the meeting time in town and the van ride to the out-of-city studio. I would not have made any difference to how it sounded; my role was always going to be the writer.) They had to completely remake themselves after that first shaky, shy attempt to make sure that they got to make another record.

At the time they didn't have a booking agent, so singer Ian Curtis would use his phone at work to book gigs for the group. They just wanted to find places to play. One gig he booked was at an old people's home, so Joy Division find themselves playing to a small audience of mainly women of a certain age as though they're the Chippendales. It had to get better after that. After all, oddly enough, it was a matter of life or death.

Their determination on the Rafters night was disrupted by the number of groups who turned up, some of them not taking the opportunity as seriously as they were. A group of non-musicians I had helped put together with Buzzcocks manager Richard Boon and photographer Kevin Cummins as a kind of playful Fluxus-inspired punk prank, the Negatives, had decided they would try their luck. When Joy Division's Ian Curtis heard we were going to play our daft non-songs before them, pushing their appearance beyond midnight, he charged towards me with a raging look in his eyes I had never seen before.

Previously, when I had a drink with him, or met him in clubs, he had seemed quiet and low-key, younger than his years, a little preoccupied but with no hint of deeper even aggressive urges, but he was so wound up by the chaos of the evening he smashed a door behind me with his fist. We were just a joke. He had far more serious, even desperate things on his mind. As Joy Division guitarist Bernard Sumner said, he was usually mild-mannered, polite and easy-going, until he didn't get what he wanted. 'Then he was like a small-sized nuclear bomb.'

By the time the group took to the stage at two in the morning, the evening already a failure as an audition for the London labels, Joy Division, folded around Ian's temper, were furiously focused, and music that had once seemed a little sluggish for all its noisy hope was now filled with targeted tempestuousness. Many of the audience had left, even, I think, the record company 'jury'; the group were doing it for themselves in front of a handful of stragglers, testing their new limits, discovering in their own way how good they were and how good they could be. There was, though, a kind of jury in the audience, more important than the London label talent scouts – two incongruous local personalities, one more known than the other, who would soon be part of the Joy Division system.

Rob Gretton was the Rafters DJ and was seeing the quartet for the first time. He'd recently lost his insurance job, his steady income. The next day, looking for work, he was queueing for a phone box that Bernard Sumner was using in Piccadilly Gardens, and recognised the guitarist from the night before. 'I want to manage you,' he bluntly announced to a surprised Sumner, adding a dose of fan flattery, verifying his status as Joy Division fan number one. Sumner invited him to one of their twice-weekly rehears-als but forgot to tell the rest of the band, who were left wondering who the fuck this stranger was watching them play.

In the pub after, as was their custom, each member of the group got their own drink, and didn't get one for Rob, who couldn't afford his own. Somehow out of this classic northern awkwardness and matter-of-fact financial embarrassment a promotion is negotiated from Rob's other gig as editor of the Slaughter and the Dogs fanzine – contributing £200 to the cost of recording their maddened rush of a debut single 'Cranked Up Really High' – to manager of Joy Division. His qualifications, per-haps, were his basic lack of conventional qualifications, a partisan south Manchester swagger, a love for music somewhere between reverent and incorrigible and access to a number of well-located payphones around town. He had his best ideas after a nap.

Tony Wilson had been at Rafters in whatever capacity – TV producer, fan, awkward hanger-on or unquenchable sensation seeker – meeting Gretton for the first time in the club's stairwell. Some girl shouted at Wilson, 'When is *So It Goes* coming back?' And he heard this flat, amused voice joke, 'He doesn't want it to come back; he wants it to disappear so he can become a fucking legend.'

Wilson and Gretton were already at odds with each other but on the same side – an unlikely bickering double act of droll, mischievous, working-class Wythenshawe and pseudo-grand Granada royalty, of City and United. Gretton's showbusiness roots were in appearing in an amateur production of *The Black and White Minstrel Show*, Wilson's were in appearing every night on live television. Perhaps the partnership worked because they were so different in appearance and sensibility. Wilson loved the notion of unity, Gretton steered away from it; Wilson gravitated towards the spotlight, Gretton shrank away from it. They bonded over respect for each other's eccentrically applied talents, and along the way shared the same successes, failures and tragedies.

At Rafters, Wilson had found himself assaulted by the irked, raging, fist-flailing Ian Curtis for not putting Joy Division on his TV show. 'You're a fucking cunt,' he seethed at Wilson, not pursuing a diplomatic route to promoting his music, not impressed by the so-called celebrity in their midst. At least, not after a few pints of bitter. 'What's your fucking problem?' replied Wilson, his first words to Ian Curtis, which, if you think about it, would be the same kind of thing he would ask immediately after Ian had killed himself.

Wilson, used to the familiar way he was greeted around town, insults regularly thrown as a very local sign of affection or to knock him off the high horse he loved riding, shrugged his shoulders and more or less told Ian to get in the queue. He had forty groups and plenty of record company pluggers from the South pestering him for TV time. He wasn't interested in a group he still thought of as Warsaw, who had sent him their scruffily packaged, extremely lo-fi 'Ideal for Living' record, lost in some murky no-man's-land between punk and post-punk – his recollection was that 'they sounded like a bunch of instruments being whirled around in a tumble dryer, but they did have an interesting and peculiar lead singer'. The singer on particularly peculiar off-stage form who was now insulting him and getting nowhere.

Perhaps Wilson's indifference was another reason – apart from me and the Negatives – why the group were so incensed that night, and suddenly Curtis was not a routinely energetic front man with little to say or show, but a front man possessed by a menacing kind of mentality, with a focused intensity, a flayed pale torso, a grey charity-shop shirt, alluding to a world beyond the material, facing down the birthday of eternity, staring through and over and around the few lingering members of the crowd, beyond himself, pushing himself somewhere forever in the future. If instinct is a memory of the future, at Rafters Ian followed some instinct, a memory of decades ahead, when he wasn't around, when it was acknowledged Joy Division had made one of the greatest debut rock albums of all time, even though at the time they had not yet fully found themselves.

And Wilson fell in love with the group now called Joy Division, all that coruscating distress. They were good enough to jump the queue and for Wilson to put them on local television, their first time on TV, four solemn, thoughtful young men in dark clothes on cute podiums, apart but together, eyes looking in different directions, framed as though they were on some 1960s pop show that never really existed, adrift in a timeline conceived by J. G. Ballard.

They were good enough to encourage Gretton to want to organise them, in his own acerbic no-nonsense way. Wilson and Gretton were now allies, a match that could only be made in Manchester, which would lead to the ambitious local graphic artist who would design their sleeve, Peter Saville, and Martin Hannett, a musician and promoter fancying himself as a producer in the style of Bob Ezrin, responsible for Lou Reed's *Berlin* and Alice Cooper's *Killer*.

With busy, pledged Gretton now helping out, Joy Division quickly recorded some songs that they used to try and interest record labels from London, including Genetic Radar, a shiny new wave pseudo-indie Warners subsidiary formed by Andrew Lauder, who had signed Buzzcocks to United Artists, where they had the most abrasively articulate of pop hits, once their singer Howard Devoto left to extend the sonic and metaphysical range of punk into the great livid beyond with Magazine, who signed to Virgin Records. The lure of a major label still outweighed the practical pressures of doing it yourself.

Wilson described his immediate involvement, apart from getting the now intriguingly disordered Joy Division to play on one of the TV shows he presented, as making sure Gretton didn't keep travelling down to London to 'talk to cunts every week' and searching for a record label that truly wanted them, for the right reasons, and paid properly for the rights. The need to avoid a major label was intensified by a depressing time spent trying to please the northern talent-scouting wing of RCA Records, which gave them some valuable studio time in return for covering the classically trained, madrigal-loving northern soul singer Nolan Porter's early-1970s 'Keep on Keepin' On', a favourite in Manchester clubs.

The session didn't work, the addition of tacky disco synthesisers making their music shallow, even gimmicky, but the meditative tension of Porter's delivery, at the opposite end of the scale from the energies of James Brown and Otis Redding, and the haunting, underplayed power of the original song, produced by 'Born to Be Wild' producer Gabriel Mekler, atmospherically seeped into Joy Division, helping break up the flat track orthodoxies of Warsaw. The combination of the obvious influences – English hard rock, experimental Bowie, wilder glam, weirder Germanic pulse, starker prog, churning Stooges, fast London punk – was disrupted by a homeopathic mutant addition of an anomalous cult soul track originally played by rock musicians, including members of Little Feat and the Mothers of Invention. 'Keep on Keepin' On' slipped through a tear in time and space and evolved into a Joy Division composition, 'Interzone', a new sound for the group, for rock, because the usual conventional equations had been accidentally short-circuited. Eruptive grandeur from an unlikely source had positively infected the system.

Making the RCA album scarred them – a cheap, drab studio miles from Manchester, recorded in a day, mixed the next, the band unceremoniously whipped into action by some guy who kept saying, 'Time is money, time is money,' almost no time to breathe, anxious, highly strung Curtis in particular completely freaked out by the soulless experience. They tacitly agreed among themselves to do it very differently next time.

One night at the Band on the Wall club, Gretton said to Wilson, 'Why don't we make the album ourselves and then take it directly to Andrew Lauder at Warners and lease it to them?' More control, more profit – Gretton had calculated it as a win–win. Wilson asked Gretton how much it would cost to record an album; he'd just released the first record on his Factory label, the 'Sample', spending £5,000 and making a profit of about £300. Gretton said Martin Hannett, making singles for Rabid, estimated about £8,000. 'Which was a complete lie,' Tony discovered. Wilson mulled the idea over, not immediately convinced by Gretton's argument that if they did it themselves they could make serious money. 'I said to him, "Are you sure?" It didn't occur to me that it was a good idea.'

The £300 Factory had made on their first attempt didn't suggest there was much of a future in releasing records, but, somewhere between sure of themselves and shambolic, between what the hell and it's the radical, necessary way forward, they fell into manufacturing and distribution. 'Somehow', said Wilson, 'we found a way of bringing out our records ourselves, without even having to involve Warners or any major label.'

Wilson would recall that conversation in the Band on the Wall as 'the dawn of the British independent movement', as if there hadn't been signs for years of other anarchically minded entrepreneurs and music enthusiasts plotting similar ventures around the country and finding ways to avoid the petty rules, annoying authority and restrictive red tape of corporate record companies. Perhaps what inspired any such independent movement was having Hannett involved, stepping out on his own path to understand how to record music, so the first Joy Division album didn't sound rough-and-ready do-it-yourself – or sounded do-it-yourself in the way that early Sun records, or Joe Meek singles, or Can albums were do-it-yourself, unprecedented adventures in sound, using original developments in technology without the interference of a compromising professional music industry contributing to a kind of committee-driven commercial balance.

Hannett had seen them play at Salford Tech, noting their mistakes as much as anything and the uneasy ways they were trying to fill the large echoey room with sound using primitive equipment. The musicians connected with each other somewhere between half-heartedly and psychically, the bassist and drummer tentatively jamming when the PA broke down, opening up tranced spaces – tender intervals – in the music that Hannett swooned over. An early exponent of drum machines, as with many modern-minded producers at the time frustrated by live drumming's even

fractionally erratic beat, he could find no fault with the metronome maintenance of rhythm from transfixed drummer Stephen Morris other than
the fact he was human.

The sound Hannett produced – found in the flickering open spaces they
left as they searched among themselves for the safety of power – switched
dynamically and yet also gently, even gingerly, between constant currents,
fixed points, background drones, found sound, inner worlds and stray
vortexes, between sped-up slow motion and serene time lapse, and calculated new possibilities for how rock music could sound, almost turning it
inside out, surrounding it with energy, dealing with space and emptiness
and shrunken infinity as much as noise and voice. He had turned the
group inwards, whereas previously they had battled vainly to make a dent
in the world, as if mere volume and aggression would get them noticed.
Through their inwardness they made more of an impact on the world as it
was and as it could be. Bass-playing Hannett made the bass a lead instrument – even as he thinned it out – as much as bass-playing Tony Visconti
had on Bowie's 'The Man Who Sold the World'. He once lost a girlfriend
because she couldn't stand him playing his bloody bass all day and night.

It wasn't exactly the tumultuous Joy Division that had transformed
themselves the night they failed one formal audition and passed another
more ad hoc one; it was some kind of X-ray of that transformation, an
amplification and yet a reduction, a divine dismantling, an unprecedented
transformation of transformation. The group had found a very different
way of working from their abortive session with RCA and a record label
that in many ways wasn't even a record label, just a loose confederacy of
individuals, including their manager and the almost madly encouraging,
positive man off the telly who was enthusing how great it was all sounding.
'You are going to be sat around a swimming pool in LA in a year's time.'
It wasn't necessarily their ambition, but it sounded good after months of
struggling, and lo and behold it would more or less come true.

Martin Hannett, with no apparent previous experience, simply by
describing himself as a producer – qualification enough at the time – had

persuaded Buzzcocks to let him produce their first record, the four-track EP 'Spiral Scratch', originally almost charmingly conceived as simply a souvenir of their appearance with the Sex Pistols, because that was more or less the beginning and end of their existence. After that, back to college, back to work. A one-off, profoundly unsullied by becoming a routine, the very ordinary everyday thing they were complaining about in their songs. Perhaps, actually, the true dawn of the independent movement Wilson talked about, as a work of art and a ferociously devious set of songs, released two years before the Joy Division debut.

During the fast few hours making the record, four tracks done and dusted in a day, a modest advance on the even more rushed Stockport demos they'd made a couple of months before, young Buzzcocks drummer John Maher, all of sixteen years old, quietly noted that Hannett 'didn't seem to know what he was doing'. Pete Shelley's father, loaning the band £250 so that they could make the record, sitting in the studio to check on his investment, also picked up that the producer seemed very new to the idea of a studio, and a mixing desk. His technique seemed to be to shove all the levels high, searching in the dark for some sort of distortion or spatial warp. The engineer they'd used on their 'Time's Up' demos, Andy McPherson, was on hand to bring a little necessary balance to proceedings.

The Buzzcocks' songs, any glory embedded in their spontaneity, didn't need much treating, much trickery, and crucially on the way to deliberately capturing their live sound, no overdubs, so Hannett, credited as Martin Zero, could get away with being a studio beginner, but he was clearly learning on the job. He was it seems a quick learner, on the way to finding more transcendent ways to get things to sound like what was in his imagination. He would also point out that he wanted to try things that the engineer, and the amount of time they had, stopped him from doing, things that were yet to become common inside the studio. Hannett was frustrated by the time limits, and especially the tech limits. There were no technological toys to play with, to create an illusion, which great recorded music always is. Toys enable the producer to come up with the most important instrument in recorded music – space.

By the time he made it to Joy Division – after his detour as house producer for Rabid Records, a local equivalent of London's Stiff run by the ebullient Manchester music operator responsible for the posters around town, Tosh Ryan, purveyor of quickly knocked-out fine Manc novelties and engaging pseudo-punk – he was well on his way to knowing what he was doing. Even as he worked on unpromising, fragile or corny music in basic studio surroundings, producing but not elevating the label's debut, Slaughter and the Dogs' headless ode to amphetamine 'Cranked Up Really High', he could experiment with the unknown possibilities of record production. Hannett had found his calling.

He discovered for himself as he went along what it meant to be one of the more mysterious but vital, controlling characters in the music business: a record producer, a constructor of sound, taking the temporary motion of music and fixing it in permanent place, a mixture of technician, teacher, therapist, dictator and illusionist, blending calculation, spirit, nerve and various forms of intoxication. Or, he was always learning as he went along, the most magical moments of a Hannett recording achieved accidentally, or for reasons not so much to do with studio knowledge as a momentary collision of tension and emotion that found its way onto tape.

Committed to releasing Joy Division on Factory, Wilson left him to get on with it in a way no traditional label would have allowed. The sleeve was also the result of Wilson allowing the person he had chosen for the task to do what he wanted. The unidentified minimal wordless monochrome sleeve for *Unknown Pleasures* conceived by Peter Saville, somewhere between incongruous quiet luxury and unsettling finality, audaciously placed Manchester at the pulsating centre of the solar system and can be read as a map of a Manchester to come, its exotic mystery, its darkest days, with all of its magnificent history merely a prologue. When something is unknown, it has a pull to it. Mystery is like a magnet.

A long way from Warsaw's flimsy 'Ideal for Living', this sleeve was a substantial piece of deluxe printing; its enigmatic black-and-white data graph set dead centre amid a landscape of deep black pulled the city into the future and pulled the future towards it. Saville had taken an image

Bernard Sumner had spotted in a physics encyclopedia, which turned out to be a signal transmitted by the first pulsar ever discovered – a rapidly spinning neutron star formed during the tumultuous death of a star many times bigger than our sun. Apart from anything else, the sleeve was a supreme act of science fiction, almost the first sound, the first beat, made by the music contained inside.

The panel floating in eternity featured 80 closely packed wavy lines representing 80 flashes of radio waves spiking at various rates representing how the neutron star had revolved 80 times in 107 seconds. The radiation had travelled across space for hundreds of years before it was recorded by radio telescopes such as the one near Holmes Chapel in Cheshire, only a few miles into the country from the Stockport studio where Joy Division recorded the album. If those lines capture a form of lightning in space, used by Saville, Joy Division and Factory as an emblem of the energy Hannett in his lust for order with his respect for disorder had assembled inside the songs, they also describe a map of the universe where the short trip between Strawberry Studios and Jodrell Bank meant along the way you took a tour of the entire universe.

It wasn't necessarily because of this that the design became as ubiquitous on T-shirts as the Ramones logo worn by those born years after Joy Division appeared, that it began to pick up speed during the twenty-first century as an image transcending context and crossing over into fashion and lifestyle, and onto the high street, different people understanding the same thing in different ways. There was its basic unknowable prettiness, its attachment to a music which didn't seem destined to date, therefore its attachment to an impermanent nameless cool, and how it had also become for many designers born long after Saville placed it into cultural space and time a kind of graphic design big bang, when their whole interest in the secret and not so secret power of design began.

It looked like a work of art, but you didn't really want to claim that – it sounded pretentious – but it wasn't clear what other term to use.

Peter Saville

I was given the challenge very early in my life because Tony trusted me, which became the inspiration to put that sleeve together. I did what I could within very great limitations, of experience, knowledge, means, everything. The key was I did what I wanted – not what I wanted to do but what I wanted to own. I now am seen as a kind of avatar for my generation, but really my social coordinates at the time were as a very white middle-class kid of the '70s. We had more information about other ideas and worlds than previous generations. The look of the world, the possibility, the style, the wealth, it was being opened to us through TV and film. In my case, I could wonder, Why can't my everyday be different, be a form of privilege that was otherwise not available to me? When I got asked to contribute an object to the everyday, I made the object I wanted to own. I thought there were things about an album sleeve I didn't need. I didn't need it to tell me what it was. I knew what it fucking was. Nobody ever bought a record needing its title displayed on it. I made something that would flatter me if I owned it rather than speaking down to me. All this was on the drawing board when I designed Unknown Pleasures, *and I wouldn't be the only person thinking this way, but my advantage was that because of the nature of Factory, which at the time had no nature, because of the way Tony worked, based on no experience, I was the last port of call prior to it going to the printers. I didn't have to present it to somebody in charge who would say, 'Fuck off, you must be joking, where's the name of the group, where is the picture of the group, make the type bigger, I can't read it.' I had the highly unusual position of being able to determine everything on that sleeve, with no possibility of anyone changing it. I had complete autonomy given to me by someone who seemed like an older brother and who essentially was paying for it out of his own pocket. Not very rock 'n' roll as such, but it allowed for something that was completely liberated and liberating. It was like, this is not an album; it's an object, it is intuitive, representing a totally new set of plans and decisions, representing a new world. Through the autonomous and again utterly*

*unprecedented opportunity afforded to me by Tony . . . the work that I
did out of my own insecurity and vanity, that funny relationship served
to introduce thousands of other people to things that struck a chord, that
spoke to them, touched them or appealed to them in some way, that their
home, their family, or their school or their state had not yet introduced
them to.*

Because this sleeve existed, because Saville the madly cerebral young local
graphic designer was given the chance by Wilson to dream something up
and embed into Joy Division these then unexplained pulsar recordings,
which turned out to be a reflection of nature at its most elemental and
extreme, Manchester became an international music city. International in
a way the city itself couldn't appreciate for decades.

It was an oblique, conceptual sign of a Manchester cultural renaissance
that was out of the mouth of Tony Wilson as much as anyone or anything,
manufactured in the space of Factory for all there being the non-Factory
workers John Cooper Clarke, the Fall, Ludus, the Passage, Smiths, Stone
Roses, 808 State and Oasis, a Manchester that wouldn't have turned out
the way it did without Joy Division – their two psycho-dramatic 1979 and
1980 albums of menace, obsession and physical unease blurring documentary and fiction, and then the dreadful Macclesfield suicide of Ian Curtis
at twenty-three putting just about everything into perspective, young life
destroyed with a catastrophic swiftness that can take your breath away.

So it goes.

Anthony H. Wilson

*I always thought of Ian simply as being very quiet, apart from that first
meeting when he was very aggressive. I remember looking at his dead
body in the chapel of rest and thinking how quiet it was in the room.
So being dead, it was the same old Ian, I guess. Very quiet and very
pale, and I was annoyed with him. I was pissed off. I thought, with
deep sadness,* You stupid bastard. You really shouldn't have done this.
What were you fucking thinking? *They'd put this suit and shirt on him*

to try and cover the telltale marks on his neck. *I wanted to see his body, because I didn't see my mother's when she died a few years before, and I regretted that.*

'And that should be it. The end. Give up. Go home,' wrote Wilson about Ian's death in his novelised autobiography. It wasn't, he didn't, Factory continued, the remaining three members regenerating as New Order.

Lindsay remembers she was struck by how much Wilson wanted to carry on after Ian died, as if nothing had happened, even though something had obviously happened. 'It didn't stop him, and I hated that. I just thought, *You're a jerk. I've always knew you were a jerk. I knew you were a jerk the day I married you and now you're proving it. How can you possibly carry on like this?'*

Mike Pickering, Haçienda booker/DJ, Quando Quango, Deconstruction Records, Sony A&R man, signing Calvin Harris

I was living in Rotterdam. I remember about three days later calling Rob, who I'd known from the football, from seeing Manchester City home and away, and going, 'What the fuck's going on?' And he told me. It was difficult to comprehend. They'd been out to Holland a few weeks before. The locals were a little shocked how rowdy they were – they thought they were arty and then they behaved like yobbos. We'd hired bikes and toured all over Amsterdam and Rotterdam. That was the last time I'd seen Ian. Rob sounded stunned. I said to him, 'What are you going to do?' He was like, 'Well, I'd like them to carry on. Maybe one of the others can sing.' I was thinking, Oh no, I've heard Bernard sing. Fucking hell. You know what I mean? But it worked, didn't it?

Gonnie Rietveld

That trip to Rotterdam was the first time I met them. Ian had scuttled off to do his thing, very depressed, not well, and the rest of Joy Division were just off the rails. They wrecked my bike, they all wanted to sit on the back of it, and the luggage rack snapped off. It was all practical jokes,

342

clichéd rock group behaviour, which you really did not expect from their music. I think it was a way of taking their mind off things. Bernard would say, 'I bet you can't do such-and-such a thing,' and then issue a challenge. 'I bet you can't put that whole plate of fried rice into your pants.' They would bet with each other who could do it. 'It's only money,' they'd say, meaning, to me, it's Manchester. Then you'd see this trail of rice going all the way up the hotel to their room. Maybe it was a way for Ian to find his way back to wherever he had gone, to be on his own.

Lindsay Reade

Tony never gave me any credit for Factory, even though I was with him all through the setting up, having people stay at our little house, because I ended up hating Factory. I just couldn't buy into it like he did. We'd been looking after Ian, after his first suicide attempt, probably not the best idea leaving the two of us together for hours at a time. Our intentions were good, but me and Ian alone together, a recipe for total disaster. I was borderline depressed, and he was extremely depressed. Ian was not well at all, he was almost catatonic, just sitting there, and I was feeling angry and confused. What a pair. Tony would be off somewhere, being Granada, doing Factory. God knows what he thought me and Ian would be doing stuck together at home. I hated Factory. I didn't want it to carry on after Ian died. I felt this thing that Factory had become is what destroyed Ian, so I wanted to destroy Factory. I did. I wanted to destroy it. This isn't worth it. It's only bloody stupid music. It's not worth losing somebody – *because I felt that's what killed him, the chaos that Factory had been built on, the weird energy of these weird men running riot, let loose on something a little beyond them. It probably wasn't, but that's what I thought – they didn't understand what they had got involved in. There was this terrible day. I remember shouting at Tony,* 'Black Factory, black Factory, death, death, death, death Factory.' *He'd brought this expensive black designer trolley home, which didn't fit in with our little two-bed terrace, rooms so small once the sofa was in there was hardly any space. I was putting it out on the street. I said,*

'I'm not having that in the house.' And he was shouting, 'Yes, we are.' We had a vicious fight about this trolley, which was of course a fight about something else.

I felt that when the punk thing came in, it was a bit threatening to our relationship. I wasn't as keen on it as he was. It didn't seem to be from where we had come from. I think that he was then keen on music for a different reason than me. Youth culture doesn't particularly excite me. Whereas for him it was thrilling. He was beside himself at being part of something when punk happened. A classic illustration of that is the closing night of the Electric Circus. He went on stage to give a speech, and as soon as he appears the audience is gobbing all over him, hurling beer at him, drenching him. He had to walk through the audience in order to get back to me. I was at the back, of course. I never went further than that. He walked back soaked to the skin, and I thought, Oh, you poor thing. You're going to need a bath. He looked ecstatic! It was like he'd had the best orgasm of his life. He said, 'Oh, that was amazing.' That moment I just thought, You and I are so different. The fact to him it was like sex that people were gobbing on him and chucking beer all over him, because I thought it was gross. Maybe I was jealous. I'd lost him. He'd found the love of his life.

Vini Reilly

I'd known Ian even before Warsaw, when we were both clerical officers. We met through a friend we had in common and we connected. We would meet up sometimes, and even if we met on Saturday we would still have our office clothes on. We both liked poetry, and he would be writing these words even then, about people he came across through work, people living odd, lonely lives. He liked a drink and I couldn't drink, but he never minded, and he never treated me as being different, which most people did. I once turned up to see him, incredibly stoned, and I felt really self-conscious about it until I was with him, and after that I was fine. We made each other relax, really – he was a lovely person to be with. I remember I was taking one sort of pill for depression, and he was *taking four or five. Taking the one made me feel very disoriented, so once he was doing all those pills he had no chance. There was no way you would be thinking straight. You would be seeing things in ways we can't begin to understand. He was very embarrassed by his epilepsy, and then when he started seeing Annik even though he was married to Debbie, well, he didn't want to hurt anyone, he just got lost between them. It wasn't sex with Annik, but in a way that was worse for Debbie – because it was love. He stayed at Tony and Lindsay's for a while, they thought it would be good to get him away from Debbie and Annik, think things through, but there was no escaping his situation really. He was going to kill himself whatever anyone did. Some states of mind are beyond earthly help. I remember once staying at Tony and Lindsay's and there was no one home. The phone rang and it was Ian. He wasn't in a good place. You can see it now, it's in every one of his fucking songs, but no one could see it at the time. It was too close. I had depression, and I could see what was happening but was in no position to help, but for Tony it just didn't translate. He'd become someone Ian was relying on, but he wasn't up to it. It wasn't his fault, maybe not even his responsibility, but he was too slow to react. He didn't understand depression, and it wasn't something people talked about then. I was angry with Tony about it, but in the end, as obvious as it was, Ian could be very secretive. His first suicide attempt wasn't secret, of course, but it made him even more secretive afterwards. Tony tried to help in his own way, but it was beyond the kind of help he could offer.*

Andy Harries

In 1980 Tony had moved on from 'What's On', from the sillier stuff – there was an attempt within Granada to use him better, give him more serious stuff. We were working together on a World in Action, *and we were doing a programme in May, what they call a fire-engine show, there's a real last-minute rush to get it on air. It wasn't a particularly interesting programme – oil money, high interest rates, companies suffering and going broke. I'd thought of a title, 'Britain Over a Barrel',*

*which gave us a hook. We filmed all the stuff we needed Thursday and
Friday, and then we went into this weekend edit, and the show had to go
out later on the Monday night. We basically worked forty-eight hours,
snatching a bit of sleep. There's a long corridor along the edit wing
in Granada, and because it was very late Sunday night, early Monday
morning, literally there was no one in there apart from us, and there was
an editor steadily chopping away at the film. It was that moment in an
edit where everything is in limbo. It's all very still. Tony came in to work
the commentary out, ready to read it the following morning. We were
looking at the rushes, and then the internal phone went in the edit suite.
The ring made quite a noise in the quiet. Made me jump. He picked it
up, listened, said nothing, put it down and just walked out of the room.
I didn't think anything of it, but after about half an hour, we were like,
'Where the fuck is he?' I thought he had gone for a piss or something,
but it was an unfeasibly long amount of time. I went to find him. I
walked down the corridor and I couldn't see any sign of him, there was
nothing, then I suddenly heard this sobbing about five or six offices
down. I pushed the door open, and he was there on the floor of an edit
room, in the foetal position, just crying his eyes out. And I didn't know
what had happened, so I went in, shut the door and said, 'Tony, what's
happened?' And without looking at me he said, almost to himself, 'Ian's
hanged himself.'*

*I don't know who called him. His missus, maybe Rob. I remember
it like it was yesterday. He was absolutely devastated. It's why I always
hated how he was portrayed in* 24 Hour Party People, *as if he took it
in his stride, glibly hearing the news in the middle of a piece to camera.
It's their right to imagine their own version, but it was so far from
the truth, as though there was something disconnected about him. I
remember speaking to Malcolm McLaren about Sid Vicious's death, and
he [McLaren] was portrayed as simply exploiting it, as though he didn't
care. In truth, he was profoundly upset by it. I think that both Tony
and Malcolm enjoyed the image of being master manipulators, creative,
flamboyant conceptualists, and I think they didn't want to show the*

truth of what they felt, as if this was too precious and private, too real,
to ruin by making it part of the story. So they encouraged the myth, they
folded it into their image. Tony was perverse like that, but it was also
a kind of defence mechanism. Of course, it meant he would run into
trouble, as though the manipulator was who he really was.

Richard Boon

He was shattered. We were all shattered. Ian was a beautifully troubled
man, or a troubled beautiful man. Wilson did have the temperament
to very quickly gloss over it. It's far too harsh to say he ever exploited
it, but it becomes an industry whether he intends it or not. It's not
necessarily in his original script. Of course, he's not very good at keeping
his mouth shut. Very soon there is a new script.

Dave Haslam, writer, Haçienda disc jockey

Nick Kent interviewed him for The Face *some time later, which naturally*
would have flattered Wilson, being interviewed by the famous rock
journalist. It seems he said that Ian dying was the best thing that had
ever happened to Factory, or to him. Which obviously gets a lot of
attention. It's something he might have said in Manchester among friends
who understood his sense of humour, who were more in tune with his
way of doing things, but it didn't travel well. And Tony wasn't at all
happy with how it looked, claiming it was taken out of context, or that
he'd never even said it. Maybe he didn't and Kent had misunderstood,
but Tony was extremely annoyed with it appearing in this way. Perhaps
Tony got carried away in the interview. He was known to show off a
little and usually not care how he appeared. This time he really did. I'd
done something for The Face, *so for some reason he decided to get me*
to ask for a retraction. I thought it was odd that he didn't know that it
didn't really work like that. Why didn't he badger the editor himself? It
was no use badgering me. I said, 'I will see what I can do,' and I think
after he put the phone down he thought it would all be sorted. It wasn't
and it dragged on and followed him around, and he floundered a little,

blamed me for not dealing with it. It was outside Manchester, and he couldn't control it like he could where he was more at home, used to running things, having production people and Erasmus and Gretton work things out for him. It shook him up, although it didn't change how he operated. He didn't learn to keep quiet sometimes. Probably the opposite.

Peter Saville

Ian's death is the point at which the proceeds of Joy Division's sales create the empowering facilitator of money. Suddenly there is money; there was no money before, so everything is on a wing and a prayer and we'll do what we can. But suddenly there's money, like it's a real business, and there is unscheduled, unimagined potential to do something like the Haçienda, which was otherwise pure fantasy. It only cost Ian's life. I say that with the utmost respect. It wasn't borrowed, there was no interest to pay on that money. The entire Factory history is based on the capital that is Ian's life, without a doubt. Tragedy that made the city happen the way it did. I once said to Howard Bernstein, the chief executive of Manchester City Council, that I believe modern Manchester stands on the investment of Ian Curtis's life. I feel that very strongly. Modern Manchester owes a lot to all of this, and at the very heart of it is that kind of . . . the sacrifice that Ian makes. That is the capital upon which everything then happens. That's the capital investment. And the first grand project is the Haçienda. That's the point at which significant impact upon modern Manchester society is leveraged.

Perhaps it was the suicide of Ian Curtis that gave Wilson the taste for dramatic change, the thrills and danger, the rush of the unknown, that comes when you keep chucking things – marriages, artists, logic, friends, family, plans – on the funeral pyre. He became addicted to crisis, and whatever else the 1980s was as a decade, as Wilson himself somehow managed to become half yippie, half yuppie, it was full of crises, self-induced, crashing in without warning.

Ian's lyrics, after all that, had not been just urgent reports and dramatic stories written by a science-fiction freak that sounded tremendous as bleak, thrilling entertainment; they were desperate transmissions from the borders of consciousness, which he was stalking like a man possessed, not one who simply danced like he was pretending that he was. He had been a man in trouble heading towards a terrible catastrophe. He didn't want to be himself any more. He was getting ready to leap into the void.

The playful, artistic distortion of space and time in the songs wasn't for mere effect; maybe the thirty-year-old Hannett understood that more than the rest of Joy Division did, none of them much more than twenty, more than those of us who were the first set of listeners, and he wanted to do justice to the burning expression of raw, desperately authentic feelings, to evoke transformative immateriality and hold on to something that was about to be lost. He combined emotion and calculation and ended up inventing a different kind of sound. It was a kind of sound he took into another new group, U2 of Dublin, Ireland, who dearly wanted it to be their sound, and for a couple of tracks it was their sound. Joy Division were their favourite group, and Martin Hannett, the maddest, scariest person they had ever met, was like Tom Baker's abrasive, forceful Dr Who. After Ian died, Martin wasn't in the mood to produce their debut album, *Boy*, as he was scheduled to, and history skipped a beat and headed off in another direction. A few albums later, U2 found another version of the Dr Who father figure they needed to help them find what they were looking for: Brian Eno, not quite as scary as Hannett, Arthur C. Clarke rather than Philip K. Dick.

Ian died just before Joy Division's enclosed, unsettling but dream-sounding second album *Closer* was released, another luminous Hannett rendering of the group's intramural dynamic, featuring a cover chosen by Curtis that solemnly presented death and a sound that seemed to anticipate unfathomable drama. Hannett is perfecting his mastery of dramatic light and dark. Destined to be a hit anyway, but given serious lift by his death, Joy Division's 'Love Will Tear Us Apart' is where Ian with maximum concentration works out how love can lead to death.

Martin himself only had eleven years left to live, many of those years lived inside the shock waves of Ian's suicide. He died at forty-two from heart failure, following years of heavy drinking and heroin use, of feeling broke and abandoned, after a few more visits to recording studios and further refinements and adjustments to his insular interpretation of the record producer, resulting in music divinely inside itself because it was from inside his head, including pop music classics by the Names, ESG, Magazine and New Order.

So it goes.

Inside the Factory, for Hannett there was a series of quarrels and rifts and basic disappointments: the disappointment of his partners opening the Haçienda rather than buying the cutting-edge sound equipment he knew he needed to make the best-sounding music of the day; firing a starting pistol at Wilson at a Factory meeting at the Manchester Gentleman's Club when they wouldn't invest Joy Division royalties in a coveted Fairlight Sampler so he could make the best-sounding records, competing with Trevor Horn and Quincy Jones. For Hannett, it was all about the records, the sounds, the presence of the musicians and singers spectacularly caught in time. That was where life was. For Wilson, it was about concept and imagination. All ideas need not be made physical. Perception of ideas leads to new ideas. He liked to leap to conclusions that logic could not reach. In defence of their respective positions, they both had a tendency to go overboard.

There were even real-world legal disputes as Hannett chased the money he felt he was due, which in his heart of hearts Wilson didn't feel was as important as the opportunities and acclaim Hannett received as the one true designer of a Manchester sound. For better or worse, Factory never had a sound once Hannett departed – and his return to produce the Happy Mondays after erratic, unfocused studio turns with John Cale, Mike Pickering and Bernard Sumner was a Strawberry Studios-mixed late-life reminder of the bizarrely achieved clarity he had brought to a wide range of Factory product.

The lawsuit was eventually resolved in 1984, when an increasingly desperate, addicted and megalomaniacal Hannett had run out of money;

the angry clash naturally received its own catalogue number, Fac 61, and a statement from Hannett that was as great as any attempt to work out how Factory, and Wilson, worked, and didn't work: 'I'm a genius, you're all fucking wankers. You'll never see me again. You don't deserve to see me again.'

Also, one day in a recording studio . . .

Silence . . .

Wilson: 'Martin, what are you doing?'

Hannett: 'Recording silence.'

Wilson: 'Recording silence?!'

Hannett: 'No, I'm recording Tony Fucking Wilson.'

Eight years later, in 1991, Rob Gretton dies, from a heart attack, at forty-six. 'He chain-smoked,' said Bernard Sumner. 'Chain-ate. Chain-drank. He didn't believe in promoting records – the music would sell itself – and he didn't believe in a healthy lifestyle.'

Some friends at the funeral see Tony cry for the first time.

It was love/hate. At times they didn't seem to have a kind word for each other. When Rob had his breakdown, he came charging down to Tony's, swearing he was going to do him in, so Tony and his wife and kids had to go and stay in a hotel.

At some meeting about something or other in Tony's house circa 1981, the meeting ends with Rob and Tony wrestling on the carpet after an argument, really hurting each other.

'What are you doing?' Rob would ask you. 'Nothing much.' 'What should you be doing?' he'd say.

Fac 253 was a bet between Gretton and Wilson that Fac 263 – 'Round and Round' by New Order – was going to reach the top five in the official UK charts. Wilson said he would resign if it didn't. It didn't. He didn't resign.

Jon Savage

I was asked to speak at the funeral by Rob's wife, Lesley. It was a very heavy day and I was very nervous, but I managed to get through it.

Bernard was in bits. Afterwards at the party, when I arrive, the first thing I see is a gurning Keith Allen, the actor who had done the 'World in Motion' England World Cup song with New Order in 1990. One of those unlikely Factory ideas that worked. You couldn't plan it, but it seemed part of a greater plan, like it was always meant to happen. He was openly sniffing cocaine, and Tony was on the coke as well. I was furious with him. I jabbed him in the chest and shouted, 'What are you doing taking that stuff at your age? You'll kill yourself.' I used to take it, stopped in 1983, perceived it as a horrible, destructive drug. It seemed insane Tony was taking it in his late forties. He said, 'Well, aren't I allowed to indulge myself?' I said, 'What about your son?' So we had a real row. Tony in some ways was very strong, but he was also very weak. And he was a hippy intellectual that got in his head he was this powerful businessman, and he scooted down into hell once the cocaine seemed part of his baggage.

Eight years after Rob dies, Tony Wilson dies, his heart giving out.
   So it goes.

Anthony H. Wilson

My final thought on how influential Factory was for Joy Division . . . I don't know. I think all one does is add enthusiasm to what people are doing and the question of whether the freedom they were given was somehow positively connected to their ability to create . . . I would like to think it was a factor. They might well have created fantastic music on a major label without us, without me. But I like to think the soil we provided was good soil to grow in, even though the surviving members who became New Order did like to whine and whine and moan and tell lies about how we ripped them off and let them down. Hooky would always say, 'Where's the money?' based on how many albums they sold. Bollocks. They had full accounting. In fact, the accounting took so long to do in 1991 the document got a Fac number, Fac 233, 'Substantial Matters'. But musicians are musicians, and I think that's one mistake we made – we actually did believe in the sanctity of musicians, not music. Musicians are complete tossers who just happen to be given this god-like gift, and we owe our lives to them, but nonetheless they are usually tossers. Sorry, Hooky. Others make the myths. There would have been no equivalent myth if Joy Division and New Order had not been on Factory. There would have been the music, but the music was more because of the myth. Factory wouldn't have been Factory without them. We were all in it together, till death did we part.

However much the city needed change, however fantastic and farcical Factory became, however determined Tony Wilson was, however good at attracting, and deflecting, attention, it needed something real and yet also ephemeral at the very centre, a massive surprise, nothing you would expect from the Manchester that emerged out of a group with two members from edge-of-oblivion Salford and two from edge-of-nowhere Macclesfield – in between was the Manchester they were said to belong to – something that was powerful enough to rip through time and place, and leave space to dream, something to be experienced rather than explained; and this was the stunning life in the music and songs of Joy Division and the stunning death of Ian Curtis.

The death advertised the life, and because the music was so vital, and suddenly it imploded, Manchester had the sort of contagious pop myth you can trace back, if you are of a mind, to James Dean. An exit to glory, an absence that is present as an after-image in the dreams of the living.

Joy Division sold records because of the life and death of Ian Curtis, which turned out to be horribly commercial, and New Order started to sell records once they'd moved on from sounding like an under-probation, grieving Kraftwerk to some kind of ecstatic, exploratory post-death disco. Because of the eccentric route New Order had taken into profit there was enough Factory money to open the Haçienda, a 'members-only' venue-cum-club-cum-arts-complex-cum-cocktail-bar-cum-arcade-cum-anomaly rising up out of the ashes of the Russell Club in nebulous, jarring Moss Side, where Factory first opened. Factory, Erasmus said, as he helped move punk music into an obscure club usually playing soul and reggae buried in out-of-town back streets, because factories in general were all closing. And cities are for people, not simply for profit. The city of factories needed a new kind of factory. A factory manufacturing pleasure and a different kind of work, and even art. Factory was given the name because of the factories that built Manchester with the intention of building a new kind of Manchester. And when they moved on, when there was nothing more for their Factory to do, they would have their own modern local factory closure. When Factory of Manchester opened, no one was paying attention to Andy Warhol.

Twenty-Four: The Haçienda (1) and the right to a city

Veritas odit moras. (Truth hates delay.)
VIRGIL

Joy Division played Factory's fourth night at a half-empty Russell Club. The posters designed by Peter Saville for the early Factory shows – closer to typographical sculptures than functional street posters – were printed after the dates of the shows they were advertising, and once the club had become a label they didn't always correct this sense of timing. The Haçienda, their next club, because Gretton and/or Erasmus urged them to invest in their own venue, helped filled the void left by the suicide of Ian Curtis.

Another variation: in the summer of 1978 Wilson travelled down to London with a few friends, including Buzzcocks manager Richard Boon and Fall manager Kay Carroll, meeting up with Geoff Travis of Rough Trade. This was when certain people, looking for a better world, were networking without realising it, supporting each other's first tentative steps into a future that was yet to be imagined or created. The networking, the fishing for ideas, was inside a very small environment where unconventionally dynamic people somehow managed to find each other.

They went to a night put on by forward-thinking Human League and Rezillos manager Bob Last, who also ran Fast Product, a stylishly self-conscious post-punk label from Edinburgh. The night at Camden's stolid, multilayered Music Machine was disappointing, the whole environment depressing, the carpet they all stood on the end of the world, and Tony said, 'If any of us ever make any money, let's have a better club than this.'

Before the Haçienda, a murmur of a movement, there was the Beach Club, a post-Russell pre-haunting in the grim maze of Shudehill, set inside a lesbian club, something underneath even the underground. It mixed music and cult film, was put together by Boon, Eric Random of Buzzcocks' Pete Shelley side-project the Tiller Boys, accountant Sue Cooper, Lindsay

Reade Wilson and Martin Hannett's girlfriend Susanna O'Hara, and was therefore known to some as the Factory Wives Club. No one thought of it as a dance venue. The name, another one of those clues to something, came from a situationist slogan: 'Underneath the paving stones, the beach.'

Erasmus thought the Haçienda was a mistake, a distraction, but what can you do? There were three votes – Saville and Hannett had no such power – and Gretton and Wilson beat Erasmus. Same when Erasmus finds a location that doesn't turn on the other two: two to one again.

After expressing interest in the more conventional venue Cornerhouse, they found a building they did like to the scruffy left of the centre of the city. Their new Factory opening, randomly, deliriously and then a little more explicitly, extended the Lesser Free Trade Hall intensity and the way new experiences, opportunities and challenges came to the city. At first a club that belonged to everyone and no one, a gigantic, custom-built version of the seedy Beach Club before the dancing started, used by locals however they saw fit – as drinking club, pick-up joint, political meeting place, arts centre, hiding place, empty tonight, music venue, last resort, once or twice, God help us, strip joint – Factory, without feeling it contradicted their essential, well-intentioned social generosity, tended to put the man into Manchester, and it was a straight man.

The location was run-down and seemed to reflect the desolate atmosphere of the areas in New York where clubs like Danceteria and the Paradise Garage were set, containing the collision of art, genre-splicing music and culture they dreamt of recreating. Architect Ben Kelly was hired via Peter Saville at the end of 1981 to manage the conversion from empty showroom to experimental nightclub and created a kind of minimalist cartoon representation of the city's industrial heritage, the idea of a functional factory workplace given an ironic visual phrasing. Cat's eyes were laid into the floor, twinkling in the direction of New York.

Carol Morley

Before the Haçienda opened we all knew it was coming and there was excitement in the air. You had to get membership in advance as I guess that was the deal with the council. It had to be a members' club. They made membership very cheap – I think it was fifty pence, but I could be wrong. The door had doormen who used to let me in for free, and who would let me jump the line. They clearly knew I wasn't eighteen, but those were the days when nobody really paid too much attention to that. When the Haçienda opened it felt like a giant youth club – it was often empty apart from nights when bands played. I remember playing Scrabble there. There was a VJ – a video jockey – and this is where I first saw a glimpse of Clockwork Orange. *Tony told me who Anthony Burgess was. He was like a professor, using the Haçienda to teach certain people about books and music.*

There were three bars, creating places to wonder, haunts to make regular, inspired by the Kim Philby Dining Club at Cambridge University, named after the infamous spies recruited at Cambridge in the 1930s to serve communism and/or fight fascism, Philby, Guy Burgess and Anthony Blunt – because, Wilson said, 'Spies like cities, they offer cover for agents, full of shady, smoke-filled meeting places, posh clubs and grubby pubs, to swap their secrets.' There was the long one on the ground floor along the dance floor, and a long one on the balcony overlooking the dance floor and the stage, but the cocktail bar – the Gay Traitor – was where you could find the most cover.

Carol Morley

The cocktail bar was my favourite. As you descended into it, there was a seated area that looked over it and you could look at who was 'in'. In the first few years after 1982 it was a fairly small room, which they later expanded. The barman would put flowers and olives on the counter. The cocktail bar, called the Gay Traitor (very Tony!), was where I had my first olive. It was also where I had my first Death in the Afternoon, a very potent cocktail. I sometimes missed whole gigs happening upstairs because I forgot there was other stuff going on. This was where it was all happening, in the moment, which was all you needed at the time. And

357

this space was often flooded as there were issues with the plumbing. You were in your element, and you were at the mercy of the elements.

The Haçienda was a preposterous venture, requiring hundreds of thousands of pounds of investment. The acoustics were challenging, and all kinds of structural and practical mistakes were made as those trying to get the basic details right battled those dreaming aloud, but in the middle of it all the Factory infrastructure didn't lose its sense of humour. 'I take the blame for everything,' Wilson said when he needed to get people off his back, as certain elements of his Manchester approached Greek tragedy, 'from people's deaths to putting the stage at the Haçienda in the wrong place to having live music on the same floor as dance music to having a restaurant with silver service in the middle to making the DJ booth too small to installing a metal detector on the door that never worked.'

Mostly, they lost all sense of reality, because it was the only way they got things done.

Andy Harries

I realised how much Tony was leading two very different lives in 1981 when for Granada Reports *we travelled out to Belle Vue Circus to make a short film. There was a boxing kangaroo, and for some absurd reason we thought,* Wouldn't it be great if we got Tony to box with the kangaroo? *Me and Tony decided to wind up the young sound man and tell him he needed to mike up the kangaroo's pouch. The poor guy believed us and tried to attach a radio mike to the kangaroo, who was not best pleased. He was kicking and flapping around. There was nothing particularly special about the piece, we cooked something up, dead silly, but Tony naturally made it work, and on the way back to Granada he says, 'I've been thinking about this club, and I think I've found a place.' He took me to the yacht showroom. I knew it, just off Oxford Road. We drove there, and it was still full of motorboats and stuff, and we pressed our noses against the window, looking in, and he said, 'Yes, this is what we are going to do.' One minute he's fronting a silly film for teatime television, the next minute he's showing me premises for this over-the-top nightclub based on some super-club in New York he wants to open. His life was divided, and I think the view at Granada was similar to the outside view – there were those that totally believed in him and those that thought he was a loose cannon of the highest order. But he was never dull. And there are some very dull people in television. And if you ever said, 'Why don't you raise some money, get some investment? Don't rely on yourselves,' he was completely dogmatic. He would almost celebrate that fact that there was no money. 'We're not going to sell out to a London record company. This is our thing. Fuck 'em.'*

Alan Erasmus

At the start I said to him about the first Factory release, 'You fund it and I'll do the groundwork.' Because he was at Granada. That was his main gig. I didn't think he would stay there once Factory started to be something. People don't realise that we pushed him for years to stop working at Granada, because it was a distraction. And Granada thought that Factory was a distraction. He wouldn't have it. I would argue about it with him all the time, I called it the artichoke argument because you had to peel away his fucking stupidity. Sometimes we'd argue for months, and then he'd reach the point where he'd go, 'OK, OK, you're right.' Silence. In the end he never really got to the point where there was enough stability in what we were doing for him to stop the TV, which didn't inspire confidence in the rest of us. He didn't really ever work full-time at Factory in terms of breaking free of the television. Granada became the safety net, but there was a point when Factory could have covered the thirty grand a year he was getting, and if he had been totally committed it would have sustained. He couldn't do it. Rob would say he was doing this because he didn't want a proper job, and that was the same for all of us. Except that Tony had a proper job. He was uncompromising ideologically and also uncompromising about these personal things. He embraced insecurity, but at the same time made sure he had security.

359

Tony could be very stubborn and pushy, and he ended up doing a lot of fucking stupid things. One of my purposes at Factory was that I would always say, 'Well, we shouldn't do that, we should try this, go this way.' Sometimes it worked, sometimes it didn't. Having someone in the middle of the fog who can point things out, point the way forward, it can be very useful. That was one of my roles. Perhaps I had too many roles for people to actually get what my role was – it wasn't a conventional role, it was about seeing things, having ideas, putting people together, bringing things to Tony's attention. Tony's writings, the way he influenced the writings about him, he somehow managed to edit it all to favour him, but then he is a grand self-publicist. That's his role. Fair enough. Everyone's role was important. But he cheated – he had this other role on the TV. He could play dangerously because he had a way out.

Peter Saville

Granada was his centre of excellence, so it was hard to imagine him leaving it even as Factory or the Haçienda is taking off. It meant his centre of excellence, the thing he was interested in, was in his home town. There was no need to leave. He had mishaps in broadcasting, an incident where he was interviewing the secretary of state for industry Sir Keith Joseph after a bad acid trip, and it could have been really bad for him, but he had Factory, so he could turn to that, the punk and post-punk world, and meanwhile the Granada thing does keep going. He can learn from his mistakes, and the direction at the time does seem to be he will be David Frost or something, with an international reputation as journalist and broadcaster. But just in case, always hedging his bets, there is Factory, which becomes an alternative way of addressing the nation, even the world. Whether he consciously knew it or not, we know the instinct was there. The attention he was getting was very seductive. He was going national, because the reviews of Factory acts were going in Melody Maker, Sounds *and the* NME, *he was speaking to more people than just the North-West. The music scene is national, so he can go national without leaving Manchester. We all had that feeling, that*

*was what motivated us, and British pop was a global concern and punk
was so important at the time it seemed like a global statement. So pop
was important to the world and punk was important to pop. It was easy
to feel you were at the centre of the world. Wilson is probably feeling
consciously or subconsciously that Factory is a platform to the world.
But for him so was Granada. He was caught between the two, and as
great as either one became he never became what he might have been if
there was only the one thing, the one demand on his time.*

'The right to the city,' announced Tony Wilson, wearing a mask of the
French Marxist philosopher and sociologist Henri Lefebvre, born in 1901,
eighteen years after the death of Marx, sixteen at the time of the Russian
Revolution, collaborator with original Dadaists and core situationists,
who once wrote an article called 'You Will All Be Situationists', sixty at the
time of the Cuban Missile Crisis, still writing as the Berlin Wall falls, 'is
like a cry and a demand. A transformed and renewed right to urban life.'

The Haçienda took its name and some of its original intentions from
poet, theorist and activist Ivan Chtcheglov's manifesto 'Formulary for
a New Urbanism', written when he was nineteen in 1953 and appearing in the 1958 *International Situationniste No. 1*, which began, 'We are
bored in the city, there is no longer any temple of the sun,' and included,
'The Haçienda must be built.' Wilson said it was fellow town planner
Gretton who found the line in one of the green situationist *Leaving the
20th Century* anthologies he liked to hand out to friends and colleagues.
Gretton asked, 'What the fuck are we going to call this place?' and fell
upon the line in the reprint of Chtcheglov's manifesto. Wilson perhaps
helped guide him towards the line; the truth might have been Gretton
saying, 'We're not going to fucking call it that.'

Chtcheglov was committed to the poetic creation of better cities: 'We
know that the more a place is set apart for free play, the more it influences people's behaviour and the greater is its force of attraction. Our first
experimental city would live largely off tolerated and controlled tourism.
Future avant-garde techniques and productions would naturally tend to

gravitate there. In a few years it would become the intellectual capital of the world and would be universally recognised as such.'

His planned spaces for his ideal city included a Bizarre Quarter, a Happy Quarter – especially reserved for living – Noble and Tragic Quarters, a Historical Quarter, a Useful Quarter, a Sinister Quarter, an Astrolarium, indispensable for giving inhabitants a consciousness of the cosmic, and a Death Quarter – 'not for dying in but so as to have somewhere to live in peace'. A few years after writing his manifesto, he was arrested for trying to blow up the Eiffel Tower because light reflected from it was shining into his bedroom and keeping him awake at night. He was arrested on his way there, having stopped at a bar with his bag full of dynamite.

The Haçienda didn't begin life as a 'rave club' but as a kind of experimental laboratory, an attempt to make real teenage Chtcheglov's inflamed envisioning of perfect city life. The Haçienda made good if unpredictable use of the space of a city according to the needs, wants and desires of Gretton, Wilson and Erasmus, their need for a social life, appropriating space for their reasons, because everyone has a right – not merely those with the power and the capital – to say how a city develops and changes, how it is formed, organised, regulated and ultimately used. Manchester, destined to be open for business, was now also open to play and the elevation of private pleasure into a public philosophy. Running the show, or at least acting like he was, or acting like he knew how, taking things seriously but giving them a vigorous, rascally spin, and arranging people around his schedule and destiny: Comrade Tony Wilson, spokesman and luminary, perhaps superficially absorbing the ideas of Chtcheglov, or claiming he had in hindsight, perhaps taking them seriously enough to change the trajectory of a city.

Twenty-Five: Anticlimax, intense young men and the next big thing

Qui non proficit deficit. (He who does not advance goes backwards.)

Tony the city planner, who can also be described as:
- 'I'm never in awe of presidents and prime ministers and major pop stars. I interview them all, it never worries me. Comedians I'm often in awe of, and I was always terrified of the late Les Dawson, because I have some weird obsession with comedians, and Les always made me nervous'
- meeting old mischief-making Malcolm McLaren collaborator and dark, sneaky journalist Fred Vermorel in 1980 with a view to releasing interview tapes with the Sex Pistols done in 1977 for a book Fred and his wife Judy had written linking the Pistols directly with situationism. Wilson fancied some Sex Pistols on Factory, for new times' sake; the eventual *Factory Records Documentary Cassette* in Saville-styled plastic wallet was viewed as a tacky cash-in, which made it both a betrayal of and in the recently displayed post-Pistols pop spirit of situationism. At the meeting an enthusiastic Vermorel accidentally spilt tomato sauce on Wilson, who leapt to his feet screaming, 'That's my new fucking suit!' The meeting ritual was complete
- an acid house rave in the grand Edwardian Victoria Road swimming baths in Longsight, he's wearing a yellow rubber designer swimsuit. It's a Sunday night in 1988. He's being filmed – naturally – in the pool with clubbers, swimming and posing, and he says something like, 'And this is what we do in Manchester on a Sunday night'
- cheerfully chairing a raucous live television debate in 1997 about the video for the Prodigy's 'Smack My Bitch Up', featuring a woman played by the model Teresa May plus drug use, vomiting, violence, vandalism, nudity and sex, with the controversial, elaborately

unpleasant art critic Brian Sewell, whom Wilson secretly loved for his vicious put-downs, an accent Sewell himself described as like an 'Edwardian lesbian' and the fact his former tutor and possibly lover was the Soviet spy Anthony Blunt

- the intellectual conscience in Manchester at the end of the twentieth century of a ragbag of musicians, designers, technicians, thinkers, comedians, disc jockeys, viewers, listeners, theorists and sundry other freedom-seeking Manckety-Manc loudmouths
- living vicariously through his friends and colleagues and collaborators
- seeing the self as a door, a threshold, a becoming between two multiplicities, from the tight jeans, Ford Escort, hippy long hair and Neil Young of the early 1970s, to the Jaguar, flowing full-length Japanese coats, copious man bags and madcap impresario flamboyance of the 1980s, to the superior self-styled style guru's conceptualist dreaming of Pennine Lancashire, a utopian upgrading of run-of-the-mill east Lancashire, in the early 2000s
- dreaming up a massive nightclub in a former-textile-factory-turned-yacht-showroom not least for himself, for something to do and somewhere to go, and coming up with all sorts of reasons for its existence when it turned out to be a mistake, then a marvel, then a mistake, then a memorial: 'We had no idea others would enjoy it. At first only we enjoyed it. If you are your own customer, you deal with yourself. If you love yourself, as you should, you make the best thing that you can. Not to make money, but because you deserve the best'
- because the table that he wanted for the Factory office was sold out at the local IKEA he got a mate's mate to make one for £1,500 and then told everyone it cost £23,000. 'Spin', he called it, as he watched his story become true, and at some points the alleged cost of 'the temporary contemporary table' (Fac 331) reaches £35,000

Once I'd left Manchester for evil London, Wilson seethed for years at my betrayal. He quickly replaced me, as though I was an employee, with a writer guaranteed to threaten my shaky sense of well-being and get under the skin of my tender boyish ego. No one local; someone brought in from elsewhere, from down south, London, from a rival music paper – *Sounds* – with a great name, great taste and a great writing style: Jon Savage. Wilson's new boy, who in fact got a researcher's job at Granada along the lines of the one I completely bungled. His qualifications, and manner, and skill in an interview were more conducive to the school of Granada, its oblique, insular clubbiness, and he made the reverse move to me, from London to Manchester, one that thrilled Tony, always anxious that the more typical move down south to the fake lights was dangerous to his vision of a Manchester at the centre of things. (Of course, he had also mercilessly plugged the Factory 'Sample' to Jon Savage, journalist, whispering, making exactly the same case to Savage as he had to me, 'The entire future of this venture relies on your review.')

In London I carried on writing about Factory's releases once the first single and album by Joy Division in 1979 had established the label. In fact, I covered Factory so extensively and favourably over the next couple of years that my editor at the *NME*, Neil Spencer, thought I must be somehow formally connected to the label rather than being a straight-forward enthusiast. I must surely work for Factory. The magazine had not allowed me to review Joy Division's debut album because I was too obviously biased – who on earth wasn't going to be, if they had ears and feelings? – and became so suspicious they eventually said it would be best if I stopped reviewing Factory acts.

Wilson was not happy, deciding I had turned my back on his label at a time when it was going through one of its difficult periods. By 1981–2, the label's distinct presence, centred around the success of Joy Division, itself centred around a tragic suicide, had faded a little. Pop music moved fast in this bygone era, because everything around it was moving slowly. Now that everything moves fast, because of the internet and social media, pop loses one of its greater purposes.

Factory's new signings looked – because of Saville, designing sleeves at some distance from the music – and to some extent sounded – because of Hannett, producing music at some distance from the musicians – like capsized versions of Joy Division, and didn't seem part of an exciting new scene with specific stories of innovation and revelation, and certainly nothing as dramatic as the violent death of their twenty-three-year-old singer. Factory were getting a reputation for signing the kind of acts no one else would want, both as an act of contrariness, but also because that's where their taste had taken them at the beginning of the 1980s. Distressed post-punk mood music emerging out of the doomier, gloomier parts of their most famous act was, for a while, their signature sound. Music that became associated with miserable-looking young men in long grey rain-coats taking life very seriously, just for fun.

Joy Division hadn't sold particularly well at the beginning. Wilson had been so sure their first single for the label, 'Transmission', was destined to sell after mostly positive music paper reviews for their first album that he manufactured 10,000 copies, which quickly turned out to be 9,000 too many. He once answered a magazine question, 'Career disappointment?' with, 'Pressing 10,000 copies of "Transmission" and selling only 1,000 – at first.' To Wilson, with all the 'dance, dance, dance' going on, and the constant mention of radio in the song, plus a focused, if fucked, Hannett getting the right equipment in place, it had sounded like an actual hit.

A riveting, disturbing, one-off performance of the song by the group on the BBC's 'youth programme' *Something Else* comes close to getting inside the just-discovered concentrated live power of the group at the time and the spiralling, demented compression of Ian Curtis's performance, hitting the future face first, still seeking light at the end of the tunnel but discovering he was standing on quicksand. They're wearing miserable modernist grey as a million colours crash around them, the moment the 'Fuck off' of the Sex Pistols snakes forward to the 'We're fucked' of post-punk. On the surface, at a time when rock music on television was still relatively rare, it seemed like the kind of appearance that if nothing else announced a new age – of something not yet specified. There was still a huge gap, though, between cult local band making a fantastic new track and them actually becoming nationally popular, a gap it would end up needing mystery and myth, and terrible disastrous chance, to fill.

I did my best to support the record, smuggling how absurd I thought it was that such a fantastic record, such a pulsating pop song, light fracturing through unquiet water, was not being played on the radio into a live review in the *NME* of the retro-mod group Secret Affair. The review was also a disguised story of how I had been attacked in the street outside the venue by a bunch of sullen skinheads lurking in the shadows. (The very British social and fashion merging that had positively filtered into punk, so there were commingled traces of skinhead, mod, ted, rocker, rude boy, reggae, glam, terrace and more elusive, unnamed tribal affiliations, had splintered within a few years, once the tabloids had forced divisions back into the mix, for their own benefit, their own ugly troublemaking tendencies.)

Presuming I was a mod, apparently their sworn enemies, the skins slashed my face with a Stanley knife; I fell to the floor in terrifying slow motion, turning the collapse into my own dance, dance, dance. Having been wounded on the bloody pop battlefield for the sake of a 500-word review in the paper about an underwhelming tribute act, I decided I could write what I damned well wanted, even if it was about Factory. So my review of Secret Affair was a poem in celebration of 'Transmission'. Wilson appreciated the sentiments, which I had written with a sliced upper lip, bleeding over my typewriter.

A couple of years later, I was unofficially banned at the *NME* from talking up Factory. Wilson never understood this, assuming I had made the decision to stop writing about Factory acts at just the time he was needing the kind of attention he had hassled me for with the 'Sample'. I became a traitor, writing about groups from Sheffield, Glasgow, Bristol and often quite simply from the pop charts and ignoring his special acts, a perceived slight he took very personally.

Factory's gloriously downcast series of post-Joy Division groups had sales more like 'Transmission' than the hit the group had in 1980 following the death of Ian Curtis, 'Love Will Tear Us Apart'. These included the not yet fully remodelled, pre-'Blue Monday' New Order, Gillian Gilbert as the new fourth member, Bernard taking over singing, a space on stage where Ian should have been, with their gorgeously dispirited, weirdly wounded debut album *Movement*, Joy Division painfully shedding their skin, shadowed by a deep and persistent melancholy, soft splendid electronic rhythms filtered through an anti-depressant haze.

Factory's newest groups, Stockholm Monsters, Crispy Ambulance, the Wake and Section 25, had the sort of names and cheerless, depleted, done-in sound that didn't trigger instant followings, which made the *NME* even more suspicious whenever I tried to slip recommendations into the paper about this austere, possibly droll new wave of Factory gothic casting its long shadow straight from an underworld Manchester. Some ghosts are so quiet you hardly know they are there.

'Intense young men with minds as narrow as their ties' was C. P. Lee's way of classifying them from the point of view of 1960s common sense – the next step on from the punks he'd described in an Alberto y Lost Trios Paranoias song as 'gobbing on life' – and my editors at the *NME* were mostly in complete agreement. They decided that to like this sort of music you needed to have a morbid personality; for a while that seemed the case with the Haçienda as well, a dark, narrow and crooked Gothic tower where the sun never shone and the dance floor was usually deserted.

The last Factory group I was permitted to cover at length for the *NME* as an intense, tie-less young man was the diligent, young, sometimes tie-less, sometimes tied-up A Certain Ratio, who, in 1980, the year Joy Division was forced to end, seemed to be marching in line to be the next great Factory group. This was when it was all working for Factory, when they seemed to be the future simply because of the way they worked and the ideas they had, not because they also needed the right accidents, coincidences, collaborations, fortune and circumstances to make things work.

I persuaded the *NME* to put A Certain Ratio on the cover, quite a coup in those days, especially for a group yet to make an album. The *NME* ultimately wasn't happy, because it soon became clear ACR weren't the new Joy Division and I might have exaggerated their appeal, even though in hindsight they had as much influence on Talking Heads, whom they had supported on some British dates, as vice versa.

The band weren't happy – but how could you tell when they were? – because they felt the cover drew too much attention to them too quickly, and that everyone would think they *were* the new Joy Division. Or they hated the piece and were irritated I had praised them so much and mentioned Wilson too much, like they were his puppets. It did alert the dole office, who assumed being on the cover of the *NME* meant you must be making money – some of the members lost their benefits.

Tony was happy because it seemed like I was still following orders and, for now, he had power enough to put his new bands on the cover of the *NME*. It seemed like he knew what he was doing. There'd been a death in the family, but the future was there for the taking. Of course, for all Wilson's planning and theories, the future would arrive as a complete surprise. The future was dance, where in fact music had been in Manchester in the 1960s. Wilson's musical taste, ranging from West Coast America to UK punk, was usually at the very opposite of dance. Few saw it coming at a time when there was still a considerable chasm, widened during the mutating disco years, between a dance audience and a rock audience. If A Certain Ratio were a dance act, the rhythms were bent around an avant-garde sensibility, any swing was charred and outlandish, the whole idea of 'Get on up' skulking and emaciated, optimism in the sewers.

A Certain Ratio were a despairing, alienated post-punk foreshadow of the Stone Roses and Happy Mondays – and the Chemical Brothers and Autechre's electronic-and-beyond reconfiguration – haunted as much by Brian Eno's experimental manipulation of repetition, itself haunted by German avant-rock, as they were by the bitter, prophetic rhythms of Sly and the Family Stone and Parliament's mind-tapping deconstruction of black traditions. From the ghettos of a drug city, growing up in a loaded dance city, with their bewitching, skeletal funk, their depraved disco, their cobbled grooves, Ratio were a phantom prognosis of the sort of music that would turn Wilson into Mr Manchester, unlikely non-dancing, non-believing lord of the dance. They were the derelict link between American electro and Manchester house. (The Happy Mondays, meanwhile, turned out to be the deviant link between the chaotic creation of Factory as thought experiment in action and the incoherent end of Factory as any kind of real-world going concern. They brought the house down.)

The ACR piece, in the murky, pre-E age before certain stray forces festively coalesced, and the Haçienda found its rhythm half a decade after Cabaret Voltaire played in its first week to less than sixty and William Burroughs as mind-altering monk read from one of his books, featured a significant cameo by Tony Wilson, who not only released A Certain Ratio on Factory but managed them as well. In the 1950s this would have seemed like dubious pop exploitation and a conflict of interest; in the late 1970s, after the rewriting of punk, it was a kind of agreeable, anything-goes-seeming music business spontaneity, and where was the money anyway? Factory's idea of the music business was that it was not a business, even as circumstances forced them to deal with it as a business, and Wilson, either sincerely or as more play-acting, eventually started to behave, mostly desperately, occasionally hysterically, as though it was a business.

Some close to him couldn't see why, but he loved A Certain Ratio from the moment he saw them make a churlish, boyish racket, awkwardly rising out of stinking concrete marshland. He fell head over heels not least because of how their disordered, depleted funkiness emerged out of the shabby, ugly funkiness of Hulme, its original industrial tenements being replaced by cheap brittle buildings unforgivingly packing people together, small-roomed dwellings doomed to repeat even amplify the deprivation they had been conceived to replace, people thrown away like trash, never consulted, never asked, the direct victims of another's often aloof convictions.

As with rap and hip hop – same time, different place – the dance of ACR emerged at the very moment neglected neighbourhoods were suffering from the worst consequences of deindustrialisation and urban renewal. At the time it was just how things were: you dealt with what you'd been dealt with and either found a way out or found whatever temporary consolation you could afford or steal.

The patched-up funk of ACR was inspired by the devastation of inspiration, finding a way to crawl out of a hole and locate a space where you could find your feet. 'There was a bombsite feel about parts of Manchester like Hulme,' Tony noted.

It was the kind of industrial dereliction that felt funky, and musically the absolute perfect response to it was A Certain Ratio. A funkiness that could have only come from one part of the world, the way George Clinton's emerged from growing up in New Jersey. When Martin Hannett was recording New Order and A Certain Ratio in New York in the summer and autumn of 1980, he always wanted to drive through a particular part of New Jersey on the way to the studio because it reminded him of Trafford Park, that sort of half-bricked, dilapidated feel.

The article shows how things seemed at the time, at the beginning of a new decade, a few weeks after the suicide of Ian Curtis, two-year-old Factory both in limbo and fulfilling unintended targets, in shock and taking things for granted, a few years before the Haçienda proposed a new world, with Wilson already ideas-deep in another project, plotting a new sound of Manchester, taking a sudden turn into his thirties, Factory going to his head, planning for a future that came true in a completely different way than he imagined. He could see things coming; he couldn't see things coming. One failure on top of another, two wrongs sometimes making a right, and always somehow getting noticed, always finding a way to explain things, find the right excuses, stretch the truth, sell the dream, stumble into glory, miss it by a mile.

A CERTAIN RATIO: FAILED CSE ROCK!
Paul Morley, *New Musical Express*, 6 September 1980 (extract)

A Certain Ratio are a crazed Mancunian unit who spent their wild youth doing some heady, posey nightclubbing at Manchester's more decadent clubs. The members gathered to make music almost out of spite.

Their sound is a derisive, decisive contemporary coalition of abnormal rhyme, the recession and no distinct reason; where funk's smouldering exuberance has been coarsened by lack of money, lack of future and a certain neurosis, and twisted viciously by an impatient post-Ubu/Pop Group spirit. It's a wretched, wrenching doppelganger to the sensual funk that reached a creative peak a couple of years back, the darkest, deepest side of disco imaginable.

And if truth be known ACR play not art-rock but failed CSE rock.

The Ratios have less than nothing to say about other groups and their attitudes; and only slightly more to say about their own group and attitude. They are not keen chatterers.

We wander along the darkening precinct. Always curious about what others think about the group and their occasional tricks, Topping asks whether I'd seen them play in khaki shorts. The time when fake tan could be seen coursing down their usual pale bodies? (A no doubt discreet reference to their manager's prediction that ACR will soon be cruising round Bel Air in Cadillacs.)

'Yeah, we got some girls to rub in that stuff, but afterwards they wouldn't take it off.'

I can't say I'm surprised.

'Did you think wearing those shorts was funny?'

Within reason. Is that why you did it?

'Not really. Tony (Wilson, Factory boss) got us them. They were only two quid. They're really practical, it gets very hot on stage.'

When a journalist writes a piece on a Factory group, he is inevitably met at Manchester's Piccadilly station by Factory's wizard Tony Wilson (to Hannett's mad professor, Gretton's jesting hooligan, Erasmus' elusive tramp and Saville's self-conscious design executive). And sure enough as we burst through the ticket barrier of platform nine there's the grinning Wilson, pushing loose hair out of his face, striding towards us in pathetic khaki balloons, happily sockless. He's skiving off more time from Granada Television.

Taking such time off has meant that Wilson by mutual agreement

has been taken off the World in Action *team. Too fast, youthful,
unpredictable within that context, he once hitchhiked to an important
interview with Sir Keith Joseph and turned up dishevelled and
disorientated, with a minute to spare.*

*Granada's respect for him as an on-screen personality – the man
who grannies used to love, who still gets recognised in Manchester
streets by teenage girls shoving each other in delight – has meant that
he's to link an upcoming Granada pop show,* The World Of Pop, *the
inevitable attempt to visualise* Smash Hits.

*The probable success of this, combined with the phenomenal and
significant success of Factory Records, suggests what the more flexible
among us have always thought: that* So It Goes *was more perceptive
and brilliant than merely being erratically entertaining. Wilson's
understanding of rock's volatile inner tension, its crude art and its
ace style, is unimpeachable. Factory Records is a success because it
perceives what is wanted and needed in 1980 pop.*

*By not limiting eccentricity, extremity or indulgence, Factory – along
with labels like Ze and Fetish – define where pop is and where it's going
as a reflection of today's turmoil. They are dragging rock forward.*

*Who else but Factory would have discovered and patiently encour-
aged A Certain Ratio, a group who in their early days were unhelpfully
primitive? And what a loss it would have been if no one had!*

*By totally lacking general rock expectations, Factory are more
likely to spot inner coherence in a superficially messy group like ACR
than in the restricted code of an average tidy rock band. By saying
that commercialism can be anything, not just this and that, Factory's
definition – rather lack of it – is best.*

*It allows ACR to be. They're continuing the punk spirit rather than
the letter of the law. Listen to them and you know what's going on all
around.*

*Tony Wilson is ACR's manager. As such he is ruthless, ever watchful
and scurrilously protective. The first time I ever saw Ratio was in
May '79, the London debut of Factory groups at Acklam Hall (along*

*with Joy Division and Orchestral Manoeuvres when there were less
than 100 in the audience). They were drummerless and I thought
cumbersome. I didn't like them.*

'We thought we'd played really well,' comments Topping wryly.
'But Tony thought we were drunk and he gave us a right bollocking
because people like you didn't like us.'

*ACR are not too sure how honest to be about their manager. They
always like to have it their way. Equally they are not too sure about
their position of relative acceptance but try to take it in their stride.*

'I think the reason that we are accepted has something to do with
Factory Records. Yeah, it's only because we're a Factory band that
we get a lot of the attention that we do. Factory bands do get a lot of
attention. Tony knows how to do things right.'

*There's a quiet respect for Wilson mixed with a tinge of suspicion.
ACR have gained a lot of attention through the Factory packages,
packages that now become slightly predictable and restrictive.*

'We don't want to do that any more. We're going to stop doing
them after America. That's where arguments have started . . . Tony
thinks that we're being arrogant. We can't understand in what way.'

*Wilson's side of it is that he hears Ratio developing the type of
crusty aloofness of latter-day Pop Group. This so-called arrogance
could be rooted in Ratio's intense desire to keep everything as
personal as possible.*

'Well, it's just we want to do things our way and they want to do
things their way. It's mainly that Tony's ideas are so different from
ours because of his age and everything, and he used to say that we
could do what we wanted but now he's trying to control us – not the
music, just the other things. It's become less of a family, Factory. It's
more of a major record company. It's gone up a stage since six weeks
ago. Some things have changed. Since Joy Division. Since the money
started coming in.'

*To some extent ACR are being mollycoddled as the next Factory
superstars: right now they're elitist press darlings, in the shadow of*

JD *but ready to leap into the glare . . . they skirt around any such pressure there may be to be the next year's successful Factory band.*

'If there is that sort of pressure we can leave. We are not chained to Factory Records.'

For all their emaciated energy and angry, mangy diffidence, Tony sees A Certain Ratio as potential pop stars, if only because he manages them and is soon planning to put them at the centre of a Factory music film, a slanted post-punk update of a groovy 1960s pop pic, *Too Young to Know, Too Wild to Care*. His unlikely choice to write the script is Liz Naylor, co-editing agitated, excited *City Fun* fanzine with Cath Carroll, she furiously articulating anxieties about their differences even after she'd failed with an early project for him, he perhaps trying to take her inside the fold as someone who couldn't begin to take him seriously and making that pretty clear at every opportunity.

As edgy enthusiast, craving space to function as herself amidst all these sarcastic hetero-boys in the city of sarcasm, fretting over what it would take to survive, she was always warily circling him and Factory, receiving her copy of *Unknown Pleasures* at the Palatine Road offices, and with cunning mate Cath Carroll becoming members numbers one and two of the Haçienda. She erred, though, on the side of not believing a word Wilson said, suspicious of the power he was beginning to wield but a little in awe. The way he blessed you with opportunity could one way or another be irresistible.

Thinking she was perfect to write the film script was one of his typically extravagant gestures, one of his zany rolls of the dice, taking a chance just to see what the results were. If it worked out when there seemed no chance, it would be an impressive sign of his unorthodox technique, his talent-spotting skills – and of course challenge those thinking it was a boys' club, a very straight zone.

He asks this kid from Hyde, where blighted 1970s Manchester really sinks into an endless no-go zone, to write a film for a group he is investing so much time and love into, perhaps seeing in her what he could in the end never understand: the crooked, cracked-up drive of the lost and lonely, some actual working-class, and whatever is below that, desperation. The desperation mixed with her need to be everywhere at once in the making-its-mind-up Manchester that came between the domestic introspective revelations of post-punk and the international dance of the Haçienda: for Wilson, well on the advantaged outside of the millstone of poverty, it is a perfect formula.

'You were forced to compete at the time with all this male energy,' remembers Naylor, 'and not show fear, not show weakness. *I can do this, because of course I can do this.* That's what you felt inside. That's why I was drawn to the music in the first place, to feel safe, and it did initially feel safe, but it starts to get tense once you engage with the scene. If I'd been a man, I might have been able to bluff it better, because that was what he was doing, what all of them were doing, bluffing the idea of belonging. It's all a front, and I couldn't understand how to put it on. I tried, which is why I ended in conflict with so many people.'

Wilson has a dual fantasy of what he believes people can do – because he has chosen them – and what they can actually do. The idea of a chippy, quick-witted, nineteen-year-old lesbian from tough, deprived Hyde writing the screenplay for an anarchically fun Factory film with a Durutti Column soundtrack turns him on, and he reluctantly hands her the most money she has ever seen in her life, £200, and sends her away. The deal is sealed in the Granada canteen, Wilson using the premises, one of his homes, as a cloak for the big time. He assumes everyone is totally in tune with his thinking and can fulfil his wants and needs; sometimes it works, sometimes it doesn't.

Perhaps what really turns him on is doing it on the cheap, and from the perceptive energy of her *City Fun* persona she would seem a smart choice. But Naylor has never written a script and feels totally out of her depth. She doesn't even have a typewriter. She scribbles a few handwritten pages in the spirit of *City Fun*; there's an idea for a comic caper where A Certain Ratio and the Distractions try some local pop terrorism, kidnapping Ian Curtis and blowing up Joy Division, but she can't take the story anywhere.

She's left feeling embarrassed, and Wilson comes to believe she can never deliver, and to some extent discards her from his thinking. When he was interested in you, he could place you at the centre of his world. If the infatuation ended, usually overnight, it was like being ejected into space. He wasn't there any more.

'He could be like a psychic black hole,' remembers Liz, 'that sucked everything in, including me. It left me bewildered more than anything. I remember him driving me near Piccadilly in the early 1980s and explaining how some run-down street was just like San Francisco. He was always putting on a show, he was always entertaining, and he needed an audience. You were there just to orbit him – he was the sun and you were some little planet. Whatever he was doing at the time, it was beyond us. It was beyond me. Even in real life I always thought of him as a screen. A television screen. You watched him at work, on television, in the city.'

The film shrinks to a series of surreal sketches; a terse Factory shareholders' update announces the schedule for it is 'No Date No Time', and then it disappears, to some extent taking A Certain Ratio with it, behind the screen into the grey skies above the city, spending most of their musical life as purveyors of stormy gloom, lovely angst and fallout dreams alone.

Twenty-Six: Morrissey, some exes, missing the boat, New Hormones discretion and the light at the end of the tunnel

Ne cede malis. (Yield not to misfortunes.)
VIRGIL

Tony Wilson the impatient mentor can also be described as:
- wrong-footing people all the time with new versions of himself
- television presenter at various times of 'What's On', *Granada Reports, Which Way, So It Goes, World in Action, Flying Start, Up Front, After Dark, The Other Side of Midnight, Sports Exchange, Workshop of the World*
- hosting Channel 4's live late-night round-table discussion show *After Dark* and, feeling bored, almost falling asleep and waking up to hear one of the guests attacking him for the fact that Joy Division were named after the prostitutes' wing in a concentration camp. He heard two words. Babies. Lampshade. 'I realised I was being accused of making lampshades from the skin of babies! I did the worst thing possible by putting my hand on her knee and calling her "love", and then explaining that no one from the National Front had ever come to a Joy Division gig'
- pop bohemian
- a dictator in his own province
- don't bother me with details
- if I always listened when people said no, life would be very dull indeed
- a very trustworthy person, with the slight exception of money
- tsar of a Manchester that was always on the verge of becoming solid and then melting away
- 'He has to make sure *he's* the biggest star in Manchester' – Morrissey
- non-stop swearer because 'One, I'm Mancunian, two, I work in music and, three, it sounds fucking cool'

378

- the missing link between a total loser and God almighty
- never far from his nervous old mother
- visiting her grave and still talking with her after she died
- ex-husband, twice
- always engaged in a feud with someone or other
- organising things without organising anything
- up to the same old scam
- cynical exploiter of rock music trends
- 'I'm obsessed with money but it's my seventy-second obsession'
- explaining why he hired misogynist loudmouth local comedian Bernard Manning for the opening night of the Haçienda by saying, pleased with himself as he is saying it, '*Pour épater les bourgeoisie*'
- slamming his fist on the desk and screaming, 'We'll deal with it ourselves. We're in Manchester. Who gives a fuck? We'll do it the way we want to do it. Our way. Fuck them'
- interviewing a cabinet minister live on TV at 6.30 p.m., then flying to Italy and before midnight mixing the on-stage sound for Stockholm Monsters in a small cinema in Tuscany

In 1981 Wilson felt that Factory had become useless, even if at the time he would never have admitted it in public. A wilful 'music above business', no-marketing philosophy that had worked at the end of the 1970s, elliptical punk and post-punk momentum still flowing forward, making massive, welcome cuts to rock's pomposity, was not so successful now that there were more independent labels and more varied, vivid and often more commercially accessible post-punk groups. Not promoting was for a couple of years the best form of promotion, and then it wasn't. Being weird and cryptic seemed the way forward, an act of genius, and then within months it seemed profoundly out of date.

He was embarrassed that he couldn't sell the sad soul music of Stockholm Monsters, the Wake and Crispy Ambulance, the elegant laments of Section 25, the weightless, reflective, troubled folk of Kevin Hewick; signing them with love, romanticising their value and putting them out as art was already looking futile, and not in a good way, in the early 1980s, a decade shaping up to have very different forms of creative energy, financial precariousness and cultural changes to the 1970s. Factory's roster was increasingly filled with strangers, and even Tony started to feel like a stranger as the times changed. There is always a moment when you start to fall out of love with a person, an idea, a cause, even if you don't realise it until years later. Something doesn't feel right. Things can never be the same again. Whatever next?

Wilson would use this depressed period – when it all threatened to become ordinary, no enigmatic sleeves able to cover it up, and Wilson potentially a minor off-beat footnote in rock history, and Factory weren't music paper favourites any more – to explain why he didn't sign the Smiths. This would have seemed inevitable from the moment in 1974 when a sickly schoolboy named Steven Morrissey had written to Wilson at Granada TV, sending him a New York Dolls album sleeve with the message, 'Dear Mr Wilson, why can't there be more bands on television like this?'

Wilson took an interest in young Steven, and encouraged his writing, including a short play about toast. He would come across him at various venues, and knew him through Morrissey's best friend, Linder Sterling, whose boyfriend at the time was Howard Devoto, temporarily of fast, smart Buzzcocks and then post-fast, even smarter Magazine. Some remember Morrissey in those last years of the 1970s as once adolescently infatuated with James Dean and the New York Dolls, somewhere between messed-up mummy's boy and eternally disappointed, sexually ambiguous attention-seeker, and with vague, far-fetched ambitions to be something that would either take him to writing scripts for *Coronation Street* or becoming a flamboyantly obscure pop singer big in a town or two in Italy. Others dismissed him as the very embodiment of a disturbed, persecuted loser. Wilson would claim he imagined Morrissey would become 'our Dostoevsky', naturally fancying that Manchester should possess such a thing, a literary genius weaned on Cilla Black and Oscar Wilde.

In 1980, as though he was a doctor specialising in non-specific anxiety, Wilson was summoned to Morrissey's mum's house in Stretford, and went up to his bedroom, his secret chamber, where, sat awkwardly on the edge of his single bed, in a small room dominated by a poster of James Dean, Morrissey solemnly informed him that he had decided to become a pop star. Steven had made a wish and seemed quite sure it would come true. Wilson indulged him, but even though he saw occult genius playing in the awkward young lad's eyes, he thought the idea preposterous. 'In my mind,' Wilson would say, 'he was the last person on the planet likely to become a pop star.'

Maybe he didn't stifle his laughter as much as he thought he did, so that when, over thirty years later, I asked Morrissey if I could talk to him for this book, he definitely couldn't stifle his laughter, or hide a look on his face as though he considered Wilson a total fraud, irrelevant to his life, nothing but a third-class villain.

Wilson once said, possibly as a compliment, 'Morrissey is the Jeanette Winterson of pop music, a woman trapped inside a man's body.' Morrissey replied, camp, cutting bully versus camp, cutting bully, heightened bitchiness tipping over into the nativist misogyny that would increasingly isolate him thirty years later, 'Tony Wilson is a man trapped inside a pig's body; the day someone shoves Wilson in the boot of a car and drives his body to Saddleworth Moor, that is the day Manchester music will be revived.'

It all started out as a fine romance. A few months after the urgent bedroom call, Wilson saw one of the early Smiths performances with Richard Boon of New Hormones, the more ethereal yet down-to-earth, cottage-industry version of Factory, who had already heard this group, which initially appeared to have a less promising name than Crispy Ambulance. New Hormones had an office in the centre of town where everyone with a thought or more in their heads about art, music and dreams would hang out, sitting on the couch often just to watch Richard try to operate the phone. Morrissey would turn up as if it was a combination of youth club for errant boys and girls and campaign headquarters for something subversively subdued, a glorious dysfunctionality that anyone wandering in could have access to.

Although the Smiths never signed to New Hormones, Morrissey as supreme awkward local outsider was nurtured and mentored by Boon, who would then work at Rough Trade – to which the Smiths did sign – and there is a world in which Boon and Wilson formed two wings of Manchester; two different interpretations of a situationist construction of the truth that itself split into factions. The New Hormones Manchester was soon overshadowed by the Factory Manchester – not least because one was running things, producing goods, strategies and illusions, and the other was a kind of judicious messenger abstractly influencing mood and behaviour.

Richard was a chaste, unobtrusive precursor of Wilson, another one paving the way, a more gentle spreader of the joy, of the discoveries he'd made, a more austere version of the way records transmitted important secret information and redirected history. Wilson had received media training, Boon hadn't. Wilson was comfortable with harassing people, Boon was more of a sidler, 'a hapless interventionist', one of those who preferred the Haçienda when it was empty, a web of quiet intrigue, dedicated to chance rather than dance, the kind of person who, when someone might say after a slice of reminiscing 'Happy days', will instantly reply under his breath, 'Some of them.'

Unlike Wilson, he would lose his train of thought when interviewed, but then, as Boon said, 'Manchester was about losing your train of thought,' as much as it was about staying focused. The experimental Beach Club he helped set up on the cusp of the 1980s, as the shock of a suicide damaged the recently energised spirit of the city, got all of its drama out of the way in a few short weeks and becomes an aside, a few on-line anecdotes, the place where a subdued, jerky New Order played their first show, in recovery, featuring a replacement for Ian Curtis who looked likely to burst at any moment into disconsolate tears. The Beach Club is a venue mentioned three times in a book that mentions the Haçienda over a hundred times, a venue that when Lindsay said to Tony she was involved, he replied with a little condescension, as if it was nice that the wife, already merging into ex-wife, had found some little project of her own.

Wilson watched Boon closely, even if just to avoid the mistakes that he was making as he worked out with New Hormones exactly what kind of label he wanted. One of the mistakes was signing Buzzcocks to a major label. 'We were like marsupials in Manchester,' says Boon, 'vulnerable creatures growing up in our own strange way far removed from the London-centric music industry. Signing to a major seemed a good move but it wasn't necessarily so. This said to Tony, with Factory, do not copy this. Keep yourself to yourself because whatever promises the majors make about your "creative control", they will forget them as soon as the work begins.'

When the major labels came north, for Joy Division, for Factory, Wilson was adamant. No deal. No corruption. (Island Records were particularly determined to sign Joy Division, but ended up with a lesser-known Factory act, the Distractions, still pop of the North with a certain local cunning, still with Peter Saville attached, but they got Gerry and the Pacemakers rather than the Beatles. When the decision needed to be made about two bands Island had signed in their attempt to compensate for missing out on punk – whose debut albums had in the end not sold perhaps any more than they would have done on independent labels – the ex-Factory group lost out to a band from Dublin. After some debate, because things weren't clear at the time, and the Distractions got some votes, Island chose U2, and the abrupt dropping of the Distractions confirmed to Wilson it might be grim up north, but it was cruel and unpredictable down south.)

Richard Boon was close to Gang of Four, to the Fall, to Cabaret Voltaire, the Prefects, the sound of where emotionally and politically the times were, and they all could have been released by New Hormones. 'I wouldn't have liked that expansion, though,' admits Boon. 'We got tapes from all of them after "Spiral Scratch", because that was the beacon, the sign that said, "This way next", but I didn't think my temperament suited a larger business. So we put them on as opening acts at Buzzcocks gigs, our way of making things happen, of supporting them, and saying, "This way next".' It's best not to tell a story at all unless you know you can do it right.

Boon had found situationism at the Isle of Wight Festival in 1968, after he'd bought a badly xeroxed copy of Bob Dylan's not yet officially published cascade of consciousness *Tarantula* from a stall run by a wild-eyed hippy.

'OK, kid, if you like that,' the hippy murmured conspiratorially, 'you might like this,' pulling a copy of Debord's *Society of the Spectacle* from underneath his table, charred with mystery. Later, Boon would buy a *Leaving the 20th Century* anthology at an anarchist bookshop in Leeds, a book making him aware very early on of how many different narratives are available. In some of these narratives there is drama based on a mistake, in some nothing much happens at all; once or twice the narrative feels completely natural, or it's a dream you keep on having. Sometimes the story being told creates its own structure and its own length, proving that human behaviour is messy and unpredictable and unconcerned with convenient symmetries; and there are narratives where some of us end up as footnotes that never get to be read, where we struggle to remain alive and not be submerged.

In this particular narrative, when New Hormones melts away into the early 1980s, a decade that didn't suit its idling, sloping form of unguided hanging-out and tricking things into motion, Boon rents their offices on Newton Street for a few more weeks to store old label material, including some of Linder's artwork. After a while he hears from Pete Shelley and Linder that the landlords have thrown out all of their carefully boxed and labelled paperwork, all their treasures – chucked into a skip. New Hormones of Manchester, opening up many of the routes for Factory, sharing similar visions but taking different decisions, is thrown away, another clue about what might have happened to Factory if it wasn't for the solicitous aggravation – and the enduring day job – of Tony Wilson.

With the Smiths, Boon knew that something unanticipated had bloomed, and splintered, inside Morrissey's bedroom at his mum's house, which turned out to be a fantasy machine, hothousing a hypersensitive mind. Wilson couldn't believe what had happened to Morrissey now that he had Johnny Marr to turn fugitive introversion and surreptitious confession into stealthy pop songs glorifying various forms of unhealthiness; despite being in a group so outside current fashions – behind and beyond – Morrissey was somehow in touch with the throbbing force of now, and suddenly more or less the first person on the planet you could imagine as a pop star. He was finding a way to belong on completely his own terms.

The Smiths would obviously have been the group to save Factory from the bleakness. Factory released the first James single in 1982, but that also seemed to confirm the label was now stuck in the shadows, stuck with sad-boy mood music, and the group needed to move on from the darkening Factory to get noticed. New Order's 'Temptation' hinted at a way of escaping the shadows – through delirious electronic thrills, a new kind of elevated, isolated mood – but creeping into the top thirty and then immediately falling away didn't cheer Wilson up.

Factory was cold, and it was periods like this which made it clear to Wilson he must never leave his Granada job, so that if and when the hits returned, he should never forget how cold it had got before New Order found the right kind of sounds and beats to give ecstatic focus to their melancholy, and even the Haçienda started to seem like it might make money. The cold could – and would – return, often combined with biting rain, howling winds, threatening police, vengeful crooks and circling creditors.

Gretton of Factory, with no particular job title but more the music man than Wilson, was telling everyone in fan mode that the Smiths were the new Beatles, but being a little tricky with the band, acting like Factory was a professional label, like he now ran things in this town but in the shadows of Wilson's mouth, saying their demos were not up to scratch, and they needed better ones. He needed to be convinced. But the Smiths would make it clear they never had any intention of signing to Factory and becoming part of a conveyor belt of Manchester product, as though there was no other way to make progress without kissing the feet of Godfather Wilson and taking whatever he offered. The Smiths were never going to follow Wilson into his Factory, and their story is they were not turned down by Factory, with its bossy, almost authoritarian ways. They knew how good they were, even if Marr and Morrissey couldn't explain how they had come across such alchemy.

Wilson's story was that he had no intention of signing something as special as the Smiths and someone he loved as much as Morrissey to a label he felt at the time was 'shit', a lost cause, and that was the reason he said no. He was doing it because he knew Steven was destined for greatness, not because he wasn't convinced. 'I said to him, "We wouldn't be of any use to you." That's my memory. Whatever. And Steven is a nightmare to work with, and if the Smiths hadn't gone to Rough Trade instead of Factory, then Rough Trade would have gone bust, and the British independent movement would have ended right there.'

When he interviewed Morrissey on *Granada Reports*, Wilson, pointing out that he knew him as Steven, kept calling him Steven. He liked Steven. His last word on Morrissey, during an interview with Ian McCulloch of Echo and the Bunnymen on his XFM 97.7 radio show in 2006, was that he was a twat. It might still have been a compliment.

At the end of the 1980s, Factory missed out on the Stone Roses. The Wilson explanation for this was that he could never shake off seeing them dressed as a bad goth band in the early '80s, and that there were a lot of his exes involved in their management – ex-wife Lindsay, determined to show him she would get the next big thing, that she was better than him at knowing what was good, ex-business partner Martin Hannett, an ex-protégé from the Haçienda, and the ex-manager of the Haçienda, now running his club's main rival, the International. 'So I completely ignored them.' He could take credit for giving them a first television appearance, when he was working on Granada's *The Other Side of Midnight*. His roving television talent-spotting eye was different from his meticulous or far too self-conscious Factory standards.

People working for Factory in the early 1990s were very keen on signing Oasis, which never happened because they came from a different Manchester – by then, Factory had the more conventional kind of A&R department, scouting bands as assiduously as many routine mainstream labels, and to some extent signing to Factory was no more exciting than signing to a more traditional label, just a lot less stable. Pulp were also of interest to his A&R people. Wilson wasn't interested – in Pulp or in Oasis. His excuse this time: 'Factory was busy going bankrupt. Anyway, Oasis and the Smiths are brilliant, but they never changed music. My bands did.'

In his own way, as an entrepreneur contriving an avant-garde aloofness and more culturally occult aspirations, he was right. No one could come close to recreating or redirecting the anomalous space of the Smiths – as freakishly singular as Velvet Underground and Nico – and there was something too obvious even ordinary about the idea and image of Oasis, who paid sweetly oafish tribute to the idea of rock 'n' roll rebellion, to the idea of pop as transcendence, but helped lay it to rest.

They were the kind of group that would have sounded exactly like they did without the sound and style of Factory, oblivious to the resonance of the two-note guitar solo of Buzzcocks' 'Boredom', Wire's twenty-one-songs-in-thirty-five-minutes debut album *Pink Flag*, the hysterically precise seven-second song packed with alert menace 'VD' that Buzzcocks' regular support act the Prefects used to start their show. Sinking back into the padded guitar consolations of Status Quo rather than the speedy agitations of the Damned, Oasis activated a different kind of more decorative, populist Manchester, a more pedestrian, sentimental, ultimately superficial model, the Hirst after the Warhol, the Harry Potter after the Philip K. Dick, the ELO after the Beatles. The clichés after the revelation.

Anthony H. Wilson

I always say that my two main groups – notice that I say 'my groups', I even say 'my songs' even though I never wrote any of them, which is a bit cheeky – both achieved something very rare: they both created classic, timeless albums back to back. I'm talking about Unknown Pleasures *and* Closer *and* Bummed *and* Pills 'n' Thrills and Bellyaches. *The rarity of that in the rock pantheon is that normally groups have to go through one or two, even three transitional albums to get to something new, but they got it straight away.*

Wilson was also always sensitive about his decisions regarding the kind of musicians he wanted to work with. It wasn't just about operating as power-broker on autopilot, signing the hottest new act, even if they were from Manchester, or the North, and it seemed to make sense, especially when it came to cash flow and balance sheets. If it was just about hits, money and working with new young Turks he didn't really rate, it would have been boring, a waste of his time. Wilson would rather suffer than go through the motions. He would get more nostalgic as he grew older, but it was a nostalgia for when he ran Factory very much in the Marxist spirit of 'not drawing poetry from the past, but only from the future'. Eventually he would against his better instincts get trapped in his past, even as he tried to escape it. He would get irritated in the early 2000s, when he was constantly reminded of what he had achieved in the 1970s and '80s, as though all that energy had dried up, collapsed into legacy, a lost militancy, but then he would spend a lot of time reminding others of what he had done.

He wouldn't have had his heart in Oasis, as much as he could have faked it. They were resetting music, and Manchester, to pre-punk times, with just a surface sheen of resistance, a formulaic sense of otherness. Working with the more obscure and capricious A Certain Ratio meant aligning himself with their record collection, more or less the only furniture they had in their run-down Hulme squat, 200-odd albums, a biography of diverse influences, the entire Parliament and Funkadelic catalogue, a brutalist chunk of German metal noise, a hot spray of Brazilian samba. These records excited him. ('Manchester kids' record collections are the best' was a theory he advanced when he was asked why Manchester was the city it was.) With Oasis, it would just have been the same old Slade, Bowie and T. Rex, and there was nowhere radically fantastic to take that, in the same way there was nowhere new to take the Smiths.

Then again, he would professionally enthuse about at best ordinary bands with at most one slightly better than average song who were signed to Factory in the early 1990s, like the Wendys and Northside, as though there actually was a 'baggy' genre triggered by the Happy Mondays and the Stone Roses that he had personally masterminded. These were the sort of underwhelming, derivative groups major labels would sign thinking that they had discovered the secrets of Madchester, or baggy, before it all turned to dust in their hands, because there was nothing there, no trend, no new genre, no money, no style.

In 1982, perhaps to make it up to Tony, moaning at me down in London that I had deserted what he was now thinking was a sinking ship, I wrote a 'manifesto' quoting Blake and Yeats about New Order for the *NME.* I had just enough star power at the paper to push my own agenda, even if it was me still sponsoring Factory. By then it seemed as though Factory had peaked, and so they allowed me my own kind of rant. It called attention to a then largely ignored New Order, still inching away from the ash, and cash, of Joy Division, their days in the pop charts over, a New Order funding an isolated nightclub, searching for a reason, a group still working out a revelatory connection between rock and electronics, between Manchester and dance, on the verge of leaping into the 1980s and a whole new future with 'Blue Monday'.

People still needed to be told, so I told them – taking their latest single, 'Temptation', as the perfect sign that a 1982 Factory release was definitely not 'pale', 'remote', 'frigid' or 'resigned', as some of my fellow writers were suggesting, writing them off. What's the point of that sort of writing, I began, if a record as heart-breaking, as enriching, as compelling slides past, floats into the mist, without being held and ultimately celebrated as a vital movement?

It was really a 1,500-word essay on a single that had not been as successful as Wilson and I thought it should have been and suggested perhaps that the Factory time was coming to a close. This was something to be taken seriously at a time when words in a music paper did have some form of influence, and there were no instant comments to distort and undermine the message, the manifesto. I must just confirm that I was not wearing a thin tie when I wrote this:

To finish where I began, with 'Temptation' – one of the most
poignant and bruising records that I can think of, a sublime secret
adventure. This record tells us much about tomorrow's New Order,
the excitement, the pressure of the unspeakable, the repulsion and
the euphoria, the gorgeous drift between sign and image. With
'Temptation' we think of all the words and all the images that I

think it is important to use when deciphering or dismantling or describing New Order . . . words that relate to the frightening honesty and treasured desire of New Order actually have animated useful meanings . . . words like 'brightness' 'life' 'generosity' 'dignity' 'beauty' 'incision' 'precision'. New Order shine a harsh white light on the devaluation of words and music, and they ask us not to lose our concentration.

I'm glad that I discovered them. I'm pleased I found the time.

What I was saying was, this is a fucking great track 'on the edge between melancholy and zest' – don't ignore it, don't let it all come crashing to an end. I then pointed out – because it still wasn't clear, in this hazy, tremulous period between 'Love Will Tear Us Apart' and 'Blue Monday' – that three of New Order's members used to be in Joy Division and its newest one was Gillian Gilbert, abstractly replacing Ian Curtis, even though Bernard Sumner was now the singer, tentatively working out how to deal with that, and how to sing a new sort of love song for the romantics who hate clichés, the dreamers still getting used to new realities, in a Manchester emerging from the mist.

Twenty-Seven: Meanwhile, a private life

Si vis amari, ama. (If you wish to be loved, love.)
SENECA

Tony Wilson being saved once again by one of Rob Gretton's groups can also be described as:
- someone not capable of doing anything that wasn't all about him
- a man of the theatre not of the theatre
- the very first person you would see with a phone in his car
- one of the first people you would see with a mobile phone, the size of a brick, which enabled him to execute at least two conversations at once
- he loved to jet-wash his car; he loved to see his car gleam
- skilled at throwing his pursuers off his trail
- yer fucking wanker
- a joke letter written printed in Manchester magazine *City Life* that began, 'I am in my mid-thirties and I go to clubs and no one seems to want to talk to me. I can't fit in with anyone no matter how nice I am to people.' It was a long list of why this person was being rejected, and at the end it was signed 'T. Wilson'

Carol Morley

I did have one night with Tony. My one night with Tony. He was thirty-two, thirty-three, not an old man but much older than me, and I remember he seemed even older because he had this jowly face. I suppose with my dad being dead he was the oldest man I knew at the time. The Haçienda was then the kind of place where I'd take the portable Scrabble game I'd got from my brother, and each night you'd go it would be filled with strange moments, Linder wandering through doing something conceptual, odd people up to odd things in all this unfilled open space. It wasn't like later, when it became one beat and one memory, simple enough to roll into mainstream culture. So I meet him for the first time in the Haçienda, when it was almost an extension of his home, his imagination, the Cambridge common room, the Granada canteen, the Factory offices.

I remember Coronation Street *stars turning up, like Bet Lynch, and it was like a local Hollywood. Tony's little centre of the world. At this time I hadn't been abroad, and the Haçienda was like going abroad, and then once he took me back to his house, and that was also like going to another country. There was another woman with us, and she might have worked at Granada because she said, 'He gets his clothes from the Granada costume department and then keeps them.' Not so much that he was frugal but that he wasn't as rich as he seemed to be.*

His house was filled with lovely things, and he made me a sambuca with the flaming coffee bean, which seemed like magic. Fire on a drink. He had a really nice modern kitchen, I guess with jars and stuff from Habitat, and an incredible avocado bathroom suite, which seemed from the future. There were lots of rooms, and at the top some kind of mezzanine, and he projected some Super 8 film of him at Cambridge. Silent, just him walking through Cambridge.

My one night at Tony's meant that on the next Valentine's Day he sent me a red rose to the boarding house my mum ran, just about, for a while, on Wellington Road, Stockport. She was convinced the van that delivered it had 'Granada' written on the side, which was hard to believe. Mum and the next-door neighbour were so excited about this red rose arriving from Tony Wilson. I did imagine on that day the van delivering loads of roses from Wilson to various houses all around Manchester. I sent him a Valentine's card quoting Sylvia Plath, because I had become known for pulling this plastic duck around the Haçienda, and there was this Plath poem, 'Child': 'I want to give you color and ducks, / The zoo of the new,' which I suppose at that point was what the Haçienda was. It was never mentioned again. He was interviewed in relation to the film I made about those times, The Alcohol Years, *and when asked about me he did admit to 'one very strange evening'.*

I remember the morning after, he gave me a lift home, and he was very irritable, driving very, very fast – he had somewhere to get to fast. I was yesterday and he now had today to contend with. He dropped me off and that was that. He'd given me a beautiful dark-maroon Factory badge in the morning – there were other colours – Fac 21. I have still got it. It felt amazing when he gave it me. My one night with Tony. And also he had a coffee machine, surely the first in Manchester to have one, and I am pretty sure there was something else in the morning I had never come across before. A croissant. Another first for Manchester.

Lindsay Reade

I did move in with him too quickly, and really Tony was into my looks – I used to be a ten, but now I'm a five – but not really my personality, so it soon turned pretty toxic. I married him as Factory was starting, a whole new set of interests which would increasingly take him away from me. I should have known when we returned from our three-week honeymoon in America and Alan Erasmus, his right-hand man, met us at the airport with a bottle of champagne. My mum was there too for some reason – she always said it would end badly – and me and Tony drove off, and Alan didn't have any money to pay for the car park and had to borrow it from my mum. I remember thinking, He's got his priorities wrong – he spent all his money on the champagne. That was a sign of things to come. He helped Tony choose the house we lived in on Old Broadway in Didsbury without me even seeing it. Once the amazing early romance wore off, there was a very different Tony. I wasn't his lover any more, unless he needed to conquer me again for his own reasons, and I wasn't even his drug-taking partner any more.

Neville Richards

He was such a romantic and couldn't really exist without a woman, or women, in his life. The truth was he was so fucking shy with women, and he'd absolutely love his women at first, and then as with Lindsay it would all sour, sometimes very quickly. For me to go into what happened

393

with Lindsay, you'd have to turn the tape recorder off. Both sides were
at fault. He didn't really get women – that scene in 24 Hour Party People
where he is in the back of a van with a hooker snorting cocaine made me
laugh, because he would not have known what to do if that happened.
Not a clue. He was modest even demure with women, oddly. Perhaps he
got too close too quick, perhaps he was keeping his distance – wanting
an impossible combination from his wives of being his mother, lover,
hedonist, friend and someone needing him to save them.

   I introduced him to Hilary when we were in the bin together, for
mental stuff. I was off my head and had been urgently taken into
Withington Psychiatric, and he'd come down to see me and we'd have a
few joints. He passed Hilary in another ward, noticed her, and I said I'd
introduce them. I mean, he's Tony Wilson off the telly, he's Tony Wilson
of Factory, but I had to make the introductions – he couldn't approach
her on his own. You wouldn't believe it, but he was nervous. And after he
spoke to her, being Tony he immediately says to me, 'I'm going to marry
her.' She was a double darling. Shame she struggled mentally, but she was
smart enough to keep up with him, and he liked that. He fell big time.

Hilary Wilson, née Sherlock, social worker, second wife

1983. I was twenty-seven, very anorexic, living in Chorlton, working for
Oldham City Council as a social worker, and I had been wheeled into
the mental ward about the same time as Neville was being stretchered
in, so we had quickly bonded. One day I was lying in the dark and not
really with it, and Neville introduces this guy to me and we chat for a
bit. They come back the next day, and later Neville says to me, 'Do you
know who that was?' He said, 'That was Tony Wilson.' And I went,
'Who?' 'You know, Granada Reports.' He was wearing a pair of plus
fours. I thought he was another psychiatric patient. He should have
been, really. But he would come in every evening and play guitar for
me and the patients, sing some James Taylor, Neil Young. He was really
endearing, and after I was released from hospital he started to take me
out on dates. He opened up the Haçienda so just the two of us were sat

there drinking cocktails. It was all very strange and surreal, and I just went with the flow. He was so kind and understanding, which was what I needed at the time. He used to come round to my house after I left hospital, and I wouldn't want to see him, because it all seemed too much. He would leave cheese and crackers on the doorstep. We'd sit on the sofa watching World at War *on Granada on Sunday morning eating the cheese and crackers. It was lovely.*

I had a friend who also knew him, and he said to her, 'Oh, I've met the woman I am going to marry,' and she asked who it was. When she heard it was me she thought, Oh no, poor Hilary. *She said it was typical Tony.*

I think he found me very interesting and mysterious, and Tony, when he wanted something, he usually got it. He saw me as, I think, quite exotic, quite unlike anyone he knew in television or music. I had a kind of extra ingredient. Anorexia was quite an exotic illness at the time. He'd always liked very thin women, and I couldn't have been thinner! I remember asking him why he wanted to marry a woman with a history of psychiatric illness, and he said, 'Because I know you're the one for me and I want you.' He made it seem inevitable. He was quite an insecure man and he was looking for someone down to earth, someone definitely not in the business like Lindsay – he wanted something to ground him a bit.

When I went to live with him, he used to say to me, 'If you wake up in the night, wake me up. Don't be on your own. Don't be on your own with any bad thoughts.' He was very, very kind, quirky, funny.

Tony was living on Old Broadway, which was funny because I used to pass those big houses and always wanted to live there. I couldn't believe it when we first went back to his home. Lindsay and he were separated, and she worked for Factory and had a room at the house. They had a really tempestuous relationship. Of the three of us, even though I had the badge of mental illness I seemed the sane one. As soon as he met me she was sacked from Factory and asked to leave the house.

Lindsay Reade

Classic Tony. He sacked me. The final coup de grâce. *He's given me this job at Factory, really sold it to me, overseas licensing, a little salary. We'd been having an open relationship, which wasn't the best idea – I'd slept with Howard Devoto to get back at him over something he'd done, because he was the one person Tony thought was even smarter than he was. It was never the same after that. Well, it was sometimes vicious. It was definitely interesting.*

Hilary Wilson

He promised me everything. I think I was looking for a bit of a saviour, and in a way who better? After a year or so, Oliver was born. I wasn't married when I got pregnant, but we got married in May and Oli came along in September. And then, six years down the line, Isabel came along, and Tony was having an affair. He left me when she was one.

Judy Finnigan

When Hilary was pregnant with Oli, she was very happy. She tried to bring a lot of order to their house. We went over one Christmas. They were having a Christmas drinks dinner. And she'd done the house. She put candles and holly and evergreens all over the mantelpiece, and it was so not Tony. It was so much a woman nesting, a woman expecting her first child and really looking forward to it. I remember when we went to see Hilary in hospital just after she'd had Oli. Tony wasn't there, but we went to see her. And Oli looked just like Tony. He still does, but dear God, when he was a baby he was a little Tony. And she was very emotional that she'd had this baby. And she held my hand and said, 'We're a family now. We're a real family now.' And it was never going to happen, really. I don't think Tony could ever have worked like that. As soon as things changed that much, or settled down in a way, he was looking in other places for something else that was new.

Oliver Wilson

I was christened at the Hidden Gem, and then the reception continued at the Haçienda, so I'm born straight into Wilson's world. For a very long time I thought my dad was the head of some secret military organisation. When I was a kid growing up – so this was the '80s and '90s – when we walked along the street there'd be people coming up to him and whispering in his ear. He'd get his pen out and he'd write something down, put it in their hand, then they'd go off. One day there was a big fire in Manchester in the city centre, and eight fire engines came roaring down the street and they went right past us, and then five minutes later they drove past and they drove slowly, all rolled down their windows and were like, 'Hiya, Tony.' And he's like, 'What's been going on?' I loved fire engines at the time. He's like, 'Don't worry about it – it was a false alarm, it was a false alarm.' So we were going back to base. Once we were walking through the park, and this jogger comes up and he sees Dad and he's like, 'All right, chief? All right, chief?' So to me this is secret messages, this is the fire and ambulance service are directly answerable to my dad, and there's people running up to him in the park calling him 'chief' or even 'colonel'. So all of these things formed the idea of what I thought my dad was when I was younger. Some kind of covert, clandestine operator. And I think sadly you get brought round to a realisation of who he actually is through people not being very nice and maybe bullying me at school. It came out in the newspapers that my dad was having an affair with Yvette and had left the family. You used to get comments about that from the kids – that your dad's fucking his secretary. You can't fathom it. So I am eight or nine, working out who he is and what he does. He's either spy or cheat.

Isabel Wilson, daughter

To be honest I never knew much about my parents' relationship, but I think they were deeply in love for quite a few years. He loved anything difficult, controversial, passionate, he was never going to live a conventional life, and for a while my mum fitted into that. But by

397

the time I was here, well, things had changed, it was a family, it needed responsibility, which wasn't really his thing, and he was an absent father. He left my mum when I was one and Oli seven. Very unreliable. We were classic kids waiting on the doorstep for four hours for Dad to turn up late on his day to look after us. The classic divorced parent story, kids used as a go-between for two adults who can't bear to be in the same room together, mostly screaming at each other. You can guess the nightmare it would be. I'm not sure he knew how to deal with the reality of a divorce with kids while he spent his life with Yvette. I'm not sure he knew how to be a father, or he made it up as he went along, as he did everything else. Saying that, though, there were a lot of good times together and a lot of good memories. He did the best he could, the best he knew how. He taught me so much, about everything, you know? We'd drive to a record shop every time we hung out, buy a new album and spend the day listening to the music and learning the history of the band.

He had this amazing thing which I half respected, half hated: that we were treated as adults almost from day one – swearing, drugs, sex, chaotic parental relationships, everything was an open book. There was no 'The children are in the room, don't talk about that, don't say that.' It was never like that, which is an incredible way to be brought up. It was definitely an alternative way to bring up your kids, like some sort of experiment, but also it was anarchic. He took Oli to the Haçienda as a baby, and then me. He would take me to big events, restaurant openings, charity dinners, aged eight, and just send me off to speak to people. He wouldn't have me sat next to him all the time, he'd go off and speak to his mates and leave me to speak to people like forty years my senior. Which on one level is amazing, but I can't say it was easy. But he loved it, it's what he wanted, so it happened. Swearing became a big part of my childhood. I remember when I was about seven Dad, Oli and I were walking up to the front door and Oli said 'shit', and even though Dad said 'fuck' a hundred times a day, he said to Oli, 'Don't speak in front of your sister like that.' And I went, 'Don't worry, Dad, I'm used to it, Oli's always calling me a sad fucking wanker.' Dad laughed so much, because

I think this is what he wanted. He wanted to be different, and this was definitely different.

Oliver Wilson

My dad took me everywhere – the Haçienda, New Order and Happy Mondays tours, music studios, video shoots, raves and Granada. It was just the most amazing experience for a young kid. But the music petrified me. It was loud acid, and as a four- and five-year-old I just didn't get acid dancing. At the Haçienda I'd hide away under his rain mac and peek out at everyone. We'd go to Factory and Haçienda board meetings and meetings in London. He'd plonk me at one end of the table with a model helicopter or something.

My dad had his office at the top of the house, where he could be himself – it was very important to him – where he could have his ideas. Oddly, he was quite solitary in his own way. It was a super-cool room, really big, Haçienda flag, Peter Saville artwork, whole wall of family photos and old photographs, and my dad always had a massive desk, this huge door on trestles, with writing implements on it. My dad loved making lists. I'd go to bed, eight, nine, and a few hours later if I woke up, midnight, four in the morning, he'd still be in his office, which would be filled with smoke. He was never shy in front of me about his drugs and his habits. He'd say, 'I've got this speech to write so I've taken some speed, I've got some cocaine,' and he made it all very natural. All the men I came across, the Factory bands, they were all doing drugs. Which was good in the sense that as a grown-up I've got no mysticism about drugs, but it also meant I wanted to take them as soon as I could. I wanted to be part of it.

I remember sometimes I wouldn't see him for weeks, and he suddenly turns up because he'd heard about me being bad or something. I remember one time I'd not been doing my GCSE revision for weeks because I'm on my computer on Cubase making drum-and-bass tracks, and my mum's gone spare, worried I'll get expelled from school because I've done fuck all, and maybe I'm reacting because I don't see my dad.

399

And it was hard, it was really hard, because I'm sure my dad, he was off in this whirlwind life, being whoever he was, not thinking about how we were dealing with it.

After not seeing him for a while, I remember you'd always hear the roar of his Jaguar coming up the street too fast. Jumping out the car, shades on, with a big fucking rain mac on so it spreads out like a cape. Coming into this house – 'Where the fuck is he? Where the fuck is he?' And he would come upstairs and rip my keyboard out of the computer and take the power lead – 'You fucking pass your GCSEs, you prick' – and take my stuff away. He then speeds off down the street with my lead. And that's all I'd see of my dad for maybe three, four weeks. But it's good parenting in a way, in his way. He said, 'I don't give a fuck what you do the night before, as long as you turn up the next day and your work's done. I don't give a fuck what you do. And if you turn up the next day and your work's not done, you're a fucking dickhead.' Word for word, that's what my dad told me. And that's what I live with still. But he gave me books and an intellectual direction – Shelley, Kafka, Marx, Engels. He had a huge influence on me, even if he wasn't around in person. That roar of the Jag, though, would get me very nervous. And I hated him picking me up from school in that bloody car. It was OK for him, but I had to deal with the fallout at school.

Isabel Wilson

I got caught with some weed at school once. And I remember we were in his Jag – most of my memories are when we were sat in his car – looking forward, not looking at each other. And he suddenly said, 'Darling, I need to talk about what happened at school.' I was mortified, I was thinking, Fuck, fuck, fuck, I'm in trouble. And he said, 'Listen, if you want to have fun, have fun. Just don't fucking get caught.' That was all he said on the matter. His other advice to me was never date a musician. Which of course I did.

Hilary Wilson

I remember once in the kitchen he seemed to completely lose it. I think he was off his head on coke or something. He was pacing up and down, saying, 'I'm at the forefront of this generation, I'm the leader of something really important.' And I remember standing there thinking, Fucking hell, he's lost it, you know. He got lost a bit in it all.

Oliver Wilson

I had the best of my dad when I was a kid, but then things just got a bit crazy for him and the rest of us. I think for a while at least he lost touch with the real world and struggled to see what was important. But I can understand that. He was in the middle of it all. It must have been a ride. And it resulted in this rock 'n' roll lifestyle that didn't always match up with being a dad. I can understand that, but it made things difficult at the time.

Twenty-Eight: The Festival of the Tenth Summer, a uniform and politics

De gustibus non est disputandum. (In matters of taste, there can be no dispute.)

The lost Tony Wilson can also be described as:
- presented with an honorary degree by the Open University in recognition of his role in promoting the North-West region and his contribution to the regeneration of Manchester
- he and Richard Madeley were ordered to read a particular news story on TV straight and without comment. Richard read the story about Granada's own journalists going on strike in support of the nurses' day of action with true professionalism. As he did so, Tony's clenched fist appeared behind him as a sign of solidarity with the workers. On the day of the strike he mounted the Quay Street steps and addressed the bemused health workers with quotations about Marx and 'dialectical materialism'
- the television reporter who did a piece to camera in 1976 at the crumbling Electric Circus punk club in unlovely Collyhurst to explain who the Clash were for viewers still catching up with the idea of the Beatles, but still really talking about himself, wearing a massive fedora while standing under a leaking ceiling below the upstairs toilets, so as he did his loose-lipped all-knowing spiel, piss was dripping onto his look-at-me hat
- posing for a cool 1976 black-and-white photograph with starting from (spiral) scratch Pete Shelley and Howard Devoto of Buzzcocks, trying to keep up with their natural deadpan artful posing but looking like their squiffy sitcom uncle
- forming a company or two made up of sceptical, self-organising revolutionaries, collaborative inventors and mischievous specialists treating the business of producing and distributing music and

associated images from a position that was somewhere between
aesthetic conviction and amiable bewilderment
- the head of Granada Television roaming the office looking for Wilson,
wondering where he was 'and what is he doing apart from using my
fucking phone to run his fucking business', because he was using his
Granada office as an extension of his Factory office
- telling an audience of local government representatives at the HQ of
a regional government agency in Warrington that the town, halfway
between Manchester and Liverpool, was 'the perineum of the
North-West'
- 'One of my worst habits is that I can talk to my bosses and betters as
if they're pieces of shit'

Some of the most awkward, embarrassing things I have done in public
involved Tony Wilson – trying to keep up with him, to compete with
him, understand him. Even if you were in one of those periods with Tony
when he was giving you the silent treatment or busy enough for years to
pass by with little contact, you would still catch yourself thinking about
some piece of writing or appearance on television, *I wonder what Tony will
think of this.*

I have been pushed into other places, because of Wilson, or my interpretation of what he was, as much as by anyone or anything, directly or
indirectly. Directly because he encouraged me if only by being interested
in what I was doing, indirectly because he set precedents and suggested
directions to take even if I only imagined them.

He always made me feel like I knew nothing about anything. This was
good in one way. I had to keep finding out. I had to keep proving to him
that I did. I had to keep remaking myself. On the other hand, it always
made me think I could never catch up. He would invite me onto live television shows he was hosting, and I was always on the back foot, not sure
whether I was competing with him or being promoted into some new
position that would help me in my professional career – thus confirming
his possibly inflated view that I 'was the finest writer of my generation',

which caused me as many sleepless nights as quiet moments of triumph, and which got me onto radio and television, like him, but without the qualities, and the qualifications.

He invited me to take part in events and happenings he was organising to mark the ten years since the Sex Pistols as a semiotic assault had played in Manchester. The Festival of the Tenth Summer in 1986 showed off what Manchester had become since 'Spiral Scratch' and New Hormones, since the unpromising Russell Club in Hulme, where Madchester was prehistorically hatched, and the avant-glam Factory 'Sample', since Joy Division and the Fall, since Magazine and Linder. It had become New Order, Buzzcocks and the Smiths off the telly, off *Top of the Pops*, from the pages and covers of the music magazines. Stored-up energies released by the Sex Pistols had become new forms, new materials, new directions, addressing themselves to new people, many of them young enough to have no idea about their beginnings.

The handful of early explorers playing at difference, venturing out to marginal, co-opted venues like the Squat and the Ranch, many with the Lesser Free Trade Hall Sex Pistols ringing and raging in their ears, had in ten years become thousands filling the G-Mex arena, round the corner from the Haçienda, which was about to become the Haçienda known around the world as an influence and a mecca, not the Haçienda that for a few years seemed more white elephant than the future of the city. The Haçienda that would eventually become the city's equivalent of the 'Yellow Submarine', a sign of old times, the past of the city, part of the tourist map, its ironic, industrialised logo colours ultimately engraved into the Puma 2019/20 away kit of Manchester City, their philosophical manager Pep Guardiola's mind-altering patterns of play one glorious far-fetched consequence of the beats that lifted the Haçienda into local legend. The black and yellow police warning colours becoming a pleasure warning, the bliss-chasing Haçienda house dance rippling through Manchester history into the elevated, mesmerising football City played. Alas for Wilson, luckily enough never living to see the day, it had no impact at all on his beloved United, who seemed to stick with being Simply Red.

The Festival of the Tenth Summer was a typical Wilsonian exercise: make something up to make something happen, and then after that make something else up, so that something else could happen. At the time it didn't seem remarkable that he had accumulated all this power to organise such events, eight or so years after the marginal, magnetic grunge of the Russell Club and the luxury limited-edition eclecticism of the Factory 'Sample'. It was taken for granted that Wilson was now somehow deep into his own Thatcher-like reign, taking power in the months after the death of Ian Curtis, embedding his face and Factory, his fake TV manner and his simultaneous indie second-life-seeking authenticity, his image and chosen images into the city. Steve Diggle of Buzzcocks said that it was as though 'you didn't have to think for yourself any more. He did it all for you. His ideas were good, but it wasn't so good that he had such force they were taking over.'

The Smiths – back in the innocent days, decades before Morrissey came out, or was dragged out, as certified nationalist mutant, his pursuit of purity turning poisonous – were for a short time the main sign of another, freer Manchester, one with a different set of issues and commandments, different ways of deconstructing the dominant meanings and simulations that saturate social space. New Order had become, after a heart-stopping pause before they worked out how to make the machines work for them, the Factory stars; the Smiths represented the New Hormones alternative, and the Fall, holding a mirror up to Manchester and then breaking it, represented the freedom that leads either to deviant new art or to nothing but itself.

By the time of the Festival of the Tenth Summer, organised by Wilson as a cultural conference, ten numbered exhibits of how much Manchester as cultural centre had moved and changed in ten years – number one in the list of ten: the fact there was a list – New Hormones had become a ghost network. Morrissey the local outsider had been replaced by someone with the same name and concerns who had become an idol to many, who appeared to see the world, and through the world, the same way. He had been handed sudden new power, because at the time – getting older robbing him of time and timing, and because of the absence of the internet, a now unimaginable emptiness that actually created shadows where you could hide – it seemed he could sort out all the mysteries known to humans through his songs and obsessions.

Morrissey was the pop star he'd wished to become; Wilson had evolved into more or less a pace-setting city leader, an unelected governor. Maybe those who bought 'Blue Monday' didn't really think about it, but they had elected him, Peter Saville's almost ruinously expensive sleeve being among other things a mysterious ballot paper. Wilson had meanwhile started to dress like a dignitary, somewhere between Zen fop and avant-garde entertainment executive. He'd found a uniform; actually, someone else had found his uniform for him.

The 1970s Wilson didn't look like he cared about his clothes, and there was a muddy professorial scruffiness about him that didn't seem like it would ever change. On television, as newsreader and reporter, he seemed vaguely scrubbed up, a presentable presenter in ill-fitting jacket and indifferently chosen tie as wide as his crowd-pleasing but slightly awry grin. On *So It Goes* he looked a little like one of his idols, son of Salford criminal turned eminent Californian dreamer Graham Nash, who'd learnt to harmonise singing the Lord's Prayer every morning at Salford Grammar. (Wilson once told me when I asked him what his role was in the whole Manchester scheme of things that he was the Graham Nash of it all, stabilising the wayward geniuses and time-bomb personalities around him, the Hannetts, Curtises, Sumners, Toppings, Ryders, Savilles, Browns, pulling it all together; he wasn't unalloyed genius like Crosby, Stills or Young, but they couldn't have done it without him. And Erasmus like Crosby had the best dope in the world.)

By the early 1980s, his dusty, shapeless, academic-hippy look had not aged well, especially now in contrast to Factory's artistically commercial enigmatic images. If his clothes were architecture, he was wearing the equivalent of a suburban semi-detached. He needed an equivalent to Peter Saville to put him in clothes that made sense for someone who had turned a record label into a multifaceted mobile gallery.

A striking-looking seven-foot-three-inch ex-Sale Grammar boy and business student, Richard Creme, after rejecting the offer of a corporate job in America, had followed his father into the garment trade, but with ambitions to open a shop featuring the kind of avant-garde male clothes that no one else in the North-West was selling. With his skills as a tailor and an intrepid artistic approach to style, he could reanimate the way-out men's boutiques that Manchester and Stockport had been famous for in the 1960s, when there were pop stars, footballers and disc jockeys to dress in lively, nonconformist new fashions.

In the early 1980s, set to become *the* designer decade, Creme was the first in the city and one of the first in the country to become aware of Comme des Garçons and Yohji Yamamoto from Japan and Jean Paul Gaultier from France. This was before anyone really knew how to pronounce these mysterious new names. He opened a small shop in Manchester's compact city-centre posh district, St Ann's Square, L'homme, inspired by the stores he had seen on Rodeo Drive, Los Angeles. It looked like a gallery – apparently you needed to ring a bell to be allowed – invited – in, but that was just for show, a little bit of theatre. Really, you just needed to push the door, and then cope with being sized up by the lightly judgemental, clearly shrewd Creme, who didn't want his clothes to head off in the wrong direction on the wrong body.

Slick, would-be flash professionals with money, or on the make with ambitions to take it or steal it, as long as you were seen by Richard to have the right attitude, up to carrying off his carefully curated clothes, you were the subject of his generous, discriminating attention. Some of his clothes featured a little addition or adjustment requested by Richard. Whoever you were, however internationally respected as a designer, if Richard made some sort of request, it usually worked and was acted on. I still have the shoes I would buy from Richard in the 1980s, including a pair by Cesare Paciotti that he had given a little twist, a little remix, getting the Italian designer to add some metal embellishments that lifted wonderful objects to another, near-sculptural level.

On early buying expeditions to fashion designers to make selections for his shop, there was initially a little amusement that he was hoping to sell these clothes in Manchester. The North of England surely was where style never reached. Richard knew better, and for three decades he influenced the look of Manchester, never wrongfooted by new trends, always in tune with changes in style, responsible for David Beckham's transformation into bold international style icon, on the way to a widespread metrosexual transformation of male style. Beginning with Beckham, Richard Creme found out about how to dress as a form of translated expression, of displaying ego.

His shops became a port of call for visiting pop superstars, including Madonna, Prince – opening up by royal command in the dark, early hours of the morning, Creme found himself 'shaking hands with a small child' – and Bruce Springsteen, who had learnt about Richard from David Bowie. Springsteen's American Express bills for shopping at L'homme – enough clothes so he wouldn't have to buy any more for months – were so steep they needed to be ratified at the highest Amex level. At Richard's you could find what he called before anyone else in town 'pieces' that you couldn't find in New York, even Paris and Tokyo. When there was Madchester, he was the reason why Ian Brown of the Stone Roses and Shaun Ryder of the Happy Mondays on their *Top of the Pops* appearances wore their usual streetwear with fuck-off easy come, easy go couture elevation. The clothes Richard sold were to him just a way of elaborating on and modifying an essential individual local style, a form of down-to-earth extravagance that could be displayed with little money or a lot of money.

His commitment to doing something special in Manchester, his pride that stars thought of Manchester as somewhere they could buy the best clothes, and his resistance to offers to relocate his shop and sensibility to London, were Wilsonian. So it wasn't surprising as a regular Haçienda client that he couldn't allow Wilson to look so sloppy. As a Manchester ambassador to the outside cultural world, surely he of all people needed to look the part.

Creme got to tell Wilson that he looked like a left back for permanently Third Division Oldham Athletic, basic code for an uninspiring, unstylish nobody. When she was his wife, Lindsay remembers ironing his shirts for him, 'and I can tell you they were not designer'.

If your personality is flat, then you wear obvious things, and Wilson's personality whatever else it was certainly wasn't flat. Creme offered his help, and Wilson found his stylist, his designer, another crucial adviser, someone to produce him in the flesh in the way he was produced as an on-screen presenter. Another member of his long-term entourage. The shift from pre-Creme to post-, from high street to post-modern, was as dramatic as the shift from the sleeve for Warsaw's 'Ideal for Living' to the sleeve for Joy Division's *Unknown Pleasures*, from the Russell Club to the Haçienda.

Creme did it by reading Wilson's philosophical dandiness and thespian instincts perfectly, directing him towards the loose-fitting, exotic but tempered black flowing shapes and sizes of the unearthly Yohji Yamamoto and imaginatively austere Comme des Garçons – about as modern and modernist as clothing was at the time – labels that approached their tailoring as though they were designing for mind as much as body, with a reverence that seemed quasi-religious.

Cryptic founder of Comme des Garçons Rei Kawakubo worked in a textile factory as a young woman, and then started styling for the factory, producing the sort of clothes she wanted to wear but couldn't find anywhere, clothes that had never been seen before. She would explain that she was not an artist, and not a fashion designer; she used fashion to make a business out of creation.

Yamamoto is a fashion radical who combined historically inspired craftsmanship and dreamy philosophy – the intellectual and the personal, the ritualistic and the sensual – and tested the boundaries between commodity and art. His Paris catwalk debut in 1981 featured an amplified heartbeat as a soundtrack, and his shows since then have generally employed an anti-advertising spirit in order to advertise his clothes. It wasn't long before Peter Saville was being commissioned to design campaign material for Yamamoto, whose approach to publicity material, if not borrowed from Factory, then shared a sensibility. The next generation of rebel designers also seemed connected to the style of Factory. Belgium's Antwerp Six graduated in 1980/81, internationally breaking through in 1986, and were

409

headed by Dries Van Noten, Ann Demeulemeester and Dirk Bikkembergs. Martin Margiela became an unofficial member of the Six, worked with Jean Paul Gaultier during his 1980s pomp, and introduced a cryptic numbering system to his clothing that seemed indebted to Factory's Delphic system of archiving its products, principles and processes.

All this was further reason why Creme was correct in diagnosing that the Factory boss needed to dress for the situations he was creating, directly and indirectly. Wilson believed his creation was an unworldly organisation producing culture. As he said, 'We are not a record company, we are an experiment in human nature.' He started to dress experimentally to more appropriately suit that definition, to underline in person that he did not want to pass through anywhere without being noticed.

The existential, sombre black that Yamamoto and Comme des Garçons favoured would become Wilson's default colour, closer to luminous Mark Rothko than the beatniks. Seen at the time as symbolising dread and hopelessness, as though Yamamoto and Kawakubo only made clothes for austere intellectuals, for insurgent or ascendant elites, or were perpetually memorialising a personal tragedy, black suited Wilson down to the ground, especially because he was quick to appreciate the designers' dark, almost mocking sense of whimsy and play. Kawakubo started using black in the early 1980s because at the time it wasn't utilised at all in the fashion world. At the time it was new, which is what she wanted to be. 'I work in three shades of black,' she said. For her, a good collection was when people were afraid of it, knowing that in ten years everyone would love it.

'Black is modest and arrogant at the same time,' Yamamoto would say. 'Black is lazy and easy – but mysterious. It means that many things go together. You need black to have a silhouette. Black can swallow light or make things look sharp. But above all else black says this: "I don't bother you – don't bother me."' For Ann Demeulemeester, it was the 'purest colour, the colour of poets and rebels and writers'.

Yamamoto saw his clothes as a romantic extension of punk – and gothic – black, and what became known as his deconstructive approach to cut, material and the positioning of pockets was his way, influenced by the revolutionary objectives of the late 1960s, of rejecting what he saw as oppressive bourgeois conformism. Kawakubo felt an affinity with punk, because 'it was against flattery'.

This was all perfect for Wilson, who also loved that the clothes immediately acted as both armour and provocation, and being colourless could pretend to be classless. They were the television presenter's neutral, near-invisible clothes militantly abstracted, with a touch of the macabre, into something that was either impressive or highly annoying, depending on where you stood regarding Wilson. A tidier new haircut confirmed the new arrangement, eventually joined by a pair of minimalist spectacles that managed to make him seem even more conceited.

Only Wilson could pull it off; only Wilson would want to pull it off, knowing of course how his appearance would draw attention. He'd found a uniform that no one else was wearing; he was a sect, a company, of one. If brands are tools for consumers to describe their personality, he'd found the perfect ones.

Suspiciously proportioned, almost asexual, obviously expensive suits – which he claimed all fitted inside his mid-'80s £2,000-a-year Granada clothes budget – long baggy coats transforming him into a surreal Batman, shirts as shrouds, a tumble of scarves, a lot of miserabilist black, the ever-present bag, a bulging Filofax: this was the new Wilson, made even bigger, louder, more energetic, styled by Richard Creme to look the part. The part being, 'Follow me to the centre of the 1980s designer universe,' which, because Wilson says so, happens to be in Manchester.

This was how Wilson was at the time of the Festival of the Tenth Summer, charging around Manchester as a venue as the man in charge, already organising anniversaries to celebrate cultural achievements as a way of promoting his new Manchester. 'I'm fond of anniversaries,' he would say, wearing a mask of the smart, irreverent Chicago journalist, critic and essayist A. J. Liebling, who influenced the New Journalism that came decades after him, 'although I do not believe in letting them get the better of me.' Wilson preferred thinking about tomorrow, or the day after tomorrow, but he was quite happy to look back if it helped with the march forward.

Celebrating ten years since 'that first Pistols gig in Manchester watched by thirty-five people with their mouths open', and how what had happened in Manchester was proof that 'punk converted everything it touched, creating a post-modern world in which everything may be transmitted into anything, and nothing is what it seems', he decided to hold it at the new arena-sized G-Mex Centre. The refurbished Manchester Central station, once one of the city's great Victorian termini, built in 1880, unused for fifteen years, was opened in March 1986 by Queen Elizabeth II, after four years of renovation, as a concert venue and conference and exhibition centre. It was Manchester's main music venue until the opening of the Manchester Arena nine years later, which was constructed as part of the city's unsuccessful bid for the 2000 Summer Olympics. When Wilson decided to use the G-Mex as a concert venue, it had yet to be used in such a way. He loved the idea of being the first and loved the building for its vast single-span arched roof, the second-widest unsupported iron arch in the country.

Wilson saw the G-Mex as the mainstream municipal equivalent of what with his stoned Factory counsellors he had done with the Haçienda, regenerating the city, with all its iconic and ruined past, because the city was worth saving and making new, because Manchester was where artistic, scientific, political and commercial things happened first, and there had to be new things happening. The renovation had been a major part of the regeneration of the Castlefield area, bordered by the River Irwell, Quay Street, Deansgate and the Chester Road connecting Chester with North Yorkshire. This is the site of the Roman fort Mamucium – meaning breast-shaped hill – or Mancunium, from which the name Manchester comes from. It was the birthplace of modern Manchester and contains the terminus of the Bridgewater Canal, the world's first man-made industrial waterway, the first working canal of the Industrial Revolution, which provoked Canal Mania around the rest of the country at the end of the eighteenth century.

Anthony H. Wilson

In the early '80s when we built the Haçienda we thought we were idiots, just individual crazies for some strange obscure reason in love

412

with our city and putting some of our money back into the city. It was only by about '84, '85 that we realised there were a lot of other people doing exactly the same thing, also individually, on their own, separately thinking they were just the same idiots. Our city fathers, the council leaders, were doing the same thing, and we all thought it was in isolation, and suddenly by the mid-'80s we realised we were all doing it in parallel, continuing a story that went all the way back to Roman days, its ruins built over by the Rochdale Canal, by the building of the viaducts for the Great Northern Railway. It all fitted together without us knowing how or why. Maybe Gretton, on the quiet, was more aware of what the city council's plans for redeveloping the area were.

For his Festival of the Tenth Summer, it was vital that Wilson had all the main Manchester bands booked to play, not just the Factory successes, or not-so-successes, and this meant he needed the Smiths, not least because even with New Order, on the cult side of pop, it was not obvious the festival would sell out the G-Mex. A full house was necessary, because in true Factory style this didn't mean profits flowing into the Factory tills, but it did mean breaking even. The Smiths turned down Wilson's invitation – they didn't need to play along with Wilson's autocratic vision of the city – even if he had issued it with the best of intentions. When Wilson did things with the best of intentions there were always those who doubted his motives, who saw political incorrectness, even political bullying.

Morrissey's story is that the Smiths turned down the festival because they felt ticket prices were too high. Wilson's story is of course different. A year before, there had been a benefit, 'With Love from Manchester', put on at the Liverpool Royal Court Theatre for Militant, a Trotskyist outpost of the Labour Party which in the 1980s, after decades of marginalised planning, had taken over Liverpool Council, causing panic even within Labour at this outbreak of unusually successful municipal militance.

Militant's deputy leader of Liverpool City Council, ex-fireman Derek Hatton, was vilified by *The Times* as a provincial self-publicising revolutionary, and Wilson naturally identified closely with another flamboyant

North-West disruptor – this one still dressing like it was the 1970s – whose notoriety peaked when he heckled Labour leader Neil Kinnock at the 1985 party conference. Although Hatton was winning elections at a time when he was losing them, Kinnock felt that the Trotskyite was the failure – for betraying socialism, for hastening the demise of the left, for heading what he described as a 'crazed council'. Wilson was obviously on Hatton's side as he desperately battled the hegemony of Conservatism, the kind of messily idealistic politician Wilson would have been if he'd entered local government, the Scouser described by the Liverpool Social Democrats as a 'gangster'. Wilson would have been flattered by such a description.

Anthony H. Wilson

I was always flattered by John Lydon because every time we met, he would ask me what I was doing. When I'd reply, 'The usual, you know, music and the telly,' he'd get hold of me, shove me up against a wall and say, 'You were the one who was supposed to go into politics.' I don't think I would be very good as a politician because I open my mouth too much. I've just read a local business paper today where I'm slagging off the city's chief executive, the emperor of Manchester basically, and I shouldn't have said those things.

The benefit, with Factory catalogue number Fac 152 and accompanying merchandise, was held to pay the legal bills of the Liverpool councillors led by Hatton who had been sacked after they set an illegal budget, triggering a fight with Margaret Thatcher's government. For working-class under-dog Liverpool, struggling more than most under the impact of Thatcher's absolutist policies, Hatton was a hero standing his ground and bringing rare passion to British local politics.

Wilson demonstrated his own local political power by being able to organise such an event, inspiring significant, not generally politicised pop talent to follow his lead: Manchester's biggest three, the Smiths, New Order and the Fall, all at key parts of their story, plus fiercely larking, one and only Salford punk poet John Cooper Clarke, ghost of Percy Shelley and George Formby, Thomas de Quincey with a lick of beat, handy for covering the moving around of equipment between acts. All played for expenses only.

Wilson would claim there was a fight about the order the groups appeared in, and New Order volunteered to start first, so that the Smiths finished the night. For Wilson, serving his own story, New Order were on top form – disputed by others – and consequently showed up the Fall – the Mark E. and Brix Smith, Karl Burns, Steve Hanley, Craig Scanlon and Simon Rogers line-up that is for many the classic Fall – and the Smiths, calming down their nervous fans after the Fall's ataxia. The Smiths apparently feeling upstaged by a superb New Order was, for Wilson, the reason they didn't want to play the G-Mex concert. 'Basically, don't play games. New Order should have gone on at the end, and Morrissey was annoyed that he was something of an anticlimax.'

Wilson pushed hard to get the Smiths to play G-Mex, 'but it was a fucking nightmare'. They agreed, then pulled out. They agreed again, and a week before decided they were definitely not going to do it. He was forced to write Morrissey one of the last-resort letters he would send people he really needed to persuade to do something for him, but ultimately to their own advantage. Such letters, before asynchronous texts and emails took over, suggest he was one of the last cohorts of the epistolary age.

'I wrote it at the Haçienda office, four pages, took me an hour. As I was writing it I thought of Steven reading it, and how superior it would make him feel. I had to go to him.' Wilson was an elaborate flatterer, knowing exactly how to appeal to the vain and worse with a little inside knowledge, and he wrote the letter in such a way Morrissey couldn't really turn down his pleas. The Smiths agreed to play and that they would go on stage before New Order, for 'technical reasons'.

Their revenge, perhaps, for having to join Tony's festival was to overrun into New Order's time. The alternative, provincial view is that Wilson was terrified the Smiths were going to show up his band and win what was not really a competition except in his head and possibly those of the two bands, and he made a fool of himself by trying to get the power shut off to bring the Smiths' set to an end. Wilson vainly trying to pull the plug on the Smiths is a true story, and not quite a true story. (Thirty years later, many would join him in wanting to pull the plug on Morrissey.) He remembers the whole incident ending in farce, involving various fights and a visit from the police. 'Fucking nightmare.' But then he loved a fracas.

Twenty-Nine: Fuck, shit and Thatcher

Nemo sine vitio est. (No one is without fault.)

I ended up having my own peripheral Festival of the Tenth Summer 'fucking nightmare' – often the result of doing something with or for Wilson. It was as though the chaos – or brilliance or frustration – produced as an inevitable by-product of the situations he devised radiated around him, knocking against those in proximity. He preferred not to do things the easy way, because where was the glory, the memorable, in that?

He had asked me as one of the Lesser Free Trade Hall 'thirty-five' to be one of the compères for the night, along with Bill Grundy, the television presenter who had played his own unintended part in the promotion of the Sex Pistols a few months after the Manchester show. What had happened in Manchester because of the Sex Pistols then happened to the nation, not because of a musical performance in front of a curious few but because of live television, because of the all-powerful, all-seeing and ultimately all-seen media. In a television world decades before the advent of reality television, the Pistols had found themselves in a setting that anticipated how stories would be carefully contrived inside a studio – a laboratory – setting and then distributed throughout the wider media.

Experienced live-TV expert Grundy, feeling a little jaded after years in television, had been faced with a rushed last-minute booking on the low-energy teatime programme he presented for Thames Television, one of those easily parodied, spookily friendly magazine shows that have important-sounding titles like *Today*. On the first day of December 1976, a few months after they had made their two significant trips to Manchester, dropping mind-changing symbols into the heart of the city, the Sex Pistols had been shunted onto the show by their record label EMI as a last-minute replacement for Queen, whose singer Freddie Mercury needed an emergency visit to the dentist. (Thames and EMI shared an owner, which for some suggested a set-up, but ultimately what happened seems more a classic English cock-up than the result of a planned piece of publicity. As Tony Wilson once said, wearing a mask of Kingsley Amis, 'Sheer muddle is an underestimated element in human affairs.')

As the Pistols arrived at the Thames studios to plug their national tour, given a punkishly short ninety-second slot, no one could have seen what was coming, even if one or two programme assistants nervously noted how easily the word 'fuck' dropped from the mouths of this loutish, unlikely-seeming pop group as they gathered in the green room before their appearance. Their ripped, stained, oddly fastened clothes and erratic grooming also seemed to suggest that their idea of fun was perhaps not the idea of fun of those who prefer life to pass without incident. They appeared a strange askew combination of not interested and charged-up.

They'd turned up for the show complete with a posse of punk poseurs – including Siouxsie Sioux of the Bromley contingent, who had quickly responded to the greater, antidote to alienation point of the Pistols – as though on the way to a party at a mate's house. They had been transported in a very un-punk – or possibly very punk – limousine, reluctant to leave their rehearsals for their forthcoming 'Anarchy' tour – their real work, they thought – until manager/foreman/enabler Malcolm McLaren threatened to dock their wages. To the outside world he would describe them as his young, sexy assassins, but as far as he was concerned they were his carefully cast hired hands, equivalent to shop workers, with few if any union privileges. If he could, he would have paid them in luncheon vouchers – perhaps a book token for the singer.

For Grundy, wily grand master of TV presenters, the Pistols were no big deal, just another pop group on the endless conveyor belt, or another bunch of ordinary people excited to be on television. This new 'punk rock' trend was surely just today's end-of-show novelty with absolutely no future. When they wandered into the studio, he vaguely noticed they appeared to have been released for the day from borstal. To the Pistols, their accompanying entourage adding to the feeling they were on a jolly day out, lizard-skinned Grundy represented the stodgy grown-up world they were dead against because it kept telling them what to do and how to do it.

Tony holding a Kevin Cummins photo of Ian Curtis
in a photo taken by Kevin Cummins, 1991.

Top: Tony at home with son Oli and daughter Izzy.

Above: Tony in Didsbury with his Jag, loving to see it gleam, plus bag, braces, sunglasses, keys, tie and trainers.

The Gay Traitor cocktail bar, downstairs at the Haçienda.

Tony and John Peel at the Russell Club for the Fall
and Echo and the Bunnymen, 1978.

Top: Dean and Martin, Burroughs and Ginsberg, Cannon and Ball,
Wilson and Ryder.

Above: Dressed for the occasion on the set of the 'World in Motion'
video with John Barnes, 1990.

Right: In his element, Tony hosting Channel 4's *After Dark*, with old friend, in 1991.

Below left: Art is never finished, only abandoned. The Haçienda is demolished, 1997.

Below right: Along the wall of Affleck's Palace on Tib Street, Mark Kennedy's mosaic of the Factory Five: Wilson, Saville, Erasmus, Gretton and Hannett.

Top: Tony and 'Tony Wilson' (Steve Coogan) at the New York
premiere of *24 Hour Party People*.

Above: Still from Anton Corbijn's *Control*, 2007: 'Tony Wilson' (Craig Parkinson)
reasons with 'Rob Gretton' (Toby Kebbell), with 'Joy Division' looking on.

Top: Manchester from the Bridgewater Canal towpath, 2016.

Above left: Flowers for Tony – and the Haçienda.

Above right: Headstone by Peter Saville.

The segment started badly, various weapons drawn – Grundy's smug, tabloid TV, 'I'm the man in charge' condescension, the Pistols' slouching amusement at the whole situation with their own youthful sense of superiority, trying to distract Grundy by reading along with him from the autocue – and didn't get any better. Grundy in some ways had met his match when it came to ad-libbed repartee, but then so had the Pistols.

Sensing danger, the studio director quickly reasoned it might be better just to get to the end of the programme rather than scrap the entire interview and try to clear the Pistols out of the way, which might have triggered a scuffle. What could go wrong in a minute? What goes wrong is Grundy cottoning on to Siouxsie Sioux, if only to avoid the unholy, meta-mocking rebel glare – somewhere between crying baby and scurrilous guerrilla – of trickster-haired, skinny, skint, scavenging Johnny Rotten, which sees directly into his sad, lonely, lascivious heart. Grundy does what came naturally to ageing male disc jockeys and television presenters at the time, as though it was part of the service they provide to the public or the only way they know how to relate to women. He starts flirting with Siouxsie, an act of misanthropic non-chivalry, which perhaps he thought was some form of gallantry, tipping him into one of the Pistols' traps.

'You dirty sod. You dirty old man,' sneered affronted Pistols guitarist Steve Jones, beginning to turn inoffensive teatime television into history.

This is what Grundy has been waiting for, and he baits his trap, ignoring the studio voice in his ear urging him to calm things down. He cannot resist seeing what happens next if he doesn't calm things down, surely better television if not the wisest. 'Go on,' Grundy grins. 'You've another five seconds. Say something outrageous.'

Jones does what he's told, which all at once is obedient, punkish, childish, bored, purposeless and possibly, his one specific purpose, drunk. Grundy, with a journalist's then almost compulsory reputation for long liquid lunches, denied being drunk, saying it was impossible to present live TV without being sober.

Jones's inevitable next few lines come from a script written by chance and accident, two of the great influences on Shakespeare – 'You dirty bastard. You dirty fucker' – and finish with a word he must have cadged from an old *Carry On* film: 'What a fucking rotter!'

Rotten, in perfect harmony, adds a couple of almost sheepish 'shits', and when Grundy in affronted-teacher mode asks what he said, there is no remorse, just a cheekily indifferent shrug. 'Nothing. A rude word. Next question.'

The appearance of the Pistols in the middle of an everyday broadcasting routine generally safely distant from the political turbulence and cultural disintegration buckling the country was like an action version of a Dada collage. It had a similar impact on rigid middle-English sensibilities as another art hoo-ha that year, when the Tate paid almost £2,300 for Carl Andre's 1966 *Equivalent VIII*, 120 builders' bricks to be arranged in a low neat pile on the floor of a gallery space. The bricks and the Sex Pistols, uncovering different physical realities but both proposing that concept was as important as talent, were the natural targets of vilification by those assuming their universe, their way of doing and seeing, and owning and running, things was the natural order of existence.

The TV event's rare beauty was its actual authenticity. No one and nothing was in charge; for a few marvellous giddy seconds there were no limits, and everything materialised with about as much unforced spontaneity and unplanned humour as television can muster – but McLaren was ready to exploit it, or even just let it play out now that the Pistols were seen by the tabloids as worthy of their prurient interest. And their constant attention, for the next eighteen months, until they had squeezed the life out of the group, rewarding them with free publicity, punishing them with contrived moral outrage, harrying them to actual death and disaster.

McLaren's more directed attempts to create a scene shaking up music, fashion and culture could never really travel beyond the music papers and ultimately cosy art margins. What the group had done in a different context in a few scruffy venues – and the posher Lesser Free Trade Hall – to a few early responders they now did to millions more. Overnight, the Sex Pistols jumped from minor cult fascination to the torrid centre of culture itself, where the jagged games McLaren fancied playing with

Establishment power made more sense. The Thames TV farce made sense of his intentions, taken from his racy interpretation of original situationist policy: to create art – and entertainment – out of 'instances of transformed everyday life'.

According to some witnesses, a jumpy McLaren initially panicked that Grundy vs the Pistols was a blow to his plans, that the resultant reaction would crush the group before they'd broken out of the small, unpromising rock venues which were never his ideal stage. McLaren claims he knew immediately from the startled response of production workers in the studio as it all happened that this was a eureka moment; signing to a record label was a significant part of the overall strategy, but upsetting mainstream cultural and social sensibilities was top of his manifesto. Making money was on the list, but making it like a pirate, like a conman conning the conmen in the miserably discriminatory and mean-spirited mainstream record industry.

The real work could begin: expose the system and demand the smashing of the state machine. Revolutionary theatre could now be played out where it belonged, in front of the masses. The revolution must be first for workers and peasants! It begins immediately, as the first few dates in their end of year 'Anarchy in the UK' punk package tour, in Norwich, Derby and Newcastle, are cancelled – the Pistols with special guests including the Clash and Buzzcocks breaking punk out of the clubs, ballrooms, colleges, discos – and prisons – and into city halls, where thousands not hundreds will be exposed to the filth and the fury. (Bill Grundy, meanwhile, is suspended for two weeks for 'sloppy journalism'.)

The tour was too much for some city councils, who banned it from their little realms fearing riots and worse. But the bans, the Pistols' tantalising absence, the tabloid-stoked myths and music-paper hyperbole that snaked around their increasingly sensational name amplified their audience to more than thousands, promoted them to the top of the charts, as they tossed obscenities from where everyone could hear them, challenging the entire notion of royalty, whether the Queen of England or Rod Stewart.

Until the *Today* fiasco, it had all been going fairly normally for the Sex Pistols as any kind of 'ordinary' hard-working band, playing gigs regularly, recording songs, getting music-paper reviews. Afterwards, it was thirteen months of smash-and-grab drama. Grundy's snide goading helped create both the beginning and the end of the Sex Pistols as a national cultural phenomenon that by its very nature could only last so long. A few months later they were in prime position, as music group with added extras, to provide a spectacular and necessary alternative to the way the Establishment would use the Queen's Jubilee celebrations to distract people from political chaos, economic breakdown and social disintegration.

If the population was to be drugged by spectacular events, the Sex Pistols suggested there could also be different drugs, different images and therefore a different reality. The mainstream would not have it their own way with the Queen's Jubilee – the most memorable images, the greatest tribute to life and society, the greatest hint that history could go in different directions were generated by those oafish punk vandals caught swearing at Bill Grundy.

Grundy was caught up in his own disgrace, his proudly assembled broadcasting career abruptly condensed into a couple of lines about his bit-part role in the scandal. Wilson as live teatime broadcaster with a certain debt to Grundy the Granada grandee, as well as McLaren-inspired experimental provocateur, appreciated how Grundy was as much collaborator in the grand scheme of punk things as he was unwitting stooge. Combining unlikely-looking man-off-the-telly Grundy and me as fan turned critic at the Festival of the Tenth Summer was Wilson's way of filling in for himself, creating a hybrid that resembled his own mix of mainstream and marginal. He should really have been the host, but he had a number of other jobs taking up his time, as promoter, organiser and self-styled avant-garde head of Manchester.

Perhaps at the Tenth Summer Wilson was looking for some convenient echo of the *Today* scandal by having Grundy introduce talentless groups that he was still convinced were, like the Sex Pistols, sick and deluded, and his introductions were mostly long, sneering, pompously delivered old-man moans about the horror he was participating in. It wasn't controversial, it was just rambling, and of the two of us he was meant to be the professional broadcaster.

It wasn't long before he slumped into a drunken stupor, leaving me on my own as the host, walking out in front of thousands of fans, most of them there for the chart music of the Smiths and New Order. The loud boos of the audience were disconcerting, but I would eventually learn that few of them could hear anything that I was saying and just thought me and Grundy – when he was functioning – were probably saying something boring, so we might as well be booed. And of course if it had been Wilson, he would have been greeted with boos, because that was the ritual, and to some extent, without me realising it, I had crossed over into Wilson territory as an *NME* writer and because of my involvement with Frankie Goes to Hollywood. I couldn't really be simply a fan any more. I apparently was sharing Wilson's power.

There were no outrageous interruptions that would give Wilson his memorable situation, just an undercurrent of discomfort emerging from how he had created a competitive edge to Manchester, built in his image, with no one really understanding what the competition was. At the end he tried to inject some controversy by pulling the plug on the Smiths, but that failed.

Before their set Morrissey passed a message to me that he did not want me to introduce the Smiths. He wanted no introduction, certainly not from an *NME* journalist who had recently aided and abetted Frankie Goes to Hollywood to the top of the charts. He wanted to stay well clear of any battle that wasn't his alone, avoid the Wilson Manchester, where rows, punch-ups, feuds and fallings-out were elevated to the status of legendary moments. He had his own affairs to watch out for, his own cult to organise, and didn't want me, acolyte of Wilson, soiling his beautiful group by introducing them. He was of his own Manchester and didn't want anyone else's to get in the way.

Backstage, where Wilson's competitive edge was most apparent, I had inherited from out-of-service Grundy the role of tipsy compère, rowed with Jon Savage and tipped a cup of sugar over the head of Liz Naylor, thinking she was someone else. I've forgotten who that was or why I had a grudge against them. This made me definitively a twat in the Wilson sense, but that was about as Wilson as I got during the event, which, apart from all the grumbles, niggles, rivalries and low-level chaos, passed without the kind of incident that would help it make the kind of history Wilson craved. Some you win, some you lose, some you win and lose at the same time.

'There was a horrid atmosphere,' said Jon Savage. 'I think it's to do with maybe people unconsciously taking off bits of Thatcher. Which I think we all did. Because we were in that world, even though we might have hated it. Everyone was super-bad-tempered.'

Thirty: A sudden violent interruption

Lupus dentis, taurus cornis. (The wolf with his teeth, the bull with his horns.)

Of course, within hours he would be up and running on his next project, seemingly untouched by embarrassment or shame or annoyance. When Wilson asked me to do some task for him, on one of his television programmes, for one of his promotions or self-promotions, I would get a glimpse inside the world he constantly inhabited, and you had to be a Wilson, able to deal with catastrophes small and large, self-inflicted and natural, to pass through it unscathed. Wilson had the fortitude to handle the consequences, often negative and unfulfilling, of setting up situations that would hopefully lead to wonderful if unforeseen results. He was a genius at taking advantage of what often happened around him without him initially seeing it, which meant taking advantage of people and their activities, which he somehow considered he owned because they were happening inside his orbit.

Inevitably, off stage, off screen, existing at the time as rumours, as uncontrollable additions to his story, his biography, there were the less malleable, less fanciful pressures of a real life he just couldn't get on top of with a vulnerable wife and young kid.

Hilary Wilson

He could be a great dad to Oli in those first few years. He used to finish Granada Reports *at half past six, and by ten to seven he would be at home bathing Oli. He was so into Oli, loved the whole new routine, but then when he was about six months the attack happened. Tony left to go to work at nine in the morning, and we didn't know but there had been someone who had been stalking him for ages and she had been hiding in the garage for about two weeks. And she just knocked on the door basically, very nonchalantly, and out of nowhere jumped on me with a*

Stanley knife and began to slash me. Basically, she held me hostage in the house with Oliver for about three hours. She cut an artery in my face, the blood was pumping out of me, it was horrific. How I didn't die I don't know. And it was the only time I've ever prayed, but I just said, 'God, if you get me out of this one, I'll never sin again.' It was like this was it. This woman was completely obsessed with Tony. She'd been watching him on television, and something clicked in her mind. He was the only one for her. She was from down south. She'd never met him, but she'd been to the Haçienda, looked him up at Companies House, went to where Lindsay was living because he was still registered there. She ended up at our house and went berserk. That was one of the worst periods of my life.

I showed her a photograph of Tony. I said, 'You can have him.' Because she was saying to me, 'What's he doing with you? I want him. He should be with me. You're a whore, you're a bitch. Show me where you sleep. Show me where you have sex.' She was a complete psychopath. And as it happens, the phone was cut off at the time because we had not paid the bill. Tony forgot – typical, he would shrug off things like that – so when I went to get to the phone it was dead. Tony! I managed to escape while she stared at this photo of Tony she'd found. She heard me open the door and she ran after me, and then ran back inside the house and the door slammed behind her. I was locked outside, and she was inside. Oliver was still inside the house with her and I thought she was going to kill him. That was one of the worst periods of my life. Silence inside the house and her with Tony's son. The police turned up, and a priest, and they managed to talk to her through the letterbox and slowly persuaded her to open the door. She hadn't hurt Oliver, he was fine. The attacker was arrested, she got ten years in Broadmoor for wounding with intent. I wanted attempted murder, but they couldn't get her on that. When they let her out of prison the police rang to tell me, and I was very scared and paranoid about the kids. She might still have been after Tony. She didn't seem like someone who would ever give up. She wanted Tony and would get rid of anyone in her way.

*Tony arrived at the hospital where I had been taken soon after
it happened, but he was very weird and quickly left to do some live
broadcast. He couldn't handle his emotions, and this was total proof.
He didn't know how to approach it, how to approach me. The incident
changed me in his eyes, which was in some ways as bad as being slashed.
I was punished, made different, by being attacked, even though it wasn't
my fault. He couldn't handle it, like it was too real. He ran away from
it, absolutely ran away from it. I came out of hospital, and he went to
Japan for two weeks. He rang me every night saying how much he loved
me, but he wasn't there for me. Publicly he could be very emotional,
but privately it was very different. He tried to stay safe by not going to
emotional places he didn't like, but he was calling me every night when
he was away, saying how much he loved me. The distance allowed him
to be emotional with me, but he couldn't do it when he was close to me.
A psychiatrist I was seeing said he was actually more concerned about
Tony's reaction to the attack than he was mine. Not that I ever really
recovered. He started to go out more and stay out of the house longer.
He had that option. Because one of his other homes was the Haçienda.
Real life didn't really impact on that. Not yet anyway.*

Thirty-One: Becoming the '80s, the Haçienda (2), missing the boat again and various bums

Panem and circenses. (Bread and circuses.)

Tony Wilson, coming and going from many homes, who can also be described as:
- 'I have come to the conclusion that one way to think of the human brain is to think of Widnes. Widnes is a town in north Cheshire, full of chemical industry, so it is the smelliest place in Europe. The human brain is Widnes and Widnes railway station is where Paul Simon wrote "Homeward Bound", and when I say that the human brain is like Widnes people think that I have lost my mind. I have forgotten the point I was making . . .'
- no one likes to remind people of their greatest failures. Except me
- wanting to rebrand St Helens as the new Milan
- broody bastard
- lover boyfriend husband
- he was besotted with his mum, said his friend, and he was besotted with the women in his life who had to take the burden as he looked for someone who could live up to being a replacement
- by the early 2000s developing a new calling as a 'regenerations consultant' and guest-editing an issue of *Building* magazine
- unruly strategist
- Blackburn, Burnley, Rossendale and Pendle, he said, were the muscle of the Industrial Revolution, Manchester was the heart and Liverpool was the mouth
- being flung against the wall by one of his Granada bosses, complaining about a programme he's made, who was shouting, 'I've never seen such fucking Trotskyite rubbish in my fucking life, you fucking acid casualty. I'm going to fucking kill you'
- don't let the bastards grind you down – *illegitimi non carborundum*

428

Carol Morley

I remember seeing a Filofax for the first time in the Haçienda. At the time I saw it I didn't know what it was, just that it was very impressive. I was in the cocktail bar, and Tony, always in a suit, opened his jacket and brought out this enormous thing. He was checking on a date. I remember being amazed it didn't cause a huge bulge in his jacket – but it didn't. Looking back, it feels the epitome of the '80s! I think now the Filofax must have been disguised by his big shoulder pads! All the spaces to go to in Manchester had been small and seedy, or if they were big (like the Ritz) they had carpets your shoes stuck to. The Haçienda was industrial glamour, and it seemed hopeful at a time when we'd all been told (at my school anyway) that if you worked hard you might get a job, but it wouldn't be a job you wanted. The Haçienda seemed to prove that anything could happen. For a while it didn't – it was just chaos really, the kind Wilson liked. It was never full, unless there was a big band on, which was rare. And then the chaos started to get a soundtrack, and it started to get full.

Mike Pickering

Loving disco in the early 1980s was still looked down upon from the rock world, like it was shallow and disposable. But there were a few of us otherwise in that NME world that were coming from punk but loving Chic, Ohio Players, Crown Heights Affair. Rob had called me back from Rotterdam to help him at the Haçienda, and at first I was booking bands, making a name for myself by getting in Culture Club just before their first hit for fifty quid, ABC, Orange Juice. I also booked the DJs, based on what we'd been seeing in New York and Chicago, where they were taking something on Rough Trade and mixing it with electro. I designed the DJ box at the Haçienda so that there was no microphone for the disc jockey, and in England the expectation was that the DJ talked between records. In New York the disc jockeys didn't talk. They did their talking with the music they played, how it fitted together, the connections they found between genres. The way they moved from James

Brown to Public Image. They had taken a lot of their attitude from independent British labels, so it seemed only right it would work in the Haçienda. It was what it was meant for really. All sorts of music from all over the place played with no standing on ceremony. I didn't want any DJ talk, especially with the acoustics.

While Erasmus is touring with some Factory bands including A Certain Ratio around 1984, he starts talking to someone whom he likes who manages the Rock City venue in Nottingham, Paul Mason. Mason has done some research on the Factory bands, knows his stuff, impresses Erasmus with his knowledge of the label, not just the obvious hit bands. Erasmus finds out how successful Mason's been running Rock City and calls a meeting – increasingly difficult – with Gretton and Wilson to recommend him as Haçienda manager. Commercially, the Haçienda is not doing well except as an idea, as a workshop for Pickering to construct a domestic manifestation of the musical blending and genre-bending of downtown New York. It's patiently, weirdly glowing with its own impertinence for a Manchester, even a music and an audience, that doesn't yet exist. The guy running it whom Rob put in has absolutely no experience of running clubs. He's opening it seven nights a week when most of them are all but empty. It's world-class but perched a little secretly on a lifeless street corner. Erasmus asks Mason if he fancies the job. 'He ripped my fucking hand off. Of course he would.'

It took months to force through – Gretton needs to get rid of his guy. Wilson would keep cancelling the meetings, always something else, or even nothing else, just not in the mood, it wasn't his idea. Eventually, they all get to meet and are as impressed with the no-nonsense Mason as Erasmus is. He starts work at the Haçienda, and Erasmus is relieved. For him, that's when the club starts to work. When it starts to make money. Because it's being managed. One of Mason's innovations is making sure there are floats on the tills. Having floats on the tills – and other running-a-business-day-to-day normalities – was as much a reason the Haçienda was saved as the house music.

Or maybe the Haçienda lived because it reversed the trend for clubs to let in people wearing suits and ties who turned out to be violent thugs but reject the guys in Tacchini tracksuits or really cool casual clothes who brought energy and movement with them, which meant the Happy Mondays and all their mates couldn't get in. Or maybe it survived after New Order, who had invested in the Haçienda as a tax write-off, were hauled in front of the Inland Revenue because it turned out that it wasn't. They were in the tax office for eight hours a day for days going through every detail of their business, and suddenly the Haçienda had to professionalise, sort out some of the early mistakes, and New Order had to play far more gigs than certainly Bernard Sumner wanted to.

Once the Haçienda became, just in time, a prime dance venue, a prototype super-club, therefore the sketchy blueprint for vibrant capitalist enterprise, inspiring a host of clubs in Ibiza, the prototype for the Ministry of Sound, Cream, Renaissance, Brooklyn's Teksupport, Wilson decided against the recommendations of friends and colleagues to do the obvious thing and create a dance subsidiary of Factory. Rob Gretton, who might have persuaded him, had resigned as a Factory director after one too many arguments turned physical. 'I thought you needed to be good businessmen to make money from dance,' said Wilson, perhaps implying a good businessman meant a bad artist, 'and I thought it would never happen commercially because there were no artists. And I always thought our forte was finding bands that no one else wanted and selling millions of albums around the world. Look at Happy Mondays. Shaun Ryder always said they signed to Factory because no one else would have them. They'd been around for years before we worked with them.'

Dance parenthetically elevated Wilson's music-paper reputation as pop culture visionary, but even as it was happening he was still sentimentally locked inside an album world suited to groups like the Wake, the Railway Children, Durutti Column and Section 25 rather than the records the Haçienda's Mike Pickering ended up releasing on what could have been part of Factory, Deconstruction. It was the atmospheric album music that Martin Hannett had excelled at that mostly generated Factory's original revenue, and the first time Hannett ever entered the Haçienda, the club he never wanted to see built, was when he mixed the sound for the Stone Roses in 1985.

A Factory unshackled by Wilson's resistance to dance music – possibly rooted in late-1970s white-rock prejudice against the disposability of disco – would have released T-Coy's 'Cariño' in 1987, one of the first British house records, recorded in a room in Didsbury as if in downtown Detroit, featuring Simon Topping from A Certain Ratio. Pickering, who'd brought the Happy Mondays to Wilson's attention and helped make 'Cariño', was working for Deconstruction, and released it there, a strong hint of a future Factory that never was. It almost made too much sense, it was just too obvious a thing to do, so it wasn't Wilson's Factory dream.

'We'd had my band Quando Quango,' says Pickering; 'we'd had dance acts like Marcel King that were going down a storm at the Danceteria in New York; we'd had 52nd Street on Factory because of me and Rob, our taste not Tony's, and it was so obvious as I was getting in all these great records before anyone else and playing them in the club that there should be a Factory dance section. Tony wouldn't have it. It simply wasn't part of his vision for the club or the city. A real blind spot. Rob was really pissed off. Alan would call me up, asking why weren't we putting them out. I was embarrassed. I had to tell him I was putting them out on my own label.'

The Haçienda became what it became through the efforts and discoveries of others, dance experts and enthusiasts trying to make sense of this drifting space, updating the lost connection with the northern soul of the 1960s and '70s, while Wilson increasingly became figurehead and mouthpiece. He was distantly aware as a fan of kinetic action how the supple bass lines of Factory's Quando Quango were reaching back into the Chicago house that originally inspired them, and then feeding back into the Haçienda, absorbed and transformed, effortlessly slipping inside Manchester's house style to be transformed once more, but was not willing or able to put that into Factory records.

Wilson didn't particularly like Quando Quango, very much a Rob signing because of his friendship with Pickering. He loved the sleeves, though,

432

which made them a Factory act. To Wilson it was Eurodisco, beyond his understanding or interest – he couldn't make Pickering's conceptual leap to see that the artist on an otherwise apparently anonymous dance record was Factory, the myth, style and mannerisms of the label itself.

Factory Records breezily headed on its road to self-destruction even as the club originally funded by album sales now existed at the centre of the dance world. Nothing would get in the way of the launch of a Factory classical music subsidiary, as if to highlight its unwavering perversity, not making money by following dance music into the charts, but losing some more with another one of Wilson's absurd advanced-guard schemes. Why make easy money getting to number one with music you don't really believe in when you can squander a fortune on the hunt for the dream concept? In any list of all-time bad music-business decisions this ranks high in the top ten, but Wilson sometimes even as he was in the psycho-pomp middle of some cultural trend he could front was still on the hunt for the worst music-business decision of all time: to challenge the assumed relationship between taste and success.

'In 1989, when Black Box got to number one on Deconstruction with "Ride on Time",' says Pickering, 'he would send me bottles of champagne. I had balloons and flowers all around my flat that he'd sent. There was a launch event for Factory Classical, and he gets me to stand up, and he said, "This is Mike Pickering, he's got a number-one single." And I thought, *This is so Tony. He's not thinking, Oh my God what have I done, why aren't we number one? Why am I launching a bloody classical label?* He doesn't seem to be even bothered a big hit could have been on Factory, that it was done by Factory people. He's relishing another wayward scheme.'

Wilson, practically or preposterously, with a playlist largely based on the moody, mordant, white-male template of pre-Haçienda Factory Records, was preparing for rock fans to get older, before it became obvious, decades before BBC Radio 6 Music and Scala, that, too sentimentally attached to their youth, they never would. Staying at the heart of the community, selling records made out of dreams in their hundreds or even tens, seemed the correct ideological counterweight to everywhere else becoming of the high street, but with all that meant in terms of potential locational and cultural obsolescence.

He could have had a spree of top-ten records, but he preferred investing in more challenging, perverse even fractious personal projects, in what he considered proper, outlandish personalities, channelling tens of thousands of pounds into Cath Carroll, his old ferociously intelligent foil/favourite, second-ever Haçienda member, convinced she was some sort of art star, or perfect cult, always on the verge of becoming some kind of Factory Patti Smith, a Manchester Dorothy Parker.

Carroll was one of those in his orbit he liked because of the way she was mean to his face, keeping him on his toes, engaging in the sort of argumentative tussles he liked from his debating days and Cambridge studies. She was one of those anomalous kindred spirits he came across on his travels through the city and its scenes – smart enough to have gone to Oxford but in the end wandering aimlessly yet with purpose through the 1980s, from postwoman to the *NME* to Chicago, gathering momentum even if in reverse, in a way Wilson loved.

In some ways, he was repeating the days of the Factory 'Sample', his response to the disappointment at how *So It Goes* had ended, an exciting, perversely optimistic time when everything was forming, in obscure clubs, during rambling meetings, before it all went right, and wrong, and required more adult negotiating, when he was helping if only in his own mind to invent an asymmetrical independent scene featuring iconoclastic indie legends. Championing the wayward, the difficult, the loved-only-by-those-in-the-know was his safe place.

Most bosses of record companies who begin labels inspired by their early taste and instincts drift out of touch with music currents as they get older, and music gets newer, and hire the kind of enthusiasts who are deeply involved in what's happening now. While Wilson carried on pursuing his own 1968-incubated interests, which had moved in and out of fashion and were in the late 1980s almost redundant, certainly distant, he hired positive, enthusiastic music fans to find new talent, but as much as he found ways to cover up for it, and even attempt to make up for it after the first Factory collapsed in the early 1990s, he was more out of touch than most. Or more in touch with doing it his way. Doing it his way was to absolutely not cash in on the Haçienda's success.

In 1988 he suggests to Mike Unger, editor of the *Manchester Evening News*, that there should be a column in the paper devoted to local music. 'He wanted there to be somewhere he could be sure would sell some of that stranger Factory stuff that he just couldn't move,' said Terry Christian.

The column becomes 'The Word', and is written by savvy, fast-thinking teenager Sarah Champion, who takes the column into her own local place, well outside the self-serving limits of Wilson. She's getting to the Stone Roses first, to the deft, askew inner-city electro-dance of Chapter and Verse and A Guy Called Gerald, writing about a Manchester where the life and soul of the city has moved on through different beats and spaces from ten years before.

The Haçienda had become a kind of laboratory for mixing outside influences with the quickness and scavenging curiosity of Manchester fans, but oddly Tony is slow to process this extension of traditional local openness to cultural change. In an interview with Champion he even suggests that 1988 Manchester is becoming a little dull. 'Have you not been to your own club recently?' she asks, thinking of the music and movement, the unruly, spectacular action inside the Haçienda. He's not yet found a way to make sense, on his terms, of what's happening there.

Still fond of fraudsters, game players, troublemakers and freakish thinkers twisting entertainment around their distressed minds, out on his own even as pop fashion is forming around and through him in Manchester, quite capable of splitting his attention into many different directions, he collaborates again with puckish post-Pistols pseudo-situationist pals Fred and Judy Vermorel. For the Vermorels, no history of pop made sense without the fan, whose taste, obsessions, often mad love completed the circuit. Their 1985 book *Stardust* was a deadpan chronicling of the sorcerous sexual connection fans have with their idols, and in the same way Fred started to stalk one of his obsessions, Kate Bush, in order to get inside the mind of such a stalker, they formed a group perhaps to see

435

what it was like to be worshipped by fans. It was all part of their research into obsession.

In Wilson's mind, it's the whimsically malicious 'tactical campaign' the Vermorels waged against the BPI – the British Phonographic Institute, which Factory never joined – and their flagship Brit Awards as a promotional campaign for their 'Stereo/Porno' single (Fac 198) that's culturally as important, if not as actively present, as the Haçienda. He'll pay attention to anything that engages him, because it all becomes part of his thinking, and his artwork, situated in a shimmering outpost of utopia.

(The BPI issued silver, gold or platinum discs for bestselling records; non-members Factory awarded New Order their own version of one of these discs when the sales of 'Blue Monday' passed 500,000. According to Peter Hook, this was actually an award for losing £50,000, as myth has it each copy of the record lost ten pence because of Saville's beautifully complicated cover replicating a floppy disk, which he saw for the first time 'as an interesting object' in their studio. The sleeve was not designed with the music in mind, but instead a piece of digital storage. Wilson claimed the loss was more likely five pence a cover, achieved by some arcane accounting strategy. Saville suggested that after a few thousand were sold a cheaper, simpler version may have been used, even though Factory was still being charged the original rate. Typical Factory – a fuck-up even as they created something special.)

Punk rock as it existed during the two years or so the Sex Pistols were present as a living work of art created around the idea of cultural hooliganism even art terrorism was still very fresh in the Vermorels' minds, accompanied by a stubborn faith in the ability of pop culture to penetrate and manipulate reality at a higher level. Their revolt against a trade body's more or less monopolistic control of the music industry was somewhere between quaint and quixotic, and therefore typical of the more oblique Factory follies.

The 'promotional campaign' for the single, which goes through the motions of attempting to disrupt the Brit Awards, included generating fake press releases stating that invitations to the awards were being sent to disabled children and the mentally ill so that they 'can see how their illnesses are exploited'. For the Vermorels, the BPI was like a medical practitioner who helps the mentally sick while repressing the dangerous nonconformist.

There was also a six-by-four-foot-poster campaign entitled 'Bums for BPI'. The posters' bum, taken from the Saville-designed record sleeve – part of the ongoing Saville series in which a radiantly precise, idealised sleeve was remote from the actual music, as usual as though he had never heard it – belonged to the musician the Vermorels' music publishers introduced to the project, which to her quiet horror was not a straightforward music project but more a gruelling piece of living theatre. Jingle/session singer Ginny Clee remembers a difficult partnership – 'It was almost the end of me' – made a little better by the fact that Saville's sublimely indifferent sleeve, and therefore her abstracted backside, became part of an exhibition at the V&A of the hundred best record covers of all time. The poster claimed the Fac number 199, which was also at one point apparently allocated to Wilson's son Oliver.

Eventually, the 'campaign' reached its presumably intended target, with an annoyed BPI taking out an injunction to stop the fake information. A punchline that is not a punchline, a group that is not a group, a single that plays at being a single, at being an art object, an obscure record packaged as if it is a deluxe transformative product both tied to and critical of being tied to capitalist production, nonsense presented seriously, the serious presented playfully, an enthusiasm for illusion – pure Factory – and Wilson's scheming, still operating as though the label is at the stage it was in 1978, in a naive space uncorrupted by success and failure. It was a space he always returned to even as he was noisily playing the role of Mr Manchester, until there was no space to return to.

The true nature of Factory, and Wilson, can be found in these divergent, often dissonant and unfinished or never-even-started projects. The Haçienda is where Factory's conspiratorial spirit fitfully penetrated into the mainstream, taking with it fragments and fibres of its more curious, irregular endeavours, but it was a more hidden Factory that functioned as Wilson's research and development department.

This was his favourite department, a permanent, unsung splinter group within a company best known for its unusual hit groups and its hyped-up community-minded venues. There was an always partially formed cell specialising in the game of events, and this Wilson-maintained insider energy never disappeared before, after and even during the bankruptcy in 1992, which for all the bad blood and shattered dreams, the embarrassment and black humour, the insults and recriminations – the conclusion to a project that came across like a cover version of the inevitable end of the Sex Pistols – was in itself a supreme Factory moment. Bankruptcy was the only way it could have ended.

For Wilson, if the unnatural-seeming experimentation, the accidental discovery of disorientating wonders and new routes through history ceased to exist, as irrelevant and illogical to those who just wanted the music, the remixes, the new rhythms, the hip young things, then the consequences ultimately would be the erosion of the hard-earned freedoms that permit such eccentric and dogmatic research. Dissent and the doubtful are the first things to be censored, sometimes through lack of attention, sometimes for ideological reasons.

This censorship, starting with the mavericks, the intelligentsia, eventually leads to the disappearance of a performance space that allows something like the Haçienda to thrive as an accessible, popular representation of freedom. Wilson never wavered from pursuing the extreme even in the middle of his imperial phases, so that at the same time as he was conventional populist emblazer, wearing his Mr Madchester sash, his madcap crown, he was also camouflaged radical interloper who never stopped believing in the revolutionising of the ordinary.

Factory as a constant spirit of influence on the city came about because of the mostly forgotten happenings and releases, the less-obvious catalogue numbers, as much as the hits, the club and the well-documented escapades. It's what happens in the corners, under the floorboards, that helps make a city, as much as the soundtrack and the headlines. When the weirder, darker, minor elements are forgotten, the city can turn to cliché.

There was a part of him that was very fond of proud northerner Pete Waterman, gregarious show runner for the Stock Aitken & Waterman 1980s hit factory that ruthlessly churned out cheap, sparkling, high-street, high-energy hit singles, who once said, 'Everything I touch turns to gold,' and a part of him very partial to Thomas Aquinas, thirteenth-century Italian Catholic philosopher and theologian, who once said, 'The things we love tell us what we are.'

Wilson accepted the plaudits and music-paper covers as the acclaimed ringmaster and chief exalter of a new Manchester, but he was as removed from the intricacies, developments and revelations of late-1980s underground dance music as you would expect a middle-of-the-road television presenter to be, or on the other hand someone more turned on by the poetics of subversion. Intellectually, he could dance his way out of looking confused by the changes, but he was always reacting in hindsight.

'He would do his walk-round of the club every Friday,' says Pickering, 'and he would come into my booth, stand and watch me, watch it all going on, big grin on his face – "Marvellous, darling, marvellous. See you later" – and leave. It was like you had just had a visit from a politician pretending he knew what was going on.'

The Haçienda was still a relatively local secret in 1987, its existence as a dance venue still taking shape. When Ecstasy, the yuppie psychedelic from America, was first shared inside the club, a new sort of party drug delivering a jolt to the city like the Pistols had a decade before, there was that era's equivalent of the few first responders, sitting in 'their' corner of the Haçienda, feeling the air change around them, feeling something that seemed real but didn't exist.

By May 1988, when the 'Hot' night was at its hottest, the club would be crammed with hundreds of worshippers, a sacred space confirmed, a materialisation of the temple of the sun, the music sounding better and better, most of the dancers on something that would more or less give them three to six hours of euphoria, emotional closeness, intense love and empathy with those around them, atoms in a galaxy of possibility. The Haçienda had set Manchester back on course, not least to being branded tabloid-friendly 'Madchester' as the crowd went wild inside a new surge of energy, a new set of beats, the nickname conjured up by Happy Mondays' video-makers the Bailey Brothers. They were in talks to make one of those films Wilson always liked the idea of, some post-modernised 1960s car-chase pop caper, this one set on the Isle of Mad, because in a meeting the one word that could quickly distil the essential point of the Mondays was 'mad'. Mad like a pop group on drugs.

Shaun Ryder was one of those early Ecstasy missionaries sat in a dark Haçienda corner, and he accepted 'Madchester' just like the punks accepted the 'punk' word they never came up with. It was OK, 'but if you were from Manchester and used it, you were a prick'. If you said that the Happy Mondays were like Mozart – as Wilson did – Ryder would also think you were a prick.

For Wilson, when the sun started shining inside and the kids were, once more, all right, in a space very much of their choosing, those Haçienda nights were more like great parties where every so often something new and unexpected would happen, before they dissolved into something else, and then around 3 a.m. Shaun Ryder would materialise in front of him, crouching like a gargoyle, staring at him with a new pair of eyes, and bamboozle him with some lines from a song that rhymed 'alibis' with 'eyes' and seemed under the circumstances as great as anything by Dylan in how they questioned the rules of the game. Wilson would be in his element. He didn't have to dance. The dancing was all around him. *Everything works out eventually*, he would think.

Thirty-Two: Tony Wilson's voice

De minimis non curat praetor. (The governor does not deal with the small stuff.)

Wilson wants to say something, which is his right. It's his book. I'm ghost-writer for a ghost finding a way to get in touch. As I write, while the TV is murmuring away, inside a few hours, on the news, Marple, his old home, is threatened with being flooded and might need to be evacuated, which is ridiculous; Shaun Ryder is on *Pointless* with his daughter, also ridiculous; 'Blue Monday' is played during an episode of *Come Dine with Me*, is the music used in the commercial for British television streaming network Britbox, is the music used for UEFA's Euro 2020 collaboration with TikTok; and *So It Goes* is being repeated on Sky Arts, looking at the same time very much from the past, looking forward to something that never quite arrived – except as a repeat – but also not out of place, pop culture still being shaped by baby-boomer and punk designs and desires.

He's trying to tell me something, reminding me . . .

1. I used to presume that everyone paid for their drinks in the early days of the Haçienda, because I paid for mine. It seemed to be the way that one should conduct one's business. It should be above board. No room for making it seem it was just a personal indulgence, not a real business. It was after about three years of running the Haçienda that we found out that everyone in Manchester was having free drinks except for those of us who owned it. Steve Morris of New Order, one of the owners, even had to pay to get into his own club sometimes. I guess we were ploughing our money into it to keep it alive. Except for Peter Hook. He always had a bar bill and ran that up and never paid it. Me and Rob certainly would pay. I could never work out who was giving the drinks away. Was everyone giving the drinks away? That's my question. I mean, it's unbelievable. Fucking nightmare.

2. The first year, we organised a taxi service for the staff, until we found out that these taxis were in operation between one and six in the morning and effectively we were running a taxi service connecting all the parties in Manchester.

3. Scenes are important in cities to make sure that there is always new energy keeping the city going. Manchester always had its scenes and its micro-scenes – the Twisted Wheel, Magic Village, the Stoneground, Pips, Rafters, the Ranch, the Beach, the Electric Circus, and of course the Haçienda. The idea of place is always important for the talk and thinking that becomes action, that becomes direction – you think of the Spanish surrealists in the Black Cat Café off the Ramblas in Barcelona, a meeting point for Picasso and Gaudí, Gertrude Stein's salon at 27 rue de Fleurus in Paris, mid-'70s CBGB in the Bowery, the Abbey Theatre in Dublin with the Irish Literary Revival, leading to W. B. Yates. Where Pete Shelley and Howard Devoto lived on Lower Broughton Street, Salford, in spring 1976 was a scene, an important place to meet and set things in motion – Morrissey, Linder, Richard Boon. Liz and Cath made a scene. The parties there were in Hulme around 1980, in rooms that had no carpet, or paint, or wallpaper. Music decorated the rooms. That's what made those parties what they were. And toast. People were always eating toast. It's how scenes begin, in rooms like that, with lots of toast, and eventually that spirit reaches deep into the future and becomes whatever Manchester became in the late '80s. At first the scene was everyone just hanging out in Hulme, rolling joints and quietly listening to music. Scenes are cultural and ephemeral, but they are always linked to bricks and mortar. What goes on inside is pure energy, but it needs the building to exist, to contain it and let it out. Great things evolve quickly from small places. There have been scenes in Manchester since the '60s – maybe the early 1970s were pretty quiet, but mostly there were overlapping scenes, new cultural groups, with distinct music a part of the scene. I think perhaps Manchester is a good size for scenes like that.

4. Strangely enough, the Haçienda was built around that central concept of skinny white kids with guitars in love with American black music. A traditional idea really, and what came out of it was not part of our original plan. I remember as we were building it in 1981, 1982, whenever it bloody was, and someone asked us who we were building it for. I didn't really have an answer, to be honest. We'd had – and by 'we' I mean Gretton and me – this idea of giving something back to the city, which no one ever really fell for, but it was true. We had made all this money from the Joy Division albums and weren't really experienced enough to know what to do with the money we were making, where to invest it. Hannett obviously wanted new equipment, because his concern was the making of the records. Gretton and me just thought everything happened because of the clubs, the meeting places. In the end, I said we were building it for the kids, those hanging around after punk had happened, post-punk, I suppose. He said, 'For Christ's sake, have you seen the kids recently? They're all wearing long grey raincoats, and you're building a 1,500-capacity New York-style disco.' We hadn't thought it through. We abhorred research. In the end the Haçienda wasn't a part of British culture; it was a part of British culture that loved American dance culture, but that became British culture. It wasn't built for them, but Manchester kids sort of reacted to it and learnt how to use it. Within a few months they weren't filling it, but they started to look great inside it. They were working out what it was because we hadn't really made it clear. Eventually realising, through no real help of mine, and working it out that it was for dance music.

5. I remember a famous artist who originally came from Oldham visited the Haçienda around 1984, and we took him down to the Gay Traitor bar, and when he saw it, he said, 'Listen, I haven't lived here for years, but I spend my life in LA and Tokyo and Paris, and I go out all the time to the best clubs, and I'm friends with Mick Jagger, and these people here, these kids in my home town, are better dressed and better looking and far cooler than anyone I've seen for years anywhere in the

443

world.' I don't think it would have been like that if it was still Rafters, the usual '70s places. The 1980s were different and needed somewhere different.

6. I adore drink like I adore food. I love the taste of alcohol, but I hate getting drunk. I haven't been drunk since I was thirteen, fourteen. The Marple Amateur Dramatics Society, which my dad was involved with, came round on Boxing Day and I had a few drinks. When I woke up next day I felt terrible and I remember thinking, *Fuck, did I behave that badly? Oh my God.* I decided I was never going to get drunk again. Gretton often bought me drinks and tried to get me drunk, but I haven't been drunk since that Boxing Day. Alcohol just doesn't work for me, which is why I take drugs. It's like Chaucer, or someone, once said, 'Where the drink goes in, the wit goes out,' and since I am very partial to wit and as an Englishman think discretion is quite cool, alcohol is the worst sort of drug for me. It's the one that provokes violence, and people tend to hurt people when they're drunk. It's like the bouncers at the Haçienda, whom I was always very fond of – they saved lives. And the number of people over the years who complained about being beaten up by the bouncers. When we got to the bottom of it, we usually found out they were pissed and were having a go, provoking the bouncer. Bouncers have enough trouble dealing with homicidal lunatics, let alone having to deal with drunks as well. So, yes, I love the taste of alcohol, but I think it's worse than cocaine, which is lovely and fun but takes away creativity and talent – it's done that to people whom I have really admired. But alcohol is worse, and on balance, including them all, it's worse than heroin, because it brings out this violence. It's a dreadful fucking drug, and it's just bizarre that it is the one that is the easiest to buy, just in any shop. It's all about money; the drug that requires capital-intensive production becomes the dominant one in society.

7. It's like my dad's boyfriend would get drunk a lot, and over the years that's twenty years of getting drunk, all the time, and I end up not

444

talking to him because it's boring, and you can have a one-hour conversation with a drunk, and the next day they have absolutely no memory of what you talked about, so it's a complete waste of time. I can be very rude even to my closest friends when they are pissed because it is all such a useless exercise. I loved my dad dearly, but his boyfriend was drunk and stupid and semi-violent. I was never bothered by my dad being gay, but I certainly did resent his relationships. I remember he got barred from the Haçienda once for taking off his trousers and simulating sex with one of the pillars on the dance floor. We barred a lot of people, but it never seemed to make a difference. There were always more people to bar.

8. I always found it strange that we had to run this club selling the worst drug on God's earth. We had to finance it really by selling alcohol. And then we were in a position when we weren't selling so much alcohol because of the drugs.

9. One of my favourite moments in life was standing in the Haçienda with Mick Hucknall of Simply Red, the most famous of all Manchester musicians, even though he never makes the list, the great list of the Manchester greats, and we're with Leroy, who was the barman at the Haçienda, and some heavy, charismatic gangster figure walks over. He completely bypasses me and Hucknall, and he shakes Leroy by the hand. 'Respect, man.' And I thought that was great – minor TV celebrity, major pop celebrity, fuck them. Leroy, man. That's Manchester.

10. We put the Haçienda into administration to try and resolve problems with the VAT, blah blah blah, basically because we ran the club like shite. Rob was one of those who created it but basically one of his faults was cronyism – he surrounded himself with hangers-on, employed about thirty of them. We went into receivership, and then the police hit us with a massive writ to close us down – we had made a deal with them, we thought, but no one could remember doing it. Anyway, we

lost the club, and then Rob said we should buy the name back, it's worth something. And as usual Alan and I didn't have any money, so Rob said, 'Me and Hooky will do it on behalf of all of us.' It cost £5,000. Eight years later, when they came to license the name for the apartments they paid £500 per apartment, which came to £42,000. Of course, Rob and Hooky alone owned the name. Nobody could be bothered getting wound up about it. I certainly couldn't. I quite like the fact that I got screwed and still get screwed, having lost millions of pounds on it, and Alan probably never knew it happened, and when I told Bernard he said, 'Yes, I know. I've told Hooky.' 'Told him what?' 'That he's a cheating swine.'

11. You couldn't make it up, except we did.

12. People never really told me what the gossip was – I was often the last to hear, if at all, what was really going on in the club. It's like that line Liz Naylor came up with, about me being the mill owner, and there's all this gossiping between the workers and the foreman, but no one ever tells you anything because you're the boss – you're outside that structure, even though you dearly want to be part of it. It can be lonely always being the boss, but of course, as the boss, you couldn't let that slip. I was not meant to be lonely. It wasn't part of the story.

13. Oh, and don't forget to mention Kevin Hewick. He was going to be my John Martyn, my Roy Harper, my Nick Drake, and I think he thinks I lost interest when I met him at Manchester Piccadilly station for the first time, and he swears I did a double take because he didn't look like a romantic troubadour but like a postman from Leicester. We got him to audition for the new group after Joy Division, because they needed a new singer, and he could sing. I think Hannett fell asleep under the mixing desk while Kevin auditioned. He wasn't the right singer to replace Ian Curtis. But then who was?

Thirty-Three: Discovering Ecstasy, acid house, Madchester and on the importance of design

Nemo enim fere saltat sobrius, nisi forte insanus. (Nobody dances sober, unless maybe they are insane.)

CICERO

Funnily enough, and Wilson must have known this, or indeed told me at some point, E was something else that came into Manchester from Germany, having gone round the houses, the first official recipe appearing in a Polish scientific journal in 1960, the first seizure of Ecstasy tablets made in Chicago in 1972, with the American West Coast being the first major centre of sensation-seeking use in the late 1970s. German chemists at Merck in Darmstadt discovered 3,4-methylenedioxymethamphetamine – MDMA – in 1912, while developing medicines that would help blood to clot, contrary to early myths that it was patented as an appetite suppressor. During research on its therapeutic properties in the 1970s, one psychiatrist described it as 'medicine for the soul'.

Wilson would buy his first tab of E in a rough dealer's house in Alphabet City, New York, a couple of years before it hit the Haçienda, another 'drug adventure in New York' to file along with the time he was tripping in a New York bar where Madonna was a waitress, which, what with one thing and another, led to a room with two guys in bondage gear. The Haçienda 'mastermind' had paid his dues. (Madonna would later appear at the Haçienda, before she was a star, frolicking on the dance floor, miming to some of her songs with backing dancers, while the early Haçienda audience stared at her, wondering how on earth to be impressed. Backstage, Rob Gretton in all 'innocence' offered her fifty quid to do a private performance at a party at his house.)

Dance was where something new would emerge, dance as a form of activism, dancing as an intrinsic and ubiquitous part of protest, standing – moving – for release, exercising the right to self-expression and freedom from conventions and prejudice. Instead of terror, violence or anxiety, the power to envision change. And the makers of dance music, even though you couldn't see it directly in the prickly, boyish militancy of A Certain Ratio, were the cheerleaders of change.

Wilson, with his comforting rock prejudices, may not have been a dancer, not since the twist when he was a kid, and the Haçienda, weirdly, even as it was inspired by the more exploratory New York venues was not conceived primarily as a dance club, but once Manchester's new dance identity started to happen, accidentally synth-drummed into being by New York-club-loving New Order, white indie kids getting used to the house tempo through the Manhattan Manchester of 'Blue Monday', white rock kids dancing to music for the first time, taken into a whole new place by the house-selecting DJs who saved and solved the Haçienda, Wilson quickly equated the demand for public happiness during the Thatcher era with dancers acting together, the public display of one's own virtuosity, performers rejecting the routines, institutions and identities of the mundane social world.

Being Wilson, always keen as part of his job to politicise sound, unstoppably defending everyone's right to beautiful, radiant things, he could easily link the dancers in Manchester and the rave parties of the 1980s to the student protests of 1968 and the emergence of an exciting, spontaneous new public space.

Hearing Dave Haslam, one of the DJs making sense of the Haçienda, say in 1987 that he had just bought some 'acid house' twelve-inch singles on import instantly intrigued him, a connection between a world he didn't really understand and one that had been part of his teenage years. Acid and Ecstasy were linked, it was still music and drugs, drugs and music. He could find a way to rationalise the way dance had taken over the world, his world, his precious Manchester, even though he never quite thought of it as music. It was culture, though, the symbiotic relationship between drugs and music, and *that* he understood. He wasn't necessarily an expert on music, but he was a world expert on the relationship between music and drugs.

448

The music and drugs took Manchester onto the cover of *Time*. Wilson might have felt old 'for the first time' when he walked into his club and saw 1,500 people dance like their dreams of freedom were coming true to a music with no guitars and few if any words, but he didn't feel so old that he failed to put himself at the centre of it all, explaining it to anyone who'd listen and those that wouldn't. He was thrilled it was happening, thrilled he could find a way to take a lot of the attention while officially taking no credit. Within weeks of hearing the label for the first time he had become the champion of the acid house scene.

Dave Haslam

There were a few times where I kind of felt a little like he was co-opting all our hard work in order to make himself look good. Which was me being a little bit bitter and twisted, I guess, because if he hadn't done it, nobody else would have done it. Nobody else would have made all the different pieces of information into one coherent story. If he hadn't said 'Madchester', if he hadn't said that the Haçienda's changing the world, if he hadn't told everyone about acid house, it might not have become anything. He didn't have the ideas, but he had the idea to make something of them, to take them further. It would have happened, but the way that he framed the story, nobody else would have ever framed it that way, instantly turning it into the news. It was like he was his own channel, reading out the headlines.

Perhaps Wilson himself was the most important Factory signing of them all, or perhaps the most important signing was the one he made before anything had really happened, as fastidious, situation-creating cool hunter – the commissioning, hiring, mentoring of Peter Saville, an act which definitely made the label a multidimensional, multi-formed vessel, a modernist Manchester design centre transferring timeless signals into a wider world that just happened to release music as well.

Factory's record sleeves were as much descriptions of experience, of the experience of experience, as they were seductive designs and sophisticated

449

visual codes transmitting elegiac or dynamic information, sleeves that often had at their heart a kind of high-Romantic yearning for wholeness, which sometimes reflected the music's own longing for something missing or unattainable, and sometimes didn't.

When you signed to Factory, and you were more on the tremulous outside with Quando Quango or the Wake than on the inside with New Order or Joy Division, you would never see any money from record royalties, not a farthing, for all your 50/50 deal, but the defence from the label would be that you had these fantastic, expensive sleeves – just the thing to take the sting out of not being able to pay the bills. You may have been poor, but God your records looked gorgeous. You'd even get a Fac number. You were part of *that* universe. What more could you want?

Joy Division records were released in sleeves that rejected ornament and represented a number of things, including the progress of technology, systems of proportion, pure elevation, personal wilfulness and a mixture of the minimalist and monumental, the playful and the deadly serious. New Order records, representing a new sort of power and self-realisation, were released in sleeves that reflected Saville's madly grand passage through the history of design and art, and his own love for perfection and high finish, his own loyalty to the artistic dimension of design, his own fascination with the exquisite, exploratory eighteenth- and nineteenth-century typefaces of John Baskerville, Firmin Didot and Giambattista Bodoni, and yet also the deluxe exhibitionism and glamour of Roxy Music and Ultravox! and the poetically droll, deadpan semiotics of Kraftwerk.

There was obsession to the point of mania in the design of the New Order sleeves: the extreme perfectionist attention to detail, the serene, determined absence of obviousness, the absorbing collection of clues to a (murder) mystery that would clearly never be fully explained, the suggestion that the sleeves themselves were the most important element in the release, the work of art, the actual point, and the music somehow secondary, merely the soundtrack to the image of the group.

At one point there was even an idea that New Order might be presented as Peter Saville's New Order, in the manner of Andy Warhol's Velvet

Underground, echoing the role of the invisible member of Kraftwerk, Emil Schult, a student of Joseph Beuys who generated much of the conceptual quality of the group, through artwork, titles, images and lyrics. Even a company that was never afraid of taking things too far thought that Peter Saville's New Order might be taking things too far.

Saville was not involved with the imagery for the Happy Mondays, because that required a misfit kind of colour-drenched, retro-surrealist, streetwise mutant psychedelia from a Manchester perspective that was either beyond, or beneath, him – fun Mancofuturistic sleeves reflecting the trouble and rumpus of the group, jarring Salford Bosch rather than Bauhaus dream-space transcended. It emphasised how central design was to Wilson and Factory, but this was irreverent, quickly dated graffiti next to Saville's grand tour of modernity, embarked on once he had Factory to design.

When the occasion demanded, Wilson and Factory would commission other designers: reclusive, high-minded 8vo, seriously perfecting the ritualistic continental Saville mindset, his obsessive attention to detail, finding expressive new ways out of Swiss and modernist typography, favouring the Unica typeface over Saville's prized Helvetica, and, handling the mucked-up, spiritually battering *joie de vivre* of the Mondays, defining the second half of Wilson's Factory story, which spilt into Madchester and *24 Hour Party People*, the painted-up Salford magic realism of Central Station Design. Central Station Design were fathomably down to earth where Saville and 8vo sometimes stalked the desolate ends of the earth, leaving occasional cryptic traces. Wilson: capitalist and socialist, Buddhist and Catholic, snob and commoner, sheriff and outlaw, obscure and populist, faithful and faithless, Joy Division and Happy Mondays, Peter Saville and Central Station Design.

Perhaps the most important signing was another Factory signing that wasn't really a signing, or something that in essence couldn't be easily defined: a building. The Haçienda as Wilson's most important decision, even if, as per usual, it was made with, even by, others, and couldn't have happened without all his other engagements, antics, stealing, schemes and mistakes.

Or it was Hannett, or Gretton, without whom none of the drama, which once or twice led to a certain form of commercial success. Or was it Pickering, finding the right record to play at the right time to what turned out to be the right audience finding the right place? Or Cath Carroll, as the ultimate symbol of the label's peeved contrariness?

Or Erasmus. There were those who asked, 'What exactly does he do?' The answer lay in the fact the question needed to be asked and had something to do with how the label worked, because its structure was so hard to pin down, and the living symbol of this unpindownability was Erasmus, the dreamer, who at some crisis meeting or another, Factory on the verge of another collapse, another lawsuit, another problem with personnel, another dispute with its musicians, another slice of chaos, was sat there staring blankly ahead, and then in the middle of some discussion about premises or cash flow suddenly sat up and said, 'You know, the weather's very cold. Do you think the sheep will be all right?'

There was perhaps something inappropriate about the fact that Wilson, the much more experienced older boss, the executive at the top of the hierarchical tree, the owner of the space, was making himself part of the Madchester scene. Then again, in his other life, his Granada home, he was a relative youngster; newsreaders or chat-show hosts could still act young into their sixties, existing in an impenetrable, self-preserved bubble of timelessness, which in his case also incorporated a real passion for arcane philosophy. It's where his double life in pop and TV really worked for him: both sides kept him younger than his years, as he plunged into the pharmaceuticals and cocaine, perks of his job, or one of his jobs, as part of research into what made Shaun Ryder tick, making him perhaps more of a jerk than usual, but one ultimately craving illuminating magic rather than simply getting wasted.

And he was the sort of boss who was not after crudely, creepily sucking the energy from the young, running things for his own seedy benefit. He was the sort of boss who would wear a mask of Wordsworth and declaim, 'Bliss it was in that dawn to be alive, but to be young was very heaven.'

He loved to have something new to work out, give conceptual coherence to, and this new scene, the dancing through the night into the ground and into heaven, and sometimes hell, was worthy of his attention. He saw the dancing as a form of demonstration. Dancing as a weapon in the revolutionary class struggle. Dancing as a supplement to revolution, an indicator of social change. A way of expressing identity as an act of defiance. The anarchy of the Lesser Free Trade Hall, where the dancing had been all in his head, you could say, was the link between the northern soul – aggressively joyous, fabulously produced American soul as the sound of resistance played in northern clubs – that began in Manchester and the acid house that poured out from the Haçienda.

The Happy Mondays – and the Stone Roses – began as closer to rock, perhaps with a psyche kink or two, early Happy Mondays close to a punkish tribute to early-'80s Factory grey-mac glum, but it was the fluid, uplifting Haçienda sounds drifting into their mixes, Detroit and Chicago house taking a detour via Ibiza all-nighters, holidaymakers bringing the word back via cheap flights, that made them hands-in-the-air pop sensations; for Wilson, there were always the racy words, the mental melon-twisting *flânerie* of Shaun Ryder, melancholic, comic and bracingly obscene, walking with a gangster's swagger but as sensitive as shit, and the wordless whimsy of ramshackle maraca-shaking bug-eyed sidekick Bez, fiendish mind with its edges knocked off by the crack and Ecstasy he took, the whole circus stuffed and shuffled with mischief, that made Wilson sure that the Happy Mondays were more psychedelic rock 'n' roll shindig than regimented dance escapism. They were the sort of outlaws, hustlers and racketeers he was drawn towards, who were never as obviously present in the dance world; when dance music showed signs of subversion it tended to be made by more abstract entities, behind-the-scenes technicians wearing masks and hiding behind machines or symbols, and increasingly videos and DJs.

Thirty-Four: Happy Mondays, hamartia, Factory sale and what the hell

Fortuna vitrea est; tum cum splendet frangitur. (Fortune is like glass; the brighter the glitter, the more easily broken.)
PUBLILIUS SYRUS

Pickering had come across the Happy Mondays when he was given a demo CD by a friend working in a local market. He thought Ryder in his 'pre-ravaged drug days' was a little like Feargal Sharkey of the Undertones. One of the Factory dogmas was that you had to see a band live before they were signed, and so Rob arranged for them to play Salford Tech. All went well, so the next stage was telling Wilson. Pickering raved about the group: 'Rob likes them, we've seen them live, I think they're great. A bunch of scallies from Worsley.' Wilson said, 'Darling, if you like it, we'll do it.'

He hadn't even heard them. But then he would sign bands like the Royal Family and the Poor based on deep conversations with them rather than their music. He'd allocate a catalogue number and a fantastic sleeve based on an intellectual crush rather than musical content, which was nice, and sometimes worked, but mostly didn't. But that was Factory – as soon as that didn't happen, there would be no Factory. Of course, there was also ultimately no Factory because it did happen. It was all part of the game he played.

Here's Wilson selling the idea of the Happy Mondays to America, where everything about the group, from clothes to language, would seem foreign enough to require subtitles and interpreters, dangerous enough in a low-lying petty-criminal way to require cops, magistrates and doctors, hedonistic enough to require antidotes and possibly psychologists. He sets out the context, expediently ignoring the extent of the group's unreliability as performers, as timekeepers, as human beings, glossing over how they were the bent side of the Sex Pistols combined with the addict side of the Meat Puppets. Then again, part of the story, of their fly-by-night genius, is

454

how singer Shaun financed the group by supplying the North of England and Scotland with Ecstasy bought in Ibiza with money made from fencing stolen stereos in Amsterdam.

'There is no great genius' – Wilson grins, wearing a mask of Aristotle, rolling a joint at the bar while in the middle distance wobbly Bez dances for hours and hours, travelling to forever in his head, death a very distant rumour – 'without some touch of madness.' Puff. He puts on a mask of Schopenhauer. 'Talent hits a target no one else can hit. Genius hits a target no one else can see.' Others might see the Happy Mondays as a clear-as-mud shambles of rhythm and rhyme that *might* only make sense if you complete the circuit by taking the right accompanying substances, but Wilson knows the real score.

He presents to polite company as a reader of cultural runes important news of a breezy casual culture that is sweeping the North-West of England, and here is a group buying their clothes at supercool Joe Bloggs, creating the crack soundtrack culled from those hazy Haçienda nights when rock and dance had their heads smashed together, driving fans out of their heads. It's going to be the sound of the '90s, it's the Ecstasy Sex Pistols, it's thug pop, poetics of the lowly high on their own improper trip to fame.

He's relishing the fact he's somehow part of all this, hitting forty, a first, or second, midlife crisis averted, another new load of local slang to learn, more cultural chaos to immerse himself into from the relative safety of his television career – what could possibly go wrong? He talks of expensively kitted-out working-class Salford and therefore Manchester males, lazy, loutish, lewd, *loco*, tripping on Ecstasy and waving three-foot inflatable bananas while watching Manchester City, to the confusion of a watching media, who assume it must have a racist element, unaware of its carefree psychedelic quality. Psychedelic football fans? Where the hell has that come from? Only Tony Wilson's Manchester, now moving almost as fast as his thoughts. 'There are decades where nothing happens,' he explains, wearing one of his favourite masks, V. I. Lenin, 'and there are weeks where decades happen.'

As his life one way or another sped up at the end of the 1980s, spilling over into the 1990s, the older he got, the faster life went, now spinning on the spot on behalf of the smutty, powdery world of the Happy Mondays, teetering on the edge of hell, he could make a great case for how new rock music that hadn't paid attention to dance music was missing the point. House had infected the kind of indie his label had helped invent; luckily, as the provocateur, the ideas salesman, he was part of the infection. But when he went home, into his study, a church, a library, a workshop he'd built for himself for the quiet, private moments when he could see if he could still find himself, or what was left of himself, check if his priorities had changed, he was more likely to play Leonard Cohen, Jackson Browne or Bruce Springsteen. Some things never change, even for someone who loves change.

Aristotle writes in the *Poetics* that the greatest tragedies involve people who are closely related. 'Whenever we achieve something good,' Wilson would say, wearing the mask of someone with an abiding love for ancient Greek plays, 'it is we ourselves who destroy it – we pluck out our own eyes, as the Greeks say.'

Here he is, explaining to his audience the meaning of 'hamartia', from the Greek *hamartanein* – 'to err' or 'to miss the mark' – an inherent short-coming in the hero of a tragedy, who is in other respects a superior being favoured by fortune, a fault which lies at the very heart of Greek tragedy. This defect in personality is also known as a tragic flaw, although some prefer to think of it as a kind of ignorance, a moral failing in an other-wise predominantly good man, and sometimes the flaw might result from overly trusting others, a basic lapse in judgement. It is perhaps a false step taken in blindness, but then there are always going to be failures in any attempts to change the course of fate.

Aristotle casually uses the word in the *Poetics* to suggest mistakes or errors in judgement, perhaps wrongdoings, even sins, which can be per-ceived as both intentional and unintentional. A classic example of hamar-tia is where a hero aspires to do something special but as he is achieving it he commits an error on purpose or accidentally and ends up achieving exactly the opposite, with horrendous results. Oedipus had a tragic flaw, Hamlet, Othello, Macbeth obviously, Dr Faustus, Pilate's ignorance of the true identity of Jesus, Victor Frankenstein's arrogant conviction he could outdo God and nature: all a mix of good and bad qualities, suffering because of their flaws.

Is Wilson a victim of fate who has no control over his destiny, or is it his own action, his lapse of judgement, which sets the events of the story on the way to their conclusion? The beginning of the end perhaps started when Factory famously lost money with 'Blue Monday', despite it becoming the bestselling twelve-inch single of the 1980s, because of the cost of Saville's immaculate, all-knowing sleeve. Perhaps it was when the Haçienda started to float free of its immediate surroundings and those outside the Manchester area started to pour in, non-Mancunians adding to the diversity, the edginess, inviting problems. Perhaps it was when in July 1989 a young girl bought some E in Stockport but took it inside the Haçienda, dying from an allergic reaction and becoming the first nationally reported Ecstasy death, causing the police to pay attention to the club, threatening its licence.

Wilson wondered if there was some kind of curse – why their dance floor, why the Haçienda? – making a rare admission that he had under-estimated a drug, didn't understand its potential for a horrible death, didn't really want to face up to the idea that there could be such a dark side to the party. The beginning of the end could have been the late delivery of Fac 1, the original Factory poster, or when Ian Curtis died, or the unreal contracts Wilson had with his signings, or maybe it was when Malcolm met Tony, or Tony looked at Johnny, or a psychopath burst through the film that separated his public life from his private life and slashed his wife, the film only he had previously been able to move through . . .

If it was a case of hamartia as an error derived from ignorance of some material fact or circumstance, then the beginning of the end was in 1991, when Factory booked their new bestselling prize act the Happy Mondays into Eddy Grant's Blue Wave recording studios in Barbados to record the follow-up to *Pills 'n' Thrills and Bellyaches*. So this might mean disaster really began when they signed the uncouth ranters and ravers Happy

Mondays, or perhaps at some stage along the way as the group went from possibly being another obscure Factory act to supporting Jane's Addiction at Madison Square Garden in April 1991, freshly signed to Elektra, with America, perhaps, theirs for the taking as the spearhead of a new sort of British invasion. The group took a detour on the way to the show to buy some drugs and arrived twenty minutes after they were due on stage. The twenty-five minutes they managed to play, more or less them tuning up, or beginning to tune in, was the sound of a group not ready for prime time in the only way America understands.

Then there was a piece in the *New Musical Express*, after Steven Wells had interviewed them in Factory's own Dry Bar, the first in-depth profile of Wilson's new northern wonders. Wells forensically framed the group's then mostly lauded lunatic laddism as nothing but sexism and homophobia, supporting the idea that Wilson's aroused, open-mouthed love for the dangerously grumbling Mondays resembled his unreconstructed love for Bernard Manning.

Ryder was like a Bernard Manning who had appeared at Woodstock and before going on stage had been handed some mescaline by Jerry Garcia. And of course Wilson had a soft spot for Pol Pot and Gaddafi, for the permission granted to extreme poets and vicious comics to puncture the membrane of decency and experiment with moral limits, so some grubby Salford chauvinism, some music-paper juvenile delinquency, was not going to dent his admiration. 'It's all good, all good,' he would say when the piece was published, as though it was all part of his masterplan. It would all go away; he had anticipated the at this point necessary alienation of *NME* readers. 'They're not being dickheads. It's all working out nicely.'

Factory Records began with desperate sadness – Joy Division – and ended with dysfunctional craziness – the Happy Mondays – but also began and ended with two very different kinds of bleakness, and began with a group that wisely more or less withdrew from interviews and ended with a group throwing up in interviews. The fluidities of queerness that seemed to materialise at the end of the 1970s, promising a wider construction of otherness, failed to reach this far into the future. Normal service, albeit in an abnormal, often grotesque setting, had resumed. Dance rhythms had carried the Mondays into the charts, but then rock continuity was to some extent straightened, preparing the way for the whitewashed, rock-steady pop conservatives Oasis.

Factory at all times being Factory was out of its depth when it came to the commercial coordination of a group edging towards the sort of stardom that requires boring professional standards rather than wild schemes. Factory was a major label in Manchester, and now had imposing offices to prove it, but in the outside world was still minor, an independent living hand to mouth, relying on random bursts of inspiration and international deals with major labels.

The idea of getting Chris Frantz and Tina Weymouth of Talking Heads and the Tom Tom Club to produce the Barbados album was inspired, if not what the group wanted, loyal to the precisely calibrated club- and radio-friendly acid rock of *Pills* producers Paul Oakenfold and Steve Osborne, and on paper it was a reasonable idea to record in Barbados, where there should only be a limited supply of heroin to help the group's lead singer kick his habit. However, Wilson was surprised to learn that actually Barbados was *the* centre for crack cocaine in the Americas. The good news: Ryder stopped taking heroin. The bad news: having broken his bottle of methadone back at Manchester Airport, he was smoking daily a Ryder-sized amount of crack, anywhere between thirty-five and fifty rocks a day, which sounds challenging even to the inexperienced onlooker.

At some point, one story goes, Eddy Grant's furniture from the studio's residence was being sold to buy more drugs, and Ryder ransomed the incomplete master tapes for a little more extra drug cash. Wilson never made it out to Barbados, another one of his regrets both because he couldn't save the situation, but also because he never got to witness the carnage, but he would brag, for the sake of the story, how as his plane was landing on the island he saw Ryder dragging a sofa along the runway on the way to selling it for more crack. It was in the script.

Ryder was unable to write a word, language an increasingly distant proposition, or even sing his parts. After a few months' work, there were some backing tracks but little else. Frantz and Weymouth reminded us that in some extreme cases the role of the record producer involves some serious babysitting, but Factory could have hired much cheaper sitters, and less extravagant premises. Meanwhile, Bez had broken his arm, twice, once crashing a jeep and four weeks later while jet-skiing against doctor's advice, and it had gone gangrenous, requiring ornate metal pinning. The cost of the recording was taking its toll on Factory's fragile finances, everyone just wanting to get the record finished, more desperate for basic product than they had ever been and unable to bring themselves to take the lead singer's real-life problems seriously.

A worried Elektra executive from New York visiting the island for an update after a few weeks of radio silence called the group's manager, Nathan McGough, who was himself struggling with personal problems in Manchester and couldn't help. The executive tried Wilson next, explaining that Ryder was in a terrible state and pretty much required urgent medical attention, or the record might not be finished but the group would be, and Shaun could well be Factory's second great rock 'n' roll casualty.

Wilson didn't have an immediate answer and for once struggled to make a decision. At the time of the call he was dealing with piled-up debts and drugs and guns and police and people dying in his club. He suggested the executive call Erasmus, who sounded like he'd just woken up and this was the last news he wanted to hear. A quietly desperate Erasmus murmured, 'Just do what you think best,' and the sessions were shut down. Factory wasn't a label being run out of a small flat with mismatched furniture in Didsbury any more – they now had swish self-conscious city-centre offices that harmonised with the look of the Haçienda – but it might as well have been.

Eventually, once Ryder had been relatively sorted, and Bez's arm saved, the album was finished as *Yes Please!* but was always going to be written into the story as a disaster album, destined for a two-word 'No thanks' review in *Melody Maker*, its awry, bombed Manc–Caribbean hybrid not what the world wanted under the circumstances, and not what Factory needed. At another time, for a small cult audience of music-paper readers, the Happy Mondays as a mashed Talking Heads making an album called *What Larks!* might have been looked on more kindly, but the 20,000 it would sell, at best, would not solve anyone's financial problems. So Wilson had thousands of copies of an album no one wanted, 'watching it rot on a pallet' in a warehouse, as Factory went into administration. New Order and Rob Gretton couldn't save the situation, late with their own album, and were themselves owed a million pounds by Factory – a nice round number they would never see.

Even Factory's and New Order's – and Tony Wilson's – only number-one single couldn't halt the inevitable. 1990's 'World in Motion', billed as Englandneworder, was a subversive, anti-hooligan, 'anti-football song' football song that could also be heard as a love song and even a comedy song. It also existed as a beguiling, stand-alone, optimistic and bittersweet New Order song and is therefore, for what it's worth, the greatest football song ever written. (Its sweeter, perkier rival for the title, 'Three Lions (Football's Coming Home)', by the Lightning Seeds and Baddiel and Skinner, could exist only because New Order first of all, somewhere between foolishly and fantastically, changed the expectation of what a football song could be.)

The official England song for the 1990 Italian World Cup, 'World in Motion' was one of those examples of how Wilson's more formal broadcasting contacts and his ability to create an anomalous even chaotic situation contributed to a strangely functioning utopian project that couldn't have happened under any other set of circumstances. It was Wilson and Factory at their best and worst, a kind of poignant and potent, and peculiar, more public, climax to the story of Factory.

In 1988, at some event, Wilson had been chatting to the head of press at the Football Association, who mentioned that he really didn't want the next England song to be another of the usual awkward pub-pop sing-alongs. It would be better not to bother than to have yet another weak, self-conscious piece of nonsense sung by the team, who would then be forced onto *Top of the Pops* in terrible suits and ties. It was a tradition that looked corny even in the 1960s and '70s, but now seemed a punishment for everyone involved, whether players or fans.

The FA man told Wilson that he would love a cool Manchester band to record the next England song, making clear the emerging connection between football and fashion, but it seemed highly unlikely anyone would want to. Wilson, sensing devilment, asked him who his dream group to write an England song would be. The answer was New Order, then at the peak of their powers as songwriters and chart regulars.

Wilson told an indifferent and even anxious New Order that the FA would like them to write a serious England World Cup song, to change the tawdry image of the standard football track. Most members of the staid and old-fashioned FA had no idea that the idea had been proposed. Wilson naturally acted like it was all a done deal, telling New Order that the FA was very much in favour of their involvement and informing the FA that New Order were flattered to have been asked and had come up with a fantastic and appropriate song.

The England footballers thought it would be another of those annoying and clichéd singalongs. Thinking of previous cheap and cheerful England songs, like 'World Cup Willie' and 'Back Home', New Order decided that writing such a song would have been the last straw in terms of their credibility, guaranteed to unsettle their hardcore followers, especially their original Joy Division fans. On paper, it seemed the equivalent of the group being asked to write the British entry for the Eurovision Song Contest. They ended up accepting the challenge, precisely because writing what is basically a novelty song seemed to be the absolute opposite of what they apparently stood for.

The actor, football fan, party animal and Haçienda-lover Keith Allen was brought into the project when a desperate Bernard Sumner needed to find a way to insert the England footballers themselves into the song – an FA contractual requirement. Allen's original idea, encouraged by an increasingly excitable Wilson, was a song called 'E for England', because 'E' was also for Ecstasy.

That idea never made it directly into the song, but enough mischief and accidental highs did to satisfy Allen's, Wilson's and the group's desire to add a little attractive, sly danger to the idea of an England football song, somehow symbolising how the English team at a football tournament can, one way or another, whether they do well or not, turn the world – or at least the nation – upside down.

Only a handful of players turned up to the recording, the rest not wanting to be associated with another flat, dated football anthem. Not even Wilson at full tilt could persuade them this one was going to be different. Those few footballers that did get to the recording session – treating it as a party, outdrinking the group – stayed for about an hour, before heading off to another engagement, with no idea that the song would be anything other than the usual weak cheerleading embarrassment.

The Jamaican-born Liverpool left-winger John Barnes ended up being the player who, with naive and accidental grace, performed a madcap rap written mostly by Allen that helped make it truly different, as a football song and a pop song – an unlikely alliance of sport and dance, electronics and tactics, the cheeky and the sublime, the hedonistic and the athletic, the laddish and the transcendent.

New Order were number one in the first two weeks of June, and England reached the semi-finals of the 1990 World Cup, bringing a new kind of hope to a nation disorientated by a decade of relentless Thatcherism, which included a certain suspicious hostility to the working-class energies of football and the motives of the fans.

England's achievement, which mixed up nostalgia and an innocent form of nationalism, offering the revelation of something new, required a song that had its own perverse, uplifting, sentimental glory, but also its own enchanting logic, a song that could reflect the history of the moment as it was happening and spin it out into the future. Weirdly, wonderfully, it got one.

Somehow, 'World in Motion' belonged with the silly old-fashioned England football songs, and at the same time with the innovative, timeless, often heart-breaking songs of New Order, which will always keep working as beautifully organised soundtracks to timely moments and emotional – and commercial – occasions. New Order's songs – perhaps because they are produced in mysterious ways, under a certain amount of stress and also of hope – turned out to be great at predicting the rhythms of the future.

Wilson had used his conniving skills, his media contacts and his messy, dark cunning to generate the perfect musical accompaniment to a special time of transformation. It was as though he knew exactly what he was doing. Sometimes his methods could create something extraordinary. It didn't mean that he'd found a solution to Factory's financial problems.

Despite scraping into the charts a couple of times and even appearing on *Top of the Pops* in June 1991, Northside weren't going to save the day either. Their one album of downtrodden druggy, baggy up-jangle – as though Factory now had a department for turning out Happy Mondays clones – was produced by Ian Broudie of the Lightning Seeds and seemed to throw some scuzzy swagger forward to Liam Gallagher and the Oasis to come, and was even considered a lost classic by some Factory completists. It could, though, have been put together by any number of record labels following a certain formula. There was a catalogue number allocated for Northside's 'Want a Virgin', the first single from a proposed second album, but circumstances turned the group into just another minor casualty in a sorry Manchester mess.

Talks with London Records to save Factory cannot survive Factory not being a label, more a state of mind, a form of performance art, as such not worth a penny, and Wilson betrays his original partner and friend Erasmus, who seethes that he didn't negotiate with anyone else, by taking an internal role at London in lieu of the original deal. He didn't say to London, 'It's me and Erasmus or it's nothing'; he took a position as some kind of mascot or consultant. He took the money. Within days of Factory collapsing Erasmus is on the dole. Erasmus lives, but the pair are estranged. Erasmus has been expelled from the group. Their friendship is dead.

So it goes.

On Monday 23 November 1992, Leonard Curtis are appointed official receivers by the National Westminster bank and issue instructions that all operations must cease. The day passes with incident, as Factory workers – Wilson, Gretton, Erasmus initially denying anything is wrong – enter and exit the four floors of the building for the final time, passing over the keys to the receivers, who take control of the property and more or less raid the offices, assessing what exactly is left. A film crew directed by Tosh Ryan, the Manchester music-business operator who went from Music Force to Rabid, paving the way for Factory, his name shrunk down from something double-barrelled and ornate as though to symbolise his opposite sensibility, is there to film the sad remains: records, New Order and Happy Mondays posters, merchandise strewn across the floor, and the sorry-looking temporary contemporary Factory office table, trashed by the Mondays, which had become a character in its own right. It hung limply from the ceiling on a few steel strings, an obvious metaphor for the demise of Factory, a table that they said cost £35,000 but was really a tenth of that which now looked like it was worth a hundredth of that. Factory eventually ends up being swallowed by the corporate Warners label, as back catalogue to play with, data to monitor and mythology to exploit.

There's a kind of wake in the traditional Victorian glazed-tile Lass O'Gowrie pub just off Princess Street, Wilson resigning himself to the end and delivering a jaunty, defiant speech because it is all over but tomorrow really is another day, and you don't get rid of him that easily. The film Tosh Ryan makes, almost relishing poring over the sorry Factory leftovers, witnessing the destruction of the label that effectively made him redundant in 1978, is called *Black Monday*.

Factory has gone bust, there's plenty on his mind, but Wilson is still helping his audience to understand 'hamartia'. His long-standing reputation provided some protection, so any punishment for facing his hamartia wasn't fatal.

'It is important in the tragic definition of hamartia that the hero does not acknowledge his or her own flaw.'

You cannot escape your own personality. No matter where you go, there you are. Events can unfold in the opposite way to what was intended or expected.

Thirty-Five: Meanwhile, more private life because that never stops

Amantes sunt amentes. (Lovers are lunatics.)
TERENTIUS

Neville Richards

The arrival of his third wife Yvette was my fault. I had introduced him to Hilary, but now I introduced him to the idea of Yvette. I'd got this young girlfriend, absolutely lovely, twenty-one, and I introduced her to Tony and he was pretty transfixed. She was drop-dead gorgeous; even Vini fell in love with her. He went home and said to a pregnant Hilary, filling out because of the baby, that he had seen my new girlfriend, and sort of not meaning it but meaning it, being a little naughty, he said, 'I want one of them!'
A few weeks later he met Yvette. He was forty. She was eighteen, a Miss Something-or-Other. It was so typical of Tony to do something like that. A bloody beauty queen. Part of what he couldn't resist was how much that would wind people up. He craved what others had sometimes, and even with a great head like Tony had you could easily go off the rails. Sometimes you had to give him a hard time to make him see, and after he met Yvette, it became more difficult to get to him. He became besotted with her.

He needed a different wife really for each part of his life. And this was the power period, and Yvette was also into power, I think, the idea of Tony as real Manchester leader rather than it being in theory. She wasn't so keen on him coming to Didsbury to see his old mates, and Tony of course wanted to please her. So we were out, really. They did become like a power couple, and that suited what he was up to in the '90s after Factory. It did get a bit kitchen sink between them, Hilary and the kids battling with this new woman taking Tony's attention, which was being taken by other things as well. There wasn't a lot left for Hilary and the children. He'd definitely left Hilary behind in the 1990s, and the children got a bit lost as well.

466

Hilary Wilson

Yvette was a very powerful woman, very forceful. I went round to her and said, 'Look, you're eighteen and Tony is forty with two young children. If you're not serious about him in the long term, please just back off.' She told me, 'Tony doesn't want to be with you any more. Get out. I'm going to call the police.' I had Isabel in my arms because she was only one. Yvette more or less threw us out. There was no negotiating with her.

Rose Marley, events manager, In the City stalwart, entrepreneur

I was always as fascinated with what made Yvette tick as I was with Tony – perhaps even more so. Which of course riled him a bit. You'd always be finding new things out about her – she was a pilot, she'd gone out with Prince Andrew for goodness' sake, she drove a convertible Bentley even when they were trying to raise money, pleading poverty. Sort of the female version of Tony in a way, with enough business sense to take that pressure off Tony. I think they loved each other incredibly, but sometimes it did seem more like as siblings. He cared for her a lot, but it never seemed particularly conventional.

Gonnie Rietveld

It wasn't like he had loads of different girlfriends. It wasn't like that. She – whoever the latest one was – she was always beautiful. But that's a different thing. Because all his relationships, I think, were always with very bright and intelligent women. But none of them were truly in the limelight, even if they wanted to be. They were always a rock for him, you know. Behind every successful man stands a surprised woman, and I think it worked quite well. For him, for a while, until the nature of the relationship changed.

Hilary Wilson

If I wrote a book about all of this, I would call it The Factory Casualties. *There was this wonderful Mr Manchester, this great glamorous figure*

467

changing things, but to get there so many people had to fall by the wayside. I had to be his ex for so many years. People would always be asking me in Didsbury village, 'How's Tony, Mrs Wilson?' 'I don't know – ask him!' To me he was just a husband and a dad and a very vulnerable person who did all he could to hide that.

Thirty-Six: Dry, the Northern Quarter, the Haçienda (3) and be careful what you wish for

Spectemur agendo. (Let us be judged by our acts.)
OVID

In 1989, Haçienda high, Happy Mondays happy, Wilson and Factory with New Order tagging along again made a move that helped alter the map of the city, coinciding with city council plans to regenerate an area that had significant historical presence but which by the 1960s and '70s had almost become a no-go zone. Nothing much had changed in the 1980s, so that over on the other side of town, as the Haçienda started to create a glow from the future, and the G-Mex centre smartly transformed one of the city's old stations, beginning an upgrade of the Castlefield area, a key part of the city was still suffering from the kind of decay that confirmed how much of the city was still in a broken post-war state.

The city council had long ignored an area centred around Oldham Street on the eastern edge of Piccadilly Gardens, therefore right in the heart of the city, that needed urgent attention. Just a few steps along Oldham Street and you would soon leave behind city-centre safety. Walking up there in the 1970s, passing through shrunken, wrinkled remnants of Manchester's industrial prime, was like heading into the heart of darkness. Manchester fell away underneath you.

Ironically, the area had suffered after an analysis performed by the city surveyor in 1962 that suggested Manchester was 'crystallised in its Victorian setting . . . A new look for the city has been long overdue . . . Its unsightly areas of mixed industrial, commercial and residential development need to be systematically unravelled and redeveloped on comprehensive lines. Only in this way can a city assume its proper place as a regional centre.' Market Street, Manchester's main shopping street since 1850, was described by the *Guardian*, whose northern offices were nearby, 'as depressing and decaying for 30 years'.

A major consequence of the council's approach to improving the city's appearance – matching the changes Stockport had made to clear its town centre of cotton mills and create the Merseyway Shopping Centre and Salford's updating of its central retail area – was the building of the American-style Arndale Centre, an act of modernisation finished after seven years of construction in 1979 that some saw as a necessary twentieth-century boost to the city's image and critics decried as replacing a characterful area with opaque if gleaming functionality.

Architects Wilson and Womersley included Jack Lynn, who with his forward-looking British interpretation of European modernism worked on the almost instantly defunct Hulme Crescents flats. They were based on his radically brutalist, post-war modernist Park Hill 'streets in the sky' development in Sheffield, built as a bright new hope for the city in the late 1950s. Hulme's flatness meant they lacked the visual drama of Park Hill, built on one of Sheffield's seven hills, rising above the city – these streets were planted firmly on the streets – and although after they were finished in 1971 they were clean and seemed nice, if a little eccentrically shaped, a year later it all started to go wrong. The ideas were positive, the engineering a disaster, construction poorly supervised. The problems soon started, as if the land was cursed, always determined to reach into the buildings and pull them apart.

Arndale also suffered from problems generated by a lack of connection between the idealism of the architects and the inevitable pressure on the council to build big and cheaply. Chaotic communications between the architects with their avant-garde visions and Manchester City Council with its unavoidable pragmatic requirements led to a mammoth structure containing over 200 shops and underground parking that seemed designed to suck the energy out of Manchester, an invading mass for the masses that was described by one critic as conceived by minds who 'seriously believe that the centre of Manchester should look like a barbaric new city borrowed from Le Corbusier'. If only it had . . . On seeing it completed, one member of the council sighed that the model hadn't looked like that. The model looked like a space-age city. This resembled a botched repair job.

Featurelessly ugly on the outside, positively shiny and new on the inside, tarted up with pot plants and even a fountain, which is all some cared about – all those lovely escalators gliding into the future, all those shops spilling over with desirables – the Arndale Centre symbolised the difficulties involved in modernising old, bombed, Victorian Manchester and deciding what the new would consist of. Many British cities were acquiring an Arndale Centre, so it was nothing particularly special, but at least Manchester was keeping up; the city was trying to take care of itself, even if it could only manage a few facelifts and deeper surgery to certain parts.

But the once eccentrically lively, forgotten narrow streets on the other side of the Arndale Centre wedged between Piccadilly, Victoria station and Ancoats withered in its shadow. It was all front, with a deadpan, un-English, very non-Manchester expression, and everything behind it carried on decaying. Around the back there was Tib Street, combining pet shops full of rabbits and puppies, boarded-up but still open adult-entertainment emporiums and random clothes shops and textile warehouses, but it was a Manchester hanging on for dear life.

In the early 1970s Virgin Records had opened shops across the country, making high-street record stores seem a little underground. Their cramped but exciting Manchester premises were a few paces up Oldham Street from the bus station in Piccadilly Gardens, about as far as you'd venture before hitting the forbidden zone; grab your Tangerine Dream double gatefold *Phaedra*, the sound of the future, and then retreat – before the nineteenth century grabbed you around your ankles – to catch your bus. By the end of the 1980s, after the few remaining shops along Oldham Street had closed and businesses fled under pressure from the commercial glamour nearby, the area had drifted into unloved neglect, few daring to explore the shadowy territory created by the arrival of the shopping centre. Some parts of the city had made it into the future; others were almost forbidden to leave the past.

Enter Wilson and his independently minded council of dreamers and talkers. Sometimes it would seem as though having made his mind up that he was never leaving Manchester permanently, he needed to add facilities he felt were missing from his kind of modern metropolitan city. What he definitely felt was missing was the kind of place where you could eat and drink all day and into the night, which was at the time in Manchester, with its rigid licensing laws, an absurd-seeming concept.

Wilson lived an ad hoc freelance life, a prototype digital nomad with hours to spare and the temperament to live and work anywhere he fancied, along with one or two of the pop stars living in and around Manchester, and he was imagining a world that no one else saw coming. He was missing a place which you could use as an office, laptop on table, mobile phone in hand, years before there were laptops and mobile phones in everyone's hands. And of course he was missing a place where not only did everyone know his name, but a place where he could hold court and be seen to be right at the centre of moving Manchester and could burst through the doors into hip central, the first person in town wearing a suit with trainers, the first person in town in his forties actually wearing trainers. He was the first person ever spotted anywhere with a USB stick. 'What's that around your neck?' 'It's my computer, darling.'

Having taken the idea of the vast nightclub from New York at the beginning of the '80s, by the end of the decade he had decided Manchester required the kind of fashionable cafe-bar you would find in progressive-minded European cities that weren't so tangled in the past.

For Wilson, the area at the edge of the Arndale with its combination of exiled spaces and ignored, deteriorating, protected buildings – plus the odd desolate car park to shovel consumers into the Arndale – was as deprived as Detroit, so naturally this is where they would site their follow-up to the Haçienda – Dry, catalogue number 201. The Russell Club had taken some getting to in the middle of one abandoned zone, the Haçienda was originally at the rarely-visited-on-foot, depressed edge of central Manchester, and Dry was going to be, for all its relative glitz and modernist charm, quite a challenge to get to. The location alone made it seem like another Factory folly, another dubious, perverse gesture, a spectacular space waiting for something to happen. It wasn't a pub, it wasn't a club – surely it was too foreign, especially stranded along the unlovely Oldham Street.

It was what you would actually call a cocktail bar, a distant rumour in most of Manchester even in 1989, and there was also going to be a food floor, christened Hungry by New Order's Bernard Sumner, which never quite made it. There was of course a manifesto – this was Factory business, part of a movement, taking itself seriously with its tongue in its cheek. 'We are establishing a new head office in Central Manchester. We see this merely as a second phase of a much larger plan . . . Dry is to be to bars what the Haçienda is to clubs.'

The Haçienda's architect, Ben Kelly, was called in. Augmenting the stripped industrial fixtures and fittings of the Haçienda style, he retained elements of the original warehouse but transformed it, using iron gird-ers to create 'drinking ledges', making sure that it had the longest bar in Manchester at the time, twenty-four metres of slate and steel, and a whole array of spaces that were obviously defined as continental.

A cash phone by the door to order various necessities for the trip ahead to the Haçienda stood in until mobile phones weren't slab-sized. Bernard Sumner, finding New Order roped into another Haçienda-like scheme, would listen to Tony marvel about the bar, the enthusiasm that would some-times get on your nerves and other times make the world a wonderful place. Remembering what the Haçienda had to go through to become something, this time it was getting on his nerves. 'He was raving about all this urban chic, and being the pessimist, of course, I just pointed out that yet again it was a massive space. "When it's half full it will look completely empty, and it's in a really crap area. Why don't we put it in Oxford Road where all the students are? It's a captive market." "No, no," he'd say. "It's a real up-and-coming area; the council are going to invest so much money in the area. Within nine months it will be the new Greenwich Village." You didn't know if he was just getting carried away again, or if he had it all worked out.'

The huge mirror behind the bar – so that Manchester could see itself being Manchester, which meant much more than it had a decade before – was soon hit with what some say was a bottle thrown by Shaun Ryder, making himself at home in what to some extent was his second home, or a bullet fired at Tony Wilson, the preferred legend that eventually made it into *24 Hour Party People*. It was also a necessary part of the marketing that Liam Gallagher was banned from the premises for some rock-star misdemeanour. Saville's suitably dry logo DRY201 would be featured on glassware, menus, aprons, matches, coasters, counter cards, flyers, posters and doggy bags, brand Factory proving Wilson's theory that there was no avant-garde; there are only people who are a little late.

Dry hadn't popped up out of nowhere like the original Factory club and the Haçienda, few understanding how it should be used, and there was enough momentum and new life in the city to make it an early success. It did turn out to be part of the larger plan claimed in the manifesto. After a tough decade fighting Margaret Thatcher's onslaught on municipal localism, planning for a Labour win in 1987 that never happened, the Labour-controlled council entered the 1990s with a determination to give the city a much-needed modernising lift.

In 1992 they started preparing an audacious-seeming bid for the 2000 Olympics, which eventually went to Sydney – the beginning of a renaissance that truly bloomed following the massive IRA bombing of the area around the Arndale Centre. The explosion was the biggest-ever terrorist attack on the British mainland, which was ultimately seen as a violent, unwanted but perversely liberating demolition of the city centre, its unloved parts and its historic landmarks.

At the time of the explosion in 1996 there were about 1,000 pioneering residents in the city centre, tucked away in small enclaves, including the sixty flats of Cromford Court, built in 1981 as a miniature concrete cul-de-sac in the sky with neat communal garden above the Arndale Centre, home to an assortment of Manchester music scenesters including Mike Pickering and Roger Eagle, and the red-brick Smithfield Estate in what would become the Northern Quarter. Twenty years later there would be close to 55,000 city-centre dwellers.

The attack and its aftermath channelled the city's growing Olympic ambitions – not to compete with the likes of Stockport and Barnsley but with Sydney and Barcelona. This had always been the thinking of Wilson and Factory – Manchester as competitive international city – but what had seemed fanciful when they talked of it was much more realistic now that the 'city fathers' had understood the aspirations.

Even before the bomb focused political attention on the city's need for change, Dry had become a kind of defiant beacon along gloomy Oldham Street, along with the alternative indoor market Affleck's Palace, which made use of the vast spaces inside the old department store Affleck and Brown. They were a symbol of what the area could become, and Wilson's audacity anticipated a council decision in 1992 to form the Eastside Association. Local artists were encouraged to use the area's buildings and walls for the kind of public art that would pick up from Dry and Affleck's how this was an area for DIY enterprise and creative entrepreneurship.

A shabby area with low rents featuring emotionally charged art on the walls implying a bohemian vibe attracts independent entrepreneurs, and the council – following the nerve of Wilson with Dry – starts to invest, and an almost deserted part of the city begins to come alive. The once lost-looking, solid but soiled warehouses are perfect – as with the Haçienda – for converting into apartments, offices, studios, galleries, bars, clubs, venues and shops. The modern finally turns up, accentuating the history of the place rather than wrecking it; old and new, messy and modern Manchester work together.

It becomes a neighbourhood and gets a name – the not particularly Chtcheglov-, more New Orleans-inspired Northern Quarter, no one bold enough to call it a Bizarre or Happy Quarter – a fifth quarter to go with the Civic Quarter around the Town Hall, the Green Quarter, the Millennium Quarter and the University Quarter, none really taking off as much as the Northern Quarter, Canal Street and Chinatown not being counted as quarters. The Dry designer style, where pop culture, local music heroes and design consciousness are infused into bricks and mortar, influences the bars and restaurants that would fill the area, becoming a part of the new Manchester, along with the relentless glass-faced skyscrapers and the return of the gliding trams.

The plans of Factory and the city council coincide; an unlikely alliance of the mainstream and the alternative, the practical and the inspired. The council can't manufacture cool, contrived, bustling cultural life, balancing grittiness with glamour, but the advanced guard that created Dry could, because they opened a venue where pop stars would hang out and play up, and the music was chosen by real experts. It meant there was for better or worse a transitional authenticity to the emergence of a cosmopolitan zone. Dry was the original source of the independent spirit that as much as possible, at least for a couple of decades, managed to resist corporate intrusion buying into the idea of a cool city.

When the council with all its responsibilities and prejudices had moved to modernise and repair, they had tended to follow a generic idea of what a city should be – leading to the Arndale Centre, reconstruction without imagination, the facilities a modern city required, but laid out with limited and limiting flair. Modernisation hadn't leaked into the city any further than the shape and size of buildings; it didn't seep into its psyche. Factory's conception of modernisation was as much abstract and fanciful as it was physical but proved that a city changes shape not only through its appearance but also as a concept, as an image. There was a splendid naivety about Factory's belief in the idea of the city, but also a kind of haphazard sophistication – an idealism, a wayward, exaggerated sense of possibility and a belief in the recuperative energies of creative knowledge that could never survive a formal committee.

The city council consistently appreciated that for the sake of economic and social survival, and eventually to fill in the holes left by the IRA bomb, there needed to be changes, but what made the changes more resonant was the fact that at the edges of their decisions, solutions and investments was the organisation set around Wilson's creative taste and knowledge. Sometimes Factory's thoughts, daydreaming and plans were ahead of the council's; other times they arrived a little late, finding to their surprise that the council were already there, commissioning proposals, engaged with artistic communities, looking for new uses for abandoned buildings, for ruined areas. Among the many collaborations the council would make with

476

architects, investors and businesses, one of their most idiosyncratic, ad hoc and ultimately most influential was with Wilson's informal collective.

The council would be doing the heavy lifting; Wilson would add a poetic architectural dimension and theoretical details, and a fascination with the language of design, that added Manchester itself to what otherwise could have been well intentioned, sometimes grand, but ultimately ordinary and even anonymous. Wilson sneaked himself into a role as a kind of futurist historian haunting the council's plans, so as Manchester redeveloped after wartime bombs and peacetime terrorism, there was a thread of subversion that ensured the delivery of a more mysterious, dreamlike city that politicians and academics never fully understand.

Wilson also taunted the council from his position on the outside, sometimes frightening the life out of the councillors with his plans – urging them to bid for the World Cup, to think as big as possible, coming across definitely in the tradition of those who crazily dreamt up the Manchester Ship Canal. When there were early suggestions that Manchester should have a mayor with real powers like London's, the council leaders were truly scared that the obvious winner of such an election would be the fiercely independent Tony Wilson, as though that was what he had been preparing for with Granada, Factory and the Haçienda.

The Lancashire-born, Cambridge-educated former Labour cabinet minister and shadow home secretary Andy Burnham was elected as mayor of Greater Manchester in 2017, having failed in his attempt to become leader of the Labour Party. Even as a seasoned professional politician, he brought into the job a sense that he'd studied how Wilson as a guerrilla activist balanced provocation and play. Some of what he was doing was carrying on the work of Wilson: how to make sure Manchester, and the North, didn't become a lost cause. Burnham would be nicknamed 'the king of the North', but even the idea there could be such a character was based on Wilson's campaigning separatist energy, refreshing bluntness and sometimes improbable-seeming aspirations.

Wilson's fascination with the metaphysical meaning of a city positively distorted an otherwise overly pragmatic conception of a working urban environment. The regeneration would happen anyway, but the unruly, uncontrollable Factory element added energetic new nonconformist fibres to a city conventionally extending its existing industrial, educational and media legacies.

It was a difficult balance between the real and the simulation once Manchester became a modernised version of itself; 'Cottonopolis becoming cool', as the articles would be headlined. Peter Saville once said to me, 'Be careful what you wish for,' as Manchester became increasingly packed with boutique hotels, carefully branded chain cafes, hipster shops, designer studios, warehouses transformed into attractive new venues and homes, billboards advertising international products, using the kind of classical typography Saville had incongruously reapplied to some of the stranger Factory acts.

Being commercially conscious of the cool is of course not cool, but the alternative was never becoming cool in the first place. Manchester without the Northern Quarter would not have made sense – its unpolished tumbledown atmosphere a necessary sign of energised resistance to the city-centre reconstruction post-IRA bombing that was regenerating the city almost to a fault – but it too became threatened with inevitable gentrification. The commercial world wants to have some of the valuable energy that first emerges in the margins, but chases away the spirit that attracted it in the first place.

When Factory lost Dry after its 1992 bankruptcy, the bar kept going, each modification and redecoration creating a more degraded version of the original, as authentic magical chaos was replaced with mere efficiency, only its name and looping soundtrack carrying with it a sense of its initial anomalous, even dangerous presence.

The cool fades away, it becomes part of the rock heritage trail, another bar among many. Dry derived from the Haçienda, which derived from a dream of experimental metropolitan life, and the Manchester bars that followed were increasingly diluted copies, often like cover versions, in the way the post-Factory Dry became a series of copies of itself until it finally closed, all used up, twenty-five years later. In 2000, just eleven years after

Dry set off a chain reaction that turned a ghostly part of Manchester into a fast-moving 'mixed use' enterprise zone holding on to the soul of the city, there were already signs that the Northern Quarter had turned into the sort of location that attracted those wanting to live in the centre of the city in brand-new apartments, but not wanting to share its lively, bohemian spirit.

Demonstrating how continually incongruous Wilson's impact on the city was, in 2000 he presents a short piece for *Granada Reports* inside the Northern Quarter, lamenting that there had been complaints from one or two of those who had moved in about the noise from the bars. He's still wearing one of his loose-fitting Comme des Garçons suits, unaware of or indifferent to how 1980s it makes him look, charging around the streets like he owns them, with no mention of his role in their post-Dry existence. (He does introduce a personal note – mentioning how the local paper accused him of being a whinging nimby for wanting to get rid of a lap-dancing club that had opened next to his own city-centre loft. He had a few choice words about the difference between red-light seediness and the playing of loud music on his doorstep, because after all 'this is a music city'. The music was fine, even welcome; sleaze was not. Broadcaster, urban theorist and music man and the phrenic, frenetic film loudmouth played by Steve Coogan combine in one place, reporting on the new Manchester.)

'It's the great contradiction,' he intones, some say through his nose, others think looking down his nose, 'that in the '80s and the early '90s the music culture of Manchester turned a dead city centre into a vibrant city centre, so much so that people are flocking into that city centre to live. The only problem is, they want to get rid of the vibes.'

He broadcasts what is a combination of a light-hearted teatime news report on the absurdity of those looking for the cool then complaining about the cool and a slightly annoyed lecture handing out advice to those who decide to live in a hip area: the liveliness is why those apartments were built in that style in the first place, so please don't look to then squeeze out those who bring and love the noise. Perhaps, he concludes, as if this is now policy, because it's him saying it with the wisdom of Solomon, even though he's doing it in the guise of television reporter, it could be a little quieter during the week, Sunday to Wednesday, and then from Thursday to Saturday, live with the action – the action of a great city.

He mentions someone he would like to ask for advice – another one of his lesser-known heroes, for seeing into the future of Manchester from the early 1970s – 'the gentleman who had the vision of inner-city living in Manchester, Allan Roberts, a great housing chairman here in Manchester, later a great MP for Bootle, who built a council estate in this area twenty years ago. He was a visionary – what would his answer be?'

Allan Roberts, one of the quieter influences on Wilson, was born in Droylsden, east Manchester, in 1943, joining the Labour Party as a teenager at the end of the 1950s, joining the Campaign for Nuclear Disarmament in 1960, three years after it had been founded. He taught in primary and secondary schools and became a senior social worker with Lancashire County Council before entering politics. Always to the left of the party, a supporter of Tony Benn and Militant, working for Manchester City Council in the 1970s, becoming chair of the housing committee, he became a specialist in council housing and was especially damning about the dehumanising Hulme estate.

It was his decision to bring council housing into the then very non-residential city centre that enthused Wilson, and after building the Smithfield Estate, which stayed as it was as the Northern Quarter materialised around it, he also persuaded Wimpey to build houses there when no one else would. One small sign of his legacy is a street, Allan Roberts Close, on an estate of council housing in Blackley, north Manchester. At the 1978 Labour Party conference he stated that the way to solve the housing crisis was through a surplus of council houses. Because of his work in Manchester he was chosen by the Labour Party to stand for the safe seat of Bootle in 1979, even though he had no connection with the town, remaining on Manchester City Council until 1980. He died of cancer in 1990, aged forty-six.

So it goes.

Wilson finishes his piece squatting in suit and tie on an outdoor table by the Rochdale Canal, in front of a brick-and-glass view of the modernisation of industrial Manchester, a middle-of-the-road TV feature presented with his urgent bonhomie given a psycho-political spin, as though he is smuggling a party political broadcast into his report. His script drifts into becoming a speech – and you realise he was always delivering a speech – as though he is touting for votes, even though he remained an unelected spokesman for an unofficial city.

'I have the answer for Manchester: no one moves into a city-centre property without signing a disclaimer that says, "I will not unreasonably object to city-centre life." You cannot want to live in the city and yet destroy the life of the city. If you want to live in one of these great new places, and they were queuing up to buy them before Christmas, then get down, or get back to the suburbs.'

It was true, though, that fifty years after a council report urged action so the city didn't fossilise into what at the time still seemed Edwardian, and therefore Victorian, Manchester had finally escaped its industrial heritage by using it as the basis for the new, with the addition of Wilson's 'vibes'. Along the way there had been the modernist disasters of the Hulme Crescents and the Arndale Centre, a terrifying terrorist bomb and an impulsive, flaky, post-modernist, maverick pop culture sect gambling on putting unlikely new premises in unlikely settings.

And Wilson could monitor the progress of the city, and transmit his questions and answers, from his apparently objective position as television reporter. The outsider with insider knowledge, or vice versa. He could transmit criticism not in the council meeting rooms where he was never invited but through his appearances as Tony Wilson of Factory, of the Haçienda. In 2002, launching his sly, cash-in novelisation of *24 Hour Party People* at a sell-out standing-room-only event at Waterstone's on Deansgate, in shirt-sleeves because he was on the campaign trail as much as he was promoting, he reminisced as protagonist, observer and fantasist about how dilapidated the city had been in the 1970s, before it was revitalised by the music scene. A history he had made damn sure wasn't silent. He spread his arms wide and gestured to the city outside. 'Of course, now it's all become *this*.' It was up to the beholder to work out exactly what he meant.

Thirty-Seven: Loss and gain: In the City and the Haçienda (4)

Quod me nutrit me destruit. (What nourishes me, destroys me.)
CHRISTOPHER MARLOWE

Wilson was a kind of gambler, spinning the wheel with nerves of steel and a classic straight face, prepared to take the losses as long as on the way there were the big wins, the occasional luck of the draw, the luck that is mere luck and comes around when you least expect it, and now and then when you most expect it. As Wilson once said, wearing a mask of Hunter S. Thompson and keeping his balance, 'Luck is a very thin wire between survival and disaster, and not many people can keep their balance on it,' and, wearing a mask of Emily Dickinson, 'Luck is not chance, it's toil; fortune's expensive smile is earned.' The more stuff you do, the more you give luck a chance to find you.

One of Wilson's methods of finding luck, good or bad, was networking. This is another way of describing his occupation. He was a hard-boiled genius at networking, operationally, personally and strategically, long before there was social networking, before LinkedIn and Facebook made it an everyday duty/plaything for millions, back when it was a lot of hard work. Networking was how he ensured he would on regular occasions be in the right place at the right time.

It wasn't enough that he had Factory, his bands, the Haçienda, Dry and his work at Granada; however much he was doing, he always felt there was something missing, especially in relation to the music industry. He fancied himself as a major player in the industry, but he didn't want to leave Manchester behind to become a bigger name, a greater presence. His solution to this conundrum was far-fetched and surely impractical.

Having had his two main unorthodox commercial successes with Factory – Joy Division/New Order and the Happy Mondays – and having abstractly contributed to the rise of rave, another new British scene turning

482

into a great music-business export, he felt he could save something he naturally thought wasn't working properly. The hippy entrepreneur weaned on punk and driven by his own maverick impulses, his motive for mixing with the industry elite was not only to join them, but to sort them out, analyse their problems, modernise a ruined system and of course goad them into agreeing with his methods. He felt the music world was too safe and formal, too orthodox and simple-minded. It needed at the very least the energising addition of his rants and raves about art and culture – his indelicate intrusions.

There were those in the industry who would say his vanity had got out of control – Simon Draper, co-founder of Virgin Records with Richard Branson, would talk of how Wilson was looked on by the music-business heavyweights he wanted to emulate as a self-important figure of fun, with his wafting Japanese suits and suggestively dangling shoulder bag. He was dressing for the part; he was actually out of his depth. None of this troubled Wilson, who was used to appearing preposterous in his home town. It was part of his strategy for getting things done. Being ridiculed never bothered him as long as it didn't interfere with his bigger aim.

His desire to be a music-industry player was not for the money; it was for the festivity and for a certain amount of leverage on the inside of proceedings. He didn't want to go to where the music industry was, so he formed another ad hoc committee and decided he would bring the music industry to him, to Manchester. In 1992, at the same time as Factory was coming to its inevitable end, stupidly or deliberately bungling a possible deal with London Records, the company's always vulnerable cash flow finally crushed by the out-of-control recording costs of the third Happy Mondays album – not the best reference for someone aspiring to act as saviour to a moribund business – he started In the City, an annual music conference. To Erasmus's annoyance, he started it with Factory money, with Factory personnel. He could have been saving Factory, but he had had his head turned by a new idea, a new place to lecture the world, and in his eyes liberate it.

The industry – managers, agents, publicists, A&R – came for the jolly, for the chance to see what the hell Madchester actually was, to pat each other on the back and perhaps to discover what on earth Wilson was on and if he actually knew something they could learn from, about what the hell Manchester had that other cities didn't.

If Factory was his 1970s beginning as self-styled music mogul, Haçienda the psychedelic '80s anointment, his '90s were built around the conference he based on the New York New Music Seminar he loved flying to and participating in. He loved the people he met at the New Music Seminar, their speed of thought seeming to match the speed of the city, the fact that the relationship between music and business seemed heavily weighted towards music, collisions of ideas and energy. It was a debating society that seemed to have emerged out of CBGB, Max's Kansas City and Andy Warhol's Factory, on the way to the appearance of TED Talks, perhaps imploding into Donald Trump's 2019 Social Media Summit. Wilson always considered In the City the bastard offspring of the New Music Seminar.

In the City softened the impact of the first and in the end only real incarnation of Factory failing at the beginning of the decade and the Haçienda crashing from its imperial heights to a messy end as a drug exchange with a reputation for violence and criminal activity – the inevitable end for such a vibrant public display of youthful liberation, blamed for all sorts of local ills and abuses by those forces paranoid about this new misfit energy. Madchester became Gunchester.

Wilson had been forced to become more administratively involved in dealing with the club's connections to the Manchester underground, the police and council alarmed at the apparent lawlessness, with real-world issues of responsibility and compliance, even protection rackets and gang warfare. It was all a long way from the early utopian flights of imagination and its founding beliefs. 'There were strange meetings and deals done with chief superintendents in graveyards on Sunday afternoons,' he remembered. 'Fucking nightmare.'

Neville Richards

He let the bouncers take over the club. There were some good guys on the door, but there were some fucking villains. There were the Salford

Crew, the Cheetham Crew, and I thought his view of it all was a bit fucked-up because he did the Tony thing of trying to glamorise it, and that wasn't the right thing to do at all. He wasn't a frontline kid from Wythenshawe used to dealing with these characters. Tony was a soft middle-class professional who let the villains take over the Haçienda. And Tony then tried to be in the two camps – the villains and the cops, like he went both ways after a while with being a socialist and a capitalist. In his heart he was a beautiful, gentle man, but he was getting lost in it all, the power of it, and also he dived into the devil's dandruff, which gave him a sense of being able to deal with it, but of course there is nothing behind it, nothing behind the front it seems to give you. He couldn't resist being in the limelight, and cocaine was the obvious extension, made him feel he was in charge, but charlie's a disease, and he really needed a clear head at this point.

Hilary Wilson

I was concerned for his safety. I thought he was going to get hurt, especially when there was shooting, but of course Tony would laugh it off. In his mind, he could deal with the gangs. I used to go down to his house to check on him, but of course it wasn't part of my life any more. I was worried for his safety, but he somehow seemed to take pleasure from it all. There was part of him that enjoyed the chaos. Part of him that didn't know what to do but could put things off to the next day.

He needed to become diplomatic, managerial grown-up as the club repro-duced many of the tyrannies it was set up to escape – egoism, power strug-gles, envy, mistrust, even fear, and definitely greed. The cunning contriver of rows, the Wilsonian charm, the slick smile, the wiles and distractions of the charismatic conman weren't enough when the club was faced with cold, calculating, criminal outside interference and found itself being shut down, as if it alone was responsible for a rise in Manchester crime. As if it was threatening the safety of the local citizens Wilson had a deep abiding love for. 'It did become violent,' says Mike Pickering, 'to such an extent

I stopped putting my sisters on the guest list. It really wasn't a place you wanted your family coming to.'

At the beginning of the life of such a venture, having an articulate figure-head is an essential ingredient of success – someone carving out a coherent vision, delegating organisational tasks among others, mostly acting as a persuasive publicist and propagandist, keeping everyone focused on what's important while overcoming the pettiness that can creep into everyday business. Towards the end of the Haçienda, Wilson was expected to be head of maintenance, not the best use of his talents, and chief negotiator, dealing with the police threat to revoke the club's licence because of the drug-taking and -selling and the presence of Manchester's indelible local criminal gangs, happy to use guns to get what they saw as their deserved cut of the business. The vivacious self-styled subversive situationist wilted when faced with a situation where art and crime actually met. He was surprised how 'shit' the guns the gangsters carried were, but that was the response of a comedian trying to make light of it all after the fact. At the time, Guy Debord – or Bernard Manning – was of no help.

The building that once functioned as an untameable hallucination excit-ing irrational emotions, a surreal self-governed retreat from the outside world, becomes more and more rooted in the dreary, punishing, frustrat-ing everyday, a classic burnt-out consequence of when imperfect humans attempt perfectibility. Its founders never imagined that a mind-altering space built with a higher purpose for dreamers and partiers would also become somewhere that addicts, criminals, drunks, scoundrels, the needy, the wounded and sundry undesirables found appealing for its promise of freedom. 'When planning the new perfect society,' explains Wilson, wearing a mask of Marty Rubin, 'be sure to take emotions into account.'

The Haçienda must be built; it must fall because of human nature. It all came down, after its naive picturing of a world where the imagination and pleasure are primary to money and decisions and the inability to manage relationships inside the group, to tiresome work. He could live with its ruin because he knew that, as a Manchester monument, it was immortal. Paradoxically, to become immortal, such cultural eruptions must first die.

486

The Haçienda lives on as spiritual tourism, as a kitsch souvenir of when Manchester officially entered a post-industrial era, as a ghostly venue that inspires sentiment because of how it served as a short-lived Petri dish for emergent culture. It began as something in the spirit of the avant-garde; it ended as decoration, its black and yellow iconography a cubist version of the worker bee that exists as a cute, council-sanctioned logo for the city of workers. 'Utopian desires,' Wilson would say, quoting someone he'd forgotten, 'all too quickly become just another tempting commodity.'

The Haçienda begins as blueprint; it ends by being reconstructed in a hyperbolic feature film that was somehow part of that blueprint. It was built by collaborative explorers reimagining the use of city space, dreaming of the city as artwork, and there was enough power for it to make splashes all over the future of the city. The artwork wasn't completed, but just the thought that such a thing could happen meant the city felt its impact, even if just nostalgically, as a contribution to its image, its history, another counter-site that succeeds and fails because it becomes simply a site. Even after it is knocked down, it is still being built, in the imagination, where it began. A map of Manchester that does not contain the Haçienda is not worth glancing at. After it was all over Wilson was happy to leave it on the map, in the tourist literature. 'Do I miss it?' he would wonder a few years later. 'What's that phrase about the hole and the head?'

Anthony H. Wilson

I would always put a brave face on things. It wasn't my place to look vulnerable. That wasn't my role in all this. Normally, everything was fun, but I do remember a period, always having to promote and push something that just couldn't be promoted and pushed, maybe it was after Ian died, or when Factory was going under, or when the Haçienda was in trouble, with the drugs, and the gangsters, the police and the council fucking us over, or when the Happy Mondays' expensive recording in Barbados led nowhere, and I thought, Am I going to go over the edge? Is something happening that actually I can't control? *There was a feeling my exuberance and whatever else was spiralling and spiralling, and it started to be a concern that this spiralling would get out of control. I can't remember what I did about it, but I do remember clearly thinking,* If it goes on like this, will my head explode, will it all explode? Will it all be over, or will I be able to begin again?

Thirty-Eight: Lawyers, managers, sundry disruptors and a love of talking

Audiatur et altera pars. (Let us listen to the other side.)
AESCHYLUS

As the Haçienda stutters to its collapse through the '90s, finally shutting down in 1997, self-dividing Wilson of course is soon up and running with another start-up that makes better use of his passions, his skill at presenting himself as visionary founder of a great idea, even if it isn't quite clear yet what that great idea is. He is heading towards no particular direction; he is on a constant journey. As long as he has got something to do, he's got something to do, because he's nothing without something to do.

He annually puts Manchester at the very centre of the music world by drawing in the great and the good, the bad and the indifferent from the international industry, creating another alternative site for debate, music, argument, gossip, workshops and Wilson's smitten idea of sex and drugs and rock 'n' roll, which punk deconstructed but never fully, profoundly revised. And he can place himself at the centre of it all, introducing into his already crowded head more and more influential and interesting people, creating more potential for things to happen. He's got used to it by now, the idea that he can make things happen. He doesn't want it to stop, even as he loses Factory and the Haçienda, which means also losing New Order and the Happy Mondays.

In the City represented his undimmed belief in the value of passionate and intelligent conversation, all things springing from talk, which become plans, which one way or another can become history. It was also set up as a marketplace, a festival, but first of all it was about panels and debates that celebrated words as one of the world's great entertainments. Perhaps nothing more defines his idealism, or his almost sweet self-delusion, than the thought that organised music-industry talk could lead to something radical and visionary.

489

He loved the grand, complex talk show that such conferences became, but then he was a talk-show virtuoso, a genius conversationalist, a natural dissenter, a sucker for ad-libbing as a way of finding out what he actually thought and what he wanted to happen next. Not many others in the music business, or any other business, were as fluent, as madcap, as argumentative as he was. A hundred Wilsons at such a conference might lead to genuinely enlightened discussion, some wider regeneration of Factory's special qualities, an ingenious analysis of cultural, social and technological challenges, to a progressive sort of mainstream recording industry that appreciated its role as being about something more than just the production of music, the follower of trends, the fast, slick dealing with an ongoing turnover of interests; otherwise it would be, for all its busy-ness, cross-talk, social mixing, nightlife, earnest enquiry, junketing and lively chatter, just the music business confirming to itself that it is the music business, looking at itself in a mirror.

Wilson would be in his element, though, as if there really were a hundred motoring minds like his up for fighting among themselves in the name of progress, for reinventing the record, which at the time was becoming a concern, and which was proving to be a necessary version of reinventing the wheel. Impossible, but it had to be done. And there were so many people to get to know and connect with – and to rudely interrupt.

As part of the conference, encouraged by Elliot Rashman of Simply Red, Wilson provides rock managers with the space to set up a forum. For the first time major managers from across the industry gather in one place to air their frustrations and share their knowledge. It becomes some form of a trade union meeting, featuring managers of all shapes and sizes. Rashman talks about organising juggernauts to carry equipment across America; managers of newer, local groups moan that there are more pressing matters. As they meet, Tony enters the room, winds them all up, gets it all kicking off, and then once he has them all arguing among themselves, abruptly leaves. Job done.

Wilson asked me to host two centrepiece interviews at the inaugural In the City, the first with the fearless, fearsome manager and protector of

Led Zeppelin, Peter Grant, and the following day with one of the most powerful and wealthy American lawyers in the music business, coarse, gregarious Brooklynite Allen Grubman. After a brief apprenticeship with the lawyer who represented Brian Epstein and the Beatles, Grubman started his own business in the early 1970s, at the beginning of disco, with George McCrae and the Village People, which led to Billy Joel and Bruce Springsteen, Elton John and U2.

Formidable, game-changing Grant and brash, feisty Grubman, with his motto 'If there's no conflict, there's no interest,' were very much from Wilson's playbook, as he rubbed himself against giant music-industry figures to absorb some of their powers and set himself deeper inside music history. The urge to become one of their pantheon seemed a long way from late-night flights of fancy in 1970s Didsbury, but for Wilson it was the logical result. The 1980s had seen to that. Business had increasingly fascinated him – maybe not the mundane business of business, but definitely the culture of business.

The In the City interviews were something that Wilson should have done, but as usual, as co-organiser, he pretended he couldn't do everything, even though he knew he could. The complex mystery of deals and advances, of artist-friendly changes in the industry system, the developing symbiosis between independent labels and the majors, all had become areas of increasing interest, and as an act of continuing mentorship, keeping me inside his northern borders after over a decade living elsewhere, or perhaps hoping for some of that conflict Grubman lived by, I ended up doing what turned out to be one and a quarter interviews.

Because of the Wilson effect, his knack of bringing out the worst behaviour in people, on the way to perhaps sometimes the best, I would always enter into one of his projects a little distracted by what he was expecting from me. Should I be Wilsonian – try to match his unruly, heat-seeking energy?

One of his greatest, outraged and outrageous performances, bringing out his propensity for insults that could be both civilised and uncivilised, often simultaneously, was at a New Music Seminar panel in 1990, assisted by skittish actor and comedian Keith Allen and Happy Mondays manager Nathan McGough, son of Wilson's first love, Thelma – a debating panel equivalent of all previous troupes, comedic and musical, called the Stooges. He called the panel 'Wake Up America, You're Dead', and was in the mood to explain to the Americans what rave was and that the house music they had invented had been positively transformed in Britain via Ibiza into compelling chart music – obviously led by one of his bands and based in 'my club' – but in America had gone nowhere. British kids were having the time of their lives. 'I don't see any kids in fucking America having the time of their lives.' Also on the panel were two producers who had helped with the invention, Derrick May and Marshall Jefferson, observing Wilson high on himself with a mixture of annoyance and amused tolerance.

Wilson introduces the speeding Allen as a 'world expert on drugs', and when the audience react in puritanical shock, he scolds them for being so 'embarrassed about drugs. It didn't do Guns N' Roses any harm.' The mainstream American industry, he rages, or the sole remaining American label still run by Americans, does not understand house because it is a producer's music. The music that was in the margins when the New Music Seminar began so that its American profile would be lifted has become – via his club, of course – the only interesting new music that 'fucking sells in large numbers. And it isn't as strong in America.'

The debate quickly turns into a debacle as old arguments about the white appropriation and dilution of black music get mangled. Allen adopts clumsy black–white positions guaranteed to infuriate May and Jefferson. Wilson sits back and enjoys the mayhem he's triggered. Jefferson walks out. May supports his decision, because English idiots have turned the panel into 'intimidating warfare'.

Wide-eyed Wilson protests his innocence. May tells him to shut the fuck up. 'You makin' a fool out of your stupid ass,' he screams, speaking on behalf of many who've felt Wilson's stinging wind-up shtick, following Jefferson off the panel. Allen claims victory – over what, it's not clear. May goes for the last word as he leaves: 'I don't have to stand up for my manhood. You can argue with yourself. You can pull out your little two-inch penis and dog yourself, OK? I'll see you later.'

Wilson smiles broadly at the carnage. There's a riot going on. All in a day's work. Eventually, America will dance to the music that comes after the music he's been selling. It just takes a little time and, of course, inter-vention from inciting speculators like Wilson. 'You cannot make a revolu-tion' – he shrugs – 'in white gloves.'

It's this Wilson you think has asked you to do something for him, the devious one that thinks this form of challenge is the only way to instigate change, when sometimes it's the more obviously professional television producer who calls up and isn't necessarily looking for a riot or even raised voices. It was just hard to tell; both characters sounded the smooth-talking same.

At In the City, the Grant interview passed with minimal incident, and I was interested enough in his life, if unsure about the excessive pre-#MeToo antics of Led Zeppelin, the 'one big boys' party', to concentrate on the interview, after a faulty introduction where I pretended I needed a body-guard to get close to Grant. Grant and Zeppelin had a history of using jour-nalists as targets for leftover food. The large audience did not seem to be aware of this detail, making my little stunt completely pointless. This was me trying too hard to please Wilson, or at least what I imagined Wilson was looking for – enthralling, scene-making differences of opinion.

Before the interview I spoke to Malcom McLaren about his fascination with Grant, a call that Wilson arranged which lasted almost as long as the interview itself. McLaren was in his Hollywood period and developing a film with Grant, based on his life story. McLaren poured out his research into my ear, one question from me generating many minutes of rant, from Grant working in circuses in the 1950s, in Soho coffee bars at the birth of pop, then as a lookalike for rotund English actor Robert Morley, then merging the management techniques of Colonel Tom Parker, Allen Klein and Don Arden, to the *Starship*, the notorious, customised Boeing 720 that Led Zeppelin used to tour America. McLaren was part automati-cally pitching a movie that ultimately would never get made and part marvelling at the way Grant helped give Led Zeppelin – his only act, turning down Queen because 'I had no interest in building an empire' – mythical qualities that were only fractionally to do with the music. McLaren – and Wilson – were obsessed with how Grant as hooligan interventionist turned life into an artwork full of audacity, power, self-assertion and single-mindedness, with great stories which he was at the centre of even as he was surrounded by lively, unrivalled personalities.

The interview with Grubman the next day was less successful. I had no interest in lawyers, even lawyers to the stars with apparent superpowers, and failed to understand Wilson's fascination with this particular one's relationship with artists and record labels. Wilson adored mingling with a disruptive, influential insider who regularly generated million-dollar fees for negotiating deals, but for me Grubman was the kind of lawyer who helped perpetuate a system that resisted the changes that would encourage true industry diversity and innovation. I was of course missing the point of the conference. To Wilson, Grubman was some sort of scurrilous champion, increasing the value of artists, even if only the elite, and tackling anti-artist contractual bias, even if again for the few. Wilson saw him as Robin Hood; I saw him as the Sheriff of Nottingham.

I also didn't appreciate how the audience was predominantly from the music industry – networkers in the very act of networking. Within a few questions, during which I loosely challenged Grubman's boisterous claim to credibility, it was clear I had lost the crowd. You could hear I had lost the crowd, because a few of them started heckling me.

I had assumed it was my role to be tough on the lawyer, a lawyer with the reputation of being the toughest and shrewdest of all music-business lawyers, but the audience had come to hear Grubman reveal his punchy, nuanced negotiating secrets and brag about his dazzling problem-solving techniques. They wanted to hear all the details of the Michael Jackson contract that Grubman had recently negotiated with Sony, hailed, without my knowledge, as 'the most lucrative arrangement ever for a recording artist', the price Sony had to pay to ensure Jackson stayed with them.

I strayed so far from the perceived reason Grubman was there the heckles soon turned into requests for me to leave the stage. One particular audience member in the front row became increasingly angry with what he saw as my inability to ask Grubman what many clearly saw as the right questions. I asked him if he could do better. 'Of course,' he said. I offered him my seat – was this the conflict Grubman was looking for, and in his own way Wilson? – and he immediately took me up on my offer.

This turned out to be Ed Bicknell, the manager of Dire Straits, in town as a leading member of the managers' forum. He finished off the interview, satisfying those looking for music-business details and apparently uninterested in ethical or even moral questions. I simmered in the audience and after it was all over I left, feeling an embarrassment I would carry with me possibly until now, and that I had learnt nothing that was of use to me, probably in the way Bicknell felt he had learnt nothing during my questioning.

For the next few conferences, Ed Bicknell would take over solidly delivered interview duties. The next year, Wilson asked me to host an awkward awards ceremony, which, still feeling the Grubman shame, I also failed to handle with racy Wilsonian skill, and after that it was decided, between Wilson and Yvette, that it might be kindest if I was not handed any specific duty, just asked to do the odd appearance on panels, in debates, where it was less likely I would lose my way.

I wasn't sure if I had let Wilson down or acted just as he expected. I don't think he even thought about it once he'd checked that I wasn't too mortified by it all. He had too much to do, to sort out, so many employees and volunteers to sort out the sorting-out, and so many people to deal with, encourage, string along, a gaggle of collaborators to marshal, a host of In the City guests and topics to monitor. My real role would come later. He was saving me up. He would get on with the living, feeling secure that as far as the collecting went, the storing of information ready for the moment his life story would be told, according more or less to his rules, it was all taken care of.

He could get on with refining his talents, reaching his targets and perfecting his theories. He could get on with making often entirely unreasonable plans and getting others to make sure they happened.

*

In the early 1990s, ambitious Rose Marley from New Moston – an ever-so-slightly posher part of north Manchester around the Harpurhey area that titillated Wilson's lofty fondness for the rough and common – was studying at Leeds University for a degree in media and marketing, then a relatively new course. As she studied she hit the pre-mobile phone boxes looking for work experience in the modest but increasingly lively Manchester music scene, in which Factory was the most prominent player.

She was desperate to work for Factory and would ring every day asking if there was anything – anything – she could do. Factory was on the verge of going into administration, but few outside its inner circle fully appreciated that, and their large city-centre offices certainly made them seem a going concern. 'I was telling them how I was friends with Northside, which considering what Factory were going through was very unhelpful.' Inevitably, there was no work.

A colleague of Tony, Jane Lemon, eventually got her a placement in a Manchester management office with Tina Simmons, who had been on the Factory board. Within a few weeks she was working for a tenner a day, cash, for other companies sharing the office, and Tony came in one day for a discussion about launching what eventually became the Heaton Park Festival. It's her first sighting of the way Tony handled a meeting. For it to be successful, for there to be some sort of conclusion, there must be some element of chaos, of argument. That would put a smile on his face. 'He made me realise pretty quick that even as I didn't know what I was doing, no one else did really, however much they pretended. But even as he loved the workings of business, he never tried to be a businessman – that was for others.'

Tony immediately liked Rose, if only because she didn't seem too impressed by him, and even if she came from the posher part of Moston, she was quite comfortable fielding his insults. She was from a newer generation that was not so enthralled – more bemused, even amused – by his often overbearing shtick.

'We rowed and clashed a lot. I was quite happy to challenge him when a lot of people didn't dare. I was very pragmatic, got the job done however many curve balls he threw at me, and for him the rows were all part of making sure the job did get done. One way or another.'

Eventually, he comes to rely on her to act conscientiously upon the vaguest of instructions. She helps out on the first In the City conference in 1992, and every summer in various increasingly more demanding capacities, until ten years later she finds out in typical roundabout Tony fashion that she has a new job.

Rose Marley

Someone congratulated me out of the blue, and then others started calling me and would say, 'Well done, I hear you're running In the City this year.' I rang Tony to find out what was going on, and he said – butter wouldn't melt – 'Isn't it fabulous? You're the first woman to be granted the honour of running In the City since Yvette.' He said, 'She wouldn't let another woman run it until you, but she's given you permission!' I imagined that was because I was married and clearly wasn't interested in Tony. And let's face it, he had fallen out with everyone else. I realised very quickly how chaotically the conference was run – they basically reinvented the wheel every year; there was no held knowledge about how it was organised. No computer, no printer, no unifying plan. There was a lot of goodwill but little else – Tony really did everything using goodwill. It cost me more to do it than the fee – and I really needed that money – but somehow you ended up doing it for Tony because it seemed important. He relied on that kind of commitment from people.

I wanted to get in some serious sponsors, and I did some data analysis on previous conferences to work out the type of people that came and why. He hated that. He said, 'The day we do that kind of research is the day I die.' I said, 'I need to know the details to get some funding, how many, gender, job title,' and he was absolutely fuming. 'Tell them the delegates all wear great trainers. That's all they need to know. Fuck demographics.' He said, 'You cannot map it, you cannot log it, you cannot analyse it.' For him it was all just a feeling, and even when that

497

feeling had all gone wrong, with Factory and Haçienda, he didn't think that was his fault. That was the fault of others.

He would somehow always imagine you knew what he was thinking and planning before he had even told you, as if it was that obvious. One day he asked me if I had booked the flights to New York. I didn't know what for. He'd decided to run a version of the In the City conference in New York four weeks after the main one. Twelve of us were meant to be going. We hadn't got any money. He didn't want to know about the details; he just wanted it done. Eventually I managed to get some flights on BMI in exchange for some stuff with the inflight magazine – an interview with Tony and Yvette. The flight was to Washington, and then I got someone to give us a minibus to get us all to New York. When I told Tony, he didn't seem impressed that I'd managed to get us there at such short notice; he just said, 'Don't forget me and Yvette only travel first class.' You'd do something for him, and he would just wilfully raise the bar! And when we landed he jumped into the van, he grabbed a bag of weed he had in his pocket, which he'd just walked through customs, chucked it to someone and cheerfully said, 'Skin up!' He had this aura of confidence, that nothing was going to go wrong, and everyone else had to fall in with it.

He taught me that blagging was a skill. A great Manchester skill. I always say that to kids I now educate about how to get things done. I tell them never to think of 'blagger' as a derogatory word. If you're blagging something, it means you've got someone to do something they didn't want to do, and you've got them to do it for free. You've made something happen. There's a big difference between blagging and bullshitting. You've got to deliver on the blag. That's a real skill. If you're born in Manchester, you're called a blagger. If you are born in Westminster or you go to Oxford or Cambridge, you're called a negotiator. Tony's art of blagging created this Manchester infrastructure which we use to this day, whether it's putting on an event after the Arena bombing or planning the bus ride through the city when United or City are showing off a trophy. That's all rooted in how Tony made In the City happen. It was mad, but in its own way there was a kind of focus.

Thirty-Nine: Every thirteen years and the opening and closing of various Factories

Mundus vult decipi, ergo decipiatur. (The world wants to be deceived, so let it be deceived.)

When it was put to Wilson at the end of a press conference for the film *24 Hour Party People* – which Wilson turned into a shambolic, extended one-man show despite the presence of cast and director – that his theory that a great pop culture revolution occurred every thirteen years was rubbish, he replied with one of his favourite quotes, bringing his show to a perfect climax: 'You are entitled to an opinion. But your opinion is shit.'

To arrive at his thirteen-year theory he worked backwards from his highly subjective estimate of the arrival of rave, 1989, to punk in 1976, to the Beatles in 1963, to the Teddy boys in 1950 all dressed up for rock 'n' roll, so that it all began, of course, in the year of his birth (and there is a case for suggesting that the end of rock 'n' roll, as someone born around 1950 would know it, occurred when the first hashtag appeared on Twitter, taking attention somewhere else, which just happened to be the year Tony died, 2007, so his life in that sense was perfectly proportioned. Perhaps the hashtag – the twenty-first century's crucifix, a techno-sedative, a grain of salt, a mess of distraction, an autocrat's mission control – was where the whole pre-digital human game itself started to play out.

Also, Wilson never had to deal with why he did or didn't tweet – he would in one way have seemed an ideal, self-dramatising user of Twitter, one of the original pulpit pundits constantly marshalling and modifying his brand with something rude, aghast and striking to say about something every hour of the day. He would also have been unconvinced by Twitter, at the dead centre of a world that was making everything, whether art, entertainment, politics, beliefs or feelings – or even revolution and definitely slogans, now becoming hashtags – into fractured, saturated content possessed and processed by corporate companies pretending they

499

were committed to freedom of speech, truth dissolving into gossip, sound-bitten into nonsense.

The great communicators of the latter part of the twentieth century, whether J. G. Ballard or Susan Sontag, would not have functioned well in a world of swarming opinionators, summarisers, commenters, complainers, whiners, nitpickers and influencers, taking themselves so seriously, assaulting the world with information, everything increasingly reduced to a title, a glance, a fleeting confrontation, a passing moment, a broken(-hearted) America. Everyone with a platform is now a situationist, without the, you know, ultra-radical desire to commence an esoteric new society. All of this helped by the iPhone, first appearing in 2007, looking like something Peter Saville might have designed as some kind of cassette package for a lesser-spotted Factory band, or something to hold an invitation to an event Wilson was hosting. It definitely looked like something predicted by a sleeve emptied of apparent detail designed by Saville for Section 25 or New Order.

Wilson was the first around Manchester to passionately alert others to the cool interiors of the boutique hotel, the first ones featuring design contributions from one of his great loves, Philippe Starck, where the front desk would get your skins for you. He was the first to get excited about the MP3 technology that would eventually lead to iTunes, and loved his iPod, but he was gone too early for an iPhone.)

Wilson's thirteen-year theory meant he was all set up in 2002 like some loft-living Nostradamus for the next great movement, still believing, because what else is there, that he could find another Joy Division, another Happy Mondays, because 'No one takes the ball home when they've scored twice.' He had boasted in 2002 that at the age of fifty-two he had finally stopped showing off and telling people about new bands. That was true – people had stopped listening to him after he raved about the Leeds group the Music and then even a Milton Keynes teen emo band that was really his son's thing – but of course it was also a lie.

By then it was the activist electronic beats of grime, another punk, another social movement for another silenced generation, which jumped out of garage, out of east London council estates, and it was London's greatest music scene, and perhaps the country's last-ever music scene. The last one to stretch time forward, not in on itself, the last one to coalesce because of music, because of rhythm, not because of an app or an upgraded device. It was from the mutant South, a South buried in London but on the outside of all the city's mainstream energies, and it wasn't apparent for a while – because it was hyper-local and so black – that this was the latest revolution, the British way of turning the whole story full circle, from appropriating black history to reasserting black history.

Wilson could make claims for this 2002 confirmation of his theory, but he was a little late to seem prescient, late enough to seem he was following cultural orders as just another music-business scout following an obvious path – Wiley's 2002 'Eskimo' was the first unofficial, effervescently beaten outline for a new hybrid from the future of the future, temporarily called eski-beat, and Dizzee Rascal was already a Mercury Prize-winner by the time Wilson announced that his next big thing was a black crew called Raw-T, coming out of the council estates of Moss Side, again recommended to him by his teenage son Oli. The recommendation was enough for him to overcome his previous typically purist hatred for 'English kids rapping'.

He was trying hard to still know the times, to continue his narrative, to fulfil Gretton's dreams of a proper black-music Manchester scene, but there was a little hint of sentimentality for estate prodigies A Certain Ratio and the underdoggedness of the early Happy Mondays, and here was another young group, twenty-five years after ACR, a little worried that they might be seen as Tony's latest pets, ruining the very urban credibility that made them interesting in the first place.

'They're real poets, geniuses,' he inevitably enthused about a group with an average age of seventeen who didn't know who Joy Division were, and had been born around the time Ecstasy was being popped as the Haçienda was setting its controls for the appearance of Madchester. Wilson founded his fourth incarnation of Factory twelve years after the first one ended with a whimper, still feeling it was his job to rectify a record industry which he decided didn't know what it was doing.

Number 2 – Factory Too – was the brief, awkward alliance with London Records as Factory faced bankruptcy, 'when they owned us and pretended to be interested', featuring the inevitable Durutti Column supplying living continuity, some live Joy Division, some post-Factory-catalogue-number fancies, a less dashing sample echo of the first 'Factory Sample', and a pre-Magnetic Fields Stephin Merritt before-the-fact tribute to himself, Merritt's mild conceptual conceit and slender synth-pop seeming to be part of the conceptual resignation note from Factory, as the champions of subversion through inefficiency became a mere designer subsidiary of a major label whose function was to supply a magic cloak of cool.

The main evidence of any lingering, or festering, original Factory adventure outside the Joy Division collectors' items and Durutti Column was some dissipated Fred Vermorel rigmarole about the holiness of fans and the unholiness of fame that always cheered Wilson up. The monsters were always the most interesting to Wilson, and Vermorel's project gave an always welcome dose of the dark side, just in case the light of his own fame started to produce too much lightness of being.

'What would an ocean be without a monster lurking in the dark?' he could still muster up the energy to say when Factory was well and truly fucked, wearing a mask of Werner Herzog. 'It would be like sleep without dreams.'

Factory introduced *The Pornucopia Experiment* audio novel as 'A recording of Obsessions created by the obsessed themselves.' Wilson and Malcolm McLaren were numbered among the project's 'governors'. A berserk fantasy imagined the saving of the record industry, in which rock 'n' roll had lost its allure and a rescue package was necessary. One of the 'shrewdest minds' in the music industry invited to head a think tank to sort things out and make rock dangerous again through extreme marketing: Tony Wilson, given a second life.

The think tank's report/manifesto would include the rousing lines 'Music should once more become a hotbed of controversy: explosive with passion, desire, malice and dissent. It must tease out our most furtive aberrations and secret inclinations and glamorise, package and normalise these as goods; acts, songs, T-shirts, mags . . .' Vermorel's infatuation with hysteria and fetishism, fan behaviours and stalking, extreme desire and sexual deviancy was blown up into a mutant music-industry porno-thriller in which the stories of the Sex Pistols and Factory Records were interbred and bent around his own crushes and hang-ups; the finished product as a film would have been a hybrid of *The Great Rock 'n' Roll Swindle* and *24 Hour Party People*, with a dash of *Hellraiser*.

At the time there was next to no nostalgia for the Sex Pistols or any sort of civil disobedience or experimental social warping in pop culture, and much more for the Beatles and the safety of a positive 1960s, filtered through its pop stars and fashions, as though this might postpone the end of the century. 'Everything is possible' became 'All sorts of fun are possible' – one mood led to the other, but it was all going in one direction.

The Vermorel project could not have been more out of step with the times, but this was nothing to bother Wilson, some of him still stuck in 1968 or 1976, stuck with his antiquated hope that the ransacking, progressive, revolutionary figure would yet return, and happy to supply some funding for a film dedicated to bringing back the danger to rock music, a great exercise in ageing wishful thinking.

For Wilson, as well as the brief Factory Too, there was what he saw as an abstract Factory 3, embedded in Too in 1994, existing just to put out the Space Monkeys – from Factory's generic, almost self-effacing indie pop period, alongside Hopper. The Space Monkeys were Wilson's doomed after-the-fact attempt to split the difference between Oasis and the Stone Roses, between Madchester and the brand-new Britpop, whom he'd been to see in a snooker club in Bury in 1995. The label by then was just the band, Wilson, an assistant, and weekly meetings consisting of sitting around talking about United, what was going on at the Haçienda and how much Tony hated acid house smiley faces. It didn't take much after that to close the curtains.

Red Cellars was the original name for what became the fourth Factory, the name plucked nostalgically, hoping lightning might strike twice, from the same section of Chtcheglov's 'Formulary for a New Urbanism' that gave Wilson and Gretton the name for the Haçienda. 'And you, forgotten, your memories ravaged by all the consternations of two hemispheres, stranded in the Red Cellars of Pali-Kao, without music and without geography, no longer setting out for the Haçienda where the roots think of the child and where the wine is finished off with fables from an old almanac.'

For money reasons, Wilson was intending to run the label from his home, as with the original Factory, but he naturally spun this as an advantage rather than a necessity. Its greatest and pretty much only release was its business plan, a kind of concrete poem quoting Hegel, James Joyce and Sam Phillips of Sun Records, discoverer of Elvis, Wilson of course putting himself in their company. The mission statement echoed, somewhere between quaintly and arrogantly, original Factory principles made up as they went along: they were going to sign one major band per annum for the first two years, and up to six 'interesting bands' through an underground subsidiary, Sticky Paw.

'We sign bands,' it claimed, somewhere between meaning it and knowing the game was up, the twentieth-century Factory fires extinguished, 'for £80,000 not £180,000. Some we sign for £30,000. No bidding wars because no one else will bid when it's that early. "I hear a hit single." – "No you fucking don't – they haven't written it yet." Cf. "Love Will Tear Us Apart." We sign bands without hit singles, because they haven't written them yet.'

Red Cellars evolved into F4 to release its first £30,000 signing, Raw-T, which ended up selling more like Section 25 than Joy Division, although there was a time when selling Joy Division was no easy matter. 'I'm working with British black music, and no one wants to buy it,' Wilson would grumble. 'Just like they didn't want to buy Joy Division. No one wanted to buy Happy Mondays for three years. I've managed to sell only a thousand albums. I'm fucking annoyed. I've got a load left on the shelf in a warehouse. It reminds me of when I had 9,000 copies of "Transmission" left over because I was convinced it was going to be a hit. Talk about not heeding your own warning. I did a vinyl twelve-inch and it sold eighty copies. I'm as pissed off as hell.'

A quarter of a century had passed since he was perfectly in tune with musical fashion. It didn't seem that long ago, and inside he still felt he could be of use, a help – which of course also meant being a hindrance – but be true to his original principles. It would have been more honest if he hadn't kept trying. Desperation had replaced inspiration. He wanted his hat-trick, but amidst the declarations of intent, he would also realistically admit, 'It probably won't happen.'

It turned out this would be Wilson's last tilt at making an impact with a continuation of brand Factory. In 2005 there was still all that heaped-up hyping Wilson energy, but he didn't have three years left to wait while Raw-T sold hardly anything on the way to suddenly breaking through, writing their hit single, caught up as a local northern version of a hyper-localised London movement in a grime wave that slowly gained momentum. He never got to see the abstractions and enigmas of grime slowly seep through to the surface of pop culture, eventually allowed in, over time, overcoming certain fears and prejudices, media perception changing from 'violent and threatening' to 'voice of a generation'.

Grime's eventual slippage into the mainstream, once the ideological sting and fundamental antagonism had been neutralised and it became relatable to a white audience, Stormzy turned into mum-loving national treasure, confirmed that his thirteen-year theory had merit after all. As unlikely as it seemed to those used to thinking of Tony as indie maverick, not quite trusting his latest infatuation, the blatant-seeming white-middle-class appropriation, he was onto something. Grime started out as the new punk, more or less still of the outside by the time Wilson with Raw-T confused those expecting convulsive white rock from him, but by the time it was part of the mainstream, it was more the new, new wave.

Wilson was right about 2002, but also at the same time, as was often the case in this story, he was very wrong.

Perhaps the beginning of streaming, the first spotting of what would become Spotify, and by the time of Jay-Z the more aptly labelled Tidal, was another sign of a 2002 revolution. More of more, with none of the context to make it anything other than a collection of sounds, a history of memories, a series of sales pitches, of adverts for themselves, an encyclopedia of poses and trends, all circling each other, making music a mere utility, something to take for granted, the internet quickly began to make everything, including music, into something else, a new, as yet unclear version of itself, of a reality slipping outside itself.

As Guy Debord had predicted in his *Society of the Spectacle*, never actually imagining how much the internet – the spectacle in one place – would fulfil all his darkest estimations, 'the reality of time has been replaced by the advertisement of time', a pseudo-experience based on fashion and consumerism.

It was the beginning of a post-boomer, even post-Gen X pop history in which there would be no more prescribed revolutions, just increasingly regular, niche evolutions broken into fragments by the technology that was where the revolutions – now known as upgrades, launches, brands – were happening, not the kind of thing for a believer in grand cultural gestures and clear shifts in emphasis, for a believer in books, in the biggest ideas.

Forty: The dream of Pennine Lancashire, chic sheds and urban theory

Salus populi suprema lex. (The welfare of the people is the ultimate law.)
CICERO

For a while, as he vainly tried to find his third great hit act, it appeared that he was attempting to follow up the Haçienda with its Dry sidekick and In the City, and complete a hat-trick of ideas that economically and abstractly transformed Manchester as an international cultural destination with his plans for a devolved North-West, and the more conventionally prepared sociopolitical plan that he conceived with Yvette to regenerate east Lancashire. The ambition was to push 'the new Manchester' north, twenty-two miles through Bacup in the Rossendale Valley to Burnley, at its mid-1860s peak one of the world's largest producers of cloth.

Wilson's usual method for influencing the direction and reputational substance of the city was clandestine, or as he would like to say, *sub rosa*. He talked to anyone who would listen, even when they didn't, about making a city where the principal activity of the inhabitants would be continually passing through zones designed to alter their moods and behaviour, and then, somehow, through activities that sometimes seemed to border on the lunatic or pre-emptory, in the face of the suspicious even furious, make his plans happen.

By the 1990s, after his time spent running things, and continuing in increasingly famous, eccentrically minded Granada Television, he was far too loud and visible – as a metaphysical mayor of Manchester, a benign civilian commander-in-chief – to work from behind closed doors, changing things from the side of the stage, from within a record/communications company. His campaigning and imagineering took on a more official tone. In 2002 he founded the Necessary Group with Peter Saville, a coalition of local politicians and celebrity influencers from Sir Alex Ferguson to Shaun Ryder campaigning for the devolution of the North-West – a serious democratic play, much more realistic fifteen years later, seeking an elected regional government. The UK's Labour government had planned English devolution by doing it region by region.

First things first for Wilson: a North-West England flag, a banner to carry into war, Saville under Wilson's orders highlighting the upper-left corner of the English flag, inspired by the Peterloo Massacre, when the army seized the flags of the protesters. Radio 4's *Today* observed that it was merely an off-centre St George's flag, but symbol-loving Wilson was as besotted with it as he was with the first Saville Factory posters. Preparing for a referendum at the end of 2004, Wilson had already spotted the value of viral marketing, using a website for fundraising and profile-building and the selling of merchandise. (In 1998, again perhaps a few years early, he had set up a music download site with his partner Yvette Livesey, Music33.com, for a few months the only such site in the world with fully operational encryption and micropayments; perhaps the very provisional, near-invisible start of a third great event.)

The Necessary Group's campaign had an anti-climactic Factory-style ending, the flag hanging limp. Due to concerns about postal ballots, the three referendums planned in the North-West, Yorkshire and Humber were postponed. (The UK had limited experience of holding referendums, as would become apparent nine years later.) The referendum in the North-East went ahead, not least because Labour assumed that this region would have the strongest support for the proposed structure and create momentum in the other areas, but after a 74 per cent against vote on a turnout of 28 per cent the other referendums were cancelled and ruled out for the foreseeable future. Among the concerns of opponents to devolution in the North-East was that whatever limited powers the devolved region would have would be centred in Newcastle, creating more problems of inequality. If Wilson was planning for Manchester as the centre of the North-West, he was also making plans for areas outside the city.

With Livesey, a love he can work with, if only to make it clear he's a modern, liberal man, he sets up Livesey/Wilson Associates Ideas Management and works on development proposals with Manchester and Liverpool city councils and the North West Development Agency. They collaborate with Elevate, the government's 'housing renewal pathfinder', which has been commissioned to consider ways to regenerate housing in the north-east Lancashire area, its ossified mill towns falling behind the cities socially and culturally, lacking imaginative input and significant investment because their industrial base has gone and they have become drifting backwaters. The area demanded different kinds of solutions to the reordering of the heritage and politics of the cities around it, which attracted most of the attention and energy. If there were new houses, what kind of place would they be built in?

This was a new Factory, something contemporary for Wilson to concentrate on, to see off the boredom that is the enemy of all utopians, dealing with communications, locations, branding and the transmission of psychology, without the music, without the fashion. It was more grown-up, but still something for the future, a way for Wilson to keep searching for the world as it is meant to be, still finding ways to send messages to the future.

It made use of Wilson's talents as a dreamer, as a persuader and as a kind of storyteller. It still made use of Peter Saville, who via the recommendation of Wilson would start working for the city council in 2005 as Manchester's creative director – as if he could continue his lapsed work on the Factory dream of Manchester, allowed to see outside reality, within the actual living city itself. Some wondered what on earth elite typographer and London-based design consultant Saville could give to Manchester that would be of any use to those living in the most deprived, declining areas, what use his aim of coordinating all of the typefaces used in the city on street signs would actually be.

For Saville, such holistic attention to detail, barely noticed by anyone, perhaps subconsciously felt, was the beginning of making a city that became part of an outside world, not stuck inside itself and its own local concerns. The road signs were the signature of the city, an introduction to its soul, telling you where to go and how to get there. They should not make a mess of information. It was his way of explaining to the city councillors, the city elders, how to begin seeing the future and meet it. *Yes*, some of them thought, *but look what happened to Factory*. But then, Saville explained, Factory may not have had the tidiest balance sheets but it influenced intelligent everyday culture, it maintained throughout a belief that the everyday should be better, and it helped create a Manchester that the outside world wanted to visit and support. It improved the city from within like a stealth weapon. Factory's influence on standards of design becomes part of the city's difference that gets transmitted around the world.

Saville sees a line from Bauhaus to Apple, with Factory in between, and Apple could not have happened in Britain, but if you give individuals a chance and let them dream, then an Apple can happen in Britain. An Apple can happen in Manchester. Ideas can create opportunity. Society has to find a way to take a chance on individuals who have ideas, no matter what their background; a place like Manchester needs those ideas, and society needs a way to support those ideas. The cynics scoffed at the arty nonsense. The dreamers applauded the practical fantasy. 'The fact we did something at Factory that could not be seen coming is the evidence that something can be done.'

Peter Saville

At the end of the twentieth century, this notion of the original modern city came to me, which I liked. It was true. It was a historical fact. Manchester was the first industrial city, it was where the idea of the modern happened first. And of course it was my home city, so whether I live there or not, I have a sense of pride in where I come from – I think most people do, whether they love the place or hate the place, they still have a pride, it's like family. And I liked the idea that my home city, my place of origin, could be described as the original modern city, and I saw the possibility that if the city, in the twenty-first century, could grasp that idea, then it would help empower it to maintain a place for itself. I was asked to be the provocateur for it, which some saw as me adopting a shadowy presence within the council, but I was very proactive in influencing the city's approach to its own image. Tony was the first person I told the idea of the original modern city to.

We were sat in a car park at the edge of the city, and I said, 'I have had this idea what to call Manchester, effectively how to brand it – the original modern city,' which he loved. The hope is that the principle behind the idea gets absorbed into policy. It's not just a slogan, a throwaway one-liner; everything is meant to come from this sentiment. If you're going to announce that you're the original modern city, transport, healthcare, education, architecture, culture, it must all follow on. It's not meant to be hype, distraction, it's meant to be a manifesto. Of course, it's easier said than done, how to explain to the council, now to the mayor, that 'original modern city' is not just a line to put on posters or promotional material. It's an instruction on how to elevate the city to international levels. It needs acting upon. From my point of view, it needs some political equivalent of Tony Wilson to take it on and make it so. But that's another story.

Saville was drawn in to help create some graphics for a loose confederation of districts and councils that Wilson called Pennine Lancashire, hoping that it would become PL just like Los Angeles was LA. Its 'upmarket connotations' appealed to the more conventional brand consultants connected to the project; Wilson just liked the way its simplicity cut through the baggage, making a mental map of movement in an area drifting through history.

This was an invented new region, and in Wilson-world, combining the utterly practical with the phantasmal, it needed its own flag to raise, to attach emotions to, and the combination of Wilson, Saville and the design company he chose, Creative Concern, produced a luscious, soft-shelled branding image that was intended to work as an aspirational symbol of the tolerant new thinking being applied to both neglected built-up areas and beautiful landscapes.

The flag was a very twenty-first-century assimilation of the nineteenth and twentieth centuries, multicoloured flowing curves symbolising hills, rooftops and meandering canals, hinting at threads of cotton, sleek enough to be given a Factory number, functional public-sector iconography given an ethereal poetic dimension. Local councillors and government officials mostly approved of it, either in some sort of shock at the way authority was presented through extreme elegance or caught up in Wilson and his new company's myth-making raptures.

For Wilson and his new team, the flag was perfect, not least because 'the disparate elements of East Lancashire need a flag to march behind, a unifying symbol to lead them to the top of the mountain known as successful regeneration'. It was perfect, but not necessarily for the immediate needs of the project, which was very Wilson and not usually something that got in the way of his enthusiasm – the flag bore as much relation to the everyday worlds of Burnley and Pendle as the first Factory posters did to the music they were advertising. Which meant it could all still work, as long as it did.

The report Livesey and Wilson came up with, proposing a mind-bending Seattle-like reinvention of the area, approached the task with the same kind of language, promises and exaggeration Factory would apply to a press release for one of its releases or follies: confidence sometimes bordering on arrogance, hopes and dreams presented as matters of fact. Its official title was 'The Dreaming of Pennine Lancashire', which was still a little wishy-washy for uptight, down-to-earth councils looking for realism, but was much more definite than their preferred title, 'A Wish List: A Series of Consummations Devoutly to Be Wished'.

The wish list included allotment sheds created by Wilson's design love Philippe Starck, who in the 1980s had helped invent the concept of the boutique hotel, as if they might attract youngsters to growing things – 'chic sheds' to replace the traditional broken-down garden hovel, a neat countryside metaphor for city regeneration, and more a provocative 'what if' call to arms than a realistic ambition. The same perhaps for a 'fashion tower' in Burnley – Weave – 'a vertical story of the industrial revolution as art installation', with a dramatic bar at the top designed by a world-class architect. But this stylish building as beacon for the town was rooted in the greater truth that this sort of modernisation required grand gestures. Get people to look up, beyond their usual horizons, to see the result of thinking big, so the past can be outwitted without being wiped out.

Here he is, arms whirling, voice rising into comfortably clad know-it-all charm, selling the idea of the fashion tower to those who think he's out of his depth in taking on such a challenge, to those who still only know him as the man off the telly, to those who wish he'd come up with another Haçienda, another Happy Mondays, and stop messing about with all this middle-class lifestyle shit.

The fashion tower is important, he announces, because there have only been two real changes in humanity's history. We were nomadic hunters and then we became farmers, and that happened in Mesopotamia and along the banks of the Yellow River in China. Then we stopped being farmers and became industrial, modern people, and that happened around Manchester and east Lancashire, which makes this the epicentre of the world at a certain point in history. So Lancashire is more important historically than the Valley of the Kings, and we should celebrate that however we can.

'Right is right even if no one is doing it,' he says, wearing a mask of St Augustine. 'Wrong is wrong even if everyone is doing it.'

More wishes included a football theme park, a 'curry mile' based on the famous one in Rusholme, the area becoming Manchester's playground, public spaces established in the centre of each town, direct trains between Manchester and Burnley, public celebrations of local heroes – all ways of attracting the creative and middle classes with close connections to Manchester.

Wilson's latest intellectual fascination, his new McLaren, was with urban studies theorist Richard Florida, who had recently published his highly optimistic unlikely bestseller *The Rise of the Creative Class*, putting the case for how creativity and the creative classes were revolutionising the global economy. Hipsterism, tech workers, arts and music were the direct route to the revitalisation of tired cities. The book was filled with references to Baudelaire, Bob Dylan, T. S. Eliot and Isaac Newton; one of the chapters was presented as a 'rant', in which he excitedly noted that 'it is hard to think of a major high-tech region that doesn't have a distinct audio identity' – pure Wilson, and to some extent post-Wilson, Manchester one of the very few cities in the world with such an audio identity, one that essentially emerged after 1976, either directly because of Factory or as a reaction against it by Morrissey, the Roses and the Gallaghers.

Wilson naturally loved the idea articulated by Florida – an extremely self-confident fan of quoting Marx – that young creative workers, whom Wilson had always championed, were the future and economically significant. Simply by moving to a location – bringing with them avocado on toast, bike paths, gallery space and the loft living of Wilson's dreams – they would cause it to thrive. Graphic designers were the twenty-first-century equivalent of eighteenth-century farm workers. 'Access to talented and creative people is to modern business what access to coal and iron ore was to steel-making.' Ideas were the new currency.

Wilson also inevitably approved of the idea that a specialist in regeneration could be described as a rock star. (Wilson wouldn't live to see the relative fall of Florida, blamed for bland gentrification, creative ghettos and the replacement of the incoming bohemians with the white middle class chasing hipness, castigated for American insularity, but could identify with how Florida's menus of ideas would increasingly be seen as dogmas sold as guaranteeing success rather than fluid thinking-aloud suggesting possibilities, triggering reactions. He could also identify with how Florida was penalised for testing out ideas in public. Florida's view, in 2002, that the creative individual should no longer be viewed as an iconoclast but as the new mainstream would have concerned him, not least because in some ways it suggested the end is nigh.)

Chic sheds and generally spending heavily on hipster-friendly cultural amenities were very Floridian solutions to the ongoing decline of east Lancashire, and Livesey and Wilson realised that the suggestion that everything could be solved by trendiness might be too much for both the policy-makers and council departments they were consulting for and those already spotting the flaws in Florida's calculations. For Wilson, the greater point was to generate initial interest, to make it clear that this was going to be a serious venture, quoting Florida not necessarily because he was supplying all the correct answers – maybe a few – and enthusing over the idea of Starck sheds, unique shops and street performers because why shouldn't east Lancashire be at the centre of such thinking?

He saw the first step to making the necessary changes was by treating Burnley and the allotments around Accrington with the same sort of intensity even glamour as the more obvious big cities. Small-town thinking only produces small-town ideas. Small Lancashire towns should be associated with 'culture' because it can no longer be seen as mere decoration but as economic energy. To some extent it worked in Manchester; the alternative, independent musical scenes and rock-star murals were essential to the city's economic future, if only by giving the city an attractive commercial hook that was more modern than old-fashioned science and industry.

The more radically thought-provoking the ideas, the more they would show how serious the councils and the local population were about seeing their part of the world taken almost in one leap from the nineteenth to the twenty-first century. Livesey and Wilson were originally asked simply as part of typical committee brainstorming to see what kind of housing and how much should be built in east Lancashire. 'Housing has always been a key to great resets,' sang Wilson and Florida in perfect harmony, the Crosby and Nash, maybe the Paul Kantner and Grace Slick, of urban theory. Their over-the-top response, imagining an almost science-fiction social and cultural reinvention of solidly behind-the-times east Lancs, was designed to get attention, but it also meant risking scaring off the politicians and their advisers and those locals who ultimately felt more comfortable in stasis than with progressive new ideas.

PL would never become the third element of a Wilson hat-trick, and by the time there was any momentum, and the soft revolutionary flag, it was the end of 2006, and he had only a few months to live. His last great project was one of the great Wilsonian unfinished projects, and whatever happened to it after he died, it could never progress with the sense of missionary verve that would lift it above the ordinary with a gentle twist.

The 'Wish List' proposal was one of his greatest pieces of writing, and one of his greatest collaborations, but it was closer to fiction than any kind of blueprint, as much as it enthused sympathetic factions at Elevate and the local councils.

The report in that sense was the finished product – what usually would be written after he had set things into motion that then entered history because they existed. If he had needed to write reports and make pitches to gain funding and support before the fact, asking for belief in Factory, Joy Division, the Happy Mondays, the Haçienda or his broadcasting career, he would never have got anywhere. The Haçienda was a great piece of fiction, but it ended up being built, and inhabited, and turned into books, films and memories.

The report deserved to be turned into a film in a series of films about Wilson, detailing all of his interests, infatuations and infuriating inconsistencies, but before it could be a film it needed to be built, and of course there is no Fashion Tower in Burnley with a Zaha Hadid bar at its peak, and no avant-garde Philippe Starck allotment sheds lifting plain, blunt Accrington into a solar system mixing luxury and lunacy. The tower was put on hold in 2011, and after that for ever. The football theme park never went beyond feasibility studies. The chic sheds were awaiting lottery funding for a while. The inspirational public spaces linking six Lancashire towns stayed stuck in blue sky. The drizzle kept falling in Accrington.

Pennine Lancashire would not be built.

Forty-One: OGs, broken dreams, reality television and a shaman's brew

Splendide mendax. (Splendidly false.)
HORACE

There would be no continuation of Wilson's thirteen-year theory in 2015, unless you count Snapchat launching its Discover and Lenses filters. The fact that in 2015, on Wilson's timeline, nothing specific really happened, other than an increase in the accumulation of more music, and an increasing collapse in the sort of standards Wilson trusted, was perhaps the next moment in line – a vague form of disintegration, the vague beginning of a post-computer pop era in which everything was available, and a version of Wilson was going to be more a Kanye West or a Jack Dorsey than a Brian Epstein or a Pete Waterman.

The ultimate version of a post-everything, dot-connecting, twenty-first-century Wilson was Virgil Abloh, architecture student, shopper as artist, former creative consultant to Kanye West, consumer revolutionary, prototype fashion influencer, founder of Off-White – with its ubiquitous quotation marks, its diagonal lines and construction iconography echoing Haçienda graphics, its devotion to Helvetica – learning from Barbara Kruger how you could evoke meaning by crashing two things together, referring to Marcel Duchamp as his 'lawyer', offering art-history precedent for the way he absorbs and copies and pastes existing intellectual property into his system. Clothes and trainers as ready-mades, his ultimate ambition to have streetwear perceived like an art movement. He saw fashion as a recording system of its time, in much the same way Factory was a recording system of Manchester time. Abloh would say, wearing a mask of Tony Wilson, 'Expressing wealth isn't the coolest thing right now. It's expressing your knowledge.'

When Abloh needs some advice or reassurance from an OG – an original/authentic – he rates, he turns to Peter Saville, who got the chance to build Factory from scratch because Wilson liked his style and who like Abloh appreciates the importance of typography, the way you can use it to completely change the perception of a thing without changing anything about it. Wilson's adviser becomes Abloh's confidant.

The ultimate version of a twenty-first-century Tony Wilson who didn't sacrifice his professional career but concentrated on his life in broadcasting, resisting the pull of music, or passing through it up to about 1980, letting his adolescent obsessions melt away, would be Christiane Amanpour of CNN. She has the same unusual ability to be able to interview anyone from wherever in the cultural and political strata with the same sensitive, penetrating precision, elegantly putting the powerful in a corner or sympathetically engaging with the less entitled. 'One of the problems with me,' Wilson said, 'is that in interviews there has to be a bit of, well, chemistry, I suppose, and my partner doesn't like it when that happens. But you have to have it.' It's all about him – more than with Amanpour, although all great interviews are really about the interviewer finding out about themselves – but he had a certain way of entering an interview as though he was already your friend. When you were his enemy, he would still have a knack of getting in close but slipping through your guard. It was another way of making everyone he met part of his collection of people who were indirectly or directly useful to him, a universe he was forever at the centre of.

Approaching fifty, when his youthful concerns and aberrant intellectual ambitions were getting stronger, he admitted he was always only at best on the verge of taking his TV career seriously – enough to have ended up as a CNN presenter or the single-minded host of *Newsnight* or *Question Time*, with *Mastermind* on the side. His agents once said to him, in his fifties, that they would be really interested in reviving his TV career, but they weren't too sure he had the slightest interest in a TV career. Which was, he said, fair enough. He was far too playful, and too much of a would-be player in cultural war zones, to concentrate on one strand of his abilities.

He'd left *Granada Reports* in the late 1980s, Haçienda issues, messy changes in family circumstances, keeping up with the hedonistic manias of the Happy Mondays making presenting increasingly tricky. He becomes slick, ornery presenter for hire across a range of programmes, mostly still within the North-West, including live late-night rough-and-tumble debate show *Up Front*, with new TV partner, TV wife, Lucy Meacock.

For this he was given a clothing allowance of £750 for the year, which he spent in one go on one of his favourite big-shouldered suits, which would become his uniform for the show. Soon he was wearing the suit with trainers, defying the orders of the chairman of Granada, who had sent a message requesting he put on some 'proper shoes'. When he presented a late-twentieth-century six-part series on the Industrial Revolution that put many of his interests into one place, his director Ged Clarke suggested that he dressed a bit differently, something a bit more tweedy university professor than Zen undertaker. Wilson, again, was unmoved. If you wanted his ability to improvise informative and insightful pieces to camera about complex historical subjects, you had to take the clothing as well, even if you thought he was wearing a funeral coat.

In 2002, perhaps readying himself for the latest Great Pop Culture Year of Revolution, he returned to *Granada Reports*. It was also a warped part of the publicity for the *24 Hour Party People* film, in which much of the elastic comedy came from the ridiculous idea that a bland, beaming, local TV presenter with daytime egregiousness should also be a philosophy-quoting, punk-loving conceptualist who founded a melodramatic record label that wanted to have a nightclub all of its own.

He sold his return yet again as it being a privilege to be the voice and face of such an important region, promoting his loyalty to the socially vital local half-hour news programme, and of course his loyalty to speaking to the North from the North, clinging on to traditional Granada values even as, more or less apart from its local news, Granada was absorbed inside the tamed national ITV beast. Even though he had never been worried about his dignity, there was something undignified about watching such a broadcasting expert with the skills of a Dimbleby having to go back to where he began, nearly thirty years later. It was like watching David Letterman in his fifties, emperor of surreal, self-conscious, emotionally experimental TV, having to start out again as a local weatherman. To function as the cheery, chatty, early-evening anchor, Wilson effectively had to lop off vast parts of his character and capability.

Many of the original Granada greats – and even not-so-greats – went on to dominate British television either on or behind the screen, as talent or as controllers, as award-winning film-makers extending their range to Netflix, embedding Granada principles into British broadcasting, influencing international productions. This Granada great with just too much on his mind to settle down traps himself as a minor, eccentric, still mostly local broadcaster, and eighteen months later finishes his final *Granada Reports* half-hour, a new era, a new regime less forgiving of his quirks and personal stylistic tics. He swears on camera, live, although he swears he had no idea he was on air, but it's enough for a quiet, final removal from the job for which he was not too unprofessional but actually completely overqualified.

He returns to what has now become his day job, campaigning for north-western self-government, and almost begins constructing a broadcasting career again. There's *The Politics Show North West* on the local BBC, which hints at what he could have been as trusted, vigilant mainstream host, and increasingly there's talk radio. He lands his own show, *Talk of the Town*, for BBC Manchester, after a senior executive hears him interviewed on the station and cannot believe it when he learns Wilson is effectively out of work. Wilson loses himself in a freer, more fluid approach to communicating his ideas and enthusiasms, and it becomes one of his best periods of broadcasting, truer to the quickness and somehow focused randomness of his mind than any of his broadcasting since *So It Goes*.

His fondly regarded experience as a music man, his love of sport and his fluency as an argumentative current-affairs operator made him a perfect radio voice, even if there was something missing. Not being able to see him in action, gauge the look in his eyes, somewhere between excessively sure of himself and light-hearted, reduced a lot of his impact. He was still a Granada boy; he promised to return, no doubt once he had delivered an independent North-West, leading from the shadows, but then Granada wasn't what it was between the 1960s and '80s, and television itself wasn't the same. He put on a brave face, but his world was falling out from underneath him.

'I could have been a network television presenter,' he told the *Guardian*, swearing in the face of *sine qua non*, shrugging his shoulders at a life that never happened, another broken dream. 'But the fact is, fuck it, really. Fuck it.'

2002 could also be read in terms of his pop culture theory as the Year of Reality Television. The star of the third British *Big Brother* series was Jade Goody, who became the very first of a certain type of reality star that lifted the genre from guilty – or quite innocent – pleasure, a television ingredient largely empty of calories, to becoming the commercial-generating future of what was left of scheduled television. The latest pop cultural breakthrough on Wilson's list shifting from music to the invention of a new kind of fame, which would lead all the way to the smartphone Insta generation and the torrent of personal brands, a different kind of fame and misfortune.

Reality television was initially not for mainstream television personalities, generally viewed as a lower form of TV life, but mostly for desperate show-offs with no apparent talent – until twenty-year-old dental nurse Jade Goody chaotically, somehow winningly, demonstrated how its stars' very real talent was their ability to perform on TV, and that being famous for being famous, for being roughly ordinary, for negotiating a toxic world dominated by populist monsters and tabloid creeps, required its own skills, abilities and judgement. 'Celebrity' versions of reality shows quickly arrived, in which those who were more or less famous for more than just being famous joined in, to exploit their fame and make sure they were part of a lucrative growing new genre.

Whatever else Wilson was, he was definitely a twenty-first-century celebrity, if only because of his association with the Haçienda, touchstone for an increasingly influential new generation, and with Shaun Ryder, himself more of a celebrity who happened to sing, as the Happy Mondays slipped back into the twentieth century or onto the vintage circuit. The role of the has-been became something else in the celebrity era; even the most minor celebrity, the most classic one-hit wonder, previously all used up as the world moved on, could generate a new life in the reality age, in which the world was so full of itself it simply couldn't move on.

Others in the devil-may-care Wilson realm, including John Lydon and Malcolm McLaren, found there might be roles, and healthy fees, in competitive, episodic reality television as the equivalent of pantomime villains, or watchable, screwed-up, old-school, know-it-all oddballs, from a time when native intelligence came from reading and listening, and ranting, more than from watching and consuming and acting dumb, before the smooth touch screen had completely replaced the needle drop as the central factor of pop culture.

Celebrity shows filled with engaging, or enraging, celebrity eccentrics of all shapes and sizes were a twenty-first-century trend that might well have been a future source of income, an extra self, for Wilson, running a little out of options as he passed his mid-fifties, or on the way to formal leadership, with a little showbusiness on the side. A glimpse of a future as a reality regular was his 2005 appearance on a Channel 4 scandal-chasing adventure reality show, *Extreme Celebrity Detox*. There was a £5,000 fee, much-needed cash, and a long, arduous journey into what could pass as the heart of darkness in the Amazon basin. He relocated to the Peruvian jungle for a while with classic reality colleagues glamour model Jo Guest and comedian Mina Anwar to try some ayahuasca, a powerful plant-based Amazonian hallucinogenic illegal in both the UK and the USA, and in most other countries.

In Peru it is only legal as part of a formally supervised spiritual ceremony, a shamanistic initiation into an altered state of consciousness, with the ultimate intention of exploiting its apparently potent healing properties. Some report that as a medicine it is like having five years of therapy in a few hours. It might also be a long way to go to eat the equivalent of magic mushrooms, but it had become a popular part of many a student's gap year, which itself was a subsection of ayahuasca tourism. For Wilson, with his own shamanic instincts and his never-ending interest in psychedelic enlightenment, a druggy ritual in the jungle – perhaps joining the dots between the Haçienda and the Hidden Gem – was an irresistible offer. He was also aware of William Burroughs' experience with the 'shaman's brew', which he first came across in the early 1950s as 'yage', a secret known to few Westerners with apparent telepathic properties.

Burroughs had consumed almost every drug under the sun, and he went on his own, non-televised quest to find a rare one he hadn't tried, a necessary addition to his repertoire, a few stressed turbulent months after killing his wife Joan Vollmer in a drunken game of William Tell. He tried to write his way out of the guilt. The last line in his first novel, *Junky*, his brutally spare investigation into heroin and its users, reads, 'Yage may be the final fix,' a less crippling post-heroin release, possibly, or the truth that there is no escape from addiction, only a cushioned slip into oblivion.

He exchanged letters with *Junky*'s editor Allen Ginsberg as he searched for the drug in 1953 – Ginsberg following in Burroughs' footsteps seven years later, the writings between the two collected as *The Yage Letters*, published in 1963, at the dawn of the psychedelic counterculture. In a way, courtesy of Channel 4, Wilson was visiting the very source of his singularity, of his early influences. (The definitive end of the counterculture is arrived at when the quest for yage has progressed from Burroughs' pioneering, reality-bending journey into his personal heart of darkness to the structured reality of a celebrity television journey or a gap-year experience. The point of all those journeys being misadventure as much as anything else.)

Following a seven-month expedition to Panama, Colombia and Peru, after being jailed, robbed and contracting malaria Burroughs eventually tracked yage down, first experiencing four hours of head-spinning delirium, convulsions of lust and regular vomiting, on a later occasion ecstatically finding it to be the most powerful drug he had ever experienced. It was space–time travel; it was the calling-up of Rimbaud and his famous derangement of the senses. One way Burroughs described it was by drawing an 'archaic grinning face', a kind of primitive precursor of the black and yellow Second Summer of Love acid house smiley face, an icon originally designed in 1963 to cheer up workers at the State Mutual Life Assurance Company during a hostile takeover.

The splintering, disordered effect on his imagination would be reflected in Burroughs' later use of cut-up techniques and a more intensely non-linear approach to writing, with its subsequent impact on songwriting, sampling and viral memes. Ginsberg's sessions with ayahuasca led to a snake-vomiting dance with death, slimy worms of pure sensate transcendency, a realisation of the illusion of separate consciousness and the poems 'Magic Psalm' and 'The Reply', written from his experience with 'the Great Being' of his visions. The perfect ingredients for some celebrity-driven reality TV shenanigans.

Wilson also felt that by taking ayahuasca he would outdo someone else on a mission to take every drug under the sun, Shaun Ryder, a recent influential figure in the cultural history of drug consumption, the tracksuit-clad rave version of Burroughs the drug user and drug dealer, a rampageous, mind-mashing Salford heir of the Beats and their role in the cultural shift towards drug-taking. To Wilson's disappointment, Ryder was already familiar with ayahuasca. 'Fucking great, isn't it?' he said casually, nodding as Wilson enthused over his amazing find. Bez had brought some back from his holidays.

Ryder's skilled description of its effects reminded Wilson why he loved Ryder's lyrics so much: he felt they spilt out from such knowledge in much the same way the drug's benefits and risks had spilt into and disrupted the language of Burroughs and Ginsberg. Bez, apparently, was a different, gentler, more accepting person for a few months, until the effects wore off. 'I suppose I was too,' reported Wilson.

After they had taken the drug under controlled conditions, his two reality-show allies felt as though they were going to die, right there and then, and were slammed into shivering panic attacks. They needed considerable help from the programme's resident expert to deal with their terrifying sight of the abyss, perhaps experiencing one of the darker unintended consequences of appearing on reality television much quicker than most. Wilson – having been relieved of his mobile phone, to achieve the correct personal settings for the experiment – was well used to staring into the abyss, whether with receivers dealing with some bankruptcy or another, with divorce lawyers, or a more Nietzschean abyss, and after a little light vomiting wandered off back to his quarters feeling fine to drink a glass of wine and listen to some music on his iPod.

The next morning he delivered a politely positive little New Age speech about how the experience, while not flinging him into the shredded, known unknowns of Burroughs or into Ginsberg's other dimension, had made him rethink his priorities. Essentially, been there, done that, but there was a feeling that he had woken up from a very vivid dream, most of which he had forgotten. Something to do with being ready for whatever happens next. Whatever will happen will happen soon enough. It may come more suddenly than you expect.

The psychedelic beginning and celebrity end of the life of the man off the telly played out in contrived reality circumstances, with a little playful hint from the local shaman that the spiritual properties of the medicine were bullshit, really, but that there were other, more practical benefits that you may have forgotten about but that hadn't forgotten you.

Yage had been the final fix. The effects lasted a few months, taking him to the very edge of another adventure and a truth that is more real than life itself.

Forty-Two: The death Factory

Nascentes morimur. (From the moment we are born we begin to die.)

And then something happens that apart from anything else does some considerable damage to his perception of time, and to the future of Anthony H. Wilson. He's pleased that he's getting more broadcasting work than he's had in a while – even without the music and Factory, the delightful cultural detours. Even if some of the work comes from his past, he's beginning to relax into the idea that there might be money and employment, and new directions, in the future.

There's the new television and radio work and directing the future as social designer of wound-down beautiful east Lancashire. He's an executive producer on the muted, meditative biographical film Anton Corbijn is directing based around how Ian Curtis, as a kind of Factory worker, in three years went from sickly, introverted Macclesfield office clerk and hyper-sensitive social worker to tragic iconic dead rock star. Perhaps there might be something in the idea of working on more films that tell stories from closer to home or that are about a more abstract concept of home, of finding and returning home. Films in which some caricature, some shadow of himself, doesn't feature. It's less vivid, or heroic, than his exploits between the mid-'70s and mid-'90s, but old age after all might yet be kind to him, the strident young know-it-all Turk becoming spiky know-it-all elder statesman, a more measured mentor.

Time both slows down and speeds up, and then there is enough strange time cut through with boredom and terror, humour and desperation for Wilson to take a pause, and take a view, until the very last minute. The separate strands of his life, all those divisions, all those different endeavours, all that juggling, the private and the public, the work and the play, the lovers and enemies, the friends and the family, conflicts and connections, flesh and mind, the secrets and the rumours, truth and lies, art and business, memories and fantasies, image and inner life, dreamer and reality, selflessness and selfishness, it all starts to gather in the one place, the one person, it turns out the one dream, because for all the different stories and the different characters inhabiting the same body, there can only be one end to one life. Everything must now come together so that the end can take shape.

It was his turn. It wasn't as though Factory, the death Factory, hadn't pointed the way, each death – Curtis, Hannett, Gretton – taking its turn, bringing him closer; the Ecstasy death, the murder of Dave Rowbotham, the end of the Haçienda, the end of Factory, the end of *Granada Reports*, each death like the death of a parent, clearing the path towards his own death. And it all started with the death of his mum and some money she left him.

He always knew it was coming; he was only passing through really. He would toy with death to the end, as part of his constant spiel, his regular cheery, accepting summary of a life lived as he passed through various age milestones, content with how his life had turned out, with the adventures he'd had, the discoveries he'd made, even with the mistakes he'd made, the missed opportunities, the schemes that led nowhere or simply round and round in circles.

Out of nowhere, finding out he was seriously ill, preparing for and experiencing death, completing the circuit from discovery to conclusion inside eight months, turns out to be the final act, the ultimate performance of Tony Wilson, announcing his presence while he can, dealing close-up with the connection between life and death. He gets to know his illness, treats it as a project, his last statement of intent, even to some extent coming up with a form of manifesto. He finds out that when it comes to his life he is definitely going to have to finish what he started; there is a definite deadline. This is why he never completely gives up on God, at least in theory, making sure that in the end there will be more than an end, and it is why he never gives up telling stories, because stories never end.

His days, like his beloved Factory catalogue collecting music, monuments and moments, were numbered. His final act of Factory business is to allocate a catalogue number, Fac 500, to the first Happy Mondays album for fifteen years, *Uncle Dysfunktional*, released on the non-Factory Sequel label during his last few weeks. The first Happy Mondays item on Factory had been in 1985, Fac 129, the 'Forty-Five EP' featuring 'Delightful', produced by Mike Pickering, when they sounded like the fast, hazy Warsaw end of Joy Division, as though one Factory success was tardily mutating into the next, obliquely mixed in the all-knowing mind of Wilson.

One moment he had all the time in the world . . . Suddenly, but not suddenly enough to stop things in their tracks and cut out the cruel, accumulative stress, Wilson finds out that he is ill, ill enough to have to take it very seriously. During the last few weeks of 2006 he feels as though he has a cold, or even the flu – shitty, stubborn symptoms he cannot shake off, interfering with his usual basic thrusting energy. Feeling bad, dodging the doctor, because you never know, 'after two weeks of incessant nagging' Yvette eventually encourages him to find out what might be wrong.

Two weeks before Christmas, with his usual capable, determined airiness, he presents his last-ever *Politics Show North West*, hosting a short debate between a local MP and a GP on the state of the NHS that brings back memories of how Salford's Hope Hospital – where he had been born – took such great care of his father in his final days. A few days later he enters a series of increasingly urgent-seeming procedures and internal examinations and learns at ten o'clock at night on the Tuesday before Christmas that his right kidney is completely consumed by cancer and will have to be removed. Before he hears the actual words, the warm, soft hand the super-calm doctor gently places on his knee says it all.

For a few years there had been small but unnerving hints that the complications, the sundry pressures, the rows and negotiations, divorces and melodramas, stalkers and receivers, rivalries and disputes, the constant live TV and the money struggles, the miscellaneous hedonistic indulgences had all taken their toll. There were a couple of mini-strokes, an aneurysm, all witnessed by Isabel – one attack when they are alone together on holiday, one of their regular New Year's Eves together, this one skiing in Morocco, when she was fifteen. They did a lot of trips together. 'Maybe because his relationship with Oli was so tortuous I sort of kept things bottled up, didn't really tell him how I felt. So we would have a nice time.'

After a meal one night in Manchester on her thirteenth birthday, his arm went completely limp when he tried to sign the bill. He lost all feeling in it. He took Izzy back to her mum's, lay down on the sofa and groaned. He ended up in hospital, warned that he must change his lifestyle, find a way of controlling his appetites. 'He kept taking the drugs, though. Nothing would stop him living his life the way he wanted to.'

Two years later, in Morocco, he's smoked a huge joint and drunk a mojito that was pretty much pure rum while Izzy is in the next room. He walks in, something clearly wrong.

Isabel Wilson

I now know as a doctor how ill he looked. He was completely grey. And he just said, 'I feel really ill,' walked into the bathroom, and I heard this almighty crash. I went in, and half the porcelain sink was off the wall, and Dad was on his back, and there's a pool of blood coming out of his head. So then I was like, 'Oh my God, are you all right?' And I just lay next to him, and he's like, 'I'm fine, I'm fine.'

And then we went to bed. It was New Year's Eve. We were meant to go and watch the fireworks, but he was too weak. So we just hobbled to the end of the road and just kind of looked at the stars and then went back in. And then I lay awake all night, checking that he didn't stop breathing. I was terrified. I needed to tell someone. And he was like, 'No. Don't tell your mum.' Nothing was to ever be told. No one must ever know.

Eventually, it was serious enough to have to tell Hilary, serious enough for others to know, in a rush of information, breaking into the usually guarded private life of Tony Wilson, which must be kept separate from the public life so that the myths and exaggerations could fly unhindered. Another ritual was Tony taking his children to Mass on Christmas Eve and having them both with him on Christmas Day. This time when they returned to their mum's house on Boxing Day they told her he had a tumour.

Hilary Wilson

I was mortified. I called him immediately, and he told me he had kidney cancer. It went on from there. We became quite close over the next few months.

He wanted experiences. At any cost. He always said he'd die young. 'I'm going to live my life, but I'm going to die young.' He thought he'd die of a heart attack like his mother, but he lived his life as he wanted to. And I think a lot of it was to escape reality, but a lot of it was just for the craic. When he died the kids found so many drugs in his apartment, so he was doing it to the end.

Alan Erasmus

I didn't know for a while. We weren't talking at the time. After Factory went bankrupt I went into a shell. I found the whole thing, how it ended, very disheartening. It affected me for years. I didn't do much, spent my time in front of a computer, games, early eBay, in a room where I would smoke, have ideas, stroll around. I thought the way he behaved as Factory ended was wrong. We didn't talk for years. Maybe once, when he rang me to tell me Rob's dead, after about seven, eight years. We kept our distance at the funeral. Nothing else after that. Until he was ill. I saw this Evening News *poster outside a newsagent on the Stockport Road – 'Music mogul dying of cancer' – and I thought,* Well, that's either going to be Peter Waterman or Tony Wilson – maybe what's-his-name, the Take That manager. *I went into the shop and there was a picture of Tony in the newspaper. So then I knew. I immediately thought maybe we should sort things out. Sort it out, and then go our separate ways. Because those last years had been unpleasant. Tony could be very unpleasant. When he loved you, it was great. When you weren't in his thoughts, it could be so cold.*

Lindsay Reade

I was actually in the John Lewis changing room and my mobile rang. He had told me a few weeks before he had a bad cold, because we'd been meeting up over the last few months, and it was one night when he said he felt too unwell to come out. I thought that was just an excuse, like you do. Then we ended up meeting halfway, in a TGI Friday, or whatever it's called, dreadful place, but it was empty when we met there. Which didn't really help. We had worked out it was halfway from his flat to where I lived, and we went for a walk with the dog afterwards. He did seem like he'd got a bit of a cold, but he always seemed like he'd got a bit of a cold, especially when he was taking cocaine. He just said he was a bit under the weather. Then in the John Lewis changing room I hear down the phone, 'Oh, by the way, it turns out I'm actually ill, seriously ill.' I said, 'Oh, what's the matter?' He said, 'Well, I have got a kidney disease.' I said, 'Oh God, what are they going to do then?' He said, 'They're going to take my kidney out. But don't worry, it will be fine.' He didn't tell me he'd got cancer; he said it was some problem and that he'll be fine, and I thought, He'll be fine. *I actually kept buying his stupid idea, I bought that. Eventually he told me he had kidney cancer, and I just burst into tears.*

Forty-Three: The Christie Hospital, the NHS and the rallying of friends

Dis aliter visum. (The Gods thought otherwise.)

2007 begins in the Christie Hospital, in Withington, one of the largest cancer centres in Europe, with a reputation for treatment world-firsts that Wilson as Manchester cheerleader was very aware of. The hospital is embedded in the vibrating, interconnected history of Manchester that Wilson relished. Sturdily set along the Wilmslow Road, which leads into Didsbury, centre of early Factory activity, it was founded using money left by Stockport-born engineer, inventor, philanthropist and entrepreneur Joseph Whitworth, who had helped with the manufacture of Charles Babbage's early-nineteenth-century mechanical calculator known as the difference engine, a mechanical calculator and precursor of the computer, and had helped found the Manchester School of Design. Whitworth died in 1887, leaving his fortune to the people of Manchester.

Wilson is eased into the hands, brains and no-fuss conscientious twenty-four-hour care of the NHS. One kidney is removed, a radical nephrectomy, an unwelcome new phrase for word-mad Tony to size up, a neat little scar the tattooed logo for his condition, and plans are made for fighting the remaining cancer. A very different kind of project . . .

Around this time I get in touch with Tony, to send him basic best wishes, sorry about the news, not imagining it was anywhere near as serious as it turned out to be, that his life was entering its final part. It didn't seem possible that Tony Wilson – all of *that* – was coming to an end. To me he issues a positive, soft-centred bulletin – he's entering another great adventure, all will be revealed, upwards and onwards, God bless. These are the last words he says to me, as they often had been at the end of a conversation over the phone, or at the end of a message he had left.

Mike Pickering calls and receives a more pissed-off assessment of his status. Buddhist and Catholic, life and death. Tony's In the City colleague

Rose Marley sends her love, and the reply is a jaunty 'Fuck off.' He hates how people are now being nice to him. He doesn't trust people being nice to him. Something must be up, for sure, it must be serious. He preferred it when people were insulting him to his face.

Immediately dealing with his new circumstances, this new rush of reality he needs to grab hold of and mould to his own resistant shape, he writes what he calls a love letter to the NHS for the *Manchester Evening News*. When in doubt, when faced with a problem, when needing to shift the balance of power back in his own direction, he loves to write a letter, with foot down on the Wilson pedal, an imaginary one-handed rolling of the spliff, the heading for the hills, on the hunt for a veil of illusion, the right thoughts to change the situation and win the day.

In his letter the NHS is a miracle, the doctors and nurses are agents of God, and Shakespeare is quoted, from *Much Ado About Nothing* – 'Converting all your sounds of woe into hey nonny nonny,' so dealing with the disaster with a what-the-heck – to 'the readiness is all' from *Hamlet*, the play about the meaning of existence forever buried in his consciousness, 'If it be not now, yet it will come,' Hamlet coming to an acceptance of his situation, where the best we can do is prepare for what comes next. 'I'll either live or die' becomes one of Wilson's mantras for his new circumstances, which have moved from Burroughs to Beckett. 'Either way I'll be fine.' There are parts of Wilson that refuse to fall away, even as there is less and less of the world, his world.

In early February he's told there's standard chemotherapy that he can have, which might help, which doesn't seem particularly hopeful, but there is also a more expensive, possibly more useful alternative called Sutent. It's not yet approved by the NHS in his district, so it would cost £3,600 for a six-week cycle, with Wilson needing the cycles to continue for as long as he lives. In other parts of the country the drug has been made available to patients, in one case in Cheshire, a few miles over the border from his local primary care trust, and Wilson finds himself suffering for being in the wrong part of the country. The great drug-taker, loving to experiment with new highs and certain refreshing lows, is denied the chance to try a new drug absolutely built for his urgent current needs.

In his frustrated, mordant *Evening News* love letter, mentioning someone paying for this treatment who had only recently made it public how much it was costing him to stay alive, he rages, on other people's behalf, against those who turn matters of life and death into bureaucratic procrastination. Here was the truth: Wilson, for all the front, designer appetites and first-class travel, was not a wealthy man, and even if his bestselling – and worst-selling – acts had felt that signing to Factory was not for all the benefits of their contracts a route to generously proportioned royalties, there had been no money siphoned off by him. Wherever the money went, it wasn't funnelled into any secret account of his.

Everyone was in the same usually sinking Factory boat. Once he stopped working, the money quickly dried up, and he was now forced to stop working. As an eminent northern socialist, not as part of some radical-chic pretence, he had always been against paying for private health insurance. He drily remarked that one of his favourite old quotes, about how he preferred to make history rather than money, was very funny until he couldn't afford to keep himself alive.

Friends, neighbours, colleagues, ex-Granada executives raised the cash to pay for some Sutent cycles in a desperate, loving attempt to extend his life. Elliot Rashman, who had made his money, a little guiltily, from Simply Red, almost the definitive, commercial, shiny anti-Factory band, immediately started a fund. 'I knew he was broke, even as he tried to bluff it. He was facing a huge VAT bill that year, he almost viewed it as a badge of honour. "It doesn't matter, it doesn't matter," he would mumble, as if he would find another way to duck and dive through it, but he was totally broke. I rang up Richard and Judy, said, "It's some awful postcode lottery thing. He has to pay for the drugs himself, he needs help, we have to raise some cash. I'll look after the music-business side if you do the television side; we can join forces." "Consider it done," they said.'

Richard and Judy

We phoned up everybody, every person we could think of that Tony had worked with, or knew, or respected. His old bosses at Granada, even the ones he might have had run-ins with. We said, 'It's not question of a tenner, we want big zeros on the end of your contribution, and we don't have long.' Some of them had a lot of money, some didn't have a lot, but everybody forked out. Every single phone call was either returned or they answered on the spot and pledged straight away, proper money. People were really wanting to help him. I remember hitting the phones and contacting everybody that we knew, that knew Tony. And there was never a 'Well, times are hard'; it was like 'Absolutely' straight away. It just showed how much love there was for Tony. Anyway, we paid for it, up to when it was clearly of no use any more. And the rest I think went to some charity.

Richard Madeley

I remember saying to him, 'Where's all your fucking money, man?' He said, 'I don't know, I've given up thinking about it.'

Richard and Judy

It kept him going a little longer and he really appreciated that there were all these people who cared.

Judy Finnigan

We cried when we got that call about how much he needed the drug. It was very upsetting. And then about two weeks later, after he had his first treatment and he called up, he was very . . . Do you remember? He called up and spoke to us both and wanted to say thank you. He'd never had to say thank you like that to us for anything before. He called up to thank us.

Richard Madeley

I remember it was quite a long conversation. I said, 'Well, how are you feeling?' He said, 'I feel like fucking death, mate, and so I've got to tell you, I think you're wasting your fucking money.' He wasn't bitter. He was just cutting through the bullshit.

He comes out of the Christie Hospital for a few weeks in May and June, a few awkward weeks with Izzy living in the loft he never managed to sell for a million pounds. Rapidly declining father, feeling guilty about the tumour, and angry, scared daughter warily coexist, but eventually he's bed-bound, increasingly trapped, and moves back into the Christie for full-time care, his final stop, a last home.

He's frustrated, furious, even ashamed that this most negative of conditions and words has got inside this most positive of humans.

Terry Christian

I was doing the breakfast show at Radio Manchester and I heard what was happening from various people. There were like monthly dinners with the senior citizens, the local treasures if you like – Bruce Mitchell, John Cooper Clarke, C. P. Lee. Tony would go, and you found out from them how ill he actually was. At first you just assumed it was something he would recover from. He would still come into Radio Manchester and do some things, walking that crazy fucking dog of his that Yvette had bought him so he would exercise. The idea of Tony of all people being ill was awkward, really, it wasn't right, but it cut through all that nonsense, all the arguments about music, about Manchester.

Alan Erasmus

I bumped into Lindsay, and she said, 'Tony really wants to see you.' It was before he was in the hospital full-time. 'Yeah, OK, I'll do it.' But I put it off. Then she called and 'He really would like to hear from you.' I said, 'Well, he's got my number.' Eventually, I did call him – he was back home – and I said, 'I'll come Sunday and bring bagels and papers.' So ten o'clock I hit the buzzer at his loft, and I went up through the entrance – you went into this long room – and at the other end of the big table there was this very frail-looking old man with a fucking beard. I thought,

536

Fucking hell. Tony with a beard. Things must be serious. *And there was a big hug and we talked, like we used to. He had stopped smoking dope.* 'You've stopped smoking as well!' *I couldn't believe it. Fucking hell, I never thought I would see the day . . . So I fucking rolled one. I thought,* Right he needs looking out for. He's not in a good way. *So that's what I did. And then I would go in some more and we'd talk every few days, and sometimes I'd go in with a newspaper, what-have-you. Just talking things through. Like we used to. We had a couple of ideas. Nothing was going to happen with them, but that was nothing new really. I like to be on the move, so maybe ten minutes and then I'd be off. More if he wanted.*

Lindsay Reade

Alan and Tony made friends again because of the cancer. Tony was absolutely overjoyed about it. He actually said it was worth getting cancer to get Alan back in his life.

Elliot Rashman

Alan said to him, 'I know you're not well, but I still think you are a conman.' Tony said, 'I'm sorry.'

Isabel Wilson

I remember sitting with my friends in a car, probably a couple of months before he died, being like, 'I don't know how to react to this because I hate him so much.' But now he's dying. Of course, I was an angsty teenager. But that's what I mean when I say my love solidified after he died. Because he had been such a twat in many ways, despite us having this epic father–daughter bond. So I avoided him for a long time when he was in at the Christie the first time. Oli went all the time. I avoided him like the plague. And I would go, and we would have nothing to talk about. Very awkward. I would just sit on the chair in his room. And then I'd get really drunk at night and leave him voicemails, like 'I don't want you to die!' and all that bollocks. And then he came out of the Christie and was at home. This must have been around June, or May/June, and my mum called me into the lounge and said, 'We decided it would be a good idea for you to go and live at your dad's.' And I thought, 'Oh fuck.' I used to hate staying at my dad's as a child. Used to have screaming temper tantrums. It didn't feel comfortable there, because we didn't spend that much time together. It felt very much like, um, a miserable place, or like, not home. So anyway, I moved in with him for I don't know how many weeks it was. He was trying to hobble with a stick, but he couldn't. And it was just me and him. I would empty the wee pots in the morning, go to school, come back, empty the wee pots in the evening, and like maybe make him dinner. And that was nice. That was a nice time. But it was awkward. We were both like, 'This is weird, because you are, you know, this big man in my life, but we're not close.' We are close, but we're not, you know? It was really complex.

Elliot Rashman

He was very dismissive of what he was going through, as a way of dealing with it. Moaning about what a fucking arsehole he was, because it had happened to him. I was always used to him keeping his self-doubt to himself, hiding whatever darkness there was, and he was trying to do it even then. The wives became a difficult thing, which was still concerning him right to the end, making sure at all costs the three of them were never in the room at the same time. One would leave, and then another would arrive. He had been living apart from Yvette for a while, what he called 'a modern relationship', but she was with him during the day and then she would go away at five o'clock and leave him, and Lindsay would step in – she cooked for him, and Hilary was cooking and sending food over and choosing her time to see him. Whatever she thought of Tony, her compassion trumped it. The three wives, Tony's women, in one door, out of another, missing each other by seconds, had a slight quality of a French farce. I think he quite enjoyed it, as long as there was no actual clash and the wives gathered in front of him.

Lindsay Reade

I think I fell in love with him again and I remember saying it to him – joking really – 'Will you marry me?' And he said, 'Well, we already did that, and look what happened.'

Alan Erasmus

He was always a very up person. He always tried not to let anything get him down. At the end, when the doctor would say, looking at him, reading his state of mind, 'I think this is depressing you,' he would say, 'I've never been depressed in my life.'

Isabel Wilson

It was really busy. His room in Christie's was lovely. He had his newspapers, he had his music, you know, I remember the sunlight, and there was everybody always coming in and out.

Alan Erasmus

He was having these tests at Christie's, and one day he called me with some news: 'Oh, the tumour's shrinking.' And I was shocked because I thought there was no chance of that happening. I thought, Well, no, you're in a bad way. I paused a little. Did he ever notice that fraction of a second when there was no response, because in my head Tony was dying because that was the only possible outcome? He knew I knew he knew. That was that. Perhaps he was trying to make me feel better as much as himself. He was always confident, full of himself, as far as he could be this close to the end. I think he was probably frightened then, though. Obviously, if you think you're going to die, that's going to make a difference, whoever you are.

Elliot Rashman

I said to him after the kidney was removed, taking on some of his positive attitude, 'You'll be fine.' 'I'm not out of the woods yet,' he said.

Lindsay Reade

He was very brave. I take it back about him being not brave, if I ever thought that, because he proved how brave he really was. There was no self-pity. He cried for his own demise, but he wasn't feeling sorry for himself. It's different, isn't it? I remember saying to him when he was in pain once, 'Have they given you anything?' 'Yes, I had a paracetamol.' 'Jesus, I take paracetamol for a headache, for Christ's sake.'

Isabel Wilson

In the hospice he said one openly nice, deep thing to me about our relationship. When he just had his shot of chemo and he was just starting to go into the shakes and the vomiting, he asked, 'Izzy, are you OK?' And I was just like . . . [silence]. And then he murmurs, 'The girl that always just doesn't say anything or smiles, even if she's really hurting inside.' That is the one deep thing he said to me about acknowledging my inner being and his inner being. But a week before he died, on 2 August my friend from school died in a car accident. And Dad was obviously in the Christie, in the last week of his life. And he sent me a text message saying, 'Darling, I'm so sorry for your tragedy.' And, um, ten capital 'X' kisses. The capital 'X' was always his way of saying, 'I love you.'

Alan Erasmus

I was upset with Factory disappearing because it was a very powerful platform. Maybe it was taken for granted – we've got this power, we can do things. We did things but never really knew what we could do. And it was only in the last week when I said, 'Do you realise the power we had, and we've lost?' And he looked at me and slowly nodded.

Terry Christian

The last time I spoke to him was about two weeks before he died. We had just published a book about The Word, *and he was in it, a not very flattering mention. I thought he would like it, though, and there was all this unbelievable behind-the-scenes production stuff which he always enjoyed. I said I'd send him a copy, and he said, 'Oh, I'd love to read it, darling.' I asked him how he was. 'Not so good, darling.' I sent it round to the hospital. I didn't go in. In the end I'm quite glad I didn't, because if he only had two weeks to live, I didn't want to take up some of his valuable time with my nonsense.*

Elliot Rashman

We talked about all sorts of things in those last weeks. I brought him a copy of the Bob Dylan documentary Don't Look Back, *for the Manchester connection. He seemed keen to watch it. He had this big TV in his room, and he said to me, 'There's only one thing worth watching on TV. Do you know what it is?' I said, 'Al Jazeera?' He went, 'You got it.' He said, 'It's the only thing, it's the only place where you're going to hear the truth.' He was still just taking it all in, still reading the world his way.*

Oliver Wilson

He said he was happy to die, that he'd done everything he wanted to with his life. Except for one thing, and it annoyed him that he'd only just started working on it – regional devolution. He said a revolution was coming, and it pissed him off he wouldn't be there.

Forty-Four: Do not be a magician – be magic!

Vocatus atque non vocatus, Deus aderit. (Called or not, God is present.)

There was one last night with Leonard Cohen. At their first meeting, an interview in 1973 for 'What's On', Cohen had taken an instant liking to the brisk, savvy and unexpectedly entertaining Tony, an unusual hybrid of passionate, sensual hippy and slick, professional newshound. When Cohen performed a new song, 'Chelsea Hotel', which he'd been working on since 1971, and which becomes 'Chelsea Hotel #2' on his 1974 album *New Skin for the Old Ceremony*, he kept Tony sitting next to him as he sang. He felt very comfortable with him. Because this was for television, he didn't deliver the line about getting head on an unmade bed, a reference to an adventure at the hotel with Janis Joplin he later admitted he regretted gossiping about through the song.

Leonard singing as Tony watches is an intimate moment, and the darkly gracious, radically self-questioning and spiritual existentialist Cohen becomes another teacher, planting some seeds of wisdom as both hedonist and Buddhist, and passing on to Tony his love for hotels as described in 'Chelsea Hotel'. He once said, 'I love hotels to which, at 4 a.m., you can bring along a midget, a bear and four ladies, drag them to your room and no one cares about it at all.'

At their next meeting, in a San Francisco bar, Wilson is impressed by how Cohen acts as they get drunk together and knock bottles and glasses over. Wilson is worried about causing a mess; Cohen doesn't give a damn. 'Leonard taught me not to give a fuck.' It reminded Wilson of when he once refused to get on a bus with his mum because she was wearing a mink coat and he thought they should be in a taxi. She said, 'Who cares what people think?' He was embarrassed, but deep down he knew she was completely correct. Never care what people think. The mink coat became his 1980s Japanese suits. The Royal Enfield motorcycle became his Jaguar.

He loved his mum. He loved life. His dad was something else. And he got to hang out with Leonard fucking Cohen.

Cohen and Wilson keep in touch over the next thirty-four years, and Tony comes to consider him an old friend. One of Tony's last appearances in public is at the Richard Goodall Gallery in Manchester for an exhibition of Cohen's art. Cohen is in town to perform and takes the opportunity to visit the gallery. A few months earlier, when the gravity of the situation was still a little more abstract, and there was more body to his body, and life in his life, Tony had written how he hoped he could get a message to Cohen asking him to dedicate 'Sisters of Mercy' to 'the wonderful people on Ward 7 who looked after me so well'.

A month before his death, looking pale, fragile and withdrawn, death visibly taking control, he needs to sit down before he speaks to preserve some last precious energy; Wilson, generous as ever, could still muster up the old flair to deliver a welcoming speech for Cohen. He seems very happy to be saying thank you to one of his great mentors and getting a last chance to regale an audience. Even this close to death, an audience helps him come alive. One or two present, not realising how close the haggard, unstable Tony is to death, imagine he must have been out the night before with Shaun Ryder.

This time it's Cohen who is close to Wilson as he performs, smiling as Tony refers to him as 'my hero' and characteristically goes over the top to explain why. He mentions how when Cohen sang 'Chelsea Hotel' for him, he was disappointed that Cohen didn't include the line about getting head. This upsets those old-time fans who are not sure who Wilson is, and don't know how ill he is: mentioning a controversial line from another lifetime, when Cohen was perceived as being less sanctified. Tony is being Wilson – swearing and cheerleading, glorifying and idealising, being careful and careless all at the same time about what he's pretending to be – to the bitter end, before his soul crosses over.

Cohen thanked him for his kind words and, chuckling, wished he were the man Wilson described – he sounded like he'd had a lot of fun. A weakened, exhausted Tony left early, disappearing into the streets of the city he had help build and become part of, going home without his costume.

As Tony, on the arm of his son Oli, slowly, painfully made his way out of the gallery, aching in the places where he used to play, Cohen – who had written radiant songs for forty years, often about strangers who turned out to be death, his recent ones boldly facing up to finality, prepare to die, the dice are loaded, the end is coming, nothing left to do, be not afraid – put his hands together and gave him a respectful final bow.

Forty-Five: The final campaign, the final documentary, the final interview

Mors certa, hora incerta. (Death is certain, the hour is not certain.)

He still does some television interviews in the last months: with his old *Granada Reports* colleague Gordon Burns, focusing on the tantalising closeness of a drug that could prolong his life; for a Chris Rodley BBC4 Factory Records rock documentary simplification of his life's work. He has scores to settle and grand claims to confirm when talking to Jon Savage for the Grant Gee *Joy Division* documentary film, filled with ghosts of landscape, people, music, where the now middle-aged participants wonder about the distant, unreliable past, everything and everyone held together by the conversational sure touch and roaming historian instincts of Wilson. He's the head of the family and somehow also the estate manager, issuing some last instructions, some final judgements. It's almost his way of doing 'My Way' – to talk about what was, and still is, and make all those connections that did and didn't exist, and through it all I took the blows, to a dramatic, defiant climax.

Jon Savage

That was the last time I saw him, to do the interview with him for the Joy Division *film. It was very weird. I knew he was ill, and just before we met I'd gone flying headlong in the car park underneath the hotel. I nearly broke both my wrists, my hands were bloody, so it was like I had stigmata, and I was hiding them behind my back and hurting like fuck. Anyway, we did the interview – it's a very good interview – and he said at the end, 'That was a really good interview, Jon,' and I thanked him. That's really great because he was a television professional, and I was really pleased about that. The pain was worth it.*

Oli discovers to his surprise that with his dad barely able to get out of bed, needing a walking stick to take a few steps before he runs out of breath, he has arranged an interview at the Sky News studios to talk about the NHS and Sutent. He's still campaigning, and he's so close to death. Oli watches him struggle for ages into his signature Wilson suit and then takes him to the studio, helps him to the chair and marvels, a little unnerved, as his dad once on air becomes rock solid, staring so strongly into the camera as if there is nothing at all wrong with him. Afterwards he can barely move.

The gregarious, persuasive loudmouth is shrinking by the week but carrying on as though, well, there's a lot to get off his chest, a lot of yesterdays to make sense of, and there's still a lot on his mind, injustices to rave on about, heroes to praise. The imagination isn't shrinking. If anything, it's getting more florid, ready to make its acquaintance with what lies beyond, which one way or another is going to be nothing like being alive in this world.

In his last appearances before a camera, he clings on to his image, the Factory man, the international Mancunian, the audacious storyteller, the reporter making up news where he is often in the headlines. There's the adrenalised sense that this is how it is, because he has thought long and hard about it, or just made something up, but it's all making perfect sense, it's all going according to plan, but the expensive suits overwhelm his fragile frame, the old forceful certainty is being chipped away, the dishevelled grace is drifting into unfamiliar gauntness.

He won't shut up until he has to shut up, wooed speechless, made silent because he hasn't the power to speak any more. The spirited monologues shrink as his body does, and then before you know it, no more valiant one-liners are issued for his own benefit as much as anyone else's. In his last days he retreats into the inner recesses of the mind, from which there is no way out.

O God save me from myself, he thinks, wearing a mask of Samuel Coleridge, lying penniless in a sweat-soaked bed in 1813, his literary career and private life in a shambles.

Forty-Six: Mr Manchester and Mr Manchester, waiting for Godot

Plaudite, amici, comedia finita est. (Applaud, my friends, the comedy is over.)

Bruce Mitchell was consistently on guard during the final weeks. Here was another busy, buoyant man-about-Manchester, another unofficial senior adviser who paved the way for Tony to become a Mr Manchester, starting out in the clubs and jazz bands of 1950s Manchester, experiencing the city's underground '60s scene, one-time drummer with tart parodists Alberto y Lost Trios Paranoias, slipping as easily as John Cooper Clarke via Rabid Records into punk and post-punk territories, becoming loyal, caring sidekick to Vini Reilly in Durutti Column, driving the van, setting up the equipment, drumming between the lines, between the whispers, offering movement and stasis and chipper northern swing.

To some extent, Durutti Column settle down as an abstract trio, three brothers connected by an aura, featuring Reilly's guitar, painting paradise, Mitchell's drumming, tense with time, and Wilson's curation, somewhere between spiritual and lordly. Sometimes patron Wilson would stand behind Vini in the studio as he searched for the right chord, the right space between notes, and suggest something, like he was standing behind Van Gogh recommending – sometimes demanding – a certain colour, a specific shade.

Bruce Mitchell

He came round on Christmas Day to deliver presents, like he always did. He'd come to us, and then he'd go somewhere else, another house, and then another. It was absolute chaos in our house, lots of family noise, complete Christmas turmoil. He sits down on the settee and he just says, out of nowhere, 'I'm going to die.' I said, 'Wow, Tony, thanks for spoiling Christmas dinner.' We had a laugh about that, as much as you could. What else could you do?

Bruce, south Manchester through and through, had become friends with Wilson as soon as he got back from the South, in 1974. He'd lived and worked with Martin Hannett, played drums in the band at Tony's wedding to Lindsay.

Bruce Mitchell

That all kicked off, of course. What do you expect? Nothing was normal in his world, even a wedding. He was fantastic company from the very beginning. He knew everything in the world, and if he didn't, he made out that he did. You couldn't really argue with him, even if you were right. If you did, he would say, 'You're interfering with a philosopher.' He supported the Albertos when few others did, loved our craziest ideas. I worked for him non-stop over the years, as a production man, on practical things. If I wasn't playing music, just to be involved in music I'd gone into promotion and managing events. I facilitated things. If you needed a PA at a moment's notice, some lighting, the workers to put it all together, I was your man. I was in charge when he wanted some laser beams in Cannes during the Midem conference to shoot a message from a boat onto a building saying, 'From Manchester with Love, In the City, the best music conference in the world'. We both enjoyed being in the middle of it all, and I'd do whatever he wanted for a show or event, even if the last thing he'd asked me to had been a major disaster. I loved getting the call – 'Mr Mitchell, it's Mr Wilson' – because what happened next was always going to be something different. Sometimes he could turn into Tony Soprano, threaten you, but you'd do more for him, whatever the stress, for the adventure. He was like no one else, and he had ideas no one else did.

One day, in his room at the Christie, Tony's moaning that Izzy cannot find him a copy of the *New Yorker*, one of his pleasures. 'He was complaining that there had to be a bloody copy of the *New Yorker* somewhere in Manchester. "What kind of city is this?" I went out and got him his *New Yorker*, and that got him vibed up, with such a short time left. He got very enthusiastic about an article on Garibaldi. That really hooked him in.'

The Tim Parks *New Yorker* piece is one of the final things Tony reads — almost perfectly, about a revolutionary Roman patriot and propagandist with an uncompromising will to win; great popular hero of nineteenth-century Italian reunification, leader of the guerrilla redshirts, who spoke in a soft, seductive voice, his schemes, urban dreams and projects often insanely grand. Glory if you follow him, shame if you don't. Wilson reads about Garibaldi emphasising the social and moral teachings of Christ while rejecting the dogma and corruption of the Roman Catholic Church, an anti-cleric who also holds sophisticated ideas on social reform. In his last years in the 1860s and '70s, crippled by rheumatism, he describes himself as a socialist, but Karl Marx is not convinced that his true aim is the liberation of people rather than patriotic aggrandisement. Wilson is still arguing about this with Bruce, with whoever attends the club that has evolved inside Tony's room, even if he cannot lift himself off his back as he lies in bed.

He also reads *The Tibetan Book of Living and Dying*, which his Cambridge friend Patrick Gaffney had ghostwritten for the disgraced Sogyal Rinpoche, a meditation on death with advice about how to die well and incorporate death into life, and how the world can seem completely convincing until death upsets the illusion and kicks us out of our hiding place. He knew that Sogyal had been exposed as a bit of charlatan; he didn't know that Gaffney would eventually be reprimanded for knowing of his teacher's lust for pleasure. He feels this is the book that should be helping him, written for exactly this time, but at the worst point possible he's beginning to see through it.

As his world falls apart, some things still hold true and some things don't.

Bruce Mitchell

Once, I'd gone in because he wanted the lightbulbs changed in his room – they were too harsh – and some artwork came through for some detail of something he was working on with Saville for the Pennine Lancashire project. He said, 'You have to look at this, Bruce – it came through this morning.' He said it was so beautiful he wept. Even as he was dying he was touched and so enthusiastic about a design, writing, a piece of art. It was what he lived for.

Bruce needs to help Tony piss into his bedpan. As the task is completed, two old pals dealing with whatever life throws at you, Wilson remembers a conversation he had with Bruce thirty years before about Aleksandr Solzhenitsyn's story of survival in a Soviet labour camp, *One Day in the Life of Ivan Denisovich*, Denisovich holding on to his dignity while faced with relentless brutality and suffering. The book is an inventory of 'small victories' that keep him going, even content – stealing a bit of food, avoiding the cells, smuggling a blade, buying some tobacco, a day without a dark cloud. 'Small victories, Bruce,' sighs Tony as he settles down again, temporary emergency averted. 'Small victories.' He was about to leave the world in extraordinary circumstances, but you had to laugh. Bruce said goodbye, and it turned out to be their last goodbye.

Wearing a mask of Seneca the Younger, Stoic philosopher, statesman, dramatist, satirist, author of 'On the Shortness of Life' in AD 49, who felt that most people waste much of their life on meaningless pursuits, Tony thought, *Learning how to live takes a whole life and, which may surprise you, it takes a whole life to learn how to die.*

A couple of days later, Bruce is sitting by the sea in Llandudno getting some air when Yvette rings to tell him Tony has died. He feels a bit guilty that he's not there, but he's still on guard and starts ringing people himself to tell them the news. Quite a few people, many of the Manchester faithful, hear the news first from Bruce.

'He's gone, kid,' he says, time after time.

Forty-Seven: The final decision, the end of the argument

Finis coronat opus. (The end crowns the work.)

Neville Richards

I saw him a couple of days before he died. He was having trouble with The Tibetan Book of Living and Dying. *I think he wanted answers that were not there for him. He had accepted death, but he wanted to know specifically what was going to happen. He wanted some sort of plan, and in the end there wasn't one. I was up in the Lakes at the very end. I really wanted to hold his hand in those last moments.*

Oliver Wilson

The day before he died he suddenly said he needs to write something. It's the last thing he ever writes. It was a note, in barely legible writing, and it said, 'Sort out the season tickets.' We had three season tickets for Old Trafford, and they needed to be renewed that week. We'd had them fifteen years, and if we didn't renew them we would have lost them. And we're going, 'Fuck the season tickets, Dad, you're dying!' And my dad started to cry then, which I rarely ever saw. I remember there was once when he saw Russell Watson at the Bridgewater Hall, and another time was when he first saw Ronaldo play for United and he did something spectacular. 'That was beautiful,' he said. 'This guy is going to be world class.'

Alan Erasmus

That Friday, waking up exhausted, I put the phone on. There were loads of calls from Oliver. And I knew, Uh-oh, we're in trouble. *Where I live is two minutes' walk from Christie's. I shot round there straight away. It was one of those swallow-swooping, blue-sky mornings that would usually fill me with joy, but not today. And the registrar was there,* and they'd done various tests. And he said to Tony, 'You've had a heart attack. It's weakened your heart, and you've got . . . basically twenty-four hours at most. Do you want to be resuscitated?' He said no. Or the kids said no, maybe Hilary.

Hilary Wilson

They would have had to open him up when he had another attack, it would be really aggressive. I thought how weird that we'd been apart, we've had our ups and downs, and yet in the very end it was me that was asked, 'Do you want him to be resuscitated?' Even if he was, he might only have another three days, or even three hours, and it would have been really gruelling. It was up to the children. Whatever they said.

Alan Erasmus

The room felt very quiet when I walked in. I asked him what he wanted; he whispered, 'Beer, music.' I maybe got four beers, so he had a choice. There was a Dutch one and a Red Stripe maybe. A Guinness. He couldn't really sip them any more, so we dabbed them on his lips with cotton buds. We listened to favourite tracks by Dylan, Springsteen, Cohen to help him on his journey. He made a humorous comment about his support for the Palestinians, but by now he was speaking with great difficulty. I could barely hear what he was trying to say, so I gave him a pencil and some paper. He scrawled, 'Best friend, so, so sorry.' I told him, 'You were a very, very difficult bastard at times, Tony. Your pyrrhic stubbornness cost us dear, but what the fuck, it was all part of the leaving-the-twentieth-century spectacle.' We grinned. 'Love you, mate.' People came, and one last time went. Father Clinch arrived to give Tony his last rites. We were left alone; Oliver and Isabel were in the corridor, Tony had asked for the ex-wives not to be there when it happened. Yvette was apparently on the phone to her boyfriend. He wanted to write, but his strength had now gone, he couldn't grip the pencil. He tried to speak, but his voice had now reached the edge of silence. Tony placed his hands together, Pope-like, and slowly gestured towards me. I was puzzled: 'You want me to pray for you?' He slowly shook his head, no, no. 'Namaste?' He shook his head, no, no, no. As he gently waved his hands, I understood. Thank you. He smiled. Last words.

I called Hooky and Bernard and Stephen and Gillian. I don't think I called anyone else; I may have done.

So me next. Well, they're all gone, aren't they? Martin, Rob, Tony.

Isabel Wilson

And that day that he died, the whole family room was full. Me, Oli, some of the wives – God knows which ones – Vinnie, Erasmus, Bruce. It was a hub of activity for sure.

Oliver Wilson

He asked me to fetch Dennis Clinch from the Hidden Gem. It was such a bizarre experience, on the day of my dad dying, to be driving down Princess Road with a canon in full dress and headgear in the passenger seat of my little car. I am not sure what they spoke about.

Elliot Rashman

He was going to go out swinging as much as he could. And he taught me how to die poor. More than anything else in life, he taught me that. Which is a fearful thing, and somehow it gave me great heart, because I would not go with such calm – not that I would not have expected it for Tony, but he showed a courage that was monumental. I think I'm going to be dragged out kicking and screaming, but he kept this incredible dignity right until the end, and I loved that. That was Tony, behind all the, you know, the Tony-ness.

We were asked to leave the room. Tony was having trouble. His heart. It was fucked up. He'd been having these TIAs, mini-strokes, and he was getting weaker. All I could say to him was, 'You're immortal, Tony, you're immortal.' He was dead an hour later.

Richard Madeley

*He was incredibly brave. Whatever flakiness people might have
previously thought there was combined with all that apparent pretence
and pretentiousness was of course not who he really was. I think
the making of a man in a way is how he dies, and he died in a most
extraordinary way, surrounded by friends as well as family to the last
moments. And right to the end he never lost his sense of humour.*

Lindsay Reade

*Whatever else he was, at the end he was certainly not cowardly. The last
conversation we had he asked me, 'What about God?' I didn't believe,
he didn't believe, but he said, 'Well, I can't simply have come from a
combination of basic elements. Maybe there is something else there.'*

Vini Reilly

*I wasn't told how ill he was immediately. People were very protective of
me and they were worried how I was going to take it. I can't remember
who told me. It was probably Bruce. I went to see him a lot in those last
days. 'Readiness is all,' he would say. 'The readiness is all.' I was there on
the day he died. I leant over and kissed him, told him I loved him. His
eyes were closed, and he couldn't speak. He managed to open his eyes
and give me a peace sign.*

Dave Haslam

Being Tony, he still held a grudge against me for that Face *article – he
still blamed me for that loss of control – but for some reason his lawyer
rang me from his room at Christie's when I was about to go on air
with my live Manchester XFM radio show. He said, 'Tony's having his
last rites read; I just thought you should know.' I told someone in the
office, and they asked, 'What does that mean?' I said, 'It means he's
going to die very soon.' I said to my producer, 'If it does happen, I hope
you don't mind if I play some appropriate Factory music.' Half an hour
later, someone calls to tell me he has died. It was a very strange feeling,*

but I wanted to play some of the records he was involved in. And then of course I discovered that the XFM playlist computer had 900 Kaiser Chiefs tracks but nothing by Section 25 or Durutti Column. I ended up playing 'Atmosphere' three times.

Isabel Wilson

I remember feeling an immense sadness. Not that my dad had died and I would no longer see him, but that I knew that he really wasn't ready to die. He was not ready to stop living. And that really stuck with me for a long time.

Oliver Wilson

The one thing that my dad promised me, made me promise on his deathbed, the only thing was to not do cocaine. He made me promise never to do that, and it's funny that he did that at the end of his life, when he probably spent years doing it. He couldn't stop himself, but he wanted to stop me.

Isabel Wilson

I remember for my A levels originally I had chosen Latin, geography, history – you know, stuff that wasn't science – and then he died, and I had to make some sort of decision about what I wanted to do. On the final day of the Cambridge applications, I hadn't put one in because I was really . . . although I was getting great marks, I was really naughty. Loads of the teachers at school said, 'You know, you're not Cambridge material.' And I was always like, 'Fuck you.' But I didn't apply. And it was the final day of applications, and I remember thinking, What the fuck? Dad, what should I do? *And I had always considered being a doctor, but his unbelievable respect for the NHS throughout his cancer care I think forced my hand a little bit. Definitely. I applied to Cambridge on the day before it closed, in like a* Fuck, what am I doing? Fuck you, Withington Girls' School. I'm going to try anyway. *And it was nothing to do with the media or music. I'm so glad I've done what I did. I see it as the safe option* to be a doctor and do medicine. To do all these really hard exams. I see it as the easier route. It's safe for me, compared to my upbringing, which was so mad and so complicated. Medicine is so straightforward, it cannot be mad and unpredictable, you have the knowledge and the skills, and you go to work, and you help people. And that simple transaction of however many times you do it that day is so pure and beautiful and comfortable for me. I feel so enormously lucky that I can do it. And it's safe. I will have a monthly income for the rest of my life, you know. I just hated that Mum never knew where money was coming from, and Dad would be bankrupt. My God, no, I can't think of anything worse! I didn't want to have to worry about going bankrupt like my dad. I want a nice family, with two children, a nice house and a monthly income. He taught me that.

Just a nice story that someone wrote after he died on a Facebook tribute page, because above it all, Tony was a dad. She wrote, 'My daughter went to early-years nursery in Didsbury with Isabel. And one day Tony dropped Isabel off. She must've been about three. And she was screaming, screaming, screaming. Didn't want to go in. And he just, he very calmly just pushed her in. Let her go, even though she's screaming. Walked away, and ten minutes later came back and peered through the window just to check that she'd stopped crying.'

I lost the phone that had his final message on, the kisses, and that killed me. I still have a Dad box, you know. Because I was seventeen, and, you know, emo, blah, blah, blah. I've got a Dad box that's his handkerchief, his glasses, all pictures of me and him and also, you know, when Granada did a half-hour tribute with Lucy Meacock. And sometimes on his anniversary I'll watch that. My desire to say 'I love my dad' came after he died. And not because of what I've learnt after he died, which I never really knew, but because of my ability to talk about my childhood now. Because you have to go through those feelings and digest it all and figure out what the fuck happened. To be able to acknowledge that, yeah, of course I loved him.

I held his hand as he died. I was on one side, Oli was on the other. He panicked a bit, but I was quite calm for some reason. I don't know

why I didn't panic. I hadn't been to medical school yet. Yvette was there.
There was one last breath, and Yvette and I hugged, which was bizarre,
and then thirty seconds later, a last gasp. Then it was over. It was so
important to me that I was there.

So it goes.

Richard Madeley

It didn't seem real. I keep saying it, even years later: it doesn't seem
real. It seems like there's been this huge mistake. It's almost as if you
expect the phone to ring or there to be a knock on the door, and you
open it, and it's Tony breathlessly saying, 'Total fuck-up, mate, complete
misunderstanding. How long have you got? It'll take me an hour to
explain it, but I'm here, darling, it's fine. No, I'm not in Southern
Cemetery as folks say I am. You can't get rid of me that quickly.'
I'd done a eulogy at his funeral. I wanted to do my best and I felt
supremely unqualified to do any kind of justice to it. He was a towering
figure.

Richard Boon

I miss him. I miss his voice, his ideas. I miss arguing with him. I miss
how frustrating he could be. I miss the difference he made in a world
that often had a problem with difference. I miss not knowing what he'd
get up to next.

Andy Harries

I remember some time after I had left Granada – around 1989, 1990,
I don't remember exactly when – I was in LA hanging out in the film
business making documentaries, trying to make contacts. That week
the Happy Mondays were playing along Hollywood Boulevard at some
trendy sports bar. This was the Mondays' breakthrough gig in LA.
I realised Tony was going to be there and I got in touch. He said,
'Yeah, yeah, come down,' and he explained how to get there and what

to do when I got there. It was electric, a real sense of excitement, and people like Keanu Reeves were there. It was a big deal. On the stage at the back there was a huge banner hanging up and it said, 'From Manchester with Love'. I was so proud. I was moved to tears. I thought, He's fucking done it. He's brought Manchester into the heart of young, indifferent Los Angeles. Manchester now means something. I could remember how it all started really. How that journey began. It began because he was bored at Granada. He wanted more. He needed more. And he was never polite about it. He just never knew how to quit until he had no choice.

Forty-Eight: 'Ceremony', 'Atmosphere', 'Sketch for Summer', 'Bob's Yer Uncle', an Irish life and the designer gravestone

Sic itur ad astra. (Thus one journeys to the stars.)
VIRGIL

Bruce Mitchell stage-managed the funeral on 20 August – 'Four hundred seats. It was a sell-out' – a requiem Mass held at the city-centre Hidden Gem, St Mary's Roman Catholic Church, where his children had been baptised. The Hidden Gem was where he would go, alone, sometimes with his children, to continue one of his longest quests: for the something he could sense in music – in Vini's guitar-playing, the visions of Ian Curtis, in the voices of Leonard Cohen and Neil Young, the lettering of Peter Saville, which could be musical.

The service was conducted by Wilson's old philosophical sparring partner, Canon Dennis Clinch, who, he would say, had a better degree than him, 'but I was cleverer', arguing with him deep into the night about whether the imagination was a continuation of God's self-consciousness, the imagination therefore emerging from a divine cause. Coleridge, Wilson would say, saw imagination as a religious act of faith which empowers one to perceive and create symbols. Imagination governs the world! The canon kept his counsel.

The coffin bearing the plaque Fac 501 – the final Fac number – entered the church to 'Sketch for Summer' by the Durutti Column, the translucent one about the subtle interplay between conscious and subconscious, and exited to the Happy Mondays' 'Bob's Yer Uncle', the bawdy one about an orgy – the band had made lewd gestures to singer Rowetta when she was recording it. On the hearse a Fac 51 floral plaque for the Haçienda, a TV set made of flowers with the *So It Goes* logo.

Inside, among the hundreds, members of the Happy Mondays and New Order, local musicians from the Smiths, Elbow and Inspiral Carpets, TV presenters Terry Christian, John Robb, Bob Greaves and Lucy Meacock, politicians including Derek Hatton, leader of Manchester City Council Sir Richard Leese and lord mayor Glynn Evans. There are flowers from the *NME*, from thirty Liverpool musicians coordinated by Pete Wylie, the floral tribute mistakenly ordered so it is many times the size it should have been. 'It's what he would have wanted' was the only answer. (The same for the stealing of the church's visitors' book.) There are flowers from Sir Alex Ferguson and the staff and players of Manchester United, from the head of Oasis's record label Creation, Alan McGee. The seating was arranged so that the paths of the three wives didn't cross. 'Why should he give a fuck about that?' said Lindsay. 'It just doesn't matter when you are dead. He really didn't like scenes, I suppose, even the thought of them, although he created enough of them himself.'

'Atmosphere' is played in all its ridiculously appropriate heaviness and lightness, and one of the final songs Ian Curtis wrote before he died, New Order's 'Ceremony', both merging seamlessly into the hymns 'Hail Queen of Heaven' and 'To Be a Pilgrim'. As well as Richard Madeley standing up and celebrating Wilson's contribution, there is Peter Saville honouring his mentor. Saville also designed and delivered on time the order-of-service booklet. 'We shared the opinion,' said Saville, 'that time on earth is short and is not about making wealth but making a difference.'

There is for some a surprise face standing up as one of the main speakers to say goodbye, Wilson still revealing hidden parts of himself even as he seemed to have given everything away about his life through his words and actions. There was so much in his head, so many people he knew and who knew him, many of whom turned up to the funeral – all these names and faces and lives would take some keeping up with – and then there is a whole other world as well, an Irish connection that goes all the way back to Marple Bridge in 1958.

Sean Boylan Sr and his wife Gertie are slowly walking up the hill after attending church – they are visiting from Dunboyne, County Meath, looking for some help from healers for Sean's Parkinson's. A car stops to give them a lift – Doris Wilson and Sydney Russell in the front, eight-year-old

Tony in the back. The two couples immediately hit it off, and Doris and Sydney invite the Boylans round for a cup of tea. Sean turns out to have been a leader of the Irish independence movement in the early twentieth century, a leading member of the IRA in Meath from 1913, jailed in 1916, joining the Free State army in 1921.

They get on so well, the next year Tony travels over with his mum and dad to meet the whole family – including four sisters and an only son, Sean Jr, born a couple of months before Tony. He meets someone also destined to be a great yarn-spinner, also with a mind stuffed with ideas, plans and stories, and they become firm friends for the rest of Tony's life. A symbolic sibling for an only child.

Tony is there, a great help, when Sean Sr dies in 1971; ill since the 1920s after testing some ammunition and being given a year to live, he had turned to herbalism to control his failing health. Sean will continue the herbalist tradition with an alternative-medicine practice. He also goes on to have his own boisterous fame as a Gaelic football manager, winning an Alex Ferguson-quantity of trophies with Meath, whom he starts managing in 1982. In 2006 he manages the national team in an International Rules Series match against Australia and becomes the first freeman of the County of Meath.

He flies over from Belfast for Tony's wedding to Lindsay in 1977, when Belfast seemed part of a dangerous world, and he has to explain bringing his hurleys into the country – he's got a match back in Ireland the day after – the unfamiliar three-foot sticks looking as much like weapons as sports equipment. The wedding is as wild as he was hoping, this being Tony and whatever madwoman is prepared to have him. They are increasingly from very different worlds, but have become as close as brothers, swapping energy, releasing each other from their real lives into another sort of space, Tony finding in Ireland what he would call a second home, that peace of mind he was seeking when he slipped into the Hidden Gem as life skidded out of control. Perhaps, also, romance and girlfriends filled this other life, this alternative world, a whole separate sphere of adventure. Sean and Tony might not see each other for a while, their different lives flourishing in very different ways, but they were always keeping an eye on each other, looking after each other across the sea. Sometimes you just need to know that someone is there.

Tony's in Dunboyne when Sean's mother is dying in 1987, calling her Mammy, and he would visit when he can, attending Mass, sometimes bringing his children; Sean is a godfather to Oliver. He sees Tony in 2007 at an annual charity event that Sir Alex Ferguson hosts and is shocked by how weak he looks. It never occurred to him he wouldn't be celebrating with Tony fifty years of unflagging, wonderful friendship.

'My dad asked for Sean just before he stopped being communicative,' says Oli. 'I rang Sean from the nurses' station, and he starts making his way from Dunboyne. When I went back into Dad's room, I wasn't sure if he could hear me, but I whispered in his ear that Sean was coming. He hung on all afternoon.'

Izzy tells how Tony, almost gone, held on for Sean Boylan to arrive. 'Definitely, and I don't believe in all of that hocus-pocus, the life force, tying up loose ends, that family keep you hanging on, but I'm convinced he held on for sure. Once Sean had entered the room, he was dead within a few hours. He needed to see Sean to die in peace.'

Outside, there are hundreds more people, the coffin almost mobbed, Wilson as a Manchester Beatle, a beloved local hero, the funeral turning into a public event. There is no booing. He's not a twat today. The funeral procession drives to the Southern Cemetery on the Barlow Moor Road in Chorlton, downtown Wilsonland, three miles south of the city centre. It's the largest municipal cemetery in the country – what else for Wilson but the best, the biggest? It's where lie John Rylands of the library, Sir Matt Busby, supreme manager of Manchester United between 1945 and 1969, Salford artist L. S. Lowry, northern comic Wilfred Pickles, who during the Second World War was the first newsreader on the radio to speak with a regional accent to confuse the Nazis attempting to imitate BBC broadcasters, and a couple of fallen Factory comrades.

Wilson had wanted to be buried near Martin Hannett. Bruce took a photo of where Martin was buried and took it to show Tony. It wasn't a very attractive part of the cemetery, but Tony said he didn't care. He wants to be near Martin, a posthumous reunion. Bruce takes Oli to have a look at the plot, and Oli says, 'I don't care what my dad fucking said, I am not having him buried there.'

They wander around with two patient gravediggers, looking for a final resting place for Tony that Oli approves of. It's absolutely pissing down, and they walk round the vast graveyard for over an hour. They look for somewhere near Rob, because he's buried in the cemetery as well, but nothing works for Oli. Eventually the gravediggers ask, 'Shall we show you where we're buried?' – it turns out the gravediggers know and choose the best areas. Oli finds somewhere he likes.

For a while, after Tony is buried, there is a temporary gravestone while Peter Saville slowly progresses designing the sort of cool, elegant edifice Wilson would have wanted. Before he's done, working as usual to his own deadline, people leave things on the makeshift grave, including joints, and once a note on a piece of A4 paper inside a plastic sleeve: 'Can someone please get Alan Erasmus to ring this number urgently.' It was the only way they could get hold of him.

It was the first burial Saville had ever attended, and he was struck by how Tony, such a huge influence on his life, was now lying inside a coffin about to be lowered into the ground. He stares around the large, beautiful Southern Cemetery and wonders how he can design something that represents Tony's modernist spirit yet fits among all the traditional, ornate and largely Victorian stones nearby. The idea that it was for all eternity was a little disconcerting. 'It took a while at the beginning to imagine what it should be, but I didn't let the length of time it was taking intimidate me.'

Coming back a few hours after the burial ceremony for some peace and quiet, to contemplate the perfect headstone, he bumps into Alan Erasmus, also coming back for some quiet time, his own personal goodbye. It was the first time they had spoken for over twenty years. The Factory five, the original family, three permanently in the cemetery, two passing through, are together once more, a final meeting chaired by Tony as he gets used to his new position.

With the help of various collaborators, including Haçienda architect Ben Kelly, Saville eventually delivers the powerfully minimal five-foot-by-three headstone, its size determined by the grave's position in the cemetery. Resembling something discreetly monumental from a Kubrick film, it's made from polished black granite, mirroring the world around it as Tony reflected things around him, a solemn symbol of infinity, an entry to somewhere else, his Japanese suits turned to stone. The font Saville uses is called Rotis, which had been used for the final Factory logotype.

It's a definite ancestor of the second poster – black and white – Saville designed for Factory, and an object of art in the spirit of Factory, the imperishable positioning of the lettering enough to please Wilson for the rest of time. It's an object from a Bauhaus graveyard, from a remote, surreal spot around the back of an exquisitely designed boutique hotel, where even after you are buried you can still order room service or put a call in to a coffin nearby and find yourself discussing with Nietzsche whether a morality of equality – and altruism – is an obstacle to human excellence, or ask George Best what the greatest goal he ever scored was. Tony can put in a call to Martin and Rob, skin up, talk about this and argue about that, make plans for whatever, deep into the long, untouchable night.

At the foot of the stone there is a quote chosen by Tony's children from *The Manchester Man*, by Victorian novelist Isabella Varley Banks, in which she remembers the city before it had been modernised by railways, viaducts and roads, where her hero is rescued Moses-like on the banks of the Irwell, grows in power as the city does around him, and ends as an enlightened master.

Mutability is the epitaph of worlds
change alone is changeless
People drop out of the history of a life as of a land
though their work or their influence remains

Rose Marley

The In the City I ran seemed to go well – I'd somehow pulled it off – but it was incredibly stressful, and I really didn't want to do another one. I had my own work to do, and it wasn't as though I had made any money. I was pregnant, my husband Lee's parents had died, I didn't want to take it on. I met Tony and Yvette at the Fat Cat on Deansgate Locks with the sole intention of telling Tony that under no circumstances was I going to do it again that year. My husband Lee had said, 'Please don't do it – it will all fall on you again.' Tony wouldn't accept it of course, but eventually he could see I wasn't going to change my mind. He went to the bar to get another round. Yvette said to me, 'Don't let him get to you.' I wasn't going to! He came back and he said, with that glint in his eyes, 'When you are doing your shitty job and you've got a shitty life and you realise that working with me was all you ever lived for and you come back to me humbly, and I do mean humbly, I might let you work for me for free in the evenings.'

After he died I helped put on a festival celebrating Tony with Jane Lemon – The Tony Wilson Experience – and I did it for free and spent most of my time working on it at night. Where I live overlooks the Southern Cemetery, and I could see the place where Tony's grave was. And as I was stressing out doing something for Tony for free yet again, I thought, Well, Tony, you have had the last laugh. Here I am working for you for free in the evenings.

So it goes.

Forty-Nine: How do you remember Tony Wilson? and other questions on live television

Omnia causa fiunt. (Everything happens for a reason.)

Tony Wilson the local hero, who can also be described as:
- negotiating in long swooping black coat with a wild-eyed Martin Hannett, who is producing the first Happy Mondays album at the nicely named Slaughterhouse Studios and holding the stoned and petrified band hostage with a loaded gun. In one hand the revolver, in the other a bottle of brandy. 'No one gets out of here alive,' he shouts, wearing a mask of Jim Morrison. This is how far pop music has travelled since George Martin produced *Revolver* for the Beatles. Hannett explains he isn't convinced by the band's music. Wilson doesn't care about that; it isn't his job to like them, just make them sound good. As though the whole situation is just one of those things, Wilson says he feels it would be better if Martin put the gun down. Eventually, after much grumbling, Hannett follows orders. Wilson tells Hannett, 'You are a fucking genius, but you need some sleep.' The band are released. Hannett calls out to Tony and fires a shot at his head, missing by inches as Tony dives behind a chair. He quietly brushes himself down. 'Very funny, Martin, now will you fuck off home?' All in a day's work
- and when things got tough when things were difficult, and everyone was flummoxed, he would say if life wasn't fucking complicated, it wouldn't be fucking life
- described in the *New York Times* in 2017 as representing the rarefied, down-to-earth soul of the city, after it is savagely turned upon by a ruined, ruinous and murderous local lad with confused, corrupted roots in Libya
- and finally . . .
- bored to death with books and films and anniversaries about Factory Records and Manchester and Tony Wilson

- getting the kind of attention celebrities can get after they've died
- spending a life borrowing against a future
- having risked his life in the name of making things happen
- because we all die, and the goal isn't to live for ever but to create something that will
- passing away on 10 August, the day a small earthquake strikes Manchester, measuring 2.5 on the Richter scale, noticeably shaking windows and doors in Stockport and Didsbury
- dead

After he died, within hours, it seemed like minutes, I was inevitably called onto live television – his element, the media man being honoured by the media – hoping I could do him, and all the insides and outsides of his being, the good things and bad things, which is what made him such a compelling figure, some kind of justice. I ended up in this position because whatever else I did or wrote or became, it was my job to write and talk about Tony Wilson; he had made sure of that.

Because I became, not least because of Wilson's abstract goading and remote guiding, a critic on the BBC2 arts review programme *Newsnight Review*, I hear of his death from the *Newsnight* presenter Kirsty Wark, who wants to discuss Tony's life on that night's show. As a performer, a grand host of random special occasions, an unusual occupation I had never thought of pursuing, he loomed above me, and I felt this whenever I was persuaded to step into his shoes. I'm not built to be like him, to hold so much in my head, and know so many people, and know so much, to put so many things together, to fail so dramatically, but there has always been part of me that wants to try and keep up, to try and match him, perhaps if only to understand what it was that made him so different and, damn him, so special.

That night there is an awkward squad gathered live on *Newsnight* in its London studios to talk about Tony – Richard Madeley, Peter Saville – and, beamed in from the North, Stephen Morris of New Order, with faces that still imagine that this might be some sort of wind-up, some bizarre rehearsal for when we really must face up to the idea that, as characters like Wilson exit stage left, we have reached the end of an era. But surely not yet, not for a decade or two.

Early next morning I appear on BBC *Breakfast* wearing my silver trainers – at fifty – for the carefree glamour of Tony, the flair and swagger, deciding at the last minute not to wear some Comme des Garçons because it might look like I am wearing mourning clothes. 'Ooh, nice trainers,' remarks presenter Bill Turnbull, with his own layer of camp sneaking through the formal suit and tie, reminding me that most BBC television presenters have absorbed large or small traces of the eccentric, playful Wilson presence, the great broadcasting shadow player. I have my script ready in my mind, sinking into the inevitability of my role, that here I am live on BBC1 talking about Wilson as though I have just left my small bedroom in Stockport having just received my first phone call from him, as though he has flattered me onto his team, into his plans, his history, into eventually writing his biography. I only have about three minutes, and somehow I am meant to introduce someone the majority of the BBC1 audience, especially those outside the North-West, know little about. This remembering of television's Tony Wilson is the media acknowledging one of its own.

Somehow, in a matter of seconds, I want to get across as much as I can about the mad, packed life of Wilson – to hint, in three minutes, on live television, that when it came to Wilson, anything was possible. I don't get to say a small fraction of what's on my mind, but hopefully the look in my eyes suggests that the following is what I really want to say about some things that haven't even happened yet, what I think thirteen years later, before Bill shuts me up and hands over to the weather:

Wilson was about fifteen people in one and each of those fifteen contained their own dazzling contradictions, secrets and peculiarities, and each one had a tremendous thick-skinned capacity for disturbing the peace.

He had a relish for revolutionary, insurgent figures and philosophers – the true legislators of the world – who gave history the kind of glamour the great rock stars would steal from, so that for him it wasn't much of a move from Spinoza to Springsteen, from 'because to understand is to be free' to 'baby, we were born to run'. He also didn't think there was too much distance between Percy Bysshe Shelley arguing that civilisation advances and thrives because of poetry and Shaun Ryder mouthing off for the joking heck of it.

Manchester has been remade since the angry, agitated 1970s, a transformation transmitted through songs, entertainment, typography, fashion, buildings, films, clubs, trends, blogs, theatre, TV, sport, football, comedy, books, arts festivals – many of these things inspired, promoted or adopted by this voracious hunter of experience. The city by the 2010s was being awarded so many grants and becoming the potential recipient of so much government investment there were those who suggested this was a Conservative plot to distract attention away from the general North–South imbalance and the fact that power still resides in London and get less-favoured regions in the North to gang up on Manchester. The city is becoming to the rest of the North what London and the South has traditionally been to the North: the South of the North, richer and more funded, its skyline rapidly changing, other northern cities and areas shrinking beneath its weight. It's a little like how within the area of Manchester, stretching out into Greater Manchester, Factory – as eccentrically, self-destructively independent as it was – became an equivalent of the major labels it was set up to oppose, blocking the light at the time and also in the future. But the light that it blocked wouldn't have been there if it wasn't for the ruinous idealist energy of Factory.

A city needs such a believer, a totally convinced advocate, in what in the end is a worldwide battle between cities for all sorts of resources and attention, and a battle between cities as targets of fundamentalist spoilsports, of jealous jihadists, or those who deplore cities as the emblem of diversity, of freedom of movement. Then there's the new competitive pressure coming from the elite multimedia virtual meta-cities of Apple, Amazon, Facebook, YouTube, Netflix, Twitter, Snapchat, Instagram and Google – cities as digital code and information, cities issuing orders and taking control, monopolising attention, leisure, reality, attention, what have you got, what do you need? Even now he's not here, Manchester spirals out from his sense of audacity, his crusade to place it with Berlin and Barcelona, Los Angeles and Lagos, a distinct state of mind that travels the world and brings the world to it.

Somehow, as he made himself known, the city came with him, with a lucid soundtrack of intelligent, swaggering pop the world would recognise. It would have been something without him, with a lively, non-stop music scene not necessarily needing his busybody antics, but his priceless determination, his show-off skill as TV celebrity and the Factory Records syndicate built in his improvising, impulsive image, run as a business with the logic of a poet, gave the city's reputation a wider focus.

The giddy, ambitious bid for the 2000 Olympics, the post-IRA-bombing regeneration of the city centre and its surroundings, long-abandoned mills transformed into city-centre canal-side apartments, an invasion of hotels ranging from the boutique to international chains, the hosting of the 2002 Commonwealth Games, the international arts festivals, the spontaneous, articulate community pride of a city that's been offensively violated: all seemed refracted through his presence, once easily tabloid-reduced into the farcical Mr Madchester and abbreviated near-affectionately as 'twat' or 'prat' as polite euphemisms for 'cunt' or 'wanker' on the *24 Hour Party People* poster. Perhaps the only character ever to feature in movie marketing for a film that celebrates, or caricatures, his life who is labelled so bluntly.

The modernising of a deindustrialised Manchester so that it competes in the twenty-first century as a cosmopolitan, multicultural 'global player' with Paris, Stockholm, Munich, Amsterdam, Madrid, Vienna, Prague and Milan, vigorous and central enough to be a terrorist's target, is not directly rooted in the mouth and mind of Wilson and the laws of cool he helped establish, except as a symbol, a mascot, of a perceived hipness. But the atmosphere and reputation of the city as a place people travel to are connected to theories he had about the relationship between popular culture and the image and identity of a city, and to how he put these theories into practice, with, among other things, the Haçienda influencing the style of the modernisation to come, and the making of a new kind of factory for creative production in what had been in the nineteenth century the city of factories. The nineteenth-century idea of a factory manufacturing goods is replaced by the twentieth-century idea of the Factory manufacturing culture; textiles replaced by mythos.

The active strategy developed by Manchester City Council to promote city-centre living was connected to Wilson's creativity script – a place people wanted to escape from must become a place people want to go to. In 1982, when the Haçienda opened, less than a thousand people lived in the city centre; by the time Tony Wilson died, over 15,000 people lived there. Within years, there would be thousands more, as the Northern Quarter pushed out east through a once-emptied, ruined Ancoats, beyond the inner ring road, which once seemed the end of the world of Manchester, all the way to Manchester City's Etihad Stadium, one of the world's great modern football teams opening out the city to the world. He believed such a thing should happen, even if he didn't have a say or even agreed with how it did.

And Factory was an influence on the changing shape of Manchester. Factory was a record label, a numbered list of things to do, think and be, a flawed system madly slammed into bankruptcy and failure, but it was also a fantastic blueprint for the idea of generating personal and artistic freedom in a world where there are many often sinister forces, systems, networks and viruses trying to remove it.

Factory, filtered through the Dylanised, punked, Marxist desires of Wilson and his unstable ersatz business partners, is the missing link between the whimsical, utopian free-thinking Apple of the Beatles and the enigmatic, controlling, persuasive Apple founded by Steve Jobs. Wilson, arrogant and bullying mix of art groupie and commodity fetishist, conjurer and conman, collaborator and individualist, was as much a North-West Jobs as he was a McLaren, a McLuhan, a Letterman, a Zappa.

He has become a great twentieth-century northern figure who left his mark, part of the map of the place, named and famed in Manchester's very institutional fabric, a post-modern update of the northern industrialist who left behind buildings, communities, museums, libraries, all those great homes of learning and discovery that Wilson loved.

There might well be an arts centre called The Factory built on the site of the old Granada studios, a well-intentioned, explicit tribute to the talents of Wilson the great broadcaster and Wilson the well-publicised player, doer and maker. There is a Tony Wilson Place, featuring a statue of Engels, another great son of Salford, underneath the railway viaduct that held above street level the railway line out of Oxford Road station heading into Lancashire, just opposite where the Haçienda used to be, near where he lived in what he called the city's first loft apartment, if only so he could sell it for a million pounds, to be the first million-pound home in central Manchester, and of course to pay a tax bill.

Tucked-away Tony Wilson Place by the Home cinema and arts centre is a nice permanent reminder, but it's not in his cryptic, cantankerous, bloody-minded spirit; it's the decoration, not the provocation, running in parallel with how sublime Joy Division songs become football chants, are played over the credits of *Come Dine with Me*, are reduced to adding wafting soundtrack glitter to *Love Island*, and bass player Peter Hook tours the world in a sort of post-punk end-of-the-pier Joy Division tribute act, draining the music of its original astonishing, mysterious suddenness for the sake of a night out, a sentimental nostalgic kick. Phantom pop turned into panto pop. Pop slipping across four decades from when it was treated as a matter of life or death to being treated as just a matter of playlists and parties.

The Wilson being memorialised in the city as one of its salt-of-the-earth great and good is not really the Wilson who changed the city. It is one of the many Wilsons, the more traceable, palatable one who was quite capable of appearing well behaved and sensible, but it removes the less knowable erratic loudmouth, the irrational opinion-former, the moody dogmatist, the insulting, insinuating controversialist, the unlikely spirit guide, the deviant comedian, the haywire professional, the first adopter of trends, the early embracer of new technology, falling fast for the latest urban theory, most of all the slippery, confounding and outrageous intellectual. The outrage and unpredictable, unclassifiable energy threaten to be buried under mundane memorialising as sanctioned by dull men in ill-fitting suits.

Yes, history inevitably forms in this careful, edited way, smoothed out and accessible to all, but what should come with the consolidation – the bland hipster texture, the insipid Haçienda nostalgia, the New Order cushion covers, Joy Division designer tables and £500 *Unknown Pleasures* hoodies, transgressive energy processed into branded muzak, illegal highs paved over, the mainstream manifestation of Manchester the renowned international city with a distinct soundtrack – is the mercurial, obnoxious, fanciful Wilson, the one that could never be pinned down, and certainly shouldn't be by simply naming a road after him, which somehow remembers him by forgetting him, fixing him slightly off the main map.

Wilson believed that worlds need to exist outside artificial, corporate, commercial, governmental culture, and the need for those worlds is even more necessary now that this culture slickly, emptily absorbs the once avant-garde and the cool, which therefore become the new conformity, the new orthodoxy. Yesterday's revolution is today's Establishment and corporate deception.

Manchester is getting richer, becoming increasingly international, a leading candidate for capital of a nation being left behind by the monstrous, mutating megacity of London as it floats outside the UK, and Wilson is a great figurehead for those keen on creating the cosmetically maverick, enterprising brand that goes with this new modern city. Roads named after him and arts centres honouring his impact at least offer some acknowledgement that the city thrives because of how Wilson and his Factory gang created fantasies in order to rearrange reality, producing a series of events and ceremonies, however obscure or arcane, that altered the innate texture of the city. But they can't acknowledge the generous, anarchic spirit that idealistically pursued the notion of art and music as a way of outmanoeuvring political and commercial interference, of negotiating a possible new reality; in some senses they bring it to a resolved, decorative halt, turning innovation and crazy thinking into the always suspect status quo. The honours on their own don't let Wilson haunt proceedings in his own image; they must come combined with other ways of representing in and beyond the city the grand, scheming, sceptical, never-satisfied romantic.

One friend of Tony's, Elliot Rashman, dreamt of a giant sculpted representation of Wilson in some form, an *Angel of the North*, a monumental megastructure that could be seen for miles around, from Wales, from the Pennines, from the peaks around Marple, from the edges of the imagination, taller than the towering, overhanging and overdetermined city-centre Beetham Tower that Manchester's council leader approved out of the blue, overruling his building department as though he had suddenly come over all 'the megastructure must be built' Wilson. The outside of a building, though, is never as important; even the most beautiful buildings need something fantastic happening inside.

A sublime giant Wilson rising above the nothing zone of Beetham, hands outstretched like a vivacious Mao Zedong, would stretch the city into an entirely new, fabulous shape, and counteract those simple-minded, standardised glass-and-metal skyscrapers and loft-lite apartments that reach into their own generic soullessness, would reject the numbing, reductive effect a terrorist attack can have on the reputation of a city, adding it to a spoiled, undermined list. That kind of wonderfully ridiculous statement gets to the heart of what the showboating, big-headed, sure-thing, weirdly literate, bragging mythic Manchester mind as excessively represented by Wilson actually is.

Or maybe the subject of 'Wilson' – a study of how things change, and how cities and people after all sorts of trauma are rebuilt as artwork as much as community, as conflicting states of mind – should be taught locally, and further afield, as a method of making sense of the world around us as it melts into another state altogether, which only the imagination at its most enterprising can ultimately deal with.

Perhaps all the mills and factories that have been turned into apartments and homes radiating out from restless inner Manchester along the once-defiled canals floating out into Cheshire and Lancashire are tributes to Wilson. Each new transformation of a once-abandoned vast red-brick building into a lived-in small village is a sculptural honouring of his life;

the buildings once left to drift for decades have unexpectedly turned up in the future, as living space, glass and metal, wooden floorboards replacing dismal flowery carpets, city homes built out of Factory's dreams, descendants of the Granada TV studios packed with modern art, of the Haçienda inserting modern architecture into the city through the back door.

What is modern, and post-modern, about the city is rooted in Wilson's haphazard civilian genius. You cannot pass by all those shiny new apartments lining once completely neglected canals now repurposed as picturesque, part of the city's attractive new ambience, without thinking of the Haçienda, which nearly forty years before brought canal-side continental architectural flair to Manchester, but within a few years as a character, a vivid presence, Wilson is already drifting back into the twentieth century. He is becoming a ghost from the previous century, like one of those great nineteenth-century industrialists whose name, outside of a street name, didn't really carry into the twentieth, even as Manchester would not be what it has become without the buildings he commissioned, the meetings he chaired, the disputes he generated, the minds he altered and the energy he for better or worse generously donated to the city.

A few weeks after he died, a large group of friends, colleagues, writers, musicians, collaborators, celebrities, interested parties and local entrepreneurs were gathered by the city council to work out how best to remember him and continue his work. The discussion petered out a little. No one managed to take charge of it and generate a plan, set out a direction, organise the troops in the way Tony Wilson would have if he had been there. The one person we really needed at such a meeting had gone missing. The thirty-odd Mancunians present could not replace him. Manchester was already a very different place without him.

Fifty: Freedom of the city and sundry other odes and honours

Non omnis moriar. (I shall not wholly die.)
HORACE

Tony Wilson was given the freedom of the City of Manchester a few months after he died, which wasn't usually allowed – the council twisting the rules slightly, coming up with a loophole, suggesting that they had already agreed to give him the honour while he was alive. Making something up, in the spirit of Wilson.

Between 1984 and Wilson's freedom in 2008, the only others to be given the city's freedom were Manchester United's Sir Bobby Charlton and Sir Alex Ferguson, and the Manchester-based Great Britain Olympic and Paralympic cycling teams, following their thirty-four medals at the 2008 Beijing Olympics. The inscription carved in marble at the Town Hall placed him next to Sir Alex Ferguson, who led United to thirteen Premier League titles, five FA Cup wins and two European Champions League titles. It was decided that Tony, United-mad since he was a kid, would have loved being next to one of his heroes.

Other previous recipients include Enriqueta Augustina Rylands, founder of the John Rylands Library, C. P. Scott, editor of the *Manchester Guardian*, Sir Matt Busby, who survived the Munich air disaster and then rebuilt United as European champions, and radio astronomer and physicist Bernard Lovell, designer and first director of the Jodrell Bank Observatory near Holmes Chapel in Cheshire, twenty-five miles from Manchester, originally intended to be located along Oxford Road in the city centre before electrical interference from trams forced him to look elsewhere.

The city changes, once it has brutally, definitely become all twenty-first-century, ten years after the very twentieth-century Tony Wilson dies, finally shaking off the previous century with the kind of violence it often needs to escape the past and establish its role in a wider history. You can see how much the city changes, and why, because it is suggested that Ariana Grande, an American entertainer performing at the Manchester Arena when it is attacked by someone committed to denying everything, be given the freedom of the city as a symbol of its defiance of that radical denial.

People coming from outside, to live, play, study, sing, plot, visit, always make a difference, from the nuclear physicist and the football manager to the pop singer and the extremist. It's a very different Manchester once the Arena has been bombed to the one desired, and abstractly designed, by Wilson in the last three decades of the twentieth century. It wouldn't be the Manchester it is without him, but it's becoming something outside his interests, other factors taking over. Some of us might lament that this newer Manchester lacks the crazy, wayward romantic, the arrogant, annoying smart-arse battering through all the respectful routines.

Some disciples of the diligently contrary Wilson make sure he is not erased, that Factory as a furtive, flamboyant statement of dissent becomes an enduring myth, even as the city becomes less and less an extension of Factory, less and less the version of a utopia dreamt up by stoned, radically minded pals believing it was possible to unite art with industrial techniques with fashion with music and direct it into social regeneration, as though urban renewal was as much hallucination as organisation. Society could be revived through design, through dreams, and there are elements of that in twenty-first-century Manchester, but without the sensuous northern surrealism, the literary vitality, Wilson's idea of rock 'n' roll as an avant-garde celebration of civilisation – without Noel Gallagher's 'artiness'.

Wilson would be the saintly subject of Mike Garry's epic, and epically flattering, poem 'St Anthony', which motors through his tumbling, show-off mind, hailing the great 'what if' of Manchester, and he would be included for 'continuing the benchmark for uncompromising entrepreneurs' in a magazine list of fifty visionaries 'that subconsciously shape our everyday actions, ethics, preconceptions and pleasures, as nominated by a cross-generational group . . .'

. . . along with the likes of Adi Dassler of Adidas, Adrian Henri of the Liverpool scene, Ai Weiwei, Andrés Iniesta, Angela Merkel, Armando

Iannucci, Bill Bowerman of Nike, Bill Drummond, Björk, Brian Cox, Brian Eno, C-3PO, Carol Kaye, Dangermouse, Diana Athill, Eminem, Evan Williams of Twitter, Greil Marcus, Ian Curtis, Ian Hislop, Ingvar Kamprad, J-Lo, Jayne Casey, J. K. Rowling, John Peel, Jonathan Ive, Lady Gaga, the Loch Ness monster, Malcom McLaren, Matt Groening, Norman Foster, Patti Smith, Paul Abbott, Pierre Morad Omidyar of eBay, Queen Elizabeth II, Ray Bradbury, Scanner, Sofia Coppola, Tim Berners-Lee, Tim Burton, Willow Smith and Zaha Hadid.

Fifty-One: Leaving a fortune

Verba volant, scripta manent. (Spoken words fly away, written words remain.)

'And one more thing,' he says, looking straight into the camera, seriousness in his voice, a smile in his eyes, or vice versa, not wanting to let go, never wanting to stop talking, never wanting the biography, the life, to end.

In 1977, the bad–good Catholic boy is on some very attractive Granada assignment meeting the smiling, embracing archbishop of São Paulo – the unstoppable, courageous Paulo Evaristo Arns, one-time cardinal of the people, champion of the re-democratisation of Brazil in 1974, a symbol of human rights, a fan of Cuba's Castro who ran the Catholic Church in South America on Marxist principles.

Arns tells Wilson that being rich in itself is a sin, but that in the achievements of revolution there were signs of the kingdom of God, which is going to have a big influence on Wilson's approach to pop culture and living a life. They talk about Castro, and how he said that any kind of revolution is not a bed of roses. It is a struggle between the future and the past.

That Jackie Collins rendition of the well-intentioned, post-hippy entrepreneur, Virgin's Richard Branson, once told Wilson he'd never make any money, as if that could be the only possible reason for his existence. He did too many things; he needed focus; he should concentrate on one thing, the single route to a fortune. Wilson preferred the bishop's message – creative revolution to balance the insanity of history, leading to a very different kind of fortune.

He was focused on himself, on his mission, on raiding knowledge, on the local waifs and strays and familiar faces he loved and supported, always best without a script, revelling in the fact that people either loved him or hated him, because he was magnificent and maddening, stamping his mind on Manchester, fully understanding how nothing improves the reputation of someone in his position more than a premature death, someone who once said that when he died, if he could come back as anyone, he would come back as himself, because he 'kind of' enjoyed being Tony Wilson.

He quietly relishes this thought at some point while driving along the rain-soaked Wellington Road, aka the A6, named after the nineteenth-century conqueror of Napoleon, in his trusty dark maroon Peugeot estate, the one his wife at the time said was like a hearse. He's always rushing somewhere, arriving, leaving, it's past midnight, he's making progress, Manchester behind and ahead of him, with all sorts of wires and amplifiers in the back, it's why he got an estate, for the needs of his boys, his musicians, for the kids he wanted to have, rushing through edgy, whimsical Stockport, in and out of Manchester, the city dissolving around him, ignoring the rear-view mirror, past the old hat factory where asbestos-sniffing mad hatters once toiled, the Pennines permanently set like fading gravestones in the distance, music blasting, fragrant smoke uncoiling, the tangled smell of hash, sweat, coffee and aftershave, Grey Flannel, his favourite, created by American fashion designer Geoffrey Beene in 1976, woody, oriental, citrussy fresh, a hint of delicately perfumed Parma violets, the fizzy sweets and the pale blue flowers, hard-wearing and covertly masculine, a love-it-or-loathe-it smell, think about it, puff puff, listen to the music, oh happy living things, speed limit smashed of course, always believing that a car with the petrol needle on empty can run about fifty more miles if you play the right music very loud, it's why he bought his Jag, under the influence, under a blue moon, one hand on the wheel, the other with a life of its own, operating as delivery man, tour guide, road warrior, racing driver, endless drifter, illicit lover, argumentative friend, glorified roadie, giving someone a lift home or giving them a detailed tour of the local sites, someone not used to it a little dizzy with the ostentatious smoke, someone thinking, *I wonder if he has a centre, if he can ever settle, ever stop, is he made up of fragments?* He's tracking down some music equipment, some special material, on the way to another brief encounter, discovering some new part of pleasure, another rapid spring of love gushing from his heart, another infatuation with a person or project, just generally on the hunt for experience, talent or some obscure, marvellous treasure. So shines a good deed in a weary world. He wonders whether Morley will hang on to him at the end of the biography – having spent so much time with him he doesn't want to let him go. He writes something on his notepad. '*Pactum serva.*' Keep the faith. He takes everything in, letting it all hang out, and thinks to himself how every actual existence is so overwhelmingly unexpected that everyone who exists at all seems like the result of some huge, improbable choice. Sat in your car at a red traffic light in the deathly quiet middle of the night, thinking secret things, savouring the loneliness, working out a piece to camera, the River Mersey magically flowing nearby like it has for ages, like a stream of consciousness, sometimes with no direction, you realise that the world need not exist. But it does. And there you have it. *There is no easy way*, Tony Wilson thinks to himself, wearing a mask of Seneca, *to get from the earth to the stars.* The traffic lights turn green. And the light comes rushing in and shows him the way.

Onwards, darling. God bless.

Acknowledgements

Acta est fabula, plaudite!

That the book is finally here – finished before the completion of the £190 million Factory arts arena in Manchester, originally due in 2019 – is thanks to many people, starting with:

Lee Brackstone, who commissioned it for Faber & Faber when 'Bad Romance' by Lady Gaga was number one, and who won't believe it's finished even when he sees it.

Cathryn Summerhayes, who represented Oli Wilson at WME when the album of the year was Jay-Z and Kanye West's *Watch the Throne* and who won't believe it's finished, etc., etc.

And then, at a later date, in another reality:

Thank you to my publisher Alex Bowler and editor Alexa von Hirschberg at Faber & Faber for keeping the faith and taking it forward, and much gratitude for the vigilance and support of those who helped turn the manuscript into a book: Hugh Davis (copy-editor), Kate Ward (production) and Ian Bahrami (proofreading and beyond). Thanks also to Mo Hafeez (editorial), Dan Papps (deputy director of music) and Hannah Marshall (marketing).

Thanks to Emily Faccini for the map of Wilsonland and Luke Bird for the cover design.

Thanks and more to those I interviewed at venues including various hotel spaces, pavements, cafes and texts (Alan Erasmus); his studio in east London as he emerged for each interview from the shower, whatever the time of day (Peter Saville); his house in Didsbury as the sun went down (Vini Reilly); a restaurant/bar in Didsbury (Hilary Wilson); another restaurant/bar in Didsbury (Neville Richards); various cafes, hotels and emails (Oli Wilson); the British Library cafe (Dr Isabel Wilson); the trendy Dean Street Townhouse restaurant (Steve Coogan); her kitchen in east London (Carol Morley); Hollin House restaurant outside Macclesfield

(Lindsay Reade); his house in Hebden Bridge (Elliot Rashman); the bar at the Edwardian, Peter Street, Manchester (Bernard Sumner); the Camden Head tavern, Islington (Richard Boon); the Villa Bianca Italian restaurant in Hampstead, with a cameo appearance by Melvyn Bragg (Richard Madeley and Judy Finnigan); many hours even days in and around his house in Leicester, which fell away into another phantom book (Kevin Hewick); the Parcel Yard, King's Cross Station (Rose Marley); Orsino's, Covent Garden, with a range of his choice of grappas (Terry Christian); Orsino's at another time (Jon Savage); his Images and Co. office in the Clarence Centre, south-east London (Malcolm Garrett); his house in Didsbury (Dave Haslam); an annex at Shoreditch Church (Liz Naylor); the Sony Records office, Kensington (Mike Pickering); the Southbank Centre cafe (Gonnie Rietveld); the Lowry Theatre cafe, Salford (Ged Clarke); the St John's pub in north London (Mark Hart); his office at Left Bank Pictures (Andy Harries); the bar at the Malmaison, Manchester (Bruce Mitchell); another part of the bar at the Malmaison, Manchester (Andy Spinoza); Carluccio's at Piccadilly Station (Ron Atkinson); B-Lounge, Manchester (Mike Garry); the Doubletree Hilton bar (Rebecca Boulton); and to those I never quite got to or couldn't find, or who said no or didn't get back to me, there is always volume two.

Thanks to AHW for bringing us all together.

Thanks to Kevin Cummins for the cover photograph and an interview remembering Tony in the Boot and Flogger in Southwark – falling away into another phantom book – which ended, in the nicest sense, in tears.

Family/school/university photographs of Tony Wilson courtesy of Hilary, Oli and Izzy Wilson.

Love and thanks to Carol Morley for Tony Wilson's voice in Section Thirty-Two. His words are mostly from an interview Carol conducted on a drive through Manchester with Tony in 2005, as part of her research for a film she was going to make about Joy Division fans who lived in China. *Shadowland* was never made but can be imagined.

Thanks to David Godwin and Philippa Sitters at my agency DGA for wise words and constant presence.

Love and thanks to my daughter Madeleine Morley for loving books, making me think and noticing things.

Love and thanks to my soulmate Elizabeth Levy for continual motivation, inspiration and insight, helping me in any number of ways while my mind filled up many times over with lives, opinions and occasional desperation.

In the end, it all led to an end, which, if you're lucky, leads to an index, a peaceful afterlife.

Index

271; DJ box, 429; dress code, 431; Ecstasy death, 457, 527; and Erasmus, 355, 356, 430; first members, 375; formation, 84–5, 353, 355–8, 362, 412–13, 443, 451, 487; free drinks, 441; and gangs, 484–6, 486, 487; Gay Traitor bar, 357, 443; and Gretton, 355, 356, 361, 362, 430, 441, 443, 445–6, 447, 504; and Hannett, 350, 432, 443; influence/legacy, 404, 412, 487, 571, 575; location, 84, 472, 572; logo, 318, 404, 487; Mason as manager, 430; naming, 361, 503–4; Oliver Wilson at, 397, 399; opening night, 379; Pickering on, 430–1; Ryder at, 440; situationism conference, 168–9; taxi service, 442; till floats, 430

Hall, Stuart, 88

Hall, Terry, 123, 125

Hallé, Charles, 30

Hallé Orchestra, 29–30, 105, 114

'hamartia', 456–7, 465

Hamill, Pete, 259

Hamlet: character, 41, 58, 457; play, 533

Hamp, Johnny: and the Beatles, 100–1, 104; at Granada, 99–100, 102–4; *I Hear the Blues*, 103

Hannett, Martin, 266, 365, 386, 452, 548; and AW, 562–3, 566; bass player, 226, 336; and Buzzcocks, 336–7; death, 350, 527; and drugs, 306, 307, 350; Factory rift/lawsuit, 350–1; and Haçienda, 350, 432, 443; and Happy Mondays, 350, 566; and Jilted John, 294; and Joy Division, 70, 335–6, 338, 339, 349, 366, 446; at Music Force, 306–7; and New Order, 371; as producer, 292, 307–8, 333, 336, 337–8, 349–50, 431–2; and Reilly/the Durutti Column, 324–5, 326; schooling 121–2; and Slaughter and the Dogs, 338; and U2, 349

Happy Mondays, 59, 66, 169, 369–70, 388, 408, 501, 504; AW as fan, 270–1, 440, 454, 455; and Hannett, 350, 566; in Hollywood, 557–8; musical evolution, 453; Pickering and, 454, 528; record sleeves, 451; sign to Factory, 431, 454; streetwear, 408, 431, 455; 'Bob's Yer Uncle', 559; 'Cowboy Dave', 294; 'Forty-Five EP', 528; *Pills 'n' Thrills and Bellyaches*, 387; '24 Hour Party People', 137; *Uncle Dysfunktional*, 527–8; *Yes Please!*, 457–61, 477

Harding, Mike, 121

Harries, Andy: on AW, 215, 285–6, 345, 358–9, 557–8; *So It Goes*, 231, 258; *World in Action*, 345–6

Harris, Bob, 108, 231, 236

Harris, Emmylou, 215

Harrison, George, 196, 215

Haslam, Dave: on AW, 347–8, 449; on AW's illness/death, 554–5; Haçienda DJ, 448

Hatton, Derek, 413–14, 560

Hazlitt, William, 58, 136–7

Head (Monkees film), 213

Heaton Park Festival, 496

Hell, Richard, 250–1; 'Blank Generation', 250–1

Hendrix, Jimi, 50, 153; AW on death of, 184, 213

heroin: and Hannett, 350; Ryder kicks, 459; vs alcohol, 444; vs Yage, 523

Hewat, Tim, 98

Hewick, Kevin, 37, 446

Hipgnosis, 318

hipsterism, 275, 480, 513, 514, 573

Hitchens, Christopher, 178

Hoffman, Abbie, 259

Hoggart, Richard, 88

Hollies, the, 50, 225–6, 321

Honeycombe, Gordon, 187

Hook, Peter, 352, 436, 441, 446, 572

Hooker, John Lee, 50–1

Hopper, 503

Howlin' Wolf, 50–1

Hucknall, Mick, 445

Hudson, Rock: *Seconds*, 39–41, 59

Hulme, 113, 288, 293, 370–1, 442, 470, 480

Huxley, Aldous, 156, 157; *The Doors of Perception*, 156

Hyett, Trevor, 208

Ibiza, 431, 453, 455, 492

Iggy Pop, 92, 188, 240, 264, 323

In the City (music conference), 140, 483–4, 489–91, 495; author interviews Grant/

Manchester, 315, 316–17; Royal Court Theatre ('With Love from Manchester' benefit), 413, 414–15; vs Manchester (1960s), 225–6, 304

Liverpool FC, 199, 200

Livesey, Yvette (third wife): and AW, 397, 398, 466, 467, 498, 536, 538, 565; and AW's illness/death, 528, 550, 557; at In the City, 495, 497; Music33.com, 508

Livesey/Wilson Associates Ideas Management, 508–9, 512–15; *see also* Pennine Lancashire

Lloyd, Clive, 247

London: Assembly Hall (Sex Pistols gig), 238–9; Festival of Britain (1951), 85; grime scene, 500–1, 505; Music Machine (club), 355; Sex (boutique), 249, 255, 261, 265; Willow Road, 85

London Records, 169, 464, 483, 502

Longsight, 113, 286, 326, 363

Lord Sutch, Screaming, 261, 263

Loren, Sophia, 36

Lovell, Bernard, 576

Lowe, Nick, 229

Lowry, L. S., 62–3, 68, 69–70, 79–80, 562

LSD, 41, 156–7, 296; and AW, 156, 181–2, 195, 212, 231, 245, 276, 292, 306, 360; and naming of psychedelics, 157; and situationism, 156, 157; vs Ecstasy, 448

Ludus, 266, 270, 341

Lydon, John, 250–1, 254, 255, 520; and AW, 414; Grundy interview, 419, 420; at Lesser Free Trade Hall, 264, 267

Lynn, Jack, 470

Macbeth: character, 457; play, 67

McCarthy, Joseph, 87, 108

McCartney, Paul, 86, 204, 215

Macclesfield, 73, 353

MacColl, Ewan: 'Dirty Old Town', 62

McGee, Alan, 560

McGhee, Brownie, 103

McGough, Nathan, 460, 492

McGough, Roger, 204

McGough, Thelma (*née* Pickles), 204–5, 492

Maciunas, George, 9–10

McKelvie, Jamie, 56

McLaren, Malcolm, 111, 245, 520; and AW,

247–8, 256–8, 500; and death of Sid Vicious, 346; on Grant, 493–4; quotes, 248; Sex (boutique), 249, 255, 261, 265; and Sex Pistols, 249–51, 252, 253, 261, 418, 420–1

McPherson, Andy, 71, 337

Madchester, 270, 388, 404, 408, 439–40, 449, 451, 452, 483–4, 501, 503

Madeley, Richard, 96; and/on AW, 132–3, 193, 194–5, 202–3, 217, 402; and AW's illness/death, 534–6, 554, 557, 560, 567–8; on book title, 192–3, 194; *This Morning*, 133, 192

Madonna, 408, 447

Magazine, 2, 233, 266, 270, 280, 333, 350, 380, 404

Maher, John, 71, 121, 337; *see also* Buzzcocks

mainstream media, 126, 155, 211; attitude to rock/pop culture, 237

Mamucium, 412

Man Who Shot Liberty Valance, The (film), 3

Manchester: Affleck's Palace, 475; Arena, 412, Arndale Centre, 470–1, 472, 474, 476, 481; and AW, 4–5, 9, 10, 11–12, 24–5, 27, 50, 63, 96, 236, 239–40, 298, 301–2, 313, 412–13, 442, 479–81; Beetham Tower, 574; Central station, 412; Chetham's Library, 24; Cromford Court, 474; Deansgate, 279, 298, 299, 412; Free Trade Hall, *see* Free Trade Hall; Granada Studios, 15, 83–4, 86–7, 575; *see also* Granada TV; Greater Manchester, 65; Hulme Crescents flats, 470; John Rylands Library, 97, 298–301, 576; Market Street, 469; Northern Quarter, 474, 475, 478, 479, 571; Oldham Street, 469, 471, 473, 475; Palatine Rd (Factory HQ), 295, 296, 460; Richard Goodall Gallery, 543; St Mary's church ('Hidden Gem'), *see* St Mary's church; Tib Street, 471; Town Hall, 289–90, 297–8; University, 51, 113–14; vs Salford, 60–1, 63; *see also individual suburbs*

history/events: Arena bombing (2017), 11, 271, 577; AW/Factory's influence, 402, 438, 510, 570–3, 575, 577; Boon on, 226, 304, 382; Copernicus

Orchestral Manoeuvres in the Dark, 234–5, 374; 'Electricity', 234
Osborne, George, 14
Osborne, Steve, 459
Osmond, Humphry, 156–7
Othello, 457
Outsider, The (Colin Wilson), 46–9

Page, Jimmy, 51
pandemic (Covid), 12, 15
Paris protests (1968), 52, 140, 148, 151, 153, 154–5, 223
Parkinson, Michael, 95–6, 97, 99, 207, 246
Parliament, 369, 388
Parsons, Gram, 107
Paxman, Jeremy, 170, 246
Peak Forest Canal, 75
Peel, John, 210, 232, 233, 265–6, 578
Pendle, 426, 512
Pennebaker, D. A.: *Don't Look Back*, 109
Pennine Lancashire, 364, 511, 512, 549–50; 'The Dreaming of Pennine Lancashire', 512–15; flag, 511–12
Pere Ubu, 308, 329
Permild and Rosengreen (printers), 72
Perry, Lee 'Scratch', 252
Peter, Paul and Mary: AW as fan, 105–6, 108; 'Blowin' in the Wind', 106; *Peter, Paul and Mary in Concert Volume 1*, 108; 'Puff the Magic Dragon', 108–9
Peterloo Massacre, 55, 300, 508
Phonogram (comic book), 56
Pickering, Mike, 284, 350, 474; and AW, 432, 433, 439, 532; on Curtis suicide, 342; at Deconstruction, 431, 432; and Haçienda, 429–30, 439, 452, 485–6; and Happy Mondays, 454, 528
Pickles, Wilfred, 562
Pilkington Committee of Enquiry into Broadcasting (1961), 82–3
Pink Floyd, 219, 251, 318
plagiarism, 128–9, 158, 163
Plath, Sylvia, 171, 392
Pol Pot, 52, 458
Poly Styrene, 296
Pop Group, the, 374
pop music, 5, 48–9, 88, 100–1, 102, 105, 109, 176, 208, 235–6, 365, 566; charts,

124; comics, 56; for youngsters, 123–4, 125, 209–10; vs rock music, 210
popular culture, 48, 125–6, 160, 164, 165, 210, 228, 248, 249, 253, 254, 285, 291; AW's thirteen-year theory, 499, 500, 505, 517; Williams on, 141–3
Porter, Nolan: 'Keep on Keepin' On', 334
Powell Enoch, 137
Prague Spring (1968), 52
praxis, 23–4, 139, 180, 239
Prefects, the, 296, 383; 'VD', 387
Prince, 56, 408
Prodigy: 'Smack My Bitch Up', 363–4
protest movement, 148, 153; *see also* Angry Brigade; Cambridge University, Garden House Riot; Civil Rights movement; Paris protests; Strasbourg University protests
psychedelics, 156–7; *see also* ayahuasca; LSD
Pulp, 386
punk: clothes/fashion, 224, 249–50, 251, 253, 265, 418; emergence, 216, 219, 221–4, 230, 233; fanzines, 225; fe-punks, 296; as movement, 224–5; music style, 224, 234; music, vs rock, 234; origin of name, 226–7; and skinheads, 367; *see also individual bands*
Purple Gang, 226

Q (TV series), 213
Quando Quango, 432–3, 450
Queen, 417, 494

Rabid Records, 268, 294, 335, 338, 547
Radcliffe, Mark, 96
Railway Children, the, 431
Ramones, 183, 227, 266, 339
Random, Eric, 270, 355
Rashman, Elliot: and AW's illness, 534, 537, 538, 539, 541, 553, 574; and In the City, 490; on Manchester, 304
Raw-T, 501, 504, 505
RCA Records, 334, 336
Reade Wilson, Lindsay (first wife), 195, 295, 297, 395; on Factory/Curtis suicide, 342, 343; on AW, 201–2, 343–4, 393, 396, 408; and AW's illness/death, 530–1, 536, 537, 538, 539, 540, 548, 554, 560; and Beach Club, 355–6, 382;

Christie Hospital, 532, 536, 539, 554; death, 550, 556–7, 567; Erasmus on, 530, 536–7, 539, 551–3, 563; funeral, 559–60, 562–4; Hilary Wilson on, 530, 538, 552; Isabel Wilson on, 528–9, 537–8, 539, 540, 552, 553, 555, 556–7; kidney cancer/removal, 528, 532; last documentaries/interviews, 545–6; last football match, 64; last reading, 549; last rites, 554–5, 554; letter to NHS, 533; Lindsay Reade on, 530–1, 536, 537, 538, 539, 540, 548, 554, 560; Mitchell and, 547–8, 549–50, 559, 562; Oliver Wilson on, 544, 545–6, 553, 555, 556–7, 562, 563; Rashman on, 534, 537, 538, 539, 541, 553, 574; Reilly on, 554; Richards on, 551; TV tributes, 567–8; Yvette Livesey and, 528, 550, 557

influences/interests: broadcasters, 187–8; Buddhism, 26–7, 167–8, 181–2, 245; cultural studies, *see* Williams, Raymond; football, 63–4, 117, 199–200, 455, 551; history, 45, 297; Marxism, 52, 361, 514; music managers, 111, 246; philosophy, 24, 139, 568–9; poetry, 122–3, 138, 204, 237; praxis, 23–4, 139, 180, 239; situationism, *see* situationism

at ITN, 185, 186, 188–90, 211–12, 237, 246; job interview, 184–5

and Manchester, 4–5, 9, 10, 11–12, 24–5, 27, 50, 63, 96, 236, 239–40, 298, 301–2, 313, 412–13, 442, 479–81; freedom of the city, 576; honorary degree, 402; influence, 402, 438, 510, 570–3, 575, 577

musical taste, 107, 234, 235, 369, 388, 448; resistance to dance music, 431, 432–4; *Rolling Stone*, 107; thirteen-year theory, 499, 500, 505, 517

post-Factory projects: Factory Too (Number 2), 502; Factory 3, 503; F4, 504; In the City, *see* In the City; Pennine Lancashire, *see* Pennine Lancashire; Red Cellars, 503–4

relationships: author, 2, 3–5, 276–7, 308, 313, 315, 364, 365, 403–4; Boon on, 196, 304, 347, 557; Carol Morley, 283–4, 357, 391, 392–3, 429; Christian on, 203, 284, 435; Coogan on, 130–1, 197–8, 283; Curtis, 6, 332, 341–2, 347–8; Erasmus on, 195, 359–60; Hannett, 562–3, 566; Harries on, 215, 285–6, 345, 358–9, 557–8; Haslam on, 347–8, 449; Hilary Wilson on, 394–5, 396, 401, 467–8, 485; Isabel Wilson on, 397–9, 400, 528–9, 540, 556; Jane Buchan, 228; Judy Finnigan on, 133, 202; Lindsay Reade on, 201–2, 343–4, 393, 396, 408; Lydon, 414; McLaren, 247–8, 256–8, 500; Mitchell on, 548, 549–50; Morrissey, 378, 380–1, 384, 385–6, 413, 415–16; Oliver Wilson on, 203, 213–14, 397, 399–400, 401; parents, 38–9, 44–5, 212; Pickering, 432, 433, 439; Reilly on, 282–3, 325–7, 345; Richards on, 119, 195–6, 393–4, 466, 486; Rietveld on, 284–5, 467; Rose Marley on, 496–8; Savage on, 131–2, 256, 285, 303, 352; Saville, 13, 14, 360–1, 449, 560; Spinoza on, 286; Sumner on, 330; Thelma McGough, 204–5; Yvette Livesey, 397, 398, 466, 467, 498, 536, 538, 565

Wilson, Brian, 41–2

Wilson, Colin: *The Outsider*, 46–9

Wilson, Doris Emily (mother), 66, 79; on AW's TV career, 212; and the Boylans, 560–1; death, 44, 245, 527; marriage, 43; motorbiker, 45; move to Marple, 64, 66; on Sydney, 44

Wilson, Harold, 46, 72, 127, 142, 206

Wilson, Hilary (*née* Sherlock; second wife), 466; attack on, 425–7; on AW, 394–5, 396, 401, 467–8, 485; and AW's illness, 530, 538, 552; and Yvette, 466, 467

Wilson, Isabel (daughter), 396, 467, 555–6; on AW, 397–9, 400, 528–9, 540, 556; and AW's illness/death, 528–9, 537–8, 539, 540, 552, 553, 555, 556–7

Wilson, Master (comic character), 57–8

Wilson, Oliver (son), 396, 426, 437, 501, 528, 537; on AW, 203, 213–14, 397, 399–400, 401; and AW's illness/death, 544, 545–6, 553, 555, 556, 562, 563

Wilson, Tony, *see* Wilson, Anthony H.